Java™
for RPG Programmers

JAVA™
FOR RPG PROGRAMMERS

Phil Coulthard

George Farr

IBM
Press™

Java™ for RPG Programmers

Phil Coulthard and George Farr

Published by IBM Press™
IBM Associate Publisher: Tara B. Woodman
IBM Press Alliance Publisher: David Uptmor, MC Press, LLC

For information on translations or book distributors outside the USA
or to arrange bulk purchase discounts for sales promotions or premiums,
please contact:

MC Press, LLC
Corporate Offices:
125 N. Woodland Trail
Double Oak, TX 75077
Sales Office:
P.O. Box 4300
Big Sandy, TX 75755-4300
877-226-5394

First edition
First printing: March, 2002
Second printing: December, 2002

ISBN: 1-931182-06-X

OS/400 V4R3 and higher

For the three beautiful ladies in my life: my wife Chris, and my daughters Cassandra and Jennifer. They are the joy of my life. Since the first edition, Cassandra has become a competitive dancer and Jennifer has got all her teeth! I remain the person tapping on the keyboard all night. I also dedicate this book to my father Frederick Coulthard, and my brother Wayne Coulthard. I thank my whole family for their encouragement, and for putting up with my "humor."

— Phil S. Coulthard

To my loving wife, Diana, for her unending support with the first, second, third, fourth ... books I wrote. Watch out! I am thinking of a new book project!

To my beautiful children: Angelica, my baseball "buddy" waiting for the next season to start! Michael, my basketball "buddy" hoping that the Toronto Raptors win the NBA! Annalisa, my little "grade 1" Barbie girl, who is starting to call me "Big Guy" instead of Dad!

To my in-laws: Kamal, Zack, Pierre, Laura, and Janette: Thanks for taking my sisters and brothers away!

To Leo, Effie, and Jim: You have to increase your shelves if I keep on going at it!

In addition, Once again, I like to dedicate this book to my big brothers: Ibrahim and Elias. They continue to lead the way in education, career success and most importantly, good family values.

Finally, for our best, my Mom, Angelica Neiman Farr: We all love you for being the best Mother!

— George N. Farr

ACKNOWLEDGMENTS

We heartily thank the following fellow IBMers who took personal time to review the book or to answer our endless questions:

- Maha Masri
- Kimberly Mungal
- Joe Sobura
- Barbara Morris
- Abe Batthish
- Cheryl Renner
- Sheila Richardson
- Kou-mei Lui

We also thank the following members of the "real world" who previously worked for IBM:

- Jon Paris and Susan Gantner
- Rares Pateanu
- Sarah Ettritch
- Paul Holm
- Clifton Nock

In addition, we wish to thank the following customers who also took an active interest in both the topic and the book:

- Estrella Tan
- Johnny Lee Lenhart
- Vincent Green

CONTENTS

FOREWORD

The AS/400, and the RPG programmers (you!) who have made it the most successful business system in the world, face the biggest change ever to occur in their intertwined histories.

As former AS/400 General Manager Bill Zeitler has said, IBM is "betting the ranch" on Java.

IBM has irrevocably linked the future success of the AS/400 to Java because:

- Java offers a way to add the graphical interface so urgently needed for AS/400 applications.

- Java provides the core technology for IBM's attempts to sell the AS/400 as an e-business server.

- Java is the only viable answer IBM has to the Microsoft Visual Basic juggernaut.

If you haven't already gotten the word, here it is: IBM is making the AS/400 a best-of-breed Java server, and is no longer basing the AS/400's future on RPG alone.

Considering IBM's bet on Java, the industry-wide rise of the Web, and Microsoft's push to capture the traditional business market, an RPG programmer has three choices:

1. Learn Java now.

2. Abandon the AS/400 for Windows and learn Visual Basic.

3. Become one of the last living RPG programmers doing maintenance on legacy applications.

If yours is the first choice, reading this book is one of the first steps you should take. Get yourself a copy of IBM's VisualAge for Java or Inprise's JBuilder, prop this book up on your desk, and follow two of the best guides you'll find to lead you into the exciting world of Java programming. You'll never turn back.

Phil Coulthard and George Farr have spent years immersed in IBM's RPG development, working with AS/400 programmers. They're also key developers in IBM's Java platform and tools. They have the perfect combination of skills and experience to explain the practical use of Java for AS/400 development. Now, they've delivered a unique book that presents Java and object-oriented programming in terms familiar to RPG programmers. No RPG programmer who wants to become proficient in Java should be without this essential resource.

—Paul Conte, Paul Conte Educational Services
Consultant, Author, Editor,
Java Advocate, WebSphere Advocate

THE WORLD OF JAVA

Since the first edition of this book in July 1998, the world of Java has continued to gain significant ground. By now, everyone is aware of the industry's commitment to Java, of IBM's commitment to Java, and especially of the AS/400's (now known as the iSeries') commitment to Java. Way back in 1998, the options for AS/400 Java programmers were exactly two: write Java applications that run on the AS/400 or on a client connected to an AS/400, or write Java applets that run in a Web browser connected to an AS/400. Now, in addition to the expanded capabilities of both of these options, there are servlets, JavaServer Pages, and Enterprise JavaBeans (EJBs). Java is now also a full-fledged option for writing Domino applications. Further, XML, with its Java affinity, has emerged as the new standard for business-to-business communication and is a favorite way to persist information needed by tools. A rapidly emerging new standard for reusable components, known as Web Services, also have tight affinity with Java.

Most vendors writing tools have switched to Java. Most package vendors have adopted Java or have a plan to phase it in. Java presentations at professional and technical conferences continue to fill rooms. Look at the agenda for the North American COMMON conference (*www.common.org*), and you'll see that Java and Java-related technologies permeate it.

So, while Java is still maturing and expanding rapidly, it is now an entrenched part of the iSeries and AS/400 application development scene. At the same time, IBM has proven it is not backing away from RPG or COBOL, and has continued to deliver significant new functionality in each release of both. Further, as of this writing, IBM has just released its new application development package, WebSphere Development Studio for iSeries (WDS), offering modern tooling for everything from RPG to Java to Web user interfaces. That tooling includes WebFacing, an exciting new option for quickly and cost-effectively converting 5250 applications into Web-enabled applications. WebFacing converts display-file DDS source into JavaServer Page source and JavaBeans (simple beans, not EJBs). The WebFacing runtime intercepts the display file input/output operations from an application and diverts them to the WebFacing runtime servlet, offering a Web refacing with no application code change. This awesome new capability is possible due to the power of Java.

The first release of WDS includes the "classic" version of WebSphere Studio for Web user interfaces authored in HTML, JavaServer Pages, and JavaScript, and includes the classic version of VisualAge for Java for applications, applets, servlets, and beans. Also included is the classic version of CODE for RPG, COBOL, C, C++, CL, and lightweight Java development, and even VisualAge RPG for writing Java applications authored in RPG IV. Exciting as this tooling package is on first release, future releases promise to be even more exciting, as all the tools converge around Eclipse, IBM's new Integrated Development Environment that is the basis of the next generation of all IBM tooling. Eclipse is a pluggable and extendable IDE, fully open and indeed open source. What is Eclipse written in, and what is used to extend it? Java, of course. Java is now the cornerstone programming language for IBM.

Evolving the languages and the tools are important enough in their own right, but IBM has also shown it clearly sees a world with both Java and RPG/COBOL by continually enhancing both RPG and COBOL to increase your ability to mix Java and RPG/COBOL code in the same application. V5R1 and later releases of RPG and COBOL bear out this commitment. While Java is clearly the glue of e-Business, IBM will ensure that both RPG and COBOL have roles in this new and exceedingly important picture, for those who prefer to use a business language for their business logic.

With all this in mind, this book will teach you Java so you can include it as another option in your programming toolbox. If you have already read the first edition, welcome back. You will find many additional topics and increased coverage of the core topics. If this is your first read, congratulations on taking the first step on the road to Java.

WHAT IS JAVA?

Java is a programming language. So are RPG and CL. You learned them, and you can learn Java. The reason Java seems like more than just a programming language is the vast number of places it can be used. Vertically, it can be used to program the smallest embedded chips and personal devices all the way up to the largest scalable, transaction-based, distributed enterprise applications. Horizontally, it can run on any operating system and almost any device. Java can be the answer for your user interface, and it can be the language of your next batch language. It can do e-Business on the Internet, and it can do back-office payroll.

However, with all of this, you must distinguish between the core Java language, which is stable, mature, and relatively small, and the Java technologies built on top of that language. These technologies are just specialized Java code written by the industry to solve specific tasks, such as programming chips, Internet Web servers, or large-scale mission-critical applications that support distribution and transactions.

The trick to learning Java is to start with the core language, including the syntax and the core Java-supplied functions. With these under your belt, you can move on to additional Java technologies with relative ease, if and when you need them.

From this book, you will learn the core Java language syntax by having it compared every step of the way to RPG. You will also learn the core Java-supplied functions that you will need to succeed with Java, again compared every step of the way to RPG. With the proper analogies, and the proper definition of terms in iSeries-speak, you'll find that Java is not mysterious and absolutely within your capabilities to learn, use, and master! Indeed, thousands of RPG programmers before you have done exactly that.

This book is not small, but neither are your RPG and DDS manuals. Do not despair, as the size is simply because we have included many examples in both RPG and Java to give you a complete introduction to as much Java as you will need to be productive. This might not be the last book you read on Java, but it should make you immediately productive with Java.

WHAT ABOUT THAT OO THING?

Java is an object-oriented language. It is inconceivable that a new language today would not be object-oriented; the benefits in productivity and quality are too great to ignore. These gains come from the capacity to reuse code and perform better problem domain-modeling. When people complain about Java's learning curve, they always refer to the OO side of things. This is typically from people who haven't learned Java, or want to promote an alternative. Don't be fooled. Yes, thinking "OO" is different than thinking procedurally as you do in RPG. But it comes quickly, and not by reading a book, frankly. That helps, to be sure, but it really starts coming home only by writing code. With a little experience, you can pick up an OO book or course, and it will all fall into place. Once it does fall into place, you will wonder how you lived without it.

Our approach to OO in this book is not to hit you over the head with it. Our primary goal is to teach you the language and the major functionality supplied with the language. As we do that, we'll be showing you many examples. You will slowly get the hang of objects simply by seeing them, and, if you follow along, by coding them. They really are not that hard. So, don't think OO means "uh oh!" It is just a tool that ultimately will make your life better. (Well, your programming life, anyway.)

WHY THE HYPE?

If Java is just a programming language, then why all the fuss? There are a number of reasons:

- *The name.* Java is a cool name! Programmers like that.

- *The Internet.* Java has much affinity with the Internet. CEOs like that.

- *Portability.* Java makes it possible to write completely portable code. CIOs like that.

- *Accessibility.* Java is free. CFOs like that.

The following sections examine these reasons a little further. We hope *you* like that.

The name

Java was originally designed by engineers from Sun Microsystems. Their intent was to create a small-scale, interpreted language for programming small consumer devices. Reportedly known as "Oak" in its early days, it was originally an embedded language that quickly found a new use for Internet-related programming. It had all the attributes a programming language for the Internet could want: it was small, simple, easy to code, platform independent, and provided support for dynamic loading of code on demand. Thus, it was renamed and made publicly available as a programming language for the Internet in 1995.

Java's big boost, however, came in early 1996, when Netscape Communications stepped up to support it as a programming language that could be processed by its Web browser. Suddenly, thousands of programmers and Web site owners wanted to learn and use Java.

What about the name? Legend has it that it came from the coffee the engineers drank in vast quantities while working so hard on the project. We guess "Donut" was ruled out.

The Internet

The original reason for Java's popularity, then, was the Internet. Specifically, Java could be used to program Web pages displayed by Web browsers·such as Netscape's Navigator or Microsoft's Internet Explorer. Web browsers display text and graphics through HTML (Hypertext Markup Language), a tag-based language similar to UIM (User Interface Manager, the AS/400 source language for writing online help).

Java adds the ability to embed Java *applets* inside HTML pages. Applets are small applications that only run inside Web browsers, using the screen real estate of the browser window. Since they have the full power of a modern programming language behind them, they can provide fully interactive, animated, live-data Web pages, which is beyond what HTML could originally offer. Java can also be used to author *servlets*, which are server-side programs for serving up Web pages dynamically and on demand.

Java also supports easy Internet communications programming, using either HTTP or TCP/IP communications protocols. Indeed, it is possible to write a Web browser entirely in Java that performs the basic tasks of finding, retrieving, and displaying HTML files. In fact, Sun has done just that with its HotJava Web browser. While this is easy enough, you have no need for communications programming as an AS/400 programmer because IBM supplies the AS/400 Toolbox for Java, a rich collection of pre-written code that makes remotely accessing AS/400 programs and data easy.

Portability

Java approaches more closely than any preceding language that elusive goal of "write once, run anywhere." It is possible to write completely portable applications in Java without too much sacrifice or pain. Here is why this is possible:

- Java (like BASIC and Smalltalk) is interpreted rather than compiled.

- Java's interpreter is everywhere, in operating systems, Web browsers, chips, and more.

- The Java is rich in functionality, so there is little need for operating system APIs.

Accessibility

Sun Microsystems makes Java available for free over the Internet for Windows and Solaris. IBM and others take that and make it available for their operating systems, Web browsers, computer chips, personal devices, toaster ovens, and so on. In most cases today, Java is actually made part of the operating system, so it is even more accessible.

Visit any Web-search site, do a search for the word *Java*, and you'll find thousands of free tutorials, newsgroups and other resources at your disposal. Of course, you *can* pay for onsite education and robust development tools, but one of Java's most alluring features is that you don't *have* to make that investment. Even your local community college will almost certainly offer a Java programming course. (Finally, the Pascal courses are being retired!)

THE ROLES OF JAVA

Java can play a role in at least three important places in your application:

- *The client.* This can be a traditional GUI application, a Web browser applet, or a Java servlet-created Web page. The user interface will run on any client operating system.

- *The server.* This can be a small part of an existing application, an entire traditional business-logic application, or a new Enterprise JavaBean application.

- *The glue.* Whatever the decisions for the client and the server, Java is a good option for tying them together. With new Web Services coming online, Java is also the glue between any two pieces of business logic running on any two machines in any two companies.

THE HOUSE OF JAVA

Java comes in its purest form as the *Java Development Kit*, or *JDK*. This kit contains a number of fundamentals, including these:

- A Java compiler that compiles Java source code into efficiently interpreted bytecode (as opposed to directly executable machine code). This is the `javac` command.

- A Java interpreter that interprets or runs Java bytecode. This is the `java` command.

- A set of Java class libraries (*packages*), similar to reusable ILE service programs, for often-needed programming tasks.

These basic elements, together with their documentation, define the Java language. The documentation is in HTML and is shipped compressed into a file that is a separate download from the JDK, so be sure to get it too. While packaged separately, the documentation is still considered part of the JDK. The JDK also includes a number of other useful command-line tools, shown in Table 1.1.

You can find Sun's JDK for Windows and Solaris at *www.java.sun.com/products*. However, be aware that the official name has changed to Java 2 SDK, Standard Edition, V1.*x*. So you have to follow the links for Java 2 SDK at Sun's Web site. Further, Java comes with the operating system on the iSeries, but is known there as the Java Application Development Kit (*ADK*). However, this book uses the simpler term *JDK*.

Table 1.1: JDK Tools	
Tool	**Description**
javac	Source-to-bytecode compiler
java	Java interpreter
javadoc	Documentation generator
appletviewer	Applet tester
jar	Java archive (compression) tool
jdb	Java debugger (Don't get your hopes up!)
javah	Java-to-C stub generator

Table 1.1: JDK Tools (cont.)	
Tool	Description
javap	Bytecode-to-source de-compiler
extcheck	Jar file conflict detector
rmic	Remote-method-invocation stub generator
rmiregistry	Remote-method-invocation registry
rmid	Remote-method-invocation daemon
serialver	Remote-method-invocation serial-version ID generator
native2ascii	Text-to-Unicode Latin-1 converter
keytool	Security certificate generator
jarsigner	Signature generator
policytool	Security-policy file manager
tnameserv	Naming-service access provider
idltojava	CORBA-IDL-to-Java stub generator

The JDK does *not* include an editor, an integrated development environment, or a visual design tool, and it provides only the most rudimentary of debuggers. Nonetheless, with a decent editor (such as CODE/400's) you have all you need for basic Java development. Figure 1.1 illustrates the pieces of the JDK.

Most programmers, however, will opt for one of the many full-scale Java development tools that are already available, such as IBM's VisualAge for Java, Inprise's JBuilder, or Symantec's Visual Cafe. These start with the basic JDK, and then add IDEs (integrated development environments), class hierarchy browsers, debuggers, visual design tools, wizards, and many more items to make the development task easier. Multiple-developer shops will also look for tools that offer built-in team

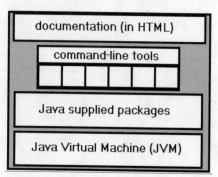

Figure 1.1: The Java Development Kit (JDK)

support and versioning control, such as VisualAge for Java offers. (Note that the name "VisualAge for Java" can mean either the classic version of this tool, or its new Eclipse-based generation known as "Java Tools" inside IBM Eclipse-based products such as WebSphere Studio Site Developer and WebSphere Studio Application Developer.)

The JDK originates with Sun Microsystems. Based on tremendous programmer feedback, the company adds enhancements and features to the language, and regularly releases a new version of the JDK. Other industry partners betting heavily on Java work with Sun to define and even implement many specialized pieces.

In February 1997, Sun released version 1.1 of the JDK. In December 1998, it released 1.2, and in February 2000, it released 1.3. Release 1.4 is scheduled for the end of 2001, as of this writing. As of version 1.2, the official generic branding became Java 2 Platform, Standard Edition. Sun's own JDK for Solaris and Sun is named Java 2 *SDK*, Standard Edition. There is also an Enterprise Edition, which is a superset of the Standard Edition and includes server-side functionality such as servlets, JavaServer Pages, and Enterprise JavaBeans. The JDK is maturing and improving very fast, but hopefully its name has stabilized!

Because this book examines the basics of Java, all its samples are written using Sun's JDK on Windows. We happened to use CODE/400 for entering the source, but you can use whatever tool you have handy. The nice thing about using CODE/400 is that you can use the same editor and debugger for both Java and RPG.

If you decide to follow along with this book's samples, you should get the JDK for Windows from *www.java.sun.com/products* (follow the link for Java 2 SDK). Also be sure to get the documentation, which is a separate download. When you install the JDK, be sure to follow the instructions in the readme file, especially those related to updating your PATH and CLASSPATH statements on Windows. Other operating-system vendors license the JDK code from Sun and port it as-is to their operating systems. The IBM Hursley laboratory, for example, licenses and ports the JDK to the IBM operating systems AIX, OS/2, OS/400, and MVS, as well as to Linux. For OS/400, the IBM Rochester lab leverages that ported base, and then integrates it deeply into the operating system for improved performance. Various Web browser manufacturers also license the JDK code in order to run Java applets embedded in Web pages.

As part of the Java license, the licensee agrees to stay current with the JDK, and must port a new release within about six months of its release by Sun. This ensures a reasonably current base across all the operating systems and Web browsers, as well as user program portability. The JDK now comes with most, if not all, major operating systems.

It has come with OS/400 since Version 4, Release 2 (V4R2) and has been significantly improved ever since. (For more details, see *www.ibm.com/java* and *www.ibm.com/iSeries/java.*)

JAVA BYTECODE

Java achieves its portability because of its bytecode architecture. As illustrated in Figure 1.2, the Java source code you enter is compiled into bytecode using the JDK-supplied javac command-line compiler. This compiler is really only the front half of a traditional compiler, in that an executable program is not produced as a result. Rather, it stops at what is referred to as the intermediate code in traditional compilers. This is a more efficient, compact version of the source, which is independent of any particular operating system.

The Java source code is contained in a file that ends with the extension .java ("dot java"), while the Java bytecode is contained in a file that ends with the extension .class ("dot class"). You can copy a bytecode .class file to any operating system or Web browser that contains the Java interpreter, and run it there without change. The hard work is performed by the interpreter itself—it has to be ported. And it is the operating system and Web browser vendors that do this hard work for you.

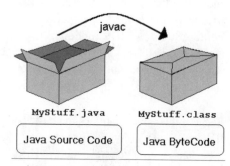

Figure 1.2: Compiling Java source code to Java bytecode

To run a Java application, you invoke the java command and pass it the name of your bytecode .class file as a parameter, as shown in Figure 1.3. For applets, you need to use something called an APPLET tag in your Web page source. (This tag will be described shortly.)

Sun and other vendors also supply a subset of the JDK called the *Java*

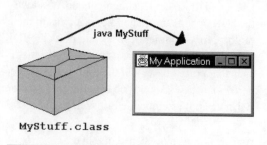

Figure 1.3: Running a Java application

Runtime Environment, or *JRE*, for the operating systems they support. The JRE consists of only the Java virtual machine (the interpreter) and the supporting runtime packages. As such, it is intended as a distribution option for applications when you do not want to assume the existence of a virtual machine on your users' computers, or if you are worried that their version of the virtual machine might not match yours.

JAVA: THE LANGUAGE

Java is based heavily on C++, with some key features borrowed from Smalltalk, Ada, and other languages. The working theme of the Java designers is always KISS ("Keep It Simple, Stupid"). To that end, the language does *not* have the following:

- Pointer variables. (It does have object references though, as you will see.)
- Memory allocation and deallocation constructs.
- Include files (copy members, in RPG parlance).
- Make files (a language for facilitating C and C++ builds).
- Multiple inheritance (an OO construct that C++ uses).
- Prototyping. In Java, you declare and define methods at the same time.
- Operator overloading, a complex function available in C++.

The biggest plus, from the point of view of programmer productivity, is the absence of memory-management functions. Instead of supplying built-in functions for getting and returning memory, Java offers automatic *garbage collection*. That is, when you declare variables, Java keeps track of where they are used at runtime, and frees up their memory when it determines your code no longer requires them. If you have written any C or C++ code or used the new memory allocation operation codes in RPG IV (ALLOC, REALLOC, and DEALLOC), you must take care to do the following:

- Allocate enough memory.
- Reallocate the memory when more is needed.
- Free up the memory when you are done with it.
- Free up the memory once and only once.

Memory management is very error-prone, and such errors are typically hard to reproduce and difficult to find. As the RPG IV reference manual states, "Misuse of heap storage can cause problems." Indeed. Garbage collection is a language feature Java picked up from Smalltalk, and one that, by itself, saves a significant amount of programmer time. (Now just imagine if someone could manage your *real* memory! You would save even more time! Maybe in the next release.)

In Java terms, KISS could also be interpreted to mean "Keep It *Safe*, Stupid" because, in addition to focusing on ease of use, Java focuses on security. An Internet language must be secure; it is not considered polite for code downloaded to client workstations to have the potential for obliterating the data maintained on those trusting, friendly little computers.

Java's extensive built-in security is designed to prevent problems that might arise from both malicious intent and poor programming. The most fundamental of these possibilities is the decision to not define pointers in the language. While this might be seen as a programmer plus (pointer programming, after all, is a battle-won skill), it also stands as a major sand trap for malevolent hackers. Many malicious programs are written by accessing memory that the program is not supposed to utilize, which is done by clever manipulation of pointers. We could tell you more about this but then, of course, we would be creating a potential security problem ourselves. Suffice it to say, "see no pointer, do no evil." (By the way, on the iSeries, pointers are not nearly as dangerous as on other systems because each one encapsulates significant security information. That's why they are 16 bytes long on OS/400, versus 4 bytes on a typical 32-bit operating system.)

THE INTERNET, HTML, AND JAVA APPLETS

Java's initial role in life was that of a Web browser language. In this form, it is used to author applets that run inside Web browsers. Applets resemble traditional applications, except that they are embedded inside HTML and share the Web browser's user-interface real estate.

HTML is a tag-based language that resembles the way UIM (User Interface Manager) is used to author online help pages or menus on OS/400. A tag has both a starting form and an ending form, and the text for that particular tag goes between them. For UIM, the tags are special symbols that start with a colon (:). Typically, the ending tag is the same as the starting tag, but with an *e* prefix. For example, in UIM, you start a list with :ul (for "unordered list") and end it with :eul (for "end unordered list"). In HTML, the principle is similar, but the syntax is slightly different. Rather than denoting a tag with a colon, HTML encloses it in angle brackets. And rather than ending a tag with an *e*, it ends a tag with a slash (/). For example, an unordered list is started in HTML by <ul> and ended with </ul>.

HTML includes many tags for partitioning and formatting text. For example, you can use tags for creating headings, paragraphs, and lists, as well as for formatting text. An example of HTML is shown in Listing 1.1. Figure 1.4 shows how this HTML appears in Netscape's browser.

Listing 1.1: An Example of HTML Code

```
<html>
<head>
<title>My First Web Page</title>
</head>
<body>
<h1>This is a header</h1>
<hr>
<p>
This is a paragraph. Well, you see how simple it is! The following is
an ordered list...
</p>
<ol>
<li>Type in the starting tag inside angle brackets
<li>Type in the body between the tags
<li>Type in the ending tag with a slash in front
</ol>
</body>
</html>
```

HTML tags are not case-sensitive. Some tags, like <hr> (horizontal rule) do not have an ending tag. Others, like <li> (list item), have an optional ending tag; the end is implied by the existence of the next tag.

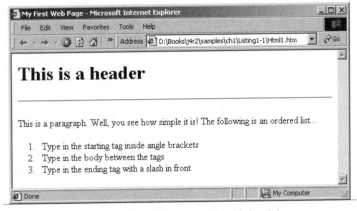

Figure 1.4: The result of the HTML example in Listing 1.1

HTML is not compiled. You simply create the source with a text editor, save the file with the filename extension `.htm` or `.html`, and then open the file directly with your Web browser. The Web browser interprets the HTML commands on the fly and displays the contents according to the instructions provided by the tags.

HTML provides plenty of tags to spice up your Web pages, including some for formatting fonts and graphics, and even some for audio. One all-important tag is used to link text or an image with an element elsewhere on the same page or on another Web page. The text or image that represents the link is highlighted in several ways, depending on how the user has configured the browser. Most often, a textual link is displayed in the browser window underlined and in a different color than the rest of the text. An image that functions as a link is usually surrounded by a black border. When you pass your cursor over the link, the cursor turns into a little hand. Clicking the mouse while over the link takes you to the referenced Web page. That is, the content of the Web browser's window changes to display the referenced page or graphic. Clicking on the left arrow in the toolbar of the browser returns you to the originating page. The ability to jump quickly from one location to another is what puts the *hyper* in *hypertext*, enabling you to author a complex web of pages that are easily traversed by the end user. An example of HTML code for a hyperlink is shown in Listing 1.2, with the result in Figure 1.5.

Listing 1.2: An Example of the HTML Anchor Tag for Creating Hyperlinks

```
<html>
<head>
<title>
My Second Web Page
</title>
</head>
<body>
<p>
To see my first web page, click
<a href="html1.htm">here</a>
</p>
</body>
</html>
```

Authoring traditional, static Web pages, then, is quite simple. You only need an editor, an HTML reference manual, and a Web browser. All of these are available for free on the Internet today. Of course, the example shown presents a link to a local file on your hard disk; you have not actually made a link to a location on the Internet. To do that, you need to connect your computer to the Internet. This is often done by paying a monthly access fee to an *Internet Service Provider* (*ISP*).

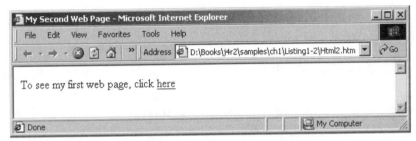

Figure 1.5: The Web page produced with the HTML anchor tag

Along with giving you access to the Internet, it's common for ISPs to allocate space where you can install your HTML source files on their servers. You then use their servers' *HTTP (HyperText Transport Protocol)* software to make your HTML files accessible from the Internet. HTTP servers serve up Web pages to Web browsers, so they are often referred to as *Web servers*. Alternatively, you can get a leased line to enable your own Web server to the Internet.

The directory on the Web server where your HTML files, graphics files, and other files are stored is assigned a universal, unique *URL (Uniform Resource Locator)* address. This URL enables your Web pages to be found by Internet surfers. They can display your page either by typing in its URL in their Web browser window, or by following a hypertext link. The important thing to remember about these links is that they can refer to any HTML file anywhere in the world, as long as that file's URL is known.

A URL address consists of several parts:

- The protocol or prefix section of the URL denotes the part of the Internet on which the file resides. Web pages use the HTTP protocol, which corresponds to the prefix `http://`, whereas `file:///` is used to identify local files.

- The protocol is followed by the domain name for the HTTP server, such as *www.ibm.com*.

- The domain name is followed by the pathname. This includes a series of file directories, separated by slashes, and ends in the actual filename of the Web page, graphic image, or other object to be displayed by the browser.

URLs can refer to many types of resources accessible through the Internet, in addition to HTTP files and local files. The Web browser knows what type of file to expect based on the protocol in the first part of the URL name. Also, Web servers can be configured to map URLs entered by a user to entirely different physical files on disk.

Here's an example of a typical URL:

```
http://www.ibm.com/software/ad/vajava.html
```

This identifies the Internet file `vajava.html`, in directory `software/ad`, at HTTP server domain *www.ibm.com*—the IBM home page. How did IBM get its domain name *www.ibm.com*? It applied for it, from a regulating body that hands out unique names.

The infrastructure and underpinnings of the Internet are beyond the scope of this book. For more information, consult any number of books published on the subject, or start with the OS/400 manual, *OS/400 TCP/IP Configuration and Reference* (SC41-5420).

HTML as an Internet user-interface language

Choosing a Web browser interface for your applications is a good idea. With such an interface, your internal applications, such as accounts-receivable files, can be served on an *intranet* that only employees of your company can access (or even only certain employees within your company). Your external applications, such as product-ordering forms, can be made available to the Internet world at large.

Such filtering of access between external Internet files and internal intranet files can be accomplished with a security device called an Internet *firewall*. A firewall is software or hardware that restricts access to a Web site to Web surfers with a particular computer IP address or within a particular block of IP addresses, or by means of passwords.

Regardless of whether you choose intranet or Internet deployment for your files, the bulk of your application runs on the server. Typically, only the user interface itself runs on the client. Furthermore, even these client- or Web-browser-hosted pieces are downloaded on demand to the Web browser from your server, by your Web server software. This architecture offers a number of advantages over the traditional client/server option for adding graphical user interfaces to your applications. Specifically, this architecture:

- Supports all clients, not just Windows

- Removes the need to install and maintain your programs on every user's workstation

- Leverages your server's scalability, security, backup infrastructure, and performance

- Expands your application's reach to potentially anyone with a Web browser

But there is a problem; these Web pages are static, which means they only display information to the user; they do not accept input from the user. This is pretty useless for interactive applications. How many AS/400 applications have you seen that are comprised entirely of UIM help panel groups, without display files to interact with the user, and that lack RPG code to process that information?

There *is* a way, using conventional HTML, to define interactive Web pages. It involves special HTML tags for defining *forms*, which allow you to create input-capable fields such as text entry boxes and drop-down lists. Here are the steps by which data on a form is received from a user and processed on the server side:

- The HTML form defines fields that ask the user for some type of input.

- The HTML form contains a Submit button that is associated with a server-side program.

- When the user presses the Submit button, the input is sent to the server-side program.

- The server-side program uses APIs to retrieve and process the input.

- The server-side program uses APIs to create and return a new Web page that is displayed to the user.

The server-side program used to process HTML form input is called *CGI*, or *Common Gateway Interface*. CGI is the standard protocol between the Web browser and the HTTP server for processing forms. CGI was, prior to Java, the only way to allow users to interact with your Web browser pages. It is a mature and pervasive technique for producing interactive browser-based interfaces. If you have ever registered a software purchase via the Internet, for example, chances are a CGI program got your purchase information to the vendor.

Various languages can be used for writing the server-side program, depending on the Web server (that is, the HTTP server) software you are using and the one on the server itself. All offer CGI support, and all of them support RPG as a CGI server programming language. Another alternative is to use a general scripting language called *Perl*. Perl is an interpreted language that works well for writing CGI programs and is available on all major operating systems, including the AS/400. It is quite an arcane language to learn, but it is available everywhere and is always freely downloadable from the Web. Perl comes from the world of shareware—UNIX. To find out more, see *www.perl.com*.

Do you have to learn CGI programming techniques to write interactive Web pages? Not anymore. There is a new option for Web server software, called Java servlets. This part of the Java initiative has been adopted by all major Web servers, including IBM's. To enable servlets, IBM offers WebSphere Application Server, which works with IBM's HTTP server and most other Web servers, including Microsoft's Internet Information Server (IIS). On AS/400, the standard edition of WebSphere Application Server is available as a free offering, at least up to version 3.5.3.

Servlets are just like CGI programs. The HTTP server calls them when the user presses the Submit button, they process input from HTML forms, and they produce new pages to be displayed in a browser. However, they are written in Java and use specific Java-supplied APIs to process input and prepare output. They are loaded into memory once and remain in memory until a preconfigured time. CGI, on the other hand, starts another job for each call to a CGI program. This means servlets offer the programming, security, and stability advantages of Java, are more efficient than calling external CGI programs and, furthermore, easily support state information between client invocations.

Servlets are exploding in popularity, especially among AS/400 programmers who are used to the screen-at-a-time user interface model that HTML offers.

Java as an Internet user-interface language

So how else does Java fit into this picture? Through a new APPLET tag added to the HTML language. This tag refers to a Java program (an applet) to be run by the browser when the tag is encountered while reading the HTML. These programs most often contain user interfaces, although they can as easily be raw logic, such as a tax calculation. If the applet involves a user interface, it has the full power of Java's very rich graphical user interface support. For example, an applet might show a multiple-column scrollable table, something not possible in HTML alone. However, applets usually do not have their own main window. Rather, they use the window of the Web browser. This is what distinguishes a Java application from a Java applet. Because these Java programs do not have their own windows and cannot be started from the command line, they are referred to as applets instead of full-fledged applications. The applet inserts user interface parts such as lists, push buttons, and entry fields into the Web browser's window at the point in the HTML where the APPLET tag is encountered.

The APPLET tag includes parameters for specifying how the HTML text will flow around the applet, and how much of the Web browser window the applet will occupy. There is also syntax for specifying hard-coded parameters to be passed into the Java program. Of course, these applets are not traditional program files at all, but Java .class files containing bytecodes that will be interpreted by the Web browser's built-in Java interpreter.

When the Web browser sees the APPLET tag inside an HTML page, it goes back to the HTTP server where the HTML page originated to find the referenced Java class. Once found and downloaded, the Java class is interpreted, or run, by the Web browser. If you have ever seen a "Java applet started" message when browsing a Web site, you have encountered a Java applet.

While Java applets have the full power of the Java programming language at their disposal, they do have some restrictions regarding access to the local client workstation's resources for security reasons. That is, an applet cannot read or write files on the local file system or call any local executables. It can do communications back to the server it came from, however. These restrictions are known as the *sandbox* that the Java applet must live within, which is a constraint not faced by a full-fledged Java application.

You can even free yourself from these constraints if you know who your users will be. The JDK comes with tools for digitally "signing" your applets so that users can be guaranteed it came from you untampered. If the users trust you, they can allow signed applets from you to access their workstation resources. This works well in intranet environments, where you can predefine who is allowed to distribute signed applets for company-wide use and you can identify which employees are allowed to run them. (The flip side of signing is the ability to preauthorize only selected users to run the applet.)

JAVA APPLICATIONS

Certainly, the prospect of being able to embed Java applets inside HTML Web pages is an enticing one. That is the fuel that has fed Java's wildfire acceptance. However, you can write full-fledged applications with Java, as well. These might be server-side applications that run on the AS/400 and do business logic or data manipulation, or client-side applications that display full-fledged user interfaces, access the AS/400 for data, or call programs on the AS/400. These applications are invoked by running the java interpreter on them. You pass to the interpreter command the name of the Java class file to be interpreted.

Java applications are portable to all Java-enabled operating systems (which means all operating systems). They have the advantage of having their own main window and user-interface real estate. They also do not have the sandbox restrictions of Java applets. However, you have the responsibility of distributing client-side GUI Java applications (versus applets or server-side programs) that communicate with server-side programs, as you would with any client/server application.

For servers such as the AS/400, you can only run Java applications that do not have a GUI. While there is technology for running graphical user interface Java applications on the AS/400 directly (via Remote AWT or JBroker technologies), it is recommended that your server-side Java applications be non-interactive and focus on the business logic. For the user interface, use either raw HTML, HTML with applets, or full-function client/server GUI applications.

This book focuses on the technology for writing Java code that can be used inside applications *or* applets *or* servlets.

JavaScript

On the client side, Java applications and applets are often used in intranet environments where there is a well-defined user population and a high-speed network. For Internet environments or far-flung intranet environments, we have seen a return to raw HTML. This is because HTML has the fewest client requirements (it can run in any Web browser) and is by far the fastest option when slow modem connections have to be supported.

As mentioned earlier, you can use Java servlets running on your Web server to dynamically create HTML Web pages and process the input from them. Since the servlet is running on your server, it has access to your data, applications, and transactions. It can draw on these resources to process the input and build the content of the pages to be displayed. For example, a customer might enter a bank account number in an HTML form, and the servlet will use that to access the account information and generate an HTML page to display that information. This could be done with all-Java business logic or by calling an existing RPG program.

The original downside of HTML as a user interface language was its weak GUI constructs and lack of programmability. Hence, the initial excitement in Java applets, which allows you, for example, to display an entry field that only takes integer numbers as input. With raw HTML, you have to use a form and send the data to the server first, where it is verified. If the user typed something incorrectly, you have to wait for an entire new page to be returned from the server in order to see the error message. A Java applet can catch syntactical errors and display the message immediately, without a round-trip to the server.

Time has moved on for HTML since the early applet days. There is now an industry-standard version of HTML called *Dynamic HTML (DHTML)*. This is a combination of HTML, something new called *Cascading Style Sheets (CSS)*, and a new embedded language called *JavaScript*. Cascading Style Sheets offer much-improved visual control over your Web page, and allow you to set corporate look-and-feel standards across your entire Web site. JavaScript offers an alternative to Java applets for writing code to run directly in the Web browser. It looks like a subset of the Java language, but is quite different. It is embedded via `<script>` tags directly into the HTML and is interpreted directly by the Web browser. It is not compiled into bytecodes like Java applets. Because it does not require another trip to the server, it tends to be much more efficient than Java applets.

JavaScript works with a *Document Object Model (DOM)*. This is an exposure of the entire Web page contents in a programmatic API that JavaScript code can access. JavaScript can be used to author functions, which are then assigned to specific events in your Web page, such as a user pressing a button. The JavaScript function can then use the DOM APIs to query and set the contents and state of the Web page, such as entry field contents. Thus, simple syntax error-checking and error-message displaying is easily done directly in the Web browser, without the need for Java applets. However, JavaScript has no communications or graphical user interface capability, so sometimes it is augmented with a few Java applets to improve the user interface or to communicate with a server.

DHTML, CSS, and JavaScript are beyond the scope of this book, but there are many great books available on these subjects. Also, they are an evolving industry standard being defined by the W3 consortium that oversees Web standards. You can read about them at *http://www.w3.org*.

JavaServer Pages

DHTML pages are usually created on the fly and served up by a Java servlet running on the server. One way to do this is to simply embed "write" statements in your servlet Java code to write out each line of HTML output as you build it. The problem with this approach, though, is that it mixes the Java business logic with the HTML user interface. It makes it impossible to use what-you-see-is-what-you-get (WYSIWYG) tools on the

HTML. It also makes it hard to reuse the business logic (which is the same problem we have today with monolithic RPG programs).

JavaServer Pages, or *JSPs*, are the answer to these problems. These are HTML or DHTML source files that have actual Java code embedded in them. Typically, a Web page has much static content; only a small amount of information in the page needs to be generated dynamically. JSPs allow you to put the static part of a page in a separate file, and leave "holes" that are filled at runtime by data supplied by a servlet. This is just like using a display file and leaving holes in the form of named fields or reference fields, which your RPG program fills in at runtime. With JSPs, these holes are in the form of Java logic that pulls data from fields in a JavaBean, which is created and passed to the JSP by the servlet.

When an HTTP server first calls a `.jsp` file, it compiles it to a Java servlet that writes out the static HTML source. The embedded Java code becomes servlet code. Typically, a hand-authored servlet gets control from an HTML form, processes the request by collecting the data needed for the output page, and then calls a JSP to display the output, passing a JavaBean containing the substitution data. There is an API supplied by Java to make the call to the JSP. The JSP contains all the static HTML, plus embedded Java code to extract the data from the JavaBean and insert it into the static HTML, forming the final page that is sent to the user. The important thing to note is that the embedded Java code in the JSP is preprocessed on the server side by the HTTP server, while any embedded JavaScript tags are sent to the client and processed there by the Web browser. This gives the ultimate in flexibility, permitting very dynamic content and behavior.

The advantage of JavaServer Pages over simply writing out the HTML from a servlet is that it allows separation of the user interface source (the HTML) from the business logic source (the servlet). This means one skill can be used to author the HTML and another skill can be used to author the business logic needed to get the data to be displayed in the Web page. Often, the former requires more artistic skills, while the latter requires more programming skills.

ENTERPRISE JAVABEANS

Server-side JavaBeans are "growing up," too. They are evolving into *Enterprise JavaBeans* (*EJBs*), which support such enterprise-scale ideas as transactions, persistence (storing their variable data in a database), and Internet lookup by name (naming and directory service). EJBs are arguably the future of server-side Java. Their goal is to provide a standard environment across all operating systems and to enable enterprise-scale JavaBeans to be built or bought and easily incorporated into any application. That is, they are intended to be the component model for line-of-business applications. To this end, all EJBs are stored in a standard server or shell, which hosts them and supplies all the ugly "plumbing" that big applications need. EJB authors focus on business logic, not plumbing.

EJBs and their shell is a standard from Sun Microsystems with tremendous input from many companies, including IBM. Many vendors supply standard-conformant shells, and the holy grail is that any EJB can be deployed in any vendor's shell. The current reality is that this is a very young technology and continues to mature. However, EJBs hold tremendous promise.

Java versus RPG

Obviously, we are strong supporters of Java. Although RPG is certainly a great language, we are here to sell you on Java and teach you Java. To that end, consider some of the areas in which Java has the advantage over RPG:

- Portability
- Syntax (arguably)
- String support (arguably)
- Date and time support
- Internationalization support
- Data structures such as arrays, vectors, hashtables, and collections
- GUI support
- Object-orientation support
- Thread support
- Communications support

To be fair, there are also areas where RPG has the advantage over Java:

- Learning curve
- Performance, especially database throughput
- Database access support
- Access to other languages
- Printing or report writing

As you read the book, you will make your own decisions, but remember that it does not have to be an either-or discussion. All languages have their strengths and weaknesses, and clearly there is a lot of room for multiple languages in applications. With Java, you have one more option.

SUMMARY

Here is a summary of the topics covered in this chapter:

- Beyond all the hype Java is, after all, a programming language.
- Java is an interpreted language (although traditional compilers for Java now exist).
- Java is free and shipped as the Java Development Kit (JDK).
- Java source code is compiled via javac into Java bytecode.
- Java applications are invoked via the java command.
- Java applets require the HTML APPLET tag.
- Java servlets are invoked by the HTTP Server software to return a Web page.
- JavaServer Pages are HTML files with embedded Java code, preprocessed on the server.
- JavaScript is embedded directly into HTML and interpreted by the Web browser.
- Enterprise JavaBeans are an evolving industry standard for large-scale server-side components.
- HTML, DHTML, applets, servlets, JavaServer Pages, and Enterprise JavaBeans are interesting, exciting, fun and popular. They are all in your future!
- IBM's strategic product offering to enable these is called WebSphere Application Server. This product is available on many platforms, including OS/400, OS/390, Windows, UNIX, and Linux.
- The tooling for WebSphere Application Server can be anybody's, but IBM's is WebSphere Studio, which includes HTML and JSP editors, and VisualAge for Java, for development of Java servlets, applets, applications, beans, and Enterprise JavaBeans. (As of this writing, these classic tools are about to be merged into a single set of offerings on a completely new technology base. These are very exciting times for tooling!)
- Both RPG and Java are great languages, and each has its own strengths and weaknesses.

We encourage you to explore all these topics, perhaps by starting at the one-stop-shopping Web site *www.ibm.com/java*. However, further exploration requires that you know the basics of the Java programming language, which is the focus of this book. We will put you well on your way to absorbing these new topics and many more in the rapidly expanding world of Java.

References

The following Web sites provide more information on the concepts discussed in this chapter:

- W3 Consortium home page: *www.w3.org*
- HTML online reference: *www.w3.org/TR/REC-html40/*
- InterNIC home page: *www.internic.net*
- Perl home page: *www.perl.com*
- JavaSoft Web page for Windows JDK (look for JSDK): *www.java.sun.com/products*
- Java for OS/400 Web page: *www.ibm.com/iseries/java*
- IBM WebServer Web page: *www.ibm.com/webservers*
- IBM WebSphere Web page: *www.ibm.com/websphere*
- Overall IBM Java Web page: *www.ibm.com/java*

THE JAVA ONION

RPG programmers who have already made the journey to Java report that the transition to Java is made far easier if you have a footing in RPG IV, rather than RPG III. This is because new constructs exist in RPG IV and its ILE (*Integrated Language Environment*) definition that are more modern and a closer match to Java and its environment than RPG III. Many of the new concepts you need to learn in Java, such as modularity, free-format expressions, methods, and method calling, are easier learned first through their counterparts in RPG IV.

You should also be continuing your code migration to ILE RPG IV from RPG III, even if you are eventually destined for Java. Moving from RPG III to IV will give you short-term quality, maintainability, functionality, and performance benefits. Such a progression will position your code base to make selective replacements with new Java code, and give you more options for intermingling RPG and Java. You will have a far better base than if you have a monolithic RPG III application model.

For these reasons, we have chosen to teach you Java by comparing it to RPG IV. However, we realize you might not have made the transition to this greatly improved version of the language yet, so the beginning of this chapter reviews the overall concepts of ILE and RPG IV. These are the "outer shell" concepts, not the internal language definition details. As we go deeper into the Java language, we will continually contrast it to appropriate details in RPG IV, and where there are new functions in the RPG language, we will briefly review them before diving into their Java counterparts. In this way, this book will make you more comfortable not only with Java, but also with RPG IV. You end up with two very important skill sets, so start thinking about that salary increase now! If you are familiar with RPG IV and ILE, you can safely skip these RPG reviews, of course. And presumably you have already received half of your deserved salary increase!

This is an extensive chapter that covers a good deal of ground, but when you are done, you will be well on your way to being familiar with the architecture and interfaces of Java applications, and of RPG IV as well. (Note that the terms *RPG IV*, *ILE RPG*, and *ILE RPG IV* terms are used interchangeably here.)

RPG IV VERSUS RPG III APPLICATIONS

In a typical, traditional RPG III application, you might have a CL program that gets initial control and then calls the appropriate RPG program or programs. The RPG program, of course, is huge. It contains mainline code and includes dozens, if not hundreds, of subroutines. For large applications, there may be dozens or even hundreds of these RPG programs, but due to the overhead of calling them, each does a significant amount of work when called, usually driving an entire piece of the application. The CL program might put up a main menu and process the selected option by calling the appropriate RPG program. It also, of course, performs file overriding and library list manipulation. The application is "scoped" to the job, so that common resources, such as open data paths and file overrides, are available and applicable to all the programs in the job.

Now, contrast this with what a typical ILE RPG application might look like. First, ILE redefines the compilation unit: rather than compiling a source member directly into a program object (*PGM), in ILE you compile a source member into an intermediate module object (*MODULE) using the CRTRPGMOD command. These modules are not shipped with your application, and you cannot call them from the command line as you call a program. Rather, they are designed to be subsequently "bound together" into a program object using the CRTPGM command.

There is also a CRTBNDRPG (*Create Bound RPG*) command for creating single-module program objects in one step, but you should only use this as a short-term solution as you convert to RPG IV. The power of ILE is that modules compiled from different languages, such as ILE CL and ILE RPG (or ILE C, ILE C++, or ILE COBOL), can be bound together to form a single program object. This program object is no different than what you are used to—you call it from the command line or via a command (*CMD) object. The question is, which module gets control from the command line? The answer is that by default, control is given to the first one specified on the CRTPGM command that created it. (You'll learn more about this later.)

Why, in RPG III, did we write such large programs? Performance, of course. It is simply too expensive to make calls between programs using the external CALL op-code. The downside to using these large programs includes the following disadvantages:

- *Maintenance.* You are new to the job, and you have been given the assignment of fixing a bug in someone else's code. (Why do "other" programmers always write terrible code? For the same reason that the driver in front of you is always too slow and the one behind you always too fast.) Your supervisor says, "Here are their 20,000 lines of source code. Go for it!"

- *Collaboration.* Suppose there are 12 of you working on a hot new project, but there is only one source member. You'll have to wait your turn to edit it.

ILE set out to improve the development and application model. It strikes at the very heart of why we write large, monolithic programs—the performance of inter-program calls. It allows us to write smaller pieces of code that get compiled into intermediate modules, which then are glued or bound together to form the final program object. These modules can call each other without the performance penalty commonly encountered with program calls. Here is how ILE solves the problems just mentioned:

- *Maintenance.* You are new, but you are good! You found the bug in that other programmer's code because you only had to look at 2,000 lines of code, not 20,000. And you did it before lunch. Take the rest of the day off.

- *Collaboration.* Each of the 12 programmers gets his or her own source member to work on. Their work is combined later by binding the 12 modules into one program object. (Of course, these programmers need to talk once in a while to know what the other is doing!)

You are probably wondering how all of these modules "call" each other. You can simply call the module by name, in which case the mainline C-specs of that module will get control. This is very much like calling another program, but faster, since the address of that module will have been determined and recorded when the modules were bound together with CRTPGM. However, you can also call directly into a specific *procedure* in another module. Procedures resemble subroutines, but unlike subroutines, they can be directly called by code in another module, as shown in Figure 2.1.

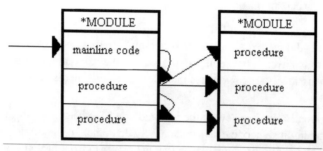

Figure 2.1: ILE modules

Procedures are "grown up" subroutines that allow multiple entry points into a module, as opposed to only a single mainline entry point. They also offer numerous other advantages over subroutines, such as local fields. (Finally, RPG has local fields!)

Once you have all your modules with their associated procedures, you bind the modules together to form a single program. If you want to facilitate reuse of your procedures by more than one program object, you can either bind the same module into multiple program objects or, preferably, put them into a *service program* instead. Service program objects (*SRVPGM) are new entities in ILE. Unlike programs, they cannot be called from the command line. Rather, they are intended to be called programmatically by code inside one or more program objects. Once again, it is the procedures inside the service programs that are called. (Note that like programs, service programs can consist of one or more modules.)

An important aspect of having these modules inside programs and service programs is that, if you change the source code for one module, you can recompile that module and selectively replace or update it inside the program or service program, using the UPDPGM and UPDSRVPGM commands. This avoids the need to recompile all of the source code that comprises the program or service program. Indeed, for service program updates, often you do not even need to re-link all the programs and service programs that use it. They get the benefit of the change without requiring a re-build or re-ship.

You can take commonly needed subroutines, turn them into procedures, and package them into a single service program object that all program objects can link to. The link is done by specifying the service program(s) on the BNDSRVPGM parameter of the CRTPGM command. Compare this to the old tricks of copy-and-paste or /COPY that lead to maintenance problems and bloated programs.

The inter-module procedure calls within the program and service programs are done using a new CALLP op-code, which provides better performance than a full external program call using CALL. This is because at bind time (CRTPGM or CRTSRVPGM) all calls between modules or service programs are resolved to actual addresses. The overhead to resolve addresses is done once at build time, rather than every time when running the application.

In traditional workstation or PC languages like C or C++, the concepts of ILE programs and service programs correspond to executables (.exe) and dynamic link libraries (.dll). The concept of modules corresponds to object (.obj) files. (All of these new ILE constructs will be described in greater detail later, as we compare them directly to their counterparts in Java.)

Finally, in your new ILE application, you have an *activation group* inside a job. These are also new constructs for ILE. You can have more than one activation group per job, and all of your application's resources can be scoped to one activation group, as opposed to the entire job. Resources in one activation group do not get shared with another activation group. This allows for more fine-grained control over important aspects, such as file overrides and open data paths. Activation groups can be named so that they persist for the life of the job; they can also be defined so that they are created and destroyed with the life of the program.

For performance reasons, it is very important to use named activation groups, which is *not* the default. You define this on the ACTGRP parameter of the CRTPGM or CRTSRVPGM commands. Activation groups are very important to understanding and mastering ILE, and all ILE books and manuals discuss them. However, they have no relevance to learning Java, so we defer detailed discussion of activation groups to these other ILE books.

THE OUTER SKIN: RPG VERSUS JAVA

The sections that follow "peel the onion," looking at RPG IV and Java from the outside in. (No crying, now!)

RPG's outer skin

In ILE RPG IV, your applications have one or more programs linked to zero or more service programs, as in Figure 2.2. Each *PGM and *SRVPGM object is comprised of one or more modules.

Java's outer skin

In Java, your application is comprised simply of a number of class files (.class). Class files contain Java bytecode, and are compiled from Java source. Recall that bytecode is not machine code that a traditional compiler produces, but simply a more efficient way to represent your source.

You will have a primary .class file that gets invoked from the command line, and many additional class files that are used by this first class file, as shown in Figure 2.3.

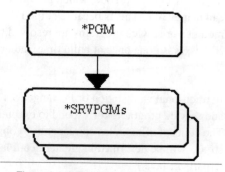

Figure 2.2: ILE service programs

Compiling RPG

In RPG IV, source members are compiled into modules (the compilation unit) using CRTRPGMOD (*Create RPG Module*). Modules are bound together using CRTPGM (*Create Program*) or CRTSRVPGM (*Create Service Program*) commands, specifying the modules on the MODULE parameter. If you use other service programs, you specify them during the bind step, on the BNDSRVPGM parameter.

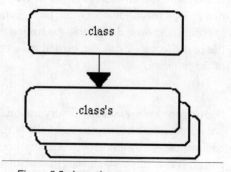

Figure 2.3: Java classes

When you link in service programs during the bind step, you are not gluing them onto your object like you do when binding modules together. Rather, you are simply recording the name and address of the service program. You still get fast calls to the procedures in the service program, but your object size does not grow. Further, if two programs use the same service program at runtime, only one copy of the service program will be resident in memory.

Compiling Java

You compile Java source code (.java) into bytecode (.class) using the javac compiler. There is no bind step equivalent to ILE's CRTPGM that benefits runtime performance, but compile-time checks are made on the referenced classes to ensure that they do indeed exist and have the referenced entry points.

In Java, there are no programs or service programs, only classes. Classes are much like ILE modules, which instead of being further processed into an executable object, are simply loaded into memory and interpreted at runtime. This is a consistent analogy to the Java compiler (javac) as only the first half of a traditional compiler. Where RPG and other traditional compilers will continue past that intermediate representation to produce machine code, Java stops at the intermediate phase, so that the result is still operating-system independent.

At runtime, when a Java class file being interpreted refers to, or "calls," another class file, that class file is searched for and found. There is no linking step at development time to perform this. This dynamic loading of referenced code might seem like a throwback to pre-ILE, and indeed, it does have performance implications. However, dynamic loading has significant productivity and maintenance advantages, and Java chooses to focus on these attributes. When you start to work with Java, you will also notice the performance overhead of finding all referenced classes at the startup time of the application. All referenced classes are found and loaded into memory up front when the first class is called from the command line. This makes startup slower, but makes the subsequent running of the application faster.

An important note about AS/400 Java is that you typically do not compile with javac. You certainly can, but this step will usually be performed on your workstation, such as on Windows using either the Sun JDK or VisualAge for Java. The resulting .class file will then be copied or transferred to the AS/400 IFS (Integrated File System), where it will reside. Thus, you do not use SEU (Source Entry Utility) to create and edit your Java source, but rather workstation-based tools.

About RPG IV procedures

Figure 2.4 shows at a high level what an RPG IV module might look like. As you can see, modules contain global fields and often one or more procedures.

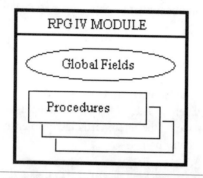

Figure 2.4: Inside an ILE RPG module

Procedures are a very important addition to the RPG language, and were introduced in V3R2. Essentially, they are beefed up subroutines. However, when compared to a subroutine, a procedure offers the following significant advantages:

- *Parameter passing.* You can pass parameters to the procedure, thus reducing reliance on global fields.

- *Local fields.* You can declare fields with the new definition specification right inside the procedure.

- *Return values.* You can return a value from a procedure. Thus, in effect, you can create your own built-in functions.

- *Recursion.* Within a procedure, you can call that same procedure again, recursively.

- *Exporting.* You can export procedures, allowing code in other modules to be able to call the procedure directly as a bound call. This allows your modules to have "multiple entry points" from the outside, which is important for service programs, for example.

- *Prototyping.* With a procedure, you first declare its *prototype,* which is its name, parameters, and return value. These prototypes are often defined in /COPY members so that callers of the procedure in other source members can include the member to aid the compiler. It will use these to verify that the number and type of parameters passed on calls to the procedure are correct, rather than waiting for a runtime error.

RPG procedures and ILE go hand-in-hand. What happened to subroutines, you might ask? Nothing! They still exist, and you are still welcome to use them. With the advantages of procedures, however, you will find using subroutines a step backward. In general, using subroutines is a *sub*-standard practice, even though it is still *routine*.

Figure 2.5 shows what a typical procedure looks like. (The terms *variable* and *field* are used interchangeably in the book, as you see in the figure.)

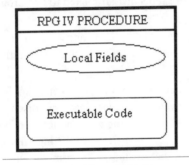

Figure 2.5: Inside an RPG IV procedure

RPG IV flow of control

You call an RPG IV program from the command line by using the CALL command and passing the parameters:

```
CALL PROGRAM1(100 200);
```

This passes control to your program. Specifically, it passes control to the *entry* module that you specified on the ENTMOD (Program Entry Procedure Module) parameter of the CRTPGM (*Create Program*) command. The ENTMOD parameter defaults to the first module specified in the MODULE parameter list, or more precisely, to the first module that does not have NOMAIN specified on the H-spec. (The NOMAIN keyword is used to create modules that have only procedures and no mainline code.) The entry module gets control from the command line in its initial calculation specifications (C-specs). These initial C-specs are referred to as the *main procedure* in the *ILE RPG/400 Programmer's Guide*. This is a bit of a misnomer, in that there is no formal procedure declaration for them. We simply refer to it as the mainline code. Further, we only use the term *procedure* for user-defined procedures, not *sub-procedure* as the manual describes them.

From the mainline code, control is passed to subroutines in the same module or to procedures in one of the following:

- The same module

- Another module in the same program object

- Modules in service programs that are linked to this program

Procedures are called using the CALLP op-code or as part of an expression in an EVAL statement. The latter is used when you are interested in the returned value.

You see that procedures can become the primary mechanism for control flow within an application. The reality, however, is that many have not discovered the joys of procedures yet, and in that case they are simply calling each module directly. When you call a module directly from another module, you are calling the mainline code of that module (or officially, the main procedure of that module). The compiler creates this main procedure for you, with the same name as the module, unless you specify the NOMAIN keyword on the H-spec. If you do so, then you can only call the exported procedures in this module. Further, you cannot call such a module from the command line.

About Java methods

We pay so much attention to RPG IV's procedures not only because they are so great, but also because they are a direct match to Java's *methods*. Methods in Java are equivalent to subroutines and procedures in RPG. They contain executable code that is callable by others. Like procedures, they have local variables (you don't call them fields in Java), they take parameters, they return values, they can be called recursively, and they can be called by code outside of the class file they are in. Further, since Java does not have mainline code like RPG does, they are indeed the only place you write executable code in Java.

Figure 2.6 shows at a high level what the inside of a Java method looks like. Unlike RPG procedures, the variables inside a Java method can be declared anywhere, as long as it is prior to their use. Given our RPG background, we prefer they all go at the top of the method. You will see the syntax of methods soon.

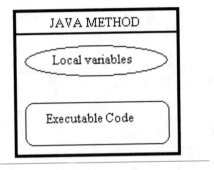

Figure 2.6: Inside a Java method

Java's flow of control

You call a compiled Java source file from the command line by using the `java` command and passing the parameters:

```
java MyClass 100 200
```

This passes control to your class file. Specifically, it passes control to the `main` method in your class file. You are required to code a method named `main` if you want to call your class file from the command line like this. We'll dissect this important method later in this chapter.

Notice the use of a PC-style call, versus an AS/400-style `CALL` command. A PC-style call is used even on the AS/400, where you have to run Java code not from the usual CL command, but from the QShell environment, which is similar to an MS-DOS prompt on Windows. However, there is also a CL `JAVA` command, if you prefer. (Using Java on the AS/400 is covered in Appendix A.)

Java class files are compiled from Java source files. What is in a class file? Methods, as you know. But these are actually inside a class, which is a Java language construct with explicit syntax that you will soon see.

Control flows from one class to another by means of method calls. The initial `main` method might call other methods in this same class, or methods in another class. Since Java has no mainline code, it is not possible to call a class directly, just a method in a class. This is different than RPG, where you can call a module directly, as long as it is not coded with the NOMAIN keyword.

Figure 2.7 shows what a class named Class1 looks like, at a high level, inside a compiled .class file. The variables declared inside the class, above the methods, are available to the code in all the methods. The variables declared inside the methods themselves are local to that method.

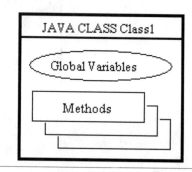

The variables inside a class can be defined before or after the methods. We prefer before, so programmers understand the context when they see the variables in use later. It is simply a style choice, though, and is entirely up to you.

Figure 2.7: Inside a Java class file

COMPARING ANATOMIES

Java classes contain *global* variables that all methods can access. They also contain *local* variables inside each method, which only that method can access. The same applies to RPG modules; they can contain global fields at the top, defined with the new definition specification (discussed in Chapter 5) and local fields inside each procedure. Table 2.1 provides an initial comparison of RPG constructs to Java constructs.

RPG	Java	Comments
*PGM	Application	Program object = Application
*MODULE	Class	Module object = Class file
Fields	Variables	Global fields or variables
Procedures	Methods	Functions
Fields	Variables	Local fields or variables
Code	Code	Executable code

Table 2.1: Comparing RPG Constructs to Java Constructs

This mapping will evolve, and it is not perfect. However, it should help you get your bearings in this new world of Java.

RPG syntax

Before delving into a comparison of Java and RPG syntax, it is important to review RPG IV's syntax at a high level, for the benefit of RPG III readers. Although we don't go into great detail here, many subsequent examples will make it all clear.

RPG IV source members are now 100 characters wide versus 80, giving more room in each area. (Comments are entered from column 80 on.) You can code blank lines wherever you wish. Further, you can enter the text in all-uppercase, all-lowercase, or mixed case, although the compiler folds it all to uppercase.

An RPG IV program consists of specifications, which must be in the correct order. The specifications are Control (H), File (F), Definition (D), Input (I), Calculation (C), and Output (O), as well as Procedure (P) specifications. The E and L specifications are gone, and there is a new D-spec. Further, the H-spec is now completely keyword driven, and you can specify keywords on the F-spec, eliminating the need for F-spec continuation lines (although keywords can continue on the subsequent line). The new D-spec is for explicitly defining fields up-front. The C-spec has been widened, and there are even a number of new op-codes that allow a very wide factor-two area and no result area. These op-codes, like the new EVAL op-code for field assignments, use free-format expressions in factor-two, which can be easily continued on subsequent C-specs without continuation characters.

There are also an exploding number of built-in functions of the form `%xxx(parameter1:parameter2)`, which you can call from inside any free-format expression. Their return values are substituted right into the expression, as in:

```
12345 *8901234567890123456789012345678901234567890123456789012345678901
      D*Name+++++++++++Ds++++++++++Len+IDc.Keywords++++++++++++
      D aField          S              9P 2 INZ(0)
      D aFieldLen       S              5P 0
      C*    Factor1+++++++Opcode(E)+Extended-Factor2++++++++++
      C                   EVAL      aFieldLen = %LEN(aField)
```

Here, two "standalone" (S in column 24) fields are declared: aField, which is packed-decimal 9,2 and aFieldLen, which is packed decimal 5,0. The former is initialized to zero using the INZ keyword. Then, we have a C-spec that uses the new EVAL op-code to assign the length of aField to the field aFieldLen, using the built-in function %LEN. Note you can also code built-in functions as parameters to the INZ keyword.

One really big enhancement to the language in V5R1 is the ability to code completely free-format calculation specifications, using the new /FREE and /END-FREE compiler directives to delimit the free-format lines of source. The details of this aren't covered here, but it is an exciting addition to the language, and you will find it makes your RPG and Java code look more similar than ever.

As well as the specifications already mentioned, there are, optionally, procedures made up of a beginning and ending Procedure (P) specification, within which are D-specs and C-specs.

The following sections show you how to define and prototype procedures in RPG. We teach this for two reasons: procedures are a very powerful and under-used tool in RPG, and learning them will help you learn methods in Java.

Prototyping RPG procedures

To use a procedure in RPG, you must prototype it first. This involves the use of the new D-spec with the PR definition-type. A prototype is essentially a pre-declaration of a procedure's name, return value (if any), and parameters (if any). This prototyping is done in your source prior to the definition of the procedure, and must be placed in the D-spec area at the top of the file. Most commonly, it is in a copy member that all users of the procedure copy into their source, using /COPY. Here is an example of a prototype for a procedure Swap that returns nothing and takes in two parameters, each length 5, internal type integer (new RPG IV type), and zero decimals:

```
D*   1          2          3          4          5          6
D*8901234567890123456789012345678901234567890123456789012345678901234567890
D*Name++++++++++++PR++++++++++Len+IDc.Keywords+++++++++
DSwap             PR
D parm1                            5I 0
D parm2                            5I 0
```

Here is another example of a prototype of a procedure Max that returns a value (packed-decimal 7,2), and which takes in two parameters (also packed-decimal 7,2). Because these parameters are not changed in the procedure, the keyword VALUE is coded to indicate they are pass-by-value:

```
D*   1         2         3         4         5         6
D*8901234567890123456789012345678901234567890123456789 0
D*Name+++++++++++++PR++++++++++Len+IDc.Keywords+++++++++
DMax              PR            7P 2
D parm1                         7P 2 VALUE
D parm2                         7P 2 VALUE
```

The name of the procedure is defined on the PR D-spec, as is the return type information (if any) in positions 36 through 42. You can specify keywords in positions 44 through 80 that apply to callers of the procedure, such as EXTPROC('name') for giving a different name for external callers. You can also specify keywords that apply to the returned type, such as DIM if it is an array. Note there is no name associated with a return value.

The parameter definitions follow. The compiler takes as parameter definitions all subsequent D-specs with blanks in positions 24 and 25 (where PR stands for *prototype*). The parameter variable names are optional, and need not be the same as those specified in the actual procedure definition. All names can float anywhere between positions 7 and 21. One or more keywords can be specified for each parameter, such as VALUE to pass a copy of the field or CONST to pass a read only reference, or OPTIONS(*NOPASS) if it is an optional parameter. (All subsequent parameters must also specify this keyword.)

The purpose of the prototype is to allow the compiler to verify, for each procedure call, that you have specified the correct number of parameters and the correct type, and are assigning the returned value to a field that has an appropriate type.

Defining RPG procedures

Having prototyped an RPG procedure with its parameters and return type, the next step is to actually define the procedure. RPG procedure definitions start with a new specification type—the P (Procedure) spec. A begin-procedure specification and an end-procedure specification are located at the beginning and end of the procedure. These are indicated by a B and an E in position 24 of the P-spec, respectively. In columns 7 to 21, you place the name of the procedure (leading blanks are okay), which must exactly match the name specified on the prototype:

```
P*   1         2         3         4         5         6
P*8901234567890123456789012345678901234567890123456789 0
P*Name+++++++++++++B+++++++++++++++++++++++Keywords+++++++++
PSwap            B              EXPORT
  * ...
PSwap            E
```

41

On the begin-procedure specification, you can specify keywords in positions 44 to 80. At this time, the only valid keyword for a procedure is EXPORT, meaning this procedure is to be accessible by code inside other modules. You'll probably use this one a lot!

Next, you simply copy all the prototype D-specifications to be after the first P-spec. However, you must change the PR on the first one to PI for *procedure interface.* It is always a complete duplication; that is, you once again define the D-spec, which identifies the return type information (and uses the procedure name again), and follow that with the D-spec for each parameter. You also repeat any keywords:

```
P*Name+++++++++++++B++++++++++++++++++++Keywords+++++++++
PSwap              B
D*Name+++++++++++++PI++++++++++Len+IDc.Keywords+++++++++
DSwap              PI
D parm1                             5I 0
D parm2                             5I 0
   *  ...
PSwap              E
```

Having defined the return value and parameters (if any) with the procedure-interface specs, you define any needed local variables with D-specs and an S (for *standalone*) or DS (for *data structures*) in positions 24 and 25. Then, the logic follows in the C-specs and finally in the RETURN statement. You *cannot* define any other specs, such as an F-spec, locally in a procedure; these are defined only at the top of the module.

Listing 2.1 shows the two procedures. (Including comment prologs; aren't we good?)

Listing 2.1: RPG IV Procedure Examples

```
P* _____
P* Definition for Swap procedure
P*  Function.: swap the values inside two integer fields
P*  Returns..: nothing
P*  Parameter: parm1 => 5 digit integer field
P*  Parameter: parm2 => 5 digit integer field
P*_____
PSwap              B                   EXPORT
DSwap              PI
D parm1                             5I 0
D parm2                             5I 0
D*Local fields
D temp              S                 5I 0
C*Local code
C                  EVAL       temp = parm1
C                  EVAL       parm1 = parm2
```

```
C                       EVAL        parm2 = temp
C                       RETURN
PSwap               E

P* ─────────────────────────────────────────────────────
P* Definition for Max procedure
P*  Function.: determine the larger of two packed fields
P*  Returns..: nothing
P*  Parameter: parm1 => 7,2 packed field
P*  Parameter: parm2 => 7,2 packed field
P* ─────────────────────────────────────────────────────
PMax                B                       EXPORT
DMax                PI          7P 2
D parm1                         7P 2 VALUE
D parm2                         7P 2 VALUE
D*Local fields
D bigger            S           7P 2
C*Local code
C                       IF          parm1 > parm2
C                       EVAL        bigger = parm1
C                       ELSE
C                       EVAL        bigger = parm2
C                       ENDIF
C                       RETURN      bigger
PMax                E
```

Procedure definitions go at the end of your mainline C-specs, but before any O-specs or array compile-time data. The procedure name can be up to 4,096 characters long! If it is more than 15, use ellipses to extend it onto the next line (using as many lines as necessary), like this:

```
PGenerateEndOfWeekPayroll...
P                   B                       EXPORT
```

If you are a CODE/400 user, you will find in the CODE/400 editor a SmartGuide or wizard that prompts you for the name, parameter, and return information, and generates the prototype and shell of the procedure for you. It also handles long names correctly.

Calling RPG procedures

How you call a procedure depends on whether you want to use the returned value or not. If not, you simply call it with the CALLP op-code. If so, you call it in the right side of an EVAL expression, much the same as you would call a built-in function. In all cases, parameters are placed inside parentheses and separated by colons. You can add spaces wherever you like. Listing 2.2 shows the mainline code to call our procedures. (For your information, the output of this program is 15, 25, and 25.99, as expected.)

Listing 2.2: Calling Procedures in RPG IV

```
 *  ======================================================
 *  Global fields
 *  ======================================================
D integer1        S                5I 0 INZ(25)
D integer2        S                5I 0 INZ(15)
D packed1         S                7P 2 INZ(25.99)
D packed2         S                7P 2 INZ(15.06)
D biggest         S                7P 2 INZ(0)
 *  ======================================================
 *  Mainline code
 *  ======================================================
C* call Swap procedure
C                   CALLP     Swap(integer1 : integer2)
C     integer1      DSPLY
C     integer2      DSPLY
C* call Max procedure
C                   EVAL      biggest = Max(packed1:
C                                       packed2)
C     biggest       DSPLY
C* end the program
C                   EVAL      *INLR = *ON
```

If the procedure does not take any parameters, no parentheses are specified. However, in V5R1 or later, you are at least *allowed* to code empty parentheses, which makes it clear to other programmers that this is a method call versus a field name.

JAVA SYNTAX

The following sections give your first introduction to the syntax of Java code. We will build on this in this chapter and subsequent chapters. Get ready, your Java journey begins...

Java class syntax

What does a Java class look like, exactly? Its syntax is shown in Figure 2.8.

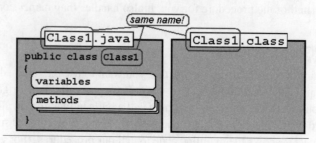

Figure 2.8: The anatomy of a Java class

You declare the class in the .java source file using explicit syntax to start and end the class. It optionally starts with the keyword public (a *modifier*), followed by the required keyword class, followed by the name you wish to give it. Finally, curly braces { and } start and end the body of the class. All variables and methods are defined between the braces, and the closing brace will always be the last non-blank line of the .java source file.

An interesting thing to note is that the name of the class must match exactly, including case, the name of the Java source file, and therefore, the name of the compiled .class file. You can legally define multiple classes per file, as long as only one is defined with public, but each becomes a separate dot-class file after using javac to compile. However, it is considered bad form to define multiple classes per source file, except when defining inner or nested classes (discussed in Chapter 14).

The public modifier in Figure 2.8 indicates this class is freely accessible to all other classes that want it. This modifier is also required for a class to be run from the command line.

Here is the syntax for defining a Java class:

```
<modifier> class Name
{
    ...
}
```

Specifically, Java class syntax involves the following:

- Optionally, one or more modifiers. You have seen public, but there are two more (abstract and final) that you'll learn about in Chapter 9. There can be more than one modifier, separated by blanks, as in public final.

- The term class is *not* optional. It defines the type of Java construct you are defining.

- *Name* is case-sensitive and totally up to you. By convention, the first character of every word in the name is uppercase, as in MyVeryFirstClass. Names in Java cannot have blanks, but practically every other character is allowed. However, since the class name must match the file name, the file system will keep you from using certain characters, such as slashes. All names in Java have no limit on length.

- The curly braces { and } define the beginning and end of the class *block*. You will see these used throughout Java for defining all blocks.

- All Java source, including class definitions, are free-format. The compiler ignores line breaks and redundant white space. Thus, you could put every word on its own line if you wanted!

Here is an example of an empty class:

```
public class SalariedEmployee
{

}
```

This class is named `SalariedEmployee` and is accessible by all other classes, since it is `public`.

Java variable syntax

Inside the braces of a Java class are the variables and methods of that class. Variables are declared using the following syntax:

```
<modifiers> type name <= initial-value>;
```

The optional modifiers include `public` and `private`, which dictate whether or not other classes have access to this variable. With no modifiers, only this class and other classes in this *package* (described later) have access.

The type is one of eight predefined data types, discussed in detail in Chapter 5. They are `byte`, `short`, `int`, `long`, `char`, `boolean`, `float`, and `double`. The first four are numeric signed integers of increasing size, while `char` is for single characters, `boolean` is for true/false variables, and `float` and `double` are single- and double-precision floating-point variables.

The convention for the name is the same as for methods, discussed in the next section. After the name, you can optionally assign an initial value. The declaration ends in a semicolon, as indeed all statements do in Java.

Here are a few example Java variable declarations:

```
private int commissionRate;
public float taxRate = 0.08;
char unitType = 'H';
```

The variable `commissionRate` is only accessible by code inside this class (`private`), and is of type integer (`int`). The variable `taxRate` is accessible by code in all other classes (`public`), with a single-precision floating-point type (`float`), initialized to 0.08. The variable `unitType` is a character (`char`) initialized to H, and is accessible by all classes in this package, which is the default if you do not specify `public` or `private`. Note that you do not declare the number of digits in Java; you just state the type. Each type has a predefined byte-length allocated for it: one byte for `byte`, two for `short`, four for `int`, eight for `long`, two for `char`, one for `boolean`, four for `float`, and eight for `double`.

In addition to these eight *primitive* data types, variable types can be the name of a class (which you will see lots of soon). Indeed, Java supplies a number of classes, to make up for the limited number of primitive data types. For example, the all-important `String` class holds character data that is more than one character long.

Java method syntax

Here is the syntax for defining a Java method inside a class:

```
<modifier> return-type name(<parameter-type parameter-name ...>)
{
    ...
    return return-variable;
}
```

Specifically, the Java method syntax involves the following:

- Optional modifiers. Again, though, you need to code `public` to allow methods in other classes to call this method.

- A return type for what this method returns, much the same as RPG procedures require. If nothing is returned, you must specify the keyword `void`.

- The method name, which can be any name you want. By convention, method names are all lowercase except the first letter of any word other than the first, as in `getName` and `getBillRate`. (Remember that all names in Java are case-sensitive.)

- The parameter list, which is a type-name pairing, with each pair comma-separated. If the method does not take parameters, you must code empty parentheses, ().

- Curly braces, { and }, delimiting the beginning and end of the method.

- The `return` statement, which is needed only if you return a parameter; otherwise, `return` with no parameter is optional. The type of variable you return must match the return-type on the method declaration, as with RPG procedures.

There are two predominant styles for Java braces delimiting a method. In the first style, the first brace is placed right on the method declaration line, like this:

```
public void myMethod() {
    ...
}
```

In the second style, the first brace is placed on its own line, like this:

```
public void myMethod()
{
    ...
}
```

We prefer the latter because it is easier to line up the braces in an editor to ensure that you have not missed one. C programmers prefer the former, though.

Note there is no prototyping of methods in Java, unlike RPG, which requires you to prototype your procedures (as C and C++ do, also). How does the compiler verify the parameters are correct on a call? It actually goes out to disk and finds the class file containing the method being called, and looks in it!

An example of a Java class

To help bring together the syntax discussions from the previous sections, let's look at a complete Java class, shown in Listing 2.3. This class, named `ItemOrder`, holds three pieces of information about an order: its ID, the quantity of the order, and the unit cost of the items ordered. This means three variables. Two methods are defined in the class, one for setting the order information, and the other for returning the total cost of the order. The former requires three parameters, one for each piece of information, and sets the values of the variables from those parameters. The latter takes no parameters, but returns the unit cost multiplied by the quantity.

Listing 2.3: A First Class in Java: ItemOrder

```java
public class ItemOrder
{
    private int    id;
    private int    quantity;
    private double unitCost;

    public void setOrderInfo(int newId, int newQuantity,
                             double newUnitCost)
    {
        id = newId;
        quantity = newQuantity;
        unitCost = newUnitCost;
    }

    public double getTotalCost()
    {
        double totalCost = quantity * unitCost;
        return totalCost;
    }
}
```

Don't worry about understanding everything about this class yet; we just want to start acclimating you to seeing Java code. It will all become clearer as you go. You should, however, be able to identify the declaration of class ItemOrder; the declarations of the variables id, quantity, and unitCost; and the methods setOrderInfo and getTotalCost. Also notice we declare and initialize a local variable named totalCost inside the method getTotalCost, and initialize it to an expression.

If you have typed this code in, you might as well finish the job by compiling it:

```
>javac ItemOrder.java
```

Please note that you must use the exact same case even here, when specifying the name of the Java file!

Of course, this class by itself is of little value. It is designed to be used by other code, not be called from the command line. You will see soon how one class in Java uses another.

Getter and setter methods in Java

It is a convention in Java and other OO languages to define all of your global variables as private (or protected, as discussed in Chapter 9) so that code in other classes are not permitted to read or write those variables directly. Rather, if you want to allow others access to them, you supply getXxx and setXxx methods. For example, you might have a private variable named name, supply a public method named getName to retrieve it (it would return name), and another named setName to set it (it would take the new name value as a parameter assigned to the private name variable).

These methods are affectionately known as *getters* and *setters*, or more officially as *accessors* and *mutators*. Variables are almost always implementation details that are best left hidden, which is what using private does. This gives you the flexibility to later change the variable type, length, name, and so on, while keeping the get and set method interface constant, and therefore not disrupting any users. Also, it is a matter of data integrity. Only *your* class code should have direct access to the variables; you do not want to run the risk of someone changing them to unexpected values. This is similar to your database—end users are not able to edit the data directly, using SEU, say. Instead, they must call your RPG program to access the data. Only by restricting access to your data and your variables can you ensure that the state of the data is always valid.

ALLOCATING MEMORY IN RPG IV

Before you learn how to use classes in Java, you should learn something relatively new in RPG IV that will make the subsequent Java discussion easier for you. We are going to define a data structure in RPG IV that will hold information about an item order, just like the Java class in Listing 2.3 does. However, we are going to use the keyword BASED when we define it. This keyword tells the RPG compiler not to allocate memory for this data structure. Instead, the memory for it will be pointed to by the pointer field passed as a parameter to the BASED keyword. So, we will also create a memory pointer field, using data type character * to identify it as a pointer. Then, we will have to actually allocate the memory and set that pointer field to point to it. With that, we will be able to access the subfields of the data structure because it will be assigned a memory location finally.

To allocate the memory, we use the new ALLOC keyword, which requires the amount of memory to allocate in factor-two, and the pointer field to set in the result field. The amount of memory we want is enough to hold the data structure, so we will use the %LEN built-in function in RPG IV to return that size, and put the result in a field, which we will then pass to the ALLOC operation. Got it? Let's have a look at it, in Listing 2.4.

Listing 2.4: Managing Memory for an ItemOrder Data Structure in RPG IV

```
D*Name+++++++++++ETDs++++++++++Len+IDc.Keywords++++++++++
D ItemOrder     DS                    BASED(order@)
D  id                          5P 0
D  quantity                    5P 0
D  unitCost                    9P 2
D orderLen       S             5U 0 INZ(%LEN(ItemOrder))
D order@         S              *   INZ(*NULL)

C*     Factor1+++++++Opcode(E)+Factor2+++++++Result++++++
C                    ALLOC     orderLen      order@
C*     Factor1+++++++Opcode(E)+Extended-Factor2++++++++++
C                    EVAL      id = 1
C                    EVAL      quantity = 10
C                    EVAL      unitCost = 35.99
```

Do you follow it? The D-specs you see are how we explicitly declare fields in RPG, and the name of the field can float anywhere from column 7 to column 21. Columns 24 and 25 require DS for a data structure, blanks for a subfield, and just S for a standalone field (that is, not a data structure and not a subfield). Columns 36 to 39 hold the length, column 40 holds the data type, and columns 41 and 42 hold the number of decimals. Keywords go in columns 44 to 80. One popular keyword is INZ for initializing the field. (More of the D-spec is covered in Chapter 5.) This example also shows the new EVAL op-code for assigning variables. The assignment expression, of the form field-name = expression, goes in free-format factor-two (column range 36 to 80).

Syntax aside, the point of this example is to show how you can define a structure with the BASED keyword and allocate your own memory for that structure. While this is not required in RPG IV, and indeed, is rarely done, it does allow you to write some interesting applications. For example, you could allocate multiple occurrences of the same data structure, and thus simultaneously store information about a number of orders. To access any one order, you would just assign the pointer field on which the data structure is based to the particular pointer field for the particular order's allocated memory, for example:

```
D* Item Orders
D order1@         S              *   INZ(*NULL)
D order2@         S              *   INZ(*NULL)

C* ALLOCATE ORDER ONE:
C                 ALLOC     orderLen          order1@
C                 EVAL      order@ = order1@
C                 EVAL      id = 1
C                 EVAL      quantity = 10
C                 EVAL      unitCost = 35.99
C* ALLOCATE ORDER TWO:
C                 ALLOC     orderLen          order2@
C                 EVAL      order@ = order2@
C                 EVAL      id = 2
C                 EVAL      quantity = 5
C                 EVAL      unitCost = 26.15
```

This is really just like using multiple occurring data structures and using the OCCUR op-code to set the current occurrence. Indeed, this is just what the RPG compiler and runtime do to support multiple occurring data structures. We show you how to do this so you understand in "RPG-speak" the idea of allocating memory and storing information in the memory according to a template or data structure.

When you think about it, this is not unlike a database. When you create a new physical file with a record format, the format is like a based data structure, in that it defines the fields that all memory (records) allocated in this database file will have. The allocation of that memory is done for you, though, each time you write a new record into the database.

Are you thinking that this code would benefit from a procedure? It would! The procedure could take as input the ID, quantity, and unit cost as parameters, and then allocate the memory, set the order@ field, and assign the parameter values to the data structure fields, and return a pointer to the allocated memory. If you named the procedure MakeOrder, the C-specs above would simply become this:

```
C                 EVAL      order1@ = MakeOrder(1:10:35.99)
C                 EVAL      order2@ = MakeOrder(2:5:26.15)
```

Yes, that's a good idea you had! We'll get to it....

USING JAVA CLASSES

Classes in action are called *objects*. With objects, we firmly leave the world of RPG and other 3GLs (third-generation languages). After discussing objects, we will describe in more detail how program flow happens in Java by way of interoperations among objects.

When you define a class, you are merely defining what the class will look like to the compiler. You have not defined something directly usable by other programmers. A class is merely a template; it does not reserve any memory or storage, just like a data structure in RPG IV with the BASED keyword, and just like a record format in a database. To use a class (put or get data in it or call methods in it), you must first allocate memory for it. You do this in two steps:

1. Define a variable to hold the memory address.

2. Allocate the memory and assign its address to the variable from step 1.

To do step 1, you simply define a variable whose type is the name of your class, like this:

```
ItemOrder order1;
```

To do step 2, you use the new operator in Java, which requires you to specify the class name to allocate memory for, followed by parentheses, like this:

```
order1 = new ItemOrder();
```

The new operator allocates enough memory for all of the variables in the identified class, and returns the address of that memory. In this example, that address is then assigned to the variable order1. The rule is that the class named on the new operator must be the same class named as the type of the variable, otherwise you will get a compiler error. Note that like all assignments of data to variables, you can do the assignment at the same time as you declare the variable:

```
ItemOrder order1 = new ItemOrder();
```

You can also define more than one variable with the same class type:

```
ItemOrder order1 = new ItemOrder();
ItemOrder order2 = new ItemOrder();
```

Here, new is used twice to create two separate allocations of memory, using the same template for the memory—the class ItemOrder. Each memory allocation is called an *instance* of the class, or an *object* of the class. Allocating the memory using new is called *instantiating* an object. In this example, because each instance is unique, you can assign one set of values to the variables in order1 and another set of values to the variables in order2. Just like each allocated data structure in the RPG example held unique data, so too does each allocated or instantiated object in Java.

Any variable you declare in Java with a type that is a class name (instead of one of the eight primitive types) is called an *object reference variable*. These variables are always four bytes long and are always destined to hold a memory address acquired using the new operator. The allocated memory is called an object, remember, and the address of that object is known as a *reference* in Java. An object reference variable, like order1, contains a reference to an object.

This concept of an object variable being a reference to an object carries the implication that you can change, on-the-fly, which instance of the class the variable points to. For example, suppose you did the following:

```
order2 = order1;
```

This copies the memory address in order1 to order2, meaning both variables now refer to the same object. Any changes made to the data in that object via order1 will be reflected when you read the data via object2. What happens to that second object in memory, originally referenced by object2? If no other references exist to it, it will be vacuumed up by the *garbage collector*, which always runs in the background, looking for dead objects like this to reclaim. This is unlike RPG IV, where memory allocated with the ALLOC op-code must be explicitly freed up when you are done with it, using the FREE op-code. This tedious but important task is done for you in Java, automatically.

You have not yet seen how to read and write the variables inside an object, or call a method inside an object, but you will soon. For now, you should be comfortable with the following ideas:

- Classes are templates describing the variable types and names in each object (and any initial values you specify for those variables).

- Objects are memory, and object reference variables hold memory addresses.

The classic analogy is that a class is a cookie cutter and an object is a cookie. From one cutter, you get as many cookies as you want, all with the same shape. Not to worry though, you won't be writing crumby code!

There are two final terms you need to know. The variables defined in a class are called *instance variables* because their value depends on the instance of the class, since each instance gets unique memory for those variables. So, the three variables id, quantity, and unitCost defined at the top of class ItemOrder in Listing 2.3 are instance variables. On the other hand, variables declared directly inside a method are called *local variables*, since their value and access is local to the method. So, the variable totalCost (of type double) in method getTotalCost in class ItemOrder is a local variable.

Remember the analogy of classes to based data structures in RPG IV? And of objects to allocated memory for a based data structure? The one thing missing from that analogy is the methods in the class. RPG data structures cannot have procedures, but objects have methods. For your information, when you allocate an object using new, the Java runtime also allocates extra memory to hold a table of pointers to the methods defined in the class. Then, when you call a method in an object, the runtime uses the pointer to find the method and run it. It also sets the registers internally, so that the method will use the unique data for this object whenever it references instance variables. (Don't worry; these concepts will become clear as you read the many examples in this book. You will be leaving a trail of cookie crumbs in no time!)

With an object, you can now access the variables and methods inside that object. Collectively, the variables and methods in a class are referred to as the class *members*.

Accessing methods

Let's go back to the ItemOrder class in Listing 2.3. It has three variables, id, quantity, and unitCost, and two methods, setOrderInfo and getTotalCost. Let's write some code to instantiate (allocate) an object of that class and call the methods in that class. First, where to write this code? Well, all code in Java must exist in a method, and all methods must exist in a class. So, let's write another class! Call it PlaceOrders, in file PlaceOrders.java, as in Listing 2.5.

Listing 2.5: Creating the Java Class PlaceOrders that Uses the Class ItemOrder

```
public class PlaceOrders
{
    public void placeAnOrder()
    {
        ItemOrder order1 = new ItemOrder();
        ItemOrder order2 = new ItemOrder();
        double order1TotalCost;
        double order2TotalCost;

        order1.setOrderInfo(1, 10, 35.99);
        order1TotalCost = order1.getTotalCost();

        order2.setOrderInfo(2, 5, 26.15);
        order2TotalCost = order2.getTotalCost();
    }
}
```

The method in the class is named, arbitrarily, `placeAnOrder`. You need a method, any method, to write the code in. Since this method does not return anything, the `void` keyword is coded for the return type, and a `return` statement is not necessary. Both the class and the method are `public`, so later perhaps you can use both from other classes. If you did not make the class `public`, you would have restricted who could use the `new` operator to instantiate this class. If you did not make the method `public`, you would have restricted who could call this method.

Speaking of calling methods, let's look inside the code to see how that is done. Two object reference variables are declared, `order1` and `order2`, of type `ItemOrder`, and set to refer to separate objects created with the `new` operator. Then, two variables of type `double` are declared, `order1TotalCost` and `order2TotalCost`, with the intention of later assigning these to the returned value from the `getTotalCost` method. That method in `ItemOrder` is declared to return a type of `double`, so it is important the variables have the same type.

Now to the actual calls. For each object, two methods are called in it. The first is a call to the `setOrderInfo` method, passing in literal values for the three parameters it expects: the item ID, quantity, and unit cost. This method returns nothing, so you don't assign the result to anything (much like using EXSR or CALLP in RPG). Notice that the parameters are passed separated by commas (versus RPG, where parameters to a procedure call are separated by colons), and you can put as many blanks between the parameters as you like (or none at all).

The second method call for each object is to the getTotalCost method, which takes no parameters, so you have to just code empty parentheses (versus RPG, where you can code no parentheses). However, this method returns a value that needs to be saved, so the entire method call is assigned to the variables order1TotalCost and order2TotalCost. Assigning an entire method call to a variable is pretty cool, and you can do the same thing in RPG when calling procedures that return values.

The syntax for calling methods, then, is to simply code the method name and qualify it by prefixing the method name with the name of an object and a dot. You do not have to set the "current occurrence" as you do in RPG, because this qualification tells Java explicitly the occurrence you wish to access. The dot between the object reference variable name and the method name is called a *dot operator* in Java.

Java parses these calls at runtime by first recognizing the method call because of the parentheses, and then finding the method by going to the memory address stored in the object reference variable used to qualify the call. This finds the method in the method table there and finds the data there as well for this instance. At compile time, Java will verify that the method named in the call exists in the target class. It does this by tracing back to where the object reference variable was declared, getting the name of the class used as the type there, and then finding that class's .class file on disk. It then opens the file and looks inside it to see if the method exists there. If not, you get an error:

```
Method badMethodName() not found in class ItemOrder.
        order1.badMethodName();
               ^
```

As with RPG procedures, you have three ways to call a method:

- As part of an assignment statement, where the returned result is saved in a variable

- As part of an expression, where the returned result is used but not saved

- By a simple direct call, which runs the method and discards the returned value, if any

Table 2.2 compares the three invocation options in both languages.

Table 2.2: Calling RPG Procedures versus Java Methods, with Parameters	
RPG	Java
EVAL myVar = myProc(p1 : p2)	myVar = myObject.myProc(p1,p2);
IF myProc(p1 : p2) = 10	If (myObject.myProc(p1,p2) == 10)
CALLP myProc(p1 : p2)	myObject.myProc(p1, p2);

While Table 2.2 shows examples that take parameters, Table 2.3 shows, for the sake of completeness, examples that do not take parameters.

Table 2.3: Calling RPG Procedures versus Java Methods, without Parameters	
RPG	Java
EVAL myVar = noParms	myVar = myObject.noParms();
IF noParms = 10	if (myObject.noParms() == 10)
CALLP noParms	myObject.noParms();

Accessing variables

You can access variables inside an object in exactly the same manner as you access methods, using the dot operator. The difference is that you don't use parentheses for variable names as you do for method names. For example, here is how you might change the variable id in the instance of ItemOrder referred to by order1:

```
order1.id = 3;
```

Because the compiler can distinguish between a method call and a variable reference by the existence or nonexistence of parentheses, you are allowed to have variable names that are the same as method names in Java. This is not true in RPG, where procedure names must be unique from field names. This is because calls to procedures in RPG do not require the empty parentheses, so they look identical to method references in an EVAL expression.

This is pretty easy stuff, we hope. If not, it will become easy! Note, however, that the line of code just shown will not compile. Do you know why? Because we happened to define all the variables in ItemOrder using the private modifier, so code in other classes is restricted from accessing it:

```
Variable id in class ItemOrder not accessible from class PlaceOrders.
```

Notice that code you write to access variables and methods in your current class does not require qualification with the dot operator. That is, the code you see in ItemOrder in Listing 2.3 uses the variables defined at the top of that class, so it just names them without qualification. When the Java compiler sees variable and method names without qualification, it looks in the current class, and only the current class, for them. If they are not found there, you will get an error.

Are you wondering how and when you are finally going to call your class from the command line? We are building up to it!

This is special

Using instance variables without qualification is equivalent to telling the compiler that you are referring to a variable in *this* class—in this class *instance*, actually. In fact, there is a special predefined object variable in Java named this. Although you can always live without it, sometimes you might want to use it to distinguish between local variables and class instance variables, if they have the same name.

You should never define variables local to a method that have the same name as instance variables declared globally at the class level, but sometimes you do give parameters the same name as instance variables. For example, in the ItemOrder class in Listing 2.3, you have a method named setOrderInfo, which defines three parameters. These parameter values are simply assigned, one by one, to corresponding instance variables for posterity. We chose in Listing 2.3 to use names for the parameters that did not conflict with the instance variables, as you recall:

```
public void setOrderInfo(int newId, int newQuantity,
                        double newUnitCost)
{
    id = newId;
    quantity = newQuantity;
    unitCost = newUnitCost;
}
```

For parameters like this, where we simply intend to assign them to instance variables, we often find it too much work to come up with parameter names that are similar to their corresponding instance variable names, yet different. Instead, these types of parameters are named exactly the same as their instance variables, with the use of the `this` qualification to distinguish the instance variables from the local parameter variables of the same name. Listing 2.6 provides an example.

Listing 2.6: Updating the Java ItemOrder Class Using the this Keyword

```
public class ItemOrder
{
    private int    id;
    private int    quantity;
    private double unitCost;

    public void setOrderInfo(int id, int quantity,
                            double unitCost)
    {
        this.id = id;
        this.quantity = quantity;
        this.unitCost = unitCost;
    }

    public double getTotalCost()
    {
        double totalCost = quantity * unitCost;
        return totalCost;
    }
}
```

When the Java compiler finds a variable name that is not qualified with anything via the dot operator, it looks for that variable first as a local declaration or local parameter in the current method. If it does not find the variable locally, it looks up to the class level to see if it is declared there. Think of parameter variables as being the same as local variables. So, in `setOrderInfo` in Listing 2.6, the use of the variable `id` results in a match with a parameter definition. To actually access the instance variable with the same name, you must qualify with this to force the compiler not to look locally.

Java overload! Java overload!

Java allows you to have multiple methods with the same name, in the same class, as long as the number or type of parameters is different. This is a key concept in object-oriented languages like Java, and it is called method *overloading*. You are effectively overloading the name of the method with multiple definitions. This allows you to imply to users of your class that in each case, the operation to be performed is the same—only the inputs are different. You might, for example, have a String class that has two methods for substring: one that takes a single "position" number and returns the substring from that position until the end, and another that takes a position number and a "length" number and returns the substring from the given position for the given length. This makes the substring method more intuitive to use than having two methods named, say, substring and substringWithLength. Under the covers, the single-parameter version of substring will likely just invoke the multiple-parameter version, with the remaining length of the string supplied as the second parameter.

Methods of the same name can be made unique by differing the number or type of parameters. For example, you might have a method named max that returns the maximum of two given integer values, and another method in the same class named max that returns the maximum of two given float values. The compiler and runtime will determine which one you mean to use on any call to max, by comparing the number and type of parameters on the call.

Method overloading is a particularly important feature of Java, since the language does not allow you to define methods that take a variable number of parameters (or optional parameters). RPG procedures do allow for this, offsetting somewhat the need for overloading in RPG.

STATIC MEMBERS

Both RPG and Java have a static keyword that can be used on variables. Java even allows it on methods. This is an important keyword that fundamentally changes the variable or method it applies to, as you will soon see.

RPG static fields

When you define local fields in your RPG procedures, you can use the D-spec keyword STATIC to change the field content's lifetime. Rather than the field being reinitialized on every call to the procedure, it retains its value from call to call. This effectively makes it the same as a global field declared at the top of your program, outside of any procedure, but this field can still only be accessed by code in this procedure. In other words, it is still encapsulated to this procedure.

When would you use static fields? Whenever you want a local field to retain its value. Let's go back to the RPG memory-allocation example in Listing 2.4. We said at the time it would be nice to turn the memory allocation code into a procedure, which allocates the memory for the ItemOrder data structure and initializes its three fields to values passed in by parameter. We will do that, but first consider the first field, id. This field is the unique identifier for this order, and really should be generated automatically. We will do that by using a static field in the procedure initialized to one and incremented after every call. The code, including the procedure and the code to call it, is shown in Listing 2.7.

Listing 2.7: Testing Local Fields versus Local Static Fields in RPG Procedures

```
D* Item Order Data Structure
D ItemOrder       DS                        BASED(order@)
D  id                         5P 0
D  quantity                   5P 0
D  unitCost                   9P 2
D* Item Order Data Structure Length
D orderLen        S           5U 0 INZ(%LEN(ItemOrder))
D* Item Order Data Structure Pointer
D order@          S              *  INZ(*NULL)
D* Individual Orders
D order1@         S              *  INZ(*NULL)
D order2@         S              *  INZ(*NULL)
D*----------------------------------------
D* Prototype for procedure: MakeOrder
D*----------------------------------------
D MakeOrder       PR             *
D  quantity_parm              5P 0 VALUE
D  unitCost_parm              9P 2 VALUE

C                   EVAL      order1@=MakeOrder(10:35.99)
C         id        DSPLY
C                   EVAL      order2@=MakeOrder(5:26.15)
C         id        DSPLY
C                   EVAL      *INLR = *ON
```

Listing 2.7: Testing Local Fields versus Local Static Fields in RPG Procedures (continued)

```
P*-----------------------------------------------------
P* Procedure definition for MakeOrder
P* Function..: Allocate and initialize a new order
P* Parameter: quantity => number of items to order
P* Parameter: unitCost => cost of each item
P* Returns..: Pointer to ItemOrder datastruct memory
P*-----------------------------------------------------
P MakeOrder       B
D MakeOrder       PI               *
D   quantity_parm                  5P 0 VALUE
D   unitCost_parm                  9P 2 VALUE
D* local fields
D nextId          S                5P 0 INZ(1) STATIC
D* local code
C                 ALLOC     orderLen       order@
C                 EVAL      id = nextId
C                 EVAL      nextId = nextId + 1
C                 EVAL      quantity = quantity_parm
C                 EVAL      unitCost = unitCost_parm
C                 RETURN    order@
P MakeOrder       E
```

Do you follow this? The procedure nicely encapsulates the effort of creating another order, given just two pieces of information: the quantity and the unit cost. The unique ID is simply derived by the procedure code itself, making this a very convenient procedure for you and your fellow programmers. The output of running this program is 1 and 2, indicating the nextId field was indeed incremented after each call. Notice, if the STATIC keyword were not specified, the field's value would be re-initialized to one on every call.

If you want to actually try this, assuming you put the source into file QRPGLESRC in library LEARNRPG, you would compile it with this:

```
CRTRPGMOD   MODULE(LEARNRPG/ITEMORDER) SRCFILE(LEARNRPG/QRPGLESRC)
CRTPGM      PGM(LEARNRPG/ITEMORDER) MODULE(LEARNRPG/ITEMORDER)
```

Java static variables

In Java, you can also have static variables, by specifying the static modifier, like this:

```
static int counter = 10;
```

However, you cannot specify this modifier on local variables in a method, the way you can for local procedure fields in RPG. Rather, it can only be specified for variables defined at the class level. The semantics of it are a little bit different, too. Static variables in Java always have only one value, regardless of the number of instances (objects) declared with that class. In other words, all objects of the class share the same value for that variable. So, rather than being a local field modifier that means to retain values between calls, in Java, static is a class-level variable modifier that means to retain values between objects.

Is this similar to RPG's STATIC keyword? Actually, it is. Let's update the ItemOrder Java class, last shown in Listing 2.6, to automatically compute and assign a unique ID value for each order. This is done by changing the setOrderInfo method, which sets this information, to only take two parameters instead of three. The new version is shown in Listing 2.8.

Listing 2.8: Updated the Java ItemOrder Class Using the static Variable

```
public class ItemOrder
{
    private static int nextId = 1;
    private int     id;
    private int     quantity;
    private double unitCost;

    public void setOrderInfo(int quantity,
                                double unitCost)
    {
        this.id = nextId;
        nextId = nextId + 1;
        this.quantity = quantity;
        this.unitCost = unitCost;
    }

    public double getTotalCost()
    {
        double totalCost = quantity * unitCost;
        return totalCost;
    }
}
```

Furthermore, static allows code in other classes to directly access the variable without requiring an object of this class. You can simply qualify the reference with the name of the class, like this:

```
int nextAvailableIdNumber = ItemOrder.nextId;
```

Of course, this won't compile because the variable is declared private, but otherwise it would.

Static variables are referred to as *class variables* rather than instance variables. The memory is allocated for them only once per class, not once per object or class instance. Indeed, Java allocates the memory for all static variables in all classes that are used at the time the application starts. Compare this to instance variables, where unique memory is allocated by you, per object, when you use the new operator.

With the latest version of the ItemOrder class in Listing 2.8, the PlaceOrders class must also be updated to only pass two parameters to the setOrderInfo method, instead of three. This is shown in Listing 2.9.

**Listing 2.9: Updated the Java
PlaceOrders Class Using the Updated ItemOrder Class**

```
public class PlaceOrders
{
    public void placeAnOrder()
    {
        ItemOrder order1 = new ItemOrder();
        ItemOrder order2 = new ItemOrder();
        double order1TotalCost;
        double order2TotalCost;

        order1.setOrderInfo(10, 35.99);
        order1TotalCost = order1.getTotalCost();

        order2.setOrderInfo(5, 26.15);
        order2TotalCost = order2.getTotalCost();
    }
}
```

Java static methods

We created the PlaceOrders class to show how to instantiate the original class, ItemOrder, so that we could show how to use that class. But then this PlaceOrders class itself will have to be instantiated by some class in order to run its placeAnOrder method. And then that class will have to be instantiated by another, and so on. If every line of code has to exist in a method, and every method has to exist in a class, and every class has to be instantiated to call any method in it, what instantiates the very first class?

The clue to answering this riddle is that not every method requires you to instantiate the class that contains it! The exception is methods defined with the static modifier. Static methods, like static variables, can be accessed by simply qualifying their names with the class name. No instantiation of the object is required. So, static methods are called *class methods*, for the same reason that static variables are called class variables. Such methods have some restrictions, though, related to the fact that they are called in the context of a class, not the context of an object. Specifically, they cannot access any instance variables because the memory for those instance variables might not exist, if no object has been instantiated.

Can either method in ItemOrder (Listing 2.8) be made static? No, because both of them use (read or write) one or more of the instance variables id, quantity, and unitCost. Can the placeAnOrder method in class PlaceOrders (Listing 2.9) be changed to a static method? Yes, it can! This method uses only local variables, not instance variables. Indeed, the class does not even have any instance variables. Listing 2.10 shows how to make the method placeAnOrder static.

Listing 2.10: Updating the Java PlaceOrders Class with the Static placeAnOrder Method

```java
public class PlaceOrders
{
    public static void placeAnOrder()
    {
        ItemOrder order1 = new ItemOrder();
        ItemOrder order2 = new ItemOrder();
        double order1TotalCost;
        double order2TotalCost;

        order1.setOrderInfo(10, 35.99);
        order1TotalCost = order1.getTotalCost();

        order2.setOrderInfo(5, 26.15);
        order2TotalCost = order2.getTotalCost();
    }
}
```

Just by adding the keyword static, code in other classes can call this method by simply using this:

```
PlaceOrders.placeAnOrder();
```

You do not declare an object reference variable and you do not instantiate an object via new. You just call the method, qualified by its class name. Thus, static methods (class methods) are just like procedures in RPG or functions in C. They are not "object" oriented; they are "procedural." If they need to act on variables, they simply take in what they need as parameters instead of relying on instance data (or use class variables). The fact that static methods are in a class at all is really just to satisfy Java's rule that all methods must exist in a class. However, we often group related static methods into one class. For example, Listing 2.11 shows a class with a couple overloaded versions of a max method that returns the maximum number of two given parameters.

Listing 2.11: Static Methods for Computing Maximums in Java

```java
public class MaxMethods
{
    public static int max(int parm1, int parm2)
    {
        if (parm1 > parm2)
          return parm1;
        else
          return parm2;
    }

    public static float max(float parm1, float parm2)
    {
        if (parm1 > parm2)
          return parm1;
        else
          return parm2;
    }
}
```

You might imagine this class having methods for all Java's numeric data types (byte, short, int, long, float, and double). However, the particular methods already exist, as you will see in Chapter 3. Java supplies a class named Math that is full of many static methods for doing mathematical operations on all Java's data types, including these max methods.

Use but don't abuse static methods

Static methods are often called "helper methods" because they offer services that are easily accessible (no object instantiation required). If your method does not use any instance variables, you should make it static so that it is easier for callers to use. On the other hand, if you find yourself writing only static methods that do not use instance variables, you are probably still thinking too "procedurally." Instead, you need to think about how you can better utilize instance variables in your class to store state information.

For example, do not design a static method named getYearsOfService that takes an employee ID and returns that employee's years of service, and another named getSalary that takes an employee ID and returns that employee's salary. Rather, design a class named Employee that has instance variables for years of service and salary, which are set once by reading the database. Then supply non-static methods that return this information for this employee instance. Users of your class would simply instantiate one instance per employee and use the methods on each instance to do all the actions related to that employee, such as getYearsOfService, getSalary, and printPayCheck.

Use and abuse objects

The true power of classes, which you will only come to appreciate with time and use, is the ability to encapsulate in one place all the data (instance variables) and all the actions (methods) that relate to one topic. The fact that you can have many instances of the same class active in memory at once is a bonus that gives you more flexibility in designing applications. You don't have to write RPG-like applications that define one data structure and then iteratively populate it and process it, then repopulate and process again for the next record of data. Rather, you have the option of having many populated instances "active" at once.

Imagine, for example, the graphical equivalent of a subfile that is listing all of your customers. Each item in that list might actually be a populated Customer object, and each of the popup-menu items (what used to be options) for the selected item in the list simply invokes a method on the selected object to perform that action, such as displayDetails, editDetails, printMailingLabel, and so on. All the data needed by that action is right there, in the instance variables. It's nice clean code and design. If all your applications use this Customer class when they need to read or manipulate customer information, then you get re-use as well. If you decide to add a new field to the customer database, such as for email addresses, you only have to subsequently change that one Customer class definition, and all code in all applications will automatically be up-to-date. They will not even have to be re-compiled! Encapsulation—'tis a good thing. Think about what classes you might design in your next application. How about Employee, Manager, Company, Customer, Address, ItemOrder, Item, and Account?

Don't worry, it is much too early in your Java journey to fully understand and appreciate this conversation now. We just want you to start thinking of classes, and their objects, as powerful ways to group in one place all data and all methods that act on that data. Now, back to the basics!

CONSOLE-ATION

The next several sections cover interacting with the console: calling programs, passing parameters from the command line, and writing to the console.

Calling a Java program: The "main" method

Now that you have been introduced to static methods, we can finally fill in the last piece of information you need to be able to "run" that PlaceOrders class you last saw in Listing 2.10. Recall that it was designed simply as a test case for the ItemOrder class last shown in Listing 2.9. You want to be able to run the class from a command line, like this:

```
>java PlaceOrders
```

However, if you try this now, you will get an error message:

```
Exception in thread "main" java.lang.NoSuchMethodError: main
```

When you try to run a Java class from the command line, the Java runtime (interpreter) will look for a specific method in that class. It will look for a method named main. Not just any method named main, but one that specifically looks like this:

```
public static void main(String args[])
{
  ...
}
```

Java looks for exactly one such method with exactly this signature. Remember, a signature is the method name, and the number and type of parameters. In this case, you even need to specify the modifiers exactly as shown. The breakdown of the main signature is shown in Table 2.4; all parts are mandatory.

Table 2.4: Required Signature for the Java main Method

Part	Description
public	This method is publicly accessible.
static	This method does not require an instance of the class to be created first.
void	This method does not return any values.
main	This is the name of the method and is case-sensitive.
String args[]	This is an array of strings, one for each parameter specified on the command line. Any name will do, but args is the convention.

Note that String is a Java-supplied class that is equivalent to RPG character fields. The square brackets, [], indicate this parameter is an array of String objects. The Java interpreter calls the main method automatically, and then the interpreter passes this parameter to you. Each element in the array represents a parameter typed in by the user on the command line.

You'll see more details about this shortly. In the meantime, since we don't care about command-line parameters yet, we now have enough information to make the PlaceOrders class "runnable." We simply have to code a main method as shown, and in it, call the static placeAnOrder method, as shown in Listing 2.12.

Listing 2.12: A Runnable Version of the Java PlaceOrders Class, with a main Method

```
public class PlaceOrders
{
    public static void placeAnOrder()
    {
        ItemOrder order1 = new ItemOrder();
        ItemOrder order2 = new ItemOrder();
```

```
        double order1TotalCost;
        double order2TotalCost;

        order1.setOrderInfo(10, 35.99);
        order1TotalCost = order1.getTotalCost();

        order2.setOrderInfo(5, 26.15);
        order2TotalCost = order2.getTotalCost();
    }

    public static void main(String args[])
    {
        placeAnOrder();
    }

}
```

Alternatively, we could have just changed the placeAnOrder method to be the main method, but it amounts to the same thing. So, now you can run the class from the command line:

```
>java PlaceOrders
```

You don't get any output because the class doesn't write any output to the console. You will soon see how to do this, though. In the meantime, rest assured the code has executed and all is well in Java land!

Command-line parameters in RPG

In RPG, you specify the parameters to your main program object on the CALL command. The RPG entry module will define the parameters that it expects, either by using the traditional *ENTRY PLIST C-spec statement, or by using the new RPG IV way of using D-spec prototyping. For example, if you have a program in which the entry module accepts a six-character string, you could define the parameters traditionally as follows:

```
C     *ENTRY      PLIST
C                 PARM                    KEYCHAR        6
```

You could also define the parameters with new ILE procedure prototyping syntax like this:

```
DMAIN           PR                      EXTPGM('PRTCUST')
D KEYCHAR                      6A

DMAIN           PI
D KEYCHAR                      6A
```

As when prototyping procedures, the PR specification defines the prototype, while the PI specification defines the actuals. Why use this technique over our trusty *ENTRY technique for defining command-line parameters? The advantage is that you could place the PR specifications inside a /COPY member and use it when calling this program from another program, using the new CALLP op-code. This gives you the advantage of letting the compiler verify that you have gotten the parameters correct in the call.

Both options are equivalent. In RPG, you can define command-line parameters to be of any valid type, and each are explicitly defined in your *ENTRY or PR D-spec.

Command-line parameters in Java

In Java applications, you pass parameters on the command line after the name of the Java class to invoke, with blank delimiters. Each word or token specified becomes one parameter. Each parameter is accessible to your Java main method as an entry in the args array of strings. Unlike RPG, every parameter is passed to Java as a string (a String object, actually), and you must explicitly convert it to the required data type yourself. (This will be covered in more detail later.) To pass a string with embedded blanks as a single parameter, you must enclose the string in quotes on the command line:

```
java Bob hi there "George and Phil"
```

This fills the String args[] array entry 0 (arrays are zero-based in Java) with hi, array entry 1 with there, and array entry 2 with George and Phil.

Writing to the command line in RPG

Very often, it is either necessary or worthwhile to write information out to the command line. It is a time-honored debugging trick, for example, to spit out "I am here" messages to track your flow of control in a program. (This is not so widespread anymore, thanks to the proliferation of source-level debuggers, but we all still do it occasionally.) Also, almost all language introduction books start with a simple little "hello world" program that writes this string out to the screen. The first page of the book is rarely the place to introduce display files or GUI constructs!

In RPG, a common way to write simple output is by using the DSPLY op-code. This has not changed for RPG IV, so we will not cover well-worn ground here. However, by using DSPLY, you could write the obligatory "hello world" RPG IV program, with the additional twist that it prints whatever is passed on the command line, as shown in Listing 2.13.

Listing 2.13: The RPG Main Entry Point Prototype

```
 * Prototype of this program main entry
DMAIN           PR                    EXTPGM('HWORLD')
D STRING                    1000A    OPTIONS(*VARSIZE)
 * Definition of this program main entry
DMAIN           PI
D STRING                    1000A    OPTIONS(*VARSIZE)
 * Global variables
DOutString      S            52A
 * Main logic
C                   EVAL      OutString = 'Input: ' +
C                             %SUBST(STRING:1:45)
C      OutString    DSPLY
 * End of program
C                   EVAL      *INLR = *ON
```

The DSPLY op-code has the nasty restriction of only being able to display a maximum of 52 characters. Using the OPTIONS(*VARSIZE) keyword when declaring the character field parameter to the program lets it accept strings of any length. To build the output string OutString, the concatenation operator (+) is used to append the literal 'Input: ' to the first 45 characters of the input parameter. We get the first 45 characters by using the %SUBST (substring) built-in function. Finally, DSPLY prints the OutString field to the console.

Calling this program with CALL HWORLD 'hi there' results in the following:

```
Input: hi there
```

To write out the values of fields that are not character type fields, such as packed decimal, you first have to convert and store their values into a character field. This can be done easily in RPG IV by using the %CHAR built-in function, which takes any field as a parameter and returns a character field value that is immediately printable.

Writing to the command line in Java

In Java, the equivalent to DSPLY is called "writing to standard output." It involves using a Java-supplied class named System, and a static object variable inside of that class named out, and finally a method of out named println, which is short for "print line." Here is an example:

```
System.out.println("Hello world");
```

By now, you are familiar with static variables, and you see here that object reference variables can also be static. In this case, out is a static object reference variable in the Java-supplied System class. You can tell it is static because it is qualified with a class name, not an object reference variable name. You can't know what the class type is, but you can deduce the System class must look something like this:

```
public class System
{
        public static XXX out = new XXX();
}
```

where XXX is the unknown class type of the out object. You know println is a method because there are parentheses after it. It must be a method in whatever class out is a type of. (You can't tell from this line of code, but it doesn't really matter.) The println method prints a line of text to a special "file" called *standard output*. This is not a file on disk. Typically, the contents of the standard output file get displayed on the invoking command line (the console). To see this output in graphical applications or in applets where there is no command line, however, you have to be running inside a shell that captures and displays it. For example, the VisualAge for Java product has a console window that displays any information written to standard output with the println method. So do Web browsers.

To write a blank line, just call println with no parameters. A similar method named print writes the given text to standard output, but without advancing the carriage return, so subsequent text will be written to the same line.

You will quickly become very familiar with `System.out.println` as you begin to learn Java—and as you continue to read this book! Most simple, starter applications use it to display dynamic information. The method `println` takes any number of strings or variables, separated by plus signs (+), and displays them. This means that `println` automatically converts variable contents from their native type (such as `int` or `float`) to string format, which is very useful. For objects, `println` does this by trying to call a method in the object named `toString`. You must code this method for this to work with objects of your classes. Most Java-supplied classes come with this method.

A Java class that echoes the passed-in string is shown in Listing 2.14. Running this class results in this:

```
>java HelloWorld ""hello world!"
Input: hello world!
```

Listing 2.14: A Java Version of the "Hello World" Program

```java
public class HelloWorld
{
  public static void main(String[] args)
  {
    System.out.println("Input: " + args[0]);
  }
}
```

There are a few things to note about this example:

- `args[0]` is the Java syntax for the first entry in array `args`. (Arrays are zero-based.)

- This example will fail if you do not pass in at least one parameter, because `args[0]` will not be defined.

- Any parameters after the first will be ignored.

- A multiple-word input string must be passed with quotation marks surrounding it.

A more robust version of the class would check to make sure that there is at least one parameter, concatenate all of the parameters in a temporary string, and then print that string. The code to do this would exceed your current knowledge of Java, but if you are interested, you can see this version on the CD-ROM included with this book, in file `HelloWorld2.java`.

To put to work what you've just learned, let's display some stuff from the PlaceOrders class. We will first enhance the evolving ItemOrder class by adding a method named displayOrder, which will write to the console the information in this object.

This updated class, shown in Listing 2.15, writes to the console all the variables and also the total cost, which is retrieved by calling the getTotalCost method. Notice that System.out.println knows how to convert anything you give it to displayable format. Also notice the string literals are double-quoted, versus single-character literals, which are single-quoted.

Listing 2.15: The Updated ItemOrder Class with the displayOrder Method

```java
public class ItemOrder
{
    private static int nextId = 1;
    private int     id;
    private int     quantity;
    private double unitCost;

    public void setOrderInfo(int quantity,
                             double unitCost)
    {
        this.id = nextId;
        nextId = nextId + 1;
        this.quantity = quantity;
        this.unitCost = unitCost;
    }

    public double getTotalCost()
    {
        double totalCost = quantity * unitCost;
        return totalCost;
    }

    public void displayOrder()
    {
        System.out.println();
        System.out.println("Order Information");
        System.out.println("----------");
        System.out.println(" id........: " + id);
        System.out.println(" quantity..: " + quantity);
        System.out.println(" unit cost.: " + unitCost);
        System.out.println(" total cost: " + getTotalCost());
    }
}
```

Next, you need to update the evolving PlaceOrders class to call this new method, in both ItemOrder objects, as shown in Listing 2.16. (This listing shows just the placeAnOrder method, as the main method is unchanged.)

Listing 2.16: The Updated PlaceAnOrder Method in the PlaceOrders Class, Now Calling the displayOrder Method

```
public static void placeAnOrder()
{
    ItemOrder order1 = new ItemOrder();
    ItemOrder order2 = new ItemOrder();
    double order1TotalCost;
    double order2TotalCost;

    order1.setOrderInfo(10, 35.99);
    order1TotalCost = order1.getTotalCost();
    order1.displayOrder();

    order2.setOrderInfo(5, 26.15);
    order2TotalCost = order2.getTotalCost();
    order2.displayOrder();
}
```

When you run the updated class, you get this:

```
>java PlaceOrders

Order Information
_____
 id........: 1
 quantity..: 10
 unit cost.: 35.99
 total cost: 359.90000000000003

Order Information
_____
 id........: 2
 quantity..: 5
 unit cost.: 26.15
 total cost: 130.75
```

Do you follow it all? If so, you are on your way! If not, don't worry, you will within a few chapters. By the way, do you see that huge number for total cost? That's a problem with using float or double numbers in mathematical computations. Chapter 5 introduces a Java class, BigDecimal, which solves this problem.

Class constructors in Java

Classes can have a special method called a *constructor*. A constructor is a method in the class, which the compiler and runtime recognize, that has the same name as the class. Unlike regular methods, constructors do not specify any return type on their definition line because they cannot return values. What does a constructor do? It is called by the Java runtime when an object is instantiated with the new operator, if it exists. This is your opportunity to initialize instance variables and do any setup that your methods assume.

Because you can initialize your instance variables when you declare them, with "= xxx;" syntax, and this initialization is also performed each time new is used, you might wonder what the value of a constructor is. There are at least three reasons why you might use a constructor:

- For complex variable assignments that cannot be easily made by simply assigning a value at the point where you declare the variable.

- For initial state operations or logic, such as opening a file.

- For user control (programmer user, that is) over the initial instance variable values. This is done by letting users pass in parameters to the constructor, which you use to initialize your instance variables.

You can also have more than one constructor. Because they must all have the same name as the class, the difference is in the number and type of parameters. A *default constructor* takes no parameters, but you can define other constructors with as many parameters as you need. Recall that Java allows you to overload methods—you can supply more than one method with the same name as long as the number or type of parameters are different. This applies nicely to constructors. You may have versions of your constructors that take differing parameters, giving users the freedom to use defaults or specify explicit initial values.

Imagine, for example, that you have defined a class named AS400, which connects to an AS/400 from a Java client. It might have a number of constructors: one that takes a user ID and password as parameters and assigns the parameters to instance variables used later in the connect method; one that takes a user ID and hard-codes the password; and the default constructor that defaults both the user ID and password. This gives users of this class flexibility in how they use it.

Users specify the parameters to a constructor as part of the new operator statement, like this:

```
AS400 myHost1 = new AS400();
AS400 myHost2 = new AS400("BOB");
AS400 myHost3 = new AS400("BOB", "ABABA");
```

One constructor can call other constructors, allowing you to abstract-out common code. You do this by calling the Java-supply method named this with the appropriate parameters, if applicable. For example, Listing 2.17 shows a common practice: one constructor takes parameters for all the instance variables you want to make user-initializable, and all other constructors simply call it and hardcode one or more of the parameters.

Listing 2.17: A Java Class with Three Constructors

```
class AS400
{
    private String userId;
    private String passWord;

    AS400()
    {
        this("QUSER", "QUSERPWD");
    }

    AS400(String id)
    {
        this(id, "QUSERPWD");
    }

    AS400(String id, String password)
    {
        userId = id;
        passWord = password;
    }
}
```

The key here is that you do not explicitly code a call to a constructor. Rather, you simply code the new operator as usual, possibly passing in parameters, and the Java runtime implicitly calls the appropriate constructor for you. That is, the runtime looks for a constructor method in your class that matches the number and type of parameters specified with the new operator and calls it with the parameters specified on the new operator. A constructor is somewhat similar to the *INZSR subroutine in RPG, in that if you code it, the runtime will call it at initialization time.

Constructors are really just a short form equivalent to supplying a method named init, say, that you would instruct users to call in order to initialize your object's state or variables. Consider, for example, the setOrderInfo method in the ItemOrder class. It really would be better to turn this method into a constructor, so that users of this class do not have to create their ItemOrder object in one step, and populate the object in a separate step by subsequently calling setOrderInfo. Listing 2.18 shows the ItemOrder class after the method setOrderInfo has been turned into a constructor.

Listing 2.18: The Updated Java ItemOrder Class with a Constructor

```
public class ItemOrder
{
    private static int nextId = 1;
    private int     id;
    private int     quantity;
    private double unitCost;

    public ItemOrder(int quantity, double unitCost)
    {
        this.id = nextId;
        nextId = nextId + 1;
        this.quantity = quantity;
        this.unitCost = unitCost;
    }

    public double getTotalCost()
    {
        double totalCost = quantity * unitCost;
        return totalCost;
    }

    public void displayOrder()
    {
        System.out.println();
        System.out.println("Order Information");
        System.out.println("----------------");
        System.out.println(" id........: " + id);
        System.out.println(" quantity..: " + quantity);
        System.out.println(" unit cost.: " + unitCost);
        System.out.println(" total cost: " + getTotalCost());
    }
}
```

Of course, having changed ItemOrder, you now have to change the PlaceOrders class to reflect the change. Listing 2.19 shows the updated takeAnOrder method, where you pass the order information into the constructor via parameters on the new operator after you have turned the method setOrderInfo into a constructor.

Listing 2.19: The Updated Java PlaceOrders Class Calling the ItemOrder Constructor

```java
public static void placeAnOrder()
{
    ItemOrder order1 = new ItemOrder(10, 35.99);
    ItemOrder order2 = new ItemOrder(5, 26.15);
    double order1TotalCost;
    double order2TotalCost;

    //order1.setOrderInfo(10, 35.99);
    order1TotalCost = order1.getTotalCost();
    order1.displayOrder();

    //order2.setOrderInfo(5, 26.15);
    order2TotalCost = order2.getTotalCost();
    order2.displayOrder();
}
```

The old calls to setOrderInfo are shown in Listing 2.19 as comments. The "//" characters in Java identify a comment: all code from there to the end of that line is considered a comment. Comments in this book appear in italics, similar to what any good editor will do.

Constructors, like methods, allow you to specify access modifiers. However, they have an additional responsibility in a constructor: they affect who is allowed to instantiate your class (that is, use new). If you specify public, this class can be instantiated by anyone. If you specify protected, this class can be instantiated only if it is extended by another class (discussed in Chapter 9). If no modifier is specified, the default is whatever is specified or defaulted for the class itself.

There is a subtlety to constructors: if you do not define any, Java will supply a default one with no parameters that does nothing. If you supply even one constructor, however, it will not do this. Therefore, the ItemOrder class now cannot be instantiated using the default constructor. Anyone who tries will get this error:

```
JAVACE No constructor matching ItemOrder() found in class ItemOrder.
```

If you want to allow a no-parameter new operation, you must explicitly supply a no-parameter constructor as well, even if it is empty. (By the way, a common short form you will see for "constructor" in the comments of code is "ctor.")

CODE REUSE AND DISTRIBUTION

The following sections discuss the constructs and mechanisms for reusable code in RPG IV and in Java, and how to distribute that reusable code.

Distributing reusable RPG code as service programs

Recall that RPG IV applications can consist of an RPG program created by binding multiple module objects together, and that service programs are also created by binding multiple module objects together. This step is done by using CRTPGM or CRTSRVPGM, specifying the modules to bind on the MODULE parameter. Programs and other service programs that use a particular service program link to it during this bind step by specifying it on the BNDSRVPGM parameter. The service programs are not physically copied into the program object; they are simply linked to it.

Suppose an ORDER program object in library ORDERLIB is comprised of the following modules: ORDERDSP, ORDERDB, and ORDERRPT. Also suppose you use a service program TAXPROCS, comprised of the modules TAXTBLS and TAXRTNS. To build the application, after all the modules have been compiled with CRTRPGMOD, you do this:

```
CRTSRVPGM SRVPGM(ORDERLIB/TAXPROCS) MODULE(TAXTBLS TAXRTNS)
EXPORT(*ALL) ACTGRP(*CALLER)
CRTPGM PGM(ORDERLIB/ORDER) MODULE(ORDERDSP ORDERDB ORDERRPT)
ENTMOD(*FIRST) ACTGRP(ORDERAG) BNDSRVPGM(ORDERLIB/TAXPROCS)
```

You create the service program first, so that you can subsequently link to it when creating the program. For the service program, you use EXPORT(*ALL) to allow all procedures in the modules in the service program to be callable from the linking programs. Well, not all procedures, only those that specify the EXPORT keyword on their beginning procedure specification. Finally, you use the *CALLER (the default, actually) for the activation group parameter, so that this service program always runs in the activation group of the program object that is using it, at runtime. Remember the same service program can be used by more than one program object, so with *CALLER, each active instance of the same service program gets its own memory for fields when multiple applications are running simultaneously.

After creating the service program, you create the program object, binding the three module objects into it. You specify *FIRST for the entry module (this is the default anyway) and give an explicit name of your choosing for the activation group. Finally, you link to the service program from the first step.

If you subsequently update any one of the modules, you can use UPDPGM and UPDSRVPGM to selectively replace it inside the *PGM or *SRVPGM objects.

Once you have an ILE RPG service program that contains a number of useful procedures (inside modules), the time will come when you want to sell it or at least package it up for reuse by others. This is easily done. For anyone who wants to use your service program in their own program, you would need to supply two things:

- The service program object itself (*SRVPGM)

- A copy member with the prototypes for the exported procedures

A user of your service program would then:

- Include the copy member in their source (/COPY) so that the compiler would be able to find the prototypes in order to perform parameter-number and type checking

- Specify the service program name on the BNDSRVPGM parameter of the CRTGPM command when creating a program that uses your service program (which calls any of the modules or procedures in it)

For your own maintenance purposes, you might want to investigate the use of the *binder language.* This is a source member language for naming all the exported procedures in your service program, and is an alternative to using EXPORT(*ALL) on CRTSRVPGM, if you do not want all procedures with the EXPORT keyword to be available outside of the service program. You can then specify this on CRTSRVPGM's SRCFILE and SRCMBR parameters. Here is the binding language source for exporting a procedure named RJUSTIFY:

```
STRPGMEXP SIGNATURE('RJUSTIFY')
    EXPORT SYMBOL('RJUSTIFY')
ENDPGMEXP
```

Actually, making procedures available to users of the service program involves two steps, and both are required:

1. Specify EXPORT on the beginning P-spec. This makes the procedure callable by code in other modules in the same *PGM or *SRVPGM object.

2. Specify the procedure in the binding source, or specifying EXPORT(*ALL) when creating the service program. This makes the procedure accessible to users outside of the service program.

Another ILE construct worth investigating is the use of *binding directories* (*BNDDIR). When creating programs and service programs, you can either specify all of the modules and service programs explicitly with the MODULE and BNDSRVPGM parameters, or externally, by specifying a binding directory on the BNDDIR parameter.

Binding directories list modules and service programs. You create a binding directory with the CRTBNDDIR (*Create Binding Directory*) command, and populate it with module and service program names using the ADDBNDDIRE (*Add Binding Directory Entry*) command. This is a good way to ensure that your programs and service programs are always recreated properly, without having to rely on all programmers knowing exactly what module and service programs are needed when recompiling and recreating the objects.

Java code reuse through packages

Java, like all object-oriented languages, is big on code reuse. Java classes are all about code reuse. As we have discussed, Java classes are like individual RPG IV modules, but can be reused simply by instantiating them multiple times. Any class in any application can instantiate any other class, assuming of course the class is accessible according to the modifiers specified for it. There is no binding step in Java, and no other file system objects like RPG's *PGM and *SRVPGM. You just use whatever class you want where and when you want! If you update a class, all applications using it will pick up the latest version the next time they run. Blissfully simple!

However, the problem you will soon run into is managing the hundreds of classes you will end up with and dealing with name collision when two classes have the same name. To help with these problems, there is a higher-level grouping mechanism in Java. It is called a *package*, appropriately enough. You can place multiple classes into a single package.

Usually, you put classes related to each other or to a certain concept into their own package. For example, the package `orders` might contain the classes `OrderGUI`, `OrderDatabase`, and `OrderReport`. This is similar to programs and service programs in RPG IV, where you group related modules into a single entity. By identifying that a class is part of a package, you add a new qualification to the class name—that is, the class name can be qualified with the package name, meaning two classes can have the same name, as long as they are in different packages. A further advantage of packages is they allow you to give classes and methods inside the same package access to each other, while restricting access by code in other packages. Indeed, if you do not specify any modifiers on a class, instance variable, or method, they have package access. This means all code in this package, and only code in this package, can access this class, instance variable, or method.

In Java, packages are a defined part of the language, as opposed to a new file system object such as *SRVPGM objects. Indeed, they actually map to directories, as you will see soon. You'll also see soon how to define what package your class is part of, and how to use or access classes in other packages. When writing production Java code, all your classes will be inside packages.

Defining a Java package

In the first line of the `.java` source file, you can optionally define the package of which the class is part, using the `package` statement. If present, this must be the first non-blank line in the source file:

```
package orders;
public class OrderGUI
{
    ...
}
```

This statement informs the `javac` compiler that this class is to be considered part of the `orders` package. You would add this `package` statement at the top of every class you want to be in this package.

Using Java packages

The opposite of defining a Java package is using it. If you have source code that needs to use classes defined in a package other than the package the class is part of, you have two choices:

- Qualify references to the class names by prefixing them with the package name, using the familiar dot notation, like this:

```
orders.OrderGUI orderWindow = new orders.OrderGUI();
```

- Import the package using the Java `import` statement at top of the source file, after any package statements, like this:

```
import orders.*; // import all classes in orders package
```

Remember, the "//" characters start a comment in Java. The `import` statement can also be used to import a single class from a package, like this:

```
import orders.OrderGUI; // just import OrderGUI class
import orders.OrderDatabase; // just import OrderDatabase class
import orders.OrderReport; // just import OrderReport class
```

There is no performance implication to importing all classes or importing one class, so in most cases, you just import them all. The only reason to import classes individually would be as a documentation aid to your fellow programmers, so that they can see what classes you are using from a package.

When you import a package, you have full, unqualified access to all its classes. This frees you from the tedium of prefixing the package name to all class names used in the package. You still can fully qualify each class name with its package name, if you wish. Why would you want to do this? If you are importing two packages, and want to use a class that has the same name in both, then you would have to qualify the references to the class name to resolve the ambiguity.

If you do not specify a package statement in your class source file, your class is considered to be part of the *default package*—that is, the "unnamed" package. All other packages are considered to be "named" packages. There is exactly one unnamed package, and all classes without package statements are placed there. This package is always imported implicitly for you by Java.

Here is a tip that will save you some grief: if your class is in a package (there is a package statement), you cannot access any classes in the unnamed package. We are not sure of the reason for the rule, but we are sure it will cause you some grief if you try to mix classes in the unnamed package with classes in the named package, in the same application. The reverse is allowed, though. That is, classes in the unnamed package can access classes in named packages.

Java package-naming conventions

Java package names are all lowercase. It is important to choose package names that are as unique as possible, to minimize the chance for collision with other package names. This becomes particularly important as Java packages become available on the market for global reuse and resale. To this end, the Java language allows package names to have multiple parts, separated by dots. This allows for some clever naming conventions for all your packages, for example:

```
accounts.receivable
accounts.billable
taxes.usa.california
taxes.usa.florida
```

Java has a standard convention for naming packages that ensures universal uniqueness. The general rule is to start all your package names with the reverse of your company's internet domain name, minus the "www." part. For example, all packages supplied by IBM start with "com.ibm," and add on to that, so AS/400 related packages start with "com.ibm.as400," and VisualAge for Java supplied packages start with "com.ibm.ivj." Your package names should start with "com.*yourcompany*," as in:

```
com.yourcompany.accounts
com.yourcompany.taxes
com.yourcompany.hr
```

As you will discover throughout this book, Java supplies all of its classes in packages, and these all start with java, as in `java.io`, `java.math`, and `java.util`. Almost all Java classes you look at will import one or more of these JDK-supplied packages. An all-important package, containing critical core classes, is the `java.lang` package. Because of its importance, this package is always imported for you, just as the unnamed package is. All JDK-supplied classes are in named packages. Other than `java.lang`, you have to explicitly import the packages containing the classes you wish to use.

Packages and the file system

When you compile a class after adding the package statement at the top to identify the package it is in, there is nothing different about the resulting .class file. No new file system object is created for you. However, there is something you have to do!

As mentioned earlier, packages are not file system objects the way service programs are. However, Java does need a way of segregating packages on disk and a way of finding classes by package, on disk. To this end, there are rules for the location where classes inside a package must exist in the file system. Each dot-separated part of a multi-part package name must correspond to a subdirectory in the file system. This is the convention that the Java compiler and runtime will follow when looking for package-qualified classes. So, for example, if you have package com.acme.orders with three classes in it, your file directory structure must look like this:

```
com
    acme
        orders
            OrderGUI.class
            OrderDatabase.class
            OrderReport.class
```

All of the classes inside com.acme.orders must exist in the directory tree \com\acme\orders. (Notice that each dot-separated part of the package name becomes a separate subdirectory of the same name.) These names are *very* case-sensitive. The Java runtime will look for subdirectories with exactly the same case as the package name, just as it does when looking for a class.

Where is this tree "anchored?" In your current directory. When you compile from your current directory, the compiler looks for these subdirectories under it when it encounters an import com.acme.orders statement, or when it encounters a package com.acme.orders statement and you reference other classes in this package. For this reason, your current directory is always the parent of subdirectory com, and you always keep your .java files there. After compiling, copy the resulting .class file to the subdirectory appropriate for its package, so compiles of other classes can find it. Who creates these subdirectories? You do! Who copies the .class files there? You do! Of course, none of this is required when using only classes in the unnamed package, or when using tools like VisualAge for Java.

A classpath versus a library list

If you followed that last discussion, you see that to successfully compile any .java file that uses classes from any other packages, those classes must exist in appropriately named subdirectories under the current directory. This is fine for a while when writing and using your own stuff, but it becomes a pain quickly. For example, it would seem to imply that you need to copy all of Java's supplied classes to directories under your current directory. Also, what happens if you want to compile code in another directory? Do you have to copy all the subdirectory trees to it? Of course, the answer is no.

Java offers a way to identify a list of directories that will be searched when it is looking for classes, both at compile time and runtime. Indeed, this is just what the library list does when compiling and running RPG.

The equivalent to the AS/400 library list in Java is the CLASSPATH environment variable. This is where you list all the directories that the Java compiler and virtual machine will search when looking for a class, separated by semicolons on Windows or colons on UNIX, OS/400, and OS/390. On OS/400, this will be a list of Integrated File System (IFS) directories, and you can use the new ADDENVVAR command to set it or the CHGENVVAR command to change it. On Windows 95 and Windows 98, you set it in the autoexec.bat file, while on Windows NT and Windows 2000, you set it via the System icon in your Control Panel folder. So in Windows 98, you might have this:

```
SET CLASSPATH = .;c:\myJava;c:\myOtherJava
```

Java searches these directories only after searching the current directory, but we still prefer to put the current directory as the first entry to be sure. When looking for classes in the unnamed package, Java simply searches all the directories in the order they are specified, looking for the .class file.

When searching for classes in named packages, however, Java searches first for the subdirectories (e.g., com\acme\orders) underneath each directory listed on the classpath, and only if it finds those will it search inside the final subdirectory (c:\myJava\com\acme\orders) for the .class file. It searches underneath each directory specified in the CLASSPATH environment variable until it finds the file in the appropriate subdirectory or reaches the end of the list of directories. Thus, you do not have to copy all package directory trees all over your system; you can put them in one spot and point to their root directory via CLASSPATH.

Distributing Java packages

When your packages are ready for distribution, you may distribute them in their directory structure. Users can then copy that structure intact (using xcopy -s, say) to any parent directory they wish. They then add that parent directory to their classpath and away they go, running your application or writing new code that uses the classes in your package.

The problem with this, though, is the inconvenience of shipping and installing many files. To make distribution easier, Java has always supported compressing many .class files into a single .zip file using ZIP compression utilities like PKWare's PKZIP or the commonly used WINZIP utility by Nico Mak Computing, Inc. (Check *www.shareware.com* for these.) The really cool thing about this is that your users do not have to unzip these files! The Java *class loader* can read classes directly out of them. We love this. Thus, you often find that companies ship their Java code in a file like classes.zip.

After copying a .zip file into the file system, users must set up their CLASSPATH environment variable to point directly to it. For example, on Windows 98, you might edit your autoexec.bat file to contain the following:

```
SET CLASSPATH = .;c:\myJava;c:\myJava\classes.zip
```

It is not enough to just point to the directory containing the file, you must point directly to the .zip file itself, fully qualified by path name.

The only downside to .zip files is that they are really a Windows-only technology, and Java runs on every operating system. It also runs in Web browsers and PDAs and toys. To solve this, Sun invented .jar files. These use the same technology to do the compression, but use an all-Java tool that comes in the JDK to compress and decompress. Like .zip files, classes can be read directly out of .jar files. Indeed, Java can read any file directly out of a .jar file, such as any image and audio files your Java code might use. As with .zip files, you simply name the fully qualified .jar file on your classpath:

```
SET CLASSPATH = .;c:\myJava;c:\myJava\classes.jar
```

The term "JAR" is short for "Java archive." While commonly used for all Java distribution requirements today, they were initially invented to speed up download time of applets by allowing all the classes and auxiliary files to be put into one compressed file and downloaded over the Internet to the Web browser. Prior to .jar files, all files came down separately, which was too slow. You do not use CLASSPATH for applets; rather, you use an APPLET tag inside your HTML Web page source, with a CODE parameter pointing to the applet class, a CODEPATH parameter identifying the host directory, and an ARCHIVE parameter naming the .jar files:

```
<APPLET code=OrderGUI.class
        codebase="http://www.acme.com/javafiles"
        archive="orders.jar + taxes.jar"
        height=500 width=300>
</APPLET>
```

Here is how you would use the jar command to "jar up" all the classes in your current directory (unnamed package) and all the classes in the com\acme\orders directory (com.acme.orders package):

```
java -cvf myClasses.jar *.class com\acme\orders\*.class
```

The -cvf options tell the command to create a new .jar file, with verbose output messages, and name the file myClasses.jar. After that, one or more file names are specified. These can be simple names or generic wildcard names. To "unjar," even though it is not necessary, you can do this:

```
java -xvf myClasses.jar
```

This extracts all the contents, preserving the relative subdirectory names, if present. To simply see what files are in the JAR file, use the -tvf (type, verbose, file) options. To see all the options, just type jar without parameters.

Because .jar and .zip files use the same technology, you can use tools like WINZIP to work with a .jar file, and the jar command to work with .zip files.

JAVA ACCESSOR RIGHTS

Now that you have seen all of the Java constructs (variables, methods, classes, and packages), we can formally summarize what the access modifiers are and what they do. You can divide the world up into the classes that make up your package, and other classes that use your package. By default, all classes, class variables, instance variables, and methods are accessible by *all* the code in this package—and *only* the code in this package. This is called "package" access control, and it's what you get if you don't specify any access modifiers. This is equivalent to specifying the EXPORT keyword on your procedures in RPG, but *not* specifying EXPORT(*ALL) on CRTSRVPGM or identifying the procedure in your binder language source. You can further qualify the level of accessibility by using access control modifiers:

- *public*. All code is allowed access to this variable, method, or class. This is the only modifier allowed for classes.

- *protected*. Only this class or classes that extend this class are allowed access to this variable, method, or constructor. (Extending a class is discussed in Chapter 9.)

- *private*. Only the code inside this class is allowed access to this variable or method. This modifier is not permitted on classes or constructors.

Table 2.5 compares each of these access rights to RPG IV procedure access rights. Remember that in RPG, all procedures (and fields) that specify the EXPORT keyword are available to all other modules in the program or service program (package access), while only the subsets listed in the binding source are available for users of the service program (public access), unless EXPORT(*ALL) is used, in which case all procedures with the EXPORT keyword are available for users of the service program. If you do not even specify the EXPORT keyword, only code in this module can call the procedure.

Table 2.5: Java Method Access Modifiers versus RPG Procedures	
Java	**RPG**
package (default)	EXPORT keyword, but not in binding source or no EXPORT(*ALL)
public	EXPORT keyword, and in binding source or EXPORT(*ALL)
protected	not applicable
private	no EXPORT keyword

SUMMARY

Phew! You've covered a lot of ground in this chapter, both from an RPG IV point of view and from a Java point of view. For Java, you have learned that:

- An application is comprised of Java source files (.java) that are compiled via javac into Java .class files containing bytecode.

- Source files contains one class (typically) with instance variables and methods that use those variables.

- Flow of control starts with a Java class containing a main method, and continues via object instantiation and object method calls through to other Java classes.

- You instantiate a class instance into an object using the new operator, which returns the address of that object.

- Variables of a class type are called object reference variables.

- To call a method or access a variable in an object, use the dot operator.

- Two Java methods in the same class can have the same name, as long as their signatures are different (overloading). A method signature is defined as the name, the number of parameters, and the type of the parameters, collectively.

- Variables that are not declared with the static modifier are called instance variables.

- Variables declared with the static modifier are called class variables and have the same value across all objects of the class. They can be accessed by qualifying with the class name versus an object reference variable.

- Methods declared with the static modifier are called class methods. They can be accessed by qualifying with the class name versus an object reference variable.

- Java classes can have constructors, which are implicitly called by the Java runtime when an object is created with the new operator. These have the same name as the class and do not specify a return type. They can be overloaded.

- The `main` method gets control from the command line, and must have an explicit signature and modifiers: `public static void main(String args[])`.

- You can pass parameters from the command line, and the `main` method gets them as entries in the `args` array of `String` objects.

- You can write to the console by passing any variable, string literal, or plus-operator-separated list to the method `System.out.println()`.

- Java classes are grouped using packages, which you identify with the `package` statement and access with the `import` statement.

- Java allows you to explicitly define who can instantiate your class: code in this package (the default) or all code (the `public` modifier).

- Java allows you to explicitly define who can call methods and who can read or write variables: all code (`public`), code in this package (the default), code in extending classes (`protected`) or code in this class only (`private`).

- You should make all instance variables `private`, and supply `get` and `set` methods to retrieve or set the value.

JAVA'S LANGUAGE AND SYNTAX 3

This chapter examines Java in more detail, focusing on the language's core syntax. It introduces you to the basics of the Java language, including the syntax of comments, statements, expressions, and operators. Subsequent chapters build on this by moving into other core areas of the language.

I WANT TO BE FREE! THE JAVA BASICS

Unlike RPG, which is column-oriented, Java is a free-form language. All redundant white space is ignored by the compiler, including line breaks. For example, this:

```
void myMethod(int parameter1) { return; }
```

is equivalent to this:

```
void myMethod(int parameter1)
{
    return;
}
```

Freedom in Java, as in other realms, is best enjoyed by observing a few rules. To aid in programmer readability, you'll probably want to set some standards in your shop regarding indentation and style. The rules themselves are not as important as using them consistently, so everyone can effectively read everyone else's code. We try to write code with a consistent style in this book, so you will get a good base, although occasionally we show some code in a compressed format, in the interest of space. Here are the loose style guidelines we "mostly" follow:

- Naming conventions:

    ➢ Package names: `all.lower.case`

    ➢ Class names: `UppercaseFirstLetterOfEachWord`

    ➢ Variable and method names: `uppercaseFirstLetterExceptFirstWord`

    ➢ Constants: `ALL_UPPERCASE`

- Brace alignment:

    ➢ Lined-up directly under the first letter of the block, except on `if` statements, where we indent by two spaces, and always on lines by themselves

- Instance and class variable locations:

    ➢ Always before method definitions

- Indentation:

    ➢ Declarations of variables and methods inside classes: four spaces

    ➢ Code inside methods: four spaces

    ➢ Code inside code: two spaces

- White space (blanks):

  ➤ Around expression operators: one

  ➤ Between parameter declarations on a method: one

  ➤ Between expressions on a for loop: one

Even RPG IV code, with its increasingly free-format syntax, benefits from style conventions. A good one can be found at the News/400 Web site, *www.news400.com.*

All statements in Java end in a semicolon. This is a result of the free-form style of the language—the compiler needs a definitive way to determine the end of one statement and the start of another. Thus, in the previous examples, the return statement ends in a semicolon. Again, white space is not important, so the following are equivalent:

```
return;
return      ;
return
   ;
```

The next pervasive syntactical note to keep in mind about Java is that curly braces are used to delimit the beginning and end of blocks. In the previous example, notice that the body of the method myMethod starts with an opening brace, {, and ends with a closing brace, }. These braces are used to delimit classes, methods, and bodies of statement blocks. Every opening brace must eventually be followed by a closing brace.

So, "brace yourself" to see many semicolons and a lot of free space.

COMMENTS

As a responsible programmer, you always document your code with meaningful comments. (Don't you?) The process of specifying comments in RPG IV has not really changed from RPG III. To specify a comment, you put an asterisk in column 7 of any RPG specification. The spec type itself in column 6 is optional for comment lines, as shown here:

```
1234567
      C*  This is one style of comments in RPG IV
      ***********************************************************
      *  This is another one                                   *
      ***********************************************************

      D* More comments
```

In RPG IV, you can also place line comments after column 80 (the RPG IV source member length minimum is 100, compared to 80 for RPG III). Further, as the example above shows, blank lines are legal and encouraged for readability in RPG IV, versus RPG III, where the compiler complained about them. In Java, you have three types of comments at your disposal, shown in Table 3.1.

Table 3.1: Comments in Java	
Comment Type	Description
/* comment */	Multi-line comments surrounded by /* and */
// comment	Single-line comments using the double-slashes
/** comment */	JavaDoc comments surrounded by /** and */

Java comments

Like C and C++, Java uses /* (a forward slash immediately followed by an asterisk, with no intermediate blank allowed) to indicate the start of multi-line comments and */ (an asterisk immediately followed by a backward slash) to end them:

```
/* this is a multiple
   line comment */
```

Everything between the comment delimiters is commented out, no matter how many lines it crosses. This form of markup is often used for comment blocks, like this:

```
/*-------------------------------*
 * Please read these comments    *
 * as they are very important!   *
 *-------------------------------*/
```

You cannot nest these block comments inside each other, as in /* outer /* inner */ outer */. Also, because it is easy to forget the ending delimiter, even the best of us have been known to accidentally comment out large chunks of code in Java. A good editor (such as those in VisualAge for Java, VisualAge for RPG, or CODE/400 on Windows) will eliminate this problem. These editors show comments in a different color than the rest of the code, so you can see at a glance when lines have been inadvertently commented out.

Two slashes, //, indicate a single-line comment. All text after // is ignored to the end of line, as in:

```
// show comment example
int myVariable = 10; // define and initialize variable
```

The final kind of Java comment is a refinement of the multi-line comment. These are called *JavaDoc comments*, and they use a double asterisk to start the multi-line comment, like this:

```
/** Hey you,    *
  * read this! */
```

This comment is identical to the multi-line type with two exceptions: it can also be used by the javadoc command to generate API documentation from the code, and it recognizes special "tags" within the code to aid the generated output. The following section describes this comment style in more detail.

JavaDoc comments

We all know the importance of documenting our code, both internally and externally. Typically, it's done as a benefit to the poor followers who have to maintain the brilliant (yet indecipherable) code we leave behind. In Java, the need is even more pressing, because Java is all about reuse of code, and such reuse is accomplished by supplying compiled classes to others for their benefit. Since the code you supply is compiled, these users have no access to the internal comments. Therefore, they must rely on some form of external documentation to tell them how to use the classes and, most importantly, what the methods are and exactly what parameters they expect. What the methods do and what they return is also of vital importance to other programmers; otherwise, how will they know when and how to call the methods. RPG IV service programs have a similar need. However, for these, we have at least the copy member that contains the exported procedure prototypes as a form of documentation. Java has no concept of copy members or included files.

With this in mind, Java supplies an easy way to embed important API informational comments right in your code where they belong, and yet extract those comments out to produce external HTML documentation. This is a very good thing! It means that these comments can double as both internal and external documentation, and that a consistent format for the information can be achieved.

The JDK includes a utility command called `javadoc` that generates API documentation from source code containing JavaDoc comments. For example, to generate documentation for a class called `Extract`, you would type the following:

```
c:\> javadoc Extract.java
```

The argument passed to `javadoc` is a series of Java package names or source files. The javadoc command parses the JavaDoc-style comments contained in the source files and produces a set of HTML pages describing the classes, interfaces, constructors, methods, and class-level variables. The output of `javadoc` depends on whether you are using JDK 1.1.x or JDK 1.2.0 or higher, since the output files changed for JDK 1.2.0. Specifically, it produces the files shown in Table 3.2 for JDK 1.1.X, all in one directory.

Table 3.2 Files Produced by the JAVADOC Command in JDK 1.1.x

File Type	Description
Main entry point	The main starting point for readers is a file named index.html.
Package list	An index list of all packages is put in a file named packages.html.
Index	An index of all classes and members found is put in a file named AllNames.html.
Class hierarchy	A list of all classes found and their hierarchy is put in a file named tree.html.
List of methods	One file per class (ClassName.html) lists the class and its methods.

For JDK 1.2.0 (which was branded "Java 2" by Sun) or higher, the output is now the files listed in Table 3.3, in multiple subdirectories (one subdirectory tree per unique package name, so `javax.swing` becomes subdirectory tree `\javax\swing`).

Table 3.3 Files Produced by the JAVADOC Command in JDK 1.2.0 or Higher

File Type	Description
Main entry point	The file index.html now uses HTML frames.
Package list	An index list of all packages is put in package-list.html.
Index	An index of all package, classes, and members is in index-all.html.
Class hierarchy	A list of all classes found and their hierarchy is put in over-view-tree.html.
List of methods	One file per class (ClassName.html) lists the class and its methods. This is found in a subdirectory tree that matches the name of the package containing the class. Each dot-separated part of the package name becomes a subdirectory, so my.package becomes my\package.

When javadoc parses a documentation comment, leading asterisk characters on each line are discarded. For lines other than the first, blanks and tabs preceding the initial asterisk characters are also discarded. This illustrates JavaDoc comments in Java source:

```
/** This is class MyClass</U>
 *   and we sure hope you like it
 *   @author  George & Phil
 *   @version 1.0
 */
```

Comments can include embedded HTML tags. In this example, the HTML text MyClass</U> produces underlined text for MyClass. The first sentence of each comment should provide a concise, yet complete, description of the declared entity. This sentence ends at the first period. It is important to be concise and describe the complete entity, because javadoc copies this to the member summary at the top of the HTML file. (Recall that the term *member* refers collectively to methods and class-level variables.) By default, javadoc only produces documentation for public classes and public or protected members, but this can be overridden with the -public, -package, or -private options to the command.

Besides parsing HTML tags, javadoc recognizes a special set of tags, called *keywords*, that starts with the at-sign (@). These tags provide additional information such as "See Also" references, an author name, or a version number for the text. The preceding used two tags: @author describes the author name, and @version identifies the version of the files. Table 3.4 summarizes the tags that javadoc recognizes.

Table 3.4: JavaDoc Tags

Tag Name	Description
@author	Formats the given author name. A comment may contain multiple @author tags. This tag can only be used in a class or interface comment, not for a method or variable.
@see	Adds a hyperlinked "See Also" entry. The class name can be qualified by the package name. To reference a method or variable's javadoc documentation, use a pound sign (#) after the class name, as in @see package.class#method.
@version	Formats the given "Version" information. A comment may contain at most one @version tag. This tag can only be used in a class or interface documentation comment, not for a method or variable.
@since	Adds a "Since" entry. This tag means that this change or feature has existed since the specified release number.
@deprecated	Identifies this as an obsolete method. You should list the replacement. If the member is obsolete and there is no replacement, the argument to @deprecated should be "No replacement."
@return	Adds a "Returns" section, which contains the description of the return value.
@param	Formats the given parameter name and its description in the parameters section of a method description. The description may be continued on the next line. Only one tag is allowed per parameter.
@throws	New in JDK 1.2, describes an exception thrown by this method, @throws class-name description. Only one tag is allowed per exception. (Exceptions are covered in Chapter 10.)
@serial, @serialData, @serialField	New in JDK 1.2, describes information related to "serializing" this class to disk, an advanced topic covered in Chapter 14.
{@link xxx}	New in JDK 1.2, identical to @see, but generates inline hypertext links versus a separate "See also" section.

Each tag except @link must start at the beginning of a line. Try to keep tags that have the same name together within a comment. For example, put all @author tags together, so that javadoc can tell where the list ends. Listing 3.1 is an example of a documented class.

Listing 3.1: JavaDoc Comments in a Class

```
/**
 * A cool class.
 *
 * @author Phil Coulthard and George Farr
 * @version 1.0
 * @see YourClass
 */
public class MyClass
{
    /**
     * Constructor
     */
    Public MyClass()
    { } // empty for now

    /**
     * Shows a message
     * @param  message The message string to show
     * @return void
     * @see    MyClass#MyMethod2(String message)
     */
    public void myMethod(String message)
    {
        System.out.println(message);
    }
    /**
     * Shows a message in quotes
     * @param  message The message string to show
     * @return String object containing quotes
     * @see    MyClass#MyMethod(String message)
     */
    public String myMethod2(String message)
    {
        String newMessage = "'" + message + "'";
        System.out.println(newMessage);
        return newMessage;
    }
} // end class MyClass
```

You create a new subdirectory to hold the results of javadoc, and run javadoc against your class source file, using the directory option (-d) to put the output in the new subdirectory:

```
C:\JAVA> md html
C:\JAVA> javadoc -d html MyClass.java
```

Then, *only* for JDK 1.1.x, you need to copy the image files that the generated HTML uses to an images subdirectory off the new html subdirectory:

```
C:\JAVA> cd html
C:\JAVA\html> md images
C:\JAVA\html> copy c:\jdk1.1.8\docs\api\images\*.* images
```

JDK 1.2.0 or higher does not use image files in its generated JavaDoc HTML, so this step is not needed.

Finally, you can open one of the generated HTML files by typing start MyClass.html. This causes your Web browser to open the file. Part of the result (for JDK 1.2.2) is shown in Internet Explorer in Figure 3.1.

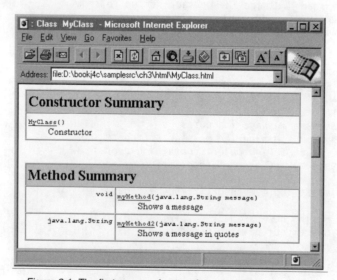

Figure 3.1: The first screen of output from JavaDoc

Due to space constraints, we can't show the whole result, but Figure 3.2 shows another part—what you see when you click the myMethod link in Figure 3.1.

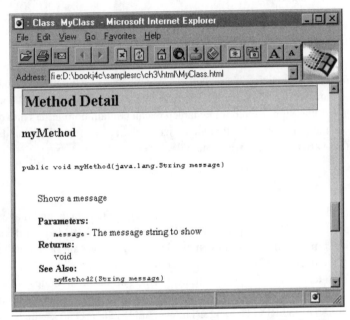

Figure 3.2: Another section of documentation produced by JavaDoc

For more information about JavaDoc, consult the JDK documentation. Specifically, look for the file \docs\tooldocs\javadoc\index.html off your JDK directory.

VARIABLE NAMING

An important feature shared by RPG and Java is the ability to reference data that is stored in memory by using descriptive symbolic names (called fields or variables) rather than numeric memory-cell addresses. Each field in your program must have a unique name. RPG IV limits field names to 4,096 characters (as of V3R7) and ignores case for field names. Java, on the other hand, allows variable names to have unlimited length, and Java names are very case-sensitive.

Case-sensitivity is a key point that the RPG programmer must consider. Its importance cannot be overemphasized. All referenced and declared names must match letter-for-letter. Furthermore, the source file name must match verbatim the defined class name inside the source file, including the case. Otherwise, the compiler will generate errors that you might not be able to diagnose easily. It bears repeating that, as a Java programmer, you must be especially sensitive!

The naming syntax for fields and variables

For RPG IV names, the first character must be alphabetic. It can include the special characters $, #, and @; the remaining characters can be alphabetic or numeric, including the underscore _ character. For Java names, the first character can be any valid letter, the underscore, or the dollar sign. Remaining characters can contain both letters and digits. Furthermore, Java names can actually include Unicode characters as well, if you desire. Go ahead, give that variable a nice Arabic name!

Keywords

Keywords are identifiers or names that are reserved by the language, and that carry special meaning within it. For example, in RPG IV, the CONST and INZ keywords on the D-spec tell the compiler that the field you are defining is a constant or that its initial value is supplied by the parameter. The RPG IV reference manual describes all of the keywords you can use on the H, F, and D specifications. Further, all of the op-codes are keywords. RPG IV also has other special words called *figurative constants*. You have used these since the inception of the RPG language. They include *ZERO/*ZEROS, which initializes a field to zeros, or *BLANK/*BLANKS, which initializes a character field to blanks. The other figurative constants are *HIVAL, *LOVAL, *null, *ON, *OFF, and *ALL.

Keywords are used by Java and all other languages. Language designers decide on their names, usage, and meanings for each specific language. Because keywords and figurative constants have special meaning, you cannot use them as names of fields or variables in your programs. Table 3.5 lists the reserved keywords in Java.

Table 3.5: Reserved Keywords in Java			
abstract	boolean	break	byte
case	catch	char	class
const	continue	default	do
double	else	extends	false
final	finally	float	for

		Table 3.5: Reserved Keywords in Java (continued)	
goto	if	implements	import
instanceof	int	interface	long
native	new	null	package
private	protected	public	return
short	static	super	switch
synchronized	this	throw	throws
transient	true	try	void
volatile	while		

The two special words const and goto are not used in Java. They may be assigned meanings in future versions of the Java language but, in truth, their reserved status is to keep C and C++ programmers from accidentally using them.

COMPARING ANATOMIES

To compare the two languages, let's review at a high level the anatomy of an RPG program and then compare that to a high-level view of a Java class. (Interesting terms we use in computer science, aren't they? *Anatomies* describe *bodies* of code. We aren't pulling your *leg*! We just want to give you a *hand*!)

The anatomy of an RPG program

An RPG IV program consists of specifications, which must be in the correct order. The specifications are Control, File, Definition, Input, Calculation, and Output. There are also procedures, which are made up of a beginning and ending Procedure specification, within which are Definition and Calculation specifications.

The interesting specifications in terms of actual executable code are the Calculation specifications, which contain op-codes defining the operation to perform, and the information required by the op-code. Generally, we refer to a C-spec that has an op-code as a *statement*. There are fixed-format op-codes and the newer free-format factor-two op-codes. The fixed-format statements you are familiar with from RPG III. The new free-format factor-two op-codes allow an expression to be coded in the expanded factor 2 in columns 36 to 80, and that expression can be continued in factor 2 of subsequent C-specs as needed. (Continuation C-specs have no op-code, and no continuation character is required unless a name or literal is split.) The free-format op-codes are CALLP, DOU, DOW, EVAL, EVALR, FOR, IF, RETURN, and WHEN.

Expressions coded in factor 2 of a free-format statement come in two flavors:

- *Computational expressions* are fields, named constants, literals, built-in function calls, and procedure calls optionally combined with binary operators (+, -, *, /, **) or unary operators (+, -). Expressions can be placed inside parenthesis for precedence, and one expression can be an operand itself within a larger expression. These are most often used to compute a value that is assigned on an EVAL statement, returned on a RETURN statement, or compared to other expressions in DOW, DOU, FOR, WHEN, and IF statements. Blanks are used mainly to resolve ambiguity, but may be used for readability.

- *Conditional expressions* evaluate to true or false, determining alternative flows of control in DOW, DOU, FOR, WHEN, and IF statements. They can be simple expressions, complex expressions combining multiple simple expressions with AND or OR, or negating expressions with NOT. Simple expressions are made of computational expressions together with relational operators (=, >, <, >=, <=,).

Now, let's look at Java's anatomy.

The anatomy of a Java Class

A Java class contains a class definition, which consists of variable declaration statements and method definitions. Method definitions consist of variable declaration statements and other statements. The interesting parts are the statements. Statements in Java come in different flavors:

- *Variable declaration statements* are used to define identifiers or variables. Variables are defined by a type, followed by an identifier name. Non-local variable declarations can also optionally start with a modifier such as public. They always end in a semicolon, and they can optionally include an initialization phrase, as in int x = 10;.

- *Expression statements* are certain kinds of expressions that become statements by ending them with a semicolon. These are assignment expressions, pre/post increment/decrement expressions, method invocation expressions, and class instance creation expressions. We will cover these as we go. Note that methods that return nothing can't be called in expressions; they must be called in standalone statements. However, even methods that do return something can be called standalone, in which case the return value is ignored. For example, `myObject.myMethod();` is a valid standalone statement.

- *Block statements* are a way to combine multiple statements into a single statement, using the block delimiters `{` and `}`. Block statements can be used anywhere single statements are allowed. Blocks can also contain variable declaration statements.

- Empty statements simply contain a semicolon and do nothing. (Hey, what's the point?)

- *Labeled statements* can be labeled by preceding them with a label identifier and a colon, such that they can become the transfer-of-control targets of the `break` and `continue` statements (covered later).

- *Other statements* in Java are subdivided into decision, loop, and transfer statements that affect the flow of control. These are covered in the next chapter.

Note there are no compiler directives as RPG has, although you can think of `package` and `import` statements as being compiler directives, if that helps. You can have more than one statement per physical line, but this is considered bad style.

Expressions in Java, unlike RPG, are divided into the following two categories:

- *Fetch expressions* are executed just for the value they result in, which is used in place of a simple variable or literal. These can be subcategorized into conditional (boolean) and non-conditional (numeric or character) expressions.

- *Computational expressions* are the three explicit expressions null, method call, and array indexing.

All these statement types and expression syntax are covered in more detail shortly. Remember, though, that white space (blanks) is not important to the Java compiler. So, X=A+B is the same as X = A + B, and you can decide what you like best.

STATEMENTS

Programmers use *statements* to control the sequence and frequency of execution of different segments of a program. Because of RPG's fixed-form nature, the compiler can easily analyze and parse the syntax of the values present in their fixed-column locations. Unlike RPG, Java is a free-form language. There is no demarcation of a line by columns. There are many more variations of what makes up an executable statement, what indicates a block of consecutive statements, and what ends an executable line of code. The following sections cover four of the six different types of statements in Java:

- Expression
- Block
- Empty
- Labeled

The other two are variable declaration statements and other statements. They're covered in Chapter 5 and Chapter 4, respectively.

The expression statement

With the simple arithmetic operators plus, minus, multiply, and divide (+, -, *, /), you can build simple arithmetic expressions in both Java and RPG. For example, X + 1 or Y + 2 / 3 are simple expressions, where X and Y are variables. The following examples demonstrate different expressions you may use in your programs:

```
1.8 / 3
X+2-3+I
amountDue > 0
```

On their own, these expressions are not very interesting, but even if you end them in a semicolon, they are not valid statements. Instead, they are used as *part* of a statement for their value. For example, you can assign expressions in a program to a variable, thus turning the expression into an assignment statement. To do this, you use a field on the left side with the assignment operator (equal sign), as follows:

```
myvalue =  1.8 / 3
result  =  X+2-3+I
```

Notice in these examples that the white space between the operators is generally not important, although consistency does aid readability. These examples show how you might code some sample expressions in your program, but they are not syntactically correct for Java statements. Can you guess why not? To make these valid expression assignment statements, you must end each with a semicolon. Obviously, RPG, as a column-oriented language, has no construct like the statement terminator. However, even for RPG, these expressions are valid only when used with one of the free-format factor-two op-codes to form a statement.

An expression statement consists of an expression that is executed for its side effects. For instance, the assignment expression has the side effect of altering the value of a variable (the operand on the left side of the statement). A method (in Java) or procedure (in RPG) call can have the side effects of the call. If you don't care about the returned value (or it doesn't return anything), you can just code the method call without assigning the result in an assignment statement. For example, this is a legal Java statement:

```
myObject.myMethod();
```

The other expression statements in Java are the pre- and post-increment and -decrement expression statements (covered later), and the new operator expression statement. You saw the new operator in Chapter 2, and almost always assign the result of it to an object reference variable to form an assignment statement. However, you can also code a call to new as a standalone statement by itself, just for the side effect of creating the object. (Maybe it starts the payroll system in its constructor!) For example, this is a legal Java statement:

```
new Payroll();
```

The block statement

A Java block statement groups together a sequence of one or more statements. The group is delimited by enclosing it with a starting brace, {, and a closing brace, }. A semicolon is used to end each statement in the sequence, as usual. There is no semicolon after either brace. Braces can be used to group declarations and statements together into a single entity, or block. They are syntactically equivalent to single braces that surround the statements of a class or method. You can also group multiple statements together after an if or while structure. For example, you can block the expression statements used in the previous example as follows:

```
{
  myvalue =  1.8 / 3;
  result  =  X+2-3+I;
}
```

This block is syntactically correct. The compiler will not issue any errors for it. However, it would be more typical for you to block a group of statements in order to make them look equivalent to a single statement. You can then apply an `if` or a loop condition before the block. The compiler will execute the block only if the condition is met. Another reason to use blocks is to define a set of variables locally in the block. If you try to reference one of these variables outside the block, the compiler will indicate that it is not declared. For example, the `if` statement syntax in Java is as follows:

```
if (expression)
   statement;
```

To condition the previous example, you would code an `if` with its expression above the block. This indicates to the compiler that you want the block to execute only when the expression evaluates to true. To use an `if` condition with a block of code, you would code as follows:

```
if (expression)
   {
   float myvalue; // declare a float type variable called myvalue
   int   result;  // declare an integer type variable called result
   myvalue   = 1.8 / 3;
   result    = X+2-3+I;
   }
```

It is important to note that the block is treated as a single statement. That is, either all or none of the statements inside it are executed. If you only had one statement to execute after the `if`, you would not need the braces. For example, the following `if` statement is syntactically correct:

```
if (x == 2)
   x = x+1;
```

You normally use a block statement when you want to execute more than one statement after an `if` or `while` condition. Braces are allowed, but optional when you have only one statement to execute. In other words, you could have coded the example as follows:

```
if (x == 2)
   {
      x = x + 1;
   }
```

In Java, the double equal sign, ==, distinguishes comparisons such as this one from assignment statements that use the single equal sign. Note also that assignment statements are not allowed inside a conditional expression like this. Only expressions that evaluate to true or false are allowed. This is different than C, and leads to many bugs in C when a single equal sign is used in a relational expression by mistake.

The empty statement

The simplest kind of Java statement is an empty one. You now know that Java statements must end with a semicolon. Consider statements like this:

```
if (x == 2)
   ;
for (i = 0; i < 10; i = i + 1)
{
   ;
}
```

Are they syntactically correct? (Do not worry about the syntax of the for statement for now.) Yes. A semicolon on its own with nothing preceding it is just another Java statement. It is called the empty statement. Empty statements are very rarely used, but they appear occasionally as the true part of an if statement when all you are interested in is the else part, for example:

```
if (x > 2)
   ;
else
   // interesting statements
```

This, however, is more elegantly coded by negating the conditional expression. Also notice that an equivalent to the empty statement is an *empty block*, for example:

```
if (x > 2)
   {}
```

The labeled statement

Java labels are similar to the RPG TAG operation code, with the tag name specified in factor one. In Java, you can have one or more labels separated by a colon. The following example shows a label definition:

```
ReturnPoint: while (x>10)
            {
               // code
            }
```

In RPG, a TAG can be specified on any line. In Java, too, any line can be labeled. However, the compiler only recognizes a label at the beginning of a loop, such as a while or for loop, when it is used as a target with the break or continue statement. Also, label names are independent of all other kinds of names used in the program. For example, you can have a variable defined as an integer and, in the same block of code, also have a label with the same name. The compiler can distinguish between both entities. The most common use of labels is with the break statement. Listing 3.2 illustrates this usage.

Listing 3.2: The Java break Statement

```
int index = 1;
int index2 = 1;

outerLoop: while(true)
{
    index = index + 1;
    index2 = 1;
    innerLoop: while(true)
    {
        index2 = index2 + 1;
        if (index2 == 3)
          break outerLoop;
    }
}
```

First, two loops are defined, one outer and one nested inner. The outer loop is labeled outerLoop, and you are then able to exit directly from that outer loop using a labeled break statement. If you did not specify the outerLoop parameter with break, you could only have exited the innermost loop. Note that you are not jumping to a labeled statement, but rather exiting from a labeled loop. (The if, for, while, and break statements are covered in detail in the next chapter.)

Listing 3.3 illustrates all of the Java statement types. To get extra credit for this lesson, take a little pop quiz by considering each statement. Decide which ones are syntactically correct and which ones the Java compiler would flag as an error.

Listing 3.3: Examples of All Java Statements

```java
public class Statement
{
    public static void main(String args[])
    {
        int x = 8;
        for (int i=0;i<10;i++)
        { }
        label1:
        while(x<0)
        {
          break label1;
          ;
        }
        if (x == 10);
          ;
        {};
        {
          System.out.println("I am in a block!");
        }
        label0:;
        label2:label3:label4:;
    }
}
```

The first structure is a `for` loop with all header information correctly specified. It includes an empty block. This is syntactically correct in Java. Next, a labeled statement has a loop that breaks out of the label. Again, this is correct. On the line after the `break label1;` statement, an empty statement is specified. Next, the statement `if ( x==10 );` is a correctly specified `if` statement with an empty body. Then, there is an empty block, followed immediately by an empty statement. Both are valid in Java, and so is the block that includes the `println` statement. Finally, several labels are defined, separated by colons. This is also correct.

As it turns out, all of the Java code in this example compiles cleanly. It is not terribly useful, but it is valid. It demonstrates many of Java's syntax rules and statement types. Feel free to use it!

EXPRESSIONS AND OPERATORS

Expressions in RPG and Java are used to fetch, compute, and store values. Those that compute and store values are referred to as *computational expressions,* and those that simply fetch a value without altering it are called *fetch expressions.* (We'll cover the latter later.)

Table 3.6 illustrates the simplest form of a computational expression. The RPG expression *IN(99) will return zero or one, and end the loop if it is zero. The Java expression (in99) will return true or false and end the loop if it is false. (The variable must be declared boolean in this case.) Both of these are *computation expressions.* They don't do much computation, however, other than return the current value in the variable and test it for truth or falsity.

Table 3.6: An RPG DOW Statement versus a Java while Statement			
RPG			**Java**
C	DOW	*IN(99)	while (in99)
C			{
C	ENDDO		}

Table 3.7 illustrates another computational expression. This expression computes the value x + 1 and stores the result of the computation back into x. Strictly speaking, in both columns of Table 3.7, only "x = x + 1" is an expression. The EVAL op-code in RPG makes it a statement, and the semicolon in Java makes it a statement. Unlike RPG, though, that expression in Java is also valid in other situations. For example, in Java, it would be legal to code this:

```
y = (x = x + 1);
```

In this case, that whole expression of (x = x + 1) is used as a sub-expression in an expression assignment statement. In this case, the nested assignment is actually performed, so the side effect of this is to not only assign a value to y, but also to assign a new value to x! This is not a good programming style, but alas, it is legal.

Table 3.7: An RPG Computational Expression versus a Java Computational Statement		
RPG		Java
C	EVAL x = x + 1	x = x + 1;

The following sections discuss computational expressions and their associated operators in both RPG IV and Java, followed by a discussion of fetch expressions.

Computational expressions

Operators are commonly classified by the number of values (operands or parameters) on which they operate. This distinction is useful because some operators have different (although related) meanings, depending on whether they are combined with two operands or only one. For example, if you remember algebra from your school days, you know that you can use -i as the equivalent of 0-i, right? In the first case, the minus sign acts on the single numeric value, performing negation; in the second, it is operating on two numeric values. An operator that acts on a single operand is known as a *unary* operator. An operator that acts on two operands is known as a *binary* operator. In this example, the minus sign can be used as either a binary or a unary operator.

Arithmetic operators

Arithmetic operators are the simplest and, probably, the most used in all languages. Table 3.8 lists all of the arithmetic binary operators used in both RPG and Java.

Table 3.8: Java Arithmetic Operators versus RPG Arithmetic Op-codes and Operators		
Java	**RPG Op-code**	**RPG Expression**
+ (addition)	ADD or Z-ADD	+
- (subtraction)	SUB or Z-SUB	-
* (multiplication)	MULT	*
/ (division)	DIV	/
% (modulus or remainder)	MVR	%REM
		** (exponent)

The binary arithmetic operators are +, -, *, and /, and the modulus operator %. In RPG, you use the MVR (*Move Remainder*) operation code or the %REM built-in function to accomplish what the modulus operator provides in Java. An important point to remember is that RPG IV, through free-form factor two, supports free-form expressions that very closely match what Java supports. In addition, to make things easier in RPG IV, many new operators have been introduced in the language, which we will use in comparison to Java. In all of the examples used in this chapter, you can still use the fixed-form operation codes provided. However, because you are already familiar with these and not the free-form operators, our examples include free-form expressions with the newly introduced operators.

Consider the examples in Table 3.9, which show different expressions using the various binary arithmetic operators in both languages, but using RPG's new EVAL op-code. In the first example, the additive operator + adds the value contained in x to one, and places the sum back in variable X. The +, -, *, and / arithmetic binary operators are similar in the way they operate.

Table 3.9: Binary Arithmetic Operators in RPG and Java			
RPG			**Java**
C	EVAL	X=X+1	X=X+1;
C	EVAL	X = X / 2	X = X / 2;
C	EVAL	A = A + 2 * 3	A = A + 2 * 3;
C	EVAL	A = (A - 3) / 2	A = (A - 3) / 2

The next example uses the division operator to divide X by two. The next two examples show expressions that use the additive and multiplicative operators. In the first case, given that the precedence of * and / are higher than - and +, the number two is multiplied by three, the result is added to the variable A, and then the result is stored back in A. In the last example, the parentheses force the addition to occur before the multiplication. As you will see later in this chapter when you learn about operator precedence, the parentheses have higher precedence than any of these arithmetic operators.

The binary modulus operator (%) produces a pure value that is the remainder from an implied division of its operands. As mentioned earlier, this is equivalent to using the DIV operation code in RPG followed by the MVR operation code.

The expressions in Table 3.10 calculate the number of minutes and seconds, given a value in seconds. If X contains the value 185 seconds, the division operation produces a value of three minutes, and the remainder produces a value of five seconds. Alternatively, in RPG, you can replace the two statements with statements using eval, minutes = %DIV(X:60), and seconds = %REM(X:60).

Table 3.10: Division and Remainder Operations in RPG and Java

RPG					Java
C	X	DIV	60	minutes	minutes = X / 60;
C		MVR		seconds	seconds = X % 60;

The only operator not yet discussed is the exponentiation (**) operator. This operator is used in RPG IV, but not in Java. Instead, Java provides a method supplied in its Math class that supports this function. This is covered later in this chapter.

Assignment operators

Once a variable has been declared, you can assign a value or a field to it using the assignment operator, =. In fact, this simple form of assignment operator was used in the previous section. To assign a value of zero to the field X, you code as in Table 3.11.

Table 3.11: The Assignment Operator in RPG and Java

RPG			Java
C	EVAL	X = 0	X = 0;

In the case of RPG, the MOVE operation code could be called an assignment operator because it accomplishes the same function. However, you should try using the new EVAL operation code instead. This way of coding is more structured and flexible.

To reduce the number of assignment statements, Java allows the stringing of variables together. If you want to assign three variables to the same value, you can string them all together in a single statement, as follows:

```
A = B = C = 25;
```

In this example, all variables will contain the value 25. RPG does not support this structure in its free-form format.

Java takes this concept of reduction one step further and introduces short forms of the assignment statement for cases when the assignee is also one of the operands. With an expression such as x = x +1; the language designers noticed that the variable on the left side is repeated on the right side of the assignment operator. They shortened this construct to x += 1; and produced a new set of variations for assignment statement, called a *contracted operator*. For example, the combination of + and = operators creates a new operator, the += operator. These operators are shown in Table 3.12.

Table 3.12: Contracted Operators in Java		
Operator	Example	Meaning
=	A = A+B	assignment
+=	A += B	A = A + B
-=	A -= B	A = A — B
/=	A /= B	A = A / B
*=	A *= B	A = A * B
%=	A %= B	A = A % B
^=	A ^= B	A = A ^ B
&=	A &= B	A = A & B
|=	A |= B	A = A | B
<=	A <= B	A = A < B
>=	A >= B	A = A > B
>>=	A >>= B	A = A >> B

Given that there are many other binary operators in Java, the language designers introduced the new x= operator where x stands for other supported binary operators. These include not only the arithmetic operators you have already seen, but *all* binary operators: +, -, /, *, %, ^, &, |, <, >, and >>.

The general rule is, if expression1 and expression2 are expressions, then expression1 x= expression2 is equivalent to expression1 = expression1 x expression2 where x stands for one of the operators mentioned. Obviously, both forms are allowed in Java (and in C and C++ as well). This format is a shorthand version that accomplishes the same thing with less typing. It hails originally from C, where the design philosophy was "less is more."

These contracted operators are not totally foreign to RPG programmers. Really, they are a shorthand that is exactly the same as using the ADD, SUB, MULT, and DIV op-codes without a factor-one value. In RPG, this means to perform the operation using factor two and the result field, and place the answer back into the result field.

Incrementing, decrementing, and unary operators

Java provides two unusual operators, also borrowed from C, for incrementing and decrementing variables. The increment operator, ++, adds one to its operand, while the decrement operator, --, subtracts one from its operand. These are most commonly used to increment or decrement the index of an array or other incrementing value inside a loop. Table 3.13 illustrates a while loop that uses the ++ operator for incrementing its index.

Table 3.13: Incrementing a Loop Index in RPG and Java			
RPG			Java
C	EVAL	IDX = 1	idx = 0;
C	DOW	(IDX <= 10)	while (idx < 10)
C*	: Some code		{
C	EVAL	IDX = IDX +1	// some code
C	ENDDO		idx ++;
			}

This example also shows an RPG DOW (do-while) loop that is similar to Java. The primary difference between them is in the way you increment the index. In RPG, a common way to do this is to use the EVAL operation code and add one to the index. You can also use the ADD operation code to increment the field by one. In Java, using the traditional assignment statement with the + operator is valid, too, as in:

```
idx = idx + 1;
```

These operators are unusual in that both ++ and – can be used as either *prefix* or *suffix* operators. In the preceding example, the ++ is used as a suffix operator; that is, the ++ is placed after the operand. To use it as a prefix operator, you would code the expression as follows:

```
++idx;
```

What is the difference between these two forms? When the ++ and – are prefix operators, the operand will be incremented or decremented by one *before* its value is used in the expression. When used as suffix operators, the operand will be incremented or decremented by one *after* its value has been used in the expression.

Consider the examples in Listing 3.4. In the first case, the ++ operator prefixes the variable a. The operand a is incremented by one (changed to six) before it is used in the expression. This value, in turn, is added to 50, and the sum 56 is placed in the variable x. In the second case, 50 is added to the content of operand b, which is five, and the sum of 55 is placed in the variable y.

Listing 3.4: Examples of Prefix and Suffix Increment Operator

```
public class PrefixSuffix
{
    public static void main(String args[])
    {
        int a = 5;
        int b = 5;
        int x = ++a + 50; // x is 56 after execution
        System.out.println("x = " + x + ", a = " + a);
        int y = 50 + b++; // y is 55 after execution
        System.out.println("y = " + y + ", b = " + b);
    }
}
```

Compiling and running Listing 3.4 gives the following (remember the `main` method is called by Java when a class is run from the command line):

```
>javac PrefixSuffix.java
>java PrefixSuffix
x = 56, a = 6
y = 55, b = 6
```

Note that `x = ++a + 50` is equivalent to this:

```
a = a + 1;
x = a + 50;
```

Something else is unique about these operators. Unlike all other arithmetic operators, they have side effects on their operands even when used in fetch expressions, such as the right side of an assignment statement. Beware of this!

In the preceding example, for instance, both a and b are affected by the statements. At the end, both have been incremented. The difference between prefix and suffix use is relative to the target of the assignment statement, but, as far as the variables a and b are concerned, both had the same effect of increasing their value by one. As part of the expression evaluation, the value of b is incremented to six; however, the increment occurs after the expression has been evaluated because the ++ operator is used as a suffix. It is because of this unique side effect that expressions with these operators can be used as standalone with a semicolon to form a valid expression statement, as mentioned earlier. So, this is valid in Java:

```
price++;
```

It has the effect of incrementing `price`. Since the other operators, like +, -, * and /, have no side effects on their operands, you are not allowed to add a semicolon and turn them into statements; they would be meaningless. The following, then, are not valid in Java (and result in "invalid expression statement" errors from the compiler):

```
price - discount;
price * tax;
-5;
```

The increment and decrement operators are similar to those in C and C++, with the exception that C and C++ do not allow the operand to be of type float. Notice also that these operators can only be applied to variable operands; they cannot be applied to expressions. For example, expressions like (a+b)++ or (a+b)– are invalid. Both of these operators are considered unary operators because they are used with one operand.

Table 3.14 lists the RPG and Java unary arithmetic operators. These operators take exactly one argument.

Table 3.14: RPG and Java Arithmetic Operators		
Operator	RPG Operator	Java Operator
Increment	N/A	++
Decrement	N/A	—
Unary plus	+	+
Unary minus	-	-

Table 3.15 illustrate how to use the unary minus and plus operators in both RPG and Java. It's interesting to note that the unary plus operator really does nothing, while the unary minus operator actually negates the given operand. Thus, if y is set to -1, then –y evaluates to 1, while +y evaluates to -1.

Table 3.15: Unary Minus and Plus Operators in RPG and Java			
RPG			Java
C	EVAL	X = -X	X = -x;
C	EVAL	x = +x	x = +x;

Relational operators

RPG and Java have several operators for testing equality and magnitude, or relationships. All relational expressions using these operators return a boolean value of true or false. For example, to test if variable X is greater than 10, you can have a simple relational expression such as X > 10 in both languages.

This expression is most useful when used in conditional or loop statements to determine the flow of control, as you will see in detail in the next chapter. For example, it is often used as the expression test in an if statement or the loop-termination test in an RPG dow loop or Java while loop. Simple relational expressions use the operators >, >=, <, <= in both languages, while RPG uses = and for equality and inequality comparisons, versus the Java operators == and !=. Table 3.16 summarizes the available relational operators in both RPG and Java, including the older RPG fixed-format op-code suffixes.

Table 3.16: Relational Operators in RPG and Java			
RPG XX	RPG Expression	Java	Description
EQ	=	==	equal
NE		!=	not equal
GT	>	>	greater than
LT	<	<	less than
GE	>=	>=	greater than or equal
LE	<=	<=	less than or equal

Table 3.17 illustrates a simple relational expression used on an if statement. This is a straightforward test of a simple relational expression that tests for equality to determine conditionally whether to execute a subsequent block of statements.

RPG		Java
Table 3.17: Relational Expressions in if Statements in RPG and Java		
C	IF prefix = 'A'	if (prefix == 'A')
C*	some code	{
C*	more code	// code
C	ENDIF	}

Logical operators

Simple relational expressions that use the relational operators listed in Table 3.16 can be combined by using logical operators to form a more complex test. The logical binary operators are AND and OR in RPG, while Java uses && and || and an additional one, ^. Java uses doubled-up characters for its relational operator ==, and its logical operators || and && . This is to clearly distinguish them from the similar-looking but different operators =, |, and &. (The last two are bitwise operators you'll learn about soon.) Negation of a simple relational expression is done with the NOT operator in RPG and the ! operator in Java.

These logical operators can combine simple relational expressions or even combine other combined expressions. As long as the sub-expressions being combined or negated evaluate to true or false, you can use the logical operators to form a larger test.

Let's look at some examples of combined simple relational expressions. If you want to test whether the variable age is greater than 10 *and* less than 20, you can have an RPG logical expression such as this:

```
(age>10) AND (age<20)
```

The Java equivalent is this:

```
((age>10) && (age<20))
```

This syntax combines the two relational expressions using the AND operator, and will only evaluate to true if both sub-expressions evaluate to true. Again, the use of blanks in the expressions is totally optional, as expressions are free-format in both languages. For example, many people prefer to code (age > 10) instead of (age>10). The use of parentheses around the sub-expressions is also optional, but often used for readability, or to be sure the compiler interprets the expression correctly. However, one difference between the languages is that Java requires parentheses around the entire expression, whether it is a simple relational expression or a combined logical expression, as you saw in the Java column of Table 3.17. RPG, on the other hand, does not force this requirement, but does allow it optionally.

If you want to test whether the variable age is less than 11 *or* greater than 19, you can have an RPG logical expression such as this:

```
(age<=10) OR (age>=20)
```

The Java equivalent is this:

```
((age<=10) || (age>=20))
```

This combines the two relational expressions with the OR operator, and will evaluate to true if *either* sub-expression is true.

Java has an additional binary logical operator that is not supported in RPG, namely the *exclusive OR* operator, ∧, for example:

```
((age <= 10) ∧ (day == 2))
```

With this operator, the expression will evaluate to true if exactly one of the sub-expressions evaluates to true. However, it will evaluate to false if they are both true! Obviously, this is a rarely needed operator, which underscores RPG's decision not to include it.

Consider the OR example: "age less than 11 or greater than 19." It really is the opposite of the AND example. That is, you could have worded the test "if it is not the case that the age is greater than 10 and less than 20." So, you could have coded that last example by negating the logical expression from the AND example. In RPG, this would be:

```
NOT ((age>10) AND (age<20))
```

The Java equivalent is this:

```
(! ((age>10)  && (age<20)))
```

Notice that the negation operator works on a single expression, not two expressions like the previous logical operators. To reflect that, we prefer to put the entire expression being negated inside parentheses, as you see. Then, for Java, we have to again put the entire expression, including the negation operator, inside parentheses as per Java's rules. Hence, all these parentheses! The negation operator negates the expression that follows it. Therefore, the entire expression results in true if the negated expression returns false. If the negated expression returns true, the entire expression returns false.

For both languages (really, for all languages), it is very helpful when using negation to know *DeMorgan's Rule* from the study of algebra. This rule describes how to negate a boolean expression of any complexity, and can save you much head-scratching when you try to manually ripple a negation through an expression, or even read a negation expression. The rule is, to negate an OR expression, negate each operand and change the OR to an AND. To negate an AND expression, negate each operand and change the AND to an OR. For example, these are equivalent:

```
if ( !( (day != MON) || (age < 65) ) )
if ( (day == MON) && (age >= 65))
```

These are also equivalent:

```
if ( !( (day == MON) && (age >= 65) ) )
if ( (day != MON) || (age < 65))
```

Don't confuse the logical unary negation operators (NOT and !) with the relational binary inequality operators (<> and !=). The former negates an expression, while the latter compares two operands, returning true if they have different values. Table 3.18 summarizes the logical operators in RPG and Java.

Table 3.18: Logical Operators in RPG and Java

RPG XX Op-codes	RPG Op-codes	Java	Description
Orxx	OR	|| or |	logical or
ANDxx	AND	&& or &	logical and
NOT		!	logical not, or negation
		^	exclusive or

You see that you can use the single & and | operators, as well the doubled-up versions. Be careful, however; the difference between these two operators is in the internal expression evaluation. For the & operator, both sides of the expression are evaluated regardless of the outcome. For the && operator, if the left side of the expression is false, the entire expression is obviously false, and the right side is never evaluated. Similarly, for the | operator, both sides are also evaluated, while for ||, the right side is never evaluated if the left side is true, as that means the whole expression is true.

We recommend always using the doubled-up version, as sometimes the right side is not valid if the left is true, for example ((x != 0) & ((y / x) > 0)). In this case, if x equals zero (the left sub-expression is false), you would be dividing y by zero in the right sub-expression.

As you will see in the following section on bitwise operators, the operators & , |, and ^ are used with bit manipulations, as well.

Bitwise operators

The RPG language only supports TESTB, BITON, and BITOFF op-codes for bitwise manipulation. Java, on the other hand, has seven bitwise operators that allow you to perform operations on individual bits in integer values, as shown in Table 3.19.

Table 3.19: Bitwise Operators in Java	
Bitwise Operator	Meaning
&	Bitwise AND
|	Bitwise OR
^	Bitwise Exclusive OR
~	Bitwise negation
< <	Left Shift
> >	Right Shift
> > >	Zero fill right shift

All of these operators are inherited from the C and C++ languages. (And, yes, you too can be a "bit wiser.") It is very important to keep in mind that bitwise operators work only on integer types. Using any other type causes a compiler error. This is different than RPG's op-codes, which only work on character fields or hexadecimal literals or constants.

The bitwise AND (&) operator is often used to mask off some set of bits. It produces a value that is the bitwise AND of its operands. The bitwise & works on bits, whereas the logical && works on boolean values. Traversing each operand bit by bit, if the corresponding bits in *both* of the operands are ones, the corresponding bit in the result variable is set to one. Otherwise, the corresponding bit in the result variable is set to zero. This is similar to the logical AND where the resulting value is true if both operands evaluate to true, otherwise false, as shown in Listing 3.5.

Listing 3.5: The Bitwise & Operator in Java

```
public class Bit
{
    public static void main(String args[])
    {
        int firstNum  = 14;
        int secondNum = 12;
        int result;
        result = firstNum & secondNum;
        System.out.println("The result is : " +  result);
    }
}
```

Listing 3.5 performs a bitwise & on two integer operands that contain the values 14 and 12. Knowing this, the internal representation of these two operand fields and of the resulting field is shown here in bit format:

```
firstNum   == 14 == '00000000 00000000 00000000 00001110'
secondNum  == 12 == '00000000 00000000 00000000 00001100'

result     == 12 == '00000000 00000000 00000000 00001100' (after &)
```

In this case, only the third and fourth bits have a one in both operands. That means that all of the values of the `result` field will be zero except these positions. This value evaluates to $2^2 + 2^3$, which equals 12. Therefore, the `println` method will print the value 12.

If you have followed the example so far, then the other bitwise operators will be just as easy to understand. The bitwise OR operator (|) traverses the operands bit by bit. A one is returned in the result value at each bit position when *either* of the two operand values have one in the same bit position. Otherwise, it is zero. By comparison, the exclusive OR operator (∧) returns a one at each bit position when the two values have *opposite* values in the same bit position. Listing 3.6 shows an example of these.

Listing 3.6: The Bitwise OR and Bitwise Exclusive OR Operators in Java

```java
public class OrxOr
{
    public static void main(String args[])
    {
        int firstNum  = 14;
        int secondNum = 12;
        int firstResult, secondResult;
        firstResult = (byte) (firstNum | secondNum);
        System.out.println("First result: " + firstResult);
        secondResult = (byte) (firstNum ∧ secondNum);
        System.out.println("Second result: " + secondResult);
    }
}
```

Listing 3.6 uses the operand values of 12 and 14 again. Here are the bit values of the operands and two results after doing a bitwise OR and bitwise exclusive OR:

```
firstNum     == 14 == '00000000 00000000 00000000 00001110'
secondNum    == 12 == '00000000 00000000 00000000 00001100'

firstResult  == 14 == '00000000 00000000 00000000 00001110' (after |)
secondResult ==  2 == '00000000 00000000 00000000 00000010' (after ∧)
```

All this talk about twiddling bits might have you wondering how to print out the binary version of an integer variable. This is jumping ahead a bit, but there are classes in Java that mimic each of the built-in data types and supply some cool methods. The one we want is the `Integer` class, and the method is the static method `toBinaryString`, which takes an integer as input and outputs a string containing its binary or bitwise value. You might want to create your own static method named `printBits` in your own helper class that, in turn, uses this `Integer` method:

```java
public static void printBits(String name, int x)
{
    System.out.println(name + " == " + x + " == " +
                        Integer.toBinaryString(x));
}
```

Calling this with the `firstNum` and `secondNum` variables you have seen so far gives the following output (note that leading-zero value bits are not printed):

```
firstNum == 14 == 1110
secondNum == 12 == 1100
```

The inverse operator (~) is similar to the logical negation operator (!), but at the bit level. That is, it negates whatever the value is in each bit of the operand. So ones become zeros and zeros become ones. Imagine, for example, that the previous examples changes to this:

```java
firstNum = ~firstNum;
secondNum = ~secondNum;
```

You would get the following before and after results:

```
firstNum   == '00000000 00000000 00000000 00001110' (before)
secondNum  == '00000000 00000000 00000000 00001100' (before)

firstNum   == '11111111 11111111 11111111 11110001' (after ~)
secondNum  == '11111111 11111111 11111111 11110011' (after ~)
```

Shift operators

The shift operators complete our discussion of bitwise operators. As you work with the bits that make up an integer number, some operations might require you to shift the bit values to the right or to the left. In Java, this operation is performed with the left bitwise shift operator, <<, and the right bitwise shift operator, >>. Listing 3.7 illustrates how these operators work.

Listing 3.7: Shift Operators in Java

```
public class Shift
{
    public static void main(String args[])
    {
        int firstNum = 2;
        int firstResult, secondResult;
        firstResult = (firstNum < 2);
        System.out.println("The first result is : " + firstResult);
        secondResult = (firstResult > 1);
        System.out.println("The second result is : " +
                                secondResult);
    }
}
```

You start by initializing the variable firstNum to two. This is represented internally by the following sequence of bits, shown for firstNum:

```
firstNum     == 2 == '00000000 00000000 00000000 00000010'
-------------------------------------------------------------
firstResult  == 8 == '00000000 00000000 00000000 00001000'
secondResult == 4 == '00000000 00000000 00000000 00000100'
```

The first operation performed on the variable shifts it left twice. Then, you use the result from the first operation to shift right once. As a result, the internal representation for each of the variables firstResult and secondResult is as shown. Notice that shifting left is equivalent to multiplying by the corresponding power of two, and shifting right is equivalent to dividing by the corresponding power of two, with possible truncation in both cases. These operations are generally more efficient than using multiplication or division, however.

Unlike the inconsistencies found in some implementations of C and C++, Java always preserves the sign bit (the leftmost bit) after performing the right bitwise shift. To handle this situation, Java introduces a new bitwise operator, the shift-right operator, >>>. The difference between >>> and the other shift-right operator, >>, is that the >>> operator does not preserve the leftmost sign bit. In other words, the operator always sets the leftmost bit to zero.

After all this, keep in mind that all these bitwise operators are very rarely used in business applications!

Conditional operators

Another of Java's short-form operators is the conditional operator (? :), also called a *ternary operator*. This operator is similar to the one in C and C++. RPG IV does not have it. This operator, a short version of the if statement, is used to choose alternate values for a variable, based on an expression that evaluates to true or false. The following example shows how to use this operator and compares its use to the if statement (explained in more detail in the following chapter):

```
result = (idx == 20) ? 30 : 35;
// same as...
if (idx == 20)
    result = 30;
else
    result = 35;
```

The conditional boolean expression, written with the ternary operator ?:, provides an alternate way to write similar constructs. The boolean expression before the ? is evaluated first. If it is true, then the expression between the ? and : is evaluated, and its value is assigned to the left-hand variable (result, in our example). Otherwise, the expression between the : and ; is evaluated, and its value is assigned to the left-hand variable.

Conditional expressions are only suitable when you want to return one of two values, depending on the value of a boolean expression. Conditional expressions are compact; they save you a few keystrokes. Once you become accustomed to their notation, as with the increment (++) and decrement (–) operators, you might find them faster to code (even if longer to read!) than their longer equivalents. However, if you don't like them, you don't have to use them.

Operator precedence

So far, you have seen all of the Java and RPG operators that you can use in expressions. This section discusses *operator precedence*: the order of evaluation of multiple operators in expressions. That is, these are the rules that govern which operator is evaluated first, second, third, and so on. Operator precedence is important in any programming language; it determines the final result of an expression, which depends on the order in which operands are evaluated. Table 3.20 summarizes operator precedence in RPG IV.

Table 3.20: Operator Precedence in RPG IV

```
( )
Built-in functions, user-defined procedures
unary +, unary -, NOT
**
*, /
Binary +, and Binary -
=, , >, >=, <, <=
AND
OR
```

In an earlier program example, you saw the expression A + 2 * 3. If the value of A is four, what would the result be after evaluation? Would it be 18 or 10? If you add first, the final value will be 4 + 2, or six, multiplied by three, which gives the result 18. However, if you multiply first, the value will be 2 * 3, or six, with 4 added, which gives the result 10. This is why operator precedence has to be established.

As you can see in Table 3.20, the multiplication operator has higher precedence, so the value of the expression is 10. Multiplication will be done first, followed by addition. In fact, this is the logic that the compiler uses to establish the evaluation of any given expression in a language. High-precedence operators are evaluated before low-precedence operators.

What happens if you have operators with the same precedence? For example, what would the expression (X / 4 * 3) evaluate to? If X is 12, would the result be 1 or 9? The result depends on how the compiler parses and evaluates the line. Is parsing done from left to right, or right to left? For the multiplication and division operators, RPG and Java parse and evaluate from left to right. This means that the expression in both languages evaluates to 9.

The Java operator precedence and associativity is shown in Table 3.21. Again, operators at the top of the table have higher precedence than those below them. For operators that have equal precedence, the "Associativity" column indicates which ones will be evaluated first. For example, in the case of the * and / operators, evaluation is done left to right, as indicated by the **L** in the column. On the other hand, the operators ++, -, ~, !, -, and (type cast) are evaluated from right-to-left. (Type casting is discussed in Chapter 5, string concatenation in Chapter 7, and the instanceof operator in Chapter 9.)

Table 3.21: Operator Precedence and Left or Right Associativity in Java

Operators	Associativity
()	L
++, —, ~, !, -, (type cast)	R
*, /, %	L
+, -	L
+ (concat operator)	L
>>	L
>, <	L
<, <=, >, >=	L
instanceof	L
= =, !=	L
&	L
^	L
&& |	L
||	L
?:	R
=, *=, /=, %=, +=, -=, <=, >=, >>=, &=, ^=, |=	R

Fetch expressions

You have learned about computational expressions, which compute a boolean or arithmetic value. The following sections discuss the other kind of expressions, *fetch expressions*, which are the most elementary type. They don't compute a value, they get, or fetch, a value. The different kinds of fetch expressions are null, method call, and array index.

Null expressions

The fetch expression null produces a special object reference value that does not refer to any object, but is assignment-compatible with all object reference types. These are simply any variable declared to be of a class type, as described in the previous chapter. The null is the default value for these types of variables before they have been assigned to an object by using the new operator. Keep in mind that, if you subsequently assigned an object reference variable to null, the object it was pointing to will be left "dangling" if no other variables point to it. Hence, the garbage collector will sweep it up. The null value is most easily thought of as a language-supplied constant, but it is actually an expression, a fetch expression. This is splitting hairs, though, and not of much consequence. (Notice, how-ever, that null is not considered a zero as it is in C and C++.)

If you need to determine whether an object reference variable has yet to be assigned to an object, you can compare it to null, as in:

```
if (myObject == null) // not instantiated yet?
   myObject = new MyClass(); // instantiate it now
```

Method call and array index expressions

A method call expression is a primary expression that invokes a method. This is similar to a procedure call expression in RPG IV. A method call expression fetches a value returned by the method or the procedure. Similarly, an array index expression produces an array element value when it is evaluated. Arrays are indexed using square brackets in Java. (Arrays are covered in detail in Chapter 6; they are mentioned here only for completeness.) In both cases, the returned or fetched value can then be used in-place in an expression, as though a variable had been used. The following illustrates both of these expressions:

```
if (stateObject.getStateTax() > 0)
   ...
if (stateTaxArray[stateIndex] > 0)
   ...
```

OTHER MATHEMATICAL FUNCTIONS

Earlier in this chapter, you saw the basic math operators that are used in expressions. These include +, -, *, /, and %. However, RPG and Java support many other mathematical functions, such as op-codes and built-in functions in RPG, and supplied methods in Java. The Java-supplied class Math contains methods for performing basic numeric operations, such as exponentiation, logarithms, square roots, and the trigonometric functions.

To help ensure the portability of Java programs, the definitions of many of the numeric functions in the Math class supplied by Java are implemented using certain accepted, published algorithms. These algorithms are available from the well-known network library NETLIB in the package "Freely Distributable Math Library" (FDLIB). These algorithms, which are written in the C programming language, were rewritten in Java and supplied as the Java Math class. The Java Math library is defined with respect to the version of FDLIB dated January 4, 1995.

Listing 3.8 shows an example of the RPG %ABS (absolute) built-in function. The fields firstNum and secondNum are zoned (4,0) and initialized to the values 40 and 65, respectively. On the C-spec, you perform two different calculations using the EVAL operation code. In both calculations, the field with the larger value, secondNum, is subtracted from the field containing the smaller value, firstNum. In both cases, the subtraction results in a value of -25. The %ABS built-in function then returns the absolute value of -25, which is 25. Thus, %ABS returns the positive value of a given negative number. It has no effect on positive numbers. The output of the sample is -25 and 25.

Listing 3.8: The RPG %ABS Built-in Function

```
D firstNum       S           4S 0 INZ(40)
D secondNum      S           4S 0 INZ(65)
D result         S           4S 0
C                EVAL        result = firstNum - secondNum
C     result     DSPLY
C                EVAL        result = %ABS(firstNum-secondNum)
C     result     DSPLY
```

The same result can be accomplished in Java by using the Math class, which is found in the Java.lang package. Listing 3.9 illustrates the same example written in Java.

Listing 3.9: The Absolute (ABS) Java
Method in the Math Class of the java.lang Package

```
public class ABS
{
    public static void main(String args[])
    {
        int firstNum  = 40;
        int secondNum = 65;
        int result1, result2;

        result1 = firstNum - secondNum;
        result2 = Math.abs(firstNum - secondNum);

        System.out.println("First result is: " +  result1);
        System.out.println("Absolute result is: " + result2);
    }
}
```

As in the RPG example, two fields of type integer are declared and initialized to 40 and 65. In the first case, we just do the subtraction. In the second case, we subtract and then use the abs method to return the absolute value. Again, this gives -25 and 25, respectively. This is just one example of the many different methods available in the Math package.

Another straightforward math function in RPG and Java involves retrieving the square root of a given number. The special RPG op-code SQRT does what you need. Listing 3.10 declares a field with the value of nine and uses SQRT to find its square root. The expected result of three is returned.

Listing 3.10: The RPG IV SQRT Op-code

```
D test             S              4S 0 INZ(9)
D result           S              4S 0
C*
C                  SQRT      test            result
C        result    DSPLY
C                  EVAL      *INLR = *ON
```

It is just as simple to do this in Java. The Math class contains the method sqrt for just this purpose. This method is available only for fields with a double data type (covered in Chapter 5). Listing 3.11 illustrates the Java way of getting the square root of nine.

Listing 3.11: The Square Root (sqrt)
Java Method in the Math Class of the java.lang Package

```
public class SqRoot
{
    public static void main (String args[])
    {
        double firstNum = 9;
        double result;
        result = Math.sqrt(firstNum);
        System.out.println("The result is: " + result);
    }
}
```

As you see can see, the static method sqrt is used with a nine as the parameter. This results in a three being returned.

We have shown you only a couple of examples of the available methods in the Java Math class. There are many more, including those in Table 3.22.

Note: These methods are all static, and therefore, resemble traditional, standalone functions in other non-OO languages. The exception is that, in order to call them, you must qualify the method name with the class name, as in `Math.xxxx()`.

Table 3.22: The Methods in the Math Class of the java.lang Package

Method	Description
abs(double)	Returns the absolute value of a double value.
abs(float)	Returns the absolute value of a float value.
abs(int)	Returns the absolute value of an int value.
abs(long)	Returns the absolute value of a long value.
acos(double)	Returns the arc cosine of an angle, in the range of 0.0 through pi.
asin(double)	Returns the arc sine of an angle, in the range of -pi/2 through pi/2.
atan(double)	Returns the arc tangent of an angle, in the range of -pi/2 through pi/2.
atan2(double,double)	Returns the rectangular coordinates (b, a) to polar (r, theta).
ceil(double)	Returns the smallest (closest to negative infinity) double value that is not less than the argument and is equal to a mathematical integer.
cos(double)	Returns the trigonometric cosine of an angle.
exp(double)	Returns the exponential number (e.g., 2.718) raised to the power of a double value.
floor(double)	Returns the largest (closest to positive infinity) double value that is not greater than the argument and returns the greater of two double values.
max(float, float)	Returns the greater of two float values.
max(int, int)	Returns the greater of two int values.
max(long, long)	Returns the greater of two long values.
min(double, double)	Returns the smaller of two double values.
min(float, float)	Returns the smaller of two float values.

Method	Description
min(int, int)	Returns the smaller of two int values.
min(long, long)	Returns the smaller of two long values.
pow(double, double)	Returns the value of the first argument raised to the power of the second argument.
Random()	Returns a random number between 0.0 and 1.0.
rint(double)	Returns the closest integer to the argument.
round(double)	Returns the closest long to the argument.
round(float)	Returns the closest int to the argument.
sin(double)	Returns the trigonometric sine of an angle.
sqrt(double)	Returns the square root of a double value.
tan(double)	Returns the trigonometric tangent of an angle.

Table 3.22: The Methods in the Math Class of the java.lang Package (cont.)

In many cases, a method listed in the table may have an equivalent RPG built-in function or op-code that performs the same function. In some cases, though, there is no equivalent RPG functionality. In these cases, it is a good opportunity for you to plug that hole by writing a procedure! For example, in the next chapter, you will see a procedure named Max that gives the same function as Java's max method.

Finally, when arithmetic operators were discussed earlier in this chapter, we mentioned that RPG has an exponentiation operator, while Java does not. Listing 3.12 illustrates an expression that uses exponentiation in RPG. The DSPLY operation outputs the value of 16, which is the result of 2^4.

Listing 3.12: The Exponentiation Operator in RPG

```
D*Name+++++++++++ETDsFrom+++To/L+++IDc.Keywords+++++++++++
D firstNum        S              4S 0 INZ(2)
D exp             S              4S 0 INZ(4)
D result          S              4S 0
C*
C                 EVAL           result = firstNum ** exp
C      result     DSPLY
C                 EVAL           *INLR = *ON
```

Although Java has no standalone exponentiation operator, it does have a static method named pow, again in the Math class. As an exercise, you might try experimenting with it.

SUMMARY

This chapter introduced you to the following concepts:

- There are three kinds of comments in Java: multiple-line, single-line, and JavaDoc.

- The javadoc tool supplied in the JDK helps you document your classes and methods. It converts the comments in a Java source file into an HTML document that can be read by any Web browser.

- Java variable names must start with a letter, an underscore, or a dollar sign.

- Java variable name length is unlimited.

- There are six kinds of Java statements:

    - Variable   - Empty

    - Expression   - Labeled

    - Blocked   - Other

- There are two kinds of expressions in Java: computational and fetch. Computational expressions use operators, compute a value and may cause side effects; fetch expressions are used to fetch values, but do not do any computation on them.

- Java's assignment operator is the single equal sign: =

- Java has seven math operators: +, -, /, *, %, ++, −

- Java has six relational operators: ==, !=, <, >, <=, >=

- Java has three logical operators: &&, ||, !

- Java has seven bitwise operators: &, |, ^, ~, <<, >>,>>>

- Java has a ternary or conditional operator: ?:

- Java allows contraction of all binary operators, as in: X += 10

- Java has a Math class in package java.lang that has methods to cover a variety of math functions, including sin, cos, tan, abs, sqrt, and many other useful methods.

STRUCTURED OPERATIONS AND STATEMENTS

Control structures control the order in which statements will be acted upon by the computer. They can be divided into four basic categories:

- *Sequence structures* (op-codes or statements) allow control, in both languages, to flow from one statement to the next in the order in which they were written in the program. That is, flow is sequential. Examples in RPG are the ADD, MOVE, SUB, and EVAL op-codes. An example in Java is the assignment statement. These statements (or op-codes) execute consecutively. They do not cause the flow of control to shift. When control comes to the end of a program, it usually terminates. These concepts are covered in Chapter 3.

- *Decision structures*, or conditional statements allow control to flow in a different path, depending on the result of a condition. You can conditionally select alternate paths for your program. Decision control structures include the following:

  ➢ The if conditional statement

  ➢ The SELECT (RPG) or switch (Java) conditional statement

- *Loop structures* allow control to flow iteratively for a specified number of times, or until a condition is met. These include the following:

  ➢ The DO (RPG) and for (Java) loop statements

  ➢ The DOW (RPG) and while (Java) loop statements

  ➢ The DOU (RPG) and do-while (Java) loop structures

- *Transfer structures* allow control to flow to another part of the program. Transfer control structures include the following:

  ➢ The GOTO (RPG) statement

  ➢ The LEAVE/ITER (RPG) and break/continue (Java) statements

  ➢ The RETURN or return statement

  ➢ The try-catch and throw (Java) statements

Table 4.1 shows structured op-codes that are available in RPG and their equivalent Java statements. Some less-common statements are not shown because they are not available in both languages.

Table 4.1: Structured Statements in RPG versus Java

Table 4.1: Structured Statements in RPG versus Java

RPG	Java	Description

IFXX/IF
ENDIF/END
	if (expression)
	{
	  // statements;
	}
		Enables you to execute a code frag-ment based on a boolean test.

SELECT
  WHENxx/WHEN
  OTHER
ENDSL/END
	switch (test)
	{
	  case value:
	  break
	  default:
	}
		Enables you to switch a case (in Java) or select when (in RPG), based ont he value of an expression.

DO
ENDODO/END
	for (init; expression; increment)
	{
	  // statements;
	}
		Loops a specific number of times based on an initial value, expression, and in-crement. Loops while the expression is true.

DOWxx/DOW
ENDDO/END
	while (expression)
	{
	  // statements;
	}
		Loops while the expression is true.

DOUxx/DOU
ENDDO/END
	do
	{
	  // statements;
	}
		Loops until the expression is false. The body is executed at least once.

GOTO and TAG		Java disallows it. RPG allows it, but our advice is do not use it!
LEAVE	break;	Transfers control out of the loop.
ITER	continue;	Ends the current iteration of the loop.
RETURN	return	Returns to the caller.
SETON LR	System.exit (0)	
*PSSR, INFSR, and error indicators	try/catch	Catches all program and file excep-tions. (See Chapter 10.)
send escape msg	throw statement	Causes an exception to be thrown (See Chapter 10.)

ALTERNATE PATHS: DECISION STRUCTURES

Let's turn our focus to the RPG op-codes and Java statements that can alter the flow of control, such as if and SELECT/switch.

If, then what? Else, of course

The IF and ELSE op-codes in RPG, and the if and else statements in Java, enable you to execute different blocks of code based on a simple test. The if/else statement in Java is nearly identical to the if/else statement in C or C++. RPG IV, on the other hand, has two forms of the IF/ELSE op-codes: a fixed form that was inherited from RPG III, and a free-format factor-two form that enables you to write more expressive expressions. The if/else structures in RPG and Java are written differently, but they are the same in function. Listing 4.1 illustrates the two forms of the RPG IV IF/ELSE operations.

Listing 4.1: RPG IV Fixed-Format IF/ELSE and Free-Format IF/ELSE

```
D* fields
D age              S              3P 0 INZ(10)
D currday          S              1B 0 INZ(MON)
D price            S              3P 2 INZ(0.0)
D* constants
D MON              C                   CONST(1)
D TUE              C                   CONST(2)
D WED              C                   CONST(3)
D THU              C                   CONST(4)
D FRI              C                   CONST(5)
D SAT              C                   CONST(6)
D SUN              C                   CONST(7)

C* Older fixed-format style of IF
C        age          IFGT      64
C        currday      ANDEQ     MON
C                     MOVE      10.00          price
C                     ELSE
C                     MOVE      20.00          price
C                     ENDIF
C        price        DSPLY
C* Newer free-format style of IF
C                     IF        (age > 64) AND
C                               (currday = MON)
C                     EVAL      price = 10.00
C                     ELSE
C                     EVAL      price = 20.00
C                     ENDIF
C        price        DSPLY
C* End the program
C                     EVAL      *INLR = *ON
```

Listing 4.1 performs the same IF/ELSE test twice, once with the classic fixed-format style, and again with the newer free-format style. We think you will agree the new style is easier to read. The details of the new D-specifications for defining fields and constants are discussed in the next chapter, but they should be easy enough to read. Three fields named age, currday, and price are defined, along with seven constants representing days of the week. It then does logic to set the price based on the customer's age and the current day. The first version of the test uses the older fixed-format IF statement. In this format, the IFxx structure is used, where xx can be EQ, GT, LT, GE, LE, and NE. The disadvantage of using the fixed-format is that there is a need for additional op-codes (ANDXX or ORXX) to build each condition.

The second version illustrates the free-format IF operation. In this format, you first specify the IF op-code and then specify the expression that you want to be evaluated in the free-format factor-two entry. The free-format expression consists of the relational operators =, >, <, >=, <=, and , the logical operators AND and OR, and the unary negation operator NOT. The entire expression and sub-expressions can optionally be parenthesized, to aid in readability and to help the compiler parse the sub-expressions. If necessary, the expression can continue on subsequent C-spec lines.

Both the fixed and free versions test if age is greater than 64 and if currday is MON. If both are true, the code executes the statement after the IF op-code and sets price to 10.00; otherwise, execution flows to the ELSE op-code and we execute the statement after it, which sets price to 20.00 if either sub-condition is false. (Expressions and their rules of construction are covered in Chapter 3.). Note that the fixed-format MOVE is used in the former and the free-format EVAL in the latter, to do the assignment of price. In both forms, the IF must eventually match with an ENDIF. You could have multiple statements after the IF or after the ELSE, versus just the one in the example.

The Java if statement, as you might have guessed, is closer to the free-format version of the RPG IF op-code. Listing 4.2 illustrates the same example written in Java.

Listing 4.2: Java if and else Statements

```
public class TestIf
{
    // constants
    static final int MON = 1;
    static final int TUE = 2;
    static final int WED = 3;
    static final int THU = 4;
    static final int FRI = 5;
```

→

Listing 4.2: Java if and else Statements (continued)

```
        static final int SAT = 6;
        static final int SUN = 7;

        public static void main(String args[])
        {
            int age = 65;
            int currDay = MON;
            double price = 0.0;

            if ((age > 64) && (currDay == MON))
              price = 10.00;
            else
              price = 20.00;

            System.out.println(price);
        }
    } // end of class TestIf
```

Again, the next chapter covers the details of defining variables and constants in Java, but briefly, constants are coded using the modifiers `static` and `final`, and must be at the class level, instead of local to methods. The `main` method (recall this gets control when you run it from the command line) declares the local variables age, `currDay`, and `price`, and follows the same logic as RPG. The variables are of type integer (`int`) and double-precision floating-point (`double`). We could have used single-precision float (`float`), but then we'd have to put an f character after the decimal-point literals to get it to compile; all decimal-point literals in Java are considered double-precision, otherwise. (All of these data types and literals, as well as a better option for decimal-point data, are covered in the next chapter.)

The `if/else` logic of Listing 4.2 really just does the same test as in RPG. Notice a couple of things, though:

- The entire expression in the `if` statement must always be surrounded by parentheses

- The sub-expressions within the expression can optionally have parentheses.

- Everything is free-format, as far as blanks are concerned.

- There is nothing like RPG's `ENDIF` terminator.

Listing 4.2 is fine, as long as you only have a single line of code for the `if` body and the `else` body. If another line is added to either body, you must put the whole body inside braces to identify it as a block. With single lines, the braces are optional; with multiple lines they are required. A problem will result if you add a second line but forget to add the braces, as in:

```
if ((age > 64) && (currDay == MON))
   price = 10.00;
   discount = 1.00
```

This will compile, but you will get an unexpected outcome. The second statement will be executed regardless of the outcome of the `if` test because it is not part of the `if` body. To prevent this type of error, always use braces, even for single-statement blocks.

Here is the official Java syntax:

```
if (expression)
   single-statement; or block of statements
else
   single-statement; or block of statements
```

The `else` is optional. Single statements end in semicolon, while blocks start and end with curly braces.

You can see that both languages allow you to specify an arbitrarily complex expression. If the expression evaluates to true, the following block of statements within the structure are executed. If the `if` expression evaluates to false, then if there is an `else` statement, the block following it is executed; otherwise, control goes to the subsequent line of code. Java only allows boolean expressions (or boolean variables, as you will discover in Chapter 5) that ultimately evaluate to true or false. If you know C or C++, be aware that Java does not support the idea of allowing numeric expressions and mapping a zero to false and any other number to true. Although Java's syntax is almost identical to C, this is one exception.

An interesting situation arises when you have more than two conditions. Let's take a look at an expanded example. Suppose you would like to have conditions perform one set of instructions if the person is at least 65 years old, a second set if the person is less than 65 but not younger than 12, a third set if the person is less than 12 but not younger than 2, and a default set if the person is 2 or less. That adds up to three different conditions (there could easily be more), plus a default condition that is processed if all three previous conditions are false. Both languages support this kind of testing by allowing you to nest the IF statements. Listing 4.3 illustrates the nesting feature in RPG.

Listing 4.3: Nested **IF** *Statements in RPG*

```
C                        IF        age > 64
C                        EVAL      price = 10.00
C                        ELSE
C                        IF        age > 12
C                        EVAL      price = 20.00
C                        ELSE
C                        IF        age > 2
C                        EVAL      price = 5.00
C                        ELSE
C                        EVAL      price = 0
C                        ENDIF
C                        ENDIF
C                        ENDIF
```

You add another IF operation after the ELSE operation, with the new condition you want to test. For more complex conditions, additional ELSE and IF structures can be added. The tricky part is ensuring you eventually have one ENDIF for every IF. By the way, in V5R1 of RPG IV, a very nice enhancement you get is the new op-code ELSEIF, which allows for easy nesting and only a single ENDIF:

```
C                        IF        age > 64
C                        EVAL      price = 10.00
C                        ELSEIF    age > 12
C                        EVAL      price = 20.00
C                        ELSEIF    age > 2
C                        EVAL      price = 5.00
C                        ELSE
C                        EVAL      price = 0
C                        ENDIF
```

Listing 4.4 is this example written in Java. Notice, as is commonly seen in Java, that the else and if statements are lumped together on the same line to aid readability. The rule to always remember, however, is that an else always matches the most previous if. Sound reasonable?

Listing 4.4: Nested **if** *Statements in Java*

```
if (age > 64)
   price = 10.00;
else if (age > 12)
   price = 20.00;
else if (age > 2)
```

→

```
      price = 5.00;
   else
      price = 0;
```

You can easily get in trouble by using if statements as the body of the if statement itself, like this:

```
if (age < 65)
   if (age > 12)
      price = 20;
else
   price = 10;
```

It might look as if the else matches the outer if, but it does not. Instead, it matches the inner if. You could fix this by using curly braces, like this:

```
if (age < 65)
   {
      if (age > 12)
         price = 20;
   }
else
   price = 10;
```

Alternatively, you could avoid the situation altogether by writing these if-if statements as single if statements with compound expressions:

```
if ((age < 65) && (age > 12))
   price = 20;
else
   price = 10;
```

Too many IFs? Time to switch!

If you use the IF op-code or if statement to code too many tests, you can end up with a deeply nested set of if-else-if conditions. This can make the code clumsy to read and hard to maintain. Both Java and RPG provide you with a more elegant way of doing multiple tests. As an alternative to if-else statements, RPG and Java offer the SELECT op-code and the switch statement, respectively. These give the same results as nested if statements, but they have a simplified structure that is more readable and maintainable. Table 4.2 shows an example using switch and SELECT.

Table 4.2: The RPG SELECT versus the Java switch	
RPG	Java
SELECT	switch (currDay)
	{
WHEN currday = MON	case MON:
IF age > 64	if (age > 64)
EVAL price = 10.00	price = 20.00;
ELSE	else
EVAL price = 20.00	price = 10.00;
ENDIF	break;
WHEN currday = TUE	case TUE:
EVAL price = 20.00	price = 20.00;
	break;
WHEN currday = WED	case WED:
EVAL price = 15.00	price = 15.00;
	break;
OTHER	default:
EVAL price = 25.00	price = 25.00;
ENDSL	}

The first important point to note is the improved readability of the SELECT/switch structure compared to the nested if statements. (For brevity, we show the RPG lines starting at the op-code column.) New for SELECT in RPG IV is that the WHEN statements use the free-format factor-two version of the C-spec, allowing you to write free-format expressions just as you do for the new IF statement, in the expanded column range 36 to 80.

You can almost map the structures one-to-one between the languages. The switch statement maps to the SELECT op-code, and the case statement maps to the WHEN op-code. One difference is that Java requires the break to indicate the end of the case statement, while RPG does not need this because the compiler finds the end of the WHEN operation body when it encounters the next WHEN or OTHER operation codes. Otherwise, the default statement in Java maps to the OTHER operation code in RPG, and the final curly brace that ends the switch statement in Java maps to the ENDSL operation code in RPG. Table 4.3 summarizes these mappings.

Table 4.3: Mapping RPG's SELECT to Java's switch	
RPG SELECT	**Java Switch**
SELECT	switch
WHEN or WHENxx	case
OTHER	default
ENDSL	end brace '}'

Although RPG's SELECT op-code and Java's switch statement seem to be very similar, they differ in the expression that is tested. Here are the details of this important distinction:

- In the Java switch statement, the expression is only specified once, as part of the "switch (expression)" syntax. The result of the expression is then compared to each of the case statement values until a match is found. If found, that case body is executed. If no match is found, the default body is executed, if it exists. Otherwise, the switch statement completes without doing anything. The expression must resolve to a value of type integer. Further, the case statements can only test for equality with the expression value.

- The RPG SELECT op-code is superior in this regard. The WHEN op-code allows you to specify any valid expression you like, and each WHEN can specify a different one. RPG simply selects the first WHEN that evaluates to true. Further, the expression is open to any data type available.

There is, in fact, an additional important difference. Did you notice that the RPG SELECT statement in the example was more compact than the Java switch statement? This is primarily because of the Java requirement to end each case statement block with a break. (Note that you can code multiple lines of code before the break without having to use braces as you do for other statement types.) RPG, on the other hand, implicitly defines the end of a WHEN op-code when it sees another one, or an OTHER or ENDSL statement.

This use of break makes Java more verbose than RPG. There are more sinister implications than size of code, however. What do you think will happen if you forget to insert the break statement in Java to terminate the case clause? Rather than implicitly ending the block of code at the next case statement, Java will continue to execute all statements until it finally finds a break statement or the end of the switch statement. This can lead to some nasty bugs that are quite time-consuming to track down. Why does it have this behavior (inherited from C, by the way)? It is actually by design. It allows you to group cases together that have common code. For example, suppose you want to execute one block of code for MON, TUE, and WED, and another one for THUR and FRI. Listing 4.5 shows how you would exploit the break-less behavior for this.

Listing 4.5: Using Breakless Behavior in a Java switch Statement

```
switch (currDay)
{
   case MON:
   case TUE:
   case WED:
       // first block of code
       price = 20;
       break;
   case THU:
   case FRI:
       // second block of code
       price = 30;
       break;
   default:
       price = 40;
} // end switch statement
```

The conditional operator, ?:

Chapter 3 introduces the ?: conditional or ternary operator. Under certain circumstances, you can use a shorthand version of the if statement to indicate alternate paths through the code. RPG IV does not support this. The advantages to using this operator are simply reduced typing. However, if you are more comfortable using the if statement, or get paid by the line of code, just use if. The same results will be produced. The following example illustrates an if statement that does a simple test of age < 2. If the test is true, a boolean variable (discussed in Chapter 5) is set to true; otherwise, the variable is set to false:

```
if (age < 2)
   freeTicket = true;
else
   freeTicket = false;
// ternary equivalent
freeTicket = (age < 2) ? true : false;
```

In some cases, this is a valid alternative to more tedious if statements. (For more details, see Chapter 3.)

Loop structures—They get around

The three most common loop structures available in all modern languages, including RPG and Java, are the for loop (DO in RPG), the while loop (DOW in RPG), and the do while loop (DOU in RPG).

Table 4.4 summarizes these different loops. The Java column of Table 4.4 shows the Java constructs for the three types of loops (loop with index, loop while true, loop until false). In all cases, the body is shown inside braces or a block. As with the if statement, however, these braces are optional if the body contains only a single statement.

Table 4.4: RPG IV Loops versus Java Loops

RPG	Java

C   start   DO   limit   index
C*   :
C   ENDDO
	for (initialization; condition;
	    increments)
	{
	  // body
	}

C   DOW expression
C*   :
C   ENDDO
	while (expression)
	{
	  // body
	}

C   DOU expression
C*   :
C   ENDDO
	do
	{
	  // body
	} while (expression);

The following sections describe all three loops. Notice that the DOW and DOU loops in RPG still have both the fixed-format form that they inherited from RPG III and the free-format factor-two form introduced in RPG IV. Because the free-format form is more structured and easy to code than the fixed-format form, and because we want to encourage you to use the free-format form in your future RPG IV programming, we only use it in the examples that compare RPG loops to Java.

Going "for" a loop—Just "do" it

The DO loop in RPG and the for loop in Java are used when a known number of iterations are required to execute a block of statements. This kind of loop structure is called a *determinant loop*. In this kind of loop, there is a starting and ending value, and an index controls the iteration steps for the loop. Here is the syntax in RPG IV:

```
C*        FACTOR 1        OPCODE      FACTOR 2       RESULT
C*        --------        ------      --------       ------
C         Start           DO          End            Index
C****                     loop body
C                         ENDDO
```

The starting value is specified in factor one and defaults to one if not specified. Factor two contains the ending or limit value, and also defaults to one if not specified. The result column contains the index field. (If not specified, RPG generates an internal field to contain your index.) To delimit the end of your DO loop block, use the ENDDO operation code after the last op-code in the body of the loop. RPG iterates the loop, executing the statements in the body, until the index field reaches the end value. Thus, if the Start field contains a one, and the End field contains a 10, the loop will iterate 10 times. The default increment value is one if you do not specify it. However, you could use factor two of the ENDDO op-code to give RPG a negative or positive increment, or a step value to add or subtract after each loop iteration. Listing 4.6 shows how to use DO.

Listing 4.6: Using DO to Compute Factorial in an RPG IV Procedure

```
D total              S              10U 0
D* Prototype for procedure: Factorial
D Factorial          PR             10U 0
D number                            10U 0 VALUE

C                     EVAL        total = Factorial(4)
C         total       DSPLY
C                     EVAL        *INLR = *ON
```

$\longrightarrow$

```
P*_____
P* Procedure name: Factorial
P* Purpose:        Test DO loop by computing a factorial
P* Returns:        Factorial of given parameter value
P* Parameter:      number=>number to compute factorial of
P*_____
P Factorial        B
D Factorial        PI              10U 0
D number                           10U 0 VALUE
D* Local fields
D index            S                5U 0
D total            S               10U 0 INZ(1)
C* Code to compute factorial
C     1            DO      number       index
C                  EVAL    total = total * index
C                  ENDDO
C* Return factorial to the caller
C                  RETURN  total
P Factorial        E
```

This example has a procedure prototype for a procedure named Factorial, mainline
C-specs code to call that procedure and display the results, and finally the Factorial procedure itself. This procedure computes the factorial of a given unsigned integer, and returns the result to the caller. The mainline code is tested by passing in the number four,
and you can verify yourself the result is 24 (4*3*2*1). The important part is the DO loop
inside the Factorial procedure, which loops from one until the given number, and for
each value of the index (from one to four), computes the factorial to be the product of the
current index times the factorial of the previous index.

The Java for statement contains all the functionality that RPG provides. Listing 4.7 is the
same example as Listing 4.6, but written in Java.

Listing 4.7: Using for to Compute Factorial in a Java Method

```java
public class Factorial
{
    public static void main(String args[])
    {
        System.out.println("Welcome to class Factorial");
        int total;
        total = factorial(4);
        System.out.println(total);
    }
```

Listing 4.7: Using for to Compute Factorial in a Java Method (continued)

```java
/** Compute and return factorial of given number */
public static int factorial(int inputValue)
{
    int total = 1;
    for (int index=1; index <= inputValue; index++)
        total = index * total;
    return total;
}
} // end of class Factorial
```

The static factorial method loops from one to the given number, computing the factorial in the same way as RPG. The difference is the syntax of the for statement, which initializes the index value to one, tells Java to loop while index <= inputValue, and increments the index by one on each iteration of the loop (using index++). Since the for loop's body has only one statement, you do not have to code the braces.

The general format of the Java for statement is as follows:

```
for (expression)
   single-statement; or block-of-statements
```

The expression consists of three parts, separated by semicolons:

```
for (initialization; condition; increment)
```

These pieces are typically used as follows:

- *Initialization* is a specification of the initial value of the index variable. (You can also declare it here.) Multiple variables can be initialized by separating each initialization statement with a comma.

- *Condition* is a boolean expression. The loop continues while the expression is not false, which is evaluated at the top of the loop on each iteration. The loop executes zero times if the expression is false on the initial run. Typically, this is a comparison of the index value to a predetermined maximum value, such as the dimension limit on an array.

- *Increment* is an assignment or increment statement of your choosing, but typically increments the index value. This part is executed at the end of every iteration. Multiple statements are permitted here, as long as they are comma-separated.

In Java, unlike RPG, all management of the loop indexing is your responsibility. The only thing Java gives you in terms of built-in support in the for loop is the promise to keep looping as long as the boolean conditioning expression is not false. Absolutely everything else is up to you. So, if you want to have an index variable and increment it per loop iteration, it is your job to take care of that.

Let's look at an example of a typical simple for loop in Java that loops through all elements of an array and prints out the contents. In Java, arrays start at index zero, and they support a special built-in variable named length, which represents the number of items in the array:

```
char myCharArray[] = new char[20]; // declare an array of 20
characters
for (int idx = 0; idx < myCharArray.length; idx++)
{
    myCharArray[idx] = ' '; // set idx'th character to blank
}
```

This first declares an array of 20 characters (arrays are covered in Chapter 6), and then loops through the array, assigning a blank character to each position in it. This example does the following:

- Declares and initializes the indexing variable: int idx = 0;

- Keeps looping as long as the indexing variable is less than the size of the array: idx < myCharArray.length;

- Increments the indexing variable by one after each iteration: idx++

The following example runs backward through the array:

```
char myCharArray[] = new char[20]; // declare an array of 20
characters
for (int idx = myCharArray.length-1; idx >= 0; idx-)
{
    myCharArray[idx] = ' '; // set idx'th character to blank
}
```

This example initializes the indexing variable to the size of the array minus one (to account for the zero-based indexing in Java arrays), and decrements the variable by one until it hits zero.

Notice how we declare and initialize the idx variable in one shot. This is handy, but because of Java's scoping rules, it does mean that the variable is not accessible outside the scope of the for loop. It *is* accessible, however, in all three parts of the for expression and in the body of the loop itself.

Another point about the for loop is that, like all Java multi-statement structures, the braces are optional if the block or body has but one statement. For example, you could write this:

```
for (int idx = 0; idx < salaries.length; idx++)
    System.out.println("Salary is: " + salaries[idx]);
```

Again, however, we caution you that not using braces risks problems when additional statements are added later. (If you forget the braces, then the first statement remains the only one executed per loop iteration.) For the sake of thoroughness, we do show you examples with and without the braces, however.

As it turns out, all three parts of the for statement are optional in Java. For example, you can legally define a for loop with none of the three parts (although the two delimiting semicolons are still required), as in:

```
for ( ; ; )
    System.out.println("looping...");
```

What does this mean? Because Java agrees to loop as long as the condition expression is not false, this loop will simply run forever. Of course, we humbly recommend not writing infinite-loop programs! What is very interesting about the for loop construct, though, is that it is a completely general construct—that is, the initialization part can contain any statement, the conditional part can contain any boolean expression, and the increment part can contain any statement. It is merely convention, although a convention we recommend you follow, that these are used for index initialization, loop termination checking, and index incrementing or decrementing. The initialization part and the incrementing part actually allow multiple statements to be specified. However, they must be separated by commas, not the usual semicolons. This gives tremendous flexibility.

For a first example of this, let's go back to the for loop, which initialized a character array to all blanks. Because the body of the loop is very small, you actually have the option of performing it in the third part of the for expression, as follows:

```
for (int idx = 0; idx < myCharArray.length; myCharArray[idx]=' ',
idx++)
{
}
```

Notice that the assignment statement is put together with the idx++ statement, separated by a comma, in the increment part. This is perfectly legal, and you will see it done often. Because all the necessary work is done in the increment part, there is no need for a body, so an empty block is used. You could also use an empty statement—a simple semicolon. In fact, to be really concise, you could also increment the idx variable right in the assignment statement, as follows:

```
for (int idx = 0; idx < myCharArray.length; myCharArray[idx++]=' ')
    ;
```

You often see this kind of compact for statement in Java code. There is a trick to its interpretation. The expression idx++ uses the current value of idx as the index into the array, and then increments it after. (This is discussed in Chapter 3.) Compact for statements are also commonly used to find the first non-blank character in a character array, like this:

```
char myCharArray[] = {' ', ' ', 'a', 'b', 'c'};
int idx;
for (idx = 0; myCharArray[idx] == ' '; idx++)
    ;
System.out.println("first blank char position = " + idx);
```

In this example, the index variable idx is declared outside the for loop so it can be accessed later. The for loop then initializes the index to zero, loops as long as the array character indexed by it is blank, and increments the index each time. In this case, the output is 2. Note that myCharArray is declared as an array of characters and initialized to contain the five characters blank, blank, a, b, and c. This implicitly sets its length to five. The number 2 that you get as a result is zero-based; in fact, it is the third position.

Of course, if the input is an array of all blank characters, this example runs into trouble. The terminating condition stays true until the index variable is beyond the limit of the array. This results in a runtime exception, which is not at all unlike an "unmonitored exception" error in RPG:

```
java.lang.ArrayIndexOutOfBoundsException: 5
```

To fix this, you need the condition expression to also check for the end of the array:

```
for (idx = 0;
     idx < myCharArray.length && myCharArray[idx] == ' ';
     idx++)
    ;
```

Now you have a robust and compact example to check for the first non-blank character. Note that each of the three parts of the `for` statement is on its own line. Because Java is a free-format language, this is perfectly legal, and is often done for readability. Your subsequent code will want to check if `idx` is greater than the array's length, which will determine if the array was all blanks or not:

```
if (idx >= myCharArray.length)
   System.out.println("All blank array!");
else
   System.out.println("first blank char position = " + idx);
```

How would you find the last non-blank character, which is another common programming requirement? You'd code it like this:

```
for (idx = myCharArrar.length-1;
     idx >= 0 && myCharArray[idx] == ' ';
     idx-)
    ;
```

In Java, as you will see in Chapter 6, you can have multi-dimensional arrays. Imagine, then, that you have a two-dimensional array named `raster`, and that you want to initialize it to one for each position. The `for` loop can handle this easily. It is an array's best friend! Two-dimensional arrays are declared using two sets of empty brackets and the new operator, which specifies the length for each dimension. Note that `arrayVariable.length` gives the length of the first dimension, and `arrayVariable[x].length` gives the length of the xth row. Listing 4.8 provides a fully compilable example.

Listing 4.8: Nested for Loops in Java

```java
public class TestFor
{
    public static void main(String args[])
    {
        int raster[][] = new int[3][2]; // matrix 3 by 2
        System.out.println();
        for (int x=0; x < raster.length; x++)
        {
            for (int y=0; y < raster[x].length; y++)
            {
                raster[x][y] = x + y;
                System.out.println("raster " + x + "," + y +
                                    " = " + raster[x][y]);
            }
        }
    }
} // end TestFor class
```

The example in Listing 4.8 results in the following output:

```
raster 0,0 = 0
raster 0,1 = 1
raster 1,0 = 1
raster 1,1 = 2
raster 2,0 = 2
raster 2,1 = 3
```

This illustrates the ability to nest for loops. That is, the body of one for loop can be yet another for loop. This means the inner loop is executed for its duration multiple times, once per iteration of the outer loop. This example is a little bit longer than necessary. Here is the smallest possible version of this nested for loop for initializing a two-dimensional array (without the println statement):

```java
for (int x=0; x < raster.length; x++)
    for (int y=0; y < raster[x].length; raster[x][y] = x + y++)
    ;
```

A FOR loop in RPG—Yes, in RPG

As of V4R4 of RPG IV, you have a free-format alternative to the fixed-format DO loop. There is a new op-code named FOR that makes it very easy to write a loop that increments a given index field from a given start value to a given end value. Listing 4.9 is the Factorial procedure originally from Listing 4.6, with the DO loop replaced by a FOR loop.

Listing 4.9: A Free-Format FOR Loop in RPG

```
P Factorial       B
D Factorial       PI             10U 0
D number                         10U 0 VALUE
D* Local fields
D index           S               5U 0
D total           S              10U 0 INZ(1)
C* Code to compute factorial
C                     FOR         index = 1
C                     BY 1
C                     TO number
C                     EVAL        total = total * index
C                     ENDFOR
C* Return factorial to the caller
C                     RETURN      total
P Factorial       E
```

The FOR op-code uses a free-format version of the C-spec that ranges from column 36 to column 80, as do the other free-format factor-two op-codes: CALLP, DOU, DOW, EVAL, EVALR, IF, RETURN, and WHEN. Not only does this give you more room for writing free-format expressions, it also allows you to easily continue that expression in the same column range of subsequent continued C-spec lines.

Here is the official syntax for the RPG IV FOR loop op-code:

OPCODE	EXTENDED-FACTOR 2
FOR	index-name < = starting-value >
	< BY increment-value >
	< TO | DOWNTO limit-value >
<loop body>	
ENDFOR | END	

The entries inside angle brackets are optional. The index field must be declared before the loop, on a D-spec, and must be numeric with zero decimal positions. The starting, increment, and limit values can be a numeric literal or a numeric expression, including a built-in function call or a procedure call. The increment value is always positive. To decrement, specify DOWNTO instead of TO, which causes the increment-value to be subtracted from the index field. Note that all three parts of the FOR op-code can be placed on one line or multiple lines. RPG exits the body of the loop when the index field's value reaches the limit value. Unlike Java, the index field is automatically incremented or decremented by the runtime.

Like the DO loop, to exit the loop prematurely, you have to either set the index field value to be the limit value, or use the LEAVE op-code. Unlike Java, there is no way to test an arbitrary expression to determine when to exit. However, this is okay because typically you'll use the DOW or DOU op-codes for loops that need to do this.

We think you have to agree this FOR loop is easy to code and easy to read, and it certainly is a closer match to Java than the older fixed-format DO loop. See the RPG IV reference manual for more examples of the FOR loop. (Here's another way to find more information: in the CODE/400 editor, position the cursor on the FOR op-code and press F1.)

Looping for a while

Now that you have mastered the for loop, you will find the while loop in Java and DOW loop in RPG IV to be a breeze. It is a subset of the for loop's functionality and brings nothing new to the table—except ease of use. The while statement is simpler than the for statement because the while loop only takes an expression for evaluation and does not have as many parameters. Its use is for those cases where the termination of the loop is not predetermined and you simply want to loop while a given condition is true. You will decide in the body of the code when to set that condition to false. (If this procedure is not performed correctly, you will have an infinite loop.) This is called an *indeterminant* loop because you can't predict when it will end. It is especially useful when reading or asking for input, since the end will be determined by the end of file marker or by a user-initiated action, for example.

The while loop for both Java and RPG executes zero or more times. This point becomes important in contrast to the next section, describing the do until loop, which executes one or more times.

In the free-format DOW operation code in RPG, you specify an expression in the free-format factor two to be evaluated each time the loop iterates. If the expression evaluates to true, the next iteration is executed. However, if the condition or the expression specified in factor two is false, the loop is terminated and control is transferred to the operation after the ENDDO op-code. Here is the syntax:

```
C*      FACTOR 1        OPCODE      EXTENDED-FACTOR 2
C*      ---------       ------      ------------------
C                       DOW         Expression
C****                   loop body
C                       ENDDO
```

To show this op-code in use, imagine your child asks you for a loan, and you want to give them a printout of the payment schedule. Because you are a softee for your kids, you don't charge them any interest. (We know—you have no "interest" in such a loan, but it is the "principal" that is important here!) Listing 4.10 shows an RPG IV procedure to calculate and print out the amount paid and amount owing after each payment. The procedure takes as input the total amount of the loan and the amount to pay each payment and returns the total number of payments.

Listing 4.10: A DOW Loop in an RPG Loan-Payment Procedure

```
P CalcPayments       B
D CalcPayments       PI              5U 0
D* Parameters
D loan                               5P 0 VALUE
D payment                            5P 0 VALUE
D* Local fields
D payments           S               5U 0 INZ(0)
D remaining          S               5P 0 INZ(0)
D paid               S               5P 0 INZ(0)
D output             S               32A
C* Calculate and display payments
C                       EVAL        remaining = loan
C                       DOW         remaining > 0
C                       IF          ((paid + payment) > loan)
C                       EVAL        payment = loan - paid
C                       ENDIF
C                       EVAL        paid = paid + payment
C                       EVAL        remaining = loan - paid
C                       EVAL        payments = payments + 1
C                       EVAL        output = %CHAR(paid) + ', ' +
C                                           %CHAR(remaining)
C        output         DSPLY
C                       ENDDO
C                       RETURN      payments
P CalcPayments       E
```

This loops while there is a remainder left to pay. Each iteration of the DOW loop first checks if the new payment will reduce the debt to or below zero. If so, it changes this month's payment to just what's left. The remaining logic evaluates the total paid so far by adding to it this month's payment, and evaluates the new amount remaining by deducting this month's payment. It also bumps up the total payments counter, and finally prints the amount paid and amount remaining. We don't show the prototype of this procedure for simplicity, but here is the mainline code to call it:

```
C                    EVAL      payments = CalcPayments(335:100)
C        payments    DSPLY
C                    EVAL      payments = CalcPayments(200:100)
C        payments    DSPLY
```

The output of this is as you would expect:

```
100, 235
200, 135
300, 35
335, 0
4
100, 100
200, 0
2
```

The equivalent in Java is the while statement, which has the following syntax:

```
while (expression)
{
   // statement(s)
}
```

Like the if and for statements, the braces around the body are required if the body is more than one statement, and optional otherwise. The expression is any boolean expression evaluating to true or false. The loop iterates as long as the expression is true. Listing 4.11 is the same code as Listing 4.10, but in OO style it is a class that uses instance variables, versus passing parameters.

Listing 4.11: A while Loop in a Java Loan-Payment Class

```
public class Loan
{
    private int loan;      // amount of loan
    private int payment;   // amount per payment
```

Listing 4.11: A while Loop in a Java Loan-Payment Class (continued)

```java
public Loan(int loan, int payment) // constructor
{
    this.loan = loan;
    this.payment = payment;
}

public int calcPayments()
{
    int payments  = 0;
    int remaining = loan;
    int paid      = 0;

    while (remaining > 0)
    {
        if ((paid + payment) > loan)
            payment = loan - paid;
        paid += payment;
        remaining = loan - paid;
        ++payments;
        System.out.println(paid + ", " + remaining);
    }
    return payments;
}

public static void main(String args[])
{
    Loan loanTest1 = new Loan(335,100);
    int payments = loanTest1.calcPayments();
    System.out.println("============");
    System.out.println("payments: " + payments);
    System.out.println();
    Loan loanTest2 = new Loan(200,100);
    payments = loanTest2.calcPayments();
    System.out.println("============");
    System.out.println("payments: " + payments);
} // end main
} // end of class Loan
```

The output of this is exactly the same as the output of the RPG version. (Note that the contracted += operator from the previous chapter is used to add payment to paid.)

In Java, the expression is very often a variable of type boolean (described in Chapter 5), which itself evaluates to true or false. This makes it a perfect match for the condition expression. The variable is usually declared and initialized to true first, then set to false inside the loop when some ending condition is met, such as reading the end of the file:

```
boolean notDone = true;
while (notDone)
{
   // read input
   if (input.eof()) // end of file for input?
     notDone = false;
}
```

In fact, you will usually see the boolean variable initialized to false and its negation checked in the condition expression, which accomplishes the same thing:

```
boolean done = false;
while (!done)
{
   // read input
   if (input.eof()) // end of file for input?
     done = true;
}
```

The while loop is actually equivalent to the for loop; each can be completely mapped to the other. All you do is move the initialization part of the for loop outside, preserve the condition expression, and move the incrementing part to the bottom of the while loop body. Here is a typical for loop:

```
for (int x = 0; x < myArray.length; x++)
   myArray[x] = 1;
```

Here is the exact equivalent, but as a while loop:

```
int x = 0;
while (x < myArray.length)
   myArray[x++] = 1;
```

So, when do you use the for loop and when do you use the while loop? It is your decision, really, because they are functionally equivalent. In general, though, the for loop is used when you can predict the number of iterations of the loop, and while is used when you cannot.

Looping until done

The last loop structure covered here is the do until loop. This is the DOU op-code in RPG, and the do while statement in Java. Here is RPG's DOU syntax:

```
C*      FACTOR 1        OPCODE       EXTENDED-FACTOR 2
C*      --------        ------       ------------------
C                       DOU          Expression
C****                   loop body
C                       ENDDO
```

Except for its name, the DOU op-code is exactly the same as DOW. In the DOU operation, just like DOW, you specify an expression in the free-form factor two. If DOW and DOU are so similar, why have two of them? The DOU operation expression is evaluated *after* the body of the structure has been executed, in contrast to *before* for DOW.

Here is Java's equivalent, the do while statement (note the ending semicolon):

```
do
{
  // statement(s)
} while (expression);
```

As with RPG's DOW versus DOU, Java's do while statement is functionally identical to the while statement. The difference is that the condition expression is not evaluated until the *end* of the loop, which guarantees at least one iteration of the loop. Our experience is that programmers tend to use one or the other of these exclusively. That underlines their equivalent functionality.

Consider the job of reading input from a file. (Hey, you've done that, right?) You have to read until the end of the file. Which loop structure is best? It's up to you. Both have pros and cons. If you use while, you must do the initial read outside the loop to initialize the end-of-file flag. Then, you must do the subsequent reads inside the loop, as follows:

```
boolean eof; // a variable that will be true or false
eof = myFile.getRecord(); // get the first record from the file
while (!eof)
{
    // ... process record
    eof = myFile.getRecord();
}
```

The disadvantage here is clear. You have to duplicate the read statement. That can create bugs later on if that statement is changed in one place but not the other. Alternatively, you could code this using do while (or DOU in RPG), and avoid the redundancy, as follows:

```
boolean eof; // a variable that will be true or false
do
{
    eof = myFile.getRecord();
    if (!eof)
      {
        // ... process record
      }
} while (!eof);
```

The disadvantage of this approach is that the if statement adds complexity to ensure that the last read does not result in the end of the file. Again, the choice is completely a personal decision. (Our preference is while versus do while, but what do we know!)

TRANSFER STRUCTURES

Let's now turn our attention to those statements that directly alter flow of control by explicitly transferring control to another statement.

If you continue, I will need a break

You have seen the looping constructs in RPG and Java, and how their termination is determined by a conditional expression at the top or bottom of the loop. The language runtime evaluates the expression at each iteration of the loop, and continues iterating as long as the expression does not evaluate to false.

Controlling when the loop ends is usually a simple matter of setting the appropriate variables to force the expression evaluation to false. This is the preferred and structured approach. However, for reasons of completeness, both languages offer alternative shortcuts to this. They take the form of the LEAVE op-code in RPG and the break statement in Java. Both of these, when used in the body of a switch, while, do, or for structure, force the immediate end of the loop. Control is then passed by default to the statement after the loop structure. The Java break statement also allows an optional tag parameter to force the exit of a loop labeled with that tag. This is for nested loops.

In addition, both languages offer a shortcut to force iteration of the loop from within the body, thus skipping all subsequent code in the body. This is done using the ITER op-code in RPG and the continue statement in Java. The continue statement, like the break statement, allows an optional tag value to explicitly identify the outer loop to be iterated. The continue statement is valid inside while, do, and for structures in Java. Both break and continue apply to the innermost loop structure by default. That is, they exit or iterate the innermost loop. In a nested loop, to exit or iterate a more outer loop, you use the optional tag value to skip to a labeled outer loop.

We caution you that both of these constructs for forcing termination and iteration offer nothing new in function over a little bit of proper if-else coding, and can be avoided. They make for some nasty maintenance problems, and are really nothing but special-case goto statements. Some people avoid them altogether. Other people insist that they can offer a more readable and elegant-looking solution than the nasty use of conditioning. Our preference is to not use them by default. In our years of experience with C and C++ programming, where they also exist, we have found them to be very rarely worth using. But then again, they make up another tool to put in your programming toolbox, so Listing 4.12 shows an RPG IV example using ITER and LEAVE.

Listing 4.12: RPG's ITER and LEAVE Op-codes in the *FindLastChar* Procedure

```
     *89012345678901234567890123456789012345678901234567890
    D* Local fields
    D pos              S              5U 0
    D* Prototype for procedure: FindLastChar
    D FindLastChar     PR             5U 0
    D inString                       32767A    VARYING CONST
    C* Mainline code
    C                  EVAL      pos = FindLastChar(' a test    ')
    C       pos        DSPLY
    C                  EVAL      pos = FindLastChar('           ')
    C       pos        DSPLY
    C* End the program
    C                  EVAL      *INLR = *ON

    P*_____
    P* Procedure name: FindLastChar
    P* Purpose:        Find position of last non-blank character
    P*_____
    P FindLastChar     B
    D FindLastChar     PI             5U 0
    D inString                       32767A    VARYING CONST
    D* Local fields
```

Listing 4.12: RPG's ITER and LEAVE Op-codes in the `FindLastChar` **Procedure (continued)**

```
D index           S                5U 0
D lastNonBlank    S                5U 0 INZ(0)
C* Code
C                     FOR           index = %LEN(inString)
C                                   BY 1 DOWNTO 1
C.                    IF            %SUBST(inString:index:1) = ' '
C                     ITER
C                     ELSE
C                     EVAL          lastNonBlank = index
C                     LEAVE
C                     ENDIF
C                     ENDFOR
C                     RETURN        lastNonBlank
P FindLastChar     E
```

In this example, a procedure named `FindLastChar` takes any character field or literal as input, and returns to the caller the position of the last non-blank character, or zero if the input is all blanks. To find the last non-blank character, it uses the new FOR op-code to loop from the ending position of the string down to one. Inside the loop, it tests if the character at the current index position is blank or not, using the %SUBST (substring) built-in function. If it is, it uses ITER to keep looping. Otherwise, it has found what it wants, and so it records the index position in `lastNonBlank` and leaves the loop. Finally, it returns `lastNonBlank` to the caller. The mainline code tests the procedure by calling it with two literals, and displays the returned value. What you get when you run this is 7 and 0.

By the way, Listing 4.12 shows how to write procedures in RPG that will accept character fields of any length: by declaring the length as the maximum character field length (32767) and by coding the keywords VARYING and CONST on the parameter D-specs for both the prototype and actual interface.

Listing 4.13 is the same example written in Java, using its `continue` and `break` statements. Notice that to get the lengths of strings in Java, we use the Java-supplied method `length`, and to extract a character at a given zero-based position, we use `charAt`. Since zero is a valid character position in Java (the first), we have to return -1 for the special case of all-blank input. (Strings are covered in detail in Chapter 7.) The input lines are `continue`, which iterates the current `for` loop, and `break`, which exits the loop.

Listing 4.13: Java's break *and* continue *Statements*

```java
public class TestBreak
{
    public static void main(String args[])
    {
        int pos;
        pos = findLastChar(" a test     ");
        System.out.println(pos);
        pos = findLastChar("            ");
        System.out.println(pos);
    }

    /** Find last non-blank character position in a string */
    public static int findLastChar(String inString)
    {
        int lastNonBlank = -1;
        for (int index = inString.length()-1;
            index >= 0; index-)
        {
            if (inString.charAt(index) == ' ')
                continue;
            else
                {
                    lastNonBlank = index;
                    break;
                }
        }
        return lastNonBlank;
    }
}
```

The break and continue statements also allow an optional label to identify the loop to exit or iterate, as shown in Listing 4.14.

Listing 4.14: Labeled *continue Statements in Java*

```java
outer: for (int classes = 0;
            classes < marksByClass.length; classes++)
{
    for (int marks = 0;
        marks < marksByClass[0].length; marks++)
    {
        if (marksByClass[classes][marks] == -1)
            continue outer;
        else if (marksByClass[classes][marks] == -2)
        continue;
```

```
          totalPerClass[classes] += marksByClass[classes][marks];
          countPerClass[classes] += 1;
      } // end inner for loop
   } // end outer for loop
```

This example is a snippet from the full sample in `TestLabeledLoop.java` on the CD-ROM included with this book. It computes the average marks for all classes, given a two-dimensional array of marks per student per class. If an array entry contains –1, it marks the end of the array for that class, and if it contains –2, it marks a student who has quit the class. Hence, while processing this two-dimensional array, we need to iterate the labeled outermost loop if we see –2, and iterate the innermost non-labeled loop if we see –1. This is done using `continue` with a tag (`outer`) that is used to label the outermost for loop. Note that loops are labeled the same as statements are labeled in CL programs. However, only loops can be labeled in Java, and only for the purpose of identifying them on `continue` or `break`.

This is typically used to force your way out of deeply nested loops, and is in contrast to the procedure of setting a variable and checking that variable in the remainder of the code in all structures.

Go to where?

The `GOTO` op-code or statement is an example of a transfer structure that does not follow structured programming design, and its use has fallen out of favor. In fact, Java designers decided to not even include it in the language, although the word is reserved. It is interesting that they took such a strong stand on `GOTO` while still advocating the use of `break` and `continue`, which are quite similar.

RPG IV, however, still has a `GOTO` op-code for historical reasons, and its syntax remains the same:

```
   C    99              GOTO      EXIT
   C         EXIT       TAG
   C                    EVAL      *INLR = *ON
```

In this example, if indicator 99 is on, you want control to transfer to the `EXIT` statement, which is identified as a target by the `TAG` op-code. Notice that the `IF` operation is a cleaner and more structured replacement for the `GOTO` and `TAG` op-codes.

Return to caller

In RPG IV, the RETURN operation code does more than its predecessor in RPG III. The RETURN op-code is used to return a value to the caller from a procedure. Listing 4.15 shows an RPG procedure named Max that returns the larger of two integers, and its proto-type. It also shows some mainline code to test it.

Listing 4.15: The RPG Max Procedure Showing the RETURN Statement

```
D* Global fields
D result          S              5I 0
D* Prototype for procedure: Max
D Max             PR             5I 0
D value1                         5I 0 VALUE
D value2                         5I 0 VALUE
 * Code to call max
C                   EVAL      result = Max(100 : 200)
C     result        DSPLY
C                   EVAL      result = Max(200 : 100)
C     result        DSPLY
C                   EVAL      *INLR = *ON

P*_____
P* Procedure name: Max
P* Purpose:        Return maximum of two integers
P*_____
P Max             B
D Max             PI             5I 0
D value1                         5I 0 VALUE
D value2                         5I 0 VALUE
C* Determine and return the maximum value
C                   IF        value1 > value2
C                   RETURN    value1
C                   ELSE
C                   RETURN    value2
C                   ENDIF
P Max             E
```

The output of running this is 200, twice. The RETURN op-code in RPG uses the free-format factor-two version of the C-spec, and you can code any literal, field, or expression in factor two. The type of that literal, field, or expression must match the declared return type of the procedure, however, which is the length, type, and decimal positions specified on the PI (Procedure Interface) and PR (Procedure Prototype) D-specs for the procedure. If these values are blank, then the procedure does not return anything, and a RETURN statement with nothing in factor two is optional.

Listing 4.16 shows the same method, max, coded in Java and called from the main method with the same inputs.

Listing 4.16: The Java max Method Showing the return Statement

```java
public class TestReturn
{
    public static void main(String args[])
    {
        int result;
        result = max(100, 200);
        System.out.println(result);
        result = max(200, 100);
        System.out.println(result);
    }

    public static int max(int value1, int value2)
    {
        return value1 > value2 ? value1 : value2;
    }
}
```

This is a very compact version of max, using the conditional operator to decide which of the two parameters to return. It tests if value1 > value2, and if true, returns value1; otherwise, it returns value2. This highlights the fact that the value returned on Java's return statement can also be a literal, a variable, or indeed an expression. The type of literal, variable, or expression must match the return type declared on the signature line, which in this case is int. If void is coded there, you can optionally code a return statement with no value.

Like RPG, there can be more than one return statement in a method. However, in general, you should strive as much as possible to only have a single return statement except for very simple procedures or methods, such the RPG Max procedure. This is because you will often need to do some coding or cleanup before returning, and if you have multiple return statements, you have to duplicate that code, which leads to maintenance problems. More theoretically, the more exit points in a procedure or method, the less structured and predicable it is considered to be.

With the above discussion in mind, and the fact that procedures are so much better than subroutines, we point out that RPG has added a new op-code in V4R4: LEAVESR. This allows you to exit a subroutine prematurely at any point in it. This was added to the

177

language simply because it was so heavily requested by programmers, but we still caution you to use it sparingly, and indeed to consider using procedures instead of subroutines.

Notice that, in the case of RPG, the RETURN operation behaves just like its counterpart Java statement only if it is used in a subprocedure. If, however, the RETURN op-code is used in the mainline code, its behavior is different than Java's. The following occurs if RETURN is used in the mainline C-specs in RPG IV:

- The program ends abnormally if a halt indicator is on.

- If the halt indicator is not on, the Last Record indicator (LR) is checked.

- If LR is on, normal termination occurs.

- Finally, if none of the above indicators is on, the return goes back to the calling routine, and all data are preserved for the next time the program is called (for better performance).

Note: This description is not a change from RPG III. Programmers used the RETURN operation code in the mainline to avoid total shutdown of the program and, thereby, increased their performance by avoiding the startup performance penalty.

In Java, you can specify a return statement in your main method as well, which signifies the end of the program. It does not have the same implications, however. The program ends whether a return statement was entered in the main, or whether the end of code was reached in main. You will see in the discussion of threads in Chapter 11, however, that there is a better way to exit your programs than to use return. We recommend using System.exit(0);. This, much like setting on the LR indicator in RPG, causes total and complete termination of the program.

SUMMARY

This chapter introduced you to the control flow statements in Java and compared them with RPG's. It covered the following points:

- RPG and Java have the most common structured statements available in most modern programming languages, including the following:

  - ➤ if and else structures

  - ➤ The SELECT and switch op-code and statement, respectively

  - ➤ Loops (including DO/for, DOW/while, and DOU/do-while)

  - ➤ LEAVE/break and ITER/continue

  - ➤ A return statement for returning from RPG procedures or Java methods

- Use an if statement if only a few expressions are to be tested. For deeply nested if-else conditions, consider using the switch statement in Java or the SELECT op-code in RPG IV.

- RPG's WHEN op-code is more powerful than Java's switch statement, since it allows you to specify any kind of expression with any data type. In Java's switch statement, the expression can only be one of the primitive data types byte, char, short, or int.

- Use the DO/for loop when you have a predictable number of iterations you want the loop to go through.

- Use the DOW/while loop when you want to iterate zero or more times through the loop.

- Use the DOU/do-while loop when you want the body of the loop to execute at least once.

- Use break and continue sparingly in Java, for forcing exit or iteration of a loop.

- The GOTO op-code is available in RPG, but not in Java.

- Java supports other transfer statements, including try/catch and throw, for dealing with exceptions. These are discussed in Chapter 10, which covers exceptions.

DATA TYPES AND VARIABLES **5**

Most languages today offer a variety of standard data types, such as binary, integer, float, and character. As with RPG fields, in Java, the type of every variable used must be declared at compile time. A data type defines the set of values that an expression can produce, or that a variable can store or contain. (Again, the terms *field* and *variable* are interchangeable.) As you will see when arithmetic and string manipulations are discussed, the data type of a variable establishes the operations that may occur on the variable. For example, if you declare a field or a variable as a character, you cannot perform arithmetic operations on it. If you declare a field as numeric (no matter what type of numeric it is), you cannot do string manipulations on it, such as substringing, concatenating, or scanning. If you attempt to manipulate a data item in a way that is inconsistent with its type, the compiler will inform you of the problem by issuing an error message at compile time. Both languages have different forms of declarations, which are discussed shortly.

Both RPG and Java are *strongly typed* languages. This means every variable and every expression has a type that must be known at compile time. This allows the compiler to determine what operations can be used with certain variables, and what values can be stored in them.

A REVIEW OF RPG TYPES

RPG has a number of data-type categories. We use the term *category* to refer to one or more data types that support the same operations and initialization characteristics. Often, there is only a single data type within a category, but for some, there are multiple data types, as shown in Table 5.1.

Table 5.1: RPG Data Type Categories, as of V5R1		
Category	Data Types	Description
Numeric	Binary, Zoned-Decimal, Packed-Decimal, Integer, Unsigned, Float	Numeric data with or without decimals
Character	Character, Character Varying, Indicator	One or more characters or indicators that hold only zero or one
Graphic	Graphic, Graphic Varying	One or more double byte (DBCS) characters
UCS-2	Unicode, Unicode Varying	Character data that holds two-byte, Universal Character Set (Unicode), standard characters
Date	Date	Date data type
Time	Time	Time data type
Timestamp	Timestamp	Date and Time combined
Basing Pointer	Pointer	A memory address
Procedure Pointer	Procedure Pointer	An address to a procedure

Within any one category, you can move data between fields of the data types and perform the same operations on fields of the data types. There is also a higher-level view called a *classification*, or *class*, which is a grouping of categories with similar characteristics and support. The classes are numeric, character, date/time, and pointer. This idea of sorting data types by operations into classifications is the heart of the term "class" in Java and other OO languages. When you define a class, you define a new classification for data. Data can be declared to be of that new class type, and any data of that type supports all the operations (methods) defined for that class type.

Table 5.2 goes into more detail on all the RPG IV data types. The Char column is the character you place in column 40 (Internal Data Type) of the RPG IV definition specification to identify the field as this type. (The D-spec is described later in this chapter.) The new data types in RPG IV are integer, unsigned, float, graphic, UCS-2, date, time, timestamp, basing pointer, and procedure pointer. Also new is the ability to specify the varying keyword on the D-spec for character, graphic, and UCS-2 data types, indicating the length given is only a maximum, and the actual length is whatever the size of the current string is in the field.

Table 5.2: RPG Data Types, as of V5R1			
Data Type	Char	Since	Description
Binary	B	V3R1	Signed, two's complement data, with or without decimals
Zoned-Decimal	S	V3R1	Signed, one byte per digit, with or without decimals
Packed-Decimal	P	V3R1	Signed, one byte per two digits, with or without decimals
Integer 5 and 10	I	V3R2/6	Signed, integer-only data, two or four bytes, no decimals
Integer 3 and 20	I	V4R4	Signed, integer-only data, one or eight bytes, no decimals
Unsigned 5 / 10	U	V3R2/6	Unsigned, integer-only data, two or four bytes, no decimals
Unsigned 3 / 20	U	V4R4	Unsigned, integer-only data, one or eight bytes, no decimals
Float	F	V3R7	IEEE standard, floating-point data, four or eight bytes
Character	A	V3R1	Fixed-length, single-byte character data

Table 5.2: RPG Data Types, as of V5R1 (continued)			
Data Type	Char	Since	Description
Character Varying	A	V4R2	Variable-length, single-byte character data, uses varying keyword to identify variable length
Indicator	N	V4R2	One-byte data, eight *on (one) or *off (zero)
Graphic	G	V3R1	Fixed-length, double-byte character set (DBCS) data
Graphic Varying	G	V4R2	Variable-length DBCS data, uses varying keyword to identify variable length
UCS-2	C	V4R4	Fixed-length, two-byte Unicode data
UCS-2 Varying	C	V4R4	Variable-length, Unicode data, use varying keyword
Date	D	V3R1	Date data
Time	T	V3R1	Time data
Timestamp	Z	V3R1	Date and time combined data
Basing Pointer	*	V3R1	Memory address from %addr or alloc operations
Procedure Pointer	*	V3R1	Memory address of a procedure, procptr keyword identifies, %paddr sets
Object	O	V5R1	Reference to a Java object for RPG-to-Java support

Integer and unsigned data types are designed to replace the binary data type when used with zero decimal places. These types allow you to hold larger integral numbers with the same memory because there is no need to hold decimal information. Note you must still hard-code a zero in the decimal position of the D-spec. The memory requirements of these are one, two, four, and eight bytes depending on whether you specify a digit length of three, five, 10, or 20, respectively.

Floating-point fields hold single-precision (four-byte) or double-precision (eight-byte) values that have variable decimal positions. Float data is made up of a mantissa and an exponent, and can hold very large positive or negative numbers. Float data is most often used in scientific applications involving real-world measurements and number crunching.

Graphic data contains pure DBCS characters. Every two bytes define a single DBCS character according to the DBCS collating sequence for a particular codepage or CCSID. DBCS graphic data is used for Japanese, Korean, Chinese, and Simplified Chinese strings, and does not require shift-out/shift-in delimiters.

UCS-2 data also contains two-byte data, but it is an industry standard that is defined to hold every character from all codepages, including DBCS and non-DBCS data. With this all-encompassing character set, commonly referred to as Unicode, all complexities involved in supporting multiple language or country character sets are eliminated. Codepages and CCSIDs disappear. As you will see, all Java characters and strings are stored internally in Unicode format.

Date, time, and timestamp fields were added to the language in the first release of RPG IV. By explicitly telling the compiler that a field will hold a date, time, or timestamp, the compiler is able to support a multitude of special-purpose operations designed specifically for dates and times. This includes intelligent comparisons, formatting, extractions, and duration calculation, as covered in Chapter 8.

Basing pointers are fields that will point to a memory address. You assign this address by using the ALLOC op-code to allocate a block of memory, or by using the %ADDR built-in function to return the address of another RPG IV field. You can also define a non-pointer field with the BASED(basing-pointer-field) keyword. With this, the compiler does not allocate memory for this field, but rather sets the memory location to be that of the basing-pointer value. You can also do math on a basing-pointer field to move its location forward or backward in memory.

Basing pointers can be used to call system APIs that require pointers to data structures as input or output, or can be used to write complex applications that manage their own memory. For example, some programmers have coded their own multi-dimensional arrays by allocating the memory themselves and managing the contents using basing pointers. Until assigned, a basing pointer points to *NULL, a special value in RPG.

Procedure pointers are fields that will hold a pointer to a procedure, which, as you recall, are new in RPG IV and what we call "grown-up subroutines." Procedures use the new P-spec, and allow parameter passing, return values, recursive calls, and local fields. You assign a pointer to a procedure by using the %PADDR(procedure-name) built-in function. Once you have assigned it, you can call the procedure pointed to by the field by simply naming the field on the CALLP operation. Procedure pointers can be used to write reusable code, where the procedure to be called is determined at runtime instead of statically at compile time. Programmers have used these to write generic service programs that can be reused in many different situations, and leave it up to the caller to pass in procedure pointers that the generic code will subsequently "call back" to do situation-specific tasks. No math is allowed on procedure pointers. Until assigned, a procedure pointer points to *NULL.

Something new and exciting in V5R1 of RPG is the ability to instantiate Java objects from RPG code, and subsequently call the methods in that Java object from RPG. We don't go into that support here, but as part of the RPG language enhancements to support it, there is a new O data type that is used to hold the Java object reference after an object is instantiated.

AN INTRODUCTION TO JAVA TYPES

Variables in Java, like fields in RPG, must be defined with a type. Java has two distinct flavors of types:

- *Primitive types* are similar to RPG's data types, in that they are predefined in the language and have built-in support in the form of operators and conversion rules.

- *Reference types* are variables whose type is defined to be that of a class in Java, either Java-supplied or user-defined. Reference variables, as discussed in Chapter 2, are equated to an instance of the class type they are defined as, using the new operator. Because they contain the memory address of a class instance or object, they are said to *refer* to an object; hence, the term "reference variable." These reference variables distinguish Java as an object-oriented language, compared to the primitive-only data types in RPG. You can think of classes in Java as a mechanism for defining your own data types, with the methods in the class being the operators supported by all data defined with that type (class). Thus, the term "class" is really a short form for "classification."

We limit our discussion in this chapter to primitive types in Java, which compare to RPG's data types. Reference types were introduced in Chapter 2, and are discussed in more detail in Chapter 9 (and indeed, all the subsequent chapters). It is interesting to note, however, that all of Java's primitive types are also available as classes in the java.lang package. These classes are wrappers of the primitive types, with methods for converting to and from them. They are of value when the code expects only objects. (These are discussed later.) Also of interest is that arrays and strings are both implemented as objects in Java, so variables of these are, in fact, reference variables. (These are discussed in Chapters 6 and 7.)

Primitive data types in Java fall into the following categories:

- *Numeric* types are divided into those that do not have decimals and those that do. The former are in the integer subcategory, and include one-byte (byte), two-byte (short), four-byte (int), and eight-byte (long) types. The latter are in the float subcategory, and include four-byte (float) and eight-byte (double) types. Note that in both RPG and Java, numeric data types are signed, which allow both positive and negative numbers. However, there is an exception to this in RPG: the unsigned data type that allows only positive numbers. Thus, although otherwise identical to RPG and Java's integer data types, it does allow larger positive numbers.

- The *character* data type, unlike RPG, is always a single character long, unless you define an array of characters. Also unlike RPG, a character in Java is actually two bytes long, as it is based on the two-byte Unicode standard that encompasses all international characters. In contrast, a character in RPG is one byte long and is based on the EBCDIC encoding standard. In Java, then, the complex use of codepages is not required to support international characters properly.

- The *boolean* data type supports two values: true and false. These are reserved words in Java and are only assignable to boolean variables. Boolean is analogous to RPG indicators, where one is true and zero is false.

Table 5.3 lists the eight primitive data types in Java. As you can see, we are missing some critical types compared to RPG. Namely, there are no types for numeric data with fixed decimals, no types for character fields with a length greater than one, and no types for pointers. Not to worry, though, these apparent holes in the language are actually filled by Java-supplied classes, versus primitive types. The exception is pointers, which were explicitly left out of the language for security and ease-of-use reasons. However, you could think of object reference variables as pointers, since both contain memory addresses. The difference is that Java does not allow math on those addresses. Also, Java does not have procedure pointers, but you will discover in Chapter 9 that you can achieve the "call back" capability of procedure pointers using something called interfaces.

Table 5.3: Java Primitive Data Types	
Java Type	Declaration
byte	Signed integers, one byte of storage, -128 to +128
short	Signed integers, two bytes, -32768 to +32767
int	Signed integers, four bytes, -2,147,483,648 to +2,147,483,647 (about two billion)
long	Signed integers, eight bytes, -2**63 to +(2**63)-1
float	Single-precision, floating-point data, four bytes
double	Double-precision, floating-point, eight bytes
char	Single alphanumeric character, Unicode based, two bytes
boolean	Either true or false, one byte.

Table 5.4 shows a brief comparison of the data types in the two languages. To make accurate comparisons, you have to consider the declared length (number of digits) of the RPG types.

Table 5.4: RPG versus Java Data Types			
RPG IV Type	RPG Len	Java	Comments
Binary (no decs)	1 to 4	short	Two bytes, signed numeric integers
Binary (no decs)	5 to 9	int	Four bytes, signed numeric integers
Binary (decimals)	1 to 9	BigDecimal	BigDecimal is a class for emulating fixed-decimal numeric data.
Zoned-Decimal	1 to 30	BigDecimal	BigDecimal is the only option for fixed-decimal numeric data.
Packed_Decimal	1 to 30	BigDecimal	BigDecimal is the only option for fixed-decimal numeric data
Integer, Unsigned	3	byte	One byte, signed/unsigned integers
Integer, Unsigned	5	short	Two bytes, signed/unsigned integers

Table 5.4: RPG versus Java Data Types (continued)

RPG IV Type	RPG Len	Java	Comments
Integer, Unsigned	10	int	Four bytes, signed/unsigned integers
Integer, Unsigned	20	long	Eight bytes, signed/unsigned integers
Float	4	float	Single-precision floating point
Float	8	double	Double-precision floating point
Character or Graphic or UCS-2	1	char	Single character only
Character or Graphic or UCS-2	2 to 32767	String	The string class is used for multiple character strings (discussed in Chapter 7).
Indicator	1	boolean	*on=true, *off=false
Date		Date	Discussed in Chapter 8
Time		Date	Discussed in Chapter 8
Timestamp		Date	Discussed in Chapter 8
Basing pointer		object reference	Memory addresses, but Java does not permit address math
Procedure pointer		interfaces	Discussed in Chapter 9

As you can see, there are some RPG types that the Java designers chose to implement as classes instead of primitive data types. These will be discussed in subsequent chapters. We will go into more detail on each of the primitive data types after covering some syntactical details.

DATA DECLARATION

Data types are put to use in two places in a language: in explicit fields or variables that you define, and in implicit fields or variables the compiler generates to process expressions. Now that you have had a glimpse of what the types are in Java, it is important to understand how to define variables of those types. The syntax is completely different from RPG's, but arguably easier. Let's review both.

Defining fields in RPG

You declare a field in RPG IV in one of three ways:

- On the C- or I-spec, by supplying length information

- Using the DEFINE op-code on a C-spec

- On the D (Definition) specification, which is new in RPG IV.

Why so many? The first two are inherited from RPG III, and the third is new for RPG IV. Before RPG IV, you had no choice other than to define fields on the I-spec, E-spec, and the C-spec. The new D-spec adds structure to your RPG code. It allows you to define all your fields, data structures, arrays, and tables in one area in your source code. So why did RPG IV not drop the other two methods? The simple answer is compatibility. Existing applications written in RPG III must run "as-is" after they are converted to RPG IV. An example is shown in Listing 5.1.

Listing 5.1: Defining Fields in RPG IV

```
    *89012345678901234567890123456789012345678901234567890
FQSYSPRT   O    F    80          PRINTER OFLIND(*INOV)
D FIRST            S              5A   INZ('PHIL ')
D AGE              S              2B 0 INZ(25)
D*─────────────────────────────────
C      *LIKE          DEFINE     FIRST         LAST           +5
C                     EVAL       LAST = 'COULTHARD '
C                     MOVE       'ONCE WAS '    AGETEXT          9
C                     EXCEPT     RESULT
C                     EVAL       *INLR = *ON
C*─────────────────────────────────
OQSYSPRT   E                     RESULT
O                                FIRST          5
O                                LAST          15
O                                AGETEXT       24
O                                AGE           26
```

The example in Listing 5.1 defines fields that use the three different methods:

- The fields FIRST and AGE are defined using the D-spec. The name goes in columns 7 to 21. Material is more readable because it is not necessary to left-justify it. Names in RPG IV can be uppercase or lowercase, although the compiler converts them to uppercase. The S in column 24 indicates this is a standalone field (compared to, for example, a data structure or constant). The length is defined in columns 33 to 39, the data type in column 40, and the decimals in columns 41 to 42. The keyword INZ is used to initialize the values of the variables.

- The field LAST is defined on a C-spec using the DEFINE op-code to pick up the attributes of the previously defined FIRST field. The length is incremented by five over FIRSTs.

- The field AGETEXT is defined on a C-spec at the time of first use by specifying a length.

The resulting output of this example is the following:

```
PHIL COULTHARD ONCE WAS 25
```

(Yes, and the AS/400 was once a new computer!) Newcomers to RPG IV are encouraged to do field definitions on the D-spec because the code is easier to read and maintain. (It is no longer necessary to hunt for field definitions because now they are all at the top of the program.) The RPG IV equivalent to the DEFINE op-code is the LIKE keyword on the D-spec; the field LAST in the example could have been declared like this:

```
     D LAST            S              +5     LIKE(FIRST) INZ(*ALL' ')
```

This example also shows how to use the INZ keyword to initialize all positions of a variable to a specified value by using *ALL followed immediately by the value.

The data type column on the D-spec is in column 40, and must be a single character entry that represents one of the RPG built-in data types, as shown in the Char column in Table 5.2. If it is blank, and there is no LIKE keyword, the type defaults to character if the decimals column is blank as well, or packed otherwise (unless it is a subfield, in which case it defaults to zoned).

The D-spec is a tremendous addition to RPG IV; you will find it makes writing and maintaining code much easier. You'll soon come to frown on implicitly declared fields on C-specs! Table 5.5 describes each of the columns of the D-spec for simple program-described fields that are standalone instead of data structures.

Table 5.5: RPG IV D-spec Columns for Standalone Fields	
Column Range	Declaration
6	The spec type, D
7 to 21	The name of the field being declared. The name can float within the column range. Names greater than 15 characters can use the whole spec line, but have to end in an ellipsis (..., and then the length, type, and decimal details go on the next line.
24	An S, indicating this is a standalone field
33 to 39	The length of the field (number of digits)
40	The data type of the field, as described in Table 5.2
41 to 42	The decimal positions in the field
44 to 80	One or more keywords that further define and describe the field

The keywords allowed for standalone fields are STATIC, INZ, EXPORT, IMPORT, ALTSEQ(*NONE), NOOPT, and BASED. If you use CODE/400 for your RPG editing, you will find a SmartGuide ("wizard") that prompts you for the information and generates the D-spec for you. Here are some examples of field declarations in RPG:

```
          1         2         3         4         5         6
123456*8901234567890123456789012345678901234567890123456789012
.....DName++++++++++ETDsFrom+++To/L+++IDc.Keywords+++++++++++
       D BinaryField      S              4B 0
       D ZonedField       S              9S 2
       D PackedField      S              7P 2
       D IntegerOneByte   S              3I 0
       D IntegerTwoByte   S              5I 0
       D IntegerFourByte...
       D                  S             10I 0
       D IntegerEightByte...
       D                  S             20I 0
       D aField           S             30A
       D namePtr          S               *   INZ(%ADDR(aField))
       D nameField        S             30A   BASED(namePtr)
```

Notice how the names start in column 8 instead of 7 to aid readability, and how the names are coded longer than 15 characters (14, if you start in column 8).

One recent enhancement (since V4R4) that you will love is the INZ(*USER) keyword to initialize a 10-character field to the current user profile name.

Defining constant fields in RPG

Good programming style dictates that you avoid hard-coding literal values as much as possible, and instead use named constants to hold these values. That way, you can subsequently change that value once by simply changing the value of the constant. RPG IV has explicit syntax for defining constants, which also uses the D-spec. The syntax is very simple: give it a name as usual (all uppercase is a good standard for constants), declare a C in column 24 (instead of an S), and define the value as the parameter to the CONST keyword. No length, type, or decimals are specified. Here are some examples:

```
D* Constants
D TYPE1          C                CONST(1)
D MAXTYPES       C                CONST(10)
D TYPENAME       C                CONST('DOORKNOB')
D DFT_DISCOUNT   C                CONST(0.05)
```

Note that the CONST keyword is optional—you can just code the value in the keyword area.

Defining data structures in RPG

You don't always declare standalone fields in RPG. Often, you define data structures made up of one or more subfields. In RPG IV, you can also use the D-spec to define data structures and subfields. Table 5.6 describes each of the columns of the D-spec for data structures.

Table 5.6: RPG IV D-spec Columns for Data Structure Fields and Subfields

Column Range	Declaration
6	The spec type, D
7 to 21	The name of the data structure or subfield being declared. The name can float within the column range. The name is optional for both the structure and each subfield.
22	An E if this is an externally described data structure. Use extname to define the name of the file and, optionally, the format name.

	Table 5.6: RPG IV D-spec Columns for Data Structure Fields and Subfields (continued)
Column Range	**Declaration**
23	An S if this is a program status data structure, a U if this is a data-area data structure, and blank otherwise
24 to 25	DS for the structure, blank for the subfields
33 to 39	The total length of the data structure (optional), or for subfields, the length of the subfield
40	For subfields only, the data type of the field, as described in Table 5.2
41 to 42	For subfields only, the decimal positions in the field
44 to 80	One or more keywords that further describe the data structure or subfield

The keywords allowed for data structures are STATIC, INZ, EXPORT, IMPORT, ALTSEQ(*NONE), ALIGN, BASED, DTAARA, and OCCURS. The keywords allowed for data structure subfields are ALTSEQ(*NONE), INZ, PACKEVEN, DTAARA, and OVERLAY. Here is an example of a data structure field declaration in RPG:

```
          1         2         3         4         5         6
123456*890123456789012345678901234567890123456789012345678901 2
.....DName++++++++++ETDsFrom+++To/L+++IDc.Keywords+++++++++++
     D* Widget Data Structure: Holds information about Widgets
     D Widget           DS                   INZ
     D  id                             5U 0
     D  type                           1A
     D  unitPrice                      9P 2
     D  name                          30A
```

Notice how we specified only the length of the subfields, not the starting and ending positions. The latter is allowed in RPG IV, but is rarely used. We also indented the subfield names more than the data structure name to aid in readability.

Two recent enhancements (since V4R4) that you will enjoy are the INZ(*EXTDFT) keyword to initialize an externally described structure to the values specified in the DFT DDS keyword, and the OVERLAY(name:*NEXT) keyword to define overlaid subfields in successive positions.

Obviously, there is much more to say about all the details of defining fields in RPG, but we leave that topic to the RPG IV manuals and the many RPG IV books.

Defining qualified data structures in RPG V5R1

Something new and exciting in RPG IV V5R1 is the QUALIFIED keyword for data structures. If you specify this keyword, you can access the subfields in the data structure by using Java-like dot notation to qualify the name of the subfield with the data structure's name. This allows you to reuse subfield names in multiple data structures, because there is no longer any ambiguity about which data structure subfield you are referring to! Further, you can define other data structures to be exactly like a previously defined qualified one, and inherit all of its subfield definitions. This is done with the LIKEDS keyword. You can also use a new *LIKEDS special value for the INZ keyword to indicate you want to use the same initial values as the inherited subfields. Here is an example from the RPG IV Reference manual:

```
D sysName        DS                    qualified
D   lib                       10A      inz('*LIBL')
D   obj                       10A
D userSpace      DS                    LIKEDS(sysName) INZ(*LIKEDS)
  // The variable "userSpace" was initialized with *LIKEDS, so the
  // first 'lib' subfield was initialized to '*LIBL'.  The second
  // 'obj' subfield must be set using a calculation.
C                eval         userSpace.obj = 'TEMPSPACE'
```

This is very interesting and useful, and very much like objects in Java, only without method support.

Defining variables in Java

In Java, variables can be defined in two places: at the class level, such that they are available to all methods (similar to RPG fields declared at the top of the file), or inside a method, such that they are available only to the code inside that method (similar to RPG fields declared locally inside procedures). Unlike RPG, Java has only a single syntax for defining variables. There are, however, a number of optional parts. In its simplest form, a variable declaration looks like this:

```
type name;
```

The data type comes first and is followed by a name of your choosing. The statement ends with a semicolon, as do all Java statements. Here is an example:

```
int myVariable;
```

This defines a variable named myVariable, of type int (integer). It is really that simple. The valid types are the eight Java reserved words for built-in primitive data types, listed in Table 5.3. Note that for object reference variables, the type will be the name of a Java class or an interface (described in Chapter 9).

To initialize a variable when you declare it, just equate it to a value, as in:

```
int myVariable = 10;
```

The value to which it is initialized can be a literal or variable that is already defined, or it can be an expression (for example, myVar + 2). In either case, the resulting type must be the same or compatible with the defined type of the variable.

Compared with defining fields in RPG, in Java, you don't deal with any of the following:

- *Columns*. Java is free-form.
- *Name length*. There is no limit to the name length in Java.
- *Digit length*. You do not specify a length for your variables in Java because the length is predefined by the type.
- *Location*. With RPG IV, your D-spec variables must be declared either at the top of the program or at the top of a procedure. In either case, they must precede the C-specs. In Java, class-level variables can be declared before or after the methods (we prefer before, but others prefer after), while method-level variables can be declared anywhere in the code as long as they are declared before use.

On the other hand, you do have to worry about case. In Java, abc and ABC are different, while in RPG IV, they are the same.

Java variable names are not shortened by convention, but are as long as necessary to be descriptive. Lowercase is used except for the first letter of words other than the first word, for example, interestRate or variablePayRate. Java variables specified at the class level, versus inside a method, can also be specified with optional *modifier* keywords before the data type. Here is an example:

```
private int myVariable = 10;
```

This example specifies the modifier `private`, indicating this variable is not accessible (either to read or to write) by code outside of this class. The modifiers are shown in Table 5.7.

Table 5.7: Variable Modifiers in Java

Modifiers	Description
public, private, or protected	Accessibility of the variable, where public means all can access, private means only this class, and protected means this class or those that extend it (as discussed in Chapter 9). The default is that this class or others in this package can access it. This default is referred to as package accessibility, but there is no language modifier keyword for it.
static	This variable is initialized only once and has only one value, regardless of the number of instances of this class. Can be accessed via classname.variable, versus object.variable. Static variables are known as class variables, since there is one value per class, not one per object.
static final	This variable is a constant and cannot be changed.

`Static` and `static final` variables can also be defined as `public`, `private`, or protected. For classes that are not extendible, you should always define your non-static and non-constant variables as `private`, which will force users of your class to go through your methods. In Chapter 9, you will see that for extendible classes, you will often use `protected` versus `private`. Local variables inside a method are always private to that method and no modifiers are needed or allowed.

There are actually two other modifiers: `transient` and `volatile`. However, you will rarely use these, and you need not worry about them. Briefly, though, the former deals with the persistence of a variable when you serialize it to disk, while the latter deals with the behavior of a variable in a multithreaded application.

Defining constant variables in Java

In Java, as with RPG IV, there is explicit syntax for defining constants. As mentioned earlier, constants are identified by the modifiers final and static, and have to be initialized to a value at declaration time. The modifier final means this variable's value cannot be changed, while static means you need not waste memory by reserving memory in every object. Since it never changes value, you need only reserve space once at the class level. Often, constants are intended to be used by users of your class, so are made public. Java's convention is that constants are named all uppercase to make it easier to distinguish them. Unlike RPG, you must declare the types of your constants in Java. Here are some examples:

```
public static final short TYPE1 = 1;
public static final int MAXTYPES = 10;
public static final double DFT_DISCOUNT = 0.05;
public static final String TYPE_NAME = "DOORKNOB";
```

Defining data structures in Java

What about data structures in Java? Sorry, but there is no syntax for defining these. Or is there? A data structure is a way to group multiple related fields into a single entity, while still allowing individual access to the subfields. This is just what a class is in Java! You group variables in Java by putting them into classes. Indeed, any one of those fields inside a class can itself be an instance of another class, so data-structure nesting is also possible. The differences between data structures in RPG and classes in Java are:

- Non-static subfields (instance variables) require you to instantiate the class before using it

- You can have multiple instances of a class active simultaneously, each with their own data for each of the subfields.

- You can include procedures (methods, in Java) directly inside classes.

- To access any subfield from another class, you must qualify its name with an object reference variable name for instance variables, or the class name for static variables. The benefit of this extra work is you can use the same subfield name in multiple classes.

VARIABLE SCOPE, LIFETIME, AND EXTERNAL ACCESS

The discussion of data types leads to the discussion of variables, which in turn leads to the discussion of *variable scope* (that is, which code inside the RPG compile unit or Java class has access to the variable), *variable lifetime* (when is the variable allocated memory and initialized, and when is that memory freed), and *external accessibility* (the question of whether code outside this RPG or Java compile unit can access the variable). The following sections discuss these three aspects of Java variables.

Variable scope

In RPG III, the question of field scope is an easy one. All fields are global to the program in which they are declared, and one source member equals one program after compiling. The only rule is that a field cannot be accessed prior to being defined, but after being defined, all code, whether global or in a subroutine, can access that field.

RPG IV now has procedures that allow local fields to be defined in the procedure itself (as discussed in Chapter 2). These fields are not accessible by any code outside of the procedure. However, global fields declared at the top of the module are accessible by all the procedures in that module, as they were for subroutines.

Compile units have also changed in RPG IV. Rather than being source members compiling into a program object directly, they are compiled into intermediate module objects, which are then bound into a program object or service program object. Code in one module cannot, by default, access global fields in another module—even if they end up in the same program object. However, you can make fields accessible outside of your module by defining them with the keyword EXPORT, and then redefining them with the keyword IMPORT in the other modules.

Remember that in Java, variables can be declared at the class level or at the method level. Basically, method-level or local variables are only accessible by the code contained in that method, while class-level variables are accessible by code in any of the methods in that class. In fact, within a method, you can also have parameter variables. These resemble locally declared variables, except that they are passed in by the caller rather than being defined within the code or body of the method. Otherwise, they are just like local variables. You can roughly equate global fields in RPG IV modules to class-level variables in Java, and local fields in RPG IV procedures to local variables in Java methods. Furthermore, since RPG IV procedures also support the passing in of parameters, you can equate RPG IV procedure parameter fields to Java method variables. (By *equate,* in this context, we are talking about the scope or direct accessibility of the variables.)

However, moving further beyond parameters, Java has blocks, which are one or more statements contained inside curly braces. You have seen these already in relation to class definitions and method definitions, which are special cases of blocks. However, you can also have blocks defined directly inside methods, and these blocks can have their own variables that are local to that block, for example:

```
int myVariable;
myVariable = 10;
{
    int mySecondVariable;
    mySecondVariable = 20;
}
System.out.println("mySecondVariable =  " + mySecondVariable);
```

In this example, the variable mySecondVariable inside the braces (or block) has its own scope, so it is not accessible to the code outside of that block. Therefore, you will get an error, since the println method call is trying to access an inaccessible variable. Notice that Java does not allow variable "hiding" in blocks—that is, you cannot redefine myVariable from the outer block, as this could lead to subtle programming errors. Blocks like this are simply to aid program readability. There are other examples of blocks, such as the for statement, and you can declare variables in them that are local to that statement block, as in:

```
for (int index = 0; index < 10; index++)
{
    System.out.println("index = " + index);
}
```

Any attempt to reference the index variable after the last curly brace of the for statement will result in an error. A variable declared inside a block is only accessible inside the block in which it is defined. RPG has no equivalent to Java's local blocks. The general scoping rule in Java, then, is that code can only directly access any variable in the current scope (block) or *higher*, up to the class level. (By *directly*, we mean without qualification.)

Variable lifetime

When do variables come to life, and how long do they live? For RPG III, as you know, they come to life when the program is first called and they live until the program is ended (by either setting the LR indicator to 1 or by ending the job). Global fields in RPG IV have the same lifetime, although you can now subdivide a job into named ILE *activation groups*, and fields will not live past the life of these. The new local fields inside RPG IV procedures only come to life when the procedure is called, and they die immediately when it ends. These are sometimes called *automatic fields*, since their death is automatic with the ending of the procedure. However, if you specify STATIC for a local field in RPG, that field's value persists for the life of the program or service program it is in.

For Java methods and nested blocks inside methods, these automatic or local variables come to life when the method is called or the block is entered. If an initialization has been specified, it is applied at that time. When the block ends or method ends, the variable goes away, just as with RPG IV procedures. (By *come to life* we really mean when the variables get allocated actual storage in memory.)

For Java class-level variables, life is more interesting. Non-static class-level variables (that is, instance variables) come to life when an instance of the class (object) is instantiated with the new operator. Each class instance gets its own memory allocation for the instance variables, so they are totally independent of each other. If your instance variable declaration includes an initializer (for example, = 10), that initial value is applied at the same time as the object is created, and its instance variables come to life.

For static class-level variables (that is, class variables), there is only one allocated memory location per variable, regardless of the number of instances of the class. Since the life and values of a static variable are not dependent on, or even related to, instances of the class, it makes sense that static variables come to life or are allocated memory as soon as the Java runtime "knows about" the class. This typically occurs at pre-runtime, when the application is starting up, as it does for RPG global fields. The important thing to remember is that static variables will be alive as soon as you first possibly need them. Recall that in Java, unlike RPG, local variables in a method cannot be static.

Variable external access

When we talk about scoping of a variable, we are talking about what code has *direct* access to it. In this case, we are talking about code in the same compilation unit as the variable. In RPG III, a compilation unit is a program object; in RPG IV, it is a module object; in Java, it is a class. However, in both RPG IV and Java, code outside of a variable's compilation unit can access that variable.

In RPG IV, this is accomplished by specifying the EXPORT keyword on the field definition specification. This allows other modules in the final program or service program to access this field, providing they define it as well, but with the IMPORT keyword. This tells the compiler that this field is allocated in another module, but that you intend to access it in this module. In a service program, you can even go further and make your exported fields (and procedures) available to other *programs*, if you specify as much in the binding source for the service program (as described in Chapter 2).

The Java equivalent to RPG's EXPORT keyword is the use of the `public` modifier on your class-level variables. This tells the compiler that you want any code in any other classes to have access to this variable. Think of this as being equivalent to exporting your variable, via EXPORT and binding source, from an RPG IV service program for all the world to use. However, good form dictates that you will rarely, if ever, do this for non-static variables; you should prefer to force users to go through your `getXXX` and `setXXX` methods to access your instance variables. To prevent such global access to your variables, you can instead not specify any modifier, giving your variable package access. This gives access to your class only to other classes in this package. Since we equate a package to a service program, this is equivalent to EXPORTing your variable in RPG, but not specifying it in the binding source. To completely restrict other classes, use the `private` modifier, indicating only your class code has access. (There is also a `protected` mode, limiting access to classes that extend or subclass this class, a topic discussed in Chapter 9.)

Assuming that you have made a variable available to outside classes, that outside code cannot simply use the variable name as-is. RPG forces the external code to IMPORT the field, and Java forces the external code to qualify the variable name. For static variables, the variable name must be qualified with the class name separated by a dot. For non-static variables, the variable name must be qualified with an object reference variable name, again separated by a dot. This dot operator tells the compiler that the variable is not part of this class, and further, tells the compiler (and actually the runtime) in which class or class instance the variable can be found. The class itself is found by looking first in the current package, and then by searching the imported packages. Alternatively, the class name can be explicitly qualified with the package name.

Variables: An example

At this point it would be helpful, no doubt, to see an example of Java variables in action. Consider Listing 5.2.

Listing 5.2: The Widget Class Example of Java Variables

```java
public class Widget
{
    public  static final int TYPE1 = 1; // constant
    public  static final int TYPE2 = 2; // constant
    public  static      int nextID= 0; // class
    private             int id;        // instance
    private             int type  = 0; // instance
    public Widget() // Constructor. Note name == class name
    {
        id = nextID; // references instance and class vars
        nextID = nextID + 1;
    }
    public boolean setType(int newType)
    {
        boolean inputOK = true; // local
        if (newType >= TYPE1 && newType <= TYPE2)
          type = newType; // references instance variable
        Else
          inputOK = false;
        return inputOK;
    }
    public String toString()
    {
        String retString; // local
        retString = "Type = " + type + ", ID = " + id;
        return retString;
    }
} // end Widget class
```

This example class has two constant variables (TYPE1 and TYPE2), one static variable (nextID), and two instance variables (id and type). It also has a constructor method (Widget) and two other methods (setType and toString). All of these access one or more class-level variables. The last two methods also declare their own local variables (inputOK and retString), while setType accepts a method parameter (newType). Listing 5.3 shows another class that uses this class.

Listing 5.3: Testing the Widget Class

```
public class TestWidget
{
    public static void main(String args[])
    {
        Widget.nextID = 1000; // set class variable
        Widget myWidget = new Widget(); // object 1
        myWidget.setType(Widget.TYPE1); // call method
        Widget myWidget2 = new Widget(); // object 2
        myWidget2.setType(Widget.TYPE2); // call method
        System.out.println(myWidget); // calls toString method
        System.out.println(myWidget2); // calls toString method
    }
} // end TestWidget class
```

Compiling and running this test class gives the following output:

```
>javac TestWidget.java
>java TestWidget
Type = 1, ID = 1000
Type = 2, ID = 1001
```

First, notice the toString method. If you supply this special method for Java in your class, Java will implicitly call it when you specify an instance of your class on the System.out.println method, which is done in the TestWidget class. This method simply creates a String object (covered in Chapter 7) that displays some interesting variable values. Including a toString method in your class is a good idea to make debugging easier, if nothing else.

This Widget class example highlights a few of the items under discussion. It represents an item that you'll need a lot of. Each unique Widget will be identified by a type (the constants TYPE1 or TYPE2 make this less error-prone) and by a unique identifier. The assignment of a unique identifier is solved by using a static variable (nextID), since there is only ever one value for a static variable. You simply use and increment this variable in a constructor so each Widget instance gets a unique value. The problem is this static variable need to be "seeded" at the beginning of the program, outside of the class. That is why it is public, and you see in the TestWidget class that it is seeded to 1000. The type is set per Widget by calling the method setType and passing in one of the defined constants for a value. Notice that the instance variable type is set to this value (if it is valid). Because id and type are instance variables, each Widget instance gets to maintain its own independent values for these, which is what you want. Also notice that these instance variables are made private, so there's no risk of external code (outside of this class) *directly* changing any of Widget's values.

Take note in TestWidget how the references to the static variables are qualified in the Widget class by qualifying them with "Widget." Without this, Java would look for these variables in the TestWidget class. Also note how two instances of Widget are instantiated by using the new operator, and then the setType method is invoked on each one to independently change the instance variables of each object.

As an RPG III programmer, you will not have used either local variables or parameters (as shown in the setType method), although as an RPG IV programmer, you have both, through the use of procedures (as described in Chapter 2). However, while RPG's global fields are directly equivalent to class-level static variables, the concept of instance variables that have different values per class instance is totally foreign to RPG. In essence, RPG gives you exactly one instance of each module in your programs.

Another thing to watch for in Java versus RPG is variable initialization. In RPG, the compiler supplies reasonable defaults for fields, on which we sometimes rely. Java has a similar supplied default value for class-level variables, but not for local variables. Rather, a local variable must be initialized or assigned a value before it is first referenced or the compiler will issue an error message. A good rule is to always initialize a variable explicitly, even if it is to zero. Even in RPG!

LITERALS BY DATA TYPE

You have already seen an example of an int (integer) variable initialization in Java, so you are familiar with the syntax:

```
int myVariable = 10;
```

However, let's round out this example with examples of initialization for each data type. It is important to know this, because any literal value you specify at initialization time (or assign later, for that matter) must be consistent with the variable's data type. Each data type, both in RPG and Java, has an explicit syntax for literal values. We humans learn by example, so we will teach the syntax of literals by example. First, the non-numeric data types are shown in Table 5.8.

Table 5.8: Examples of Literals for Non-Numeric Data Types

RPG Type	Example	Java Type	Example
character 1	'a' or X'7D'	Char	'a' or '\''
character n	'abc' or 'Bob''s Store'	String	"ABC" or "c:\\mydir" or "Bob's Store"
graphic	G'oK1K2i'	String	"K1K2" where K*n* is a DBCS character
indicator	'0' or '1' or *OFF or *ON	Boolean	false or true
date	D'2001/12/11'	Date	Discussed in Chapter 8
time	T'11:33;01'	Date	Discussed in Chapter 8
timestamp	Z'2001/12/11.33. 01'	Date	Discussed in Chapter 8
basing pointer	*NULL or %ADDR(myVar)	Object reference	null or new MyClass()
procedure pointer	*NULL or %PADDR(myProc)	n/a	

The character data type takes a literal enclosed in single quotes. In Java, this can be only a single character, while in RPG, it can be multiple characters. RPG allows hexadecimal numbers if they begin with the letter x. Java also allows special character values if they are preceded by a slash, which is called an *escape sequence*. Examples are shown in Table 5.9.

Table 5.9: Java Escape Sequences

Escape Sequence	Description
\n	Newline character
\t	Tab
\b	Backspace
\r	Carriage return
\f	Form feed
\\	Backslash
\'	Single quote
\"	Double quote
\ddd	Octal number, not to exceed 377
\uxxxx	Unicode number, must be four digits

For numerics, some examples are shown in Table 5.10. The non-float values in Java are simple integers that must not be larger than the capacity of the data type. However, long data type literals do allow an optional L character (either uppercase or lowercase) after them. This tells the compiler that these are indeed long values, which can be important in expressions, where casting between data types can happen implicitly. By default, these literals are assumed to be base-10 decimal numbers, but you can also specify octal (base-8) or hexadecimal (base-16). For octal, use a leading zero, as in 035. For hexadecimal, use a leading 0x or 0X, as in 0x1d.

Table 5.10: Examples of Literals for Numeric Data Types

RPG Type	Example	Java Type	Example
integer 3	120 or -120	byte	120 or -120
integer 5	20000 or -20000	short	20000 or -20000
integer 10	1000000 or -1000000	int	1000000 or -1000000
integer 20	9000000 or -9000000	long	9000000 or -9000000L (optionally ends in l or L)
unsigned	10 or 20000		
binary, package, zoned	10 or 10.12		
float 4	10 or .12 or 1234.9E12	float	10f or 12.1f or 1.234E12F (always ends in f or F)
float 8	10 or .12 or 1234.9E12	double	10 or 12.1D or 1.234E12 (optionally ends in d or D)

Float-type literals in Java are decimal numbers, followed by an optional decimal point, followed by an exponent. The literal can be followed by an F for single-precision float or a D for double-precision float. If no F or D is specified, any literal with a decimal point is assumed to be double-precision. You can also force an integer literal to be a float literal by simply appending an F or D to it, as in 123F. The exponent part consists of an E or e, followed by a positive or negative decimal number.

NUMERIC DATA TYPE RANGES

When programming with numeric data types, it is important to know the limits to each data type, so that you can choose the appropriate data type to avoid overflow or truncation.

In RPG, when you define a numeric data type field and specify a length or decimal type, you do so by specifying how many decimal "digits" the field will hold. You do not specify how many bytes of memory to allocate—that is done implicitly by the compiler, based on the number of digits you indicate (the exception to this rule is the float data type, where you do specify the number of bytes, either four or eight). This digit length is a rather unique means of describing length, and underscores RPG's role as a business language, as opposed to a scientific or general language. Java, on the other hand, does not burden you with the business of specifying lengths at all. Rather, it supplies a number of different numeric types for you, each of which represents a different predefined length or capacity. This implies, however, that you need to know the limit for each data type, in order to choose the correct one for your particular case. You could simply always choose the largest—long for integers and double for floating-point—but for large numbers of variables, this will be a waste of computer memory, as these take up more space than their smaller cousins.

To determine the limits for each data type, you have to know the underlying size of each in bytes. Thus, in the end, you are forced to think in terms of numerical limits, rather than the number of digits, as you usually do in RPG. Let's review, then, the RPG data type ranges in Table 5.11.

Table 5.11: RPG Numeric Data Type Ranges

Type	Bytes	Range
binary 4,0	2	-9,999 to 9,999 (four 9s)
binary 9,0	4	-999 ,999, 999 to 999,999,999 (nine 9s)
zoned 30,0	30	-30 9s to +30 9s
packed 30,0	16	-30 9s to +30 9s
integer 3	1	-128 to 127
integer 5	2	2^{15} = -32,768 to 32,767
integer 10	4	2^{31} = -2,147,483,648 to 2,147,483,647
integer 20	8	2^{63} = -huge to +huge
unsigned 3	1	0 to 255
unsigned 5	2	2^{16} = 0 to 65535

Table 5.11: RPG Numeric Data Type Ranges (continued)

Type	Bytes	Range
unsigned 10	4	232 = 0 to 4,294,967,295
unsigned 20	8	264 = -huge to +huge
float 4	4	1.175 494 4 E-38 to 3.402 823 5 E+38
float 8	8	2.225 073 858 507 201 E-308 to 1.797 693 134 862 315 E+308

Note how integer types allow a maximum value of 2^{n-1}, where n is the number of bits in the allocated memory length. For unsigned types, since one bit is not required to store the sign, it is 2^n. Thus, if you are still using a binary data type but specifying zero decimal positions, it is to your advantage to switch to the integer data type. Furthermore, it is more efficient in internal expression evaluations than is binary.

Let's now compare these ranges to those of Java's built-in numeric types, in Table 5.12. (Note that the ranges given for float and double in both languages are positive numbers. The negative number range is the same.)

Table 5.12: Java Numeric Data Type Ranges

Type	Bytes	Range
byte	1	2^7 = -128 to 127
short	2	2^{15} = -32,768 to 32,767
int	4	2^{31} = -2,147,483,648 to 2,147,483,647
long	8	2^{63} = -9,223,372,036,854,775,808 to 9,223,372,036,854,775,807
float	4	1.402 398 64 E-45 to 3.402 823 47 E+38
double	8	4.940 656 458 214 465 44 E-324 to 1.797 693 134 862 315 70 E+308

FLOAT VERSUS PACKED

What are floating-point fields, and why would you use them? You can see that for Java, `float` and `double` are the only primitive data types that support decimal points. Since your

RPG code is riddled with packed decimal fields, your first inclination might be to use `float` or `double` in your Java code, or to use `int` or `long` for zero-decimal packed numbers.

Indeed, for zero-decimal fields, this is exactly what we recommend, but floating-point fields (whether single-precision or double-precision) are somewhat less efficient than packed fields. This is because floating-point fields are designed to hold arbitrary values without benefit of previous knowledge about the number of decimals. That is, you do not tell the compiler at definition time how many decimals the data will contain; you simply specify whether it is to be four or eight bytes long. Any valid floating-point number can be assigned to that variable during runtime. This makes for great flexibility, but it also means that the internal storage of these numbers has to be flexible. That means, as always with flexibility, a performance cost in order to interpret the data at runtime; the internal format of the data essentially must be converted every time it is referenced. Compare this to packed decimal, where you tell the RPG compiler at field-definition time exactly how many decimals any data contained in the field will have. This allows the compiler to store the data in a fixed format every time, and allows mathematical operations to exploit this knowledge for very fast evaluations. (Mind you, most hardware today offers built-in support for floating-point manipulation.)

Therefore, in cases where you are dealing with a predetermined number of decimals (such as with amounts of money), floating-point is not a good choice. Floating-point fields *are* a good choice when dealing with data for which you cannot predict the exact decimal precision, such as with scientific data, real-world measurements like the size of a human hair, and so on. It is also of value even when the number of decimals can be hard-coded, but the size of the number cannot. For example, if the number may become extremely large or extremely small (well below one), `float` or `double` can handle it. It is hard to imagine what type of data would need to allow for numbers bigger than $1.7 * 10^{308}$!

However, this refers to RPG, where you have a choice between packed and float. In Java, you have no such choice, as there is no equivalent data type to packed. For business applications that deal with pay rates, unit costs, unit prices, and so on, it is hard to imagine the need for the power of floats, with their attendant costs. It is too bad Java did not see fit to support a built-in packed decimal data type, but clearly the designers were not coming from an RPG background!

On the surface, then, it appears you are stuck with Java's `float` or `double`. However, these have other, perhaps more serious, concerns than performance—that is, their propensity to produce high-precision results after a mathematical operation. You do not want to be billing your customers in ten-thousandths of a cent, for instance. Let's look at a Java example. Imagine you have widgets to sell for $1,234.56, and you decide to have a sale where you offer 23 percent off. What might the calculations for the new price look like? Try the code in Listing 5.4.

Listing 5.4: Using a Float for Monetary Math

```
public class TestFloat
{
    public static void main(String args[])
    {
        double unitCost = 1234.56;
        double discount = 0.23;
        System.out.println("unitCost = " + unitCost);
        unitCost = unitCost - unitCost * discount;
        System.out.println("saleCost = " + unitCost);
    }
}
```

The result of the code in Listing 5.4 is the following:

```
unitCost = 1234.56
saleCost = 950.6111999999999
```

Can you imagine sending this bill to your customers? To circumvent this problem, you might try writing your own complicated code to force the decimal precision and make some decision on rounding, but this is ugly code. Really, then, float and double are not good choices for monetary values.

However, all is not lost! The Java designers did supply, at least, a Java class to emulate the mathematical behavior of a packed-decimal data type. While not a built-in type, it is at least something that can offer accurate results with methods for easily setting the decimal precision. The class is named BigDecimal, and you find it in the java.math package. This class offers you complete control over rounding behavior on divide and decimal-point adjustments, and offers a very complete set of mathematical and conversion functions in the form of methods. We recommend that you use this class, and in fact the AS/400 Toolbox for Java product maps packed-decimal database fields to this class in its two database packages. If your packed decimal operations on the AS/400 use half-adjust, then even that rounding option is available to you.

To understand this class and its documentation in the JDK, you have to be familiar with its terminology and architecture. An instance of a `BigDecimal` class is really the following:

- An integer value like 123456, with no limit on the number of digits (*precision*) in that integer value.

- A decimal position (*scale*) within that integer value. This is specified in terms of the number of digits to the right of the decimal point.

When you create a new `BigDecimal` object, you have three choices for the initial value: a string like 1234.56, a `BigInteger` object (another class in `java.math`), or a double value. If you get your value from the user, it will probably be as a string. Using a string sets both the integer value (123456) and the scale (two, in this example, since there are two decimal positions). Alternatively, you can use the static method `valueOf(long val, int scale)` to return a new `BigDecimal` object with the integer value and scale you specify:

```
BigDecimal unitCost = BigDecimal.valueOf(123456, 2);
```

Once you have a `BigDecimal` object, you can perform all the usual mathematical operations on it via methods like `add`, `subtract`, `divide`, `multiply`, `abs`, and `negate`. You can also use comparative methods like `compareTo`, `min`, and `max` to compare it to another `BigDecimal` value. (Note that `compareTo` ignores trailing zeros in the decimal portion, so 1234.00 is considered equal to 1234.0000. If you do not want this, use the `equals` method.) There are also methods for converting a `BigDecimal` object to other data types such as integer (`intValue`), long (`longValue`), double (`doubleValue`), `BigInteger` (`toBigInteger`), and, of course, string (`toString`).

How does `BigDecimal` deal with the precision problem, as in the example involving the 23 percent discount? It will, by default, give you more decimal points after a multiplication than you started with. (Specifically, it will give you back the sum of the decimal points of the two operators.) However, it supplies a very useful method named `setScale` to set the number of decimal points after an operation like `multiply`. This method simply moves the decimal point, but leaves the non-decimal part of the number unchanged. For example, if you start with 1234.5678 and call `setScale(5)`, you will get 1234.56780. But what if you call `setScale(2)`? This will give you back either 1234.56 or 1234.57, depending on the rounding behavior you ask for. This behavior can be specified as the second parameter to `setScale`, and must be one of the eight constants defined in `BigDecimal`. It's likely that you will only ever use two of these, however—either

BigDecimal.ROUND_DOWN (which gives you 1234.56, i.e., a simple truncate), or
BigDecimal.ROUND_HALF_UP (which gives you 1234.57, i.e., it rounds up if truncated
digits are greater than five). Let's revisit the discount example in Listing 5.5, this time using BigDecimal instead of double.

Listing 5.5: Using BigDecimal for Monetary Math

```
import java.math.*;
public class TestBD
{
    public static void main(String args[])
    {
        BigDecimal unitCost = new BigDecimal("1234.56");
        BigDecimal discount = new BigDecimal(".23");
        System.out.println("unitCost = " + unitCost);
        // unitCost = unitCost - unitCost * disCount
        unitCost = unitCost.subtract( unitCost.multiply(discount) );
        System.out.println("unitCost after discount = " + unitCost);
        unitCost = unitCost.setScale(2, BigDecimal.ROUND_HALF_UP);
        System.out.println("unitCost after setScale = " + unitCost);
    }
}
```

This gives the following result:

```
unitCost = 1234.56
unitCost after discount = 950.6112
unitCost after setScale = 950.61
```

There are only two methods in BigDecimal that may cause truncation of data from the
decimal part of the number: setScale and divide. All other operations increase the
number of decimal digits, if required. Note that the non-decimal part of the number is
never truncated, but rather simply grows as much as necessary to hold the result. For
setScale and divide, you should choose BigDecimal.ROUND_HALF_UP if you normally
use the half-adjust operation modifier in RPG; otherwise, you should choose BigDecimal.
ROUND_DOWN. However, there are six additional rounding options for you as well:
ROUND_CEILING, ROUND_FLOOR, ROUND_HALF_DOWN, ROUND_HALF_EVEN, ROUND_
UNNECESSARY, and ROUND_UP.

Note in the previous example a BigDecimal method call was nested as a parameter to another BigDecimal method:

```
unitCost = unitCost.subtract( unitCost.multiply(discount) );
```

This is possible because the `multiply` method returns a new `BigDecimal` object, which is then passed in as a parameter to the `subtract` method. This method also returns a new `BigDecimal` object, which equates back to the original `unitCost` object reference variable. In fact, all the mathematical methods in `BigDecimal` return new objects rather than changing the object on which they are invoked. That is why you must code `object = object.method(xxx)` when using the `BigDecimal` class. It is read-only or, in Java-speak, *immutable*. No method has any impact on the object on which it is directly invoked; rather, the method returns a new object altogether. If the returned object is equated to the source object variable, then the very original object in memory is lost and will eventually be swept up by the garbage collector. (You will learn about another immutable class, `String`, in Chapter 7.)

THE BOOLEAN DATA TYPE

Since the boolean data type in Java is somewhat foreign to you as an RPG programmer, we believe that it is worth a brief description. In both RPG and Java, you have expressions that evaluate to true or false, and so affect the flow of control in your program, like this:

```
if (amountDue > 0)
   // do something
```

The notion of true or false is intrinsic to computing, and is the end result of any conditional expression, no matter how complex. In RPG and DDS, this notion is embedded in indicators, with their zero or one states (or *OFF or *ON). The Java boolean data type is roughly equivalent to RPG indicators, but rather than using zero or one to indicate state, the special keywords `true` and `false` are used. Therefore, you can initialize and set boolean variables like this:

```
boolean myFlag = true;
myFlag = false;
```

This is very similar to RPG indicators. Indeed, in both cases, they can be used directly as expressions. For example, in Java all of the following are valid:

```
if (myFlag == true)
   // ....
if (myFlag)
   // ...
if (myFlag == false)
   // ...
if (!myFlag)
   // ....
```

In RPG IV, you can do something similar:

```
D myFlag          S            N   INZ(*ON)
C                 IF      myFlag
```

This is quite handy. Boolean variables can be used wherever an expression or sub-expression is allowed, including while and for loop conditionals. Most interestingly, a boolean variable can be assigned an expression. That is, it can be assigned the resulting true or false value of an expression, as in:

```
myFlag = (amountDue > 0); // will be true or false
```

You can do the same with indicator data types in RPG IV:

```
C                 EVAL    myFlag = *INLR  *OFF
```

This can all make for elegant and compact code.

Finally here is a little example to show how to convert between integer and boolean values:

```
// boolean test
int y = 0;
if (test)
  y = 1;                // Boolean to integer
y = (test) ? 1 : 0; // Boolean to integer (option 2)
test = (y!=0);        // Integer to boolean
```

CASTING AND NUMERIC CONVERSIONS

Casting is the process of converting a variable's value from one data type to another. RPG's way of converting numeric fields from one type to another is very straightforward, as Listing 5.6 illustrates.

Listing 5.6: Moving Data between Fields of Different Types in RPG

```
FQSYSPRT   O    F   80        PRINTER OFLIND(*INOV)
D DS1              DS
D   INT5                      5I 0 INZ(25)
D   BIN9                      9B 0 INZ(22)
D   ZONE9                     9S 0 INZ(30)                    →
```

Listing 5.6: Moving Data between Fields of Different Types in RPG (continued)

```
D   PACK9                             9P 0 INZ(40)
D*----------------------------
C                     MOVE      BIN9        INT5
C                     EXCEPT    RESULT
C                     MOVE      PACK9       INT5
C                     EXCEPT    RESULT
C                     MOVE      ZONE9       INT5
C                     EXCEPT    RESULT
C                     EVAL      *INLR = *ON
C*----------------------------
OQSYSPRT    E              RESULT
O                          INT5              15
```

This example declares a number of fields with different types, and initializes them. In the body of the code on the C-specs, you see multiple moves from one numeric field to another, followed by an exception output. The compiler determines the types of these fields and does the appropriate conversion as needed. In this example, then, each instance of binary, packed, and zoned is converted to integer. This example works the same if you use EVAL for the assignments, versus MOVE. What happens if the value being moved will not fit in the result? It is truncated.

Java is somewhat similar to RPG in this respect. That is, in most cases, you can simple move data between data types with no unique syntax required other than an assignment statement:

```
short myShort = 10;
int   myInt = 20;
long  myLong;
myLong = myShort;
myLong = myInt;
```

This is a perfectly legal and common practice. However, you will notice that we are only doing safe conversions here, from a smaller type to a larger type. Thus, the result will always safely fit in the target variable. What if the target type is smaller than the source type? For example, consider this:

```
long myLong = 40000;
short myShort = myLong;
```

This will fail. In fact, it will not even compile. Contrast this to RPG, where it is legal at compile time, and at runtime the result is simply truncated if necessary. Sometimes, though, you'll want to do this because you know that the resulting value will fit in the target. There is a way to force Java to allow the conversion and simply truncate the result if necessary (but, of course, you should avoid these situations). It involves some simple casting syntax, which looks like this:

```
long myLong = 20000;
short myShort = (short)myLong;
```

The syntax specifies the resulting type in parentheses before the variable or operation:

```
(target type) source-value
```

This is simply a directive to the compiler that you know what you are doing and you will take responsibility for the risk of truncation. Casting like this is required, as mentioned, for any conversion from one data type to another of lower precision. It is allowed in all other cases as well, but not required.

Table 5.13 summarizes where casting is necessary in numeric type-to-type conversions. Read this table by scanning across the rows. You see that converting from a data type specified in the left column to any data type in the columns across the top does not require a cast for those target data types that have higher precision. There are two apparent anomalies: a cast is required from byte to char and from char to short. The first anomaly occurs because, while char is two bytes and byte is one, byte is signed while char is not. Hence, the sign of the byte value could be lost. The second occurs because char is unsigned and byte is signed, even though they are both two bytes, there is potential for corruption with negative or large positive values. So, these are not actually anomalies after all. To be safe, always cast—you have nothing to lose, if you know truncation will not occur.

	byte	Char	short	int	long	float	double
byte		Cast					
char	Cast		Cast				
short	Cast	Cast					
int	Cast	Cast	Cast				
long	Cast	Cast	Cast	Cast			
float	Cast	Cast	Cast	Cast	Cast		
double	Cast	Cast	Cast	Cast	Cast	Cast	

Table 5.13: When to Cast in Java

> **Note:** If you are using a `BigDecimal` object, you cannot use this primitive type casting technique. Instead, use the supplied methods in the `BigDecimal` class named xxxValue(), where xxx is each of the numeric primitive types, for example:`double myDouble = myBigDecimalObject.doubleValue();`

Now that we have demonstrated how RPG does conversion with the MOVE operation code, what about other operations, such as numeric operation codes or the EVAL op-code that allows expressions in factor two? Take a look at Listing 5.7

Listing 5.7: Expressions Involving Fields of Different Types in RPG

```
FQSYSPRT   O    F   80           PRINTER OFLIND(*INOV)
D DS1                DS
D INT5                      5I 0 INZ(25)
D FLT4                      4F   INZ(10)
D FLT8                      8F   INZ(10)
D BIN9                      9B 0 INZ(28)
D ZONE9                     9S 0 INZ(80)
D PACK9                     9P 0 INZ(40)
D*--------------------------------------------------------------
C                   EVAL     INT5 = ((BIN9+ZONE9/PACK9)*2)+FLT4
C                   EXCEPT   RESULT
C                   EVAL     *INLR = *ON
C*--------------------------------------------------------------
OQSYSPRT   E                 RESULT
O                            INT5                    15
```

As with the MOVE operation code, you do not have to tell the RPG compiler of your intentions for field conversions. The compiler will do the conversion and expression evaluation internally before placing the result into the target field. In this case, the target is INT5, an integer of length 5. Actually, RPG introduced in V3R7 a new set of built-in functions to allow you to have more control over converting fields. For example, the %INT and %INTH built-in functions convert a field to an integer value without and with half-adjust, and %FLOAT converts a numeric field to float.

What happens in Java? Suppose you want to add integer, short, and byte field values together, and divide the result by a float number, and perhaps even assign the result of the expression to a double field. This is shown in Listing 5.8.

Listing 5.8: Expressions Involving Variables of Different Types in Java

```
public class TestEXPR
{
    public static void main(String args[])
    {
        byte    byt  = 30;
        short   sht  = 20;
        int     int1 = 20;
        double  dbl  = 10.0d;
        float   flt = (float)(((byt+sht-int1)*2.0)/dbl);
        System.out.println(flt);
    }
}
```

This example declares different numeric fields. The highlighted line defines the final expression. It consists of adding the byte and short fields and then subtracting an integer field from the result. It then multiplies by 2.0, which is a double literal, and finally divides the result by a double field. The most important thing in this example is that it casts the final result to a float. The result of executing this is the value 6.0, which is the result of the operation. Had we not cast the result, the compile would have failed.

Under the covers, a series of rules is used to convert the intermediate results to a common format, usually that of the highest precision of all the operands:

- If at least one of the operands is of type double, the intermediate result is double (if the other operand is not also double, it is implicitly cast to double), and eight-byte math is used.

- If at least one of the operands is of type float, the intermediate result is float (if the other operand is not also float, it is implicitly cast to float), and four-byte math is used.

- If at least one operand is of type long, the intermediate result is long (if the other operand is not also long, it is implicitly cast to long), and eight-byte math is used.

- If none of the above, the intermediate result is integer (all operands are implicitly cast to integer), and four-byte math is used.

Casting is done often, both implicitly and explicitly, in Java. Another place this happens is on the return statement of a method. If you define a method's return type to be integer, your actual returned value can be a byte, character, short, or integer value without explicit casting. However, if you return a long value, you must explicitly cast it:

```
public int testThis()
{
    long retValue = 20000;
    return (int)retValue;
}
```

JAVA DATA-TYPE CLASS WRAPPERS

Java supplies class *wrappers* for its primitive data types. These are classes in the java.lang package that allow you to work with each of the data types as objects instead of primitives. All of the operators are emulated via methods in the class. Furthermore, the classes supply some interesting and worthwhile additional methods and constants. The classes are as follows:

- Boolean

- Byte

- Character

- Double

- Float

- Integer

- Long

- Short

They come in handy when an object is needed, yet you have a primitive. For example, you might have an array of mixed values—some integers and some objects. This is not legal, of course, so you would instead use the class wrappers to produce objects from your integer values. You would define the array to hold objects of class Object, a generic class discussed in Chapter 9.

All of these classes contain constructors that accept a primitive type value as input for conversion to an object. Most importantly, they all supply methods to convert to and from a string, such as the methods parseInt and valueOf in the Integer class. You will use these often, as Java only accepts user input in the forms of strings, so conversion is essential. Table 5.14 shows the methods supplied by each class to convert from a string, convert to a string, and convert to a primitive type.

Table 5.14: Java Class-Wrapper to/from Methods

Class	From a String	To a String	To a Primitive
Boolean	valueOf(String)	toString()	booleanValue()
Byte	valueOf(String) decode(String)	toString()	byteValue(), doubleValue(), floatValue(), intValue(), shortValue(), longValue()
Character		toString()	charValue(), getNumericValue()
Double	valueOf(String)	toString()	doubleValue(), byteValue(), floatValue(), intValue(), longValue(), shortValue()
Float	valueOf(String)	toString()	floatValue(), byteValue(), doubleValue(), intValue(), longValue(), shortValue
Integer	valueOf(String) parseInt(String)	toString() toBinaryString(long) toHexString(long) toOctalString(long)	intValue(), byteValue(), doubleValue(), floatValue(), longValue(), shortValue()
Long	valueOf(String) parseLong(String)	toString() toBinaryString(long) toHexString(long) toOctalString(long)	longValue(), byteValue(), doubleValue(), floatValue(), intValue(), shortValue()
Short	valueOf(String) parseShort(String)	toString()	shortValue(), byteValue(), doubleValue(), floatValue(), intValue(), longValue()

Note that the valueOf(String) methods all throw the exception NumberFormat Exception if the input string is not valid. This is Java's equivalent to sending an escape message on the iSeries, and you must "monitor" for these using try/catch-blocks. Although this concept is not discussed in detail until Chapter 10, we mention it now so that we can show you the example in Listing 5.9. It accepts a float value as a string from the command line, then converts it to a primitive float using the Float class.

Listing 5.9 Converting a String to a
Float Object, and a Float Object to a float Primitive

```
public class TestConvertFloat
{
    public static void main(String args[])
    {
        Float floatObject;
        if (args.length != 1)
          return;
        try
        {
            floatObject = Float.valueOf(args[0]);
        }
        catch(NumberFormatException exc)
        {
            System.out.println("Invalid input!");
            return;
        }
        float floatValue = floatObject.floatValue();
        System.out.println("input = " + floatValue);
    }
}
```

Note that args[0] represents the first parameter string passed in the command line. The result of compiling this and running it with various inputs is as follows:

```
>javac TestConvertFloat.java
>java  TestConvertFloat 1.2
input = 1.2
>java  TestConvertFloat 1.02
input = 1.02
>java  TestConvertFloat 0000.12
input = 0.12
>java  TestConvertFloat 1.2e4
input = 12000.0
>java  TestConvertFloat -1.2e4
input = -12000.0
>java  TestConvertFloat abcdef
Invalid input!
```

Another useful thing about these classes is that there are constants for the minimum and maximum values these data types allow—for example, Integer.MAX_VALUE and Integer.MIN_VALUE. Numerous other useful methods exist, including a number of isXXX() methods in the Character class, such as isSpaceChar. Many of these methods are static and take their target as a parameter, so they do not require an instance of the class. The class then just becomes a convenient place to group these related traditional-style functions. It is worth your time to peruse the JDK documentation pertaining to these classes.

SUMMARY

This chapter introduced you to the following concepts:

- Java has two categories for data types: primitive and reference.

- Java has eight primitive data types: boolean, char, byte, short, int, long, float, and double.

- Java does not have an equivalent data type to RPG's binary, packed, or zoned. However, the class java.math.BigDecimal works well as a packed-decimal replacement.

- The character data type in Java represents one character, whereas RPG's character data type can be looked at as an array of one-byte characters. The equivalent in Java is the String class.

- Character and string data in Java is Unicode based, versus RPG's EBCDIC base. (Information on the Unicode standard can be found on the Web at *www.unicode.org*).

- The syntax <modifiers> type *name*; defines a Java variable.

- In both RPG IV and Java, you can declare a variable as either global or local.

- Only class-level variables can specify modifiers.

- The modifiers for variables are public, private, protected, static, final, transient, and volatile.

- In Java, you can initialize a variable when it is declared, using the assignment operator (=) and a literal, variable, or expression. This compares to the INZ keyword in RPG.

- Without qualification, code can access local variables, parameters, or class-level variables of the containing class only.

- With qualification, class-level variables in other classes can be accessed, depending on the modifiers specified for them.

- Static variables have a single value per class, whereas non-static variables have a unique value per class instance or object.

- Constants are defined in Java by specifying the modifiers `static` and `final`.

- Casting in Java is implicit when converting to a higher-precision data type, but requires explicit cast syntax when converting to a lower-precision data type.

- There are class wrappers for each of the primitive data types that offer string conversion and other useful methods.

ARRAYS AND VECTORS

As discussed in earlier chapters, Java programs contain two types of variables:

- *Primitive types* are defined to be one of the eight primitive data types `boolean`, `byte`, `char`, `short`, `int`, `long`, `float`, or `double`. These are similar to RPG fields. They support the operators such as +, -, / and *.

- *Reference types* are defined to be of a class type. They can be declared as one of the following types:

  ➢ *Class type*. This can include any of the classes Java supplies in its `java.xxxx` packages, or one of your own classes. This can also be the Java-supplied `String` class described in Chapter 7. Here are some examples:

    ```
    MyClass myVariable;
    String myString;
    ```

➢ *Interface type.* Interfaces are much like the prototypes for RPG IV procedures, and are discussed in Chapter 9. They are special kinds of classes that define only method names and parameters (*signatures*) without supplying the code for them, for example:

```
MyInterface myVariable;
```

➢ *Array type.* In Java, arrays have special syntax and, perhaps surprisingly, are actually objects. An array variable is an object reference variable. Array objects contain multiple occurrences of a primitive data type or of other objects. All occurrences or elements of a single array must be of the same type, and that type must be declared on the array object-reference variable declaration.

Once you have declared a reference type variable, it can be assigned values as follows:

■ *Null.* This is the initial default value assigned to reference variables until such time as they are assigned to an instance of a class or array. You can also explicitly assign null to an object reference if you wish to "free" the object to which it currently points, and you can compare it to null, for example:

```
if (myObject == null)
    myObject = new MyClass();
...
myObject = null; // done with the object, free it up
```

■ *Object.* These are instances of classes that are created by using the new operator, like this:

```
myObject = new MyClass();
```

As discussed in Chapter 2, new allocates memory for the object, and assigns the address of that memory location to the reference variable. Parameters can be specified with the new operator, like this:

```
myObject = new MyClass(100, true, "My Name");
```

In this case, both the Java compiler and the Java runtime will search the class MyClass for a constructor with the number and type of parameters (*signature*) that matches those

226

specified—one integer, one boolean, and one String. If found, this constructor is called. Otherwise, an error occurs.

OBJECT REFERENCE OPERATORS

Once you have declared and instantiated an object reference, you can perform operations on the object, including these:

- Access class-level variables inside the object, using dot notation, for example:

```
myObject.limit = 100;
```

- Invoke methods on the object using dot notation, for example:

```
myObject.setLimit(100);
```

- Cast between object types (discussed in Chapter 9)

- Use the instanceOf operator to determine if the object is an instance of a specified class name (also discussed in Chapter 9)

- Compare memory addresses of two object references, using ==, !=, or the conditional operator ?:, for example:

```
if (myObject == myOtherObject)
  ...
else if (myObject != myYetAnotherObject)
  ...
myNewObject = (myObject==myOtherObject) ? myObject :
myOtherObject;
```

In summary, variables in Java are either primitive (or base) data types like integer or object references. These object references are, in fact, pointers to instances of classes. Arrays, which are covered here, are cases of object references that are used heavily in Java programs, and so have special support in the language.

> **Note:** There are no explicit pointers or pointer arithmetic in Java. This is unlike RPG, where pointers and pointer arithmetic is supported. Java just contains reference type variables, which are like pointers in that they hold memory addresses. However, you cannot increment, decrement, or otherwise mathematically manipulate these memory addresses; they can only be assigned and compared. This gives you most of the benefits of pointers but with added security, ease of use, and strong type checking.

ARRAYS

As a seasoned programmer, you know you need a raise. Sorry—we meant to say *arrays*. Both RPG and Java support arrays, but with some noticeable differences. Table 6.1 highlights the differences and similarities between the two languages in terms of their support for arrays.

Table 6.1 RPG Arrays versus Java Arrays	
RPG	Java
One dimension only	Multiple dimensions (no limit)
Fixed in size at compile time	Size set at runtime, but fixed once it is set
Declaration time initialization (a compile-time array)	Declaration time initialization
Runtime initialization (a runtime array)	Runtime initialization
Pre-runtime initialization from a file	
(a pre-runtime array)	No built-in support for initializing from a file
Older-style "tables"	Supplied Hashtable class for fast-lookup arrays, or new JDK 1.2 Arrays class in java.util with binary search methods
Multiple occurring data structures	Arrays of objects
Dynamic memory APIs for sizable arrays	Supplied Vector class for sizable arrays

There is similar functionality in both languages, especially when we include not only Java arrays, but the additional utility classes Java supplies in the `java.util` package: `Vector`, `Hashtable`, and `Arrays`. Really, we have to give the edge to Java on this, though, because, as you will see, it has more array functionality and capability than RPG. The biggest difference is Java's support for multi-dimensional arrays. On the other hand, RPG has its little-used but wonderful support for pre-runtime arrays, which are initialized from a file just as the program first starts running. However, you will learn how you might code this functionality into Java yourself. RPG also has its "mature" support for tables, which have fallen out of favor since the introduction of arrays and multiple occurring data structures in RPG.

To refresh your memory, tables are like array fields but have names starting with "TAB" and are only indexable using the `LOOKUP` operation. Multiple occurring data structures are data structures that can be repeated, which make them effectively arrays of structures. Like tables, though, and unlike arrays, there is no explicit way to index into a multiple occurrence data structure. Rather, you have to implicitly index into it by using the `OCCUR` operation to identify and set the "current occurrence." While Java does not have an exact syntactic match for either tables or multiple occurrence data structures, you will soon see that hashtables are a good functional match for tables, and arrays of objects are a good functional match for multiple occurring data structures.

Java has explicit syntax for arrays, and generally they could be used for all of your requirements for repeating items of the same type. Indeed, as of JDK 1.2.0 (also called "Java 2"), you have even greater array support, in the form of a set of static helper methods in the `Arrays` class in `java.util`. This includes methods for searching, sorting, comparing, and filling (with the same value) arrays. However, Java also gives two other options beyond arrays: vectors and hashtables. Vectors are growable and shrinkable one-dimensional arrays. Hashtables are key-plus-value pairs, designed for easy storage of a value by key and efficient retrieval of a value by key. Arrays, the `Arrays` class, vectors, and hashtables are covered in this chapter.

If all this is not enough, you also got a whole batch of new options in JDK 1.2.0. There are a number of new classes in `java.util` for specialty data structures (well, that's what we call them). Specifically, there is support for lists, maps, stacks, and sets, as shown in Table 6.2.

Table 6.2: Specialty Data Structure Classes Available in java.util as of JDK 1.2.0	
Class	Description
ArrayList	A resizable array. It Supposedly replaces the Vector class, but most people still use Vector.
HashMap	A fast-access list of key-value pairs. It supposedly replaces Hashtable, but most people still use Hashtable.
HashSet	A list of unordered but unique elements.
LinkedList	A doubly linked list of unordered elements.
Stack	A last-in, first-out list of elements. Actually, it has been available since Java 1.0.0.
TreeMap	A very efficient way to store elements via a unique sorted key.
TreeSet	A list of unordered but unique elements, indexed by a sorted key. It uses a TreeMap.

These classes are not covered here because you don't usually need them; arrays, vectors, and hashtables can serve all your needs. Their main role is for efficiency. If you do find yourself coding a very large array, vector, or hashtable, and you are concerned about the performance of finding or inserting items into it, it will be time to go to the JDK documentation and research which of the classes in Table 6.2 increases that performance.

Having completed this fast introduction, let's take a closer look.

Declaring arrays

In Java, the syntax for declaring an array variable is essentially the same as declaring any variable, but with the added notation of square brackets to identify it as an array versus a simple scalar variable. Here is a simple example:

```
int numberOfSalesByItem[];
```

This shows you how to declare an array named `numberOfSalesByItem`, whose elements will all be of type `int`. Perhaps this is an array of sales volumes indexed by item number. The fact that it is an array is indicated by the square brackets, `[]`. Thus, the presence of brackets in Java is the same as the presence of the DIM keyword in RPG IV: it denotes an array. Note that these square brackets can come after the name, or after the type:

```
int [ ] numberOfSalesByItem;
```

Both are legal, and there is no clear consensus on which is better. We generally prefer to place the brackets after the name, but even we aren't always consistent in our code. Notice also the addition of white space (blanks) before and inside the brackets. This is just to highlight once again that Java ignores white space.

How many dimensions are in this array? One. You know this because there is only one pair of brackets, regardless of where they exist. What is the size of this array (how many elements)? You don't know yet!

Here is the tricky part compared to defining arrays in RPG: we have not created an array at all here—we have only created an object reference variable that will eventually refer to an array object. Yes, arrays in Java are in fact objects. So, even though the type is primitive (int), this is an object reference variable because the added brackets made it an "array" type. Really, all array variables have a type that is a class you never see, a special Array class that Java supplies. The type you specify is not for the variable itself, but rather for all the elements in the array.

You will soon learn how to actually create the array object. For now, here is another example:

```
int numberOfSalesByItemByPerson[][];
```

This defines numberOfSalesByItemByPerson as a two-dimensional array variable that again will contain elements of type int. Perhaps it will contain sales volumes indexed by item number and salesperson ID. You know it is two-dimensional because there are two pairs of square brackets; each pair indicates a dimension. That is the rule in Java.

Here is an interesting example for you:

```
char[] accountCodes[];
```

This defines accountCodes as a two-dimensional array whose elements are all of type char (character). Perhaps this will contain account codes indexed by country and type of expense (note that indexing is always via integer indexes). As you see, you can mix the bracket pairs between the type and the name, and the rule remains the same: the total number of bracket pairs equals number of dimensions. We do not recommend this style, however!

Finally, just as you can declare multiple scalar variables at once, you can declare multiple arrays at once:

```
boolean arrayOne[], arrayTwo[][], arrayThree[][][];
```

This declares three arrays of type boolean. The first (arrayOne) is one-dimensional, the second (arrayTwo) is two-dimensional, and the third (arrayThree) is three-dimensional. Alternatively, if you put brackets on the type, all names become arrays. This declares three one-dimensional arrays of type boolean:

```
boolean[] arrayOne, arrayTwo, arrayThree;
```

Creating or instantiating arrays

In Java, there is a big difference between declaration and creation. We cannot overstate that in Java, arrays are objects. Not only must you *declare* them, you must also *create* them using the familiar new operator. Until you do so, the array variable contains the special value null. Any attempt to reference declared array variables that are not yet created will result in a compile time error. The following lines expand the previous examples to create arrays:

```
int numberOfSalesByItem[] = new int[1000];
int numberOfSalesByItemByPerson[] = new int[1000][100];
char accountCodes[][] = new char[20][20];
```

The main difference here is the use of the new operator to create the arrays at declaration time. Notice the syntax of the new operator for arrays:

- It requires the element type to be specified again, even for primitive types.

- It uses square brackets instead of parentheses.

- It requires an integer number between the brackets, which is the number of elements this array will hold (the size, or length).

In the example, numberOfSalesByItem contains 1,000 elements; numberOfSalesByItemByPerson contains 1,000 rows by 100 columns, giving it 100,000 elements; and accountCodes contains 20 elements in both dimensions, giving it 400 elements.

You do have a choice here. You can use the new operator at declaration time, just shown, or you can declare the array in one statement and create the array with the new operator in another statement, as shown here:

```
boolean arrayOne[], arrayTwo[][], arrayThree[][][];
arrayOne = new boolean[100];
arrayTwo = new boolean[100][200];
arrayThree = new boolean[100][200][300];
```

It's your choice. Either way, after the new operation has been done, you have actual array objects whose elements can be assigned, referenced, and compared. You will learn how to do this shortly.

The examples specified an integer literal for the length (or size, which is the same thing) of the array. In RPG III, you must specify a literal number in positions 36 through 39 of the Extension specification. In RPG IV, you must use a literal number, constant, or built-in function for the DIM keyword. The key is that the number, which represents the size of the array (its number of elements), must be known at compile time. This is different than Java, where the size of the array is determined at runtime. You can use any variable or expression you wish for the size of the array. Once the array is created, its size is fixed, but at least you can defer creation until you have done some calculations to determine how big to create it. Since you can declare it first and instantiate it later, even arrays declared at the class level as instance variables can defer their creation until later, possibly deep inside a method, after determining how big the array should be.

This is very, very good. It means, in many cases, you can first determine exactly how many elements the array should hold, and then use that number to create the array with the new operator, with exactly the correct number of elements. So, there's no wasted space. It is for this capability the Java engineers decided to implement arrays as objects.

Compile-time initialization of arrays

Both RPG and Java support compile-time arrays. In these arrays, the elements are initialized at the same time as the array is declared. The syntax of initializing array elements as part of the declaration clearly differs between the two languages. In RPG IV, with compile-time arrays, you define the array with its dimension on the D-spec and initialize it using the **CTDATA keyword following the RPG source code, as shown in Listing 6.1.

Listing 6.1: A Compile-Time Array in RPG IV

```
D days           S              3A  DIM(7) PERRCD(7) CTDATA
D idx            S              9 0

C   1            DO         7              idx
C   days(idx)    DSPLY
C                ENDDO

C                EVAL       *INLR = *ON
**CTDATA  days
MONTUEWEDTHUFRISATSUN
```

Note that the name of the array is specified after the **CTDATA keyword. Compare this to RPG III, where compile-time arrays are identified by the per-record number in columns 33 to 35 of the E-spec, and the data is identified with ** instead of **CTDATA. The main D-spec keywords used with compile-time arrays are listed in Table 6.3.

Table 6.3: RPG IV Compile-Time Array Keywords on the D-Spec

D-Spec Keyword	Explanation
DIM	The number of elements the array is to contain
CTDATA	Compile-time data records
PERRCD	Number of elements per record

All RPG IV arrays use the DIM keyword. It tells the compiler the number of elements in the array. As mentioned earlier, RPG supports only one dimension, so only one parameter is supplied. (However, it is designed to allow multiple parameters in the future, in the event RPG IV steps up to supporting multi-dimensional arrays). The example in Listing 6.1 shows an array of seven elements named days. The CTDATA keyword indicates to the compiler that the array is a compile-time array, and therefore, the compiler should be looking for the **CTDATA days record at the bottom of the RPG source code. Finally, the PERRCD keyword tells the compiler that each line (record) of data consists of seven elements. In this case, the one data record supplies the data for all seven elements in the array. Since each element is three characters long and the one data record is 21 (7*3) characters long, you get the following:

```
days(1) = 'MON'
days(2) = 'TUE'
days(3) = 'WED'
days(4) = 'THU'
days(5) = 'FRI'
days(6) = 'SAT'
days(7) = 'SUN'
```

Compare this to what Java offers in terms of compile-time arrays. Here is the same example in Java:

```
String days[] = {"MON", "TUE", "WED", "THU", "FRI", "SAT", "SUN"};
```

Notice that in Java, character variables are only of one length, while the supplied String class is used for strings of multiple characters. (String objects are covered in detail in Chapter 7.) This example uses an array of String objects. The syntax shown here is the special syntax Java supports for defining, creating, and initializing arrays in one step. This is the only way you can initialize compile-time arrays in Java. In this case, the initial values are supplied between curly braces, with each element's initial value separated by commas. The literal values supplied must be consistent with the declared element type of the array. String literals are always surrounded by quotes. Also, don't forget the ending semicolon, as always.

When you specify initial values within an array declaration in this way, Java performs the new operation and defines the array size for you. The array size is implicitly determined by the number of comma-separated elements in the initialization part. These types of compile-time arrays are often used to hold constant data, and so are defined as final. Also, since they are unchanging, we can live with one instance per class versus per object, and so make them static as well to save memory (as we do with all constants in Java):

```
final static String days[] =
        {"MON", "TUE", "WED", "THU", "FRI", "SAT", "SUN"};
```

Runtime initialization of arrays

If you have used arrays in any language, then you already know what runtime arrays are. These are perhaps the most common type of array. With runtime arrays, you initialize the values of the elements in a separate step from declaring the array.

Thus, as the name implies, runtime arrays are loaded (or initialized) at runtime during program execution. Your program code initializes them by assigning values to the elements, typically in a loop that stops at the size of the array. Listing 6.2 shows how this is done in RPG IV.

Listing 6.2: A Runtime Array in RPG IV

```
D factorials      S              9P 0 DIM(10)
D total           S              9P 0 INZ(1)
D idx             S              9P 0
D value           S              9P 0

C     1           DO        10            idx
C                 EVAL      total = total * idx
C                 EVAL      factorials(idx) = total
C                 ENDDO
C     1           DO        10            idx
C                 EVAL      value = factorials(idx)
C     value       DSPLY
C                 ENDDO

C                 EVAL      *INLR = *ON
```

This example first declares the array factorials to contain integer values of length 9, with 0 decimal points and size 10. (Note that you can tell this is a runtime array in RPG IV because it does not use the keywords PERRCD, CTDATA, FROMFILE, or TOFILE.) It then declares a working sum total field named total and the array index named idx, and another working field named value that will display each array element's value. Finally, it loops through the array, computing and then storing into each element the factorial of its index number. For example, entry 3 will contain 6 (3 * 2 * 1). The final loop through the array is simply to display each element's value.

As you can see, in RPG, array indexing starts at 1. In RPG IV, array elements are referenced using arrayName(index) notation, versus the RPG III syntax of arrayName,index. Note also that blanks are not important in RPG IV EVAL statements, so this is valid:

```
EVAL        factorials ( idx ) = total
```

The Java equivalent of this example is shown in Listing 6.3. This code accomplishes the same result as the RPG code. Notice the difference in the indexing of the array. In RPG IV, you use parentheses, while Java uses square brackets. Using array elements in your source code is no different than using any other regular field, except that with arrays, you have to index them. An important difference that you might have noticed between the RPG and Java examples is that you initialize the index field to 1 in RPG and to 0 in Java. In Java, the index of the first element of an array is 0, and the last location is the size of the array -1. Officially, RPG arrays are *one-based* and Java arrays are *zero-based*. Therefore, to loop through all the elements of the array, the RPG program uses the loop index value 1 to 10, whereas Java uses 0 to 9.

Listing 6.3: A Runtime Array in Java

```java
int idx;
int total = 1;
int factorials[] = new int[10];

for (idx=0; idx < 10; idx++)
{
    if (idx > 0)
       total = idx * total;
    factorials[idx] = total;
    System.out.println(factorials[idx]);
}
```

Again, in both RPG and Java, the size of the array is fixed. While it is fixed at compile time for RPG, it is fixed at runtime for Java. Once set, however, it is set for good. If for any reason the index value being used is less than one or greater than the size of the array, RPG generates a runtime error, index out of bound. Similarly, if it is less than zero or greater than or equal to the size of the array, Java generates an IndexOutOfBoundsException error and terminates the program.

Since arrays in Java are objects, Java supplies arrays with a length public instance variable in order to retrieve the size of the array (that is, the number of elements). Knowing this, the previous example could have (and should have) been coded as this:

```java
for (idx=0; idx < factorials.length; idx++)
```

Notice that you specify the name of the array first and follow it with a dot, and then specify the instance variable `length` to retrieve the length of the array. Personally, we wish the variable was named `size`, not `length`. Indeed, it shouldn't be a variable at all but a method named `getSize`. Oh, well.

RPG IV has something similar to the length variable in Java arrays. It is the `%ELEM` built-in function, which returns the declared size of a given array. You can use it instead of hard-coding array sizes. So, for example, you could change the hard-coded limit of 10 on the `DO` loop in Listing 6.2 to this:

```
D arraySize       S              9P 0 INZ(%ELEM(factorials))
C*     1        DO        10            idx
C      1        DO        arraySize     idx
```

Initializing multi-dimensional arrays

Now that you have seen the different types of arrays and the different ways to declare and initialize them, let's look at a few examples of array manipulations. Each value of an array is called an *array element*. To access an array element, you specify the name of the array followed by a comma and the index number for RPG III, with the index number between parentheses for RPG IV, and with square brackets for Java. Since Java also supports multi-dimensional arrays, you specify as many sets of square brackets as there are dimensions in the array. For example, if array `numberOfSalesByIndexByPerson` is two-dimensional, then to access the first element in it, you specify `numberOfSalesByIndexByPerson[0][0]`.

It is important to think of multi-dimensional arrays as arrays of arrays. For two dimensions, each element of the first dimension is like another array. When using compile-time initialization, each element's initial value for the first dimension will be a valid initialization value for another array. You will then have nested sets of curly bracket values. Furthermore, when using the `length` variable, you use it per dimension. Listing 6.4 is an example of initializing a two-dimension array in Java using compile-time initialization syntax, and then looping through the array to print out the values.

Listing 6.4: A Two-Dimensional Compile-Time Array in Java

```
class TestMultiArray
{
    public static void main(String args[])
    {
        int ctArray[][] = {{ 1 , 2 , 3 },
```

```
                          { 4 , 5 , 6 },
                          { 7 , 8 , 9 }};
        for (int xIdx=0; xIdx < ctArray.length; xIdx++)
        {
            for (int yIdx=0; yIdx < ctArray[xIdx].length; yIdx++)
            {
                System.out.print(ctArray[xIdx][yIdx] + " ");
            } // end inner for-loop
            System.out.println();
        } // end outer for-loop
    } // end main method
} // end TestMultiArray class
```

This example illustrates a 3x3 array, using a compile-time array and assigning it the values one to nine. Note that curly braces surround each row of the array's initial values. Because there are two dimensions, two levels of braces are needed, and each set is comma-separated, just as each element inside is comma-separated. The body of the code has two different loops to go through the three rows and three columns in the matrix. Notice that ctArray.length is used for the length of the first array dimension, as usual, but the second dimension uses ctArray[xIdx].length. This is because you want to determine the length of the "sub array" that is the column for the xIdx row. Again, a two-dimensional array is really an array of arrays.

The example simply loops nine times, printing all of the elements of the array. The statement following the inner loop is a print of a new line in order to force the output to a separate line. The following output is produced by running the example:

```
>java TestMultiArray
1 2 3
4 5 6
7 8 9
```

Listing 6.5 is the same example as a runtime array, which gives the same result as output.

Listing 6.5: A Two-Dimensional Runtime Array in Java

```
class TestMultiArrayRT
{
    public static void main(String args[])
    {
        int rtArray[][] = new int[3][3];
        int value = 1;
        for (int xIdx=0; xIdx < rtArray.length; xIdx++)
        {
            for (int yIdx=0; yIdx < rtArray[xIdx].length; yIdx++)
```

Listing 6.5: A Two-Dimensional Runtime Array in Java (continued)

```java
        {
            rtArray[xIdx][yIdx] = value++; // assign and increment
            System.out.print(rtArray[xIdx][yIdx] + " ");
        } // end inner for-loop
        System.out.println();
        } // end outer for-loop
    } // end main method
} // end TestMultiArrayRT class
```

Are you getting the hang of it? This example creates the same loop, but uses it to initial-ize as well as print out the value of each element. Note the use of value++. As you might recall, it assigns the current contents of variable value to the left-hand side, then incre-ments that variable by one.

Think you could handle expanding this example to three dimensions? Or using com-pile-time arrays? Any guess as to what the initialization statement might look like? List-ing 6.6 gives a look.

Listing 6.6: A Three-Dimensional Compile-Time Array in Java

```java
class TestThreeArray
{
    public static void main(String args[])
    {
        int ctArray[][][]
            = { { { 1 , 2 , 3 }, { 4 , 5 , 6 }, { 7 , 8 , 9 } },
                { { 10, 11, 12}, { 13, 14, 15}, { 16, 17, 18} },
                { { 19, 20, 21}, { 22, 23, 24}, { 25, 26, 27} } };
        for (int xIdx=0; xIdx < ctArray.length; xIdx++)
        {
            for (int yIdx=0; yIdx < ctArray[xIdx].length; yIdx++)
            {
                for (int zIdx=0; zIdx < ctArray[yIdx].length; zIdx++)
                {
                    System.out.print(ctArray[xIdx][yIdx][zIdx] + " ");
                } // end inner for-loop
                System.out.print("  ");
            } // end middle for-loop
            System.out.println();
        } // end outer for-loop
    } // end main method
} // end TestThreeArray class
```

The output of this is the following (keeping in mind that it's difficult to show three dimensions):

```
1 2 3    4 5 6    7 8 9
10 11 12    13 14 15    16 17 18
19 20 21    22 23 24    25 26 27
```

Arrays are objects

As mentioned earlier, Java uses references (or, if you like, pointers) to point to objects. Array references are no different than any other Java object. For example, you can point to one array object with an array reference, and later point to another array object using the same reference. Listing 6.7 illustrates this.

Listing 6.7: Proving that Java Array Variables Are Object Reference Variables

```java
class TestArrayObjects
{
    public static void main(String args[])
    {
        int arrayOne[][] = { { 1 , 2 }, { 3 , 4 } };
        int arrayTwo[][] = { { 5 , 6 }, { 7 , 8 } };
        int tempArray[][];
        tempArray = arrayOne;
        for (int xIdx = 0; xIdx < tempArray.length; xIdx++)
        {
            for (int yIdx = 0; yIdx < tempArray[xIdx].length; yIdx++)
                System.out.print(tempArray[xIdx][yIdx] + " ");
            System.out.println();
        }
        tempArray = arrayTwo;
        for (int xIdx = 0; xIdx < tempArray.length; xIdx++)
        {
            for (int yIdx = 0; yIdx < tempArray[xIdx].length; yIdx++)
                System.out.print(tempArray[xIdx][yIdx] + " ");
            System.out.println();
        }
    } // end main method
} // end TestArrayObjects class
```

This example declares and initializes two arrays, arrayOne and arrayTwo. It then declares, but does not create, a third array, tempArray, of the same dimensions as the first two. The body of the code first assigns tempArray to arrayOne and loops through to print the contents, and then reassigns `tempArray` to `arrayTwo` and loops through again, printing the contents. This results in the following output:

```
1 2
3 4
5 6
7 8
```

You might be inclined to think that each assignment of `tempArray` to another array results in a copy of the contents from one array to another. This is not the case, specifically because arrays are in fact objects in Java, and array variables are, therefore, reference variables. Thus, assigning a reference variable is the same as changing the object it points to in memory. So, the `tempArray` assignments simply change the array to which the `tempArray` variable points, with no copying of array contents. This means changes made to the array elements of `tempArray` will also affect the original array to which it points. That's because after an array assignment, a statement like `tempArray = arrayTwo` results in one array in memory, but with two variables referencing the array.

If you did want to copy the contents of an array, you would first have to instantiate a new instance of an array for the target using the `new` operator, then loop through both arrays, copying the contents. While this is easy enough to code, there is actually an easier way to create a duplicate copy of an array. In fact, there are two easier ways. The first is to use the `clone` method that arrays have, which returns a copy of the array, like this:

```
int arraySrc[] = {1,2,3,4};
int arrayTgt[] = (int[])arraySrc.clone();
```

Note how this casts the result to an integer array using (`int[]`). Yes, you can cast objects, and arrays are objects. Casting objects is discussed in more detail in Chapter 9, but for now, just remember you must use this syntax to cast the result of `clone` to an array of the target array type.

The second option is to use the Java-supplied static method `arraycopy` in the `System` class to handle this for you. It takes as input a source array, an index position from which to start copying, a target array, an index position in the target array where the copying starts to go, and a length indicating how many elements to copy. Here is an example for a single-dimensional array:

```
int arraySrc[] = {1,2,3,4};
int arrayTgt[] = new int[4];
System.arraycopy(arraySrc, 0, arrayTgt, 0, 4);
```

These both work well for single-dimensional arrays, but for multi-dimensional arrays, you must be careful to call them per dimension, in the right order. For those, we recommend you simply use your own code loop instead, for peace of mind.

Pre-runtime arrays in RPG

RPG supports pre-runtime arrays, whereas Java does not. Nevertheless, since we are comparing arrays between RPG and Java, we'll touch on this to make our comparison complete. If you know at compile time what data you want stored in your array, then the answer is clear as to which RPG array type to use—compile-time arrays are the best choice (for both languages, actually). If your data is not known at compile time, the answer will be to use either pre-runtime or runtime arrays. What's the difference?

If the initialization data being read resides in a file on disk, use pre-runtime arrays, since the main feature of this kind of an array is to read the data from a file at the start of runtime (i.e., at load time) and write it back to the file at termination time. However, if the source of the data is coming from the keyboard or any other input medium, then your best bet is a runtime array. Listing 6.8 is an example of a pre-runtime array in RPG IV.

Listing 6.8: A Pre-Runtime Array In RPG

```
FSTATE      UF  F   70        DISK
D STATEARR        S           2A    DIM(20)
D                                   PERRCD(1)
D                                   FROMFILE(STATE)
D                                   TOFILE(STATE)
```

This example illustrates how you can load the two-character prefix of a state into a pre-runtime array. The main keywords used with pre-runtime array are listed in Table 6.4.

Table 6.4: RPG IV Pre-Runtime Array Keywords	
D-Spec Keyword	**Explanation**
DIM	Specify the number of dimensions.
FROMFILE(filename)	Read from this file at program load time.
PERRCD	Indicate the number of elements per record in the file.
TOFILE(filename)	Write to this file at termination of the program.

The list shows that, as with compile-time arrays, you use the DIM keyword to define the dimension and number of elements in the array, and the PERRCD keyword to tell the compiler the number of elements per record in the file. The two other keywords, FROMFILE and TOFILE, specify the file name from which you want to load the data to the array you are defining, and optionally the file to which you want to write the data at termination. As you see in the example, other than specifying these extra keywords, the actual definition of the array is the same as a compile-time array. You first define the file STATE, which holds the data with which the array will be initialized. Following that, on the D-spec, you define the array STATEARR as a 20-element array of two characters each, using the DIM keyword.

While Java does not have built-in support for RPG-style pre-runtime arrays, it is possible to code your own. You do this by defining a class that will simulate the main keywords that RPG supports for pre-runtime arrays, namely, FROMFILE, TOFILE, and DIM. Assume a PERRCD of one, for simplicity. Listing 6.9 shows one possible implementation.

Listing 6.9: Simulating a Pre-Runtime Array in Java

```java
import java.io.*;
public class PreRuntimeArray
{
    private String array[];
    private String fromFile, toFile;
    private int    size;
    public PreRuntimeArray(String fromFile, String toFile, int size)
    {
        this.fromFile = fromFile;
        this.toFile   = toFile;
        this.size     = size;
        try // open and read input file
        {
            BufferedReader instream = new BufferedReader(
```

Listing 6.9: Simulating a Pre-Runtime Array in Java (continued)

```
              new InputStreamReader(new FileInputStream(fromFile) ));
          array = new String[size]; // instantiate array
          for (int idx=0; idx < size; idx++)
             array[idx] = instream.readLine();
          instream.close();
      } // end try
      catch (IOException exc) {
          System.out.println("Error Reading File " + fromFile
                             + ": " + exc.getMessage()); }
  } // end of constructor
  public String[] getArray()
  {
      return array;
  }
  public void writeToFile()
  {
      if (toFile != null)
        {
          try // open and write output file
          {
            PrintWriter outstream = new PrintWriter(
                             new FileOutputStream(toFile) );
            for (int idx=0; idx < size; idx++)
               outstream.println(array[idx]);
            outstream.flush();
            outstream.close();
          } // end try
          catch (IOException exc) {
            System.out.println("Error Writing File " + toFile
                                 + ": " + exc.getMessage()); }
        } // end if toFile != null
  } // end writeToFile
  public void finalize()
  {
      writeToFile();
  }
} // end of class PreRuntimeArray
```

Listing 6.9 supplies a class that takes in as its constructor the name of the from-file (FROMFILE), the name of the to-file (TOFILE), and the size of array to create (DIM). The size of the array also indicates how many records to read from the from-file. Note the file names are for flat files or stream files, such as you find on Windows or in the Integrated File System, versus a relational database such as DB2/400. (We leave support for DB2/400 to you to add after reading Chapter 13.) This example also does not implement the PERRCD capability of RPG IV, in the interest of brevity. Instead, it assumes only one array entry per file record. You can add support for multiple entries per record yourself after reading Chapter 7 and learning how to substring `String` objects.

The example class will instantiate the array, open the from-file, and read the records from it into the array, all in the constructor. (Reading and writing local flat files are discussed in Chapter 14; for now, just take our word for it that what is coded here will work.) Users of the class can subsequently retrieve a reference to the array by calling `getArray`. Note this returns a `String` array or `null` if the open of the from-file failed in the constructor.

Finally, the code supplies a `writeToFile` method that, when called, will write out the contents of the array to the to-file named in the constructor. (We saved the name in an instance variable so it could be accessed later by any of our methods.) Again, the details of writing to a flat file are discussed in Chapter 14, so we won't dissect this here. Note, however, that if the user of the class passed `null` for the `toFile` parameter to the constructor, then nothing would be written out.

The example also supplies a `finalize` method. As you will learn in Chapter 9, this special method will be called by the Java runtime whenever an object of this class is reclaimed by the garbage collector. You supply it and code it to call `writeToFile` method. This way, if your users forget to call `writeToFile`, it will still be called automatically for them. Note that you should also put in logic to ensure you don't write out the file twice, for performance reasons.

How would you use this class? Listing 6.10 provides an illustration.

Listing 6.10 Using the Pre-Runtime Array Simulation in Java

```
public static void main(String args[])
{
    PreRuntimeArray daysPRA =
        new PreRuntimeArray("days.txt","daysNew.txt",7);
    String days[] = daysPRA.getArray();
    if (days != null)
      {
        for (int idx=0; idx<days.length; idx++)
            System.out.println(days[idx]);
      }
    daysPRA.writeToFile();
} // end main
```

The `main` method in Listing 6.10 was actually coded in the same class, as a test case for the class. Thus, you can simply call the class from the command line to see the results. We create an instance of the new class and pass it a from-file named `days.txt`, a to-file named `daysNew.txt`, and an array size of seven. Since we did not fully qualify the file names, Java will look in the current directory for them. We have created our input from-file to contain this:

```
MON
TUE
WED
THU
FRI
SAT
SUN
```

If this file is found successfully in the constructor code, then, after instantiation, the object will contain a populated `String` array with the contents of the file. To test that it worked, we call `getArray` to get the array object, and then loop through the array, printing each element to the console. Finally, we call `writeToFile` to write out the array contents to the to-file (`daysNew.txt`). If we run this class from the same directory containing the `days.txt` input file, we get the expected output:

```
MON
TUE
WED
THU
FRI
SAT
SUN
```

Indeed, we also find a new file in our directory, `daysNew.txt`, which contains this data. This file was created and populated by the call to `writeToFile`.

This example reads `String` values from the file. If you wanted to support integer values, say, you would convert the read-in `String` values to integers using the `Integer` class discussed in Chapter 5. Specifically, you would use the static method `parseInt` to convert the `String` object to an `int` value. To write the `int` values back out as `String` literals, you would use the static method `toString`, which takes the integer value as input and returns a `String` object. To read numeric data with decimals, use the `BigDecimal` class in `java.math`, passing the read-in `String` to the constructor. To write out a `BigDecimal` object in text format, use its `toString` method.

This example is coded in such a way that the user has to pass in the size of the array to the constructor. A nice enhancement would be to not ask for the size, but rather have the constructor programmatically determine it by scanning through the file first, counting and then creating an array of the appropriate size, and reading the records into it.

Unbalanced arrays

So far, the multi-dimensional arrays have been rectangular, meaning they have the same number of elements in each dimension. Java's multi-dimensional arrays are actually arrays of arrays, however, so each dimension does not have to be the same length. In fact, each element in a given dimension, if it is another array, can have differing numbers of elements. This is an *unbalanced array*. The main restriction in unbalanced arrays is for the dimensions to be specified left to right. If you are declaring, say, an array of 10 elements, and each element of the array is actually another array of unknown length, you can do that as follows:

```
int myArray[][] = new int[10][];
```

In this case, you specify the first left dimension as 10, but you leave the second unknown dimension to be declared or created after in the body of the code. This example is perfectly legal in Java. However, you cannot do the opposite and specify the second dimension before the first, like this:

```
int myArray[][] = new int[][10];  // NOT VALID!
```

This is the *left-to-right rule* in Java. It is legal to specify the left dimension and leave the right, but not legal the other way. The fact that multi-dimensional arrays in Java are arrays of arrays explains this restriction. You create the left array first, and as you proceed in the code, you create the rest, left to right. The following example uses unbalanced arrays:

```
boolean ubArray[][] = new boolean[3][];
for (int idx = 0; idx< ubArray.length;idx++)
{
    ubArray[idx] = new boolean[idx+1];
}
```

This example creates an array of size three for the first dimension, and unknown for the second dimension. It loops three times, building up the second dimension of the array. The body of the for loop uses the new operator to create the second dimension. This is, in fact, a new array for each element. The result of this is an array containing the following values:

```
false
false false
false false false
```

As you can see, it starts with the first row having only one element, the second row having two elements, and finally the third row with three elements. This is a result of using idx+1 as the size parameter when creating the new array for each row.

When and why might you use such a thing? Well, imagine you run a store with five departments, and each department has differing numbers of salespeople. To track the employee IDs of each salesperson by department, you could declare a two-dimensional array, with the first dimension's size being the number of departments, and the second dimension's size being unique per department. This will save some space, but it could be argued that the extra effort in maintaining it is not worth it.

Arrays of objects

RPG not only has arrays of single values, it also has *multiple-occurring data structures* (*MODS*), which effectively are arrays of data structures. For example, suppose you have MODS of departments. Each data structure might contain the following:

- The number of the department

- The name of the department

- The employee ID of the department manager

- A count of the number of employees

- An embedded array of the employee IDs

For example, look at Listing 6.11. Notice the new RPG IV unsigned data type, which is a nice match for data that is only positive integer numbers. While we don't show it here, to position to a given entry in a multiple occurring data structure, use the OCCUR op-code. The full file on the disk included with this book (DEPART.IRP) includes procedures to populate the Department MODS with sample data and to display the data in each occurrence to the console.

Listing 6.11: Multiple Occurring Department Data Structures in RPG IV

```
D* Track information about each department
DDepartment         DS                      OCCURS(5)
D Dept_Nbr                       5U 0
D Dept_Name                      10A
D Dept_Mgr_Id                    10U 0
D Dept_Nbr_Emps                  5U 0
D Dept_Emps                      10U 0 DIM(20)
```

How do you do this in Java? Well, you don't have data structures in Java, *per se*. You do have classes, however, and classes really are just data structures that also contain methods, as discussed in Chapter 5. So, you would create a class for an individual department, then in another class, you would declare an array of department objects and instantiate each department element. The constructor for the Department class would probably take as a parameter an open database connection object, use it to read the values for the next department record from the database, and populate the instance variables with the results.

Let's look at an example, but since database access isn't covered until Chapter 13, that part is not shown yet. First, take a look at the Department class in Listing 6.12. Notice that the variables are made private, with "getter" methods supplied to retrieve the values. That is good practice, as it allows you to change the attributes of those variables later and minimize the impact on other code using the class.

Listing 6.12: A Department Class in Java

```
public class Department
{
    private int    deptNbr;
    private String deptName;
    private int    deptMgrId;
    private int    deptNbrEmps;
    private int    deptEmps[];

    public Department() // constructor
    {
        // read next department record from database
        // populate above instance variables from database
        // instantiate deptEmps array once we know how many in dept
    }
    public int getDeptNbr()
```

Listing 6.12: A Department Class in Java (continued)

```java
    {
        return deptNbr;
    }
    public String getDeptName()
    {
        return deptName;
    }
    public int getDeptMgrId()
    {
        return deptMgrId;
    }
    public int getDeptNbrEmployees()
    {
        return deptNbrEmps;
    }
    public int[] getDeptEmployees()
    {
        return deptEmps;
    }
} // end class Department
```

The other class that creates the array of Department objects is shown in Listing 6.13. For arrays of objects, you have to instantiate the array object itself, as usual. You also have to instantiate the objects in each element in the array, as usual for objects whether they are in an array or not. The full example on disk of the Department and Departments classes contain methods to populate the Department objects with dummy data and display the contents of each Department object to the console, for testing purposes. You can run the Departments class from the command line to see the results.

Listing 6.13: An Array of Department Objects in Java

```java
public class Departments
{
    private Department depts[] = new Department[5]; // create array

    public Departments() // constructor
    {
        // open database connection. Not shown
        for (int idx = 0; idx < depts.length; idx++)
        {
            // create Department object for each array element.
            // note passing DB connection is not shown
            depts[idx] = new Department();
        }
    }
} // end class Departments
```

There are a number of other things in this example that we would turn into separate classes as well. For example, we would make a class named `EmployeeID` that would hold the six-digit employee ID per employee. This way, we could easily change that to seven digits later and not affect anyone. We'd also have a class named `Employee` and an array of `Employee` objects in our `Department` class, instead of just employee IDs.

Helper methods for arrays

In RPG, you often search tables or arrays using the `LOOKUP` operation. This is nice functionality that saves you writing your own redundant search algorithm every time. Here is an example of using `LOOKUP` in RPG IV:

```
C        searchString  LOOKUP    days(idx)                         26
C                      IF        %EQUAL = '1'
C        'found it!'   DSPLY
C                      ELSE
C        'not found'   DSPLY
C                      ENDIF
```

This example searches for an element in the array. If found, the `EQ` indicator is turned on, and the `%EQUAL` built-in function returns a one. To find the previous or next element when no match is found, the `LO` or `HI` indicators can be set, and `%FOUND` will be set to 1 if a non-equal match is found. For this though, the array must be sorted. (For the full example, see the file `LOOKUP.IRP` on the included disk.)

It would be nice if Java gave similarly capabilities, would it not? Well, if you are using Java at a JDK level prior to 1.2.0, the unfortunate answer is that Java does not. You have to code your own search algorithm, as shown in Listing 6.14.

Listing 6.14: A Helper Method for Searching Integer Arrays

```java
public static int searchArray(int searchArray[],
                              int searchArgument)
{
    int matchIndex = -1;
    for (int idx=0; idx<searchArray.length && matchIndex < 0; idx++)
        if (searchArray[idx] == searchArgument)
            matchIndex = idx;
    return matchIndex;
}
```

This method is `static` because it doesn't depend on any instance variables, but instead takes what it needs as parameters. This example will only work with an integer array, and as such, an integer search argument. This is because it declares the two parameters to the method to be of type `int`, and so only type `int` parameters can be passed. To support arrays of other types, like the other seven primitive data types, you would create overloaded versions of this method. Recall that overloaded methods are methods with the same name but different numbers or types of parameters. So, you could copy this `searchArray` method and produce versions that accept a `float` array plus `float` search argument, a `double` array plus `double` search argument, and so on. This is something you might want to do if you need to search arrays often.

If you use JDK 1.2.0 or higher, a series of such helper methods is already supplied for you in the class `Arrays` in the package `java.util`. Table 6.5 lists the methods (all static) in this class. (Note that this is not a complete list.) The `binarySearch` method is like RPG's `LOOKUP` op-code. Similarly, `fill` is like RPG's `MOVEA` op-code, and `sort` is like RPG's `SORTA` op-code.

Table 6.5: Array Helper Methods in java.util.Arrays

Method	Description
binarySearch	Provides overloaded methods for searching the given array for the given key. There are methods for seven of the primitive types, but not boolean, and for arrays of objects. The array must already be sorted. It returns the zero-based index position of the match if found; else, it returns (-(insertion point)-1), where insertion point is where the item should be inserted.
equals	Compares two given arrays, returning true if they have the same number of elements and the element values are the same. There are overloaded methods for all eight primitive types plus arrays of objects.
fill	Fills all elements of a given array with a given value. There are overloaded methods for all eight primitive types plus arrays of objects.
sort	Sorts the given array into ascending sequence. There are overloaded methods for all eight primitive types plus arrays of objects.

Note that all the array methods work on objects and primitive types. How is this possible, you might wonder? What possible type will work for all classes instead of just the one that is specified on that overloaded version of the methods? The answer is `Object`, a class in the `java.lang` package. It turns out that if you specify a type of `Object` for a method parameter, you can actually pass in objects of any class. You will see why this is so in Chapter 9, but for now, it is a very useful truth you should remember.

Another thing to think about is, given an array of objects, how can Java sort it? How does it know how to compare any two object elements, in order to sort them? It does not know what it means for one object to be greater than another object. The answer is that it leaves this decision up to the objects themselves! When comparing two objects, Java will try to call a particular method named compareTo in one of the objects, passing in the second object as a parameter. That method has to return a negative number, zero, or a positive number if the second object is less than, equal, or greater than the target object. So, to sort an array of objects of your class type, your class must have that method in it. Most Java-supplied classes, like String, already supply this method. For you to supply it in your classes, you will have to implement an interface named Comparable, but you will have to wait until Chapter 9 to learn about interfaces.

You might have noticed there are no search methods, only binarySearch methods. This is a bit of surprise for us, too, and it means if you have arrays that are not sorted, you will have to write your own search methods as shown in Listing 6.14. However, the good news is that it is easy to sort an array using the sort methods.

You might also have noticed that these methods all work only on single-dimensional arrays. That is true, but multi-dimensional arrays are actually arrays of arrays, so with only a little bit of extra work, you could call these methods on all the dimensions of a multi-dimensional array. For example, the following will fill all entries of a 1010 integer array with -1:

```
import java.util.*; // for Arrays class
    . . .
int myArray[][] = new int[10][10];
for (int rows=0; rows < myArray.length; rows++)
   Arrays.fill(myArray[rows],-1);
```

These methods are all pretty straightforward to use, so we just show in Listing 6.15 an example of using the sort method, followed by the binarySearch method.

Listing 6.15: Testing, Sorting, and Searching Arrays in Java

```
int sortedArray[] = {48,25,12,34,10,52,70,16,35};
Arrays.sort(sortedArray);
for (int idx=0; idx < sortedArray.length; idx++)
   System.out.print(sortedArray[idx] + " ");
```

Listing 6.15: Testing, Sorting, and Searching Arrays in Java (continued)

```
System.out.println();
int newpos = Arrays.binarySearch(sortedArray,15);
if (newpos < 0)
  {
    newpos = -newpos - 1;
    System.out.println(newpos);
  }
```

This simple example declares a compile-time array of unsorted integers, sorts the array, and prints the sorted results to verify it worked. Note that System.out.print (versus System.out.println) prints the given data without advancing the console by a new line. Finally, binarySearch is used on the array and the number 15 to see what we get back. The results of running this code snippet is the following:

```
10 12 16 25 34 35 48 52 70
2
```

Why did we get a two back for the index position of 15? Because while not found, that is the zero-based position of the next highest element. This is similar to using LOOKUP in RPG on an ascending array, and specifying a HI indicator.

In RPG, you can have alternating arrays or tables. These allow you to define two arrays that are complementary, such as an array of employee IDs and an array of employee names. Then, you can do a LOOKUP operation on the primary array, say on an employee ID, and get back the position of the matching entry in the alternate array, say the employee name. There is nothing like this in Java, so in the worst case, you have to do the second search yourself, using the results of the first search. However, in reality, you can combine these arrays into a single array of objects, where the objects are of a class that contains both pieces of information. For example, you might have an Employee class that contains both the employee ID and the employee name. If you supply a compareTo method, you can use the binarySearch method from above on the array of Employee objects and get the resulting Employee object, which contains both the employee ID and the employee name. There is an example of this on the included disk, in Employee.java.

Finally, RPG has a very handy XFOOT op-code for summing the contents of a numeric array. Although Java does not have any such function, we bet you could write one!

Got your *fill* of arrays? *Sort* of? Then let's *search* for something new....

VECTORS

The previous sections discussed single- and multi-dimensional arrays. One important restriction in arrays that applies to both RPG and Java is that their length, once set, can never change. In Java, you can dynamically declare an array, which is more powerful than what is allowed in RPG, as it allows you to defer creation until you know the length. However, once you create an array, you cannot change its length. In other words, an existing array has a fixed length and cannot grow or shrink.

As you tackle more complex applications, you sometimes do not know at any time, whether at compile time or runtime, how many elements you will want to store. To help with this, Java supplies a utility class named `Vector` in its `java.util` package. Java has vectors as an alternative when you need to use single-dimensional arrays that can grow or shrink dynamically. As you will see later in this section, RPG supports this as well, but more coding is required to dynamically allocate and manipulate storage.

> **Note:** Vectors are adjustable arrays that can increase or decrease their size in response to the number of elements they need to store. Vectors use the term "size" instead of "length" to define the number of elements.

Variables of the `Vector` class are (you guessed it) objects in Java, just as arrays are. However, unlike arrays, they have no hard-wired language support such as special syntax for instantiating and indexing. The `Vector` class is just a regular class, just as you could write on your own. Luckily, though, the Java engineers took the time to write it and include it in their utility package. The `Vector` class contains many methods to help you add, remove, and search elements. Listing 6.16 illustrates a simple `Vector` with three elements.

Listing 6.16: A Simple Use of the Vector Class

```
import java.util.*; // import all classes in java.util package

class TestVector
{
    public static void main(String args[])
    {
        Vector myFirstVector = new Vector();

        myFirstVector.addElement(new String("Ford"));
        myFirstVector.addElement(new String("GM"));
        myFirstVector.addElement(new String("Chrysler"));
```

Listing 6.16: A Simple Use of the Vector Class (continued)

```
        for (int idx = 0; idx < myFirstVector.size(); idx++)
            System.out.println(myFirstVector.elementAt(idx));
    }
} // end TestVector class
```

This example first defines and creates the Vector variable myFirstVector. It then adds elements to the variable. Notice the use of the String class as the elements are added. (Not to worry; we have not covered strings yet. They are discussed in the next chapter.) For now, all you need to know is that the new keyword with the String class creates a String object, and the addElement method adds that string to the Vector. For example, the first case sends the string "Ford" as the parameter to the String class constructor to build a *new* string object with that value. The reference of that object is used as the input parameter to the addElement method of the Vector class. This same thing happens three more times, adding three strings to the Vector, after which the for loop prints the content of the Vector. The loop ends when idx reaches myFirstVector.size(), which in this case is 3.

Note: Vectors can only contain objects, not primitive type values. To use primitive values, you must create an instance of their wrapper classes, such as addElement(new Integer(5)).

The example in Listing 6.16 uses two methods that the Vector class supports: the addElement method and the size method. There are many more methods that Vector supports. The most commonly used ones are listed in Table 6.6. For a complete and up-to-date list of these methods, look up the online documentation in the JDK.

Table 6.6: Common Methods in the Vector Class

Method	Description
addElement(Object)	Adds the specified object to the end of this vector and increments the size.
capacity()	Returns the current capacity of this vector. Capacity is the potential size of a vector, versus its actual size or element count.
clone()	Returns a copy of this vector. All elements are copied.
contains(Object)	Tests if the specified object is an element in this vector.

Table 6.6: Common Methods in the Vector Class (continued)	
Method	**Description**
copyInto(Object[])	Copies the elements of this vector into the specified array.
elementAt(int)	Returns the element at the specified index (zero-based).
elements()	Returns an enumeration of the elements of this vector. (Chapter 9 discusses enumerators.)
ensureCapacity(int)	Increases the capacity to the given number.
firstElement()	Returns a reference to the first element.
indexOf(Object)	Searches for the first occurrence of the given parameter, testing for equality using the equals method on each element.
indexOf(Object, int)	Searches for the first occurrence of the first parameter, beginning the search at the zero-based index specified in the second parameter. Again, it tests for equality using equals.
insertElementAt(Object, int)	Inserts an object at the specified index.
isEmpty()	Tests if this vector has no elements.
lastElement()	Returns the last element of the vector.
lastIndexOf(Object)	Returns the index of the last occurrence of the specified object in this vector. This is useful for repeated elements.
lastIndexOf(Object, int)	Searches backwards for the specified object, starting from the specified index, and returns an index to it.
removeAllElements()	Removes all elements from this vector, and sets its size to zero.
removeElement(Object)	Removes the first occurrence of the argument from this vector.
removeElementAt(int)	Deletes the element at the specified index.
setElementAt(Object, int)	Sets the element at the specified index to the specified object.
setSize(int)	Sets the size of this vector.
size()	Returns the number of elements in this vector.
toString(	Returns a string representation of this vector.
trimToSize()	Trims the capacity of this vector to be the vector's current size.

You have seen a straightforward and simple example of a vector. Let's look at a slightly more complex example that uses a few Vector methods. Suppose you are writing the software to register attendees at an event of some kind, maybe a sporting event. You want to track everyone who enters and leaves, and because you can't predict the exact number of attendees, you decide to use a vector to hold the list of names. The program will accept commands from the console and will act appropriately on the commands entered. So, your first requirement is for a static method that will write a prompt string to the console and return what the user typed in. Name this method readFromConsole and put it in a class by itself named Console, so that you can easily reuse it whenever you need to do this common requirement, as shown in Listing 6.17.

Listing 6.17: The Console Class with a Reusable ReadFromConsole Method

```java
import java.io.*;

public class Console
{
    /**
     * Write out a prompt and then read a line from console
     * @param the string to write out first for the prompt
     * @return the string read in from the console
     */
    public static String readFromConsole(String prompt)
    {
        System.out.println(prompt); // write prompt
        String userInput = "";
        BufferedReader inFileStream =
                new BufferedReader(
                    new InputStreamReader(
                        new DataInputStream(System.in)) );
        try
        {
            userInput = inFileStream.readLine();
        }
        catch (IOException exc)
        {
            System.out.println("Error: " + exc.getMessage());
        }
        return userInput;
    } // end readFromConsole method
} // end of class Console
```

You have seen System.out many times for writing to the console; this method shows how to use its opposite, System.in, for reading from the console. Using it involves nesting it inside a number of "stream reading" classes from java.io, and calling the readLine method of one of those classes (BufferedReader). Because this call can throw an exception, you have to monitor for it by placing the call inside a try block and putting the exception-case code inside a catch block. Exceptions aren't discussed in detail until Chapter 10 and the stream-reading classes until Chapter 14, so for now, we simply ask you to accept that this method will work to prompt the user and return what he or she types. Tuck this method away; it is a keeper.

Now, let's return to the task at hand. You want to prompt the user for a single-letter command to tell the application what to do: *R* to register an attendee, *U* to "unregister" an attendee, *D* to display registered attendees, and *E* to exit the program. The code loops until the user types an *E*. If the command is to register or unregister, you will need to subsequently prompt the user to type the attendee's name. You will need a class named AttendeeList to contain the list of attendees, including methods to register a new one given a name, unregister an existing one given a name, and display the current list of registered attendees. You will also need a class named Registration that does the looping and prompting, using an instance of AttendeeList.

The Registration class

Let's discuss the Registration class first, in Listing 6.18. This is pretty straightforward, especially given the readFromConsole method created earlier, so let's move on to the AttendeeList class, which encapsulates our list of attendees. Internally, it will use a Vector for the list, but you can nicely hide that detail from users of the class so you are free to change it later.

Listing 6.18: A Registration Class that Prompts the User for Commands

```
public class Registration
{
    private AttendeeList attendeeList = new AttendeeList();

    public void run()
    {
        String command = "Not set";
        while (!command.equalsIgnoreCase("E"))
        {
            command = Console.readFromConsole(
                "Enter command (R=Register, U=Unregister,
                            D=Display, E=Exit)");
            if (command.equalsIgnoreCase("R"))
```

```
            {
                String name = Console.readFromConsole("Enter name:");
                attendeeList.register(name);
            }
            else if (command.equalsIgnoreCase("U"))
            {
                String name = Console.readFromConsole("Enter name:");
                attendeeList.deRegister(name);
            }
            else if (command.equalsIgnoreCase("D"))
                attendeeList.display();
        } // end while loop
    } // end run

    public static void main(String args[])
    {
        System.out.println("Welcome to class Registration");
        Registration register = new Registration();
        register.run();
    } // end main

} // end of class Registration
```

Before we show you the class, let's assume that you have decided not to simply store String objects in the vector, one per attendee name. Rather, you encapsulate the notion of an Attendee into its own class, which takes the attendee name in the constructor and stores it away in an instance variable that is retrievable with a getName method. The reason for this new class is that, some time in the future, you might want to capture more information about the attendee than just their names. By using a class to represent each attendee, this becomes a simple matter of adding more instance variables to the class.

The AttendeeList Class

We will show this Attendee class shortly, but first, Listing 6.19 is the AttendeeList class that will instantiate an instance of Attendee for each attendee who is registered, and store that instance in a private Vector object.

Listing 6.19: The AttendeeList Class that Tracks Attendees at an Event

```
import java.util.*;

public class AttendeeList
{
    private Vector attendees = new Vector();
```

Listing 6.19: The AttendeeList Class that Tracks Attendees at an Event (continued)

```java
public void register(String name)
{
    Attendee newAttendee = new Attendee(name);
    if (!checkForAttendee(newAttendee))
      attendees.addElement(newAttendee);
    else
      System.out.println("An attendee with this name
                               is already registered");
}
public void deRegister(String name)
{
    Attendee theAttendee = new Attendee(name);
    if (!checkForAttendee(theAttendee))
      System.out.println("Sorry, that name is not registered");
    else
      attendees.removeElement(theAttendee);
}
public boolean checkForAttendee(Attendee attendee)
{
    return attendees.contains(attendee);
}
public void display()
{
    Attendee currAttendee = null;
    for (int idx = 0; idx < attendees.size(); idx++)
    {
        currAttendee = (Attendee)attendees.elementAt(idx);
        currAttendee.display();
    }
}
} // end class AttendeeList
```

This is also pretty straightforward, except for the error-checking. To register an attendee, it first creates an Attendee object, passing the name into the constructor. Then, it checks to see if there is already an attendee with that name registered, in which case it issues an error message. If not, it uses addElement of the Vector class to append the Attendee object to the list. To unregister an attendee, it also first creates an Attendee object using the name as input, and again checks to see if that attendee is already registered. If he or she is, it uses removeElement of the Vector class to remove that element; otherwise, it is an error. To display all registered attendees, the class walks the vector, extracting each element (Attendee object) and calling its display method.

Note that the Vector class only thinks it is storing instances of the generic class Object, so you have to cast the result of an element extraction to the actual class type that element is of, using the casting syntax: (Attendee). Yes, you can cast objects too (discussed in more detail in Chapter 9). For now, take our word this step is required. Otherwise, the call to method display would fail because the Object class does not have a method named display in it.

As you can see, both registration and unregistration require a check for the existence of a given Attendee object in the list, so this code is abstracted out into its own method, checkForAttendee, which the other two methods call. This check is done using the contains method of the Vector class. To determine if a given object is in a vector this way, the Vector code will call the method equals on each element of the list, passing the given object as a parameter. If any one of these calls returns true, then contains returns true. Thus, the classes must code this equals method for this to work, and you will see that the Attendee class does do this. This is also the technique used by the removeElement method call in Vector, to determine which element to remove.

The Attendee class

Finally, it is time to see the Attendee class, in Listing 6.20. This is a reasonably straight-forward class. The only interesting method in it is the equals method. You must supply this method in your class if you want to store objects of your class in a vector. You must define the method to take one parameter of type Object, but you can always assume that object will actually be the same type as your class, and so do whatever you want to decide if the current object and the passed-in object are "equal." Note that all Java-supplied classes already come with an equals method.

Listing 6.20: The Attendee Class that Represents an Attendee at an Event

```java
public class Attendee
{
    private String name;

    public Attendee(String name)
    {
        this.name = name;
    }
    public String getName()
    {
        return name;
    }
    public boolean equals(Object other)
    {
        Attendee otherAttendee = (Attendee)other;
        return name.equals(otherAttendee.getName());
```

Listing 6.20: The Attendee Class that Represents an Attendee at an Event (continued)

```
    }
    public void display()
    {
        System.out.println("-------------");
        System.out.println("Name........: " + name);
        System.out.println();
    }
}
```

So what happens when you run Registration and register a few attendees, display the list, and unregister an attendee? Let's have a look at a partial run:

```
Welcome to class Registration
Enter command (R=Register, U=Unregister, D=Display, E=Exit)
R
Enter name:
Phil Coulthard
Enter command (R=Register, U=Unregister, D=Display, E=Exit)
R
Enter name:
George Farr
Enter command (R=Register, U=Unregister, D=Display, E=Exit)
D
-------------------------
Name........: Phil Coulthard

-------------------------
Name........: George Farr

Enter command (R=Register, U=Unregister, D=Display, E=Exit)
u
Enter name:
George Farr
```

This little application can be modified to add more information for each attendee, such as phone number, to avoid name collisions.

Simulating vectors in RPG

So far, we have been talking only about Java. What about RPG? Does RPG have anything similar to what Java offers in terms of dynamically allocating and de-allocating storage? The answer, perhaps to your surprise, is yes. In RPG IV, you can perform the same functions as in the event-attendee example. To do this, you would need to first create a function to emulate Java's Vector class. That is, you would have to have the ability to maintain a list of items that can grow on demand. To do this, you would have to use the memory management operation codes ALLOC and DEALLOC. In V5R1 of RPG, these are also available as built-in functions. In either case, they allow you to allocate a specific amount of memory, store the result in a pointer data type (*), free up that memory, and resize that memory.

To emulate the Vector class, you would create a service program with procedures to:

- *Create a vector.* This allocates some initial memory and returns the pointer. This pointer would subsequently be passed to each of the following procedures as the first parameter, to indicate which vector is being manipulated. It would point to memory containing a data structure of information about the vector, such as the current element count, and pointers to the first and last element in the list.

- *Add an element to a vector.* This takes a vector pointer as a parameter, and calculates how much memory is required. It would allocate that much memory and return the pointer to it. It would also allocate a new element for the list and add the element to the list. The element would point to the allocated user memory. Upon return, the caller would put the data it wants into the allocated memory. The memory might be for a single field or a data structure with numerous subfields. This is the opposite of Java, where you allocate and populate your objects first, then add them to the vector by calling a method. However, it is preferable to forcing the callers to do their own ALLOC operation.

- *Remove an element from a vector.* Given a pointer to user memory allocated with the procedure above, this would free up that memory and also remove its element from the list. Note that it would be up to the user to get that pointer to the user memory by iterating through the list and doing the compares. This is different from the contains and removeElement methods in the Vector class, which know how to compare the given object with each object in the vector to find a match, by calling the equals method in each object. Without OO, there is no easy way to magically do the compares when you don't know what the caller is storing in allocated memory. If you wanted to get fancy, though, you could ask the caller to supply a procedure pointer to its own procedure for doing element compares. Indeed, this is exactly what Java does! It just happens the Java-supplied classes come with this method already (equals), and your own classes have to supply it in order for contains and removeElement to work.

- *Return an element from a vector.* Given an index position, this would return a pointer to the user data at that position in the list.

- *Find an element in the vector.* Given a pointer to user memory allocated with the allocation procedure, this would return its position in the list.

- *Return the current size of the list.* This just returns the number of elements currently in the given vector.

Let's have a look at what the copy member containing the prototypes to implement all of those functions might look like, in Listing 6.21.

Listing 6.21: The Copy Member VECTORPRS with Prototypes for the RPG IV VECTOR Service Program

```
/* Returns a pointer data type that needs to be passed
/*  to all subsequent Vector procedures for this vector
DVectorAllocate    PR                      *

/* Allocates memory and adds a pointer to it to vector.
/*  Also returns this pointer so caller can populate.
DVectorAddElem     PR                      *
D vectorHeader@                            *     VALUE
D dataSize                               5U 0 VALUE

/* Returns pointer to user data at given position nbr
DVectorElemAt      PR                      *
D vectorHeader@                            *     VALUE
D position                               5U 0 VALUE

/* Returns position of given user data in vector
DVectorIndexOf     PR              5U 0
D vectorHeader@                            *     VALUE
D userData@                                *     VALUE

/* Returns current number of elements in vector
DVectorGetSize     PR              5U 0
D vectorHeader@                            *     VALUE

/* Removes user data pointer from vector and frees mem
DVectorRmvElem     PR
D vectorHeader@                            *     VALUE
D userData@                                *     VALUE
```

Really, writing the code to implement this service program amounts to writing a linked-list program in RPG. The twist, though, is that the memory for the list and all the user data pointed to by the elements in the list is dynamically created with the ALLOC operation. While this is a bit of work, it not only allows you to have a dynamically growable list, it also allows you to have more than one of them in a single program. That is because each list gets its own unique memory, just like Java with its objects. So now, you can code an RPG program that has a vector of employees and a vector of customers, if you want. This is good.

We don't show you all the ugly code for a vector here, just a couple of the procedures and all the global fields, in Listing 6.22. You can find the complete code on the included disk in the VECTOR.IRP source file in the LISTING6-22 directory. Put this file and the VECTORPRS.IRP copy member in a QRPGLESRC source file on the AS/400, compile the VECTOR module with CRTRPGMOD, and create from that a service program with the CRTSRVPGM command, specifying *ALL for the EXPORT parameter.

Listing 6.22: Part of the RPG IV VECTOR Module for Emulating Java Vectors

```
D* Declare the structure for the Vector header information
D g_vectorHdr@    S                  *   INZ(*NULL)
D g_vectorHdr     DS                     BASED(g_vectorHdr@)
D  g_vhElemCount                  5U 0
D  g_vhFirstElem@...
D                                  *
D  g_vhLastElem@                   *
D g_HdrSize       S               10U 0 INZ(%SIZE(
D                                         g_vectorHdr))

D* Declare the structure for each vector element
D g_vectorElem@   S                  *   INZ(*NULL)
D g_vectorElemDS  DS                     BASED(g_vectorElem@)
D  g_elemData@                     *
D  g_elemDataSize...
D                                 10U 0
D  g_elemNext@                     *
D  g_elemHeader@                   *
D g_elemSize      S               10U 0 INZ(%SIZE(
D                                         g_vectorElemDS))

PVectorAllocate   B                     EXPORT
DVectorAllocate   PI                  *
C                 ALLOC    g_HdrSize      g_vectorHdr@
C                 EVAL     g_vhElemCount=0
C                 EVAL     g_vhFirstElem@ = *NULL
```

Listing 6.22: Part of the RPG IV VECTOR Module for Emulating Java Vectors (continued)

```
C                       EVAL      g_vhLastElem@ = *NULL
C                       RETURN    g_vectorHdr@
PVectorAllocate   E

PVectorAddElem    B                         EXPORT
DVectorAddElem    PI                   *
D vectorHeader@                        *     VALUE
D dataSize                           5U 0 VALUE
C* Local fields
D newUserData@    S                   *
D newElement@     S                   *
C* Local logic
C                       EVAL      g_vectorHdr@  = vectorHeader@
C                       ALLOC     dataSize         newUserData@
C                       ALLOC     g_elemSize       g_vectorElem@
C                       EVAL      newElement@ = g_vectorElem@
C                       EVAL      g_elemHeader@ = vectorHeader@
C                       EVAL      g_elemData@ = newUserData@
C                       EVAL      g_elemDataSize = dataSize
C                       EVAL      g_elemNext@ = *NULL
C                       EVAL      g_vhElemCount =
C                                     g_vhElemCount + 1
C                       IF        g_vhLastElem@  *NULL
C                       EVAL      g_vectorElem@ = g_vhLastElem@
C                       EVAL      g_elemNext@ = newElement@
C                       ENDIF
C                       EVAL      g_vhLastElem@ = newElement@
C                       IF        g_vhFirstElem@ = *NULL
C                       EVAL      g_vhFirstElem@ = newElement@
C                       ENDIF
C                       return    newUserData@
PVectorAddElem    E
```

With these procedures in a service program, you could then code a registration program similar to the one in Java. Listing 6.23 shows you the mainline code for this program.

Listing 6.23: The Mainline RPG IV Program REGISTER that Uses the VECTOR Service Program

```
D attendees       S                   *     INZ(*NULL)
D name@           S                   *     INZ(*NULL)
D attendeeName    S                   30A   BASED(name@)

D  command        S                   30A   INZ(*BLANKS)
D  prompt         S                   22A   INZ(
```

Listing 6.23: The Mainline RPG IV Program REGISTER that Uses the VECTOR Service Program

```
D                                        'Command: R,U,D,E')
D   name           S            30A   INZ(*BLANKS)
C                  EVAL         Attendees = VectorAllocate

C                  DOW          (command  'E') AND
C                               (command  'e')
C                  EVAL         command=ReadFromConsole(prompt)

C                  SELECT
C                  WHEN         (command = 'R') OR
C                               (command = 'r')
C                  EVAL         name =
C                                  ReadFromConsole('Enter name:')
C                  CALLP        RegisterAttendee(name)
C                  WHEN         (command = 'U') OR
C                               (command = 'u')
C                  EVAL         name =
C                                  ReadFromConsole('Enter name:')
C                  CALLP        DeRegisterAttendee(name)
C                  WHEN         (command = 'D') OR (command = 'd')
C                  CALLP        DisplayAttendees
C                  ENDSL
C                  ENDDO

C                  EVAL         *INLR = *ON
```

This uses procedures that mimic the Java version. Listing 6.24 shows those procedures. You allocate a vector and store its pointer in the attendees field. You then pass it as the first parameter to each call to the vector procedures. To register an attendee, you call the VectorAddElem procedure and give the size of the memory to allocate for this entry, which is the length of the simple field to store: name. To unregister an attendee, you have to loop through the elements of the vector using the VectorElemAt procedure until an element is found whose content (a simple name) matches the name given. If found, you use that element's address as the input to the VectorRmvElem procedure. To display attendees, you simply walk through all elements of the vector and display the contents of each element.

Listing 6.24: The Rest of the RPG IV Program REGISTER that Uses the VECTOR Service Program

```
PReadFromConsole   B
DReadFromConsole   PI           30A
D prompt                        22A    VALUE
D retField         S            30A
C      prompt      DSPLY                   retField
C                  RETURN       retField
P                  E
```

Listing 6.24: The Rest of the RPG IV Program
REGISTER that Uses the VECTOR Service Program (continued)

```
P RegisterAttendee...
P                 B
D RegisterAttendee...
D                 PI
D name                        30A   VALUE
C               EVAL      name@ = VectorAddElem(attendees:
C                                   %len(name))
C               EVAL      attendeeName = Name
C               RETURN
P               E

P DeRegisterAttendee...
P                 B
D DeRegisterAttendee...
D                 PI
D name                        30A   VALUE
D  currPos        S            5U 0 INZ(1)
C               EVAL      name@ =
C                           vectorElemAt(attendees:currPos)
C               DOW       (name@  *NULL) AND
C                         (attendeeName   name)
C               EVAL      currPos = currPos + 1
C               EVAL      name@ =
C                           vectorElemAt(attendees:currPos)
C               ENDDO
C               IF        name@  *NULL
C               CALLP     vectorRmvElem(attendees:name@)
C               ENDIF
C               RETURN
P               E

P DisplayAttendees...
P                 B
D DisplayAttendees...
D                 PI
D  currPos        S            5U 0 INZ(1)
D  dummy          S            9 0
C               EVAL      name@ =
C                           vectorElemAt(attendees:currPos)
C               DOW       name@  *NULL
C  attendeeName  DSPLY               dummy
C               EVAL      currPos = currPos + 1
C               EVAL      name@ =
C                           vectorElemAt(attendees:currPos)
C               ENDDO
C               RETURN
P               E
```

The full source for this example is in `Register.irp`, which you can upload to a QRPGLESRC file on the AS/400. Compile it into a module first, and then into a program object using CRTPGM and specifying VECTOR in the BNDSRVPGM parameter. To run it, just issue CALL REGISTER from the command line and follow the prompts, as in the Java version. You'll see it behaves identically to its Java equivalent.

This is one use, but indeed, you could use this vector service program in all kinds applications. To write your own programs that use VECTOR, just include the VECTORPRS copy member and link to the VECTOR service program as you have seen with REGISTER. Notice we are only storing a simple character field in each element. More interesting would be to store a data structure. Just remember that whatever you store has to be defined with the BASED keyword so you can set its memory address via a pointer field.

HASHTABLES

You have seen how to create single- and multi-dimensional arrays and even arrays of objects. You also saw how another class, `Vector`, is better suited than arrays when you want to dynamically grow and shrink the list on demand. It turns out that there are other times in a programmer's life when perhaps an array is not the best choice to store a list of items. For example, what about "lookup tables" like you have in RPG in the form of tables and the LOOKUP operation? Java has a special class for situations when data needs to be efficiently found using a key value. The class `Hashtable` in the `java.util` package is for this.

Hashtables are used to map keys to values. Any object can be used as a key or as a value. Like the `Vector` class, the `Hashtable` class does not permit primitive types, so to store integers, for example, you must use the `Integer` wrapper class, as in `new Integer(5)` to store the number five, and then `integerObject.intValue()` to return the primitive value out of the object later. The reason to use a hashtable over an array or a vector is strictly performance. Hashtables can offer good performance benefits when searching for a key in a large number of values.

With a `Hashtable`, you add elements using the `put` method and pass in two parameters, the key and the value for that key, like this:

```
Hashtable attendees = new Hashtable();
attendees.put("5551112222","Phil Coulthard");
attendees.put("5551113333","George Farr");
```

This examples puts two entries in the hashtable; one has the key "5551112222" and the value "Phil Coulthard," and the second has the key "5551113333" and the value "George Farr." Although this example uses String objects for both the key and values, any object is valid. Further, you do not have to use the same object type for all keys or all values.

Internally, the key value is "hashed" into a number within a particular range, which is then used as the index into an internal table. The given value is then stored at that table position. To subsequently retrieve a value, use the get method and supply the value's key, like this:

```
String name = (String)attendees.get("5551112222");
if (name != null)
  System.out.println(name);
```

Notice the output of the get method has been cast to the actual class type of the value stored for that key, which is String in this case. Again, casting of objects is covered in Chapter 9, but it has to be used here because Hashtable only knows generically about Object objects, and so to use retrieved values, you have to tell Java exactly what the type of that value is. If no value is found with that key, get will return null, which you should test for.

To retrieve a list of all the values in a Hashtable, use the elements method. This returns an object of class type Enumeration (found in java.util as well). Enumeration objects are lists with two simple methods for traversing the list: hasMoreElements returns true while there is more elements in the list, and next returns the next element in the list. Here is an example:

```
Enumeration names = attendees.elements();
while (names.hasMoreElements())
  System.out.println((String)names.next());
```

You have to cast the result of next like get, since Enumeration is also a generic helper class that works generically on objects of any type. There is also a keys method in Hashtable for similarly returning an Enumeration of the keys. You will find that many Java-supplied classes that contain lists have an elements method that returns an Enumeration object, including the Vector class. You'll see more of Enumeration in Chapter 9.

There are lots of methods in the Hashtable class, beyond the put, get, elements, and keys methods shown here. For example, there is clear to clear the table, isEmpty to test if it is empty, remove to remove an entry given its key, size to return the size of the table, and containsValue and containsKey to simply test if a given value or given key exists in the table.

In our registration example, we may choose a hashtable if we decide to ask not only for the attendee names, which are not unique, but also their phone numbers which are unique. We basically want to store key-value pairs, where the phone number is the key and the attendee name is the value. Given any key, we want to efficiently find its entry in the list and extract the name. This is exactly what the Hashtable is for, so let's evolve the example to use it.

The first thing we need is a new class to represent the key objects (phone numbers) that will be stored in the hashtable. Once again, we could just use a raw String or Integer object, but we instead prefer to wrap that value inside our own class so that we have more flexibility in the future to change what we define as the key. Listing 6.25 shows the AttendeeKey class.

Listing 6.25: The AttendeeKey Class that Represents a Key Value for an Attendee at an Event

```java
public class AttendeeKey
{
    private String phoneNbr;

    public AttendeeKey(String phoneNbr)
    {
        this.phoneNbr = phoneNbr;
    }
    public String getNbr()
    {
        return phoneNbr;
    }
    public boolean equals(Object other)
    {
        AttendeeKey otherAttendee = (AttendeeKey)other;
        return phoneNbr.equals(otherAttendee.getNbr());
    }
    public int hashCode()
    {
        return phoneNbr.hashCode();
    }
}
```

This is a simple class that stores the given phone number String object as an instance variable and offers a getNbr method to return it. Again, an equals method must be supplied for the Vector and Hashtable search code to work correctly. In addition to equals, though, a hashCode method must also be supplied to store objects of this class in a Hashtable. This returns an integer value that is unique for each unique object. Typically, we code this method to simply return the hashCode of the key instance field. This works because all Java-supplied classes, like String, already code this method.

Now that we have the key field class, let's update the Attendee class. We want to store a reference to the key field object (the phone number) for this attendee and print it in the display method. The updates are shown in Listing 6.26.

*Listing 6.26: The Updated Attendee Class
that Stores and Uses a Reference to AttendeeKey*

```java
public class Attendee
{
    private String name;
    private AttendeeKey key;

    public Attendee(String name, AttendeeKey key)
    {
        this.name = name;
        this.key = key;
    }
    public String getName()
    {
        return name;
    }
    public AttendeeKey getKey()
    {
        return key;
    }
    public boolean equals(Object other)
    {
        Attendee otherAttendee = (Attendee)other;
        return name.equals(otherAttendee.getName());
    }
    public void display()
    {
        System.out.println("---------------");
        System.out.println("Name........: " + name);
        System.out.println("Number......: " + key.getNbr());
        System.out.println();
    }
}
```

This simply adds a new parameter to the constructor to take in a key object and subsequently remember it in an instance variable. We want this for our updated display method so that we can display the phone number from the key object. A getKey method is also supplied as a convenience, although it isn't needed here. Notice that the equals method is unchanged. We still consider two Attendee objects to be equal if their name matches, which is important for the containsValue method in the Hashtable class: it searches for a match on a given value object, versus a key object.

Finally, it is time to update the AttendeeList class to use a Hashtable versus a Vector and to accept the phone number in its methods. The updated class is shown in Listing 6.27.

*Listing 6.27: The Updated Attendee Class
that Stores and Uses a Reference to AttendeeKey*

```java
import java.util.*;

public class AttendeeList
{
    private Hashtable attendees = new Hashtable();

    public void register(String number, String name)
    {
        AttendeeKey newKey = new AttendeeKey(number);
        if (!checkForAttendee(newKey))
          attendees.put(newKey, new Attendee(name,newKey));
        else
          System.out.println("An attendee with this number
                              is already registered");
    }

    public void deRegister(String number)
    {
        AttendeeKey theKey = new AttendeeKey(number);
        if (!checkForAttendee(theKey))
          System.out.println("Sorry, that number is not registered");
        else
          attendees.remove(theKey);
    }

    public boolean checkForAttendee(AttendeeKey key)
    {
        return attendees.containsKey(key);
    }

    public void display()
    {
```

Listing 6.27: The Updated Attendee Class
that Stores and Uses a Reference to AttendeeKey (continued)

```
        Enumeration elements = attendees.elements();
        Attendee currAttendee = null;
        while (elements.hasMoreElements())
        {
            currAttendee = (Attendee)elements.nextElement();
            currAttendee.display();
        }
    }
}
```

The changes versus the Vector version are shown in bold. Notice the register method now requires both a number and a name. The number is used to create an AttendeeKey object, and that object is used to check for existence in the list. If that key is not found, put places the key object and an instance of the Attendee class into the hashtable. The deRegister method now takes a phone number as the key to search for and, if found, to remove from the list. The display method now uses the elements method described earlier to iterate the list of value objects, which in this case are instances of Attendee.

Finally, it is time to show the updated Registration class in Listing 6.28, which is simply updated to prompt for a phone number and name for registration, and just a phone number for unregistering.

Listing 6.28: The Updated Registration Class that Prompts for a Phone Number

```
public class Registration
{
    private AttendeeList attendeeList = new AttendeeList();

    public void run()
    {
        String command = "Not set";
        while (!command.equalsIgnoreCase("E"))
        {
            command = Console.readFromConsole(
              "Enter command (R=Register, U=Unregister,
                        D=Display, E=Exit)");
            if (command.equalsIgnoreCase("R"))
            {
                String number = Console.readFromConsole(
                            "Enter phone number:");
                String name = Console.readFromConsole(
```

Listing 6.28: The Updated Registration Class that Prompts for a Phone Number (continued)

```
                                "Enter name:");
                attendeeList.register(number,name);
            }
        else if (command.equalsIgnoreCase("U"))
            {
                String number = Console.readFromConsole(
                                "Enter phone number:");
                attendeeList.deRegister(number);
            }
        else if (command.equalsIgnoreCase("D"))
            attendeeList.display();
        } // end while loop
    } // end run
} // end of class Registration
```

The main method isn't shown because it is unchanged. Running this a few times gives this result:

```
Welcome to class Registration
Enter command (R=Register, U=Unregister, D=Display, E=Exit)
R
Enter phone number:
5551112222
Enter name:
Phil Coulthard
Enter command (R=Register, U=Unregister, D=Display, E=Exit)
R
Enter phone number:
5552221111
Enter name:
George Farr
Enter command (R=Register, U=Unregister, D=Display, E=Exit)
D
_____

Name........: George Farr
Number......: 5552221111


_____

Name........: Phil Coulthard
Number......: 5551112222
Enter command (R=Register, U=Unregister, D=Display, E=Exit)
U
Enter phone number:
1112223333
Sorry, that number is not registered
Enter command (R=Register, U=Unregister, D=Display, E=Exit)
E
```

What you should take out of this example is not just how to use hashtables, but also a common design pattern you will see often, where separate classes are used to represent the key values versus the non-key values. The latter class often holds a reference to the former, for convenience. Further, a third separate class is used to represent a list of objects. If the list needs to be searched by key, you use a hashtable of key and value pairs. If it does not need to be searched, you use a simple list such as a vector, containing just the value objects. Basically, separating the key into its own class gives more flexibility.

For fun, we also updated our RPG IV equivalent program for registering attendees to record not just the name of each attendee, but also his or her phone number, and to use that phone number as the key for finding a particular attendee. You can see this on the included disk in the file REGPHONE.IRP, in the LISTING6-28 subdirectory. You will see we also beefed it up a bit to add some error-checking to ensure the phone number entered is syntactically correct, and to check for attempts to register already-registered numbers and unregister never-registered numbers.

PARAMETER PASSING

How do you pass arrays as a parameter? Or can you even do that in RPG and Java? The answer is yes you can, for both languages. The only difference between the two languages is whether they allow passing arrays by value, reference, or both. *Pass-by-value* means that the calling program passes the array and its values to a called procedure. If the called procedure alters the values of the array, the original values in the calling program will not be affected. This is not the case for *pass-by-reference,* where the address of the array is passed to the called procedure, and therefore any alteration to the array values will be reflected in the original program.

Parameter passing in RPG IV

Let's take a look at RPG IV, where both calls by value and reference are allowed. Listing 6.29 illustrates pass-by-value.

Listing 6.29: Pass-by-Value in RPG

```
D Week             S              9A    DIM(7) CTDATA PERRCD(1)
D PASSBYV          PR
D                                 9A    DIM(7) VALUE
 *
D i                S              1P 0  INZ(1)
 *
```

Listing 6.29: Pass-by-Value in RPG (continued)

```
C                    DOW        i<=7
C        Week(i)     DSPLY
C                    ADD        1              i
C                    ENDDO
C                    CALLP      PASSBYV(Week)
C                    MOVE       1              i
C                    DOW        i<=7
C        Week(i)     DSPLY
C                    ADD        1              i
C                    ENDDO
C                    ADD        1              i
C                    ENDDO
C                    MOVE       *ON            *INLR
P PASSBYV        B
D                PI
D weekp                          9A   DIM(7) VALUE
C                    DOW        i<=7
C                    Move       *Blanks        weekp(i)
C                    ENDDO
P                E
** CTDATA week
Monday
Tuesday
Wednesday
Thursday
Friday
Saturday
Sunday
```

This example declares an array, Week, to be a compile-time array. As you can see, in the prototype definition, the keyword VALUE is specified to indicate passing by value. This example initializes the array to the days of week and starts by displaying the values in the array before calling the procedure to indicate the initialization value. Once that is done, it calls the procedure PASSBYV, which is defined in the same example. In the procedure, it tries to clear out the array values by moving blanks to it. Once the call is returned to the caller, it does the same loop to display the content on the array.

Notice that the original values of the array are unchanged, as expected, since the array was passed by VALUE. This would not be the case if you simply removed the keyword VALUE from the example. This one slight change would suddenly make the clearing of the array in the procedure affect the array in the mainline code, such that the second display-ing of the elements would result in all blanks. This decision to use VALUE or not in RPG affects all parameter types the same way, whether they are arrays or not.

In Java, this is not the case. As mentioned in Chapter 2, Java does not support pointers. Therefore, Java methods normally cannot change a parameter's value. In other words, Java normally passes parameters to methods using pass-by-value, similar to indicating the VALUE keyword for RPG parameter passing. As it turns out, Java does pass non-primitive types such as objects, arrays, and vectors by reference. This lets the method change the content of the parameter.

If you like, you can even think of the object reference itself as being passed by value. That is, object reference variables are, after all, memory addresses. Therefore, when you pass an object—including an array, which, after all, is an object—you are passing a memory address. That address itself is passed by value, and so if you reset the object to which the variable points, perhaps by equating it to another object or a new object created with the new operator, that address change will not be reflected in the calling code. However, any changes made to the object the variable points to, by invoking methods on the object or changing elements in an array, *are* reflected to the caller.

Listing 6.30 is an example to illustrate all of this. It has a main method that first declares an array named arrayBefore and initializes it to a set of five numbers. Next, it prints the values as with the RPG example to show that initialization works as expected, but it does this by calling a little helper method named printElements, which is shown at the bottom of the class. Next, it calls another supplied method named changeArrayElements that, as you can see, changes each element by multiplying it by 10. To see if that affected the mainline array, printElements is called again. Next, another supplied method named changeArrayReference is called. This method changes not the elements this time, but the actual array variable itself, pointing it to an entirely new array. If this affects the calling code, you would expect the last call to printElements to show all zeros, since it is a new array.

Listing 6.30: Passing Arrays as Parameters in Java

```
public class TestArrayParameters
{
    public static void main(String args[])
    {
        int arrayBefore[] = { 1,2,3,4,5 };
        printElements("before", arrayBefore);
        changeArrayElements(arrayBefore);
        printElements("after element changes ", arrayBefore);
        changeArrayReference(arrayBefore);
        printElements("after reference change", arrayBefore);
    }
```

Listing 6.30: Passing Arrays as Parameters in Java (continued)

```java
    public static void changeArrayElements(int givenArray[])
    {
        for (int idx = 0; idx < givenArray.length; idx++)
            givenArray[idx] *= 10;
        return;
    }
    public static void changeArrayReference(int givenArray[])
    {
        givenArray = new int[5];
        return;
    }
    public static void printElements(String prompt, int array[])
    {
        System.out.print(prompt + ": ");
        for (int idx = 0; idx < array.length; idx++)
            System.out.print(array[idx] + " ");
        System.out.println();
    }
} // end TestArrayParameters class
```

Here is the result of running this test case:

```
C:\JAVA>javac TestArrayParameters.java
C:\JAVA>java TestArrayParameters
before: 1 2 3 4 5
after element changes : 10 20 30 40 50
after reference change: 10 20 30 40 50
```

You can see that the call to changeArrayElements did, in fact, change the contents of the array in the mainline code. However, the call to changeArrayReference had no affect on the mainline array variable arrayBefore—it still points to the same array in memory as it did before the call. Thus, you see that array contents can be changed, but array addresses cannot. Again, the address of the array itself is passed by value.

Using arrays instead of primitives for simulated pass-by-reference

Remember that primitive values, like integers, are always passed by value in Java. That means you cannot write a method to swap the values of two integer variables, for example. The swap will have no affect on the caller's values of those variables. Pass-by-value effectively means a copy of the parameter values is passed to the method. However, there is one possible way to circumvent this: instead of passing primitive values, you could pass array objects—arrays with only one element, since you have just seen that array elements can be effectively changed by methods. Listing 6.31, then, is a swap method that works in Java.

Listing 6.31: Simulating Pass-by-Reference in Java

```java
public class TestSwap
{
    public static void main(String args[])
    {
        int value1 = 10;
        int value2 = 20;
        int value1Array[] = new int[1];
        int value2Array[] = new int[1];
        value1Array[0] = value1;
        value2Array[0] = value2;
        System.out.println("value1 = " + value1 + ", value2 = " +
value2);
        swap(value1Array, value2Array);
        value1 = value1Array[0];
        value2 = value2Array[0];
        System.out.println("value1 = " + value1 + ", value2 = " +
value2);
    }
    public static void swap(int value1[], int value2[])
    {
        int temp = value1[0];
        value1[0] = value2[0];
        value2[0] = temp;
        return;
    }
} // end TestSwap class
```

The important method here is swap, which takes two single-element arrays and swaps the first element of each. The trick to using this method with primitive values is to first move those values into the first element of a couple of arrays created for this purpose, and then, after calling swap with those arrays, move the values back into the primitive variables from the arrays. This is shown in the main method of the example. While this is not a pretty thing to have to do, it does work, as you can see in the following output:

```
C:\JAVA>java TestSwap
value1 = 10, value2 = 20
value1 = 20, value2 = 10
```

SUMMARY

This chapter introduced you to the following concepts:

- Arrays, vectors, hashtables, and strings are objects in Java.

- Java has two kinds of arrays: compile-time and runtime.

- You can delay instantiating arrays until after you have determined their sizes.

- Java supports both multi-dimensional and unbalanced arrays.

- The main rule for unbalanced arrays is to define them left to right.

- The class `Arrays` in `java.util` contains static methods to search, sort, and fill arrays.

- Vectors in Java can shrink and grow on demand.

- Vectors can only contain objects, and you must cast when retrieving an element object.

- To use a vector, the contained objects must implement the `equals` method.

- Hashtables in Java can store values indexed by a key, and then easily and quickly find a value given its key.

- Hashtables can only contain objects, and you must cast when retrieving an element object.

- To use a Hashtable, the contained objects must implement the `equals` and `hashCode` methods.

- All Java-supplied classes implement both the `equals` and `hashCode` methods.

- Parameters are passed by value in Java.

- To circumvent the pass-by-value problem for primitive type variables, you can use single-element arrays.

STRING MANIPULATION

The discussion of primitive data types in Chapter 5 mentions that you can create a string using an array of type char. However, Java has a better way of dealing with strings—the String class in the java.lang package, which is always imported, and hence always available to you. You have already seen examples that use this String class, so now we will discuss it in more detail, as well as the methods that are supplied with it.

Why does Java use a class for strings instead of a built-in data type? This is because built-in data types or primitives are restricted to the few operators built into the language for math and manipulation purposes (like + and -). You spend so much time preparing, converting to and from, manipulating, and querying strings, that you gain significant programmer productivity from a class (versus a built-in primitive data type) given all the methods that can be supplied with it for common string operations.

For example, how many times have you written justification, trimming, and conversion code for text strings? Why not have language-supplied methods to save you the drudgery? In RPG, such language-supplied functionality comes in the form of op-codes and built-in functions. In an object-oriented language, it comes in the form of methods on a simple self-contained class. Indeed, it is through string classes in object-oriented languages that you first start to appreciate the power and elegance of objects. This great ability to encapsulate the useful methods or functions commonly needed by programmers into a class data type drives home the potential of objects and OO. For example, to support a new operation, you need only add a new method, versus designing a new operator into the language.

JAVA STRING BASICS AND PITFALLS

An important note about strings in Java is that the language designers slightly relaxed their strict object-oriented rules to allow strings to be concatenated directly with a built-in operator—the plus operator (+). They also allowed an intuitive means of instantiating strings that does not force you to use formal object-instantiation syntax (as they did for compile-time arrays).

This underlies the importance of strings and string manipulation to every programmer and their invariable prominence in every program. The more intuitive and convenient it is to use strings in a language, the more accepted that language is by programmers. Certainly, Java's goal is to "keep it simple." If you prefer to stick to more formal rules, though, you can do that, too. In other words, if you prefer to instantiate a string in the formal way and use a method call, concat, to concatenate two strings, instead of just using the + operator, that's fine. For example, you can use an intuitive style like this:

```
String text1 = "George";
String text2 = "Phil";
String finalText = text1 + " and " + text2;
System.out.println(finalText);
```

Alternatively, you can use a formal style like this:

```
String text1 = new String("George");
String text2 = new String("Phil");
String finalText = new String(text1);
finalText = finalText.concat(" and ");
finalText = finalText.concat(text2);
System.out.println(finalText);
```

The output of both examples is "George and Phil," as you would expect. These examples show that there are two ways to initialize strings—by implicitly equating them to string literals or by explicitly allocating an instance of the String class using the new operator. Once you create your strings, you can manipulate them using the many methods supplied with the String class. These samples also highlight the two means of adding strings together in Java, either via the intuitive plus operator or via the concat method of the String class. Note that in the latter, the string passed as a parameter is appended to the string represented by the String object. The actual String target object is not affected. Rather, a new String object is created and returned. Thus, the method call has no side effects.

Can you guess the output of the following?

```
String finalText = "George";
finalText.concat("and Phil");
System.out.println(finalText);
```

The answer is "George", not "George and Phil" as you might initially expect. Do not get caught by this common mistake. Another important consideration is string equality in Java. You cannot use the equality operator (==) to compare two string objects, like this:

```
if (text1 == text2)
```

Rather, you must use the equals method, which returns true if the target string and the passed-in string are equivalent, like this:

```
if (text1.equals(text2)) ...
```

This is the single most common mistake when using the String class. The problem is that the use of natural instantiation and the plus operator for concatenation tend to make you think of strings as primitive data types in Java. However, they are actually objects of the String class—that is, object reference variables. Like all object reference variables, they actually contain a memory address of the class instance, and as such, the equality operator only tells you if the two variables refer to the same address, which they almost never do. The operator does not have the intelligence to make a decision about whether all characters are the same and the strings are the same length. Rather, the code inside the equals method is required for this. You are all the more prone to this pitfall as an RPG

IV programmer, because RPG IV has a free-form IF op-code syntax that does allow you to compare two strings (alphabetic fields) using the equality operator, as in:

```
IF          STRING1  =  STRING2
```

Take care in your Java coding to avoid this bug, as you will not notice it for a while, given that the compiler will not complain about it. Equality testing of object references is legal, after all, for those cases when you want to know if two variables actually do refer to the same allocated instance in memory.

STRINGS IN RPG

RPG does not have a pure string data type similar to the String class in Java. In fact, in RPG III, you were quite restricted in character field functionality. You only had room for six character literals, and so you often had to resort to compile-time arrays to code longer literals. You had the MOVE, MOVEA, and MOVEL op-codes, and the CAT, CHECK, CHEKR, COMP, SCAN, SUBST, and XLATE op-codes.

In RPG IV, life is much better! You define a string field as a fixed-length character field:

```
DmyString          S              20A   INZ('Anna Lisa')
```

In this example, the first field, mystring, is defined as a 20-character alphanumeric field, and is initialized to an initial value of 'Anna Lisa' using the INZ keyword for initializing. The keyword area of the D-spec is from column 44 to 79, giving lots of room, and literals that don't fit even in this can be continued by placing a plus or minus character in the last position and continuing the literal on the next line.

Once you have defined a character field, you can perform operations on it by using the same op-codes as in RPG III, plus the EVAL and EVALR op-codes, and many handy built-in functions, as you shall see. Also, you can use the plus operator for concatenation and the free-form IF statement can do comparisons of strings. You can assign a string to a variable using the traditional MOVE and MOVEL op-codes or the new free-format EVAL or EVALR op-codes with the assignment statement, as shown in Listing 7.1.

Listing 7.1: Assigning Strings with EVAL and EVALR in RPG IV

```
D string1        S              10A
D string2        S              10A
C                EVAL      string1 = 'abc'
C                EVALR     string2 = 'abc'
```

The EVAL op-codes are only for assignment, but are preferred to the older MOVE op-codes because they have a free-format factor-two from column 36 to 79, and can continue onto the next lines, where they get all columns from 8 to 79. This means you can write expressions that are as long as you want! The difference between EVAL and EVALR is that the latter right-justifies the target string into the source field. So, in the example in Listing 7.1, string1 contains 'abc   ' while string2 contains '   abc'.

In addition to assigning literals or other fields to string fields, you can assign special figurative constants to them to initialize the values. Specially, you can assign *BLANKS to blank out the whole field, or *ALL'X...' to assign and repeat whatever literal you specify for x..., for example:

```
C                EVAL      string1 = *BLANKS
C                EVAL      string2 = *ALL'AB'
```

In this example, string1 becomes '   ' while string2 becomes 'ABABABABAB'. Note that these figurative constants can also be specified at declaration time on the D-spec as the parameter to the INZ keyword.

RPG III and IV use single quotes to delimit a string literal, while Java uses double quotes. Also, strings in RPG are fixed in length and always padded with blanks if needed to achieve this length. So, if you display the contents of the myString field in the example, you would see 'Anna Lisa   '. This is different than Java, where the size of the string is always exactly as long as the text last assigned to it. You never explicitly specify the length of a string in Java, this is done implicitly for you, for example:

```
String name = "Phil"; // new string, length four
name = "George"; // assigned to a new value, length six
```

The length of a string is exactly the length of its current contents, which can be changed with an assignment statement. The new value is never padded or truncated by Java. If you want padding with blanks, you have to explicitly specify the blanks in your literal, like this:

```
String myString = "Phil    "; // new string, length eight
```

In fact, the idea of dynamically sized string fields that always hold the exact text they have been assigned, instead of being padded, is so wonderful that RPG itself now supports it as well. As of V4R2, you can code the VARYING keyword on a character field to have it behave similar to Java, as in:

```
DmyString       S              20A   INZ('Anna Lisa')
D                                     VARYING
```

You still have to code a length, but that is used only as the maximum so the compiler knows how much memory to allocate. If you used DSPLY to print the contents of this field to the console and put quotes around the result, you would see 'Anna Lisa'—exactly the value it was initialized to, with no padding. This is nice.

In both RPG and Java, you might want to include an embedded quote. Since these are the delimiters, you have to use special syntax to embed them. In RPG, you double-up the embedded quote, like this:

```
DwithQuote      S              20A   INZ('Phil''s name')
```

In Java, you use the same backslash escape sequence you saw in Chapter 5:

```
String withQuote = "Phil says \" do you get it? \"";
```

Finally, remember that every character in Java requires two bytes of storage, even in String objects. This does not affect you as a programmer, other than to make life much easier when supporting multiple languages or countries, since you do not have to worry about codepage conversions or CCSIDs. We mention it because RPG IV also now has this capability, as of V4R4. Rather than using an A for the data type column, you can code a C, identifying this field as containing Unicode characters. You can convert between character and Unicode fields, and vice versa, using regular EVAL, EVALR, MOVE, and MOVEL operations, or the new %UCS2 built-in function. We don't cover the details of Unicode fields in RPG IV here, but if you are writing international applications, you should have a look. Further, if you are planning to have RPG code that calls Java code, or vice versa, then the Unicode data type is a perfect match for Java's String objects when passing parameters between the languages.

Table 7.1 compares all available string-manipulation op-codes and built-in functions in RPG IV to those methods available in Java. Java offers more functionality than shown here, as you will see shortly.

Table 7.1: RPG String-Related Op-codes and BIFs versus Java String Methods

RPG Op-code	RPG Built-in	Description	Java String Method(s)
CAT (or + operator)		Concatenate two strings	concat method or + operator
SUBST	%SUBST	Extract a substring from a string	substring method
SCAN	%SCAN	Scan for a substring	indexOf method
	%TRIM	Trim beginning and ending blanks	trim method
	%TRIML	Trim leading blanks	Not available
	%TRIMR	Trim trailing blanks	Not available
	%LEN	Return length of string	length method
XLATE		Translate a string	No xlate match, but there are toUpperCase and toLowerCase methods
CHECK		Check for characters	Not available
CHECKR		Check in reverse	Not available
	%CHAR	Convert various types to an outputable string.	valueOf method
	%REPLACE	Allowsreplacement of a substring with another	replace method, but only replaces individual characters

291

STRING MANIPULATION

The next sections examine each of the operations listed in Table 7.1 and give examples of them for both RPG and Java. Where there is no matching method in Java, as in the case of XLATE and CHECK, you will learn how to write a method yourself to simulate the function.

Concatenation

Let's start with string concatenation for both RPG and Java, looking at an example to illustrate the use of this function. Suppose you have two fields: one contains a person's first name and the other contains the last name. You need to concatenate the two fields and print out the result. This is easy to do in both languages, since both support concatenating strings. In RPG, you use the CAT op-code, as shown in Listing 7.2.

Listing 7.2: Concatenating Strings in RPG Using the CAT Op-code

```
D  first          S              10A   INZ('Mike')
D  last           S              10A   INZ('Smith')
D  name           S              20A   INZ(' ')
C*      Factor1         OpCode    Factor2       Result
C       first           CAT       last:1        name
C       name            DSPLY
```

This example uses two fields, first to represent the first name and last to represent the last name. It declares and initializes these fields right on the D-spec. However, in more complex applications, these fields may be read from the screen or from a file on disk. They can even be passed in via the command line. The C-spec uses the CAT op-code to concatenate field first to field last in factors one and two. The result of the concatenation is placed in the field name, which is specified in the result column. Notice also that :1 is specified in factor two in order to tell the compiler to insert one blank between the field values when concatenating them. The DSPLY op-code displays the value of name, which is "Mike Smith", as you would expect.

Listing 7.3 illustrates the same example written in Java.

Listing 7.3: Concatenating Strings in Java Using the CONCAT String Method

```
public class Concat
{
    public static void main(String args[])
    {
```

→

```
        String first, last, name;
        first = "Mike";
        last  = "Smith";
        name = first.concat(" ").concat(last);
        System.out.println("The name is: " + name);
    }
} // end class Concat
```

This example uses the String object to declare all the string variables, namely: first, last, and name. As mentioned earlier, by declaring the string variables and initializing them, all three string objects are created and initialized (that is, no new keyword is required to instantiate the object). Because you want to append a blank to the first name and then add the last name to that, two concat operations are necessary; there is no equivalent to RPG's :1 trick. The double concatenation could have been done in two steps, but we chose to do it in one. We can do this because the concat method returns the concatenated string, which can then be used directly as the object of a subsequent concat operation. Notice that we use the string to be concatenated as the object in the concat call, and pass in as a parameter the string to concatenate to it. The result is returned from the call, which is placed in the name variable. Then, the result is displayed using the println method. Double quotes are used around the blank literal, but because it is only one character, single quotes could also have been used, as there are two overloaded concat methods—one that takes a string and one that takes a single character.

Did you notice another concatenation in the previous example? If you did, you have a sharp eye. The println method concatenates the string literal "The name is :" to the object reference variable name using the plus operator. This is another way of concatenating two strings. In fact, this is a fast way of concatenating two strings in an expression for both RPG and Java. RPG supports the same + operator for concatenation in an expression. Table 7.2 replaces the CAT op-code of the previous example with the EVAL op-code, and the concat Java method with the + operator.

Table 7.2: Comparing the RPG and Java + Operator for String Concatenation

RPG IV		Java
C	EVAL	name = first + ' ' + last	name = first + " " + last;

Clearly, the use of the plus operator is a plus for programmers!

Substrings

Next, let's take a look at the substring op-code in RPG and the corresponding substring method in Java. In RPG, you use the SUBST operation code to extract a substring from a string starting at a specified location for a specified length, as shown in Listing 7.4.

Listing 7.4: Substringing Strings in RPG Using the SUBST Op-code

```
D*
123456789012345678901234567890123456789
DWhyJava          S             30A    INZ('Because Java is for RPG
pgmrs')
D  first          S              4A
D  second         S              6A
D  third          S              3A
D  sayWhat        S             15A
C        4         SUBST    WhyJava:9      first
C        6         SUBST    WhyJava:14     second
C        3         SUBST    whyJava:21     third
C                  EVAL     sayWhat =
C                               first+' '+second+' '+third
C        sayWhat   DSPLY
C                  EVAL     *INLR = *ON
```

This example takes a string with the value "Because Java is for RPG pgmrs" and retrieves different strings from it to make up the string "Java is for RPG". To do this, it declares three different character fields and a field to store the results. As the example illustrates, the SUBST op-code takes the number of characters to substring in factor one, and takes the source as well as the starting position for the retrieval in factor two. For example, the first SUBST operation receives the value Java and places it in the result field first. When all of the values have been retrieved, the concatenation operator concatenates all fields. Finally, the result of the field is displayed using the DSPLY operation code. The result is "Java is for RPG".

Because of RPG's fixed-field padding rules, we had to declare all the fields to be the exact length needed to hold the result. As an alternative, we could have coded them all to be a maximum length, such as 20, and then used the VARYING keyword on their D-spec definitions.

Listing 7.5 illustrates an equivalent example, written in Java, using the substring method of the String class. The parameters for the substring method have the beginning index value as the first parameter and the ending index as the second parameter. There are some subtle differences compared to RPG:

- The parameters are zero-based, not one-based as in RPG.

- The second parameter is the ending position, not the length.

- The second parameter is one past the actual ending position you want!

Otherwise, the logic is similar to RPG's and easy enough to follow. There is also a second version of the substring method, which takes as input only one parameter—the starting position (again, zero-based). This returns a string containing all characters from that starting position to the end of the target string.

Listing 7.5: Substringing Strings in Java Using the SUBSTRING String Method

```
public class Substring
{
    public static void main(String args[])
    {
        String whyJava, first, second, third, sayWhat;
        //        01234567890123456789012345678901234
        whyJava = "Because Java is for RPG Programmers";
        first   = whyJava.substring(8,12);
        second  = whyJava.substring(13,19);
        third   = whyJava.substring(20,23);
        sayWhat = first + " " + second + " " + third;
        System.out.println(sayWhat);
    }
} // end class Substring
```

Why is it that the second parameter has to be one past the actual ending column? It turns out this makes some processing easier. For example, you don't normally know exactly what column to start the substring operation in, and what column to end it in. Instead, you will often determine this programmatically, by searching for a specific delimiting character such as a blank or comma or dollar sign. This is done in Java using the indexOf method that you'll see shortly, but it is very simple to use. You give it the character to find, and it returns the zero-based position of that character (and you can specific what position to start the search). Well, when you are searching for the ending delimiter, you will subsequently be substringing up to the character position right before that delimiter, so this funny rule of Java's substring method makes it a little easier. For example, we could have written the first substring example from Listing 7.5 as this:

```
first = whyJava.substring(8,whyJava.indexOf(' '));
```

We don't want to *string* you out, so we'll move on now to the next topic.

In RPG IV, you can also use the %SUBST built-in function to accomplish the same thing in expressions. The syntax of this is %SUBST(string:start{:length}). The parameters are the same as the op-code SUBST, as you see in the following example:

```
EVAL        secondWord = %SUBST('RPG USERS':5:5)
EVAL        secondWord = %SUBST('RPG USERS':5)
```

In both cases, the result is "USERS". Note the similarities to Java's substring method, notwithstanding the "gotcha's" mentioned.

Searching for a substring

One of the more commonly used functions in almost all languages is the ability to search one string for the occurrence of another. For example, you might have a string like "Java is for RPG users" and you want to find the position of the substring "RPG". Once you know this, you can simply extract the characters found after it. By searching for substrings, you can avoid hard-coding the substring parameters when you don't know the positions at compile time. You can use the SCAN operation code for this, as Listing 7.6 illustrates.

Listing 7.6: Scanning Strings for Substrings in RPG Using the SCAN Op-code

```
D*                                      12345678901234567890
Dstr              S            40A  INZ('Java is for RPG users')
Didx              S             3P 0
C       'RPG'      SCAN        str              idx
C       idx        DSPLY
C                  EVAL        idx = %SCAN('RPG':str)
C       idx        DSPLY
C                  EVAL        *INLR = *ON
```

This example defines a string field named str and initializes it to "Java is for RPG users". It finds the location of the substring "RPG" in the main string using SCAN, placing the desired substring in factor one, the source string in factor two, and the resulting field to contain the numeric index value in the result column. When the operation is executed, idx will contain the position where the substring was found, which is 13 in this example. Note that RPG allows you to specify the start location for the search in the second part of factor two. If the start location is not specified, as in this example, the default is to start at the first character. This example also shows the %SCAN built-in function, which offers the same functionality as the op-code, but can be used in free-format expressions. The second DSPLY operation also results in 13. You could specify an optional :start parameter on the %SCAN function.

For Java, this is a simple operation, since Java supplies an indexOf method in its String class, as shown in Listing 7.7. This method takes one or two parameters. The first is the string you are looking for, and the optional second is the start location of the search (the character position). Again, this is a zero-based position, not a one-based position as in for RPG. If you do not specify the start location, as with RPG, the default start value will be set to the first character position (that is, zero). In the example, the value that is printed is 12 (zero-based, again, so 12 is the thirteenth character). The indexOf method returns -1 if the given substring is not found in the input String object.

Listing 7.7: Scanning Strings for
Substrings in Java Using the indexOf String Method

```
public class Scan
{
    public static void main(String args[])
    {
        //                      012345678901234567890
        String str = new String("Java is for RPG users");
        int idx = str.indexOf("RPG");
        System.out.println("RPG occurs at: " + idx);
    }
}
```

In addition to indexOf, Java also supplies a handy lastIndexOf method, which will search backwards for a given substring. Again, it has an optional second parameter for specifying where to start the search, but this time the search continues backward from that start position.

Finally, both indexOf and lastIndexOf support either a string parameter, as you have already seen, or a single character parameter when searching for an individual character, as in:

```
int dollarPos = myString.indexOf('$');
```

Trimming blanks

Trimming is the process of removing leading or trailing blanks from a string, and both languages have built-in support for it. In RPG, three built-in functions make it easy to trim blanks. Listing 7.8 shows the %TRIM built-in function.

Listing 7.8: Trimming Blanks in RPG Using the %TRIM Built-in Function

```
D leftright       S              40A   INZ('    Java is for -
D                                      RPG users       ')
D temp            S              40A
C*
C                 EVAL           temp = %TRIM(leftright) + '.'
C       temp      DSPLY
C                 EVAL           *INLR = *ON
```

This example uses %TRIM on the EVAL op-code to trim both leading and trailing blanks in the field leftright, placing the result in temp. Note that it concatenates a period to the trimmed string so that you can see the trimmed result before RPG pads it back out to the declared length of 40. After the operation, the field contains the following:

```
"Java is for RPG users. "
```

In Java, this task is also easy to accomplish, using the appropriately named trim method, as shown in Listing 7.9.

Listing 7.9: Trimming Blanks in Java Using the trim String Method

```
public class Trim
{
    public static void main(String args[])
    {
```

```
        String str = "    Java is for RPG users    ";
        str = str.trim();
        System.out.println("Trimmed: '" + str + "'");
    }
} // end class Trim
```

The result is "Trimmed: 'Java is for RPG users'". Note again that Java does not pad strings out to some pre-declared length, so we did not have to concatenate a period.

Easy stuff. However, what if you only want to remove leading blanks? Or trailing blanks? In RPG it is very easy, since the language supports two additional built-ins, %TRIML and %TRIMR, for trimming left (leading) and right (trailing) blanks. However, Java has only the TRIM method, and unfortunately, no TRIML and TRIMR methods. It is not brain surgery or VCR programming to write your own code to do this, however, and you will do so by the end of the chapter, after learning about the StringBuffer class.

Determining string lengths

Determining the length of a string, to decide if it is empty or needs truncation or padding, is a simple task in both languages. In RPG IV, you simply use the %LEN built-in function, specifying a field or string literal or built-in function as a parameter, as shown in Listing 7.10.

Listing 7.10: Getting the Length of a Field in RPG IV

```
D aString         S             40A   INZ('      Java is for -
D                                      RPG users         ')
D len1            S              9 0
D len2            S              9 0
C*
C                   EVAL      len1 = %LEN(aString)
C                   EVAL      len2 = %LEN(%TRIM(aString))
C         len1      DSPLY
C         len2      DSPLY
C                   EVAL      *INLR = *ON
```

This code shows two examples of the %LEN built-in function—one takes a character field as input and the other takes a nested built-in function call %TRIM as input. The displayed output of this program is 40 and 21. Why 40 for the first one, even though the string on the INZ keyword is 35 long? Because the field is declared as 40 characters long. If you were to add the VARYING keyword to the definition of aString, you would get 35 from the %LEN built-in function.

In Java, you invoke the length method, as shown in Listing 7.11. When you run this example, you get 35 and 21. Remember that in Java, characters are two bytes long, because they are Unicode characters. However, the length returned by the length method is the number of characters, not the number of bytes—the latter is actually two times the former. The same is true for RPG Unicode fields and the %LEN built-in function. All String class methods that take or return an index number deal with the character position, not the byte offset, so you rarely need to worry about the fact that characters are two bytes long.

Listing 7.11: Getting the Length of a String in Java

```
public class Length
{
    public static void main(String args[])
    {
        String aString = "      Java is for RPG users        ";
        int len1 = aString.length();
        int len2 = aString.trim().length();
        System.out.println(len1);
        System.out.println(len2);
    }
} // end class Length
```

Translating characters

So far, you have seen RPG op-codes compared to *available* Java methods. As you recall from Table 7.1, a few RPG op-codes or built-ins are simply not available in Java. For example, the XLATE op-code in RPG has no apparent equivalent in Java—at least, not yet. What to do in this case? Write your own method! First, let's review the RPG support. Listing 7.12 shows an example of the RPG XLATE op-code.

Listing 7.12: Translating Characters in RPG Using the XLATE Op-code

```
D from            C                   CONST('GPR4')
D to              C                   CONST('VAJA')
D source          S             4A    INZ('RPG4')
D target          S             4A
C     from:to      XLATE     source        target
C     target       DSPLY
C                  EVAL      *INLR = *ON
```

As you know, XLATE translates the source string in factor two to another sequence of characters, depending on the *from* and *to* strings specified in factor one. The result of this translation is placed in the result field. In particular, all characters in the source string with a match in the *from* string are translated to the corresponding characters in the *to* string. The rule is that the lengths of the *from*, *to*, and source strings must all be the same. The example translates R to J, P to A, G to V, and 4 to A, respectively. With the value RPG4 in the source string specified in factor two, the result is JAVA after the operation. Note that we decided to make the from and to fields constants, using RPG IV's syntax for constants.

Java has no corresponding method in its String class, but it does have a related method named replace, which takes two character parameters as input. It replaces all occurrences of the first character in the target string object with the second character. It sounds similar to RPG's XLATE, except that replace only replaces a single character, not a string of characters. Not to worry—you can write your own Java method that emulates RPG's XLATE op-code by using the replace method repeatedly, once for each character in a given string of *from* characters.

What is interesting is that you cannot extend String (discussed in a later chapter) because the Java language designers made it final, preventing this. Thus, String augmentation methods like this will be created as traditional, standalone functions—that is, they will be defined as static, and take as parameters whatever they need. But even static methods must exist in a class, so we create them in an arbitrary class named RPGString, which is where all of the remaining methods in this chapter will go.

Listing 7.13 is the Java equivalent to RPG's XLATE op-code. (For consistency, we have named the method xlate.) The required parameters are, of course, the source string to be translated, followed by the *from* and *to* strings, and finally the start position, where the translation should start. To be consistent with Java's string methods, this start position is zero-based. To be consistent with RPG, the start position value should be optional, defaulting to the first character if not passed. To support an optional parameter at the end of the parameter list in a Java method, simply supply a second method with the same name that does not specify or accept that last parameter, which we have done. This second overloaded method can simply call the first full version of the method and pass in the default value for the missing parameter. In this case, this is zero for the first character.

Listing 7.13: Translating Characters in Java Using the xlate Method

```java
public class RPGString
{
    public static String xlate(String source,  String fromChars,
                              String toChars, int     start)
    {
        String resultString;
        // minimal input error checking
        if (fromChars.length() != toChars.length())
          return new String("BAD INPUT!");
        if (start > source.length() || start < 0)
          return new String("BAD INPUT!");
        // first off, get the substring to be xlated...
        resultString = source.substring(start);
        // xlate each fromChars char to same pos in toChars
        for (int i = 0; i < fromChars.length(); i++)
            resultString = resultString.replace(fromChars.charAt(i),
                                                toChars.charAt(i));
        // now append xlated part to non-xlated part
        resultString = source.substring(0,start) + resultString;
        return resultString;
    } // end xlate method

    public static String xlate(String source,  String fromChars,
                              String toChars)
    {
        return xlate(source, fromChars, toChars, 0);
    } // end xlate method two
} // end RPGString class
```

The code in the first and primary xlate method is reasonably straightforward—you first check to make sure the input is valid, then create a substring of the source that excludes the characters before the given start position. Next, for every character in the *from* string, you use the String class replace method to replace all occurrences of that character with the character in the corresponding position of the *to* string. Finally, you append that to the substring of the source up to the start position, and return this resulting string. To get an individual character out of a string, you must use the charAt method and supply the zero-based index of the character.

To test this, we supply a main method in our class so that we can call it from the command line and see the results. (This idea of supplying a main method for test cases for of your handwritten classes is a good idea, by the way.) Listing 7.14 shows the test case, which tests both versions of the method—first without specifying a start position, and then with specifying a start position.

Listing 7.14: Testing the xlate Method

```
public static void main(String args[])
{
    /*_____*/
    /* Test xlate method               */
    /*_____*/
    //              "012345678901234567890";
    String src  = "RPGP is for you Joo!";
    String from = "RPG";
    String to   = "Jav";
    System.out.println("Input string  : '" + src + "'");
    src = RPGString.xlate(src, from, to);
    System.out.println("Output string1: '" + src + "'");
    from = "J";
    to   = "t";
    src = RPGString.xlate(src, from, to, 16);
    System.out.println("Output string2: '" + src + "'");
} // end main method
```

Note the calls to xlate are qualified with the class name RPGString. Because this method is in the same class as the method being called, this is not necessary. However, we did this to illustrate how code in any other class would have to look. The example translates the characters in RPG to the corresponding characters in JAVA, and then translates the character J to the character t, starting at position 16 (again, zero-based). If we started at zero, the first J would be translated, which is not what we want. The final result is as follows:

```
Input string  : 'RPGP is for you Joo!'
Output string1: 'JAVA is for you Joo!'
Output string2: 'JAVA is for you too!'
```

Translating case

One function you'll often require is string translation to uppercase or lowercase. There is no language-supplied function for this in RPG, but there is in Java. However, you can accomplish this task in RPG using, once again, the XLATE op-code, using all lowercase characters for the *from* string and all uppercase characters for the *to* string, as shown in Listing 7.15.

Listing 7.15: Translating Case in RPG Using the XLATE Op-code

```
D LOWER           C                          'abcdefghijklmnopqrstuvwxyz'
D UPPER           C                          'ABCDEFGHIJKLMNOPQRSTUVWXYZ'
D string          S              30A         INZ('Java is for rpg users')
C       string          DSPLY
C       LOWER:UPPER     XLATE      string               string
C       string          DSPLY
C                       EVAL       *INLR = *ON
```

Two named constant strings, LOWER and UPPER, are defined to contain all the lowercase characters and their matching uppercase characters. To illustrate how this works, a field named string is defined containing the string "Java is for rpg users". Next, the XLATE op-code is used with the value 'LOWER:UPPER' in factor one and the string variable in the result column. After executing this operation, the result is the whole string in uppercase: 'JAVA IS FOR RPG USERS'.

Need we say this is a great opportunity for a procedure? It could be named, say, Upper-Case, and take a string as input and return the uppercase version. Of course, it would only support single-length character fields unless you used VARYING length fields and specified the OPTIONS(*VARSIZE) keyword for the procedure parameter.

In Java, converting strings from uppercase to lowercase and vice versa is even simpler, as Java supplies intuitive methods to do this. The first is toUpperCase, which translates the target String object to all uppercase. The second is toLowerCase, which translates the target String object to all lowercase. For example, see Listing 7.16.

Listing 7.16: Translating Case in Java
Using the toUpperCase and toLowerCase Methods

```
String str = new String("Java for RPG Programmers");
str = str.toUpperCase();
System.out.println("String in uppercase: " + str);
str = str.toLowerCase();
System.out.println("String in lowercase: " + str);
```

Compiling and running this example results in the following:

```
String in uppercase: JAVA IS FOR RPG USERS
String in lowercase: java is for rpg users
```

Note: The RPG example does not handle international characters, such as those containing an umlaut, while the Java methods do. That is because Java characters are Unicode-based, so they inherently support international characters.

Checking for characters

As with translating characters, RPG has language support to easily handle checking for the existence of characters, while Java does not have a supplied method. RPG has two op-codes, CHECK and CHECKR. These operations verify that each character in a given search string specified in factor one is among the characters in the base string specified in factor two. Each character in the given search string is compared with all of the characters specified in the base string. If a match exists, the next character is verified. Otherwise, the index value indicating the position of the unmatched character in the search string is placed in the result field, and the search is stopped. If a match is found for all characters in the search string, zero is returned in the result field. In the case of CHECK, verification of characters begins at the leftmost character, whereas for CHECKR, verification starts at the rightmost character. Listing 7.17 shows two examples, one for CHECK and the other for CHECKR.

Listing 7.17: Verifying Character Existence in RPG Using the CHECK and CHECKR Op-codes

```
D  NUMBERS      C                      CONST('0123456789')
D  pos          S              9 0
D  base         S              7A   INZ('*22300*')
C        NUMBERS     CHECK     base:2          pos
C        pos         DSPLY
C        NUMBERS     CHECKR    base:6          pos
C        pos         DSPLY
C                    EVAL      *INLR = *ON
```

Checking characters is most commonly used to check if a numeric field contains alphanumeric characters or vice versa. The example in Listing 7.17 checks to see if a string of numeric digits contains any alphanumeric characters. It starts by defining the set of numeric digits, zero through nine, and storing them in the constant field NUMBERS. The character field base is initialized to string "*22300*" and is the field to be checked. After executing the CHECK operation, the value in the result field is 7. It is not 1, as you may have expected, because the second part of factor two, which is the start position, contains 2. This tells the compiler to start verification at the second position.

The following CHECKR operation code uses similar parameters as the CHECK op-code, except that the start position is specified to be six, which is the position to start from. If a start position was not specified, it would default to the ending character position. The result after executing the CHECKR is one in the pos result field. Note also that the result field for both operations can be a numeric array.

As mentioned earlier, Java does not have methods similar to CHECK and CHECKR for character verification. As with character translation, you need to write your own methods to take care of this. Listing 7.18 contains the code to accomplish character verification. (Note that the same class name RPGString is used as in the previous example, thus building up a number of useful static string methods in this same class.)

Listing 7.18: Verifying Character Existence in Java Using check Methods

```
public static int check(String search, String base, int start)
{
    // minimal error checking
    if (start >= base.length() || start < 0)
      return -2;
    // scan each char of base for match in search...
    for (int idx = start; idx < base.length(); idx++)
        if (search.indexOf(base.charAt(idx)) == -1)
            return idx;
    // return constant indicating match found for all
    return -1;
}

public static int check(String search, String base)
{
    return check(search, base, 0);
}
```

Two check methods are defined to simulate RPG's CHECK op-code: one takes a starting position index and the other does not. The latter simply calls the former with zero for the starting position. The algorithm first checks the validity of the input parameters, then scans each character in the given base string for an occurrence in the given search string. If all characters have a match, the special constant -1 is returned. Otherwise, the index position of the first non-matching character in the base string is returned. To be consistent with Java String class methods, the methods accept a zero-based starting position and return a zero-based index position. Because of this, they cannot return zero when all characters match, as RPG does, because zero is a valid index position. For this reason, they return -1.

Listing 7.19 defines two more methods, this time to simulate CHECKR with and without a starting position parameter. These are similar to the check methods; the only changed lines are shown in bold. Basically, you need to loop backwards through the base string, and you need to default to the last character position when no start position parameter is passed.

**Listing 7.19: Verifying Character Existence
from the Right in Java with checkR Methods**

```java
public static int checkR(String search, String base, int start)
{
    // minimal error checking
    if (start >= base.length() || start < 0)
      return -2;
    // scan each char of base for match in search...
    for (int idx = start; idx >= 0; idx-)
       if (search.indexOf(base.charAt(idx)) == -1)
          return idx;
    // return constant indicating match found for all
    return -1;
}

public static int checkR(String search, String base)
{
    return checkR(search, base, base.length()-1);
}
```

Listing 7.20 shows the code in main to test these methods.

Listing 7.20: Testing the check and checkR Methods in Java

```java
String digits = "0123456789";
String test   = "*22300*";
int    result;
result = RPGString.check(digits, test);
System.out.println("result is: " + result);
result = RPGString.check(digits, test, 1);
System.out.println("result is: " + result);
result = RPGString.checkR(digits, test);
System.out.println("result is: " + result);
result = RPGString.checkR(digits, test, 5);
System.out.println("result is: " + result);
```

Compiling and running it gives the following:

```
result is: 0
result is: 6
result is: 6
result is: 0
```

The usual purpose in using the RPG CHECK op-code is to verify that a given string contains numeric data. This is possible in Java with our new check method. However, for completeness, we show you another way. The Character class discussed in Chapter 5 is a class version of the char data type in Java. You will find in this class a number of worthwhile methods, including one named isDigit. This is a static method that takes any single character and returns true if the character is a digit from zero to nine. So, to test a whole string, you can simply call this method for each of the characters, as shown in the isNumeric method in Listing 7.21.

Listing 7.21: A Method for Testing if a String Is All Numeric Digits

```
public static boolean isNumeric(String inputString)
{
    boolean allNumeric = true;
    for (int idx=0; idx<inputString.length() && allNumeric; idx++)
        if (!Character.isDigit(inputString.charAt(idx)))
            allNumeric = false;
    return allNumeric;
}
```

PERFORMANCE CONSIDERATIONS: THE StringBuffer CLASS

Recall the discussion at the beginning of the chapter about the concat method, and how it does not affect the String object on which you invoke it, but rather returns a new String object. You have seen that this is also true of other string manipulation methods like toUpperCase and replace. This is because the String class is *immutable*—that is, you cannot change a String object, you can only use methods that return new String objects. In many cases, the original string object is no longer used and is swept up by the garbage collector.

This read-only behavior of strings can have performance implications for calculations that do a lot of string manipulating. For example, this is true of any code that builds up a string by concatenating characters inside a loop. For this reason, Java supplies a second string class named StringBuffer that is *mutable*—it can be changed directly using supplied methods. This class is completely independent of the String class. That is, although some methods are common between the two, StringBuffer also has its own unique set of methods for altering the object directly, which you will see shortly.

If you need to dynamically change the strings in your method, you should use StringBuffer instead of String. Both classes support methods to convert back and forth

between them. For example, you can use a StringBuffer object to do your string manipulation, and then, once the string is complete, convert it back to a String object using the
toString method supplied in StringBuffer for this purpose. In fact, this conversion
back and forth between String and StringBuffer classes has the added advantage of allowing you to use methods available in both classes by simply converting from one class
to the other. You will almost always want to accept and return String objects, not
StringBuffer objects, from your methods, so this conversion is often done at the beginning and end of your method. For example, methods for significant string manipulations
might follow this format:

```
public String workOnString(String input)
{
    StringBuffer workString = new StringBuffer(input);
    // do manipulation work on the workString variable
    return workString.toString();
}
```

How do you declare a string using the StringBuffer class? You must use the formal way,
with the new operator, optionally specifying a string literal or String object as input:

```
StringBuffer aName = new StringBuffer("Angelica Farr");
```

There are no language extensions to allow intuitive instantiation like '= "this is a
string"' as there are for Strings. Similarly, there are no language extensions for easy
concatenation of StringBuffer objects using the plus sign as there are for Strings. (Of
course, use of + is allowed between StringBuffer objects inside the Sys-
tem.out.println parameter string, as it is for all data types.) To concatenate strings to a
StringBuffer object, use the append method:

```
StringBuffer quotedName = new StringBuffer("George");
quotedName.append(" and ").append("Phil");
```

Notice how this method does have a side effect on the object it works against, so you do not
need to equate the result to another variable as you would with the concat method in the
String class. This method returns the current StringBuffer object, so you can string together multiple method calls in one statement, as shown here. The append method is also
convenient in that there are many overridden versions of it supporting all the primitive data
types as the parameter, and conversion to a string literal is done for you, for example:

```
boolean flag = true;
StringBuffer output =
  new StringBuffer("flag value = ").append(flag);
System.out.println(output); // "flag value = true"
```

This results in the output "flag value = true". The append method also accepts String objects as input. In fact, it will accept any object as input! For objects, it simply calls the object's toString method to convert it to a string.

You do not always want to change your string by appending to it, sometimes you want to insert new strings into the middle of it. The StringBuffer class supports this with an insert method, with a number of overridden methods similar to append, allowing all manner of data types to be inserted after being converted to string format. All versions of the insert method take an integer insertion-point index as the first parameter and the actual string or other data type to be inserted as the second parameter, as in:

```
StringBuffer string1 = new StringBuffer("GORE");
string1.insert(1,"E");
string1.insert(4,"G");
System.out.println(string1);
```

This results in the output "GEORGE". Notice the insertion point given is the character position *before* the desired insertion point. In addition to append and insert, there are setChar and getChar methods for changing a particular character value in place and retrieving the character value at a specified zero-based position. A method named getChars can return a substring, but in the form of a character array, not a String. This could, however, be converted to a StringBuffer by using the version of append or insert that accepts a character array as input.

There is also an interesting method named reverse that reverses the content of a string, such that "Java" would become "avaJ". Presumably, there is a use for this somewhere! Maybe it's used for writing out the letters "ECNALUBMA" on the front of ambulances!

StringBuffer objects support the notion of *capacity*—a buffer length that is greater than or equal to the length of the string literal contained in the StringBuffer. Behind the scenes, the StringBuffer class uses an array of characters to hold the string. The array is given an initial default size, and as the string grows, the array often needs to be reallocated with a bigger size. This behind-the-scenes work is done for you, but there are methods to explicitly set the size (i.e., the capacity) of this buffer. You can thereby optimize performance by predicting the final size you will eventually require, minimizing the need for costly reallocations. It is by judicious use of capacity planning that you can most benefit from using a StringBuffer as a scratchpad to build up a computed string.

When instantiating an empty StringBuffer, you can specify the initial capacity by passing in an integer value, like this:

```
StringBuffer largeString = new StringBuffer(255);
```

Note that the default capacity for an empty StringBuffer object is 16. Aside from setting the initial capacity at instantiation time, you can also use the ensureCapacity method to ensure that the current buffer is at least as large as the number you pass as an argument. If it is not, the buffer size or capacity is grown to the size you specified. Despite the method name, ensureCapacity does not return a boolean value—in fact, it does not return anything. There is also a method for returning the current capacity, which is named capacity. It takes no arguments, and returns an integer value. This notion of capacity and its two methods is also available in other classes in Java that contain growable lists, such as the Vector class discussed in Chapter 6.

While you have ensureCapacity and capacity methods for working with a StringBuffer object's buffer size, you also have setLength and length methods for working with the actual string's size. This is always less than or equal to the capacity. You can use setLength to grow or shrink the string's size, effectively padding it (with null characters, which are hex zeros) or truncating it. Note that if you set the length of the string to be greater than the capacity, the capacity is automatically grown, just as it is when you grow a string past its capacity using append. On the other hand, if you truncate a string, the capacity is not reduced. Listing 7.22 will help you see the difference between capacity and length.

Listing 7.22: The Difference between Length and Capacity in the StringBuffer Class

```
public class TestStringBuffer
{
   public static void main(String args[])
   {
      StringBuffer test1 = new StringBuffer(20); // capacity
      test1.append("12345678901234567890"); // string
      System.out.println();
      System.out.println("String   = \"" + test1 + "\"");
```

Listing 7.22: The Difference between
Length and Capacity in the StringBuffer Class (continued)

```
            System.out.println("Capacity = " + test1.capacity());
            System.out.println("Length   = " + test1.length());
            test1.setLength(50); // string length
            System.out.println("------------------");
            System.out.println("String   = \"" + test1 + "\"");
            System.out.println("Capacity = " + test1.capacity());
            System.out.println("Length   = " + test1.length());
            test1.setLength(10); // string length
            System.out.println("------------------");
            System.out.println("String   = \"" + test1 + "\"");
            System.out.println("Capacity = " + test1.capacity());
            System.out.println("Length   = " + test1.length());
        } // end main method
    } // end TestStringBuffer class
```

Running this class results in the following:

```
String   = "12345678901234567890"
Capacity = 20
Length   = 20
------------------------------------
String   = "12345678901234567890
Capacity = 50
Length   = 50
------------------------------------
String   = "1234567890"
Capacity = 50
Length   = 10
```

The length is always the current number of characters held in the buffer, while the capacity is the maximum number of characters the buffer can hold without having to be resized internally. Notice how calling `setLength` with a value of 50 extends the actual string itself to be 50 characters long, but it uses the null character (all zeros) to pad, so you never see the ending quote. You'd have to subsequently replace all those null characters with blanks to get what you probably wanted. Also notice how the capacity always increases in size when needed, while it never decreases in size automatically.

IMPLEMENTING trimr AND triml IN JAVA

Now let's go back to the `trim` operation and see how to implement trim-right and trim-left functionality in Java. A previous section showed how both RPG and Java have built-in functions for simultaneously trimming both leading and trailing blanks. It also mentioned that RPG has built-in functions for explicitly stripping either trailing-only or leading-only blanks, using the %TRIMR or %TRIML functions. In Java, however, you must implement this functionality yourself if you need it, which you will see shortly. First, Listing 7.23 reviews these built-in functions in RPG.

Listing 7.23: Trimming Leading and Trailing Blanks in RPG with %TRIML and %TRIMR

```
D input            S                 16A    INZ('   Java for U    ')
D result           S                 16A
C                        EVAL        result = %TRIML(input) + '.'
C       result           DSPLY
C                        EVAL        result = %TRIMR(input) + '.'
C       result           DSPLY
C                        EVAL        *INLR = *ON
```

The input string is "   Java for U   ". Predictably, the result after %TRIML is "Java for U   .", and the result after %TRIMR is "   Java for U." Note that the concatenating of the period after the trim right lets you see the result before RPG pads the result field back to its declared length. That would not be necessary if the VARYING keyword had been defined on the result field. It is that easy to trim leading or trailing blanks in RPG, since the language directly supports it.

Java, on the other hand, has no supplied methods in either its String or StringBuffer classes, so you must write your own. With the use of the StringBuffer class previously discussed, however, this is not very difficult. You again create two methods as static, pass in as a parameter the string to operate on, and place the methods in an RPGString class. To be consistent with RPG, call the two methods trimr and triml. Because you will be doing a reasonable amount of manipulation on the strings, start out in both cases by creating a StringBuffer temporary object from the given String object, and in both methods end by using the toString method of StringBuffer to convert the scratchpad object back to a String that can be returned. The trimr method is the easiest, as you just need to find that last non-blank character and truncate the StringBuffer at that point, using the setLength method. Listing 7.24 shows this. Note that this method has to test for the case when it is given a string that is all blanks, in which case it just does setLength(0).

Listing 7.24: Trimming Trailing Blanks in Java with a trimr Method

```
public static String trimR(String input)
{
    if (input.length() == 0) // error checking
        return input;
    StringBuffer temp = new StringBuffer(input);
```

Listing 7.24: Trimming Trailing Blanks in Java with a trimr Method (continued)

```java
    int idx = temp.length()-1;
    // find last non-blank character
    while ( (idx >= 0) &&
            (temp.charAt(idx) == ' ') )
      idx-;
    // truncate string
    if (idx >= 0)
      temp.setLength(idx+1);
    else
      temp.setLength(0);
    return temp.toString();
} // end trimR method
```

The `triml` method is a little more complicated because it involves shifting the characters left, from the first non-blank character. This is best accomplished by brute-force, character-by-character copying. The most efficient way to do this is to use a `StringBuffer` object that has been initialized to a sufficient capacity, as with the `temp2` variable in Listing 7.25.

Listing 7.25: Trimming Leading Blanks in Java with a triml Method

```java
public static String trimL(String input)
{
    if (input.length() == 0) // error checking
      return input;
    StringBuffer temp1 = new StringBuffer(input);
    int idx, idx2;
    // find last non-blank character
    idx = 0;
    while ( (idx < temp1.length()) &&
            (temp1.charAt(idx) == ' ') )
      idx++;
    // truncate string
    if (idx < temp1.length())
      {
        // copy characters to new object
        int newSize = temp1.length() - idx;
        StringBuffer temp2 = new StringBuffer(newSize);
        for (idx2 = 0; idx2 < newSize; idx2++, idx++)
            temp2.append(temp1.charAt(idx));
        return temp2.toString();
      }
    else
      {
        temp1.setLength(0);
        return temp1.toString();
      }
} // end trimL method
```

Again, some additional complexity is added by the need to handle the case when an all-blank string is given as input.

As usual, we write test-case code in the `main` method to drive and demonstrate these new methods, including the all-blank test case, which is shown in Listing 7.26.

Listing 7.26: Testing the triml and trimr Methods

```
System.out.println("------------------------");
System.out.println("Testing trimR method...");
System.out.println("------------------------");
String paddedString = "   Java For RPG Programmers   ";
String trimmedRight = RPGString.trimR(paddedString);
System.out.println("\"" + trimmedRight + "\"");
String blankString = "                              ";
trimmedRight = RPGString.trimR(blankString);
System.out.println("\"" + trimmedRight + "\"");
System.out.println("------------------------");
System.out.println("Testing trimL method...");
System.out.println("------------------------");
paddedString = "   Java For RPG Programmers   ";
String trimmedLeft = RPGString.trimL(paddedString);
System.out.println("\"" + trimmedLeft + "\"");
trimmedLeft = RPGString.trimL(blankString);
System.out.println("\"" + trimmedLeft + "\"");
```

The result of compiling and running this is what you would expect:

```
------------------------
Testing trimR method...
------------------------
"   Java For RPG Programmers"
""
------------------------
Testing trimL method...
------------------------
"Java For RPG Programmers   "
""
```

Easy enough? Not really, we admit, but then again, now you can simply call these methods. However, for completeness, we should also mention there are alternatives that are more inefficient but easier to code. To trim only leading or only trailing blanks, for example, you could use the `String` `trim` method if you first take care to add a non-blank character to the appropriate end of the string before the trim operation, then remove it after, like this:

```
String input = "   a test   ";
String trimmedLeft, trimmedRight;
trimmedLeft = (input + '.').trim();
trimmedLeft = trimmedLeft.substring(0,trimmedLeft.length()-1);
trimmedRight = ('.' + input).trim();
trimmedRight = trimmedRight.substring(1);
```

TOKENIZING STRINGS: THE StringTokenizer CLASS

Often, when writing string-parsing code, you will want to extract individual words. Java recognizes this need and supplies a utility class in the java.util package named StringTokenizer that does this automatically. This is a good class to know about, as it can save significant coding effort in those cases where a word-by-word extraction of a given string is required. It is instantiated by specifying the String object to parse. Subsequent iteration through the words, or *tokens*, is accomplished by the two methods hasMoreTokens and nextToken, as shown in Listing 7.27.

Listing 7.27: Testing the StringTokenizer Class in Java

```
public static void main(String args[])
{
    String inputString = "Mary had a little lamb";
    StringTokenizer tokens = new StringTokenizer(inputString);
    String nextToken;

    System.out.println();
    while (tokens.hasMoreTokens())
    {
        nextToken = tokens.nextToken();
        System.out.println(nextToken);
    }
}
```

Running this gives the following:

```
Mary
had
a
little
lamb
```

What delimits or separates words or tokens? By default, it is blank spaces, but this can be explicitly specified at instantiation time, by entering all delimiting characters as a string, for example:

```
String sample = "  $123,456.78 ";
StringTokenizer words = new StringTokenizer(sample, " $,.");
```

This specifies four delimiter characters: the blank, dollar sign, comma, and period. You can also specify delimiters as part of the nextToken method call, in the event they are different per token. For your information, the above little example yields the tokens "123", "456", and "78".

This same functionality requires a little more work in RPG, as you have to write it yourself. However, the code is not so difficult, as shown in Listing 7.28. Since you are a seasoned RPG IV programmer by now, we will not dissect this example, but rather leave that to you. In fact, we recommend that you turn this into a reusable procedure.

Listing 7.28: Scanning for Delimiter Characters in RPG

```
D formula         C                      'A * 2 / 3 - Num'
D tempstr         S             10A
D start           S              2P 0 INZ(1)
D end             S              2P 0 INZ(0)
C                 DOW       (start <= %LEN(formula))
C                 EVAL      end = %SCAN(' ':formula:start)
C                 IF        end = 0
C                 EVAL      end = %LEN(formula)+1
C                 ENDIF
C                 EVAL      tempstr=
C                               %SUBST(formula:start:end-start)
C       tempstr   DSPLY
C                 EVAL      start=end+1
C                 ENDDO
C                 EVAL      *INLR = *ON
```

THE STRING CLASS: MORE METHODS

There are a number of remaining methods in the String class that offer additional functionality beyond what RPG supplies. Rather than describe them all, we leave them to your own discovery. However, Table 7.3 provides a brief summary of some of the more interesting ones. Refer to the JDK documentation for the java.lang.String class for more detailed information.

Table 7.3 Commonly Used String Methods	
Method	**Description**
compareTo(String)	Compares two strings lexicographically.
copyValueOf(char[],int,int)	Returns a string that is equivalent to the specified character array.
endsWith(String) and startsWith(String)	Tests if this string ends with or starts with the given substring.
equals(String) and equalsIgnoreCase(String)	Compares this string to the specified object.
getBytes()	Convert this string to a byte array.
getChars(int, int, char[], int)	Copies a substring into the destination character array, starting at the given offset.
regionMatches(int,String, int,int)	Tests if two string regions are equal.
toCharArray()	Converts this string to a new character array.
toLowerCase() and toUpperCase()	Folds all of the characters in this string to lowercase or uppercase.
valueOf(xxx)	Takes as input a primitive data type value and converts it to a string.

SUMMARY

This chapter introduced you to the following concepts:

- Strings are objects in Java and instances of the `String` class.

- There is built-in language support for defining and concatenating strings.

- To test for equality of strings, you do not use the equals operator (==) in Java. Rather, you use the `equals` or `equalsIgnoreCase` method supplied as part of the `String` class.

- A number of `String` class methods offer similar functionality to RPG's string op-codes and built-ins. However, there is also some missing functionality relative to RPG, for which you can write your own code. On the other hand, strings in Java offer much new functionality.

- The `StringBuffer` class can be used to write efficient code for changing or manipulating strings. This is necessary because the `String` class is read-only, or immutable.

- The `StringTokenizer` class offers a quick and easy way to parse out words, or tokens, from a given string.

We hope this discussion of strings did not tie you in knots!

DATE AND TIME MANIPULATION

Chapter 6 mentions that programmers need arrays (not to mention "a raise"). Dare we say that programmers need a date, too? Well, maybe, but only if there's time!

Functions that manipulate dates and times are among the most important in any application. These functions include retrieving the current date and time, and manipulations such as adding a duration to a date, subtracting a duration from a date, extracting parts of a date, and formatting a date or time. Both RPG and Java require this fundamental functionality, and both languages include built-in support for it.

Before RPG IV, RPG programmers had a special set of keywords to retrieve a date, day, month, or year. These are the UDATE, UDAY, UMONTH, and UYEAR keywords, respectively. In addition, to retrieve the time from the system, the TIME op-code was used with a variable in the result field. The specified field could be six digits long, indicating that only the time should be retrieved, or 12 digits long, indicating that both the date and time should be retrieved.

In V2R2 of RPG III, IBM introduced a new set of keywords: *DATE, *DAY, *MONTH, and *YEAR. These keywords offered four-digit years versus the two-digit years of their predecessors. Given a four-digit field, *YEAR and *DATE return the century portion of the date in addition to the year. For example, if the date is July 22, 1961, then *DATE returns 07221961, whereas UDATE returns 072261. The *DAY and *MONTH keywords are identical to UDAY and UMONTH and were added simply to provide consistency with their predecessors. With this introduction of four-digit years to RPG, the TIME operation has also been modified to accept a field 14 digits long. This tells the compiler that you want the century portion of the date retrieved, as well as the year.

RPG IV DATE AND TIME ENHANCEMENTS

With RPG IV in V3R1, new data types were introduced, namely D, T, and Z (for date, time, and timestamp, respectively). These are consistent with the same data types added to the database DDS languages in V2R1.1 of the operating system.

With this new set of data types, the language also added support for op-codes to allow the RPG programmer to easily manipulate dates and times. The ADDDUR and SUBDUR operations allow you to add and subtract a specific duration from a given date or time. The EXTRCT op-code allows you to extract a portion of a date or time from a field and place the result in the result field. In addition, the TEST operation code validates the contents of a date, time, or timestamp data type field. Further, RPG IV adds support for many known international date, time, and timestamp formats through keywords on the D (Definition) and H (Header) specifications. For example, you can tell the compiler that you want to use the *DMY date format for day/month/year representation (dd/mm/yyyy), or you can specify you want to use the *USA format for month/day/year representation (mm/dd/yyyy). You will learn about this in more detail later in this chapter.

JAVA DATE AND TIME SUPPORT

Java does not offer primitive types for dates and times, as you might have noticed in the discussion of primitive types in Chapter 5. Rather, it offers classes to represent dates and times. These classes are rich with methods to retrieve, compare, add, subtract, extract, format, and test both dates and times. Again, you will see here the power and elegance of classes and objects in their ability to encapsulate in one place all the algorithms and functions needed to fully support a particular concept—and the ability to easily reuse that well-tested code, forever, in all applications. It happens that the Java engineers designed and wrote these classes for you, but you should be thinking by now of other classes you could write to encapsulate other code you have found yourself writing and rewriting time and again.

Java's support for dates and times can be broken down into the areas shown in Table 8.1, which also shows the classes supplied to address those areas, and the comparable RPG functionality. Note that Java does not separate date and time into different classes, but rather encapsulates them into a single object and gives you the ability to set, extract, and manipulate just the parts you are interested in.

Table 8.1: Java Date/Time Support at a Glance

Date/Time Function	Java Class	RPG Function
Raw time in milliseconds	currentTimeMillis method in System class in java.lang	Not available
A simple date and time object	Date class in java.util	*DATE and TIME
Advanced date and time with support for manipulation, comparison, and extraction	GregorianCalendar class in java.util	D, T, and Z data types, plus ADDDUR, SUBDUR, TEST, and EXTRCT op-codes
Date and time formatting	SimpleDateFormat class in java.text	DATFMT and TIMFMT keywords
Multiple time-zone support	TimeZone class in java.util	Not available

This chapter shows you some of the date and time capabilities of Java, which hint at the rich functionality it supports.

RAW TIME

Every computer contains a built-in clock as part of its hardware, which (surprise) keeps track of time. This clock is used by the CPU (Central Processing Unit) for hardware purposes, as well as by the operating system to establish the current date and time when you turn on your machine. In fact, if you have ever wondered how the clock stays accurate while your machine's main power supply is off, it typically uses a battery. The clock, unlike the one you have hanging on the wall, keeps track of time in milliseconds. Such precision is necessary for computers, of course, while your kitchen clock can easily live without it (depending on the precision of your recipes).

What are these milliseconds based on? If you write a little program to read the clock from your hardware, you will end up with numbers such as 6874732864982. These are the total number of milliseconds that have elapsed since a universally recognized time and date in history, called the *epoch*. In the case of RPG, the base year, or epoch, is January 1, 1940. In the case of Java, the base year is January 1, 1970. The number returned means that the clock inside your computer is continually incrementing its count of milliseconds. When your program asks for that value, the clock returns the number of milliseconds it has counted, in the case of Java, since January 1, 1970.

This base-line epoch date provides a standard from which computers or programming languages do their date and time manipulation. For example, the `currentTimeMillis` static method in the class `System` in package `java.lang` returns the number of milliseconds from the computer clock. An example of it is shown in Listing 8.1.

Listing 8.1: Retrieving the Current Time in Milliseconds, in Java

```
public class MyTimeMilliseconds
{
    public static void main(String args[])
    {
        long timeInMil;
        timeInMil = System.currentTimeMillis();
        System.out.println("Time is: " + timeInMil);
    }
}
```

This example calls the method `currentTimeMillis` in the Java-supplied class `System` to retrieve the number of milliseconds elapsed from the base date. Notice that this method returns a long primitive value containing the number of milliseconds. Is this useful? Well, sometimes it is, such as when you want to calculate the elapsed time for a particular operation. You can simply record this value at the beginning of the operation, and again at the end of the operation, and then take the difference to determine how long it took. You could divide the difference by 1,000 to get the number of seconds, if you wanted.

Here's an opportunity for your own little utility class! Assuming you might need to record elapsed time during the performance-tuning part of your development, why not design a little class that will do this? It will have two instance variables to record the start and end times, and two methods to set them. It will also supply a method to subsequently return the elapsed time in terms of milliseconds. It would also be nice to return the elapsed time in the form of a string in the format "hh hours, mm minutes, ss seconds, nn milliseconds." This will make it easy to write the elapsed time in a human-readable format. The ElapsedTime class for this is shown in Listing 8.2.

Listing 8.2: A Class for Recording Elapsed Time

```java
public class ElapsedTime
{
    private long startTime;
    private long endTime;

    public void setStartTime()
    {
        startTime = System.currentTimeMillis();
    }
    public void setEndTime()
    {
        endTime = System.currentTimeMillis();
    }
    public long getElapsedTime()
    {
        return (endTime - startTime);
    }
    public String toString()
    {
        long deltaMillis = getElapsedTime();
        // deltaMillis = n + s*1000 + m*60*1000 + h*60*60*1000;
        long millis      = (deltaMillis) %1000;
        long deltaSeconds = (deltaMillis) /1000;
        long deltaMinutes = deltaSeconds   / 60;
        long deltaHours   = deltaSeconds   / (60 * 60);
        long hours   = (int)(deltaMillis    / (60 * 60 * 1000));
        long minutes= (int)(deltaMinutes - (hours*60) );
        long seconds= (int)(deltaSeconds - (hours*60*60) -
                            (minutes*60));
        String result = "Elapsed time: "
                        + hours   + " hours, "
                        + minutes + " minutes, "
                        + seconds + " seconds, "
                        + millis  + " milliseconds";
        return result;
    }
} // end class ElapsedTime
```

This class is simple enough that we don't need to dissect it. However, note that it does not use static methods because you want to allow for multiple objects of this class simultaneously, each recording different times in their instance variables. The interesting method is the toString method, which is a standard method in Java. If you supply it, then the System.out.println method will call it when it is given an object of this class as a parameter. To use this class to record elapsed time, simply instantiate an object of it, then call setStartTime before the operation starts, and setEndTime after the operation ends. You can then call System.out.println, passing the object, to see the results printed to the console. Listing 8.3 shows an example.

Listing 8.3: Putting the ElapsedTime Class to Use

```
public class TestElapsedTime
{
    public static void main(String args[])
    {
        ElapsedTime timeRecorder = new ElapsedTime();

        // how long to append 1,000 blanks to a String
        timeRecorder.setStartTime(); // start recording
        String bigString = " ";
        for (int idx=0; idx<10000; idx++)
            bigString += " "; // append a blank to the string
        timeRecorder.setEndTime(); // end recording
        System.out.println(timeRecorder);

        // how long to append 1,000 blanks to a StringBuffer
        timeRecorder.setStartTime(); // start recording
        StringBuffer bigStringBuffer = new StringBuffer(" ");
        for (int idx=0; idx<10000; idx++)
            bigStringBuffer.append(" "); // append a blank
        timeRecorder.setEndTime(); // end recording
        System.out.println(timeRecorder);
    }
}
```

When we tested this class, we got the following:

```
Elapsed time: 0 hours, 0 minutes, 1 seconds, 963 milliseconds
Elapsed time: 0 hours, 0 minutes, 0 seconds, 10 milliseconds
```

This proves that StringBuffer is much more efficient than String! You can also time multiple operations simultaneously, simply by instantiating as many instances of the class as you need. (This is the beauty of objects.) One enhancement you might want to make is to define a default constructor that calls setStartTime, so that users don't have to explicitly call it when they instantiate the object at the right time.

GET ME A DATE, AND GIVE ME THE TIME!

Getting the current time in terms of milliseconds from the epoch is nice, but certainly not a usual thing to do. Rather, the most pressing requirement is to get the current date and time from the system in a form that is meaningful—a form that lets you extract or display it in terms of the year, month, day, hour, minute, and/or second. This is what you have always done in RPG using the TIME op-code, as shown in Listing 8.4.

Listing 8.4: Retrieving the Current Date and Time in RPG with the TIME Op-code

```
C       GETDATTME    BEGSR
C                    TIME            DTTM           14 0
C                    ENDSR
```

As mentioned earlier, the TIME op-code retrieves the time as well as the date. This example creates a simple subroutine that retrieves the date and time and puts them in the field DTTM. Notice the length of the field. It has a length of 14 to indicate to the system that you need not only the time, but the date as well. This also tells the compiler and the system that you need the date to have a four-digit year. You can also specify a date, time, or timestamp field (D, T, or Z) in the result field. Of course, this subroutine would be better coded as a procedure!

Java supplies you with the Date class in package java.util, which retrieves the current date and time when instantiated. Listing 8.5 shows an example.

Listing 8.5: Retrieving the Current Date and Time in Java with the Date Class

```
import java.util.*;
public class MyTime
{
    public static void main(String args[])
    {
        Date today = new Date();
        System.out.println("Date and time is: " + today);
    }
}
```

This example defines and instantiates an object of type Date named today. The object is used directly in the call to println, which results in something like this:

```
Date and time is: Wed Aug 08 21:44:52 EDT 2001
```

Note that the class must have its own toString method that returns a String with a default format. In fact, this format will be different depending on the time zone your computer is set for.

In RPG, once you retrieve the date and time fields, you "manipulate" them using the various supplied date- and time-specific op-codes. The same applies to Java applications, but instead of op-codes, you use supplied methods in either the Date class or (as you will see) the GregorianCalendar class, which is also in the java.util package.

The Date class is the basic class in Java for representing a date and time in terms of years, months, days, hours, minutes, seconds, and milliseconds. It was supplied in the original class version of Java, and it is still used when all you want is a simple date object, and you do not need to manipulate it. However, since JDK 1.0, this class has been *deprecated*, meaning it is no longer preferred when the intention is to manipulate or compare dates. Instead, a new class named GregorianCalendar specializes in date manipulations, like adding or subtracting durations. Internally, GregorianCalendar still uses a Date object to store the actual date, and supplies the method getTime (strangely) to get it. This is still needed because the Date object is still the preferred object to use for displaying dates with System.out.println, since it formats them nicely (a topic covered in more detail later). Thus, the preferred way to get the current date is to instantiate GregorianCalendar, and the easiest way to display that date is to use getTime to display the resulting Date object, as shown in Listing 8.6. This results in the same output as Listing 8.5.

Listing 8.6: Retrieving the Current Date
and Time in Java with the GregorianCalendar Class

```
import java.util.*; // for GregorianCalendar class

public class GetDate
{
    public static void main(String args[])
    {
        GregorianCalendar today = new GregorianCalendar();
        System.out.println("Date and time is: " + today.getTime());
    }
}
```

You can also use other constructors in Date and GregorianCalendar to create specific date and times versus the current date and time. For example, Date has a constructor that takes a long value that represents a number of milliseconds from the epoch, such as System's method currentTimeMillis returns. Using this will create an object for the date and time that the millisecond value represents. The Date class also has a method getTime that returns the milliseconds from the epoch value this object represents. The GregorianCalendar class has constructors for specifying (as integer values) the year, month, and day, or the year, month, day, hour, minute, and second, as shown in Listing 8.7.

Listing 8.7: Using the GregorianCalendar Class to Represent Any Date

```
GregorianCalendar xmas01    = new GregorianCalendar(2001,11,25);
GregorianCalendar xmas01noon = new GregorianCalendar(2001,11,25,12,0,0);
System.out.println(xmas01.getTime());
System.out.println(xmas01noon.getTime());
```

Note that the month, and *only* the month, is specified as zero-based. The result of Listing 8.7 is this:

```
Tue Dec 25 00:00:00 EST 2001
Tue Dec 25 12:00:00 EST 2001
```

There are also constants defined in GregorianCalendar for the months, so you do not have to remember to zero-base them. The constants are the actual English names for the months, all in uppercase as per the standard for names of constants, for example, GregorianCalendar.DECEMBER. The JDK documentation does not actually show these constants, as they come from the parent class Calendar, which you have to look up to see all the handy constants defined there, such as the constants for days of the week. (This concept of parent and child classes is discussed in Chapter 9.)

While GregorianCalendar does not have a constructor that takes a Date object, it does have a setTime method that takes one and sets the internal date from it. There might be times when you have a Date object and wish to make it a GregorianCalendar object. This can be done using this method after instantiation, as in:

```
Date dateObject = new Date();
GregorianCalendar gcObject = new GregorianCalendar();
gcObject.setTime(dateObject);
```

One last and important thing to note about date objects is how to store them in a database. In the discussion of database access in Chapter 13, you will see that you can retrieve database date, time, and timestamp fields directly into objects of class type `Date`, `Time`, and `Timestamp` in package `java.sql`. These are all child classes of the `Date` class, so they can be used directly as though they were `Date` objects. This means you can turn one into a `GregorianCalendar` object, for example, by calling the `setTime` method. To go the other way, and create these objects from your `GregorianCalendar` objects (for the purpose of writing to the database), one option is to use the constructor in these that takes a long value representing the milliseconds from the epoch. You can get this value from a `GregorianCalendar` object by calling its `getTimeInMillis` method, like this:

```
GregorianCalendar gc = new GregorianCalendar();
java.sql.Date databaseDate =
  new java.sql.Date(gc.getTimeInMillis());
```

Note how this example uses class names qualified with the package name, versus importing the package. As discussed in Chapter 2, either way is okay.

DATE AND TIME MANIPULATION

We've spent enough time on how to get a date! The next sections discuss how to compare and manipulate our dates.

Date/time math and duration

RPG introduced the ADDDUR and SUBDUR op-codes with the introduction of the new language definition of RPG IV in V3R1. These op-codes enable you to add a specific duration to a date or subtract it from a base date. You can add or subtract days, months, or years from a given date by specifying the second part of factor two. In addition to subtracting a number from a date by extending factor two to indicate the type of number being subtracted, you can subtract one date from another date, and indicate in the result field what units to give the results in. This saves a lot of math on your part, as shown in Listing 8.8.

Listing 8.8: Date Durations with the SUBDUR and ADDDUR Op-codes in RPG

```
DstartD           S              D    DATFMT(*ISO) INZ(D'2001-08-18')
DendD             S              D    DATFMT(*ISO) INZ(D'2001-08-28')
Dresult           S             10P 0
DresultD          S              D
```

Listing 8.8: Date Durations with the SUBDUR and ADDDUR Op-codes in RPG (continued)

```
C*
C        endD         SUBDUR     startD          result:*D
C        result       dsply
C        endD         SUBDUR     10:*D           resultD
C        resultD      dsply
C        startD       ADDDUR     10:*D           resultD
C        resultD      dsply
C                     eval       *inlr = *on
```

This example first subtracts the end date (endD) from the start date (startD), and stores the difference in a numeric field (result) that will hold the number of days, as specified by the *D in the second part of the result. (The result is 10.) Next, it subtracts 10 days from the end date (endD) and stores the result in a date field (resultD). Finally, it adds 10 days to the start date (startD) and stores the result in a date field (resultD). The results of these last two operations are 2001-08-18 and 2001-08-28, respectively.

Table 8.2 lists the different options you can specify in the second part of factor two or the result field to indicate the type of the addition or subtraction you would like to accomplish. For example, if you wanted to determine the difference in number of months between two dates, you would specify *MONTHS or *M in the second part of the result field.

Table 8.2: RPG Keywords for Specifying the Date/Time Parts to Add/Subtract

Date Part	Keyword	Short Form
Year	*YEARS	*Y
Month	*MONTHS	*M
Day	*DAYS	*D
Hour	*HOURS	*H
Minute	*MINUTES	*MN
Second	*SECONDS	*S
Microsecond	*MSECONDS	*MS

Java uses the GregorianCalendar class to do date duration. Indeed, manipulating dates is the primary purpose of the GregorianCalendar versus its simpler cousin the Date class. While Date objects just store a date and allow simple operations such as displaying it,

GregorianCalendar objects allow for complicated operations such as date comparisons and duration computation. To do this, of course, it has to have complicated, built-in algorithms that have a deep knowledge of the Gregorian calendar. (Versus, say, the Chinese calendar, which would require a different set of algorithms. There is no calendar other than Gregorian supported in Java today, but the architecture is there to easily allow others to be written. They are expected in the future, and may exist by the time you read this.)

The GregorianCalendar class has the method add, which allows you to add a date part, such as days or months or years, to a date. This will change the internal date value appropriately, as shown in Listing 8.9.

Listing 8.9: Date Durations with the add Method in Java's GregorianCalendar

```
import java.util.*;

public class AddDateDurations
{
    public static void main(String args[])
    {
        GregorianCalendar gc = new GregorianCalendar(2001,11,31);
        System.out.println();
        System.out.println("Before addition.....: " + gc.getTime());
        gc.add(GregorianCalendar.DATE,2);
        System.out.println("After adding 2 days : " + gc.getTime());
        gc.add(GregorianCalendar.YEAR,2);
        System.out.println("After adding 2 years: " + gc.getTime());
    }
} // end AddDateDurations
```

This example uses the GregorianCalendar class to do the date manipulation. It first instantiates the GregorianCalendar class with parameters to give an object representing December 31, 2001. Next, it does some date manipulation using the GregorianCalendar class. After printing the current date in the calendar, it uses the add method supplied in the GregorianCalendar class to add two days to the current day, and then adds two years to that. The result is printed after each addition:

```
Before addition.....: Mon Dec 31 00:00:00 EST 2001
After adding 2 days : Wed Jan 02 00:00:00 EST 2002
After adding 2 years: Fri Jan 02 00:00:00 EST 2004
```

What, then, tells the add method which part of the date you are adding? For example, how does it know you want the day, not the year? As you can see from the example, this is the purpose of the first parameter used in the call, which is a Java-supplied constant.

Java uses the constants YEAR, MONTH, DATE, HOUR, MINUTE, SECOND, and MILLISECOND to distinguish the type of addition. This is equivalent to the second part of factor two entered in RPG IV. As you recall, RPG uses *D, *M, or *Y in the second part of factor two to distinguish the type of addition. In both languages, the hard work of rolling all affected date parts is done for you.

Here is another example that illustrates this date "rolling" behavior in Java:

```
GregorianCalendar gc = new GregorianCalendar(2001,10,30);
System.out.println("The date before addition: " + gc.getTime());
gc.add(GregorianCalendar.DATE,2);
System.out.println("The date after addition:  " + gc.getTime());
gc.add(GregorianCalendar.MONTH,2);
System.out.println("The date after addition:  " + gc.getTime());
gc.add(GregorianCalendar.DATE,26);
System.out.println("The date after addition:  " + gc.getTime());
gc.add(GregorianCalendar.DATE,1);
System.out.println("The date after addition:  " + gc.getTime());
```

This gives exactly the results you would hope for:

```
The date before addition: Fri Nov 30 00:00:00 EST 2001
The date after addition:  Sun Dec 02 00:00:00 EST 2001
The date after addition:  Sat Feb 02 00:00:00 EST 2002
The date after addition:  Thu Feb 28 00:00:00 EST 2002
The date after addition:  Fri Mar 01 00:00:00 EST 2002
```

Table 8.3 compares the keywords available in RPG to the constants available in Java.

Table 8.3: Java Versus RPG Constants for Identifying Date/Time Parts

Date Part	RPG	Java
Year	*YEARS or *Y	GregorianCalendar.YEAR
Month	*MONTHS or *M	GregorianCalendar.MONTH
Day	*DAYS or *D	GregorianCalendar.DATE
Hour	*HOURS or *H	GregorianCalendar.HOUR
Minute	*MINUTES or *MN	GregorianCalendar.MINUTE
Second	*SECONDS or *S	GregorianCalendar.SECOND
Millisecond	*MSECONDS or *MS	GregorianCalendar.MILLIS ECOND

If the add method is equivalent to the ADDDUR op-code, what is equivalent to the SUBDUR op-code? The answer is the add method again! Adding a negative number is equivalent to subtracting. For example, adding the following two lines of code to the previous example will result in subtracting four years from the current date (be careful—you might go back in time!):

```
gc.add(Calendar.YEAR,-4);
System.out.println("The date after deletion:  " + gc.getTime());
```

How do you get the number of years, days, or months between two given dates? Unfortunately, there is no method supplied by Java to do this (which is a shame). However, it is possible to write the code yourself. Just call the currentTimeInMillis method on both of the GregorianCalendar objects, and subtract the larger from the smaller. Then divide the difference by 1000*60*60*24 to get the number of elapsed days, for example. If you want to print the difference in a nice way, use the ElapsedTime class from Listing 8.2.

Comparing dates

In RPG, you can simply use comparative op-codes like IF to find out if a date is before, after, or equal to another date value. How is this done in Java? Remember that dates are objects in Java, not primitive types, so operators like ==, <, and > will not work to compare to objects. These operators would only compare the memory addresses, which is not what you want. Instead, the GregorianCalendar class provides the methods equals, before, and after to perform these comparisons. Listing 8.10 shows how the before method determines whether a date is before another date.

Listing 8.10: Comparing Dates with
the before Method in Java's GregorianCalendar

```
import java.util.*;
public class CompareDates
{
    public static void main (String args[])
    {
        GregorianCalendar gc1 = new GregorianCalendar(2000, 11, 31);
        GregorianCalendar gc2 = new GregorianCalendar(2001, 0, 1);
        if (gc1.before(gc2))
          System.out.println("Yes it is");
        else
          System.out.println("No it is not");
    }
}
```

This example creates two GregorianCalendar objects, gc1 and gc2, representing December 31, 2000, and January 1, 2001, respectively. (Once again, only the month is zero-based.) It then uses the before method to determine if the gc1 date is before gc2. As a result, the program prints "Yes it is", as you would expect. If you substituted the after or equals method, the result would be "No it is not".

Extracting parts of a date or time

What if you have a variable that contains a date or time value, and you would like to retrieve only the day or the year portion of it? In RPG IV, a new operation code was introduced for this specific purpose. The EXTRCT op-code allows you to specify a field of type date, time, or timestamp in factor two, followed by the duration code that specifies the specific information you want to extract or retrieve. For example, specifying a time field in factor two followed by a colon and *H tells the compiler that you want to retrieve only the hour portion. The extract op-code can be used with any date, time, or timestamp field, and can return one of the following values depending on what you specify in the second part of factor two:

- The year, month, or day of a date or timestamp field

- The hours, minutes, or seconds of a time or timestamp field

- The microseconds of a timestamp field

The result field must be specified to be assigned the value returned. The type of the result field can be numeric or character. The constants for determining what to extract are the same as those in Table 8.2 for the ADDDUR and SUBDUR op-codes, for example:

```
C                    EXTRCT    TStamp:*H    temp1            4 0
```

As another example, what if you would like to print the actual name of the day instead of a number? For example, how would you determine which day October 22, 2000 fell on? (It was a Sunday, FYI.) For RPG, you would do this as shown in Listing 8.11.

Listing 8.11: Retrieving the Day Name as Text in RPG

```
D days           S              9A   DIM(7) CTDATA PERRCD(1)
D*
D CurrentDate    S              D
D OneSunday      S              D    INZ(D'2000-08-06')
D Temp           S              7 0
```

Listing 8.11: Retrieving the Day Name as Text in RPG (continued)

```
D TheDay            S            1P 0
C*
C        'enter date'  DSPLY                  CurrentDate
C        CurrentDate   SubDur    OneSunday    Temp:*d
C        Temp          DIV       7            Temp
C                      MVR                    TheDay
C                      IF        TheDay = 0
C                      EVAL      TheDay = 7
C                      ENDIF
C        days(TheDay)  DSPLY
C                      MOVE      *ON          *INLR
** CTDATA days
Monday
Tuesday
Wednesday
Thursday
Friday
Saturday
Sunday
```

The code starts by establishing a base line to deal with the calculation. This example de-clares the field OneSunday to represent any past Sunday. In this case, you simply pick Sunday August 6, 2000. When the user enters the date he or she wants to know about, the code simply subtracts it from the base date to calculate the number of days elapsed, using the SUBDUR op-code. Once you have the difference, you divide by seven, which is the number of days in a week.

The next line in the code uses the MVR (*Move Remainder*) op-code to move the remainder to the index that will be used later to retrieve the actual name of the day from the com-pile-time array. For example, if a user entered a date of August 8, 2000, the difference be-tween the dates is two. Dividing by seven also gives a remainder of two, so the day was a Tuesday.

However, what if you entered the date August 13, 2000? The difference this time is seven. Dividing seven by seven gives a remainder of zero. If you directly used this as the index to the array, you would get an "index out of range" error. This is why in the code checks for that condition. If the remainder is zero, the day was a Sunday, and the in-dex needs to be set to seven.

To accomplish this with Java, you can use a Java-supplied method in the GregorianCalendar class that gives the day of the week as an integer. The get method returns an integer from one to seven that represents the days Sunday to Saturday, respec-tively. The same example written in Java is shown in Listing 8.12.

Listing 8.12: Retrieving the Day Name as Text in Java

```
import java.util.*;

public class GetDayOfWeek
{
    public static final String days[] =
        {"SUNDAY","MONDAY","TUESDAY","WEDNESDAY",
         "THURSDAY","FRIDAY","SATURDAY"};

    public static void main(String args[])
    {
        GregorianCalendar today = new GregorianCalendar();
        int dayOfWeek = today.get(GregorianCalendar.DAY_OF_WEEK);
        String dayAsString = days[dayOfWeek-1];
        System.out.println(dayAsString);
    }
}
```

As in the RPG example, the Java code declares a "compile-time" array days and initializes it to the names of the days. It then creates a GregorianCalendar object to retrieve today's date (versus prompting for a date, like RPG example did). Once it has a date, it can call the get method to retrieve the number of the day, which, after subtracting zero to make it zero-based, is used as the index of the array days. The println method prints the name of the day as a string.

Note that you have to pass a constant DAY_OF_WEEK to the get method to tell it which part of the date to extract. You can also extract other parts of the date by specifying a different constant. The list of constants available is shown in Table 8.4.

Table 8.4: Java Constants for Extracting Date Parts via get in GregorianCalendar

Constant	Description
DATE or DAY_OF_MONTH	The one-based day in the month (one to 31)
DAY_OF_WEEK	The one-based day in the week (one to 7)
DAY_OF_WEEK_IN_MONTH	The ordinal day of the week in the month (one to five), for example, a two if this is the second Friday in the month
DAY_OF_YEAR	The day within the year (one to 365)
ERA	The era as a constant, either AD or BC
YEAR	The year (four digits)
WEEK_OF_YEAR	The week number within year (one to 52)

Of course, GregorianCalendar objects also capture time, not just dates, so there are constants for extracting time parts as well, as shown in Table 8.5. Not only is there this very handy get method, there is also a set method, which takes the same constants, as well as a second parameter which is the value to set that date or time part.

Table 8.5: Java Constants for **Extracting Time Parts via get in GregorianCalendar**	
Constant	Description
AM_PM	The morning or afternoon as a constant, either AM or PM
HOUR	The 12-hour number (one to 12)
HOUR_OF_DAY	The 24-hour number (one to 24)
MINUTE	The minute within the hour (zero to 59)
SECOND	The second within the minute (zero to 59)
MILLISECOND	The millisecond within the second (zero to 999)
DST_OFFSET and ZONE_OFFSET	The millisecond offset from Daylight Savings Time and Greenwich Mean Time

While the approach shown here works fine if you are writing an English-only application, a better approach would be to use the SimpleDateFormat class described in the following sections, with the E special character.

FORMATTING DATE FIELDS

In RPG, there are many ways to format your date fields. You can simply use the new keyword DATFMT(*format{separator}) to tell the compiler the format you want your date fields to have. You can specify this keyword in two places: on the H-spec to establish global default formatting for your date fields, or on specific fields on the D-spec to indicate specific formatting for those fields. If no keyword is specified on either, the default *ISO is used. Table 8.6 illustrates the different date formats available in RPG.

		Table 8.6: RPG Date Formats		
Date Format	Name	Format	Length	Separator
Month/Day/Year	*MDY	mm/dd/yy	8	/-.,&
Day/Month/Year	*DMY	dd/mm/yy	8	/-.,&
Year/Month/Day	*YMD	yy/mm/dd	8	/-.,&
Julian	*JUL	yy/ddd	6	/-.,&
USA Standard	*USA	mm/dd/yyyy	10	/
European Standard	*EUR	dd.mm.yyyy	10	.
International Standard Organization	*ISO	yyyy-mm-dd	10	-
Japanese Standard	*JIS	yyyy-mm-dd	10	-

For example, to tell the compiler that you want all fields in the program to have the *MDY format, you would code this:

```
H     DATFMT(*MDY/)
```

Not only does this tell the compiler the format to use (MDY), it also specifies the actual separator to use between the day, time, and year (/). As you see from Table 8.6, you can specify any separator you like, depending on the actual format used and whether that separator is allowed or not. You can continue in the RPG code and specify the same keyword on certain fields, but with a different format. This would indicate to the compiler that the *MDY format is to be used globally on all fields in your program, except those fields that have this keyword specified on their D-spec. The rule is very simple and, in fact, applies to both date and time formats. Listing 8.13 illustrates this.

Listing 8.13: Using the DATFMT Keyword to Format Dates in RPG

```
H       DATFMT(*ISO)
D*----------------------------
DstartDate       S          D   INZ(D'2001-08-18')
DUSADate         S          D   DATFMT(*USA)
DEURDate         S          D   DATFMT(*EUR)
DJISDate         S          D   DATFMT(*JIS)
DdefaultDate     S          D
D*----------------------------
C                    EVAL      USADate = startDate
C       USADate      dsply
C                    EVAL      EURDate = startDate
C       EURDate      dsply
C                    EVAL      JISDate = startDate
C       JISDate      dsply
C                    EVAL      defaultDate = startDate
C       defaultDate  dsply
```

In this example, the keyword DATFMT is inserted on the H-spec to indicate that the overall default date format for the program is *ISO. This format will be used if no other format is specified on the D-spec, or in factor one of a C-spec. The example declares five different date fields. The first, startDate, just holds the initial date, and uses the default *ISO format. The next four will hold the value of startDate after a move. Each uses a different one of the four-digit year formats: *USA, *EUR, *JIS, and *ISO (inherited from the H-spec). The C-specs do four moves to illustrate the date conversion from one format type to another, giving the following results:

```
08/18/2001
18.08.2001
2001-08-18
2001-08-18
```

V4R2 of RPG IV supports three new external date formats, but only on the MOVE, MOVEL, and TEST op-codes: *CMDY, *CDMY, and *LONGJUL. You cannot use these formats when defining new internal fields. If you specify a DATFMT keyword on the H-spec, then all date literals you specify, such as on the INZ keyword for date fields, must conform to this format. This is true even for date fields declared with their own DATFMT keywords.

In Java, it is perhaps even easier to format a date field. The JDK supplies a SimpleDateFormat class in the java.text package to accommodate this. This class is very powerful and supplies functionality superior even to RPG IV. It allows you to choose any user-defined pattern for formatting. For example, see Listing 8.14.

Listing 8.14: Using the SimpleDateFormat Class to Format Dates in Java

```
import java.text.*;
import java.util.*;
public class TestDateFormat
{
    public static void main (String args[])
    {
        Date date = new Date();
        System.out.println("Before formatting: " + date);
        String fPattern = new String("MM/dd/yyyy");
        SimpleDateFormat test = new SimpleDateFormat(fPattern);
        String dateString = test.format(date);
        System.out.println("After formatting:  " + dateString);
    }
}
```

This example first instantiates a `Date` object with today's date. It then builds the pattern, which is equivalent to the RPG IV date format of *USA, by initializing it to the `String` object `fPattern`. Once that is established, it can then instantiate a `SimpleDateFormat` object and pass your pattern to it as a parameter. This is now a date formatting machine! You can simply call its `format` method with any `Date` object, and that date will be formatted according to the originally supplied pattern. The `format` method returns a formatted `String` object, which you can directly output with `System.out.println`, as with the current `Date` object in the example. If the current date is December 24, 2001, for example, you'll see this:

```
After formatting: 12/24/2001
```

If you are using a `GregorianCalendar` object instead of a `Date` object, recall you can use the `getTime` method to return a `Date` object from the `GregorianCalendar` object, which you would then pass to your `SimpleDateFormat` object's `format` method.

The only thing you need to change to establish a new format is the value of the pattern, either by instantiating a new object or using the `applyPattern` method of the `SimpleDateFormat` class. The `SimpleDateFormat` class allows you to specify various (case-sensitive) characters as part of the string to indicate different formatting patterns. Table 8.7 lists the predefined characters for specific date parts.

Table 8.7: Java Special Characters for Date Formatting

Character	Meaning
G	The era designator—text
y	The year—a number
M	The month in the year—text or a number
d	The day in the month—a number
E	The day in the week—text
D	The day in the year—a number
F	The day of the week in the month—a number
w	The week in the year—a number
W	The week in the month—a number
‘	The escape character for text—a delimiter
"	Single quotes around literals

As you have seen, the M, d, and y characters are used for the pattern in the example. Notice that it uses an uppercase M to show the month in the year, but a lowercase d and y to show the day in month and the year, respectively. What do you think the result would be if you used an uppercase D? As shown in the table, D displays the day's number in the year. This means that if today's date were December 24, 2001, the formatted result when using the pattern MM/DD/yyyy would be 12/359/2001. Listing 8.15 shows a few more examples of date formatting.

Listing 8.15: More Examples of Formatting Dates in Java

```
import java.text.*;
import java.util.*;

public class TestDateFormat2
{
    public static void main (String args[])
    {
        GregorianCalendar gcDate = new GregorianCalendar(2001,11,24); →
```

Listing 8.15: More Examples of Formatting Dates in Java (continued)

```
SimpleDateFormat formatter =
          new SimpleDateFormat("dd.MM.yyyy G 'JAVA4RPG'");
String dateString = formatter.format(gcDate.getTime());
System.out.println("Formatted date: " + dateString);

formatter.applyPattern("'Day of week:' EEEE");
dateString = formatter.format(gcDate.getTime());
System.out.println("Formatted date: " + dateString);
    }
}
```

This gives the following output:

```
Formatted date: 24.12.2001 AD JAVA4RPG
Formatted date: Day of week: Monday
```

Notice the use of G in the format to display the era, and the use of a literal 'JAVA4RPG'. Pay particular attention to the use of single quotes around the 'JAVA4RPG' literal. When specifying string literals in the format, you must enclose them in single quotes; otherwise, Java assumes that each letter is meant to be one of the substitution variables. The exception to this rule is the separator characters slash, dash, period, ampersand, and comma—they need not be enclosed in quotes.

The second pattern in Listing 8.15 uses the E character to display the day of week. Recall that, earlier in this chapter, you saw a technique to display the name, in text, for the day of the week. It used the get method in the GregorianCalendar class, indexing into an array that listed the names of all seven days. As it turns out, the SimpleDateFormat class can do that for you, using the E pattern.

As a comparison, Table 8.8 lists all the date formats available in RPG and their equivalent patterns in Java. You might be wondering why we use multiple characters in our patterns, such as yyyy, MM, and dd. One reason is that it helps other programmers easily see at a glance precisely the pattern, including lengths for the constituent parts. Of course, it is also more than this. The number of repetitions of the symbols has precise meaning to the SimpleDateFormat class. Well, sort of precise. Notice in Table 8.7 that some of the symbols expand into numbers, such as 1999, while some expand into text, such as Friday. For numbers, the count of repeated symbols in the pattern string tell Java exactly how many digits to show. If the count is greater than the resulting number, the number is zero-padded on the left. For example, for June, you would see 06, not 6, if you used MM in the pattern. If the count is too small to hold the result, however, it will not be truncated, so using one M for the month will show 12 for December and 6 for June. The year is an exception to this rule, as it will truncate to two digits (but no less) if only two digits are given.

For text-resulting symbols like E for day in week, there are usually two forms of output possible: a short form such as Fri and a long form such as Friday. Java uses the long form only if the symbol is repeated four or more times. For symbols that can be text or number, such as M for month, Java uses text (such as January) if the symbol is repeated three or more times, and the number (such as 01) otherwise.

Table 8.8: Comparing RPG Date Formats to Java Format Patterns

Date Format	Name	Format	Java Pattern
Month/Day/Year	*MDY	mm/dd/yy	MM/dd/yy
Day/Month/Year	*DMY	dd/mm/yy	dd/MM/yy
Year/Month/Day	*YMD	yy/mm/dd	yy/MM/dd
Julian	*JUL	yy/ddd	yy/DDD
USA Standard	*USA	mm/dd/yyyy	MM/dd/yyyy
European Standard	*EUR	dd.mm.yyyy	dd.MM.yyyy
International Standards Organization	*ISO	yyyy-mm-dd	yyyy-MM-dd
Japanese Standard	*JIS	yyyy-mm-dd	yyyy-MM-dd

Note: Java allows all of the separators you can use with RPG IV, namely, the slash (/), dash (-), period, ampersand (&), and comma.

FORMATTING TIME FIELDS

RPG has just as many optional formats for your time fields as for dates. To format time fields, you use a keyword similar to that for dates, namely TIMFMT(*format{separator}). This tells the compiler the format you want your time fields to have. Table 8.9 lists the possible parameters you can specify.

Time Format	Name	Format	Length	Separator
Hours:minutes:seconds	*HMS	hh:mm:ss	8	:.,&
International Standards Organization	*ISO	hh.mm.ss	8	.
USA Standard	*USA	hh:mm am/pm	8	:
Europe Standard	*EUR	hh.mm.ss	8	.
Japanese	*JIS	hh:mm:ss	8	:

Table 8.9: RPG Date Formats

Again, as with date formatting, you are allowed to specify this keyword in two places: the H-spec (as a global default) or the D-spec (field-specific). If you like to format your times in a format similar to hh:mm:ss, for example, specify the format '*HMS:' as the parameter to the TIMFMT keyword. All optional separators are indicated in the table for each format type. Listing 8.16 shows an example of time formatting.

Listing 8.16: Using the TIMFMT Keyword to Format Times in RPG

```
H      TIMFMT(*HMS.)
H*----------------------------
DstartTime     S              T   INZ(T'10.25.30')
DUSATime       S              T   TIMFMT(*USA)
DEURTime       S              T   TIMFMT(*EUR)
DJISTime       S              T   TIMFMT(*JIS)
DISOTime       S              T   TIMFMT(*JIS)
DdefaultTime   S              T
D*----------------------------
C                   EVAL      USATime = startTime
C     USATime       dsply
C                   EVAL      EURTime = startTime
C     EURTime       dsply
C                   EVAL      JISTime = startTime
C     JISTime       dsply
C                   EVAL      ISOTime = startTime
C     ISOTime       dsply
C                   EVAL      defaultTime = startTime
C     defaultTime   dsply
```

This example inserts the keyword TIMFMT on the H-spec to indicate that the overall time format for the program is *HMS with the period separator (.). Five moves on the C-specs illustrate the time conversion from one format type to another:

```
10:25 AM
10.25.30
10:25:30
10:25:30
10.25.30
```

Note that if you specify a TIMFMT keyword on the H-spec, then all time literals you specify, such as on the INZ keyword for time fields, must conform to this format. This is true even for time fields declared with their own TIMFMT keyword.

In Java, the SimpleDateFormat class, in addition to formatting a Date object for date display, can also, of course, format it for time display. This is because a Date object incorporates both date and time values, as Listing 8.17 shows.

Listing 8.17: Using the SimpleDateFormat Class to Format Times in Java

```java
import java.text.*;
import java.util.*;
public class TestTimeFormat
{
    public static void main(String args[])
    {
        Date date = new Date();
        System.out.println("Before formatting: " + date);
        SimpleDateFormat test = new SimpleDateFormat("hh:mm:ss");
        String timeString = test.format(date);
        System.out.println("After formatting:  " + timeString);
    }
}
```

This is identical to the date formatting in Listing 8.14 except that it specifies "hh:mm:ss" for the format instead of "MM/dd/yyyy". Because only letters pertaining to time are specified, you get results showing only a formatted time. Thus, if the current time is 10:25:30, after running the program, the timeString object will contain the value 10:25:30. The letters you can specify in the format pattern pertaining to time are shown in Table 8.10.

Table 8.10: Java Special Characters for Time Formatting

Character	Meaning
h	The hour in am/pm form—a number from one to 12
H	The hour within the day—a number from zero to 23
m	The minute within the hour—a number
s	The second within the minute—a number
S	Milliseconds—a number
a	The am/pm marker—text
k	The hour within the day—a number from one to 24
K	The hour in am/pm form—a number from zero to 12
z	The time zone—text
'	The escape for text—a delimiter
''	Single quotes around literals

As with date formatting, the characters you specify in the pattern are case-sensitive, and the rules relating to the number of repetitions of a symbol apply the same way. Let's look at another example, in Listing 8.18.

Listing 8.18: More Examples of Formatting Times in Java

```
import java.text.*;
import java.util.*;

public class TestTimeFormat2
{
    public static void main(String args[])
    {
        Date currentTime = new Date();
        SimpleDateFormat format1 =
            new SimpleDateFormat("'Time is:' hh:mm:ss:SS a zz");
        SimpleDateFormat format2 =
            new SimpleDateFormat("'Time is:' kk-mm-ss");
        SimpleDateFormat format3 =
            new SimpleDateFormat("'Time is:' KK-mm-ss");
        String timeString1    = format1.format(currentTime);
```

Listing 8.18: More Examples of Formatting Times in Java (continued)

```
        String timeString2    = format2.format(currentTime);
        String timeString3    = format3.format(currentTime);
        System.out.println(timeString1);
        System.out.println(timeString2);
        System.out.println(timeString3);
    }
}
```

This gives the following:

```
Time is: 09:43:52:35 PM EST
Time is: 21-43-52
Time is: 09-43-52
```

This example uses SS for milliseconds, a for am/pm, and zz to indicate the time zone. It also shows a couple of the different options for expressing the hour, namely the lower-case k and the uppercase K. The former gives the number 21 instead of nine, as expected, but the latter gives nine, while the documentation implies you should get eight. Possibly this is a bug, since it seems to be the same as lowercase h.

For comparison, Table 8.11 lists the time formats available in RPG and their equivalent patterns in Java.

Table 8.11: Comparing RPG Time Formats to Java Format Patterns

Time Format	Name	Format	Java Pattern
Hours:minutes:seconds	*HMS	hh:mm:ss	hh:mm:ss
International Standards Organization	*ISO	hh.mm.ss	hh.mm.ss
USA Standard	*USA	hh:mm am/pm	hh:mm aa
Europe Standard	*EUR	hh.mm.ss	hh.mm.ss
Japanese	*JIS	hh:mm:ss	hh:mm:ss

THE DEFAULT FORMATTER

You have seen how to create your own formats using SimpleDateFormat and specify the format on the constructor or via the applyFormat method. The Java documentation recommends you do not typically create your own formats, though. Rather, there are static methods in the DateFormat class (SimpleDateFormat's *parent* class, a concept covered in the next chapter) that, when called, will return to you a SimpleDateFormat object. Well, actually these methods are defined to return you a DateFormat object, so you have to *cast* them to a SimpleDateFormat object, another concept covered in the next chapter.

These methods are getDateInstance, getTimeInstance and getDateTimeInstance. They are designed to give you preset formats for dates, times, and date plus time, respectively, that are culturally correct for the country and language of the computer where your Java program is running. As you know, each country has its own preferred method of formatting dates and times, and if you are writing international software, it is polite to adhere to these standards versus forcing your own country's standard on others. Java gives you a nice easy way to do this, as shown in Listing 8.19.

Listing 8.19 Getting Default Date, Time, and Date/Time Formatters in Java

```
import java.text.*;
import java.util.*;

public class TestDefaultFormats
{
    public static void main(String args[])
    {
        Date currentTime = new Date();
        SimpleDateFormat datefmt =
            (SimpleDateFormat)DateFormat.getDateInstance();
        SimpleDateFormat timefmt =
            (SimpleDateFormat)DateFormat.getTimeInstance();
        SimpleDateFormat dttmfmt =
            (SimpleDateFormat)DateFormat.getDateTimeInstance();
        System.out.println(datefmt.format(currentTime));
        System.out.println(timefmt.format(currentTime));
        System.out.println(dttmfmt.format(currentTime));
    }
}
```

This example tests each of the three static methods to retrieve culturally correct format objects for date, time, and date plus time. The result of running this on Windows NT set for USA and English is the following:

```
Jul 4, 2001
5:16:33 PM
Jul 4, 2001 5:16:33 PM
```

You get a short form for the month, which might not be what you want, even if otherwise you can accept the format given. Well, there is a way to change this, by specifying a parameter on the method calls indicating whether you want a short, medium, long, or full format. The constants defined in DateFormat for these options are, logically enough, SHORT, MEDIUM, LONG, and FULL. Listing 8.20 tests each of them to see what you get.

Listing 8.20: Using Different Default Formatting Styles in Java

```java
import java.text.*;
import java.util.*;

public class TestDefaultFormats2
{
    public static void main(String args[])
    {
        int styles[]    = {DateFormat.SHORT, DateFormat.MEDIUM,
                            DateFormat.LONG,  DateFormat.FULL};
        String names[] = {"SHORT", "MEDIUM", "LONG", "FULL"};
        SimpleDateFormat datefmt, timefmt, dttmfmt;

        Date currentTime = new Date();
        for (int idx = 0; idx < styles.length; idx++)
        {
            System.out.println("Style: " + names[idx]);
            datefmt = (SimpleDateFormat)
                    DateFormat.getDateInstance(styles[idx]);
            timefmt = (SimpleDateFormat)
                    DateFormat.getTimeInstance(styles[idx]);
            dttmfmt = (SimpleDateFormat)
             DateFormat.getDateTimeInstance(styles[idx],styles[idx]);
            System.out.println(datefmt.format(currentTime));
            System.out.println(timefmt.format(currentTime));
            System.out.println(dttmfmt.format(currentTime));
            System.out.println();
        }
    }
}
```

The syntax (SimpleDateFormat) casts an object from one type to another in Java (covered in Chapter 9). For now, it is enough to know that DateFormat is defined to return a DateFormat object, but actually returns a SimpleDateFormat object, so you need to tell Java this.

Note that getDateTimeInstance requires two parameters, one for the date style and one for the time style. Running this gives the following:

```
Style: SHORT
7/4/01
5:17 PM
7/4/01 5:17 PM

Style: MEDIUM
Jul 4, 2001
5:17:55 PM
Jul 4, 2001 5:17:55 PM

Style: LONG
July 4, 2001
5:17:55 PM EDT
July 4, 2001 5:17:55 PM EDT

Style: FULL
Wednesday, July 4, 2001
5:17:55 PM EDT
Wednesday, July 4, 2001 5:17:55 PM EDT
```

We recommend you use these static methods to produce your formats for dates and times, versus creating your own formats. It is, of course, your choice, however.

TESTING DATE AND TIME

So far you have compared, manipulated and displayed dates. What is left but to test them? A function we often use in our programs is testing the validity of a given date, time, or timestamp. That is, quite often, we ask the user to input a date, or we read a date from a database file, and we wish to ensure that it is a valid date. Frequently, it comes in the form of a character field, and our intention is to convert it to a real date (or time) for the purpose of recording it permanently in a database or using it in comparisons or manipulations.

RPG, of course, has our friend the TEST op-code. This op-code allows you to test that a given character, date, time or timestamp field contains a valid date. You specify in factor one the date format to test against (as shown in Table 8.6), and in the result field, you specify the field to test. Note that for date tests, we have to specify the D extender, and if you want to use the new-for-V4R2 %ERROR built-in function instead of an error indicator, you also have to specify the E extender. Listing 8.21 is an example of how you can use this to test if a given character field contains a date that is valid for the *USA format (mm/dd/yyyy).

Listing 8.21: Using Different Default Formatting Styles in RPG

```
D DateField1      S            10A   INZ('12/25/2001')
D DateField2      S             8A   INZ('12252001')
D DateField3      S             8A   INZ('99999999')
C*
C       *USA        TEST(DE)               DateField1
C                   IF         %ERROR = '0'
C       'good date' DSPLY
C                   ELSE
C       'bad date'  DSPLY
C                   ENDIF
C       *USA0       TEST(DE)               DateField2
C                   IF         %ERROR = '0'
C       'good date' DSPLY
C                   ELSE
C       'bad date'  DSPLY
C                   ENDIF
C       *USA0       TEST(DE)               DateField3
C                   IF         %ERROR = '0'
C       'good date' DSPLY
C                   ELSE
C       'bad date'  DSPLY
C                   ENDIF
```

Three fields are tested here. The last two have no separators, so you have to specify zero after the *USA value in factor one. The result of running this program is the following:

```
good date
good date
bad date
```

Let's compare this to Java. To test that a String in Java contains a valid date, you actually use the parse method of the SimpleDateFormat class. This is the functional opposite of the format method! Rather than formatting an existing date into a String, it parses a given String and returns a Date. The String must match the format of the pattern specified for the SimpleDateFormat. If it does not, then null is returned instead of a Date object. Listing 8.22 shows a Java class that prompts for a date from the user (via the console) and attempts to parse it into a date. If that fails, an error is issued; otherwise, the resulting Date object is printed.

Listing 8.22: Parsing Strings into Dates in Java

```java
import java.util.*;
import java.text.*;
public class TestDateParsing
{
    public static void main(String args[])
    {
        System.out.println("Enter a date in mm/dd/yyyy format:");
        /* prompt for, and read, user input from console... */
        String inLine = null;
        java.io.BufferedReader d = new java.io.BufferedReader(
            new java.io.InputStreamReader(System.in));
        try { inLine = d.readLine(); }
        catch (java.io.IOException exc) {}
        // try parsing it...
        SimpleDateFormat parser = new SimpleDateFormat("MM/dd/yyyy");
        Date date = parser.parse(inLine, new ParsePosition(0));
        if (date == null)
            System.out.println("You entered an invalid date!");
        else
            System.out.println("Date created is: " + date);
    } // end main
} // end of class TestDateParsing
```

Note that parse requires not only the String object to attempt to parse into a date, but also a ParsePosition object. Just always pass new ParsePosition(0), as shown here. Let's run this and see what we get with different inputs:

```
>java TestDateParsing
Enter a date in mm/dd/yyyy format:
12/25/2001
you typed: 12/25/2001
Date created is: Tue Dec 25 00:00:00 EST 2001

>java TestDateParsing
Enter a date in mm/dd/yyyy format:
12252001
You entered an invalid date!

>java TestDateParsing
Enter a date in mm/dd/yyyy format:
9999999999
You entered an invalid date!
```

We think this is pretty cool! Can you imagine the ugly parsing code you would have to write to do this otherwise?

LOOK BEFORE YOU LEAP

One of the other methods available in the GregorianCalendar class that is worth mentioning is the isLeapYear method. Listing 8.23 shows an example of how you use it.

Listing 8.23: Using the isLeapYear Method in the GregorianCalendar Class in Java

```java
import java.util.*;
public class TestLeap
{
    public static void main(String args[])
    {
        GregorianCalendar date = new GregorianCalendar();
        System.out.println("1600 a leap year? " +
date.isLeapYear(1600));
        System.out.println("1900 a leap year? " +
date.isLeapYear(1900));
        System.out.println("1976 a leap year? " +
date.isLeapYear(1976));
        System.out.println("1999 a leap year? " +
date.isLeapYear(1999));
        System.out.println("2000 a leap year? " +
date.isLeapYear(2000));
    }
}
```

You simply supply the method with the year as an integer parameter. This gives the following:

```
1600 a leap year? true
1900 a leap year? false
1976 a leap year? true
1999 a leap year? false
2000 a leap year? true
```

Calculating a leap year is not as straightforward as you might initially expect. For example, it is not as simple as determining if the year is divisible by four. If you need to know if a given year is a leap year, you can simply rely on this method.

TIME ZONES

You'll sometimes need to establish the current date or time in an explicit time zone other than the one in which the program is currently running. This functionality is not available in RPG, but Java does offer it. Java supports a TimeZone class in the java.util package, which can be used to instantiate an instance of a particular time zone, as in:

```
TimeZone tz_GMT = TimeZone.getTimeZone("GMT");
TimeZone tz_EST = TimeZone.getTimeZone("EST");
```

Notice how the constructor parameter is simply a string representing a valid, known time zone ID, such as EST for Eastern Standard Time. To see all the supported time zones, use the static getAvailableIDs method:

```
String tzs[] = TimeZone.getAvailableIDs();
for (int idx = 0; idx < tzs.length; idx++)
    System.out.println(tzs[idx]);
```

To get the current time zone for your computer, use the TimeZone.getDefault method. Finally, once you have a TimeZone object, you can use it in both your GregorianCalendar object to affect manipulations, and in your DateFormat object to affect the time displayed. In both cases, simply use the setTimeZone method. For example, if you have a Date object, say from instantiating the Date class explicitly or from using the getTime method of a GregorianCalendar object, you might want to display that object's time value for each of your offices around the world. To do this, you create a SimpleDateFormat object as usual, but before using its format method, you first call the setTimeZone method with the TimeZone object you wish to use. Listing 8.24 shows how this is done.

Listing 8.24: Using the TimeZone Class in Java

```
import java.util.*;
import java.text.*;
public class TestTimeZones
{
    public static void main(String args[])
    {
        Date      today = new Date(); // Current date/time
        TimeZone tz1    = TimeZone.getTimeZone("PST");
        TimeZone tz2    = TimeZone.getTimeZone("EST");
        TimeZone tz3    = TimeZone.getTimeZone("GMT");
        TimeZone tz4    = TimeZone.getTimeZone("JST");
        TimeZone tz5    = TimeZone.getDefault();
```

Listing 8.24: Using the TimeZone Class in Java (continued)

```
        SimpleDateFormat formatter =
            new SimpleDateFormat("hh:mm:ss - 'TimeZone = ' z");
        formatter.setTimeZone(tz1);
        System.out.println( formatter.format(today) );
        formatter.setTimeZone(tz2);
        System.out.println( formatter.format(today) );
        formatter.setTimeZone(tz3);
        System.out.println( formatter.format(today) );
        formatter.setTimeZone(tz4);
        System.out.println( formatter.format(today) );
        formatter.setTimeZone(tz5);
        System.out.println( formatter.format(today) );
    } // end main method
} // end TestTimeZones class
```

This results in the following:

```
    11:15:31 - TimeZone =  PST
    02:15:31 - TimeZone =  EST
    07:15:31 - TimeZone =  GMT
    04:15:31 - TimeZone =  JST
    02:15:31 - TimeZone =  EST
```

Note how the displayed time is different depending on what time zone is used, which is what you want.

Use the getDefault method to return a TimeZone object representing the time zone of the machine on which the program is running. In Windows, you might have to ensure your time zone is set properly on your machine.

SUMMARY

This chapter discussed the following aspects of date and time manipulation:

- RPG IV date and time support is far superior to its predecessor in RPG III.

- The Java method currentTimeMillis in the System class returns the total number of milliseconds since the base time or *epoch*.

- Java has a Date class for retrieving and representing basic dates. In comparison, you use the TIME op-code to retrieve the time and/or date in RPG.

- Java has a GregorianCalendar class for performing date and time manipulations. In comparison, RPG has the SUBDUR and ADDDUR op-codes, combined with the date, time, and timestamp field types.

- To extract parts of a date in Java, use the get method on a GregorianCalendar object. In RPG, use the EXTRCT op-code.

- Java has a SimpleDateFormat class for formatting any Date object. RPG has the DATFMT and TIMFMT keywords.

- For culturally correct date formats, use the getDateInstance, getTimeInstance, and getDateTimeInstance static methods.

- Use the isLeapYear method found in the GregorianCalendar class to test whether a year is a leap year in Java.

- Java supplies TimeZone and SimpleTimeZone classes for international support.

AN OBJECT ORIENTATION

Java is an object-oriented language. You have seen the object part by now—classes are instantiated into one or more objects, each with its own unique memory yet with common variable definitions and methods. This alone is a great thing, but there is more to being object-oriented than just this. There are more capabilities in OO and more syntax in Java to support those capabilities. You will find the syntax easy, but you will probably struggle with the question of why, and the question of how best to design code to exploit the power of OO. Not to worry: we all do this when we go from procedural to OO design. The most important thing for you to know now is the syntax, so that you can read and use other people's code effectively, and so that you can start writing code today. With time, experience, and more reading, the questions of why, when, and how will simply fall into place.

Let's start right here, by listing the additional syntax in Java, followed by some examples and some discussion to help you understand how to use it. (We will also take a shot at helping you understand why it is all goodness.) Java's additional object-oriented syntactical capabilities are these:

- You can create a new class by *extending* an existing class, inheriting all non-private methods and variables in the existing class. You can then define new methods and variables and override inherited methods by redefining them. You can only extend one class, but that class can, in turn, extend another. The extending class is the *child class*, while the extended class is the *parent class*.

- Methods in a child class that redefine methods in the parent class can call the overridden method in the parent class by using the `super` keyword.

- All classes implicitly extend the Java-supplied class `Object`, hence they inherit its methods.

- Constructors are not inherited, but there is a Java-supplied special method named `super` that can be used to call the extended class's constructor.

- You can specify two additional class modifiers that affect extending classes: `abstract`, meaning this class must be extended, and `final`, meaning this class can't be extended.

- You can also specify additional method modifiers that affect extending classes: `abstract`, meaning this method must be overridden; `final`, meaning this method can't be overridden; and `protected`, restricting access to only this class and child classes.

- Classes that are abstract cannot be instantiated.

- Methods that are abstract have no code in their body. They have only a signature, and must be overridden by child classes.

- You can specify an additional non-local variable modifier, `protected`, that restricts access to the variable to only this class and classes that extend this class.

- You can declare an object reference variable to be of one class type, and assign it to an object of that class or any child of that class.

- You can define *interfaces*, which are really classes that have only constant variables and abstract methods.

- You can define a class to *implement* an interface, which requires you to override all of the methods declared in the interface. You can implement more than one interface in any class.

- You can define an object reference variable to be of an interface type, and you can assign such a variable to an instance of any class that implements the interface.

- You can test at runtime what class type an object reference variable actually refers to.

- You can cast an object reference variable to a particular class type, as long as the object really is of that type at runtime.

That's the entire OO story of Java in a nutshell. Here, in a nutshell, is what OO and these Java syntactical capabilities are designed for:

- Writing highly reusable, highly adaptable code

THE THREE TENETS OF OO

It is generally agreed that for a computer language to be considered object-oriented, it must support the following concepts:

- Encapsulation
- Inheritance
- Polymorphism

The Java OO syntax listed supports these, in Java's own way. That is, all the items listed in the previous section are simply Java constructs to enable these three tenets. These tenets, in turn, are what enable OO languages to support highly reusable, highly adaptable code. The following sections describe these tenets and expand on the Java constructs that enable them.

Encapsulation

You get encapsulation in Java just by having classes. These allow you to put all the variables and methods that define a particular concept in one place, such as `Employee`, `EmployeeId`, `Customer`, `Item`, `ItemOrder`, `Account`, `Department`, `Loan`, `Attendee`,

String, Vector, and Date. These are like record formats or data structures, but the difference is they contain not only data, but also all the necessary code to access and manipulate that data. You can then reuse this anywhere you want. Subsequent changes are isolated to one class, which instantly affects all code using this class.

The ability to restrict access and hide implementation details is done using modifiers such as private and protected.

There are objects on the AS/400, such as *FILE and *PGM, but they do not encapsulate supporting code inside them. Rather, you must call that code externally and tell it the object to work on, as in RNMOBJ, DLTOBJ, GRTOBJAUT, and CRTDUPOBJ.

In RPG, you can declare data structures, but not the related code inside the data structure. Rather, you end up creating subroutines and procedures that act on a given data structure. And that code often ends up scattered and duplicated throughout many applications. With RPG IV service programs, you now have the capability to encapsulate in one place at least all the data and procedures related to a particular concept. Indeed, you can think of a module with exported procedures as being very similar to a single object. The only difference is you can only have one instance of that module, so that data active at once, unless you get into the complex use of memory management via the ALLOC op-code.

Inheritance

The ability to create one class that extends another, thus inheriting all the capability of the first class, is where you get inheritance in Java. Having inherited those capabilities, you are able to refine and extend them via method overrides and new methods. This is how to get highly adaptable code. Write a solid, reusable base, and then extend it to accommodate additional situations.

When was the last time you wrote a new RPG program completely from scratch? Chances are, not in years. Rather, you use the poor man's version of inheritance: copy and change. You have a number of RPG programs that do specific functions, such as order entry, subfile processing, and customer maintenance. For each new application, you copy the appropriate common program and then change it as much as needed to deal with this particular application and database. This works, but what happens as you improve the common base program? Nothing. All programs written using it as a base do not benefit from that change. You might have discovered this when you did your Y2K work!

With inheritance, those common base programs would become classes, and each new application you write reuses those classes as is, or else extends them and refines their behavior for this particular application's need.

Let's get into the specific syntax for creating new classes by extending existing classes. As you'll see, this syntax is very easy. For a base class, start with the ItemOrder class from Chapter 2, shown in Listing 9.1.

Listing 9.1: A Base Class, ItemOrder

```java
import java.math.*; // for BigDecimal class

public class ItemOrder
{
    protected static int nextId = 1;
    protected int        id;
    protected int        quantity;
    protected BigDecimal unitCost;

    public ItemOrder(int quantity, double unitCost)
    {
        this.id = nextId;
        nextId = nextId + 1;
        this.quantity = quantity;
        this.unitCost = new BigDecimal(unitCost);
        this.unitCost =
          this.unitCost.setScale(2,BigDecimal.ROUND_HALF_UP);
    }

    public BigDecimal getTotalCost()
    {
        BigDecimal quantityBD = new BigDecimal(quantity);
        BigDecimal totalCost = unitCost.multiply(quantityBD);
        totalCost = totalCost.setScale(2,BigDecimal.ROUND_HALF_UP);
        return totalCost;
    }

    public void displayOrder()
    {
        System.out.println();
        System.out.println("Order Information");
        System.out.println("---------");
        System.out.println(" id........: " + id);
        System.out.println(" quantity..: " + quantity);
        System.out.println(" unit cost.: " + unitCost);
        System.out.println(" total cost: " + getTotalCost());
    }
}
```

The modifier on the instance variables was changed from `private` to `protected` in this example. This allows code in classes that extend this class to access these variables directly, but still restricts any other code from direct access. Now, finally, you can see the reason for having four different access options. In Java, you can divide the users of your method or variable into:

- Other methods in this class (`private`)

- Other methods in other classes in this package (the default)

- Other methods in any subclass in any package (`protected`)

- Other methods in any class in any package (`public`)

To restrict the use of your method or variable to one of these four categories, choose the indicated modifier keyword. This restricts any method in a lower category (that is, any category below the chosen one on the list above) from your method or variable. However, it allows access from any method in the chosen or higher category.

The code from the version in Chapter 2 was also changed to use `BigDecimal` instead of `double`, which nicely solves the problem of huge decimal places.

Listing 9.2 shows an updated version of the `PlaceOrders` code from Chapter 2, which tests this `ItemOrder` class. This class declares a `Vector` instance variable named `orders` to hold all `ItemOrder` objects. The `main` method creates an instance named `orderList`, and then calls the method `placeAnOrder` twice, to create two orders stored in `Vector`. It then calls the method `processOrders` to process that `Vector` of orders, which in this example simply calls `displayOrder` on each `ItemOrder` element in the `Vector`.

Listing 9.2: A PlaceOrders Class to Test the Base Class

```java
import java.util.*; // for Vector class

public class PlaceOrders
{
    private Vector orders = new Vector();

    public void placeAnOrder(int quantity, double unitCost)
    {
        ItemOrder order = new ItemOrder(quantity, unitCost);
        orders.addElement(order);
    }

    public void processOrders()
```

➔

Listing 9.2: A PlaceOrders Class to Test the Base Class (continued)

```
    {
        ItemOrder currentOrder;

        for (int idx=0; idx < orders.size(); idx++)
        {
            currentOrder = (ItemOrder)orders.elementAt(idx);
            currentOrder.displayOrder();
        }
    }

    public static void main(String args[])
    {
        PlaceOrders orderList = new PlaceOrders();
        orderList.placeAnOrder(10, 35.99);
        orderList.placeAnOrder(10, 26.15);
        orderList.processOrders();
    }

}
```

Running `PlaceOrders` from the command lines results in this output:

```
Order Information
------------------
 id........: 1
 quantity..: 10
 unit cost.: 35.99
 total cost: 359.90

Order Information
------------------
 id........: 2
 quantity..: 10
 unit cost.: 26.15
 total cost: 261.50
```

Notice in Listing 9.2, the `processOrders` method has to cast the output of `orders.elementAt(idx)` to a type of `ItemOrder`, which is the class type of the objects in the `orders` `Vector` object. The reason for this is that the method `elementAt` in class `Vector` is defined to return a type named `Object`. This is a class supplied by Java, which all classes implicitly extend. Whenever you wish to write generic code that will work with objects of any class, such as the `Vector` class does, you use the class type `Object`. However, in order to call methods defined in the class, you must cast the object to an object reference variable defined with the class type first, as Listing 9.2 does. (You'll see more about the casting of objects later in this chapter.)

Now, let's have some fun by creating a new class that extends ItemOrder, inheriting all of its instance variables and methods, and then changes the behavior of one of the methods and adds a new method. Assume you have a special kind of order that is like the common ItemOrder except that it supports discounts. The new class is named DiscountedItemOrder, and it extends ItemOrder. Figure 9.1 shows what this class hierarchy will look like, with each box representing a class and the up-arrows indicating an "extends" relationship.

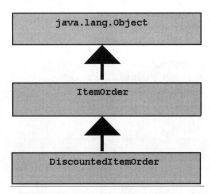

Figure 9.1: The class hierarchy diagram

The constructor for DiscountedItemOrder will have to take a third value, for the discount amount as a percentage. The getTotalCost method will have to be overridden in the new class to accommodate the discount amount in the total cost. A new method will also be added for returning the total amount of the discount, which the revised getTotalCost method will have to call. The displayOrder method can be left alone, inheriting it as-is. Listing 9.3 is the new class.

Listing 9.3: The DiscountedItemOrder Class Extending the ItemOrder Class

```
import java.math.*; // for BigDecimal

public class DiscountedItemOrder extends ItemOrder
{
    protected BigDecimal discountPerCent;

    /**
     * Constructor
     */
    public DiscountedItemOrder(int quantity, double unitCost,
```

Listing 9.3: The DiscountedItemOrder Class Extending the ItemOrder Class (continued)

```
                              double discount)
   {
       super(quantity, unitCost);
       discountPerCent = new BigDecimal(discount);
       discountPerCent =
           discountPerCent.setScale(2,BigDecimal.ROUND_HALF_UP);
   }

   /**
    * Override of method getTotalCost from parent class
    */
   public BigDecimal getTotalCost()
   {
       BigDecimal totalCost = super.getTotalCost();
       BigDecimal discountAmount = getDiscountAmount();
       totalCost = totalCost.subtract(discountAmount);
       totalCost = totalCost.setScale(2, BigDecimal.ROUND_HALF_UP);
       return totalCost;
   }

   /**
    * New method unique to this class
    */
   public BigDecimal getDiscountAmount()
   {
       BigDecimal totalCostWithoutDiscount=super.getTotalCost();
       BigDecimal discountAmount =
           totalCostWithoutDiscount.multiply(discountPerCent);
       discountAmount =
           discountAmount.setScale(2,BigDecimal.ROUND_HALF_UP);
       return discountAmount;
   }
}
```

There are some syntactic details to discuss about this new class. First, notice that you create a class that extends another class by simply using the extends keyword on the class definition, identifying after it the class you wish to extend:

```
public class DiscountedItemOrder extends ItemOrder
```

You can only extend a single class in Java (unlike C++), but another class could subsequently extend this one, and another extend that, and so on. As mentioned, any class that does not explicitly extend another always implicitly extends class Object in package java.lang.

The new child class automatically starts with all the class variables, instance variables, and methods of the parent class it extends (and those any classes the parent extends). However, you are only allowed to directly access those variables and methods that are not `private`. The same applies to users of the new class: they cannot access any of the inherited variables or methods that are `private`. However, they also cannot access any of the variables inherited or explicitly defined that are `protected`. These are reserved only for classes in this family tree (that is, classes that extend this one).

The `DiscountedItemOrder` class defines a new instance variable named `discountPerCent`, which is a `BigDecimal` object reference variable that will hold the discount amount as a percentage. Next, it defines the constructor for the class, which takes three parameters now, versus the two that the parent class constructor takes. The third parameter is the new discount value, taken as a `double` so that callers can specify literal numbers.

You must define a constructor in your child class because constructors are not inherited. However, there is an easy way to reuse the code in the constructors of a parent class. You simply call the special method named `super`, which always represents a call to the constructor in the parent class. Which constructor gets called depends on the usual rules of parameter numbers and type matching. If you call `super`, it must be the first line of code in your child class constructor. You should *always* call `super` in your constructors, because there is usually important initialization work done in constructors. Yes, call your super parents more often!

After calling `super`, Listing 9.3 records the given `discount` value, but converts it to a `BigDecimal` object and sets the scale to two, so math can be kept to two fixed decimal places. After the constructor, it redefines or overrides the method `getTotalCost` from the parent class. This is an override because the method has the same name, same number of parameters, and same type of parameters (signature) as a method in the parent class. In this case, `getTotalCost` has to take into account the discount amount before returning the total cost. However, you do not want to duplicate the code from the parent class to calculate the initial total cost prior to the discount. Instead, simply call that method in the parent class and record the returned value, which will subsequently have the discount applied.

To call a method in a parent class that has been overridden in this child class, you have to tell Java you want the parent's version of the method, not the child's version. You do this by using the `super` keyword again, but this time as a qualifier for the name of the method to call, as in:

```
BigDecimal totalCost = super.getTotalCost();
```

The rest of the method calls a new method, getDiscountAmount, which returns how much the discount is off the total cost, and subtracts that amount from the original total cost. After taking care to force the decimal places (scale) to two, the code then returns the final BigDecimal object to its callers.

The getDiscountAmount method is a new method that is not an override of a method from the parent class. It is straightforward, but notice that it qualifies the call to getTotalCost with super to ensure it calls the parent's version. Otherwise, it would call the local override version, which in turn calls it back, and you'd have an infinite loop.

The displayOrder method is not overridden from the parent class, so it is simply inherited as-is. Notice, though, that the code in that method calls getTotalCost. It will be interesting to see which version of getTotalCost gets called when you use an instance of this child class. Let's do that now! Listing 9.4 shows the PlaceOrders class updated to test the child class as well as the parent class.

Listing 9.4: The Updated PlaceOrders Class Using the New DiscountedItemOrder Class

```
import java.util.*; // for Vector class

public class PlaceOrders
{
    private Vector orders = new Vector();

    public void placeAnOrder(int quantity, double unitCost)
    {
        ItemOrder order = new ItemOrder(quantity, unitCost);
        orders.addElement(order);
    }

    public void placeAnOrder(int quantity, double unitCost,
                             double discount)
    {
        DiscountedItemOrder order =
          new DiscountedItemOrder(quantity,unitCost,discount);
        orders.addElement(order);
    }

    public void processOrders()
    {
        ItemOrder currentOrder;

        for (int idx=0; idx < orders.size(); idx++)
        {
```

*Listing 9.4: The Updated PlaceOrders Class Using the New
DiscountedItemOrder Class (continued)*

```
                    currentOrder = (ItemOrder)orders.elementAt(idx);
                    currentOrder.displayOrder();
            }
        }

        public static void main(String args[])
        {
            PlaceOrders orderList = new PlaceOrders();
            orderList.placeAnOrder(10, 35.99);
            orderList.placeAnOrder(10, 26.15);
            orderList.placeAnOrder(10, 26.15, .10);
            orderList.processOrders();
        }

    }
```

Well, not much changed here, only what is shown in bold. A new overloaded version of
placeAnOder is created, which takes three parameters versus two, and it instantiates the
new child class DiscountItemOrder instead of the parent class ItemOrder. The main
method is then changed to simply add a single call to the new method, passing a discount
value of ten percent (.10). Remember, when you have two methods with the same name
in the same class, the runtime determines which one you want to call by matching up the
number and type of the parameters.

Before dissecting the interesting aspects of this, let's run it and see the output:

```
Order Information
------------------
 id........: 1
 quantity..: 10
 unit cost.: 35.99
 total cost: 359.90

Order Information
------------------
 id........: 2
 quantity..: 10
 unit cost.: 26.15
 total cost: 261.50

Order Information
------------------
 id........: 3
 quantity..: 10
 unit cost.: 26.15
 total cost: 235.35
```

As you can see, the third order is in fact discounted by 10 percent. This is all very exciting isn't it? (Okay, so maybe *you* have a life outside of computers.) The new class appears to have inherited and leveraged all the code of its parent class, yet extended it only as necessary to refine its behavior. The calling code simply uses the new class interchangeably with the old class. Notice that the vector of orders named orders holds two objects of type ItemOrder and one object of type DiscountedItemOrder. Also, notice that the method processOrders did not need to be changed at all. You might have expected the casting to type (ItemOrder) to fail on that third object, since the rule is supposed to be that you can only cast an object to its actual runtime type, and for the third object the runtime type is DiscountedItemOrder, not ItemOrder. Well, the rule has a caveat: you can cast to the actual runtime type *or any parent class* of that type.

Let's look closer at the method processOrders from Listing 9.4:

```
public void processOrders()
{
    ItemOrder currentOrder;
    for (int idx=0; idx < orders.size(); idx++)
    {
        currentOrder = (ItemOrder)orders.elementAt(idx);
        currentOrder.displayOrder();
    }
}
```

This method iterates through the elements of the orders vector. These elements are objects, and for each, it calls the method displayOrder in that object. What class is that method in? Well, the Java compiler has to know that answer, too, so that it can verify the method actually exists. This is why the code had to declare a local variable of type ItemOrder and assign each element of the vector to it before being allowed to call method displayOrder. The compiler accepts this because it looks inside the ItemOrder class and discovers it does, indeed, have a method in there with the same signature as the displayOrder call.

This is all fine, except in the example, the third object is not of type ItemOrder at all! It is of type DiscountedItemOrder. Wow, you fooled the compiler! So what happens at runtime, then, when you actually make that call to displayOrder? It should fail, since you do not have a method named displayOrder in class DiscountedItemOrder. Or do you? Well, you do, in fact! You inherited it from the parent class ItemOrder, remember. So, luckily, this works.

In fact, there was no luck whatsoever here, and you did not fool the compiler. This is a legal loophole that you are encouraged to exploit. The compiler and runtime let you call any method on an object, as long as that method exists either explicitly or by inheritance.

Did you follow this example of inheritance? As usual, the syntax is very easy. Appreciating its true power, though, comes with time.

Inheritance is what separates "object-based" from "object-oriented."

One crude AS/400 example of inheritance is reference fields in DDS. Maintaining a field reference file of field definitions, is somewhat like having a base class. Each database file that you define by using or referencing your field reference file (FRF) fields is somewhat similar to a child class that extends its parent class (the FRF). You define new fields (simple reference), override existing fields (by redefining a reference field's length, for example), and remove (by omission) other fields. The difference is we are only talking data, not methods or code.

Note that there is no way in Java to remove methods you inherit. The best you can do is to overload them with empty methods, as in:

```
public void aMethodWithSameSignatureAsParentsVersion()
{
}
```

Polymorphism

No, polymorphism is *not* denture cream! In fact, you have already seen this concept in action. When you define a class that extends another class and then override one of the inherited methods with a new implementation of that method, you are practicing *polymorphism*. (Aren't you naughty?!) Polymorphism refers to the fact that calling the same method on two objects can have different results if the objects come from different classes in the same hierarchy. (There's a mouthful!)

Let's look again at the code in method processOrders in Listing 9.4:

```
ItemOrder currentOrder;
for (int idx=0; idx < orders.size(); idx++)
{
    currentOrder = (ItemOrder)orders.elementAt(idx);
    currentOrder.displayOrder();
}
```

If you just looked at this code without the rest of the class as context, you would have to conclude, as the compiler has to conclude, that all the objects in the orders vector are of type ItemOrder, and you are always calling the method displayOrder in that class. The reality is different at runtime, where the third object is of type DiscountedItemOrder and you are in fact calling the inherited version of displayOrder in that class. So, the method that the compiler thinks is being called is one thing (displayOrder in class ItemOrder), while the method that gets called at runtime is another (either displayOrder in class ItemOrder or displayOrder in class DiscountedItemOrder). This is polymorphism, which is from the Greek for "many shapes."

This example is not very interesting because both versions of displayOrder are the same. Let's look at a more interesting example, one you've seen already. Consider the code in the method displayOrder itself:

```
public void displayOrder()
{
    System.out.println();
    System.out.println("Order Information");
    System.out.println("---------");
    System.out.println(" id........: " + id);
    System.out.println(" quantity..: " + quantity);
    System.out.println(" unit cost.: " + unitCost);
    System.out.println(" total cost: " + getTotalCost());
}
```

This code seems straightforward enough, but look at that last line, where you call getTotalCost. This method exists in ItemOrder and is overridden with a new version in DiscountedItemOrder as shown in Listing 9.3. So which version gets called by the line of code in displayOrder? It depends on the object type at runtime.

As you saw when Listing 9.4 was run, when the target object is an ItemOrder instance, it calls the version in ItemOrder, and when the target object is a DiscountedItemOrder, it calls the version in that class. In other words, you can write totally reusable code both here and in the processOrders method that calls one of two possible methods depending on the runtime type of the object. The result you get is correct for that type. Notice, also, that there is no code anywhere that says "if order is of type ItemOrder call this method, else if it is of type DiscountedItemOrder call this method." The decision about which version of the overridden method getTotalCost to call is made for you. It is polymorphic magic.

The syntax rule that makes polymorphism possible is this:

You can declare an object reference variable to be one class type, and yet assign to it at runtime an instance of a different class type, as long as the runtime class type extends the declared compile-time class type.

For example, this is legal:

```
ItemOrder anOrder = new DiscountedItemOrder();
```

This rule also applies to parameters, so you might have a method defined to take an object of type `ItemOrder`, and at runtime pass it an object of type `DiscountedItemOrder`:

```
public static void verifyOrder(ItemOrder anOrder)
{
    ...
}
...
verifyOrder(new DiscountedOrder);
```

The reverse is not true, however. You cannot assign an object that is of a class type higher in the hierarchy tree. That is, you cannot do this:

```
DiscountedItemOrder anOrder = new ItemOrder();
```

More examples? Here is a fun one. Let's declare a parent class named `Animal`, and give it one method named `talk`. Then, let's define a child class of `Animal` named `Cat`, which overrides the method `talk` to write out "meow" to the console. Let's also create other child classes named `Dog` and `Cow`, which similarly override the `talk` method. Then, let's can create a little `Zoo` class that instantiates an array of `Animal` objects, populating it with instances of randomly chosen classes. Finally, let's walk that array and call the method `talk` on each object to see what we get.

Listing 9.5 shows all four animal classes together, one after another, in the interest of space. In reality, of course, they must all be in their own files.

Listing 9.5: The Animal Class and Its Children

```java
public class Animal
{
    public void talk()
    {
        System.out.println("I'm an animal");
    }
}

public class Cat extends Animal
{
    public void talk()
    {
        System.out.println("meow");
    }
}

public class Dog extends Animal
{
    public void talk()
    {
        System.out.println("woof");
    }
}

public class Cow extends Animal
{
    public void talk()
    {
        System.out.println("moo");
    }
}
```

Listing 9.6 shows the Zoo class.

Listing 9.6: A Zoo Class to Test the Animal Classes

```java
import java.util.*; // for Random class

public class Zoo
{
    protected Animal animals[]  = new Animal[10];
    private    Random randomizer =
        new Random(System.currentTimeMillis());

    public void createAnimals()
```

→

Listing 9.6: A Zoo Class to Test the Animal Classes (continued)

```
    {
        for (int idx=0; idx < animals.length; idx++)
        {
            int randomNbr = randomizer.nextInt(3); //between 0 and 2
            if (randomNbr == 0)
              animals[idx] = new Cat();
            else if (randomNbr == 1)
              animals[idx] = new Dog();
            else if (randomNbr == 2)
              animals[idx] = new Cow();
        }
    }

    public void allTalk()
    {
        for (int idx=0; idx < animals.length; idx++)
            animals[idx].talk();
    }

    public static void main(String args[])
    {
        Zoo theZoo = new Zoo();
        theZoo.createAnimals();
        theZoo.allTalk();
    }
}
```

What we have done is define an array of Animal type as an instance variable, then defined two methods: createAnimals to populate the animals array with objects of randomly chosen Animal child classes, and allTalk to walk the array and call the talk method on each object element. Note that arrays, unlike vectors, allow you to explicitly set the class type every element has, so you do not need to do casting. The main method instantiates things and calls the two methods. Here is the output of running this class:

```
moo
woof
meow
meow
moo
woof
meow
moo
woof
moo
```

This is why you got into programming, isn't it? It's fun! Notice because the Random object is seeded with the current time, you get a different result every time you run this.

What you should take out of this example is the power of polymorphism to replace if/else coding with elegant, simple logic that knows how to do the right thing for each object, because the objects themselves know how to do the right thing. For example, look at the simplicity of the allTalk method in Listing 9.6. It simply calls the method talk on each element of the array, which is defined to hold objects of type Animal. Yet, when you run the code, you end up calling the method talk in one of three different classes, "automagically." There's no need to test what type the array element is and hard-code the decision about which method to call. That is done for you, by the Java runtime.

Depending on your occupation and the nature of your co-workers, this example might not apply in your next business application. However, the design pattern will. That is, imagine that instead of Animal, Cat, Dog, and Cow, you have Employee, SalariedEmployee, Hourly Employee, and ContractorEmployee, as shown in the class hierarchy in Figure 9.2.

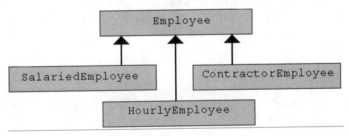

Figure 9.2: The Employee class hierarchy diagram

Instead of the overloaded method talk, you have an overloaded method printPayCheck, which has a unique pay-calculation algorithm for each type of employee. Now, imagine instead of Zoo you have a class named Payroll, which has an array of type Employee and is populated by reading the database and creating the appropriate object type for each employee. Now, the talk method in Zoo becomes a doPayroll method in Payroll:

```
public void doPayroll()
{
    for (int idx=0; idx < employees.length; idx++)
        employees[idx].printPayCheck();
}
```

Do you see the elegance of polymorphism now? It allows you to write very concise code that can deal magically with many different object types at runtime. Further, the code is very adaptable to change, without change! If in the future a new employee type is identified, such as `MaternityLeaveEmployee`, you simply create a new class that overrides the appropriate methods in `Employee`. Then you only have to change the code that decides which object type to create, and all the rest of the code remains untouched. The entire `HumanResources` and `Payroll` systems will work perfectly with the new employee type. As far as they know, they are calling methods in the `Employee` class. The reality that they are calling methods in child classes of `Employee` is polymorphic magic.

Now you can see why no formal language construct exists for a child class to remove methods from its parent class. The concept of polymorphism requires the compiler to assume that a method defined in one class is always available in its lower, or child, classes. That is why you are allowed to declare an object reference variable using a parent class type, and assign to it an object of a child class, and subsequently call methods in that child class. Via inheritance rules, you are guaranteed the child classes have at least all the methods the parent class has. You also cannot restrict a method's access rights beyond what is defined at the parent level. For example, you cannot override a method in a child class and change it from a `public` method to a `private` method, as that effectively would make it available in parent objects, but unavailable in child objects. The reverse, however, is permitted.

There are many examples of polymorphism in the Java-supplied classes in the Java Development Kit. For example, in Chapter 6, you saw the list utility classes `Vector` and `Hashtable`. These classes are designed to hold objects of any class. Generally, they do not know or care about the class type of these objects. However, there are some operations in `Vector` and `Hashtable` that cannot be done without calling methods in each of the elements. For example, the `contains` method allows you to search the list for a given object. To determine if the given object "matches" any particular object in the list, the code walks the list and calls the `equals` method of each element object, passing the given object as a parameter. If any of the objects return true from this call, then the `contains` method returns true to the caller.

In order for this code to compile, the `equals` method has to exist in every object in the list. This is, in fact, the case, because the engineers put an `equals` method in the `Object` class that all classes implicitly extend, therefore guaranteeing it exists in every object in Java. However, this method, by default, only compares the memory addresses of the two objects, so you almost always have to override it to get the correct behavior. The `String` class overrides it to compare the string content lengths and each of the characters. The

Attendee class in Chapter 6 overrode it to compare the attendee names. An Employee class might override it to compare employee numbers.

You can find examples of polymorphism in OS/400, such as PDM (Programming Development Manager). In PDM's list screens, you are presented with a list of libraries, objects, or members; you can enter options beside them to invoke actions on the items in the list. These options (like option 5 to display) are polymorphic in that the resulting action depends on the type of object you use it against. You get a different result for each object type, and yet you, as a user, always use the same simple option; PDM takes care of determining the appropriate action for the selected object's type. PDM is acting like the Java runtime in this case, deciding which command (method) to call based on the object's type.

Yet another example is the WRITE op-code in RPG. You use it the same way whether you are writing to a database, display, or printer file. The RPG runtime keeps track of which one is actually being written to, and handles each uniquely, under the covers.

One input, one of many possible outputs.

INHERITING MORE OR LESS

There are a couple of new method modifiers to introduce to you now, which relate to method overriding. One (final) prevents child classes from overriding this method, while the other (abstract) forces child classes to override this method.

Preventing inheritance

There are times when you will want to completely restrict the ability for another programmer to extend your class and override or replace certain methods. From a security point of view, you might have very sensitive methods that you want to ensure cannot be maliciously or unwittingly replaced. The getPay() method for an employee object might be an example of a sensitive method.

Notice the difference here between *using* and *overriding*. You do not mind child classes using this method—in fact, you want this, because it hides all the sensitive calculations. What you do not want child classes doing is overriding the implementation of this method. For integrity and security, it is important that all code that invokes this method get to the one and only implementation of it, and not some other implementation farther down the inheritance chain (thus preventing a *Trojan horse* kind of attack).

You can prevent child classes from overriding a specific method in Java by using the `final` modifier keyword on the method:

```
protected final int getPay()
{
    ...
}
```

This modifier tells the compiler that no child *subclass* (as they are sometimes called) is allowed to override this method with its own implementation. The compiler will enforce this, as will the runtime. In addition to security benefits, `final` also offers potential performance benefits. It is a clue to the compiler that this method will not be participating in polymorphism, so the compiler has the option of *inlining* the method. Inlining involves turning calls to the method into static instead of dynamic ones (that is, determining and recording the address of the method at compile time, rather than waiting for runtime).

You can also specify `final` at the class level, in which case all methods inside the class are automatically designated as `final` by the compiler.

Enforcing inheritance

The previous section discussed how to prevent child classes from overriding a particular method or prevent child classes altogether for a particular class. There are times, however, when precisely the opposite is required. Sometimes, methods are coded in a parent class just so you can ensure they exist via inheritance in your child classes. Consider the method `talk` in class `Animal` in Listing 9.5. A dummy block of code was created for it, but the reality is that this code will probably never be exercised. Rather, every child class should override this method with a more meaningful implementation for that particular animal type. If you forget to override this method in a child class, then at runtime, you will end up executing the dummy version of the method, getting unexpected results.

To turn this loose contract into a more binding contract, code the modifier `abstract` on the method in the parent class. When you do this, every child class must override the method, or the compilation of that class will fail. This is just what you want. When you specify `abstract` on a method, you do not have to bother with dummy placeholder code in its body. Indeed, you are not even allowed to code a method body! You must place a semicolon after the signature, like this:

```
public abstract void talk();
```

If you specify this modifier on any method in a class, then you must also specify it on the class, as in:

```
public abstract class Animal
{
    public abstract void talk();
}
```

Why is this, and what does it mean? A class with even one abstract method is not instantiable directly. That is, you cannot use new to instantiate it. The reason, of course, is that this would allow you to call that abstract method, which would be a problem because it has no code in it! Thus, you must identify the whole class as abstract so that the compiler can prevent attempts to use new on it. The assumption is that this is a class that is only used as a parent for one or more child classes that extend it. These classes will *have* to override and implement that method, else their compile will fail (unless you flag them as abstract, too).

Why would you want abstract classes? For abstraction. Use them as the base class as you saw with Animal. You would never ever expect someone to instantiate an Animal object directly, since clearly every animal is an instance of some concrete child class, such as Dog.

Are you clear on why we even created that Animal class, and that we could not have written the elegant Zoo code without it? We needed a base class to use as the declared type for the generic "work with any type of animal" code. If we instead used Dog for the type of the animals array, we would have been prevented from putting Cat objects in there, as these do not have a parent/child relationship. We could, alternatively, have used the root parent of all classes, Object, as the type, but that would have made the compiler fail on the call to the talk method in the Zoo code, as the Object class is not defined with this method.

Remember, the compiler is trying to help by ensuring the methods called really do exist in the declared class type. Even if you declare an object reference variable as a parent class type and subsequently assign an object of a child class to it at runtime, you are ensured that the method exists in the children because *all* non-private methods are inherited.

You will see lots of examples of abstract classes in the Java Development Kit. One such example is an abstract class named JComponent in the GUI packages (java.awt and javax.swing). This class represents a generic GUI widget, and all concrete widget child classes such as JButton and JCheckBox extend it. The JComponent has abstract methods that all widgets are required to support, such as setBackground for setting the background color and `repaint` for painting the widget after it becomes visible. Certainly, there is no way to write generic code in the parent class that will work for all possible widgets, so that job is left to the child classes, who are forced to override these methods. By abstracting out the idea that all widgets must have these methods, Java was able to write elegant and generic code for frame windows that contain one or more GUI widgets. When a frame window is restored from minimized state, for example, its logic simply walks its array of `JComponent` objects and calls the `repaint` method in each object. What that does depends on what type of object it is, but the important thing is every GUI widget object is guaranteed to have this method. The `repaint` method in `JComponent` is declared `abstract`, and hence so is the class, because there is simply no reasonable default code that can be done to paint a pretend component.

This GUI class hierarchy, the `Animal` class hierarchy in Listing 9.5, and the `ItemOrder` class hierarchy from earlier in this chapter are all highly adaptable. To support new GUI widgets, new animals, and new types of orders, you simply create new classes that extend the respective parent classes and override the required methods (`repaint`, `talk`, and `getTotalCost`, for example). Suddenly, then, objects of these new classes will work with all the existing infrastructure code that only uses object references variables defined with the parent class type. That is, the frame window code, the `Zoo` code, and the `PlaceOrders` code will all work with the new classes, without any change or even recompile needed.

Finally, you can think of field reference files on the AS/400 as being similar to abstract classes. They have no "implementation" (in this case, they never hold data), but are designed explicitly to abstract-out common field attributes for use in child or populated databases.

THE FACTORY METHOD-DESIGN PATTERN

At this point, you have seen the core tools in the Java language for writing highly reusable and highly adaptable code. The syntax is easy: the `extends` keyword and some optional modifiers like `protected`, `final`, and `abstract` simply help you get the compiler to enforce some rules. The tricky part for RPG programmers moving to an object-oriented language is never the "how," it is the "why" and subsequently the "how best to do this."

The latter two questions are part of a larger domain of study called *object-oriented analysis and design* (*OOA and D*). The idea is to offer some insights to help you to design an effective solution for a given problem, one that maximizes reuse and adaptability. There is no single right answer for most decisions relating to designing classes and class hierarchies, but by following some proven rules or methodologies, you can usually get some guidance. You'll learn more about OOA and D later, although in-depth discussion of that domain is beyond this book. Further, not all of your team need to be geniuses at deciding which classes to create and which classes should extend other classes. Only one person needs this skill, and he or she can subsequently assign the task of writing each class to other team members.

We do want to give you one big tip, though:

> Whatever it is you are trying to design the class hierarchy for, someone some-where has probably done it before!

Order entry, payroll, human resources, inventory management, accounts receivable, and even wine-list management have all been around for a long time. Your details are no doubt unique, but many of the overall design approaches won't be. You can do yourself a favor by looking at existing solutions to similar problems. Indeed, often the pattern asso-ciated with a solution applies to many problem domains. For example, you saw that the `Animal` class hierarchy and the Zoo class had similar "design patterns" that you could use for employee payroll, at a very high level.

The idea of scouring many successful solutions to common programming problems and documenting what emerges as common patterns was first made immensely popular by Eric Gamma, Richard Helm, Ralph Johnson, and John Vlissides in their watershed 1995 book *Design Patterns: Elements of Reusable Object-Oriented Software* (Addison-Wesley). The book is based on C++, but it can also be applied to Java. The only difference to keep in mind is that C++ supports extending multiple classes simultaneously, while Java does not.

One pattern from this book that is important for you to know is called the *object factory*. Taking a great deal of liberty on the explicit details of this pattern, it is roughly this: whenever you have a class hierarchy involving an abstract parent or base class, and a number of child classes that extend it, somehow and somewhere you have to eventually decide which child class to instantiate. The more you can encapsulate this decision pro-cess and hide the details of the decision, the less code you will have to change when you subsequently invent new child classes.

Consider the Zoo class in Listing 9.6 and the `createAnimals` method in it, which popu-lates the animals array with instances of various `Animal` child classes. If you add a new child class that extends `Animal`, you must come back to this method and add code to instantiate it. Normally, this is based on some reasonable criteria, not just a random deci-sion. Indeed, it is very often based on one of the fields read from a database, or one of the fields in a user interface. So, the pattern is this: you create a class that has the same name as the parent class, but with "Factory" appended to it, and in it you supply a static method named createXXX that returns an instantiated object. The decision about which child class to instantiate is isolated to that method, using whatever criteria you need. Any pieces of code that want an object from this class hierarchy are encouraged to call this createXXX method, versus coding new themselves.

Applying this design pattern to the Animal class hierarchy gives the class AnimalFactory with its createAnimal static method, as shown in Listing 9.7.

Listing 9.7: The AnimalFactory Class

```
import java.util.*; // for Random class

public class AnimalFactory
{
    private static Random randomizer =
      new Random(System.currentTimeMillis());

    /** Factory method to create appropriate child object */
    public static Animal createAnimal()
    {
        Animal animalObj = null;
        int randomNbr = randomizer.nextInt(3); //Between 0 and 2
        if (randomNbr == 0)
          animalObj = new Cat();
        else if (randomNbr == 1)
          animalObj = new Dog();
        else if (randomNbr == 2)
          animalObj = new Cow();
        return animalObj;
    }
}
```

Notice the declared return type for the createAnimal method. It is defined to be just Animal, the parent class. However, we always return an object of a child class. The rules of polymorphism allow us to do this. (An object reference variable declared of class type X can be assigned to an object of class X or any child class of X.) Listing 9.8 revises the Zoo code that uses the AnimalFactory method.

Listing 9.8: The Revised Zoo Class, Using the AnimalFactory Class

```
public class Zoo
{
    protected Animal animals[]  = new Animal[10];

    public void createAnimals()
    {
        for (int idx=0; idx < animals.length; idx++)
            animals[idx] = AnimalFactory.createAnimal();
    }

    public void allTalk()
    {
        for (int idx=0; idx < animals.length; idx++)
            animals[idx].talk();
    }

    public static void main(String args[])
    {
        Zoo theZoo = new Zoo();
        theZoo.createAnimals();
        theZoo.allTalk();
    }
}
```

The Zoo code is smaller because the details of object instantiation are delegated to the factory method. The Zoo class is now completely class-agnostic! It only refers to the parent class Animal, not any child class. So, if you define a new animal type by creating a new child class of Animal, you need only change the AnimalFactory class, and the Zoo code will work magically with it! This is nice.

Hopefully, you work at a zoo! Actually, even if you don't, you will probably use this design pattern. Consider the Employee class hierarchy, described earlier. Its factory class might look like Listing 9.9.

Listing 9.9: Another Factory Example: The EmployeeFactory Class

```
import java.io.*;
import java.util.*;

public class EmployeeFactory
```

Listing 9.9: Another Factory Example: The EmployeeFactory Class (continued)

```java
{
    public static BufferedReader fileConnection = null;
    public static final String EMPTYPE_SALARY = "S";
    public static final String EMPTYPE_HOURLY = "H";
    public static final String EMPTYPE_CONTRACTOR = "C";
    public static final String EMP_FILENAME = "empdata.dat";

    public static Employee createNextEmployee()
    {
        StringTokenizer empInfo = getNextEmpFromDB();
        Employee empObj = null;
        if (empInfo != null) // not end of file?
          {
            // parse record into constituent fields
            String recType    = empInfo.nextToken();
            String empId      = empInfo.nextToken();
            String empPayType = empInfo.nextToken();
            String empPay     = empInfo.nextToken();
            String empDept    = empInfo.nextToken();
            String empHours   = empInfo.nextToken();
            String empName    = empInfo.nextToken();
            while (empInfo.hasMoreTokens())
                empName = empName + " " + empInfo.nextToken();
            // Convert String info to appropriate types
            int    employeeId=0, employeeDept=0;
            double employeePay=0, employeeHours=0;
            try {
                employeeId   = Integer.parseInt(empId);
                employeeDept = Integer.parseInt(empDept);
                employeePay  = Double.parseDouble(empPay);
                employeeHours= Double.parseDouble(empHours);
            } catch (Exception exc) {}
            // Create appropriate object
            if (empPayType.equals(EMPTYPE_SALARY))
              empObj=new SalariedEmployee(employeeId,
                        employeePay, employeeDept, empName);
            else if (empPayType.equals(EMPTYPE_HOURLY))
              empObj=new HourlyEmployee(employeeId, employeePay,
                        employeeDept, empName, employeeHours);
          }
        return empObj;
    }
} // end EmployeeFactory
```

Although the getNextEmpFromDB method is not shown here, it is available on the CD-ROM included with this book. It simply reads from a flat file, since you have not yet seen relational database access. An example Payroll class that uses this, as well as the parent Employee class and its two child classes SalariedEmployee and HourlyEmployee, can also be found on the CD-ROM. You'll see they are very similar in design to the Animal classes.

Your factory code can do whatever is required to get the information to make the decision about which class to instantiate. If the information is supplied by a user, then your factory method will probably take the input as one or more parameters.

While the term *object factory* hails from the referenced book and this explicit design pattern, these days you will find it used generically to refer to any static method that instantiates and returns an object.

INTERFACES

You have seen that the syntax for creating a class that extends another class is very simple, but appreciating and realizing the full power and potential of that simple construct comes with time. That is also the case for the next construct you will see: the *interface*.

Recall that RPG IV procedures require you to write prototypes. For example, consider the simple VECTOR service program from Chapter 6, and the copy member supplied to users, which is shown again in Listing 9.10.

Listing 9.10: RPG IV Procedure Prototypes for the VECTOR Service Program

```
/* Procedure prototype for VectorAllocate
DVectorAllocate    PR              *
/* Procedure prototype for VectorAddElem
DVectorAddElem     PR              *
D vectorHeader@                    *    VALUE
D dataSize                         5U 0 VALUE
/* Procedure prototype for VectorElemAt
DVectorElemAt      PR              *
D vectorHeader@                    *    VALUE
D position                         5U 0 VALUE
/* Procedure prototype for VectorIndexOf
DVectorIndexOf     PR              5U 0
D vectorHeader@                    *    VALUE
D userData@                        *    VALUE
/* Procedure prototype for VectorGetSize
DVectorGetSize     PR              5U 0
```

Listing 9.10: RPG IV Procedure Prototypes for the VECTOR Service Program (continued)

```
D vectorHeader@                    *    VALUE
/* Procedure prototype for VectorRmvElem
DVectorRmvElem       PR
D vectorHeader@                    *    VALUE
D userData@                        *    VALUE
```

These particular prototypes are for procedures that allow you to:

- Allocate a growable list or vector (VectorAllocate).

- Given a length, allocate that much memory and store the pointer to that memory in the vector (VectorAddElem). The pointer is also returned to the caller.

- Given a one-based element position, return the memory pointer in that position in the vector (VectorElemAt).

- Given a memory pointer, return the one-based position of that element in the vector (VectorIndexOf).

- Return the number of elements in the vector so far (VectorGetSize).

- Remove an element from the vector and free up the memory associated with it (VectorRmvElem).

The prototype for a procedure is a complete duplicate of the procedure interface D-specs, identifying the name of the procedure, the attributes of the return type (length, type, decimals, and any keywords), and the name (optional) and attributes of the parameters. The reason for prototypes is so that the compiler can verify that callers of the procedure get the name right, pass the correct number of parameters, and pass the correct type of the parameters. That is the purpose of a strongly typed language: to catch as many errors at compile time as possible. If any of this information is wrong and the compiler lets it pass, it would lead to a runtime error or function check, and you have probably learned from experience that your users don't seem to like these!

Java however does not require you to prototype your methods, even though the compiler still does verify that the method name, the number of parameters, and the type of the parameters are correct for any calls. It can do this because of the compiler's unique ability to find on disk the file containing the class containing the method, and read (*introspect*) the signature information for that method. That information is compared to the information on the call, and an error is issued if they are not compatible. All this is good, as you enjoy the benefits of prototyping without the productivity hit.

Nevertheless, there still is something in Java vaguely similar to prototypes:

> You can separate your class from its interface, which includes the signatures of all the public methods you want to expose to other programmers.

Let's get right to the syntax. Listing 9.11 shows an interface named Displayable that defines a single method, display.

Listing 9.11: A Java Interface: Displayable

```
public interface Displayable
{
    public void display();
}
```

You declare an interface the same way as you declare a class, substituting the keyword interface for the keyword class. Inside the interface however, you have only method signatures, but no method bodies. These signatures look identical to the signatures you saw for defining abstract methods. In fact, are identical! The keywords public and abstract are implicit for all method signatures in an interface, although they can also be redundantly coded. Indeed, an interface is just special syntax for an abstract class that contains only abstract methods. Well, abstract methods or constants, since Java also allows you to define constant fields in an interface, but these are the only field definitions permitted.

Now to the syntax of using an interface. (We'll get to the "why would I use them?" question shortly.) As mentioned, an interface is similar to an RPG IV copy member that contains prototypes of procedures. In RPG IV, you ultimately have a module somewhere that actually implements those procedure prototypes. For example, the prototypes from Listing 9.10 are implemented in the VECTOR module, which was discussed in Chapter 6 in Listing 6.21.

Java is similar. The methods inside an interface are implemented by some class. If the interface really were defined as an abstract class with abstract methods, you know from the earlier discussion that those methods would be implemented by one or more child classes that extend the abstract class. With interfaces, the abstract methods are implemented by one or more classes that "implement" that interface. This is any class that specifies the "implements XX" phrase and contains actual implements for the methods defined in interface XX. For example, the class in Listing 9.12 implements the Displayable interface.

Listing 9.12: A Java Class that Implements an Interface: ItemOrder

```
import java.math.*; // for BigDecimal class

public class ItemOrder implements Displayable
{
    protected static int nextId = 1;
    protected int       id;
    protected int       quantity;
    protected BigDecimal unitCost;

    public ItemOrder(int quantity, double unitCost)
    {
        this.id = nextId;
        nextId = nextId + 1;
        this.quantity = quantity;
        this.unitCost = new BigDecimal(unitCost);
        this.unitCost =
          this.unitCost.setScale(2,BigDecimal.ROUND_HALF_UP);
    }

    public BigDecimal getTotalCost()
    {
        BigDecimal quantityBD = new BigDecimal(quantity);
        BigDecimal totalCost = unitCost.multiply(quantityBD);
        totalCost = totalCost.setScale(2, BigDecimal.ROUND_HALF_UP);
        return totalCost;
    }

    public void display()
    {
        System.out.println();
        System.out.println("Order Information");
        System.out.println("----------");
        System.out.println(" id........: " + id);
        System.out.println(" quantity..: " + quantity);
        System.out.println(" unit cost.: " + unitCost);
        System.out.println(" total cost: " + getTotalCost());
    }
}
```

Does this class look familiar? It comes from Listing 9.1. The only difference is that the name of the method `displayOrder` is changed to `display`, which is more generic and is also the name of the method inside the interface. The phrase "`implements Displayable`" is also added to the class definition at the top. This is all there is to it.

For any class, you can pull one or more of the method signatures out and put them into an interface, and then add the phrase "`implements xxx`" to the class definition. Why do this? Stay tuned. When you code this phrase on a class, you must implement every one of the methods in that interface, using the same signatures as specified in the interface. Otherwise, the compile of the class will fail. Of course, you are free to code additional methods as well, beyond what the interface dictates.

Back in RPG IV, you have a copy member and a module that implements the prototypes in the copy member. This compares in Java to an interface and a class that implements that interface. You have something else in RPG IV, however: other modules that /COPY the copy member and call one or more of the procedures identified by the prototypes in the copy member.

Java has this, too! You can write code that uses methods prototyped by an interface by simply declaring object reference variables whose type is the name of the interface. However, you are not allowed to assign these variables to instances of interfaces because you are not allowed to instantiate interfaces. Remember, interfaces do not have constructors or non-abstract methods. You can, however, assign them to instances of classes that implement that interface. For example, the following line of code will compile only if the class `ItemOrder` implements the `Displayable` interface.

```
Displayable myVariable = new ItemOrder();
```

Listing 9.13 is an example of a few static methods that use the `Displayable` interface. This class has two overloaded versions of a `displayAll` method. The first takes as input an array of objects whose elements are defined to be of type `Displayable`, which is the interface. It then walks through the array, and for each element, it calls the `display` method. The second method does the same thing, but is designed for cases when you have a vector instead of an array. It takes a vector of objects as input, but because the `Vector` class is defined to only hold items of type `Object`, you have to cast each element to an object reference variable defined to be of type `Displayable` before you can attempt to call the `display` method on that element. Remember from Chapter 6 that vectors offer great flexibility, but do require you to cast the objects as you pull them out of the vector, if you want to call any of the methods in that object.

Listing 9.13: Java Code that Uses the Displayable Interface: The Helpers Class

```java
import java.util.*;

public class Helpers
{
    public static void displayAll(Displayable objects[])
    {
        for (int idx=0; idx < objects.length; idx++)
            objects[idx].display();
    }

    public static void displayAll(Vector objects)
    {
        Displayable currentObject = null;
        for (int idx=0; idx < objects.size(); idx++)
        {
            currentObject = (Displayable)objects.elementAt(idx);
            currentObject.display();
        }
    }
}
```

Listing 9.13 is designed to be a helper class, so let's put it to use to help us. The class in Listing 9.14 uses one of the methods from the Helpers class.

Listing 9.14: A Revised Version of PlaceOrders that Uses the Helpers Class

```java
import java.util.*; // for Vector class

public class PlaceOrders
{
    private Vector orders = new Vector();

    public void placeAnOrder(int quantity, double unitCost)
    {
        ItemOrder order = new ItemOrder(quantity, unitCost);
        orders.addElement(order);
    }

    public void placeAnOrder(int quantity, double unitCost,
                             double discount)
```

$\longrightarrow$

```
    {
        DiscountedItemOrder order =
            new DiscountedItemOrder(quantity, unitCost, discount);
        orders.addElement(order);
    }

    public void processOrders()
    {
        Helpers.displayAll(orders);
    }

    public static void main(String args[])
    {
        PlaceOrders orderList = new PlaceOrders();
        orderList.placeAnOrder(10, 35.99);
        orderList.placeAnOrder(10, 26.15);
        orderList.placeAnOrder(10, 26.15, .10);
        orderList.processOrders();
    }

}
```

This class should look familiar, too. You last saw it in Listing 9.4, and all that's changed is the body of the processOrders method. Rather than do your own loop through the orders vector, you now simply call the displayAll method in the Helpers class to do this for you, passing your vector into it as a parameter. If you compile and run this, you get the same output as in Listing 9.4.

Here are some details on interface declarations:

- Interfaces can only contain constants and method signatures.

- Interfaces can extend one or more other interfaces, comma-separating the names.

- More than one class can implement the same interface.

- Classes can implement one or more interfaces, comma-separating the names.

The syntax is almost trivial: interfaces are just like Java classes with method signatures (and optionally constants) only; classes that implement the method signatures in an interface do so by declaring the phrase "implements xxx"; you can use an interface name as the type for an object reference variable; and you can assign objects of any class that implement the interface to that object reference variable.

Where does all this leave you? It might seem that you're just back where you started, with code that runs the same as it did before the interface. However, you aren't just back where you started. You have pulled out some of the functionality that was hard-coded in PlaceOrders class and put it into another class (Helpers) that is now reusable in many different situations. You don't get that reuse, however, until you have more than one class that implements the same interface.

Remember, the goal of OO is highly reusable and highly adaptable code. Interfaces enable finer-grained code reuse than inheritance does. With inheritance, you reuse an entire class. With interfaces, you typically reuse just one or two methods. Further, the reuse comes not from the interface code, and not from the one or more classes that implement the interface. Rather, the reuse comes from the code that works with classes that implement the interface, such as the displayAll method in Listing 9.13. This happens when more than one class implements the same interface, enabling code written to use that interface to work with more than one class.

Let's look at another example to see how the displayAll method can be reused in another, entirely different, situation. Chapter 6 had an example of a registration program that tracked attendees at an event by recording their phone numbers and names. One of the functions of that program was to display the current list of attendees. Do you think you can reuse one of the displayAll methods above, as is, to do this? You bet!

Consider the Attendee class in Listing 9.15, which is identical to Listing 6.20 except for the implements Displayable phrase. This class implements the Displayable interface and subsequently supplies a display method (if it didn't, you would get a compile error). As it turns out, this class already has the display method, so no additional work is needed.

Listing 9.15: The Attendee Class Implementing a Displayable Interface

```
public class Attendee implements Displayable
{
    private String name;

    public Attendee(String name)
    {
        this.name = name;
    }
    public String getName()
    {
        return name;
```

```
    }

    public boolean equals(Object other)
    {
        Attendee otherAttendee = (Attendee)other;
        return name.equals(otherAttendee.getName());
    }

    public void display()
    {
        System.out.println("-------------");
        System.out.println("Name........: " + name);
        System.out.println();
    }
}
```

Next, there is the class `AttendeeList` from Chapter 6, which records `Attendee` objects in a vector. It already has a `display` method to walk the list and call the display on each element, so you simply change the method to call the `displayAll` method in the `Helpers` class, and add a `main` method so you can quickly test this. The resulting class is shown in Listing 9.16.

Listing 9.16: The AttendeeList Class
Reusing the displayAll Method in the Helpers Class

```
import java.util.*;

public class AttendeeList
{
    private Vector attendees = new Vector();

    public void register(String name)
    {
        Attendee newAttendee = new Attendee(name);
        if (!checkForAttendee(newAttendee))
          attendees.addElement(newAttendee);
        else
          System.out.println("An attendee named " + name +
                             " is already registered");
    }

    public void deRegister(String name)
    {
        Attendee theAttendee = new Attendee(name);
        if (!checkForAttendee(theAttendee))
          System.out.println("Sorry, name " + name +
```

Listing 9.16: The AttendeeList Class
Reusing the displayAll Method in the Helpers Class (continued)

```
                                    " is not registered");
        else
          attendees.removeElement(theAttendee);
    }

    public boolean checkForAttendee(Attendee attendee)
    {
        return attendees.contains(attendee);
    }

    public void display()
    {
        Helpers.displayAll(attendees);
    }

    public static void main(String args[])
    {
        // test attendee code
        AttendeeList attendeeList = new AttendeeList();
        System.out.println();
        attendeeList.register("Phil Coulthard");
        attendeeList.register("George Farr");
        attendeeList.register("George Farr");
        attendeeList.display();
        attendeeList.deRegister("Phil Coulthard");
        attendeeList.deRegister("Phil Coulthard");
        attendeeList.display();
    }
}
```

If you run this class, you get the following:

```
An attendee named George Farr is already registered
-----------------------------------------
Name........: Phil Coulthard

-----------------------------------------
Name........: George Farr

Sorry, name Phil Coulthard is not registered
-----------------------------------------
Name........: George Farr
```

The important thing to take out of this is that it you successfully reuses the `displayAll`
method in an entirely new situation. By leveraging interfaces, you can write generic code

like displayAll in Listing 9.13, which works with objects of any class. By contrast, by leveraging inheritance and polymorphism, you are only able to write generic code, which works with objects of classes that extend a particular parent class.

These examples don't save much code due to the small size of the displayAll method. However, there are cases where the code saved by doing this abstraction would be significant. For example, imagine an interface like this:

```
public interface Billable
{
     public boolean prepareBill()
     public Object getBill();
}
```

This has two methods that classes like Customer, Client, PurchaseOrder, PhoneBill, and RentalTransaction might implement quite differently. The more classes that implement the same interface, the more reuse you get. The common code in this case might be a helper method printBills that calls these methods on a given list of Billable objects, and then does the necessary code to send the bill to the customer via fax or email. Keep in mind that the list of objects can consist of different objects. That is, the same list might contain some PhoneBill objects, some RentalTransaction objects, and some PurchaseOrder objects. The generic printBill code will handle all of them correctly because it defers the hard part to the objects themselves, by simply calling the commonly named methods prepareBill and getBill in each.

So, interfaces allow you to write generic infrastructure code such as displayAll, printBills, or doMonthEnd that works with any classes from any hierarchy, as long as those classes implement the appropriate interfaces. That lets you reuse the infrastructure code and easily adapt to new situations by simply creating new classes that implement the common interfaces. It also has a great side effect of forcing everyone on the team to use exactly the same method names for doing the same operation uniquely in different classes. Otherwise, you end up with many variations like displayOrder, displayAttendee, and printInformation. A consistent naming convention that is enforced by interfaces makes it much easier to read, understand, maintain, and adapt your code. The enforcement comes from the fact that any class that implements an interface must code all the methods defined in the interface or face a compiler error:

```
TestClass.java:1: class TestClass must be declared abstract.
It does not define void display() from interface Displayable.
```

Because of this enforcement, an interface is often called a *contract*. It is a contract between the designer of the interface and the coder of the class. The contract states that the coder agrees to implement methods in his or her class that match the name and parameters of all the methods in the interface.

Once you have some interfaces designed and implement them in all appropriate classes, you will start to discover more and more infrastructure and helper code that can be written to exploit it. For example, you might state that all GUI widgets that accept text from the user support a `verify` method, which is enforced by writing an interface named `Verifiable` and insisting all coders implement it in such classes. You might have various classes that extend the entry-field GUI widget in Java (`JTextField` in `javax.swing`, as you'll see in Chapter 12), and support specific inputs, such as `ZipCodeEntryField`, `PhoneNumberEntryField`, `CountryEntryField`, and `EMailEntryField`. They would all code their own unique versions of `verify` to test that the current input is a valid zip code, phone number, country name, or email address.

Now your validation code when the OK button is pressed on the window containing all these entry field objects is easy:

```
Verifiable allEntryFields[] = getAllEntryFields();
String error = null;
for (int idx=0; (idx<allEntryFields.length) && (error==null); idx++)
  error = allEntryFields[idx].verify();
if (error != null)
  // display error message window
```

This just iterate through all of the objects, calling the `verify` method until one returns a non-null error-message string. If none do, all the input is valid. Otherwise, it displays the error-message text in an error-message window. Nice, no? Think of all the if/else code this saves! Interfaces, then, enable generic helper code that works on all objects that implement the interface.

Interfaces versus inheritance

You might have noticed that implementing interfaces is similar to extending classes, except that the methods in an interface are all abstract, and hence must be overridden. Also, code that uses objects whose type is declared to be an interface name is similar to code that uses objects whose type is declared to be a parent class name. If you can force all the classes that implement an interface to instead extend a common parent class, you can simply live without interfaces.

Consider the example of the verify method in the Verifiable interface. (Interface names usually end in "able.") If you instead declared a parent class named BaseEntryField and placed in it an abstract method named verify, and coded the xxxxEntryField classes to each extend BaseEntryField, you would achieve the same results. But you can't.

Why not? Because all the xxxEntryFields already extend the JTextField class, which is Java's entry-field widget class. You have to do that because you want these to actually be just entry fields with some extra functionality added. To "be an entry field" means, in OO terms, to "extend the entry-field class." And remember, you can only extend *one* class in Java, so you are not able to create a new parent class.

So, interfaces really are a way to give the polymorphic behavior of inheritance, even in cases where you simply can't extend a common parent class. They do this by refining the rule of polymorphism to this:

> You can declare an object reference variable to be one class type *or interface type*, and yet assign to it at runtime an instance of a different class type, as long as the runtime class type extends the declared compile-time class type *or implements the declared compile time interface type.*

You use interfaces only when you can't use inheritance. For example, you saw how Java uses inheritance to support its utility classes Vector and Hashtable, by calling the equals method that all classes inherit and optionally override from Object. This allows any generic code to search any list of objects for a match. However, there is other generic code in Java that supports the notion of sorting a list, such as the sort methods in the java.util.Arrays class. These sort any given array.

In order to do a sort, or even a binary search, there must be a way to compare two elements and determine if one is greater than the other. What "greater" means for an object is subjective, as is the notion of equality, so it is left up to the objects themselves to decide. The sort methods work by comparing all the elements to each other by calling the compare method in each of them. This method is defined to take two objects, and the expected result should be -1 if the first is less than the second, zero if they are equal, and +1 if the first is greater. If you have a class such as Attendee and you want to support the ability to sort an array of these, you must implement the interface Comparator and implement this method that it dictates. The engineers decided not to put this method in the Object class, cluttering it up, and so instead had to go with the interface. If you try to sort an array of objects whose class does not implement Comparator, you will get an error.

Interfaces are callbacks

The interface examples in this chapter are all examples of *callbacks,* the most popular use of interfaces. (We mention this briefly so you understand the term when reading other Java books.) Callbacks involve generic helper code or infrastructure code that has no pre-defined knowledge of the objects it is working on, which are all defined to be an interface type. All it knows or cares about is that those objects support a method with a particular signature (as defined in the interface). The infrastructure code is simply trying to do its job, such as display information or print bills or sort objects, but it can't do it without help from those objects it is working on. So it "calls them back" by invoking the methods it knows exist in them (because they exist in the interface). It defers to the objects to do object-specific tasks.

Callbacks exist in any language that supports function pointers or inheritance of some kind. RPG IV has procedure pointers, so you could write callbacks. Consider the VECTOR service program from Chapter 6, for example. It contains memory allocation code that maintains a growable list of fields. The fields could be scalar fields or data structure fields. The key the service program allocates their memory, and a pointer to it is maintained in a linked list by the service program. Procedures make it easy to add, iterate, and remove from the list. However, this VECTOR code has no idea about the contents of each element in the list. It doesn't know if the element contains a single packed-decimal number or a structure with 12 sub-fields of different types. This is good, as it keeps the VECTOR code generic enough that any program can use it for anything.

This is bad, though, when it comes to supporting the ability to search for a given element. Suppose you'd like to be able to search by some key field for an element. For example, if you are storing structures of event attendees, you would like to easily search for an element in the vector that has a given phone number. You can't easily write generic code to do this, because you don't know what the memory map is for each element, so you don't know that it contains a phone number in the first 10 bytes. Indeed, another program might use this to store structures of information about orders, and might have an item-number key in the first four bytes.

You simply can't write generic code to do this search. However, you could write a generic procedure in VECTOR, named Search, say, that took a pointer to the item to search for (you don't want to hard-code the type of the key), and a procedure pointer to a procedure that the caller would supply. This Search procedure would walk the list of elements, and for each one, it would call the procedure pointer to compare that element's contents to the given key field, and would expect the called procedure to tell it if this is a match or not. The procedure pointed to would be supplied by each program that uses this, and so each program would know how to map the given structure, find the given subfield that is the key value, and compare it to the given key value. It would return *ON for a match and *OFF for no match. The generic search code would end the iteration at the first match, returning the element pointer.

You could similarly support a procedure Sort in VECTOR that sorted the list. To do this, it would need the callers to supply a pointer to a procedure to compare any two elements from the list, and return a number indicating if the first one is less than, equal to, or greater than the second one. Again, each caller would code this procedure differently depending on the contents being stored in the list. Comparing two data structures containing order information, for example, is different from comparing two data structures containing customer information.

Interfaces and constants

Interfaces can contain constants, so one other great use of interfaces is as a place to put constants needed throughout an application. By putting constants in an interface, any code that needs to reference them can simply implement the interface and access the constants directly, without qualifying their names with a class name. This can save much tedious typing.

Java-supplied interface examples

Java itself makes significant use of interfaces, for example:

- Comparator in java.util. Implement this interface when your object supports sorting. A number of Java-supplied helper methods use this interface, including the sort and search static methods in the java.util.Arrays class.

- Cloneable in java.lang. Implement this interface when your object supports cloning or duplicating. This allows you to write code to make copies of an object.

- Enumeration in java.util. Implement this interface when your object contains a list, and you want to support iterating through that list. There is much Java code that uses this.

- Runnable in java.lang. Implement this interface and supply the run method it dictates to support running code in a thread (discussed in Chapter 11).

■ Graphical user interface (GUI) event callbacks. These are a series of interfaces in java.awt.event and javax.swing.event to implement if you want to be informed of certain user-initiated events. For example, your GUI class would implement ActionListener and supply its actionPerformed method to be called back by the Java runtime when the user clicks a button. (This is covered in Chapter 12.)

■ Java Database Connectivity (JDBC) framework. This is an interrelated set of interfaces that database vendors implement to supply JDBC drivers for Java-access to their database. As a Java programmer, you simply code to the methods in the interface, and your code magically works with any vendor's JDBC driver. (This is covered in Chapter 13.)

The Cloneable and Enumeration interfaces are particularly important to know about, due to their pervasiveness in most Java applications.

The Cloneable interface

The Cloneable interface is defined in the java.lang package. It is an interesting case—a completely empty interface! It highlights the fact that interfaces are really tags for the compiler. The java.lang package class named Object, from which all classes inherit, has a method in it named clone. The purpose of this base method is to create a new instance of a given object that is identical to the current instance:

```
ClassA objA = new ClassA();
ClassA objB = objA.clone();
```

It is important to have this method, because otherwise you might be tempted to use this:

```
ClassA objB = objA;
```

This does not copy objA at all! Rather, it copies the memory address in objA to objB, thus creating a second reference to the same object. To create a second copy of an object, it is up to the object itself to supply a method. This is what clone does. It essentially instantiates a new instance of this class (using the default constructor only) and copies bit-by-bit all the instance variables in the current class to the new class.

Sounds straightforward? Well, it is not! The problem is that you may have objects as instance variables, and as just discussed, copying an object variable only produces a second reference to the same object—not a second copy of that object, as you would expect in this case. That is, nested objects need to be cloned, too. This job is not something that the base `clone` method inside `Object` can take on by itself. It needs to be carefully implemented by each class—by you. So, Java makes the `clone` method in `Object` protected; it can only be called by you in your class. Thus, `objB = objA.clone()` will always fail with a "`method not accessible`" error message unless you do the following:

- Override and implement the `clone` method in your class

- In that override, change the access to `public`

And that's not all. The language designers were so anxious that `clone` only be supported by classes that really think they have implemented it properly, that they force you to also tell the compiler explicitly that you support this method. How? By defining your class to implement the `Cloneable` interface. Only if all this has been done can a user invoke the `clone` method on your class.

By the way, if you do decide to support this useful function, your `clone` method would do the following:

- Invoke your parent's `clone` method: `super.clone();`

- Invoke the `clone` method on all of your object instance variables (if they are not `null`) and do a simple assignment copy of all primitive instance variables

This is a case where an interface is used in a unique way, as a tag to identify this class's support for a particular function. Can you do this, too? Yes, you can. There is a way to determine programmatically if the class type of a given object implements a particular interface—by first using the `Object` method `getClass` to return the object's `Class` object, and then calling `getInterfaces` on the `Class` object. This returns an array of `Class` objects, one for each interface implemented by this class. You can then loop through this array, invoking `getName` on each entry looking for the interface name you are interested in. Better yet, you can simply use the `instanceof` operator, which you will see soon.

The Enumeration interface

The Java utility package `java.util` includes an interface named `Enumeration`. This is a convention that classes should use when they want to support the idea of *enumerating* or walking through a list of items. Suppose you have a class that is obviously a collection of something, such as the AttendeeList class from Listing 9.16. If you want to support the ability for users to iterate through each item in the list, do so by implementing the Enumeration interface. This will make it easier for users who are used to this convention from other Java-supplied classes, such as Hashtable. The Enumeration interface contains two method signatures, both taking no parameters:

- The hasMoreElements signature returns true if there are more elements in the collection.

- The nextElement signature returns the next element in the collection.

The intended usage for these is this:

```
while (obj.hasMoreElements())
  nextObj = (MyClass)obj.nextElement();
```

Because the nextElement method is defined to return Object, you have to cast the result to the actual object type in the enumeration.

Let's update the AttendeeList class to support this interface. You could do this directly in your AttendeeList class, but by convention, the preferred way to do this is to write a second class that implements this. We will describe why this is preferred, and what you need to do in the first class to use the second class, shortly. First, the new class named AttendeeEnumeration is shown in Listing 9.17.

Listing 9.17: The AttendeeEnumeration Class

```
import java.util.*;
/**
 * Helper class to enumerate the attendees at an event
 */
class AttendeeEnumeration implements Enumeration
{
    private AttendeeList list;
    private int pos = 0;

    AttendeeEnumeration(AttendeeList list)
    {
        this.list = list;
    }

    public boolean hasMoreElements()
    {
```

```
        return (pos < list.getSize());
    }

    public Object nextElement()
    {
        Object retobj = null;
        if (hasMoreElements())
          retobj = list.getAttendeeAt(pos++);
        return retobj;
    }
}
```

This class supports the two methods from the Enumeration interface. To do this, it requires an instance of AttendeeList, which is passed into the constructor, and it requires an instance variable pos to remember the current position. To support hasMoreElements, it simply compares the pos variable to the total number of elements, which it gets by calling a new method getSize in AttendeeList. To support nextElement, it returns the element at the current position and increments the current position. To get the element, it calls a new method getAttendeeAt in the AttendeeList object.

This class is a helper class, in that the intention is for users to never see it. That is why it is not defined as public. Rather, you create a new method in the AttendeeList class, named elements by convention, which returns an instance of it. However, the return type is defined to be Enumeration instead of the class name, to hide the details (class name). Remember, when you define a return type to be an interface name, you can return any object that implements that interface. The updated AttendeeList class, then, is shown in Listing 9.18.

Listing 9.18: The Updated AttendeeList Class

```
public class AttendeeList
{
    public int getSize()
    {
        return attendees.size();
    }
    public Attendee getAttendeeAt(int pos)
    {
        return (Attendee)attendees.elementAt(pos);
    }
    public Enumeration elements()
    {
        return new AttendeeEnumeration(this);
```

Listing 9.18: The Updated AttendeeList Class (continued)

```
    }

    public static void main(String args[])
    {
        // test attendee code
        AttendeeList attendeeList = new AttendeeList();
        System.out.println();
        attendeeList.register("Phil Coulthard");
        attendeeList.register("George Farr");
        attendeeList.register("George Farr");
        attendeeList.display();
        attendeeList.deRegister("Phil Coulthard");
        attendeeList.deRegister("Phil Coulthard");
        attendeeList.display();
        // test the Enumeration support...
        System.out.println("Testing Enumeration Support");
        Enumeration elements = attendeeList.elements();
        while (elements.hasMoreElements())
        {
            Attendee nextAttendee =
                (Attendee)elements.nextElement();
            nextAttendee.display();
        }
    }
}
```

For brevity, this listing shows only the three new methods and the updated main method that tests the new Enumeration support. Note that the getSize and getElementAt methods were only added to support the code in AttendeeEnumeration, but they were made public anyway, in case others find them of value. The important new method is elements, which returns an instance of the new class, passing this into its constructor. Finally, the main method shows code to demonstrate how users will use this Enumeration support.

A separate class is used to support Enumeration so that the users can support multiple enumerations simultaneously. For example, because each call to elements returns a new object with its own pos instance variable, this is possible:

```
Enumeration elements1 = attendeeList.elements();
Enumeration elements2 = attendeeList.elements();
while (elements1.hasMoreElements())
  ...
while (elements2.hasMoreElements())
  ...
```

If you implemented the Enumeration interface directly in your AttendeeList class, this would not be possible. Whether you do it this way or not is up to you, of course.

The Enumeration interface is widely used in Java. (There is a replacement for it in JDK 1.2.0 and higher, named Iterator, but most people still use Enumeration.) Indeed, all the work you just saw to support Enumeration in the AttendeeList class is actually a waste of time! Why? Because AttendeeList uses a Vector object for the list, and the Vector class already supports an elements method that returns an Enumeration object. So, you can get the same functionality by simply coding the elements methods in AttendeeList as this:

```java
public Enumeration elements()
{
    return attendees.elements(); // return Enumeration obj
}
```

This certainly makes it easier! You simply delegate the call to the Vector object, which has done the work for you already. You really only have to code your own Enumeration class if you are using arrays. Even Hashtable, as mentioned, already has an elements method.

This gives an opportunity to both expand the usefulness and simplify the Helpers class from earlier in this chapter. Currently, it only supports arrays and Vector objects in its overloaded versions of displayAll. Let's change it now to support only arrays and Enumeration objects. This will be sufficient, because users wanting to call it with a Vector or a Hashtable can simply call elements on their Vector or Hashtable object and pass in the result. We hate to write redundant code however, so even for arrays, let's internally convert them to an Enumeration object first, and then call the Enumeration version of displayAll under the covers.

To do this, you first need a very handy class that implements Enumeration for any array. It is shown in Listing 9.19. This is a handy class. We suggest you keep it around, since it will work with any array.

Listing 9.19: The ArrayEnumeration Class

```java
import java.util.*;

public class ArrayEnumeration implements Enumeration
{
    private Object list[];
```

Listing 9.19: The ArrayEnumeration Class (continued)

```
private int pos = 0;

public ArrayEnumeration(Object list[])
{
   this.list = list;
}
public boolean hasMoreElements()
{
   return (pos < list.length);
}
public Object nextElement()
{
    Object retobj = null;
    if (hasMoreElements())
      retobj = list[pos++];
    return retobj;
}
}
```

The new and improved (how can something be both new *and* improved?) Helpers class is shown in Listing 9.20.

Listing 9.20: The Updated Helpers Class

```
import java.util.*;

public class Helpers
{
    public static void displayAll(Displayable objects[])
    {
        displayAll(new ArrayEnumeration(objects));
    }

    public static void displayAll(Enumeration objects)
    {
        Displayable currentObject = null;
        while (objects.hasMoreElements())
        {
            currentObject = (Displayable)objects.nextElement();
            currentObject.display();
        }
    }
}
```

With this change, it is very easy to change the Hashtable version of the AttendeeList class from Chapter 6 to also use this Helpers class, if you wanted. You'd simply have to add "implements Displayable" to the Attendee class, and change the display method in AttendeeList to call your new Helpers method:

```
public void display()
{
    Helpers.displayAll(attendees.elements());
}
```

Chapter 11 revisits this Helpers class and the updated Hashtable version of AttendeeList that uses it.

O2O—OBJECT TO OBJECT: CASTING OBJECTS

You have seen already that you can cast objects using syntax similar to that used for casting primitive types (discussed in Chapter 5). You do this to tell the compiler that an object reference variable declared as one type is in fact of another type. For example, many Java-supplied classes are generic utility classes that are defined to return an object of type Object, the root parent of all objects. You have to cast the returned object to your class type to call methods defined in your class. You saw this for the elementAt method in Vector, the get method in Hashtable, and the nextElement method in Enumeration.

By now, you can appreciate why this is necessary. On the one hand, since you want to write utility code that is generic and reusable with objects of any type (such as the Vector and Hashtable classes), you use the base Object as the defined type of parameters and return types, so as not to restrict use to objects of specific classes. On the other hand, Java's strong typing means you are prevented by the compiler from calling methods in an object that are not declared in that object's type. So, after getting an object out of a Vector via elementAt, for example, you can't call any methods except those defined in Object. Casting tells the compiler that this object's type is not actually Object, but really XXX. This allows you to subsequently call any methods defined in class XXX.

Here are the explicit syntactical details of this casting:

- Casting is done using the cast syntax: Type1 result = (Type1)object;

- Casting can only be to a target class type that extends the source class type (lower in the hierarchy)

- Casting can only be to the actual type of the object at runtime or a parent of that type

The last rule is the most important one. When you cast primitive values, you actually morph the data type from one to another. However, when you cast objects, the object type is not changed! In reality, the object must already be of that target type at runtime, and you are simply telling the compiler that this is the case. If you do try to cast an object to a type that is different than the object's actual runtime type, you will get a cast exception error at runtime. Well, the object must not be different from the actual runtime type or a *parent* of that runtime type, although as you know, you do not legally need to cast in order to assign an object of class C1 to an object reference variable of class C2, if C2 is a parent of C1. In other words:

```
C2 myVariable = new C1(); // legal if C1 extends C2
C2 myOtherVariable = (C2)new C1();  // legal but not required
```

You can also cast to an interface if that actual runtime type implements that interface, but once again, this is not necessary because you can legally assign an object to an interface reference variable if the declared type of that object implements that interface:

```
I1 myVariable = new C3; // legal if C3 implements I1
I1 myOtherVariable = (I1)new C3; // legal but not required
```

Because of the third rule, it is often good to test whether the object type is what you think it is before attempting the cast. This can be done using the `instanceof` operator, which is a binary operator that takes an object and a class name or interface name as operators, and returns true if the object is of that class type or implements that interface. Here is an example:

```
Object obj = myVector.elementAt(0);
Employee emp = null;
if (obj instanceof Employee)
  emp = (Employee)obj;
```

Note the class name to the right of `instanceof` is not in quotes. The object must be of the given class type or child of that class to get true as a result. For interfaces, the object must implement that interface. The `instanceof` operator is only used in expressions, since it has no side effects.

The typical need for this operator is when you have a list (such as an array or vector) of different objects. For example, you might define an array of `Employee` objects and then populate it with objects of various child classes of `Employee`. If every method you want to call is in the `Employee` parent class, you do not need to cast. However, if you want to call a method that only exists in one of the child classes, you would need to test the type and subsequently do the cast, like this:

```
Employee emps[] = getAllEmployees();
for (int idx = 0; idx < emps.length; idx++)
    if (emps[idx] instanceof SalesEmployee)
        ((SalesEmployee)emps[idx]).printSalesCommission();
```

With the proper design of class hierarchies, you will find the need to use instanceof is rare. For example, you could have placed that method in the Employee class and only uniquely overridden it in SalesEmployee. If the method is in the parent class, you need not cast.

COMMON METHODS TO OVERRIDE

You know now that all classes you create in Java implicitly extend the Object class. This gives users of your class access to all the non-final, non-abstract, non-private methods in this universal class. However, there are a few methods, shown in Table 9.1, that you should consider overriding in your new class every time. This is not to say that every class you create needs to support all of these methods, but you really should make an explicit decision in every class whether to implement these methods or not.

Table 9.1: Methods that Are Frequently Overridden

Method	Description
finalize	This method is called by Java when an object of your class is "swept up" by the garbage collector. If you have any finalization or cleanup code to be done when the object is destroyed, such as closing any possibly still open files, put it here.
clone	You have seen this already; it is a convention to supply this method if you want to enable object duplication.
equals	By convention, users will invoke this method to compare two objects of your class. If you want to support the idea of equality testing, you must supply this method, as the default implementation returns false unless you are comparing an object to itself.
hashCode	This returns a hash code, or unique key, derived from this object. If you implement the equals method, you probably need to override this one too, so as to return a unique hash value for different objects, usually based on instance variable values.
toString	This method is called whenever someone tries to convert an object of your class to a string, such as by specifying an object name in the System. out.println method. This should return a string with something useful in it.

THE OO WAY OF LIFE

By this time, you have seen all the language tools for object-orientation, as well as all the terminology. So, are you ready to design your first object-oriented project? Probably not. Using these tools efficiently is a skill that comes with time. The process of designing a good object-oriented system is different from the procedural systems that you are used to. It involves a somewhat new way of thinking—thinking in terms of objects.

Consider how you design or develop now with RPG. Everyone is different, but chances are your up-front design centers first around the functionality (subroutines, procedures, and calculation specifications) that you will need to solve the problem. The data (data structures, arrays, and so on) that you will need to support this functionality come in at a secondary stage. We are not talking about the database design here, although, for many, that design emerges from this function-centered thought process. This design process leads to functions throughout the application that access common data, whether data structures or external database files.

With OO, the design process is reversed. Rather than first thinking about the functions required to get the job done, you are required to first consider the *objects* needed. And what are objects, again? Instances of classes. And what are classes, again? Data (variables) and supporting functions (methods). You need to start thinking of data and functions as a single unit in order to grasp OO. Then, you start thinking about how to partition your "problem domain" into such units (objects). This design process leads to encapsulation, minimizing the number of places that code accesses particular data. Instead of accessing data directly, most code instantiates common objects and calls methods on that object to read, change, or insert data.

You will be surprised at some of the things that become objects in an OO world—for example, who would expect a color like red to be an object? Who would expect a two-dimensional point (with x and y coordinates) to be an object? In Java, they are. Indeed, because in Java executable code can only exist inside of objects, you'll find that everything is an object—well, to be precise, everything is either an object or a primitive variable inside an object.

In search of objects

There is no magic formula to help you begin thinking in terms of OO, but there are many books that describe the up-front part of an OO project—the analysis and design phases (OOA and OOD). You will want to read one or two. All of these books at least discuss the following:

- How to clearly articulate the "problem domain" by writing use cases.

- How to "find" objects in your problem domain.

- How to find and define the "roles" of your objects (that is, the methods).

- How to find and define the "relationships" between your various objects (that is, who uses what, and who extends what).

- How to consistently document your design. That is, most books introduce a language for writing down your object-oriented design, with conventions for depicting classes, objects, relationships, and so on.

The collective approach that a book uses to describe all this is known as a *methodology*. Such methodologies are usually named after the person or persons who defined them. Is there a "best" methodology? Certainly there is: the one that you decide to use. Pick one, roll up your sleeves, and dig in. Or, ultimately, you can hire or contract-in experienced OOA/D programmers and go with their recommendation.

One methodology of which you should be aware, however, is *UML* (*Unified Modeling Language*). It is a convergence of a number of leading methodologies, and it appears poised to become the industry standard. It was predominantly defined by highly regarded methodologists (Grady Booch, Ivar Jacobson, and Jim Rumbaugh) at Rational Software, the makers of the immensely popular OOA/D tool Rational Rose. For more information on UML, see Rational's Internet Web site: *www.rational.com/uml*.

In an OO project, you spend much more time at the beginning, thinking about the problem to be solved, than you do in the later stages. This is a good thing, because as you know from experience, the more time you spend in the design stage of the project, the less time you have to spend coding and testing the project. The objectives of OO are to reduce maintenance efforts and increase code reuse. By spending time analyzing the problem domain in the search for objects, you typically improve your final time-to-market and ongoing quality, because you:

- Drive out a better problem statement (a crisp list of requirements)

- Derive a system that better models the real-world problem, leading to end-user satisfaction and higher quality

How do you find problem-domain objects? The usual trick is to start with your requirements statement and look for nouns. These are the "low-hanging fruit"—they will almost always become objects. Examples are *car*, *employee*, *manager*, *bank account*, *customer*, and *service*. Your system will also require many implementation objects, in the end, to do the job. These are helper objects with commonly needed functions, like *tax calculations*, *date manipulations*, *string manipulations*, and *monetary calculations*. After some experience, you will get better at finding these up-front. Initially, though, you might have to stumble into them as you go.

How do you find roles? These affect what methods and variables your objects will have. The usual trick is, again, to start with your requirements statement and this time look for verbs. For example, you might expect to have methods to do *printing*, *sorting*, *calculating*, *ordering*, and *billing*. Establishing which roles are played by which objects is also important at this early stage.

How do you find relationships? This requires you to address design issues like class hierarchies, object parameters, object instance variables, and collections of objects. How objects will use each other, including quantitative metrics ("how many"), is important to consider at this early stage. This is where you typically have to make some tough decisions, which will be affected by such real-world things as performance.

In our experience, some of the more interesting decisions that programmers have to face center around inheritance. The trick is to know when to inherit from another class rather than do one of the following:

- Declare an instance of the parent class as an instance variable in your class. This is known as *containment*—your class "contains" an instance of another class.

- Pass in an instance of the parent class as a parameter to the methods that need it. This is known as *usage*—your class "uses" an instance of another class.

Again, there are general rules that cover inheritance. The idea in OO is to define objects that model, as closely as possible, the real world you are interested in. This means you rely on the real world to make decisions for you wherever you can. Therefore, to decide if a class should inherit, contain, or use another class, ask yourself some questions about the real-world relationships between the two classes:

- *Is the new class an example of the first class?* This is the classic "is a" relationship, and if you answer yes, your new class should extend the first class. Is a dog an animal? Yes, so the Dog class should extend the Animal class. Is a purchase order an order? Yes, so PurchaseOrder should extend Order.

- *Does the new class have objects of the first class?* This is the classic "has a" relationship, and if you answer yes, your new class should contain an instance variable of the first class. Does an employee have a salary? Yes, so the Employee class should contain an instance of the Salary class. Does an order have a purchase item? Yes, so the Order class should have a PurchaseItem object as an instance. Indeed, it probably should have a list of PurchaseItem objects.

- *Does the new class use an object of the first class?* This is the classic "uses" relationship, and if you answer yes, your new class should accept as a method parameter an instance of the first class. This is typically a case where you are defining a helper or utility class that performs some commonly needed function on any given object. Does a payroll system use employee objects? Yes, so Payroll needs a list of Employee objects as input. Does a reporting system use reportable objects? Yes, so Report needs a list of Reportable objects as input (where Reportable is probably an interface).

OO design tips

Here are some simple tips about OO programming:

Tip 1: Separate, separate, separate

Keep each class small, and separate each functional aspect of your application into its own class or classes. For example, notice how the registration application earlier in this chapter uses a class for each attendee, a class for the list of attendees, and a class for the user interface. This design pattern will apply to many situations; many of your applications will have a class representing an entity key, a class representing an entity that contains an entity key, a class containing a list of entities searchable by key or sequentially, and one or more user interface classes.

Tip 2: Leverage your database skills

As a good starting point in designing your new application, consider making a class for every field in the database you are using, such as EmployeeId, Salary, OrderAmount,

ShipDate, ZipCode, PhoneNumber, and Country. You will find it handy to have constructors for these that accept primitive values, and also to supply methods to verify that a given primitive value is syntactically valid. At a minimum, the constructor and verify methods should take a String object, as that is what you get from the console and from GUI fields. All these classes should supply an equals method.

Look for grouping opportunities that reduce complexity. For example, you might want to have an Address class that groups the various objects that make up an address. This will make it easier to prompt for and print an address.

Look for common basic types that can become parent classes. For example, you might find it saves many headaches to have a Money class that knows how to do math on a monetary value, such as applyDiscount. Then, Salary, UnitCost, and OrderAmount will extend this class.

For each record format, especially in logical files, define a class that contains one or more of the field classes, for example, Department, Employee, Order. For keyed record formats, create a class with the same name but with Key appended, as in DepartmentKey, EmployeeKey, and OrderKey. This class should contain appropriate objects from the field classes defined above. This class should also supply equals and hashcode methods and should implement the Comparator interface.

If the record format has fields that contain "type" information that affects processing, such as employee type, salary type, order type, or customer type, make separate child classes for each possible type. For example, you might have SalariedEmployee and HourlyEmployee child classes, or PurchaseOrder and ServiceOrder child classes. Put the unique processing required in overridden methods in the child classes. Supply an object factory class to read the next record of the database, create an instance of the appropriate child class, and return that to the caller.

For logical files, especially join logical files, the corresponding class is often referred to as a *business object*. This represents an entity that is a composite of information from other files (objects). The cool thing about business objects is that they hide inside them all the complexity involved in reading all the database files necessary to populate them. Indeed, with enough coding, you could support update operations by writing to the physical files yourself. Once you have business objects like Order, Policy, and Contract, all remaining code in the application becomes quick and easy to write. There's no database access to be concerned with, as it is all nicely encapsulated behind a wall.

Tip 3: Use the "is a" rule with a grain of salt

Despite the "is a" rule, do not inherit from an existing class unless you intend to override one or more methods in the parent class. This saves you from using up your single allowance for extending. Also, sometimes you want to extend, but can't. For example, you probably want to consider writing a Money class that is a refinement of BigDecimal that forces the scale (decimal place) to two after every operation. You can't do this by extending BigDecimal, though, because it is an immutable class. You have the same problem if you want to extend String and add more methods. In both cases, your new class will have to contain an instance of the original class as an instance variable, and the methods will operate on it. Be sure to include a method to return the contained BigDecimal or String object, though, so callers can get to the methods in those classes.

Tip 4: Create child classes that add functionality

Despite the terminology, subclasses should offer a superset of functions compared to their parent class. If you find yourself wanting to remove methods from your parent class because they do not apply to your child class, you probably should not be inheriting from that parent. Even if in real life there is an "is a" relationship, there might not be one in the actual code.

For example, a manager might not be an employee, if class Employee has methods dependent on hourly wages versus salary. You might have to abstract-out a third common class named HR (for "Human Resource") from which Employee and Manager both inherit. (Of course, many would argue that the "is a" relationship does not apply to managers and humans!) Another option here is to have a class named JobDescription that ManagerJob extends, and then to contain an instance of ManagerJob in the appropriate Employee objects. This gives you the flexibility of defining additional employee job descriptions and supporting multiple job descriptions per employee.

Tip 5: Strive for easy and elegant user code

When designing your class hierarchies and classes, keep in mind the users of your classes. You want to minimize their efforts. The main part of your application should be as simple and elegant as possible. This means letting your classes do as much as work as possible. For example, it might be as simple as this:

```
TheApp app = new TheApp();
app.run();
```

Tip 6: Strive for small methods

If you find yourself with a very large and complicated class that has some really outrageous methods, look hard at it. You might need to abstract-out some code into a base or helper class, and use more and smaller methods. This makes the code easier to maintain and understand.

Tip 7: Balance anticipated function versus bloat

The trick for long-lasting classes is to embellish them with as many methods as you predict might ever be needed. But don't go overboard! Do all private variables really need setXXX methods? Will someone really want to change these variables? Do you need a particular new method, or can the result be achieved by using a combination of existing methods?

Tip 8: Be wary of large numbers of instance variables

If your class has dozens of instance variables, consider grouping those variables into classes of their own and instantiating instances of them. Remember, classes do not have to have methods. Moving related variables into their own class will make your code more elegant, and you might then discover those helper classes have other uses, too. You might even discover that some of the manipulations you were doing directly on those variables can be moved into methods of the new class.

Tip 9: Watch for static candidates

Do you have methods that do not act on any of your class instance variables? Maybe some utility method you wrote takes all its information as parameters? If so, either forgo the parameters and use instance variables instead, or make the method static so it can be used by others without requiring an instantiation of your class.

SUMMARY

This has been a whirlwind "introductory" chapter to object-orientation. This chapter briefly introduced you to the following OO terminology:

- Encapsulation, inheritance, and polymorphism

- "Has a," "is a," and "uses" relationships

- Methodologies for specifying and documenting object-oriented systems.

It also introduced some new specific Java constructs:

- The `extends` keyword
- The `protected`, `abstract`, and `final` modifiers
- Interfaces and the `implements` keyword
- The `instanceof` operator

You also learned about:

- The `java.lang.Object` and `java.lang.Class` superclasses
- The `java.lang.Cloneable` interface and the `java.lang.clone()` method
- The `java.lang.Enumeration` interface
- Design patterns, object factories, and business objects.

You should feel more "acclimatized" to OO now and be ready to pursue it further with other books, like those in "References," below. Subsequent chapters will continue to help you get familiar with OO.

REFERENCES

Gamma, Helm, Johnson, and Vlissides. 1995. *Design Patterns: Elements of Reusable Object-Oriented Software*. Addison-Wesley, ISBN 0201633612.Gilbert, Stephen, and Bill McCarty. 1998. *Object-Oriented Design in Java*. Waite Group Press, ISBN 1571691340.

Larmon, Craig. 1997. *Applying UML and Patterns: An Introduction to Object-Oriented Analysis and Design*. Prentice Hall, ISBN 0137488807.

EXCEPTIONS **10**

This chapter discusses an aspect of Java that you will think has been lifted right off the iSeries. You are, no doubt, plenty familiar with the concept of exceptions on the AS/400. They were part of the original architecture of the AS/400 (and System/38) that was a harbinger of things to come. Well, now their time has arrived! Let's begin by briefly reviewing the OS/400 exception architecture.

AS/400 EXCEPTION MODEL OVERVIEW

On the AS/400, the idea of sending messages from one program to another is a long-established part of the programming model. All operating system APIs and functions send messages when something unexpected happens—something "exceptional." These are sent both explicitly when you code a call to these APIs, and implicitly when they are invoked by a language runtime (such as an RPG database input/output operation). Language runtimes themselves also send messages when a programming error such as "divide by zero" or "array index out of bounds" happens.

Messages on the AS/400 embed two important pieces of information:

- Error-message text, often with runtime substitution variables to pinpoint the problem (such as a source sequence number or error code).

- The severity, which for program-to-program messages is either *ESCAPE, *STATUS, or *NOTIFY.

All error messages have a unique seven-character *message identifier* that can be explicitly monitored for.

The AS/400 message-exception model is most obvious when you are writing CL (Control Language) programs and you code explicit MONMSG (*Monitor Message*) statements for each command call. It is possible to monitor for explicit messages (such as MCH0601), a range of messages (such as by using 0000 for the numeric part of the message ID), or *function checks* (CPF9999). The function check monitors typically give sweeping "if anything at all happens, tell me about it" messages. Notice also that CL programs often send their own messages for diagnostic, status, or exceptional situations by using the SNDPGMMSG (*Send Program Message*) command. Programmers have learned that messages, when used properly, can be an effective way out of a troublesome situation such as receiving unexpected input.

The OPM exception model

In the *Original Programming Model* (*OPM*, meaning pre-ILE) days, exception messages were handled like this:

1. Does the program call-stack entry that received the message handle it (monitor for it or have code waiting to receive it)?

2. If yes, done.

3. If no, send a function check (message CPF9999) to that same program call-stack entry.

4. Does the program call-stack entry that received the message handle CPF9999?

5. If yes, done.

6. If no, blow away that program and send (*percolate*) that CPF9999 to the previous entry in the call stack.

7. Repeat the previous step until the CPF9999 is handled. (Ultimately, the job ends or the interactive command line returns control.)

The ILE exception model

When writing new ILE programs, the exception model is changed in the following ways:

- The original exception message is passed all the way up the call stack until a handler is found for it (that is, code that is willing to receive it). It is not converted to a function check right away.

- If nobody on the call stack (to the *control boundary*, which is an activation group, an OPM program, or the job boundary) handles this message, it is converted to a function check (CPF9999) and the process is repeated for the function check.

- If the original message is handled by somebody on the call stack, the entries above it are terminated.

- If nobody handles the original message, each is then given a chance to handle the function check, starting at the original call-stack entry that received the message.

Each entry in the call stack that does not handle the function check is typically removed from the call stack (depending on the user's answer to an inquiry message), and the next entry is given a chance to handle it. Further, the call stack itself is different in ILE. Not only does it contain programs, but it also contains procedures, which can have their own unique exception-handling support.

RPG III exception-handling

Now that you have seen the generic system support for exceptions, let's look closer at what is involved in RPG itself. As you recall, RPG III divides exceptions into two camps:

- *File errors.* These can occur when processing files, such as "record not found."

- *Program errors.* These are programming errors, such as "divide by zero."

RPG III offers three ways to handle exceptions:

- Error indicators (*Resulting Error Indicator*) on many op-codes. These are set by the language at runtime if the op-code fails.

- The INFSR error subroutine for file errors.

- The *PSSR error subroutine for program errors.

You can also code special data structures (INFDS and PSDS) that the language will update at runtime to indicate the error that occurred (in the *STATUS subfield). When returning from an error subroutine, the value of factor two on the ENDSR (*End Subroutine*) op-code can be used to determine where control returns. We will not bore you with further details because we assume that you are already intimately familiar with this process and architecture.

ILE RPG (RPG IV) exception-handling

How have things changed for RPG IV? That is a good question, but the answer could easily fill an entire chapter on its own. For more detailed information, consult the *ILE RPG/400 Programmer's Guide* (SC09-2074). However, in a nutshell, the basics follow:

- You still have error indicators, INFSR and *PSSR subroutines, and INFDS and PSDS data structures.

- The INFSR subroutine and INFDS data structures are identified on the F-spec with the new INFSR(xxx) and INFDS(xxx) keywords.

- The INFSR subroutines apply only to the mainline code, *not* to procedures. You will have to rely on error indicators for file-processing in a procedure.

- The *PSSR subroutines are local to the procedure where they are declared. (Yes, you can define subroutines inside procedures.) This means you need one for every procedure (although they could all call a common subprocedure) *and* one for the mainline code.

- The *PSSR subroutines inside procedures must have a blank factor two on the ENDSR statement—and if control reaches that far, the procedure will end there. Unfortunately, you have to rely on GOTO prior to ENDSR to continue processing.

- The INFDS and PSDS data structures are global in scope. That means that they are accessible by all procedures.

- There is an entirely new option: an ILE exception-handling bindable API, CEEHDLR. This registers an ILE exception handler for this procedure, and its undo cousin (CEEHDLU) "unregisters" an ILE exception handler. Using these APIs gives you a language-neutral way of dealing with exceptions in ILE. Typically, then, you code a call to CEEHDLR at the beginning of your procedure and a call to CEEHDLU at the end.

- As of V4R2, there is a new %ERROR built-in function to replace error indicators. If you specify an error extender on your op-code (by adding E in parentheses after the op-code), you can test if %ERROR returns one after the operation to establish whether an error occurred. You can also use the new %STATUS built-in-function to return the status code of that error. Other related built-in-functions are %OPEN to test if the given file is open, and %EOF, %EQUAL, and %FOUND to test if the previous operation resulted in an end of file, an exact record match, or a record match, respectively.

New MONITOR operation in RPG V5R1

Worth noting is an awesome new capability in V5R1 of RPG that makes exception-handling in much easier, and offers support very much similar to the Java exception support you will see shortly. As of V5R1, you can place one or more operation statements that may result in errors between a MONITOR and ENDMON set of op-code statements. The idea is that if any of the statements inside the monitor group results in an error, control will go to a particular ON-ERROR group.

You code one or more ON-ERROR operations within the monitor group, but after the statement you are monitoring. Each ON-ERROR op-code specifies a colon-separated list of status codes in free-form factor two, for which it is responsible. If an error happens during execution of any of the monitored statements, control will flow to the ON-ERROR statement that matches the status code of the error. You place your statements for handling the error after the ON-ERROR statement. All statements up to the next ON-ERROR or ENDMON statement are executed in this case. To handle the "otherwise" cases, you can specify special values in factor two instead of status codes. These are *FILE, *PROGRAM, and *ALL, which match on any file error, program error, or any error at all, respectively.

The following example is from the RPG IV reference manual:

```
*  The MONITOR block consists of the READ statement and the IF group.
*  - The first ON-ERROR block handles status 1211 which
*    is issued for the READ operation if the file is not open.
*  - The second ON-ERROR block handles all other file errors.
*  - The third ON-ERROR block handles the string-operation status
*    code 00100 and array index status code 00121.
*  - The fourth ON-ERROR block (which could have had a factor 2
*    of *ALL) handles errors not handled by the specific ON-ERROR
*    operations.
*  If no error occurs in the MONITOR block, control passes from the
*  ENDIF to the ENDMON.
C                   MONITOR
C                   READ      FILE1
C                   IF        NOT %EOF
C                   EVAL      Line = %SUBST(Line(i) :
C                                   %SCAN('***': Line(i)) + 1)
C                   ENDIF
C                   ON-ERROR  1211
C                   ... handle file-not-open
C                   ON-ERROR  *FILE
C                   ... handle other file errors
C                   ON-ERROR  00100 : 00121
C                   ... handle string error and array-index error
C                   ON-ERROR
C                   ... handle all other errors
C                   ENDMON
```

If you have not discovered MONITOR and ON-ERROR yet, check them out!

EXCEPTIONS IN JAVA

The AS/400 and RPG exception model has taught discipline when it comes to proactively designing support for error situations. If you don't follow this practice, you risk exposing those ugly function checks to your users. So, doing more work up-front prevents problems in the long run. You produce more robust, fault-tolerant code that is cheaper to maintain. (So, it is safe to say that RPG programmers are *exceptional*!) The Java designers have taken these noble goals to heart. (Actually, they are a reasonably standard OO thing.)

Java also provides the feature of exceptions for unexpected situations, and it has language constructs for sending and monitoring them. The consequences of ignoring them are even more frightening than on the AS/400. In fact, Java goes a step further than simply ending your program at runtime if you fail to monitor for an exception that happens. It actually tries to catch, at compile time, where you missed coding in monitors for potential exceptions. To accomplish this, it has further language syntax for defining, for each method, the exceptions that callers of this method need to monitor for.

The Java exception model at a glance

In a nutshell, Java's exception support includes the following:

- Exceptions in Java are simply objects of classes that extend the Throwable class.

- Java comes with many predefined exception classes, which can be found in the JDK documentation.

- System errors extend the Error class, while your own exceptions extend the Exception class. Both of these classes extend the Throwable class.

- Exception objects include message text retrievable via the getMessage method.

- Any code can throw an exception when it detects an error, by using the throw operator and passing it an exception class object.

- Any method that throws an exception must identify all exceptions it throws on the throws clause of the method definition.

- Many methods in Java-supplied classes throw exceptions.

- To call any method that throws exceptions, you must put the method call inside a try block, followed by one or more catch blocks.

- The catch block defines a parameter that is an object of an exception class. If an exception of that class or a child of that class is thrown, this catch block gets control.

- The catch block for a given try block can optionally be followed by a finally block, which is always executed whether an exception is thrown or not.

- As an alternative to putting an exception-throwing method call inside a try block, you can percolate the exception up the call stack by just defining the throws clause for those potential exceptions in your own method.

- Constructors can throw exceptions, too. If they do, the new operation is cancelled, and no object is created.

The following "exceptional" sections expand on these concepts.

Exception objects in Java

In contrast to RPG, Java does not have error indicators. It provides only the concept of exception messages, such as the AS/400 exception model. What are these messages? They are Java objects, of course! There is a Java-defined class named Throwable, which all Java exceptions inherit from. This class is in the Java-supplied package java.lang, which all Java code implicitly imports. Any Java class that directly or indirectly extends Throwable is an "exception" in Java, whether that class is Java-supplied or written by you. You use unique language syntax to send these exceptions back up the method call-stack, and to monitor for them in code you call.

Objects of the Throwable class contain a string describing the exception, which is retrievable with the getMessage method. Another useful method in this class is printStackTrace, which prints out a method call-stack trace from the point where this exception was sent. Java programmers are particularly fond of this method because it is very useful in debugging. Here is an example of printStackTrace:

```
java.lang.NumberFormatException: abc
   at java.lang.Integer.parseInt(Integer.java:409)
   at java.lang.Integer.parseInt(Integer.java:458)
   at
ShowPrintStackTrace.convertStringToInt(ShowPrintStackTrace.java:20)
   at ShowPrintStackTrace.main(ShowPrintStackTrace.java:8)
```

This is from the exception NumberFormatException that the method parseInt in class Integer throws when it is given a string to convert to integer and that string contains non-numeric characters. You see that the stack trace starts with the name of the exception class, followed on the same line by the message text from the exception object (in this case abc, which is the invalid input used). Following that is the method-call stack, starting with the method that threw the exception (parseInt, in this case). Note the same method is listed twice in the example, indicating it calls itself recursively. The stack trace ends with the method that called printStackTrace. In this case, this is the main method in class ShowPrintStackTrace, shown in Listing 10.1. (The syntax of the try/catch blocks shown in Listing 10.1 is discussed later in this chapter.)

Listing 10.1: The Class ShowPrintStackTrace,
which Generates an Exception and Stack Trace

```
public class ShowPrintStackTrace
{

    public static void main(String args[])
    {
        try
        {
            convertStringToInt("abc");
        }
        catch(NumberFormatException exc)
        {
            System.out.println(exc.getMessage());
            exc.printStackTrace();
        }
    }

    public static int convertStringToInt(String stringToConvert)
                      throws NumberFormatException
    {
        return (Integer.parseInt(stringToConvert));
    }
} // end ShowPrintStackTrace class
```

AS/400 exceptions have a severity associated with them, as well as a unique message ID. Java exceptions (or Throwable objects) have this information, too. The severity and unique ID is implicit with the particular class of the exception object. In other words, there are many exception classes (that extend the Throwable class), so the exact error can be determined by the exact exception object used. This means the class, itself, is equivalent to a message ID because it uniquely identifies the error.

There really is no explicit severity associated with an exception in Java, but you can think of the child classes of Error as being critical, of RuntimeException as being severe, and all others as being normal. (These child classes are described shortly.) There are no informational or warning exceptions, since all Java exceptions can cause a program abend if not prevented or handled. Regular return codes are used instead of exceptions for informational and warning situations.

In addition to the implicit ID and severity that the class type implies for Java exceptions, message text is associated with each exception object, retrieved using `getMessage`, as mentioned earlier. This is also true of AS/400 exceptions, of course.

The primary subclasses of `Throwable` are `Error` and `Exception`. The `Error` exceptions are typically non-recoverable system errors, such as "out of memory." The `Exception` errors are further subclassed by `RunTimeException` and other classes, as shown in Figure 10.1. The `RunTimeException` errors are programming errors you make, such as an array index out of bounds. (Hey, it happens.) The other subclasses of `Exception` are, typically, related to preventable user-input errors.

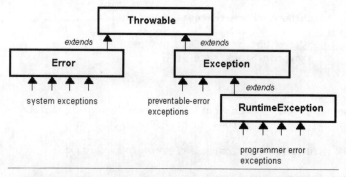

Figure 10.1: The major child classes of the Java `Throwable` class

You typically do not monitor for `Error` exceptions or subclasses in Java. For one thing, you usually can't do much about them. What's more, you will never send one of these exceptions yourself. These exceptions are sent only by the system. What you need to be concerned with are `Exception` exceptions (good name, is it not?) and their subclasses—both for sending and for handling. You have our permission to also ignore `RunTimeException` and its subclasses. These are used by Java to tell *you* that you made a programming error, not for you to tell *others* that you made a programming error. So, your code will probably send and handle only subclasses of `Exception`, except those that subclass `RuntimeException`.

There is little point in listing all of the subclasses here because, as you will see, every class you use clearly documents the `Exception` subclass objects it might send. You will learn them as you need them. (After all, it's probably safe to say that you don't know all the AS/400 system and language runtime exception message IDs by heart.) We have no doubt that you will need them!

The last point to make about `Throwable` objects (it is only `Exception` objects that you really care about) is that you can define your own. You will probably need to do this in Java if you are writing robust code or, more precisely, *when* you are writing robust code. If you discover an unexpected error situation in your error-checking code, such as bad input or an expected resource not found, you should send an exception, not a return code. Return codes, such as an integer value, should be used to identify valid possible results, not to identify exceptional situations. For example, "end of file" is a valid possible result, while "file not found" is an exceptional situation. The first will almost always happen; with good input, the latter should almost never happen. It, in other words, is a frequency call. Having decided that you should send an exception, your next step is to peruse the Java documentation for an existing `Exception` subclass that applies to your situation.

Searching Java documentation for classes

It is time to learn how to find the JDK documentation for a particular class. In this case, you are interested in seeing a list of the classes that extend the `Throwable` class in the `java.lang` package, since that will show all the available predefined exceptions in Java. This will be important when you write your Java code, so you can look for existing exceptions for your own code to throw. Hopefully, the name of the exception class will give a clue to its intended use; from there, you can drill down to the detailed documentation about that class.

First, you must have downloaded and unzipped the JDK documentation file. (When using WinZip to do this, just specify the `c:\` drive or the drive you installed the JDK itself on, and select the "use folder names" checkbox from the WinZip Classic interface.)

Once your JDK documentation is properly expanded, navigate to the `docs\api` subdirectory of the `jdk` folder. This is where all your JDK documentation searches start. Typically, when looking for documentation for a particular package, class, or method, you simply double-click or open the `index.html` file in this `docs\api` directory. However, in this case, you are looking for something special: a list of all the JDK classes that extend `Exception`. To find this (for JDK1.2.0 or higher), go into subdirectory `java\lang` and open file `package-tree.html`. Scroll down until the `java.lang.Exception` class, and you'll see something like this:

```
class java.lang.Exception
   class java.lang.ClassNotFoundException
   class java.lang.CloneNotSupportedException
   class java.lang.IllegalAccessException
   class java.lang.InstantiationException
   class java.lang.InterruptedException
   class java.lang.NoSuchFieldException
   class java.lang.NoSuchMethodException
```

This shows you a nice tree view of how classes extend each other. Remember, every class that extends `Exception` (but not `RuntimeException`) is an exception you might potentially use. To get more detail on any one class, just click its name. Mind you, this is only of limited value, as it does not show you all the child exception classes in other packages. We suggest you also open this file in the `java\util` and `java\io` directories, as they contain most of the useful and reusable exception classes.

If you find an existing exception that meets your needs, such as `IOException`, use it by throwing an object of that class. If you cannot find one that will work in your situation, or you prefer your own exceptions, create a new class that extends `Exception` (or one of its children), and design the constructor to call the parent's constructor with a string to be used as the error text. You can either hard-code this string or accept it as a parameter to your own constructor. An example of such a custom exception is shown in Listing 10.2, designed to report a string that is not a valid United States zip code (postal code).

Listing 10.2: An Extension of the Exception Class

```
public class BadZipCode extends Exception
{
    public BadZipCode(String errorText) // constructor
    {
        super(errorText);
    }
} // end class BadZipCode
```

This is the simplest possible exception class. The constructor simply takes a string and passes it to its parent (`Exception`), which will store it so code can later retrieve it via the `getMessage` method. You could elaborate on it though, and store additional information accessible with new `getXXX` methods, if you wanted. For example, you could ask the code that throws this exception to pass to the constructor a string telling the name of the method and class it is being thrown from, and log this information in a file. Since it is your class, you can do whatever you desire. However, at a minimum, you need to call the parent's constructor and pass a string.

Remember, all your new exceptions will automatically inherit the `getMessage` and `printStackTrace` methods of the root exception class `Throwable`.

Sending Java exceptions with the throw operator

Having decided that you will send an exception in your error-checking code, how do you do it? First, you have to instantiate an instance of the particular `Exception` child class, which almost always requires a string parameter that is the text extractable with a `getMessage` call later. Then, you use the Java `throw` operator:

```
BadZipCode excObj = new BadZipCode("Zip code is not all numeric");
throw (excObj);
```

These steps can be combined into one statement, of course:

```
throw (new BadZipCode("Zip code is not all numeric"));
```

The `throw` operator is similar to CL's SNDPGMMSG command on the AS/400. You can either send an instance of one of Java's predefined exception classes (such as `IOException`), or you can send an instance of your own exception class (such as `BadZipCode`). This choice is comparable to deciding whether to use a supplied CPF or MCH message on the AS/400, or to create your own new message in your own message file. By the way, the generic message CPF9898 ("&1") that many of us use on the AS/400 is similar to the generic `Exception` class in Java. On the AS/400, you substitute your own message text in CPF9898. You can do the same in the constructor of `Exception`, as shown below:

```
throw (new Exception("You made a big mistake there pal!"));
```

It is important to remember that you never throw exceptions that are of type `Error`. You use `Exception` because `Error` exceptions are for dramatic system errors and are thrown only by the system.

What does using `throw` do? It ends your method! Any code following the `throw` statement is not executed. You have done the equivalent of sending an escape message in a CL program. The current method is removed from the stack, and the exception is sent back to the line of code that called this method. If that code does not monitor for this exception, the method it is in is also terminated. The exception is sent back to the caller of the method, just as in RPG function-check percolation. It continues until it finds an entry in the call stack that monitors for this exact exception (or one of the parents of this particular exception class, as you will see).

Who throws what

In Java, callers of your method must monitor for any exceptions that you throw. They do this using a `try/catch` block, identifying the exception to monitor for in the `catch` block parameter. This is not unlike AS/400 programming, where calls to CL programs must take care to monitor for any messages sent by the called CL program.

If you have done any CL programming, you know how painful it can be to get those `MONMSG` statements just right. You typically have to examine the CL reference manual for each CL command you call, to see what messages that command might send. And you can only hope that the list includes any messages that its nested command or program calls might send.

How many times have you wished for an automated way to determine this list? For example, it would be nice to have a tool that, given a CL command as input, returns a list of all the possible messages that particular CL command might send. OO language programmers face a similar problem when trying to determine the exceptions any particular method call might result in. Java designers thought about this problem. They knew that if they didn't come up with a solution, the exception architecture in Java would suffer two real-use problems:

- Programmers would not use it enough, which would lead to too much error-prone code (human nature being what it is). This would lead to a bad image of Java.

- Programmers who did decide to place sensitive method calls inside `try/catch` blocks would find it painful to determine what exceptions each method could possibly throw. Programmers would be dependent on all methods having proper and up-to-date documentation about what exceptions they throw (much as you are dependent on this for AS/400 commands).

The Java designers decided to force method designers to specify up-front, in the method signature, what exceptions are thrown by that method. This is done by specifying a `throws` clause on your method signature, like this:

```
public void myMethod(ZipCode zipcode) throws BadZipCode
```

You *must* specify this if you explicitly throw an exception or your compile will fail. If you throw multiple exceptions, they must all be specified, comma-separated, as in:

```
public void openFile(String filename) throws FileNotFound,
                                             FileNotAvailable
```

 By putting this information into the method declaration, it automatically ends up in the JavaDoc documentation, which solves the documentation problem. Further, it explicitly tells the compiler what exceptions your method throws, so the compiler can subsequently force all code that calls this method to monitor for those exceptions. If any calling code does not have a `catch` block for each of the exceptions listed, then that calling code will not compile. This solves the lazy-programmer problem.

It may be that the calling code does not know how to handle the error indicated by the exception. If so, there is a way out. As an alternative to monitoring for exceptions with a `try/catch` block, the method containing the called code can simply repeat the `throws` clause on its own signature. If this is the case, if the called method throws an exception, the calling code simply percolates it back up to its own caller. The stack is peeled at the line of code that called the exception-throwing method. This can continue all the way up the stack to the root method—`main` in the first class. If it does not specify a `try/catch` block, you have a problem, as `main` is the root of the call stack, so it has no calling-method to percolate to. In this case, if `main` does not specify a `try/catch` for the offending exception, that code will simply not compile. If there were a way to compile it, though, the program would die at runtime in much the same way an AS/400 program dies with an "unmonitored exception." Isn't it nice that the compiler works so hard to eliminate all these errors up-front, before your users get the chance to?

Let's bring this all together with an example. Listing 10.3 shows a class designed to encapsulate a United States zip code. It takes the string with the zip code as input in the constructor and stores it away. As a convenience, it also offers a static `verify` method to ensure that a given string is a valid United States zip code. (Note that it handles both versions, with and without a box office code.)

Listing 10.3: The ZipCode Class to Encapsulate a Zip Code

```
public class ZipCode
{
    protected String code;
    protected static final String DIGITS = "0123456789";

    public ZipCode(String zipcode) throws BadZipCode
    {
        if (verify(zipcode))
          code = zipcode;
    }

    public static boolean verify(String code) throws BadZipCode
    {
        code = zipcode.trim();
        int codeLen = code.length();
        StringBuffer codeBuffer = new StringBuffer(code);
        BadZipCode excObj = null;
        switch (codeLen)
        {
          case 10: // must be nnnnn-nnnn
              if (code.charAt(5) != '-')
                {
                  excObj = new BadZipCode("Dash missing in
                          6th position for '" + code + "'");
                  break;
                }
              else
                codeBuffer.setCharAt(5, '0');
                // deliberately fall through remaining case
          case 5: // must be nnnnn
              if (RPGString.check(DIGITS, codeBuffer.toString())
                  != -1)
                  excObj = new BadZipCode("Non-numeric zip code '"
                                  + code + "'");
              break;
          default:
              excObj = new BadZipCode("Zip code '" + code +
                          "' not of form nnnnn or nnnnn-nnnn");
        } // end switch
        if (excObj != null)
          throw excObj;
        return (excObj != null);
    } // end verify method

    public String toString()
    {
        return code;
    }
} // end ZipCode class
```

In the interest of reuse, this class uses the static check method from Chapter 7 to verify that the string has only digits. Alternatively, you could have walked the string, calling the static method isDigit (from the Character class) on each character.

The verify method throws the BadZipCode exception from Listing 10.2 if it detects an error. It simply places different text in the exception for each error situation. The constructor calls the verify method to ensure it has been given a valid string. Because this call to verify is not encased in a try/catch block, the throws clause must be re-specified on the constructor itself. This means all code that tries to instantiate this class must put the call to new inside a try block, followed by a catch block for BadZipCode. If the constructor does throw the exception, the new operation will be aborted. (You will see an example of this after the try/catch syntax is discussed in the next section.)

Sometimes, your calling code might decide to handle a thrown exception, but then throw it again anyway. This is legal, and can be done with a simple throw exc; statement in your catch block. In this case, because you are throwing this exception (albeit, again), you must define it in your method's throw clause.

In summary, if your method code does not monitor for an exception it might receive, you must specify that exception in your method's throws clause in addition to any exceptions your code explicitly throws, or re-throws.

Monitoring for Java exceptions with try/catch blocks

Now that you know how to send or throw an exception to the callers of your code when you have detected an error, let's discuss what those callers do to monitor for or process it. To monitor for an exception, there is additional Java language syntax. The Java syntax for monitoring for messages builds on this, allowing you to specify a try/catch combination, as follows:

```
try
{
  // try-block: one or more statements of code
}
catch (Exception exc)
{
  // catch-block: code to handle the exception
}
```

The idea is to place any method call statement that might throw exceptions inside a try block. Because it is a block, you can actually place one or more statements inside it. If any of the statements inside the try block do throw an exception, the catch block will get control, and any code after the exception-throwing call will not be executed. The control flows immediately to the catch block upon receipt of a thrown exception.

The catch block defines a parameter, which is the exception it will handle. Java passes that exception object at runtime if an exception is thrown. Your catch block code can use methods on the object to display information to the end-user, if desired. For example, you may do something like the following inside your catch-block:

```
System.out.println(exc.getMessage());
```

Recalling the zip code example, Listing 10.4 is a method included in the ZipCode class for testing purposes. Given a string, it will try to instantiate and return a ZipCode object. Also included is a main method that uses this method.

Listing 10.4: Testing the ZipCode Class

```
public static ZipCode testZipCode(String code)
{
    System.out.println("Testing '" + code + "'...");
    ZipCode testCode = null;
    try
    {
        testCode = new ZipCode(code);
    }
    catch (BadZipCode exc)
    {
        System.out.println(" ERROR: " + exc.getMessage());
    }
    return testCode;
}
// For testing from the command line.
public static void main(String args[])
{
    // test two valid zip codes, 3 invalid zip codes...
    testZipCode("12345");
    testZipCode("12345-6789");
    testZipCode("1234567890");
    testZipCode("abc");
    testZipCode("123");
}
```

If you want to see this in action, here is the output of running this class:

```
Testing '12345'...
Testing '12345-6789'...
Testing '1234567890'...
 ERROR: Dash missing in 6th position for '1234567890'
Testing 'abc'...
 ERROR: Zip code 'abc' not of form nnnnn or nnnnn-nnnn
Testing '123'...
 ERROR: Zip code '123' not of form nnnnn or nnnnn-nnnn
```

As another example of the same problem (verifying an input string and, if valid, creating an object to wrapper it), Listing 10.5 is a PhoneNumber class that throws a PhoneNumberException exception.

Listing 10.5: The PhoneNumber Class that Throws PhoneNumberException

```java
public class PhoneNumber
{
    protected String number;
    protected static final String PHONEDIGITS = "0123456789.- ";

    protected PhoneNumber(String number)
    {
        this.number = number;
    }
    public String toString()
    {
        return number;
    }

    public static PhoneNumber createPhoneNumber(String number)
                        throws PhoneNumberException
    {
        PhoneNumber numberObject = null;
        if ((RPGString.check(PHONEDIGITS, number) != -1) ||
            (number.length() < 10) ||
            (number.length() > 12))
          throw new PhoneNumberException("Phone number '" +
                    number + "' does not appear to be valid");
        else
          numberObject = new PhoneNumber(number);
        return numberObject;
    }

    public static void main(String args[])
    {
```

Listing 10.5: The PhoneNumber Class that Throws PhoneNumberException (continued)

```
                System.out.println("Testing...");
                testPhoneNumber("5551112222");
                testPhoneNumber("555-111-2222");
                testPhoneNumber("555.111.2222");
                testPhoneNumber("555 111 2222");
                testPhoneNumber("a");
                testPhoneNumber("1");
                testPhoneNumber("555/666/7777");
                testPhoneNumber("123456789012345");
        }
        private static void testPhoneNumber(String number)
        {
            PhoneNumber nbr = null;
            try {
                nbr = createPhoneNumber(number);
                System.out.println(nbr + " is valid");
            } catch (PhoneNumberException exc) {
                System.out.println("Error: " + exc.getMessage());
            }
        }
    }
```

Notice that Listing 10.5 takes a slightly different approach with the constructor. Rather than making the constructor public and defining it to throw exceptions, this code makes it protected so that only family members can instantiate it, and designs it not to throw exceptions. You don't want the public using new to instantiate PhoneNumber objects; rather, you want them to call your createPhoneNumber factory method, which will return a new PhoneNumber object. However, it won't do that unless the input string is a valid phone number, so you can guarantee the input to the constructor is always valid. If it is not, then the PhoneNumberException exception object is thrown. (This is not shown, but it is very similar to BadZipCode in Listing 10.2.) There is some code in main to test this, and running it gives this:

```
5551112222 is valid
555-111-2222 is valid
555.111.2222 is valid
555 111 2222 is valid
Error: Phone number 'a' does not appear to be valid
Error: Phone number '1' does not appear to be valid
Error: Phone number '555/666/7777' does not appear to be valid
Error: Phone number '123456789012345' does not appear to be valid
```

Note that the class doesn't pretend to know a universal syntax for phone numbers. We're sure you can improve on the validation routine.

Monitoring for multiple Java exceptions

The `catch` statement, not the `try` statement, is actually equivalent to CL's MONMSG. Although both `try` and `catch` are necessary syntactically, it is the `catch` statement that tells Java which exception type you are monitoring for. If your `try` block gets an exception that the `catch` statement did not identify in its parameter, it is as though you never had the `try`/`catch` block. Your method is ended, and either the exception is sent back to the previous call-stack entry, or compile will fail if you don't identify the missed exception on your `throws` statement on your method signature.

What if you call a method that throws more than one possible exception? How do you define the `catch` statement when you need to monitor for multiple possible exceptions? Two options exist:

- Suppose it does not matter to you which exception happened; it only matters that some exception happened. You can define a parent exception class type on the `catch`. The `catch` will actually get control of any exception that is of the defined type or lower on the hierarchy chain. This is similar to specifying MCH0000 on the CL MONMSG command. Alternatively, to catch all exceptions, specify the root parent of all catchable exceptions: `Exception`. (Some people use `Throwable`.) This is equivalent to specifying CPF9999 on the CL MONMSG command.

- Define multiple `catch` blocks after the `try` block. This is perfectly legal. The exception object received will be compared to each `catch` statement's parameter, in turn, until a match on type is found (or the `catch` defines a child of the thrown exception class type). Use this technique when it is important to your error-recovery code to know exactly what exception was thrown. The need for unique error-handling code is also a good criterion to use when deciding whether you need to define your own exception classes.

Here is an example:

```
try
{
    someObject.callSomeMethod();
}
catch (FileNotFound exc)
{
   . . .
}
catch (FileNotAvailable exc)
{
   . . .
}
```

Finally, there is `finally`. This is an optional block you can define at the end of all your catch statements:

```
try
    block
catch (exception-type-1 identifier)
    block
catch (exception-type-2 identifier)
    block
finally
    block
```

You might think this is what will get control in an exception situation if none of the catch statements handled a particular exception type. This is only partly correct, however. The `finally` block, if present, is *always* executed. That is, it is executed whether or not an exception was received in the `try` block, and whether or not a `catch` block processed it. For example, if a `BadZipCode` exception is thrown by code in the `try` block, the code inside the `BadZipCode` `catch` block will be executed as well as the code inside the `finally` block.

The `finally` statement is typically used to do code that has to be done no matter what, such as closing any open files. No statement inside a `try` block, not even a `return` statement, can circumvent the `finally` block, if it is present. If the `try` block does have a `return` statement, then the `finally` block will be run and the `try` block's `return` statement will be honored. (It is, however, possible to override the `try` block's `return` in the `finally` statement by coding another `return` statement.)

SUMMARY

This chapter covered the following:

- A review of the AS/400 and RPG exception model

- An introduction to the Java exception model

- The Java Exception class hierarchy

- The Java throw operator, which is like CL's SNDPGMMSG

- The Java try/catch/finally statement, which is like CL's MONMSG

- The catch block, which catches the defined exception or any exception that is a child of it

- The finally block, which if present is always executed

- The Java throws clause for method signatures

- The fact that throwing an exception in a constructor is legal, and cancels the instantiation

- The two popular methods all exceptions have: printStackTrace and getMessage

- How to write your own exception classes by extending the Exception class or one of its children.

- The two hierarchies into which Java-supplied exceptions are divided: those that extend Error and do not need to be monitored, and those that extend Exception and do need to be monitored

THREADS

Threads, in contrast to exceptions (covered in Chapter 10), are absolutely foreign to an RPG program. Therefore, this chapter focuses mainly on Java, without providing many RPG comparisons. However, we predict that you will find this utterly new concept interesting. In fact, we predict that there will be increasingly more discussions of threads on the AS/400, especially since they have been introduced to the operating system starting with V4R2, and can now be used directly by code written in C, C++, and Java.

SYNCHRONOUS VERSUS ASYNCHRONOUS

In RPG, you call subroutines, procedures, and programs synchronously. The code that makes the call does not get control back until the called code has completed. For example, let's say that program P1 calls program P2 using the CALL op-code. Execution of P1 will stop at the CALL op-code to wait for the execution of P2 to end and return, before the code *after* the CALL statement is executed. A similar situation exists with the EXSR and CALLP op-codes for subroutines and procedures. This is also true of Java method calls, such as `myObject.myMethod()`, as you have seen. But Java also has built-in support for asynchronous calls. They are calls that *spawn* a second *thread of execution* and return immediately. Both the calling code and the called code run at the same time (concurrently). Imagine that, with enough threads of execution, you could have a whole *suit* of execution. Spun by the *collar*. (Sorry, bad pun. Really, it's a *knit*.)

In order to distinguish between traditional synchronous calling and threaded *asynchronous* calling, the latter is often referred to as *spawning* instead of calling. A timeline graph that shows which method is currently executing would look something like Figure 11.1.

It is important to note that when a method is invoked as a thread, it runs at the same time as the code after the call statement. You can't predict which one ends first, and your calling code does not get the return value from the thread. This is because the call statement returns immediately—before the callee has even run. This is quite similar to submitting a program call to batch in RPG via the `SBMJOB` command, and is in contrast to using the `CALL` op-code.

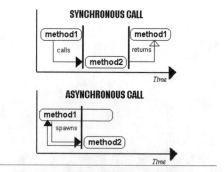

Figure 11.1: A timeline graph of synchronous versus asynchronous calls

THREADS VERSUS JOBS

Asynchronous execution is not totally foreign to AS/400 programmers. In fact, it is done quite often. Many interactive applications have a `PRINT` function key or menu option that submits a job to batch, instead of performing it interactively. This allows the user to get control immediately while the print job runs quietly in the background. This is a *disconnected job*; the application does not care when it ends. It merely submits it and forgets about it.

Some applications that involve several screens of input for a single transaction run a job in the background, gathering information from the database, so this information can be shown to the user by the time he or she reaches the final screen. This is a *connected job* because the main interactive job must synch up with the background batch job by the final screen. This is usually done using data areas, data queues, or some other form of inter-job communication.

Jobs on the AS/400 are synonymous with processes on other platforms. How do they differ from threads in Java? In the amount of overhead. Starting a new job requires a significant amount of system resources, as you well know. Calling another program in the same job is expensive enough, which is why ILE significantly reduces the need to do this. Starting another job altogether is considerably more expensive. There is overhead in allocating storage, setting up library lists, setting up job attributes, loading system resources, and so on. You would not do this without due consideration, and certainly not for frequently repeated application functions. In Java, the equivalent of starting another job would be starting another Java Virtual Machine. Via the system's command analyzer, you would invoke another Java program via Java MySecondClass, for example. (Invoking another job from within Java is discussed in Chapter 14.)

Threads, on the other hand, have relatively little overhead because they share everything with the other threads in that job or process. This includes all instance-variable data. No new memory is allocated for the secondary threads. Even if you do not spawn a thread, your main code is considered to be running in a thread (the *primary* or *main* thread). Each method invoked in another thread gets its own copy of local variables and parameters, as you would expect for a method. On the other hand, instance variables, which are defined at the class level and are equivalent to RPG global fields, are shared. If you spawn two methods for the same instance of a class, they both have the same copies of the global variables in that class. Figure 11.2 depicts this sharing.

To do threads efficiently, of course, the underlying operating system must have true built-in support for them, versus just jobs or processes. Java cannot do this on its own. All major operating systems today support native threads (as opposed to simulated threads or lightweight jobs). This includes OS/400 as of V4R2, as part of its new built-in robust Java support. Typical operating-system thread support includes the ability to start, stop, suspend, query, and set the priority of the thread. For example, you might give a print job low priority so that it gets only idle CPU cycles

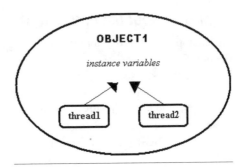

Figure 11.2: Threads in Java sharing instance variable data

versus the user-interactive threads. The Java language has built-in support for all of this in its thread architecture.

Questions arising at this point might include the following:

- How do I call a method asynchronously (that is, spawn a thread)?

- How do I stop a thread?

- How do I get back information from that thread?

- If necessary, how do I wait for that thread to end?

- How do I temporarily suspend a thread?

- How do I change a thread's priority?

- How do threads exchange information with each other?

All of these questions will be answered in this chapter. Don't worry. We won't leave you hanging by a thread!

CALLING A METHOD ASYNCHRONOUSLY: SPAWNING THREADS

The following sections start with an example that is not threaded and show you the code and its output. Then the exampled is changed to run in a thread, using the first of two ways to do this. Finally, the example is changed again, using the second way to run in a thread.

Calling without using threads

The example used throughout the following sections will be the `AttendeeList` class from Chapter 6, in Listing 6.27. That version uses `Hashtable` to manage a list of `Attendee` objects. We have revised it to support an `elements` method to return an enumeration of objects, which just calls the `elements` method of `Hashtable`. We have also revised the `display` method, which calls `display` on each `Attendee` object to print out the current attendee list. Rather than code these changes manually, we call the `displayAll` method in the `Helpers` class from Chapter 9 (Listing 9.20), shown here in Listing 11.1.

Listing 11.1: The Helpers Class for
Calling Display on a List of Displayable Objects

```
import java.util.*;

public class Helpers
{
  public static void displayAll(Displayable objects[])
```

```
        {
            displayAll(new ArrayEnumeration(objects));
        }

        public static void displayAll(Enumeration objects)
        {
            Displayable currentObject = null;
            while (objects.hasMoreElements())
            {
                currentObject = (Displayable)objects.nextElement();
                currentObject.display();
            }
        }
    }
}
```

This version of displayAll accepts an Enumeration, passing the output of a call to the new elements method. To do this, we had to change the Attendee class to implement the Displayable interface, as shown in Chapter 9. The revised AttendeeList class is shown in Listing 11.2.

Listing 11.2: The Revised AttendeeList Class that Uses Hashtable and Helpers

```
import java.util.*;

public class AttendeeList
{
    private Hashtable attendees = new Hashtable();

    public boolean register(String number, String name)
    { // register method code not shown }
    public boolean deRegister(String number)
    { // deRegister method code not shown }
    public boolean checkForAttendee(AttendeeKey key)
    { // checkForAttendee method code not shown }
    public boolean checkForAttendeeName(String name)
    { // checkForAttendeeName method code not shown }

    public void display()
    {
        System.out.println();
        System.out.println("* * * ALL ATTENDEES * * *");
        System.out.println();

        Helpers.displayAll(elements());

        System.out.println("* * * END OF REPORT * * *");
```

Listing 11.2: The Revised AttendeeList Class that Uses Hashtable and Helpers (continued)

```
    }
    public Enumeration elements()
    {
        return attendees.elements();
    }

    public static void main(String args[])
    {
        AttendeeList attendeeList = new AttendeeList();
        attendeeList.register("5551112222","Phil Coulthard");
        attendeeList.register("5552221111","George Farr");
        attendeeList.register("5552223333","Sheila Richardson");
        attendeeList.register("5554441111","Roger Pence");
        attendeeList.display();
    } // end main
} // end AttendeeList class
```

The code for the methods is not shown here since it hasn't changed since Chapter 6. Focus on the display method, which now leverages the displayAll method in the Helpers class. The main method here is simply for testing purposes. It populates the list with four attendees and then calls the display method to show the result of printing the list. (This is what we will be converting to a thread shortly.) Here is the output from this class:

```
* * * ALL ATTENDEES * * *


  _____
  Name........: Sheila Richardson
  Number......: 5552223333


  _____
  Name........: Roger Pence
  Number......: 5554441111


  _____
  Name........: George Farr
  Number......: 5552221111


  _____
  Name........: Phil Coulthard
  Number......: 5551112222

* * * END OF REPORT * * *
```

A nice header and footer are printed at the beginning and ending of the report. This is done in the display method of the AttendeeList class.

Now let's convert that displayAll method in Helpers to run in a background thread. If the number of attendees is large, and the report is being printed to a file or printer instead of to the console, running the thread in the background will improve user response time and give control back to the user immediately. Remember, while not shown here, the example in Chapter 6 had a Registration class that drove this AttendeeList class by accepting commands and input from the user, via the console.

There are two ways to run a method asynchronously in Java. The one you choose depends on whether the class containing the method to be run asynchronously is free to inherit from another class or not. If it already inherits from one, then it cannot inherit from another. Java does not allow multiple inheritance.

Using threads, option 1: The extends thread

The method you wish to run asynchronously might be part of a class that is not already extending another class. Or it might not be written yet, which leaves you free to put it in a new class definition. In these cases, you may choose to extend the Java-supplied class Thread from the java.lang package, using these steps:

1. Add extends Thread to your class definition.

2. Define a method with signature public void run(). Because it takes no parameters, the input to it must be passed in through class instance variables.

To run the code, create an instance of the class and invoke the start method on it. This method is inherited from the Thread parent class. Behind the scenes, it uses the operating system to create a thread and then invokes your overridden run method, which is defined as abstract in Thread (so you must override it).

Why not just invoke run directly? Because that would be a synchronous call! The start method Java supplies in the Thread class does the work of creating the asynchronous thread. Figure 11.3 depicts this process.

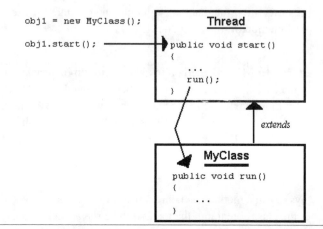

Figure 11.3: How a thread's *start* method invokes your run method

Let's put this to work in the Helpers class. The revised class is shown in Listing 11.3. As you can see, the code is changed inside the Enumeration version of displayAll. The real work is still only done in one place, but now that is the non-static run method. The code is simply moved from the old displayAll method to the run method. Because run is non-static, the class has to be instantiated first.

Listing 11.3: The Helpers Class with New Methods for Running in a Thread

```java
import java.util.*;

public class Helpers extends Thread
{
    private Enumeration objects;

    public Helpers(Enumeration objects) // constructor
    {
        this.objects = objects;
    }

    public void run() // overridden from parent class
    {
        Displayable currentObject = null;
        while (objects.hasMoreElements())
        {
            currentObject = (Displayable)objects.nextElement();
            currentObject.display();
```

```
        }
    }

    public static void displayAll(Object objects[])
    {
        displayAll(new ArrayEnumeration(objects));
    }

    public static void displayAll(Enumeration objects)
    {
        Helpers helpersObject = new Helpers(objects);
        helpersObject.start();
    }
} // end class Helpers
```

Because run by definition (as defined in the parent Thread class) must not take parameters, the most difficult change is getting the Enumeration object to that method from the displayAll method. This is done by passing the Enumeration object as a parameter to the constructor, which in turn stores it away in an instance variable. The code inside run simply uses that instance variable. The displayAll method, after instantiating the object, simply calls the inherited start method on that object, which in turn calls the run method.

In summary, the following changes make this class run the displayAll method asynchronously:

- The class is changed to extend Thread.

- An objects instance variable is defined, so the run method has access to it.

- A constructor is added that takes an Enumeration object as a parameter.

- A run method is added that preserves the signature dictated by the abstract method in the Thread class. The logic to do the real work is moved from the displayAll method to this run method. The Enumeration variable objects is now the instance variable versus a parameter as it was in the displayAll method.

- The displayAll method is changed to instantiate an instance of this class, passing the Enumeration object as a parameter. It then calls the start method on the new class instance. This is inherited from the parent class Thread, and will implicitly invoke the run method.

Not too bad! With only minor changes, suddenly anybody who calls displayAll will get the resulting work done in a thread instead of synchronously. This means that the displayAll method call will now return immediately after it calls start, and both the calling code and the run method will execute simultaneously.

You don't even have to recompile the AttendeeList class. Just re-running it shows the result of this new behavior:

```
* * * ALL ATTENDEES * * *

* * * END OF REPORT * * *
_____
Name........: Sheila Richardson
Number......: 5552223333


_____
Name........: Roger Pence
Number......: 5554441111


_____
Name........: George Farr
Number......: 5552221111


_____
Name........: Phil Coulthard
Number......: 5551112222
```

This is interesting! Because the calling code in AttendeeList's display method executes before the run method executes in the background, you actually get the end-of-report footer printed before the report itself. This output is not guaranteed, though. It is possible that run will execute first, after, or at the same time. It depends on the operating system's *time-slicing* algorithm for assigning CPU cycles to each running thread. The code that spawned the thread is referred to, by convention, as the *main thread of execution*.

Of course, in real life, you would move the code to print the header and footer into the run method so that it is printed at the right place, but we wanted to show you the asynchronous behavior of threads.

Using threads, option 2: implements Runnable

You might not have the option of changing your class to extend Thread because your class already extends another class. In this case, you can choose to implement the

Java-supplied interface Runnable (also defined in the java.lang package). This option is just as easy to implement:

1. Add implements Runnable to your class definition.

2. Define a method with signature public void run().

To run the code, create an instance of the class Thread, passing an instance of your class to the constructor, and invoke the start method on that Thread instance. Figure 11.4 depicts this architecture.

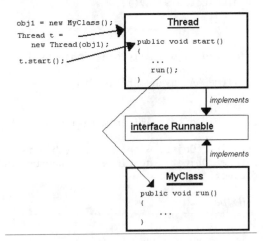

Figure 11.4: How the start method in the Thread class calls your run method in a runnable class

Listing 11.4 shows the Helpers class re-coded to support this second option. The changes made for this version, versus the version in Listing 11.3, are highlighted in bold.

Listing 11.4: The Helpers Class with
Different New Methods for Running in a Thread

```
import java.util.*;

public class Helpers implements Runnable
{
  private Enumeration objects;
```

Listing 11.4: The Helpers Class with
Different New Methods for Running in a Thread (continued)

```
public Helpers(Enumeration objects)
{
    this.objects = objects;
}

public void run()
{
    Displayable currentObject = null;
    while (objects.hasMoreElements())
    {
        currentObject = (Displayable)objects.nextElement();
        currentObject.display();
    }
}

public static void displayAll(Object objects[])
{
    displayAll(new ArrayEnumeration(objects));
}

public static void displayAll(Enumeration objects)
{
    Helpers helpersObject = new Helpers(objects);
    Thread threadObject = new Thread(helpersObject);
    threadObject.start();
}
} // end class Helpers
```

As you can see, very few changes are required:

- The class definition is changed to `implements Runnable`.

- The `displayAll` method is changed to also instantiate a `Thread` object, passing the `Helpers` object as a parameter. (The object passed must implement `Runnable`.)

- The `start` is called on the `Thread` object instead of the `Helpers` object.

Running the `AttendeeList` class now gives exactly the same output as from Listing 11.3. This shows that the two options are extremely similar. It also shows that, if you first choose to `extend Thread`, changing it later (if you decide you now need to extend another class) to `implements Runnable` is very straightforward.

STOPPING A THREAD

You will find that your primary use of threads will be for putting long-running jobs in the background. This will improve the response time to your end-users. You will also find that, in most such cases, you will want to give users the option of canceling that long-running job. This is good user-in-control design, and your users will expect that kind of control. How many times have you decided to kill a compile job because you discovered an obvious bug in the source while waiting for the job to complete?

Let's say that you want to allow a long-running thread to be stopped. The typical mechanism is to use an instance variable that both the running threaded method and the controlling thread (usually just the main or default thread) have access to. The controlling thread waits for a user indication that the running thread should be killed, and then sets the common instance variable to indicate this. Meanwhile, the method running in the thread periodically checks that variable, and, if it is set, voluntarily ends itself by returning.

Suppose you have (admittedly contrived) code that loops for a given number of seconds and displays the elapsed seconds during each iteration. This code will be in method run, as usual. The number of seconds is passed in on the command line, and then the user can cancel the loop by pressing the Enter key on the command line. Listing 11.5 shows this code.

Listing 11.5: A Class Stoppable by the User

```
public class TestThreads extends Thread
{
    private long seconds; // how long to run
    private boolean stop = false;

    public TestThreads(long seconds) // constructor
    {
        this.seconds = seconds;
    }

    public void run()
    {
        for (int secs=0; (secs < seconds) && !stop; secs++)
          {
            try
            {
              sleep(1000L); // sleep for one second
              System.out.println(secs + " seconds");
            } catch (InterruptedException exc) { }
          } // end for-loop
```

Listing 11.5: A Class Stoppable by the User (continued)

```
        if (stop)
          System.out.println("... thread stopped");
      }

      public static void main(String[] args)
      {
        TestThreads thisObject;
        long        longValue;
        if (args.length != 1)
          {
            System.out.println("Please supply number of seconds");
            return;
          }
        try
        {
          longValue = Long.parseLong(args[0]);
        }
        catch (NumberFormatException exc)
        {
          System.out.println("Sorry, " + args[0] + " is not valid");
          return;
        }
        TestThreads thisObject = new TestThreads(longValue);
        System.out.println("Running... ");
        thisObject.start();
        Console.readFromConsole("... press <Enter> to stop");
        thisObject.stop = true; // Enter pressed. Signal stop
      } // end main method
    } // end TestThreads class
```

If you run this program from the command line and pass in a maximum number of seconds, you will see that it prints out the current seconds count every second and is stoppable by pressing Enter key:

```
>java TestThreads 30
Running...
... press <Enter> to stop
0 seconds
1 seconds
2 seconds
3 seconds
... thread stopped
```

Here is the breakdown of this class:

- It inherits from Thread so that it can run a thread.

- A constructor takes in a given number representing the maximum number of seconds to loop, and stores it in a class instance variable.

- A run method loops for a given number of seconds. In each iteration, it calls its inherited method sleep, which takes a number of milliseconds to sleep (a long value) as a parameter. This can throw an exception, so you must monitor for it. The sleep method is a friendly way to pass time, as it lets other threads run. If you chose to implement Runnable versus extend Thread, you would code Thread.sleep(1000L).

- A main method validates the input, creates an instance of this class, and calls its inherited start method to spawn its run method as a thread. It then uses the Console class from Chapter 6 to wait for the user to press Enter. When this happens, the object's instance variable stop is set to true. Keep in mind that you can try this example as non-threaded by swapping the start method call with a direct call to run. You will see that, without the use of threads, the loop cannot be interrupted and canceled.

- The run loop will stop either when the maximum seconds is reached or when the stop instance variable gets set to true.

This convention of using a mutually accessible variable to control the stopping of the thread works well in most situations. There are times, however, when it will cause a problem:

- You have no convenient, mutually accessible variable to use for communications.

- You have no easy way in the long-running code to check a variable in a timely manner.

These are examples of cases in which you might find it necessary to forcefully "kill" a running thread. This is possible with the method stop inherited from the Thread class.

Let's try this method in the example, instead of the mutual variable method. You change the `main` method line of code from this:

```
thisObject.stop = true;
```

to this:

```
thisObject.stop();
```

and then recompile and run. After a few seconds of running, press Enter to get the expected results:

```
>java TestThreads 30
Running...
... press <Enter> to stop
0 seconds
1 seconds
2 seconds
```

In fact, this time it is even more responsive. Pressing Enter results in an immediate end to the program. The other method can take up to a second to respond, while the run method waits to wake up from its "sleep."

The one potential downside of using `stop()` is that the run method does not get a chance to do any cleanup that it might require (in this case, to simply print out "thread stopped"). The need for this is rare. For example, you might need to close an open file as part of your cleanup.

There is a way to get control when your code dies. The `stop` method works by sending an exception of class type `ThreadDeath` to the thread object it was invoked on (`thisObject`, in the example). Because this exception extends `Error` instead of `Exception`, you do not normally monitor for it. However, if you do want to know when your code is being "killed" by the `stop` method, you can put the entire body inside a `try/catch` block, catching `ThreadDeath`. You must put the whole body inside the `try` because you do not know which instruction will be running when the death knell comes. Listing 11.6 shows the body of the `run` method in a `try/catch` block.

Listing 11.6: Placing the Entire run
Method Inside a try/catch Block for ThreadDeath

```
public void run()
{
    try
    {
      for (int secs=0; (secs < seconds) && !stop; secs++)
        {
            try
            {
              sleep(1000L); // sleep for one second
              System.out.println(secs + " seconds");
            } catch (InterruptedException exc) { }
        } // end for-loop
      if (stop)
        System.out.println("... thread stopped");
    }
    catch (ThreadDeath exc)
    {
      System.out.println("... thread killed");
      throw(exc);
    }
}
```

Now, when you run and cancel, you see the following:

```
>java TestThreads 30
Running...
... press <Enter> to stop
0 seconds
1 seconds
2 seconds
... thread killed
```

Notice that the code re-throws the ThreadDeath exception after catching it. This is important so that the thread continues to die as expected (with dignity!). You might say, then, that you should *try* to *catch* your *body* before it dies!

If you implemented Runnable instead of extending Thread, you would invoke stop on the Thread instance instead of the class instance: threadObject.stop(). This is because stop is a member of the Thread class. When you extend Thread, you inherit stop.

We warn you that as of JDK 1.2.0, the use of the `stop` method has been "deprecated," meaning it is no longer recommended. When you compile code that does use it, you get this warning message:

```
Note:  TestThreads.java uses or overrides a deprecated API.
Recompile with "-deprecation" for details.
```

Apparently, this is due to the concern that cleanup code could too easily be skipped over, leading to hard-to-find bugs. It is recommended that you always use the first option—setting an instance variable and checking it regularly in your asynchronous code.

Stopping multiple threads: The ThreadGroups class

The previous example was easy, in that only a single thread was running. What if you instead started multiple threads running and wanted to stop all of them at the same time? You could, of course, invoke `stop` on each of them in turn. In real life, however, this can get messy, since you might not know how many threads are running and do not have a convenient way of enumerating all of them. This is common enough, especially in Internet programming where, for example, you might have numerous threads, downloading images, and resources. In fact, Java designed-in support for *thread groups*. This is a mechanism for partitioning threads into a uniquely named group, and allowing individual actions such as `stop` to be easily applied to all threads in the group.

To create a thread group, you create an instance of the `ThreadGroup` class and pass in any unique name you want for the group:

```
ThreadGroup groupObject = new ThreadGroup("longRunning");
```

To identify that new threads are to be created as part of a particular thread group, you pass in the `ThreadGroup` object as a parameter to the `Thread` constructor:

```
Thread threadObject = new Thread(groupObject, thisObject);
```

This works best for the `implements Runnable` option, versus the `extends Thread` option. However, the latter can be used, as long as you create a new `Thread` object and pass an object of your class as the second parameter, as shown. Listing 11.7 revises the TestThreads class to test this. (Only the changes are shown in the listing.)

Listing 11.7: Using ThreadGroup to Stop Multiple Threads

```
public class TestThreads implements Runnable
{
    public static void main(String[] args) // cmdline entry
    {
        // existing unchanged code not shown
        thisObject = new TestThreads( longValue );
        ThreadGroup groupObject =
            new ThreadGroup("longRunning");
        Thread threadObject1 =
            new Thread(groupObject, thisObject);
        Thread threadObject2 =
            new Thread(groupObject, thisObject);
        System.out.println("Running... ");
        threadObject1.start();
        threadObject2.start();
        Console.readFromConsole("... press <Enter> to stop");
        groupObject.stop();
    }
}
```

To test ThreadGroup, the code is changed to use implements Runnable instead of extends Thread, the main method is changed to create a thread group, and two Thread objects are put in that group. Then, both threads are started, and the thread group's stop method is used to stop both of them. Running this gives the following result:

```
>java TestThreads 30
Running...
... press <Enter> to stop
0 seconds
0 seconds
1 seconds
1 seconds
2 seconds
2 seconds

...thread killed
...thread killed
```

You see each line twice because two threads are running.

This ability to control multiple threads as a group is a welcome addition that Java offers above the typical operating-system support for threads. You will find it can save much ugly code. Note that the same object (thisObject) is used in this example and two threads are spawned on it. This is quite legal and quite common.

Note: The example shown here only catches ThreadDeath, so it only runs cleanup code when threads are stopped—not when they die for other reasons or run cleanly. If cleanup really is important regardless of how the thread ends, you should put it in a finally clause, as discussed in the previous chapter.

Once again, though, the recommendation is to not use the stop method, but rather to iterate through each thread in the group and set its instance variable to make it voluntarily stop. We wish they would have added a method signature in the Runnable interface for this voluntary stop idea (for example, setStop(boolean)), but that would have affected too much existing code to do in a 1.2.0 release. You will see later in this chapter how to iterate through the threads in a thread group.

Ending programs with Java running threads

At this point, you might be wondering what happens when the main method ends and threads are still running. You saw that, after spawning the threads, the main method regained control immediately. The threads then started running asynchronously in the background. What happens when the end of the main method is reached, and there are still background threads running? When execution reaches the very end of the main method, the Java Virtual Machine will queue up its "exit" until all active threads have finished running. That is, the program will remain running until those background threads have all finished. You will notice this because you will not get control back at the command line where you issued "java xxx" and you will see Java listed as one of the programs still running in the call stack.

There are times when you simply want to force an exit. That may involve killing any rogue threads still running. You can do this by exiting your program with System.exit(0);. Unlike an implicit or explicit return statement, this does not wait for running threads to end. Sometimes this is necessary for idle background threads, as you will see when using the AS/400 Toolbox for Java classes, for example.

DAEMON THREADS

The statement about programs not ending until all threads have finished does have a corollary: When you create a `Thread` object, you can invoke the `setDaemon(true)` method on it to identify this thread as a *daemon* (pronounced "dee-mon").

This doesn't mean you've sold your soul! It means this thread is a *service thread* that never ends. At program end time, Java will not wait for daemon threads before exiting. Instead, it will just kill those threads. An example of a daemon thread is a timer that just runs in the background and sends out "tick" events, say. Another example might be a thread that watches a data queue or phone line. Marking these types of threads as daemons saves you the trouble of explicitly killing them when you are ready to exit your program.

Even if you do not use threads yourself, Java considers your non-threaded code to be part of a main thread. There are other default threads in any Java program, notably the garbage collector. This a daemon thread that always lurks in the background, waiting for an opportunity to vacuum up an unused object. Using a graphical user interface causes another thread to run as well to watch for user events like mouse movements. However, this is not a daemon thread, so you must explicitly code `System.exit(0)` to end a GUI application.

THINKING ASYNCHRONOUS — DANGER LURKS...

The examples of threads so far have been used to allow long-running code to be interrupted. In a real-world application, you will also use threads in other ways. For example, you will use them for any potentially long-running operation to ensure overall system efficiency and higher throughput. Just as a bank has multiple tellers and a grocery store has multiple checkout counters, your programs will often have multiple asynchronous *transaction* threads. Often, this design will involve one common repository class, such as a bank or store class, and a separate transaction class that is threaded. You will spawn multiple transaction threads, each taking as input an object in the repository, and acting on that object. The transaction thread class will take an instance of the repository class as a constructor parameter, and its run method will invoke one or more of the methods on that repository object. This is illustrated in Figure 11.5.

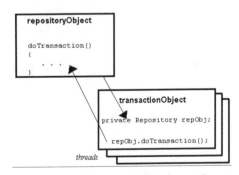

Figure 11.5: Multiple threads of execution acting on a single object

In this design, you will end up with many simultaneous threads using a single instance of an object (a *singleton*). The implication is that they will be attempting to view and change the variables in that object simultaneously. Consider an RPG IV module that is used in a *PGM object. It has global variables, just as a Java class has instance variables. Like threads, you can have multiple users running your program simultaneously. However, each user gets his or her own copy of those global variables. With threads, they all share the same copy! This can be dangerous, of course. The threads might "step on each other," with one changing a variable that undermines another.

As an application programmer, you are used to this. You already have to deal with the problems of simultaneous access to your database, and you religiously use locking mechanisms to ensure the integrity of the database. Thus, to build "thread safe" Java programs, you have to learn the Java syntax and idioms necessary to do with instance variables what you already do with database records.

The role of threads in a complex multi-user application

Will you have to worry about complex, multithreaded applications? Perhaps not, if all you are doing initially is adding a Java GUI onto your host RPG application. In this case, your Java user interface will run on the client, and each concurrent user will invoke independent instances (jobs) of your RPG backend code as needed. Your existing database logic in the RPG code will be as robust as always. However, as you delve deeper into writing and running Java server code on the AS/400 itself, you might come to a design like the one in Figure 11.6.

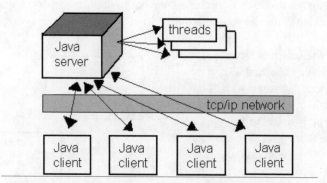

Figure 11.6: The threaded server application architecture with one or more threads per client

In this scenario, instead of having separate AS/400 jobs servicing each client, you have only one server job running, with one or more threads per client. This scales better (although admittedly the AS/400 does an exceptional job of handling many thousands of jobs) because threads have less overhead than separate jobs. Combined with *RMI (Remote Method Invocation)*, *CORBA (Common Object Request Broker Architecture)*, or servlets, this can offer an effective new way to design large-scale applications with thousands of concurrent users. To do this, however, you will have to delve deeply into threads and thread safety.

How single objects can have multiple threads of execution

You might be a tad unclear as to how one object can have multiple threads of execution. Think of a bank object. At any one time, it may have thousands of individual threads calling its `transferFunds` method. It might seem confusing to have so many executing threads, perhaps all on the same method. Do not mix up objects with executing threads. One is about memory, and the other is about instruction pointers.

It might help to think of the object as a database file, the methods as RPG programs that use that database, and the threads as users running the RPG programs. You have only one database file but, at any one time, you have many users running the RPG programs that manipulate that database.

Multithreaded danger: An inventory example

To see how multiple threads using a shared object can be dangerous, consider a system where orders of an item are accepted and fulfilled. The in-stock inventory of the item is also monitored. You might have a class named `Inventory` that manages this, as shown in Listing 11.8.

Listing 11.8: An Inventory Class that Fulfills Orders and Manages Inventory Stock

```
public class Inventory
{
  private static final int AMOUNT_INCREMENT = 2000;
  private int onHand = 5000;   // amount in inventory
  public boolean stop = false; // stop whole thing

  /** method to fulfill an order */
  public void takeOrder(int howMany)
  {
    int old = onHand;
```

→

Listing 11.8: An Inventory Class that Fulfills Orders and Manages Inventory Stock (continued)

```
        String error = "";
        if (stop) // have we been stopped?
          return; //  exit now
        if (howMany > onHand)
          {
          // increase inventory
          addToInventory(howMany);
          error = "Order: " + howMany + ", old: " +
                  old + ", new: " + onHand;
          }
        onHand = onHand-howMany; // actually take order
        if (onHand < 0) // should never happen, but still...
          {
          System.out.println("Error-onHand less than zero! " + onHand);
          System.out.println(error);
          stop = true;
          }
    } // end takeOrder method

    /** method to increase inventory stock, taking into
     *  account the size of the current order */
    private void addToInventory(int howMany)
    {
        if (howMany > AMOUNT_INCREMENT)
          onHand +=(howMany-onHand)+1;
        else
          onHand += AMOUNT_INCREMENT;
    }
} // end Inventory class
```

This is a very simple class. It starts with an initial amount of inventory onHand (5,000), and each order taken (takeOrder method) decrements the amount of the order from the inventory. First, however, a check is made to ensure the size of the order will not deplete the current inventory. If this would be the case, the inventory is increased before the order is filled (addToInventory method). Note that it checks the stop instance variable before even bothering to enter the body of the method. You will see where stop is set at the end of the method.

This is very basic stuff—what could go wrong? Look at the takeOrder method. Because the inventory is bumped up to cover the current order whenever necessary (admittedly a non-robust algorithm), it seems ludicrous to have the "if (onHand < 0)" check. How can it get below zero if the lines of code just above it ensure that it does not? In a synchronized world, of course, it cannot. But in a threaded world, it can. To see this, you need another class—a thread class— whose run method will call the takeOrder method on an instance of Inventory. This typical "transaction" thread class is shown in Listing 11.9.

Listing 11.9: A Class to Place a Single Order in a Thread

```
public class OrderThread implements Runnable
{
   Inventory inventoryObject; // passed in to us
   int       howMany; // how many items to order
   /** constructor */
   public OrderThread(Inventory inventoryObject, int howMany)
   {
       this.inventoryObject = inventoryObject;
       this.howMany = howMany;
   }
   /** "run" method, called by using Start().
    *  This method places the order for the given amount */
   public void run()
   {
       // place the order
       inventoryObject.takeOrder(howMany);
   }
}
```

An instance of this class will be created for every order, and it will be run as a thread. However, there will be only a single instance of the Inventory class. That instance will be passed in via the constructor to every instance of this OrderThread class. This makes sense; while you get many orders, there should never be more than one inventory.

A final class, shown in Listing 11.10, is needed to test this little system. It contains the main method to get control from the command line. This will create a single Inventory object, but many sample OrderThread objects, to really stress-test Inventory.

Listing 11.10: Code to Run and Test the Inventory Class

```
public class TestInventory
{
   public static void main(String[] args) // cmdline entry
   {
     Inventory inv = new Inventory();
     java.util.Random random = new java.util.Random();
     int idx;
```

Listing 11.10: Code to Run and Test the Inventory Class (continued)

```
        System.out.println("Running... ");
        for (idx = 0; (idx <= 1000) && !inv.stop; idx++)
        {
            int nextRandom = java.lang.Math.abs(random.nextInt());
            nextRandom = (nextRandom % 10000) + 1;
            OrderThread newOrder = new OrderThread(inv,nextRandom);
            Thread newThread = new Thread(newOrder);
            newThread.start();
        }
        if (inv.stop)
          System.out.println("...stopped at: " + idx);
        else
          System.out.println("...all orders placed.");
    } // end main method
} // end TestInventory class
```

This test creates a thousand order-taking threads, and each one asks for a random number of items that ranges up to 10,000. Potentially, all of these threads will run simultaneously, really testing the logic that is designed to never let the inventory fall below zero. This code creates a single instance of the Inventory class and passes it into every instance of OrderThread, so that all threads are operating on a single object. The Random object from the java.util package generates random numbers for the simulated orders. If the inventory ever does fall below zero (seemingly impossible, but still...), the code notices this and stops creating new threads because the system has obviously degenerated and is now unstable.

If you compile and run these classes, you get output similar to the following:

```
Running...
Error-onHand less than zero! -12814
Error-onHand less than zero! -20960
Error-onHand less than zero! -30707
Error-onHand less than zero! -38948
Error-onHand less than zero! -47915
Error-onHand less than zero! -57462
Error-onHand less than zero! -64871
Error-onHand less than zero! -67549
Error-onHand less than zero! -68902
Error-onHand less than zero! -76587
Order: 6277, old: 2004, new: -6537
Error-onHand less than zero! -79915
Error-onHand less than zero! -84342
Error-onHand less than zero! -94274
Order: 8146, old: 577, new: -12814
Order: 9747, old: 1263, new: -20960
```

```
Order: 8241, old: 4602, new: -30707
Order: 8967, old: 7394, new: -38948
Order: 9547, old: 8968, new: -47915
Order: 7409, old: 5518, new: -57462
Order: 2678, old: 991, new: -64871
Order: 1353, old: 512, new: -67549
Order: 7685, old: 2512, new: -68902
Order: 3328, old: 589, new: -76587
Order: 4427, old: 2805, new: -79915
Order: 9932, old: 385, new: -84342
...stopped at: 86
Error-onHand less than zero! -6537
Order: 9088, old: 5323, new: 2551
```

There are a number of very interesting (scary?) things about this output:

- The inventory falls below zero despite explicit code to check and prevent that!

- Even after the stop variable stops new threads from executing the takeOrder thread, numerous Error outputs are returned, indicating these threads were already past the "if (stop) return;" code at the beginning of the method.

- The Error and Order lines are not always synchronized in the output, even though they are issued one line after another in the code.

- The Error and Order lines both print out the value of the onHand variable (look at the "new" value for the Order lines), just at different points in the takeOrder method. However, while no changes are made to the variable in the intervening code, the variable value has still changed between the two.

All of this clearly indicates one thing: computers cannot be trusted! Actually, it demonstrates that there are multiple threads of execution running inside the takeOrder method simultaneously. The switch from one thread to another can, and does, happen quickly (from one line to the next) and arbitrarily. This causes a problem because of the common variable (onHand) that these lines of code are sharing and manipulating.

Another thread is gaining control between the line of code that checks the onHand balance:

```
if (howMany > onHand)
```

and the line of code that decrements the balance:

```
onHand = onHand-howMany;
```

It is running the same decrementing line of code. As shown in Figure 11.7, the check is passing for a particular thread, but by the time it actually does the onHand variable decrement, another thread has already decremented the variable.

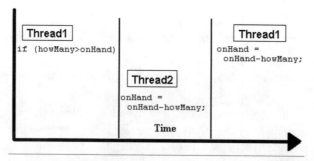

Figure 11.7: Thread time-splicing

This causes the variable to be decremented twice without the check, letting it go below zero. Threads work by *preemptive time-slicing*. That is, each thread is given a small amount of CPU time to perform a few *atomic* instructions, then it is preempted, and another thread is given a similar amount of CPU time to perform a few of its instructions. This continues until each thread is complete (by reaching the end of the run method). An atomic instruction is essentially one line of bytecode. Generally, a single line of Java source code compiles into numerous Java bytecode instructions. This is not unlike RPG, where a single C-spec statement can compile into multiple underlying machine-code instructions. This means you cannot guarantee that an entire line of source code will run before the next thread is given control.

The solution: Synchronizing asynchronous execution

This might sound hopeless. If you cannot guarantee the order of execution, how can you possibly guard against these unexpected *concurrency* errors? The answer to providing thread safety is elegantly simple. It involves merely adding one Java keyword to one line of code!

You need to be able to guard against this unexpected interruption whenever you have code that depends on a common variable remaining stable from one line to the next. The magic keyword in Java to do this is synchronized. When specified as a method modifier, it tells Java that the entire method needs to be executed without interruption by other threads. Effectively, it allows only one thread to execute this method at a time. All waiting threads get queued up "at the door." As each thread finishes executing the method, the next waiting thread is let in.

Let's simply change the takeOrder method definition to include the modifier synchronized, as shown in Listing 11.11.

Listing 11.11: Specifying the synchronized Method Modifier

```java
public synchronized void takeOrder(int howMany)
{
    int old = onHand;
    String error = "";
    if (stop) // have we been stopped?
      return; //  exit now
    if (howMany > onHand)
      {
        // increase inventory
        addToInventory(howMany);
        error = "Order: " + howMany + ", old: " +
                old + ", new: " + onHand;
      }
    onHand = onHand-howMany; // actually take order
    if (onHand < 0) // should never happen, but still...
      {
        System.out.println("Error-onHand less than zero! " + onHand);
        System.out.println(error);
        stop = true;
      }
}
```

Now, after compiling, run the test again. You should get no unexpected errors:

```
>java TestInventory
Running...
...all orders placed.
```

This code will run more slowly slower because you have considerably reduced the amount of asynchronous execution. However, it will run *correctly*, and that, after all, is the fundamental requirement.

Fine-grained synchronization

Instead of synchronizing the entire takeOrder method, you could actually synchronize just the lines of code you need to guard instead. Java defines a synchronized block as a block of code that can be placed inside a synchronized statement so only that block is protected from interruptions by other threads.

To use this fine-grained synchronization, you have to think carefully about what code is exposed by multiple concurrent threads of execution. At a minimum, it is any code that changes a common instance variable. If you have code that tests the current value of the variable and then does work based on that current variable value, you will need to synchronize the entire block. For each line of code, you need to always be thinking, "What if the value of the variable changed right now?"

In the case of the example, the onHand variable check and the onHand variable decrement need to be treated as a single unit of operation. This guarantees that no other thread can decrement the variable in between, which would cause an underflow. So, remove synchronized from the takeOrder method declaration and instead place it around this sensitive block of code, as in Listing 11.12.

Listing 11.12: Using a synchronized Block Versus a Method

```
synchronized(this)
{
    if (howMany > onHand)
      {
        addToInventory(howMany); // increase inventory
        error = "Order: " + howMany + ", old: " +
                old + ", new: " + onHand;
      }
    onHand = onHand-howMany; // actually take order
} // end synchronized(this)
```

In this example, there will be no appreciable difference in total execution time, only because you have to put almost the entire method's code into the synchronized statement anyway. However, if there were a significant amount of other code outside of the synchronized block, you would see overall throughput improvements.

In general, you should simply use synchronized at the *method level* (as a modifier) on any methods that manipulate common variables, unless:

- You are very sure about the minimum set of code that needs to be synchronized. In this example, moving the line that decrements onHand out of the synchronized block causes the unexpected error situations to happen again. If you were not checking for this in the code, you would have ended up with a very serious bug that could have gone undetected for a long time, or until a supplier received a negative-amount order!

- The synchronized versus unsynchronized code ratio is worth the extra risk.

Was it even worth using threads in this example? Maybe not, since you ended up having to synchronize the majority of the code. However, threads are usually a good idea because your code per transaction is usually complex, and the synchronized part—even if it is an entire method—is relatively small. That is, usually, the thread will involve more code than a single method call.

The use of threads can give very busy applications at least the chance for individual transactions to be completed in a shorter time than if they all had to wait for the previously submitted transactions to complete. Further, by spawning threads, you give control back to the user immediately, rather than forcing him or her to wait an indefinite amount of time for the transaction to complete. This reason alone dictates that threads should be used more often than not for user-initiated transactions. "Leave the customer in control" is a maxim to live and code by.

Threaded application design alternatives

The example puts each transaction in its own thread. This is not the only possible design, of course. Another option would be to instead give each user his or her own thread and let it perform the transactions synchronously *within* the thread. This is a reasonable alternative because users will expect their own transactions to be performed in the order they are submitted anyway. It might, thus, reduce the overall number of threads running and improve response time. If you have too many threads competing for processor time, however, you might run into *thrashing*—a situation where so many threads are running that each one gets only enough time to do a minuscule amount of work each slice.

Another option would be to create a fixed-size *thread pool* of transaction or service threads. In this design, a predetermined number of threads—say, a dozen or so—are spawned at application start time, and each transaction or thread-qualifying request is fed to the next available thread. If no thread is available, the request is queued up and the next transaction thread to become available reads it from the queue and executes it. Or the thread-pool grows by one thread to a pre-set maximum. Again, this can reduce the amount of thread-switching and improve performance for very heavy-use applications.

MORE ON THE Synchronized KEYWORD

You have now seen the basics of threads in Java. The remainder of this chapter goes into more detail, and can be safely skipped if you are only looking for an introduction to Java or to threads. If you are ready for more detailed information on threads, however, read on.

The synchronized keyword, as you have seen, can be specified as a method modifier or as a code-block keyword. In the latter case, you saw in the example that it requires a parameter. In the example, the keyword this represented the current object. The synchronized keyword is actually equivalent to the AS/400 command ALCOBJ (*Allocate Object*) with the *EXCL (Exclusive, no read) parameter. That is, it locks an object so that you have exclusive access to it. It always locks some Java object. When used as a method modifier, it locks the object the method is part of. When used as a code-block keyword, it locks the object you specify as a parameter. In both cases, the entire object is locked, not just the method or code block. Thus, at runtime, when a thread (including the main thread) calls a synchronized method or tries to enter a synchronized block, the algorithm is this:

- Is the specified object locked? (Is another thread running any synchronized code for this object right now?)

- If yes, wait in this object's queue.

- If no, lock this object, run the code.

When the code is done running (execution reaches the end of the method or block), the object is unlocked, and the next thread in the queue is allowed in. Just as with ALCOBJ, nested synchronized methods or blocks on the same object bump up the lock count for the object. It is not until the current thread that has the lock reduces the lock to zero that the object is finally unlocked for others to use, as shown in Figure 11.8.

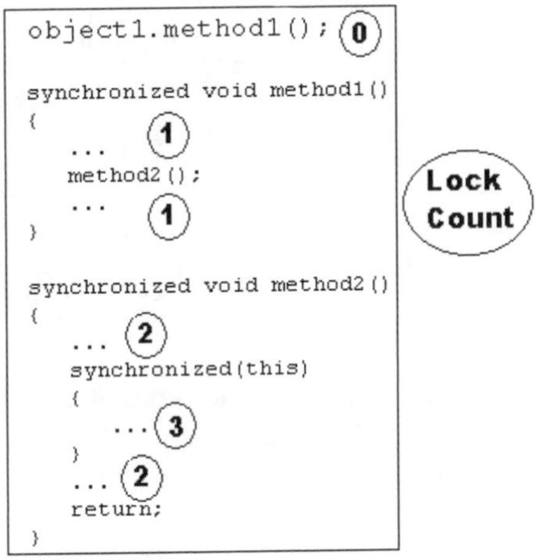

```
object1.method1();  (0)

synchronized void method1()
{
    ...   (1)
    method2();
    ...   (1)
}

synchronized void method2()
{
    ...   (2)
    synchronized(this)
    {
        ...  (3)
    }
    ...  (2)
    return;
}
```

Lock Count

Figure 11.8: Synchronized lock count

The use of synchronized as a method modifier is actually equivalent to putting the entire method body in a synchronized(this) block. It is, to be sure, the safest and easiest way to synchronize sensitive code that changes common variables in this object. However, there will also be times when code in one method changes variables in *another* object (either directly or through setXXX methods). In these cases, you have to use synchronized(object) blocks around the sensitive code, where object is the object reference variable that will be changed.

When you lock an object via the use of synchronized (either as a method modifier or a code-block keyword), it is important to know that you do not block other, unsynchronized methods from running in that same object. This means you can have one thread running an unsynchronized method that reads the common variables at the same time another thread is running inside a synchronized method that perhaps changes those variables. Locking an object only affects other threads that attempt to run synchronized code on that object. Normally, code that reads only a common variable is okay to leave unsynchronized, unless it is doing multiple lines of code that depend on the variable not changing from one line to the next. For example, if you have something like this:

```
if (account < 0)
    sendNotice("You have an outstanding account of " + account);
```

you will clearly have to be careful that the account value does not go above zero by the time the sendNotice method is called in the second line. These two lines should be placed inside a synchronized(this) block to ensure the common variable does not change from one line to the next.

Synchronizing producer/consumer relationships with wait/notify

There are times when you will have one synchronized thread that needs to wait on another thread. Java supplies two methods, each one part of the base java.lang.Object class, which are available to all. They are named wait and notifyAll. These methods can only be used inside synchronized methods or blocks. The wait method will wait indefinitely or (optionally) for a specified number of milliseconds, until another thread calls notifyAll. The wait method is always used inside a loop that is checking for some condition on which the thread depends. After waiting, the condition is rechecked:

```
while (variable < threshold)
    wait();
```

The thread that calls wait gets put on a wait queue for the current object, until the object is unlocked. That allows another thread to get in for this object. The threads on a wait queue are only released when notifyAll is called by some other thread for this same object.

There is actually a method named notify as well, which explicitly releases the thread that has been waiting the longest. NotifyAll will release all waiting threads. What does it mean to be *released*? It means this thread is put back in the queue, waiting to get into the synchronized object. Another thread might have gotten in because wait resets the lock count to zero in the meantime. When it does finally get back in, it starts executing again where it left off at the wait method call. The lock count is then restored to the value it had when the thread call originally called wait.

In Figure 11.9, Tn represents Thread n. If there were more threads in the wait queue, notifyAll would move them all to the lock queue, while notify would move only the first one (T1, in this case). Note that a thread will also move from the wait queue to the lock queue if it specified a number of milliseconds in the call to wait(mmmm), and that time limit has expired.

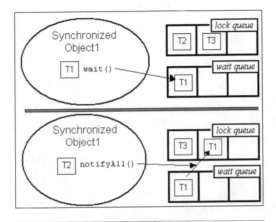

Figure 11.9: A lock queue versus a wait queue

You will use the wait/notify pair when one section of code produces some output that another section of code (perhaps the same method, perhaps a different method) depends on. For example, you might have a queue object with synchronized methods for reading and writing the queue. The read method would wait until the queue is non-empty:

```
// inside read method
while (isEmpty())
    wait();
```

The write method would notify or notifyAll after adding the entry to the queue:

```
// inside write method
addEntry(newItem);
notify();
```

When do you use notify and when do you use notifyAll? That's a good question. If only there were a good answer. In this case, only one item was added to the queue. Because you know only one thread will be able to use it, notifyAll is not appropriate. If there were an append method that added numerous items to the queue, you would use notifyAll so that all waiting threads would get a chance. The worst that will happen is that one or more threads will return to life only to find their condition still is not met. They will redo their wait call.

A thread calling the read method in this case would be a good candidate for a daemon thread. You would typically not want the application to be prevented from exiting if that read method was still waiting for an entry on the queue.

Deadly embrace

Synchronization is a great tool to ensure correctness in your multi-threaded applications. However, it is dangerous tool, as well. You can very easily arrive at a situation where all running threads are blocked because they are waiting for each other. This is like stating "When two trains meet at an intersection, neither can leave until the other is gone."

Consider a situation where thread T1 runs synchronized method obj1.method1(), locking obj1. Thread T2 runs synchronized method obj2.method2(), locking obj2. Now, obj1.method1 tries to call obj2.method2, and so thread T1 is put in the lock queue for obj2 while it waits for thread T2 to finish. But obj2.method2 calls obj1.method1, and so thread T2 gets put in the lock queue for obj1 while it waits for thread T1 to finish. As shown in Figure 11.10, each is now blocked, waiting for the other, and will wait forever. No other threads needing these objects will ever run. Also, unless these are daemon threads or System.exit is used, the program will not end unless it is forcefully killed.

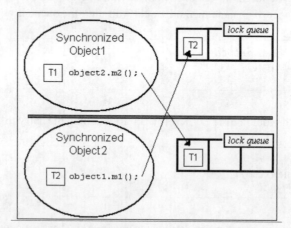

Figure 11.10: Deadlock!

This is a deadly embrace known as *deadlock*. There is nothing that Java can do to help you here! If you hit this problem, it will manifest intermittently (because it is timing dependent) and be a complete bear to debug. You need to avoid the problem completely by careful design—that is, by avoiding mutual calls from one object's synchronized method to another's and back again. If necessary, use a third object with a synchronized method that makes the necessary calls to the other two objects via unsynchronized calls.

The wait/notify pair neither helps nor hinders deadlock, but it does add the risk of a thread waiting forever if another thread does not someday notify it. However, because the waiting thread unlocks the object, at least other threads have a chance to run. If it is important for the waiting thread to eventually run (say, if it is waiting on resources in order to place a customer order), then this will still be a serious problem. You might want to specify a time-out limit, even if it is 10 minutes, on the wait method to indicate when something appears to be stuck. Of course, there is a risk that it is waiting on itself:

```
public synchronized void waitOnMe()
{
    while (variable < threshHold)
      wait();
    variable += threshHold;
    notify();
}
```

In this case, the code that notifies waiting threads is clearly unreachable. There is no point in waiting on a situation your subsequent code will address. Just go ahead and address it!

THREAD PRIORITIES

The discussion about synchronization uses the terms *lock queue* and *wait queue*. They are misnomers, however, in that they imply that threads are put into and taken off queues in a deterministic manner—say, first in, first out. In fact, they are randomly chosen by the *thread scheduler*. The algorithm used to choose them is not programmatically predictable. It may vary from platform to platform, depending on the underlying operating system's scheduling support for threads. Better terms might be "lock set" and "wait set," but these create their own aura of confusion.

One of the criteria Java tries to enforce in the scheduling of threads (and all multithreaded operating systems support) is *thread priority*. By default, your threads will all have normal priority and, thus, the same relative weighting for this criteria. However, by using the Thread method setPriority, you can set the priority to any number between one (lowest) and 10 (highest). The default is five (normal). For convenience, there are predefined constants in the Thread class for MIN_PRIORITY (one), NORM_PRIORITY (five), and MAX_PRIORITY (10).

New threads inherit the priority of their parent threads (the main thread has normal priority), or that of their ThreadGroup, if one is specified. Using ThreadGroups is a convenient way to set the priorities of all similar-role threads.

When the thread scheduler needs to pick another thread for its turn to run, get off the locked queue, or get off the wait queue, it will use an algorithm involving both the thread's priority and its time waiting so far. Higher-priority threads, all things being equal, will get more CPU time than lower-priority threads. It is a general rule of thumb that user-interface threads run at a high priority to improve response time, and daemon background threads run at a low priority to take whatever cycles they can steal.

LOOSE THREADS

We conclude this chapter by discussing some other aspects and functions available to you as a threaded programmer:

- *Named threads.* When you create a new Thread object, you can specify a new unique name for that thread, and query it at any time. This can be helpful for debugging or logging purposes.

- *Yield.* This is a friendly static method in Thread that you can use in your code to voluntarily give up your current CPU slice and let another thread run. If all your threads consist of the same synchronized method, there is no point in invoking yield because no other thread can run anyway. Until you finish the method and, hence, relinquish the lock, the other threads remain stuck on the lock queue. Unlike wait, yield does *not* unlock the object and does *not* put your thread on the wait queue.

- *Suspend and resume.* One thread can suspend another by calling its suspend method (good choice of method name, no?), and subsequently bring it back to life by invoking its resume method. This could be useful when you want to confirm a user's cancel request, for example. While asking the user to confirm, you suspend the thread (or ThreadGroup), and if the decision is not to cancel after all, you resume it. These also make a Pause push-button easy to implement.

- *Join.* This is an interesting method! It is easy to wait for a thread to finish. You simply call join on its Thread object. This will not return until that thread has finished (by returning from its run method). An example of where this is very useful follows shortly.

- *Checking the pulse.* You might occasionally need to determine if a given Thread object has finished running or not. The Thread method isAlive will return true if the thread has not yet finished (not returned from its run method). Be careful, though—if you have not yet called start on this thread, you will get false from this query.

TIMING THREADED APPLICATIONS

When writing applications, you often want to measure the elapsed time, to gauge the performance impacts of changes you make. This is especially true in a multithread application, where you want to ensure that adding a wait here, a yield there, and a synchronized statement over there does not seriously degrade the overall throughput of the application.

To measure an application's time, an easy trick is to change the main entry point to record the current time in milliseconds at the very beginning, and record it again at the very end. Then, take the difference and spit it out to standard-out (that is, the console) or a log file. Make a number of test runs through the application and average the total elapsed time. If you change something, you can rerun the test cases and compare the average elapsed time. Of course, this will be very dependent on the current load of the system, so it has to be taken with a grain of salt. For code running on the workstation, the usual trick is to run the test cases after a fresh reboot, so that memory is in as consistent a state as possible between runs.

To measure the elapsed time in the inventory example, change the main method in the TestInventory class to print out the elapsed time in milliseconds that the entire process takes. This is easy using the ElapsedTime class from Chapter 8 (shown in Listing 8.2). Just instantiate this class and call its setStartTime at the beginning of the code in main, and its setEndTime at the end of the code in main, and write the result out to the console.

There is a trick, though! You can't just take the time at the end of the main method because at that point, the threads are still running. Thus, you need a way to wait for all active threads to complete and then record the ending time. Do this by creating all the threads in a single ThreadGroup and then waiting for them all to finish. This is a good strategy, anyway, because it also gives an easy way to stop all these threads when something untoward happens or is detected: just use object.stop() on the ThreadGroup object.

How do you wait for all the threads in the group to finish? Painfully, as it turns out! You have to *enumerate* all the threads in the group, then invoke the Thread method join on each of them. The method join "waits" on the thread to finish, and only then do you get control back. (If it is already finished, you get control back immediately.)

A join method for the ThreadGroup itself is missing from Java, but the code is not intellectually taxing. We wrote a helpful static method named waitOnThreadGroup to do this, shown in Listing 11.13. You simply code in a call to it and don't get control back until all threads in the given ThreadGroup have completely. Note that join may throw an InterruptedException exception, so you have to catch it.

Listing 11.13: The Revised TestInventory Class with Time-Recording Logic

```java
public class TestInventory
{
  public static void main(String[] args) // cmdline entry
  {
    Inventory inv = new Inventory();
    java.util.Random random = new java.util.Random();
    int idx;

    ElapsedTime timeRecorder = new ElapsedTime();
    timeRecorder.setStartTime();

    System.out.println("Running... ");
    ThreadGroup orderGroup = new ThreadGroup("Orders");
    for (idx = 0; (idx <= 1000) && !inv.stop; idx++)
    {
        int nextRandom = java.lang.Math.abs(random.nextInt());
        nextRandom = (nextRandom % 10000) + 1;
        OrderThread newOrder = new OrderThread(inv, nextRandom);
        Thread newThread = new Thread(orderGroup, newOrder);
        newThread.start();
    }
    if (inv.stop)
      System.out.println("...stopped at: " + idx);
    else
      System.out.println("...all orders placed.");

    waitOnThreadGroup(orderGroup);
    timeRecorder.setEndTime();
    System.out.println("Elapsed time: " + timeRecorder);

  } // end main method

  public static void waitOnThreadGroup(ThreadGroup group)
  {
      Thread allThreads[] = new Thread[group.activeCount() + 10];
      group.enumerate(allThreads);
      for (int idx = 0; idx < allThreads.length; idx++)
      {
```

```
        if (allThreads[idx] != null)
          try {
            allThreads[idx].join();
          } catch (InterruptedException exc) {}
      }
   }
} // end TestInventory class
```

With accurate elapsed-time checking in place, you can make a few sample runs and record the average time:

```
>java TestInventory
Running...
...all orders placed.
Elapsed time: Elapsed time: 0 hours, 0 minutes, 0 seconds, 440
milliseconds

>java TestInventory
Running...
...all orders placed.
Elapsed time: Elapsed time: 0 hours, 0 minutes, 0 seconds, 460
milliseconds

>java TestInventory
Running...
...all orders placed.
Elapsed time: Elapsed time: 0 hours, 0 minutes, 0 seconds, 420
milliseconds
```

The average time in this case is 440 milliseconds (your mileage may vary). Interestingly enough, for the first edition of this book, on a slower machine and an earlier JDK, this took 6.5 seconds!

SUMMARY

This chapter covered threads in Java, including the following concepts:

- There are two ways to define threads: extend the Thread class or implement the Runnable interface.

- Once you have a Thread object, you start it by calling start, which in turn calls the run method in your class.

- The ThreadGroup class is for grouping similar-function threads.

- To stop a thread, either set an instance variable that the threaded code checks occasionally, or use the deprecated stop method from the Thread or ThreadGroup class.

- When the main method reaches the end or a return statement, the exit is queued up until all non-daemon threads run to completion. To force termination, use System.exit(0);.

- Call setDaemon on the Thread object to identify it as a background that is to be stopped when the main method ends.

- Use the method modifier or block statement synchronized to avoid common variable corruption by forcing only a single thread at a time into the synchronized code.

- Use Thread's wait and notify methods as a means of waiting and triggering co-dependent synchronized threads.

- Deadlock is a deadly embrace where two methods are waiting for each other to finish before continuing.

- Threads have a priority, set by Thread's setPriority method. The higher the priority, the more CPU cycles the thread gets.

- The Thread class has methods sleep, yield, suspend, resume, and isAlive for managing the non-synchronized thread state.

- The Thread method join is used to wait for a running thread to finish.

USER INTERFACE

So far, the Java examples in this book have interacted with the user via command-line parameters and `System.in` and `System.out`. This is not the real world of application programming, of course. Even traditional RPG applications use display files, which offer a more compelling user interface than the console. In Java, you use a graphical user interface (GUI) to interact with the user. Indeed, there are a number of GUIs to choose from.

USER INTERFACES IN RPG IV

Processing display files has not changed much from RPG III to RPG IV. The operations are still the same (`EXFMT`, `READ`, and `WRITE`), but the syntax of the F-spec for declaring workstation files is different, due to the redesigned F-spec. Here is what the F-spec for a workstation file looks like in RPG IV:

```
6789012345678901234567890123456789012345678901234567890123456789012
FFilename++IPEASFRlen+LKlen+AIDevice+.Keywords+++++++++++
FDISPLAY    CF   E              WORKSTN SFILE(sflR:currRRN)
```

Note the use of the new keyword SFILE to tell RPG that this display file contains a subfile. The first parameter is the name of the subfile record format, and the second is the name of a field that will be updated with the subfile's current RRN after a READC or CHAIN operation. Up to 12 SFILE keywords are permitted per workstation file. There is also a SLNO keyword for record formats that support variable starting-line numbers.

Display files typically contain many record formats that can cause naming collisions. A number of other keywords can help with this: IGNORE/INCLUDE, PREFIX, and RENAME. These are for dropping or including whole record formats, renaming fields, and renaming records, respectively. Green-screen applications still use display files that are defined external to the RPG program, with "holes" left in them (named fields) for the RPG program to write and read at runtime.

There are also a number of GUI options now for RPG, such as VisualAge for RPG. This product, like others on the market, allows you to design and run your GUI on a client, together with the RPG code that processes the user interface. The business logic can and should remain on the AS/400, but it is called from the client RPG code via CALL operations. These GUIs are event-driven, like all GUIs. Interestingly enough, VisualAge RPG now allows you to compile your client GUI and RPG code into Java code. This allows you to run the client part of your application on any operating system that supports GUI and has a Java Virtual Machine, or as applets in a Web Browser.

USER INTERFACES IN JAVA: OPTIONS, OPTIONS, OPTIONS

In Java, you have at least three options for your user interface:

- *Abstract Windowing Toolkit* (*AWT*) is the original GUI package (java.awt) that still ships with the JDK. It has a core set of functionality and uses operating-system GUI widgets under the covers. AWT code can run as an application or as an applet in a Web page.

- *Swing* is the AWT replacement GUI package (javax.swing) that also ships with the JDK (as of 1.2.0). It is a superset of AWT, and significantly richer in function. It is written in 100% Java, so it is more portable and consistent from system to system (yes, and somewhat slower). Swing code can run as an application or as an applet in a Web page.

- *Servlets and JavaServer Pages* are not GUI classes that you write Java code to render. They aren't even part of the JDK. Their purpose is to write out an HTML Web page that is displayed in Web browser. A servlet runs the business logic or application to get the data, and then passes it to a JSP, which, in turn, merges it with the static HTML template to produce the new page. This is very much like display files and RPG.

AWT is seldom used anymore for new Java applications, so really your choice is between Swing and servlets. You decide which to use based on whether you want a rich (read "thick") GUI that results in a traditional client/server application, or a more humble (read "thin") GUI that is distributed on demand to clients as they use it. As we write this, most people are using servlets, but Swing is still popular for people who don't mind distributing their applications, such as tool writers. As Internet bandwidth explodes over the coming years, applets written in Swing will probably become popular again, but historically their download time has been a handicap.

We can't cover all these in one chapter, so we only cover Swing here. Even if you don't plan to use Swing for end-user applications, you should read this chapter, because you will find yourself using it for your own little utilities. (We did!) Also, Swing really helps bring all this OO stuff home. Its GUI classes use it all: inheritance, abstract methods, interfaces, and design patterns.

The "classic" AWT package is still used quite a bit directly by Swing, as you will see, but if you want to learn just AWT, any Java book will cover it. However, we can't even cover Swing in much detail here, because it is simply too large. Books dedicated to it typically exceed a thousand pages. This chapter simply introduces you to the basics and gives you enough information in a recipe-style fashion to get you productive. It itemizes, but does not cover, the advanced capabilities. If you need them, you can read about them in the JDK documentation or another book. Our goal then is to teach you how to write typical Swing GUIs and make you aware of all the additional capabilities, should you decide to pursue them in more detail.

This chapter teaches how to code Swing by hand, but you don't have to. Just as you usually use SDA to design your display files, you will usually use a graphical layout tool to design your Swing user interface. For example, the Visual Composition Editor in VisualAge for Java makes writing GUIs in AWT or Swing relatively easy. However, in our experience, knowing the underlying Swing functions helps you use any of the layout tools more effectively. This is no different than SDA, which is easier to use if you know DDS. Further, some of us just prefer coding this stuff by hand! Sad, isn't it?

JAVA GUI

Java has no externally described language for defining your user interface independent of your code. This is in contrast to what AS/400 display files allow. Rather, your user interface is built up dynamically with Java code. This programmatic approach to the user interface offers some advantages, for example, use of conditional logic versus hard-to-maintain indicator conditions. It also has some disadvantages relative to reuse and code size. However, the reuse disadvantages can easily be overcome through good object-oriented principles. For example, common window and dialog styles, and common window parts, such as a customer number prompt, can be encapsulated in classes that can be easily reused and extended as needed, leading to code savings and consistent standards. Indeed, this approach helps immensely with code-size reduction.

There are a number of fundamental differences between the display-file programming model and Java's dynamic, event-driven programming model for user interfaces. They are summarized in Table 12.1. Each of these differences is covered in the following sections.

Table 12.1: Display-File User Interfaces versus Java User Interfaces

Display File	Java
Enter- or Function-key driven input.	Event-driven input.
Modal display of records. (Processing waits on the user.)	Modeless display of windows. (Processing does not wait on the user.)
Screen sizes of 24x80 or 27x132.	Programmer-defined screen sizes, by pixels.
Row, column field addressing.	Relative field addressing, depending on the window's "layout manager."
Attributes are set using indicators.	Attributes are set and queried by method calls.
Built-in support for online help.	No built-in help support. Most people code their own using HTML, or the optional JavaHelp package available from Sun.

AN OVERVIEW OF JAVA SWING

Writing Java user interfaces with Swing generally involves the following steps:

1. Import the necessary packages.

2. Write new window classes that extend the JFrame class for primary windows or the JDialog class for secondary dialog windows.

3. Write code to prepare and present the window in the constructor of your class.

4. Write all the code to instantiate the GUI objects and place them in your window, again in the constructor of your class.

5. Identify to Java which events you are interested in for which GUI objects (e.g., window close or button press), and supply the required methods to process those events. Java will call those methods at runtime.

6. In your main method, instantiate your window class, which starts the whole thing running. Control returns immediately, but the window is displayed and responds to user input until some event logic explicitly disposes of the window and exits the application via System.exit(0). Because the Java GUI runtime starts a non-daemon event thread to process user events, the application does not end by reaching the end of main.

All the following examples import the same list of packages to ensure access to all the Java GUI classes:

```
import java.awt.*;         // base AWT classes
import java.awt.event.*;   // base AWT event classes
import javax.swing.*;      // base Swing classes
import javax.swing.event.*; // base Swing event classes
```

Since Swing reuses much of AWT, you have to import both. The classes can be categorized as follows:

- *Basic components*, such as JButton and JCheckBox implement individual GUI parts as you would see in a typical GUI application. You instantiate instances of these and optionally use methods to tailor them, then finally add them to your window.

- *Containers*, such as a JFrame, JDialog and JPanel contain basic components. A JPanel is a sub-window square box for grouping basic components together into a composite component, which can then be added to any window as though it were a basic component.

- *Layout managers* define how added components to a container are to be displayed, or "laid out."

- *Events* are used to process input from each of the components. The Java runtime calls specific methods in your class when a user event happens and passes those methods event objects that contain information about the event, such as the GUI part it applies to.

The idea is to create or extend a container object, such as a JFrame window, and add instances of the basic components to it. This is done using the add method of the container class.

Consider the example in Listing 12.1. This class, when run, displays a main window with a text field, as shown in Figure 12.1. All the windowXXX methods are required because they are defined in the WindowListener interface being implemented. We only care about and hence code a body for the windowClosing method, which Java calls when the user presses the X key to close the window. Notice that you can't just call the add method directly, but rather have to first call getContentPane, and then call add on the result of that. This is a requirement in Swing for both JFrame windows and JDialog windows.

Listing 12.1: A First Java Swing Window Class

```
import java.awt.*;          // AWT components and common classes
import java.awt.event.*;    // AWT/Swing events
import javax.swing.*;       // Swing components and classes
import javax.swing.event.*; // Swing specific events

public class FirstWindow extends JFrame
                          implements WindowListener
{
    public FirstWindow()
    {
        super();
        setTitle("First Window");

        JLabel label = new JLabel("Hello world!");
        label.setHorizontalAlignment(SwingConstants.CENTER);
        getContentPane().add(label);

        addWindowListener(this); // we want window events!
        setSize(300, 100); // width, height
        setVisible(true);  // this method inherited from parent
    }

    // methods required by WindowListener interface
```

```
    public void windowActivated(WindowEvent e) { }
    public void windowDeactivated(WindowEvent e) { }
    public void windowIconified(WindowEvent e) { }
    public void windowDeiconified(WindowEvent e) { }
    public void windowOpened(WindowEvent e) { }
    public void windowClosed(WindowEvent e) { }
    public void windowClosing(WindowEvent e)
    {
        dispose();
        System.exit(0);
    }

    // Test this thing
    public static void main(String args[])
    {
        FirstWindow window = new FirstWindow();
    }
}
```

Any questions? No doubt. More details are presented in the following sections. First, however, Figure 12.2 shows the class hierarchy for the major classes involved in GUI programming in Java. This diagram will come in handy when you start using Swing. What is important to note about this diagram is that many classes inherit methods from parent and grandparent classes. For example, the component classes inherit methods from JComponent, Container, and Component.

The boxes with dotted lines in Figure 12.2 are abstract classes. The up-arrow lines indicate the lower class extends the higher classes. (This is UML diagram syntax.) The classes shown in the gray area are from the java.awt package, while the rest are from the javax.swing package. Notice that all Swing class names start with the letter J.

Figure 12.1: A simple window display with a text (JLabel) component

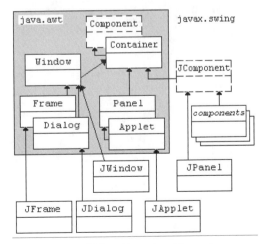

Figure 12.2: A class hierarchy of the major Java-supplied Swing classes

493

BASIC GUI COMPONENTS IN JAVA

Table 12.2 lists the basic components that Java supports. These are the basic building-block classes that you will use repeatedly throughout your Swing programming. These classes all extend JComponent, so they share many common methods.

Component	Description
Table 12.2: The Basic Java GUI Components	
JButton	Push buttons
JCheckbox	Check boxes (for multiple selection)
JRadioButton	Radio buttons (for single selection)
JComboBox	A combination of an entry field and a drop-down list box
JList	A selection list (single column only)
JLabel	A text constant
JTextField	An entry field (a named field in DDS)
JPasswordField	An entry field that masks input (usually for password prompts)
JTextArea	A multiple-line entry field (a field with the CNTFLD keyword in DDS)
JScrollPane	Wraps a Jlist or JTextArea so it has scrollbars

Table 12.3 provides a quick summary of typical ways to instantiate and initialize objects of these classes.

Table 12.3: Examples of Instantiating Basic Swing Components

Instantiation	Parameters
button1 = new JButton("Cancel");	The text on the push button.
cbFish = new JCheckbox("Italic");	The text on the check box.

rbg = new ButtonGroup();
rb1 = new JRadioButton("Option1",true);
rb2 = new JRadioButton("Option2");
rbg.add(rb1);rbg.add(rb1);
	The text on the button, with an initial selection state. Only one button is selectable among all in any single ButtonGroup object.

String itemArray[] = {"Item 1","Item 2"};
dropdown = new JComboBox(itemArray);
dropdown.setSelectedIndex(0);
	A JComboBox can be populated by passing an array or a vector to ctor, but can't be changed after.

dropdown = new JComboBox();
dropdown.addItem("Choice 1");
dropdown.addItem("Choice 2");
dropdown.setSelectedIndex(0);
	A JComboBox can also be created empty and populated by calling the addItem method.

String itemArray[] = {"Item 1","Item 2"};
listbox = new JList(itemArray);
listbox.setSelectedIndex(0);
	A Jlist can be populated by passing an array or a vector to the constructor, but cannot be changed after.

listModel = new DefaultListModel();
listbox = new JList(listModel);
listModel.addElement("Item1");
listModel.addElement("Item2");
	A Jlist can also be created with a DefaultListModel object, and can be changed by using methods in this class.

prompt1 = new JLabel("Enter name");	The text to display as the constant.
entryName = new JTextField("yourname", 10);	The default text to display and the maximum size in characters (used only for determining display size).
passwordEntry = new JPasswordField(10);	The maximum size in characters (for the display size).
entryComments = new JTextArea("comments", 5, 1);	The default text to display, and the number of rows and columns (used only for determining the display size).
jsp = new JScrollPane(listbox);	A component to be shown with scrollbars.

Figure 12.3 shows what these components look like.

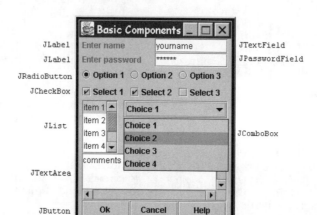

Figure 12.3: All the basic Swing components, at a glance

Note that the JList and JTextArea entries in Figure 12.3 have been placed inside JScrollPane objects to get the scrollbars, like this:

```
JScrollPane jspList = new JScrollPane(listbox);
```

When you do this, you subsequently add the JScrollPane object to the window, versus the component placed inside the JScrollPane. By default, a JScrollPane object only places scrollbars around the object if it needs it. If you prefer to always see scrollbars, use the setVerticalScrollBarPolicy and setHorizontalScrollBarPolicy methods, passing in the constant HORIZONTAL_SCROLLBAR_ALWAYS or VERTICAL_SCROLLBAR_ALWAYS from JScrollPane.

Common inherited methods

All these classes inherit from the class JComponent. They pick up important methods from this parent class, some of which are listed in Table 12.4.

	Table 12.4: Common Swing Component Methods Inherited From Jcomponent
Description	**Method**
Enabling/disabling ("graying out")	setEnabled(true/false), isEnabled()
Showing/hiding	setVisible(true/false), isVisible()
Setting focus to this component, or the next component, and querying if in focus	requestFocus(), transferFocus(),hasFocus()
Setting the background and foreground color	setBackground/setForeground(Color),
Setting the text font	setFont(Font)
Setting the border	setBorder(Border)
Setting fly-over text	setToolTipText(String)
Adjusting display characteristics	setAlignmentX/Y, setMinimumSize, setMaximumSize, setPreferredSize
Repainting after making changes (not normally needed, except that occasionally Swing doesn't repaint properly)	repaint

Colors

The colors you are allowed to use as predefined constants in `java.awt.Color` are self-explanatory. They are listed in Table 12.5.

Table 12.5: Color Constants in the java.awt.Color Class			
Color.black	Color.blue	Color.cyan	Color.darkGray
Color.gray	Color.green	Color.lightGray	Color.magenta
Color.orange	Color.pink	Color.red	Color.white
Color.yellow			

For example, to change a text constant's colors, you might code this:

```
JLabel constant = new JLabel("**overdraft**");
constant.setBackground(Color.red);
constant.setForeground(Color.white);
```

By default, the user-specified system colors are used. You can explicitly specify these as well by using the predefined constants in the SystemColor class. Because this class extends Color, you can substitute these anywhere a Color is allowed. If you are artistically inclined, you can create your own unique colors by specifying the red-green-blue components on the constructor of a Color object, or by using the brighter and darker methods.

Fonts

For each font, you have to create a new Font object by specifying a font name, style, and size, like this:

```
constant.setFont(new Font("sansSerif",Font.BOLD,12));
```

Font names are like you see in your Windows control panel, such as "sansSerif," "Courier New," "Times Roman," and "Helvetica." Font styles are the constants Font.PLAIN, Font.BOLD, and Font.ITALIC. These can be OR'd together as in Font.BOLD | Font.ITALIC. New for Swing (versus AWT) are borders and tool-tip text, which are covered in the next section. (See the java.awt.Font class documentation for more details on creating fonts.)

Borders

Borders allow you to give your component a nice-looking edge. The parameter to setBorder is a Border object from the package javax.swing.border. You can create your own borders by instantiating the Border class directly, but you rarely will. Rather, you will usually use the factory methods inside the BorderFactory class, as shown in Table 12.6.

Table 12.6: Methods of the BorderFactory Class for Creating Borders

Component	Description
createEmptyBorder(int top, int left, int bottom, int right)	Just reserves white space (sizes in pixels) around the component
createEtchedBorder()	Creates an etched ("burned in") border
createLineBorder(Color color, int size)	Creates line of a given color and size (pixels)
createLoweredBevelBorder()	Creates a beveled edge that appears to go "in"
createRaisedBevelBorder()	Creates a beveled edge that appears to go "out"
createMatteBorder(int t, int l, int b, int r, Color color)	Creates a line border of the given size per edge (pixels) and the given color
createTitledBorder(String)	Creates a thin line border with the given text in the upper left
createCompoundBorder(b1, b2)	Create a new border from two other borders

You can nest borders to get a combined effect, using the `createCompoundBorder` method. Also, `createTitledBorder` allows another border to be titled by specifying another border as the first parameter to the `createTitledBorder` method call. For example, to get an etched border with a title, you would do this:

```
Border border1 = BorderFactory.createEtchedBorder();
Border border2 = BorderFactory.createTitledBorder(border1, "My Title");
myComponent.setBorder(border2);
```

To show what these borders look like, each of them is applied to a different `JLabel` in Figure 12.4.

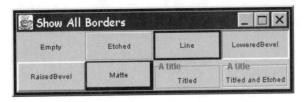

Figure 12.4: Examples of the different borders available in Swing

Borders can really improve the appearance of your application. For example, you can put a non-editable JTextField component at the bottom of your window as a message line. To make it stand out, use the lowered bevel border for it. Similarly, you might find the raised bevel border a great improvement in the look of push buttons. Also, a titled and etched border can be applied to a JPanel that contains related components, to visually group them on the screen.

Tool tips

It is very common in GUIs now to offer fly-over or bubble help, or what Java calls *tool tips*. A tool tip is a short description that pops up when the cursor hovers over a component. This is supported in Java by simply calling the setToolTipText method on your component and supplying the text to display in the pop-up. For example, you might code this tool-tip text for a push button:

```
JButton registerButton = new JButton("Register");
registerButton.setToolTipText("Select this to register a new attendee");
```

This would look like Figure 12.5 when the user hovers the mouse over the button.

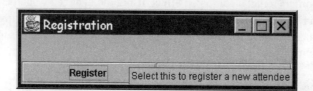

Figure 12.5: An example of tool-tip text in Swing

Common non-inherited methods

You have seen some of the most popular methods that all Swing component classes inherit from their ancestor classes. In addition to these, a number of other methods are not inherited, but are reasonably consistent among a number of the classes. Because they are not applicable to every component, they were not defined in the base class JComponent, but many of them are defined in *most* of the individual child classes. They are important enough that you will use them very often in Swing programming. These commonly used non-inherited methods are listed in Table 12.7.

Table 12.7: Common Swing Component Methods Not Inherited from Jcomponent	
Method	**Description**
setText/getText	Set label or input text, and query label or input text. For Jlabel, JRadioButton, JCheckBox, JTextField, JPasswordField, and JTextArea.
setHorizontalAlignment/set VerticalAlignment	Specify whether text is left/top justified, centered, or right/bottom justified. Specify one of the following constants from SwingConstants: LEFT, CENTER, RIGHT, TOP, or BOTTOM.
setMnemonic	Select a character from the display text to be underlined. The user can select the component by pressing Alt+character. The character should be unique per window. For Jbutton, JRadioButton, and JCheckBox.
setDisplayedMnemonic and setLabelFor	For a Jlabel used as prompt text for an entry field, this allows you to specify a unique mnemonic character, such that when it is selected by Alt+character, the entry field gets focus. The parameter to setLabelFor is any component, such as a JTextField.
setIcon and setHorizontal/Vertical TextPosition	Specify a .gif or .jpg image file to display on a Jlabel, Jbutton, JCheckBox, or JRadioButton. This also allows you to specify the position of the text relative to the image.

In addition to the methods in Table 12.7, there are common methods that are specific to JTextField, JPasswordField, and JTextArea. All of these extend the abstract class JTextComponent, which in turn extends JComponent. These are shown in Table 12.8.

Table 12.8: Common Swing Text-Component Methods

Method	Description
select/selectAll/ getSelectedText/ replaceSelection	Set and query selected text in the JTextField, JPasswordField, and JTextArea components.
setCaretPosition/ getCaretPosition	Set and query cursor character position (zero-based) for JTextField, JPasswordField, and JTextArea.
setEditable/isEditable	Set and query if the user is allowed to enter text into JTextField, JPasswordField, and JTextArea.
cut/copy/paste	Perform clipboard operations relative to the selected text.
read/write	Allows the contents to be populated from or written to a stream (i.e., a flat file).
append/insert/ replaceRange/ getLineCount/setWrap/ setWrapStyleWord	Specific functionality for JTextArea for working with the text, and for setting the word-wrap option (true or false). If you set word-wrap to true, you can use setWrapStyleWord(true) to force wrapping only at a word boundary versus a character boundary.

There are also common methods that are specific to the buttons (JButton, JRadioButton, and JCheckBox.) All of these extend the abstract class AbstractButton, which in turn extends JComponent. They are shown in Table 12.9.

Table 12.9: Common Swing Button-Component Methods

Method	Description
setSelected/isSelected	Select or query the selected state of JCheckBox or JRadioButton.
doClick	Simulates the user clicking on the button. Causes any code you have registered for this event to be executed.

Finally, there are common methods specific to JList and JComboBox. These are shown in Table 12.10.

Table 12.10: Common Swing List-Component Methods	

Method	Description
setSelectedIndex/ getSelectedIndex	Select a list item by its zero-based index number or query the current selection index number for Jlist and JComboBox. The getSelectedIndex method returns -1 if nothing is selected.
setSelectedValue/ getSelectedValue	Select a Jlist item by object reference variable, or query the selected item's object reference (or null if no selection).
setSelectedItem/ getSelectedItem	Select a JComboBox item by object reference variable, or query the selected item's object reference (or null if no selection).
setSelectionMode	Specify how many items can be selected in a Jlist: SINGLE_SELECTION, SINGLE_INTERVAL_SELECTION, or MULTIPLE_INTERVAL_SELECTION
getSelectedIndices/ getSelectedValues	Query all selected item indices or objects, for a multiple-selection JList.
clearSelection	De-select all items in a JList.
ensureIndexIsVisible	Scroll a JList to display a given item, by index number.
addItem	Append a new item to a JComboBox list.
((DefaultListModel)get Model()).addElement or insertElementAt	Append or insert a new item to a JList created with new JList(new DefaultListModel()); There is also a setElementAt method to change a list entry.
removeAllItems/ removeItem/ removeItemAt	For a JComboBox, remove all items, remove an item by a given reference, or remove an item by a given index number.
((DefaultListModel)get Model()).removeAllElem ents/removeElement/ removeElementAt	For a JList, remove all items, remove an item by reference, or remove an item by a given index number.
getItemCount	Return a count of how many items are in the JComboBox.
getModel().getSize()	Return a count of how many items are in the JList.
setVisibleRowCount	Set how many rows are displayed at a time in a JList. (The default is eight.)
setMaximumRowCount	Set how many rows are displayed at a time in a JComboBox.

Most of these methods are for setting and querying attributes such as text, text alignment, and selected item. Keep these tables handy; you will find yourself referring back to them often as you start coding Swing. Of course, this is a very small subset of the methods you will commonly need to use for each component, so the JDK documentation will become your best friend as well.

Mnemonics

It is a very good policy to always supply mnemonics for your GUI button components (push buttons, checkboxes, and radio buttons), so that power users and those who can't use a mouse can easily select those buttons. This is easily done in Swing by calling the setMnemonic method and supplying to it a character to act as the mnemonic. If this character exists in the text for the button, it will be underlined. Users can select that button by pressing Alt plus the underlined character. Figure 12.6 shows examples of buttons that have mnemonics (the underlined characters).

Figure 12.6: Examples of mnemonics

Note that a raised bevel border is also used for the push buttons. This is the code for Figure 12.6:

```
rb1.setMnemonic('O'); rb2.setMnemonic('P'); rb3.setMnemonic('T');
cb1.setMnemonic('1'); cb2.setMnemonic('2'); cb3.setMnemonic('3');
button1.setMnemonic('O');
button2.setMnemonic('C');
button3.setMnemonic('H');
button1.setBorder(BorderFactory.createRaisedBevelBorder());
button2.setBorder(BorderFactory.createRaisedBevelBorder());
button3.setBorder(BorderFactory.createRaisedBevelBorder());
```

It is slightly more work if you want to set a mnemonic for a JLabel so that when it is selected, a JTextField (or any component) is given focus. However, this is so handy for users, it's worth it. To do this, first call setDisplayedMnemonic to set the mnemonic character, and then call `setLabelFor` and identify the component to get focus when this mnemonic is selected. Here is a partial example, resulting in Figure 12.7:

```
prompt1 = new JLabel("Enter name ");
entryName = new JTextField("your name here", 20);
prompt1.setDisplayedMnemonic('n');
prompt1.setLabelFor(entryName);
```

Figure 12.7: Examples of mnemonics for a JLabel prompt

See how the letters *n* and *p* are underlined in the prompt text? If a user selects Alt+n, the entry field with "your name here" gets input focus. Similarly, if Alt+p is selected, the entry field with "your phone number here" gets focus. Cool! By the way, if you choose a letter that is not among those in the displayed text, there is no visual clue to the user as to which letter is the mnemonic. However, it will show up in the tool-tip text (if you specify tool-tip text). Java will append *alt+x* to the tool-tip text for each component with a mnemonic, where *x* is the mnemonic character.

Clearly, the tricky part to mnemonics is to select a character that is unique for this window, since having two buttons with the same mnemonic renders the second one inaccessible. This can be quite tedious and error-prone, and is even more difficult if you translate your screens to different languages. To help you with this, we have written a class that will automate it. The `Mnemonics` directory on the CD-ROM includes a class named `Mnemonics`. It has static methods `addMnemonicsForJFrame` and `addMnemonicsForJDialog` that, if called with a `JFrame` or `JDialog` object, will walk through all the components in the window, find a unique character among their text (if possible, else a unique character not among their text), and assign that as the mnemonic. This means adding a single line of code to the end of your constructor will give you mnemonics, uniquely chosen, for every component. This is a keeper if you are going to do any Swing programming.

Images

Another function we find very nice in Swing is the ability to place images in buttons, radio buttons, checkboxes, labels, and (as will soon see) menu items. To place a `.gif` or

.jpg image into one of these components, start by creating an ImageIcon object, passing in the name of the .gif or .jpg file:

```
ImageIcon burgerImage =
    new ImageIcon(getClass().getResource("burger.gif"));
```

This loads the image into the memory of the ImageIcon object. The use of getResource from the Class object ensures Java will find this file even if it is packaged with the code inside a .jar file.

You can now place your ImageIcon object inside a component by specifying it as the second parameter of the JLabel, JRadioButton, JCheckBox, or JButton constructor (or the only parameter, if you don't also want to show text). Alternatively, you can call the setIcon method and pass it there. If you have both text and an image, you can also specify how the two are placed relative to each other by calling the setHorizontalTextPosition and setVerticalTextPosition methods. They take a constant from the SwingConstants interface: LEFT, RIGHT, CENTER, LEADING, TRAILING, TOP, or BOTTOM. For example, Listing 12.2 shows just the constructor of a class named TestButtonImages. When you run TestButtonImages, you get Figure 12.8.

Listing 12.2: A Class to Display Text and Images

```
public TestButtonImages() // constructor
{
    super("Test Button Images");
    ImageIcon buttonImage1 =
      new ImageIcon(getClass().getResource("burger.gif"));
    ImageIcon buttonImage2 =
      new ImageIcon(getClass().getResource("hotdog.gif"));
    ImageIcon buttonImage3 =
      new ImageIcon(getClass().getResource("fries.gif"));
    JButton b1 = new JButton("center,top",    buttonImage1);
    JButton b2 = new JButton("center,center",buttonImage2);
    JButton b3 = new JButton("center,bottom",buttonImage3);
    b1.setHorizontalTextPosition(SwingConstants.CENTER);
    b1.setVerticalTextPosition(SwingConstants.TOP);
    b2.setHorizontalTextPosition(SwingConstants.CENTER);
    b2.setVerticalTextPosition(SwingConstants.CENTER);
    b3.setHorizontalTextPosition(SwingConstants.CENTER);
    b3.setVerticalTextPosition(SwingConstants.BOTTOM);
    b2.setForeground(Color.white);
    getContentPane().setLayout(new GridLayout(1,3));
    getContentPane().add(b1);
```

→

```
        getContentPane().add(b2);
        getContentPane().add(b3);
        pack();
        setVisible(true);
        addWindowListener(this);
}
```

By the way, if you don't like having to qualify the constants with the interface name SwingConstants, you can always just add implements SwingConstants to your class definition. As mentioned in Chapter 9, this is one way to use interfaces: place common constants in them and implement them in your classes to get unqualified access to the constants in the interface.

Figure 12.8: Examples of images in buttons

Specifying an ImageIcon in the constructor or setIcon method gives you one image. For JButton, JRadioButton, and JCheckBox, however, you can specify six other images if you want to show a different picture for different states of the button. The methods to specify these are given in Table 12.11.

Table 12.11: Button Methods for Specifying Images for Different States

Method	Description
setDisabledIcon	Image to show when button is disabled
setSelectedIcon	Image to show when button is selected
setDisabledSelectedIcon	Image to show when button is disabled and selected
setPressedIcon	Image to show when button is pressed
setRolloverIcon	Image to show when mouse is over the button
setRolloverSelectedIcon	Image to show when mouse is over the button and button is selected

Lists can have images, too. You can put any object inside a JList or JComboBox, and Java simply calls the toString method to get the text for this element. However, you can also add ImageIcon objects to get a list of images. If you want to have both image and text, however, you have to do more work. You have to create a class that extends JLabel and implements ListCellRenderer, including the all-important getListCellRendererComponent method. Then, you have to call setCellRenderer on the JList or JComboBox object, passing an instance of the new class. This is beyond this book, but an example you can copy and change is on the CD-ROM, in the files TestImageList.java and TestListCellRenderer.java. If you run the former, you will see the output shown in Figure 12.9.

Figure 12.9: Examples of images in a JList

Model view controller

While not often used for these basic components, one aspect of Swing you will often read about is the notion of *model-view separation*. Strictly speaking, Swing components all follow the model-view-controller design pattern, which stipulates that you separate the data (model) from the view (user interface) and the controller that binds the two together.

In Java Swing, the component classes are a combination of the view and the controller. They all support a separate class for holding the data that is displayed in the view. There is a different model class for each component. You have the option of first creating an instance of the model class (or your own class that extends it), and passing that object to the constructor for the component. Indeed, the same model object can be specified in more than one UI component, and if the data in the model changes, all UI components will reflect that change. You can also subsequently query or re-set the model object for any UI component by calling the getModel or setModel methods. The model class for each basic component is shown in Table 12.12.

Table 12.12: Model Classes for Each Basic Component Class	
Component Class	**Model Class**
JLabel	Not applicable (no user input)
JTextField	javax.swing.text.PlainDocument
JPasswordField	javax.swing.text.PlainDocument
JTextArea	javax.swing.text.PlainDocument
JButton	javax.swing.DefaultButtonModel
JRadioButton	JToggleButton.ToggleButtonModel (nested class)
JCheckBox	JToggleButton.ToggleButtonModel (nested class)
JList	javax.swing.DefaultListModel
JComboBox	javax.swing.DefaultComboBoxModel

You don't have to use the M-V-C power of Swing very often, and indeed almost never for the basic components. When you create a component object and do not specify a model object in the constructor, Java creates an instance of the correct model class for you and uses it. All the methods for setting and querying content (getText, setText, addItem, etc.) that are supplied by the component classes are simply fast paths to the same methods in the underlying model object. The calls are simply passed through.

The only exception to this is the JList class, which does not supply a default model. You are forced to create an instance of DefaultListModel and pass it to the constructor of JList. To manipulate items in the list, you have to use the methods in the DefaultListModel class. As a result, using JList requires a bit more work than the rest of the basic components, unfortunately.

Events

When you write display-file applications on the AS/400, you are writing modal code. This means the processing involves writing the record formats and reading them (or both in one step, with EXFMT). The READ or EXFMT operation does not return control to your application until the user presses Enter or a function key.

This is different in GUI programming. When you write a GUI application, the processing involves preparing and then displaying windows. At that point, you get control back immediately, but the Java runtime also gets control, via its event thread. Because this is a non-daemon thread, the program does not end when execution reaches the end of the main method. Rather, it will run forever until you issue a call to the System.exit method. The Java event thread watches for users to perform events, such as pressing a button or selecting a list item. Anything the user does, including simply moving his or her mouse, is tracked. If you decide that you wish to do processing for any of the events Java tracks, you can.

Unlike some other GUI systems that simply try to call a particular method in your class for each event, and do nothing if you don't code that method, Java tries to be a little more robust. First, to reduce traffic, it only tries to call you for each event if you have registered an interest in that event for a particular component. It supplies a method in every component, which you can call to do this registration. Further, to allow the compiler to verify you are ready to process that event, it forces you to implement specific interfaces for specific events. Thus, the interface rules force you to code the methods dictated by that event. Let's look at the details of this framework for the basic components.

Because of the sheer number of event types, Java groups them, and supplies a single method call for registering interest in each group. Further, each group has a single interface you must implement for the events in that group. The individual event types within the group are distinguished by different methods within the interface, and you simply code empty methods for those specific events you are not interested in. Table 12.13 lists each event group, the method you call per component to register interest in these events, and the name of the interface you must implement to process these events.

Table 12.13: Basic Event Groups and Related Registration Methods and Interfaces

Event Group	Interface; Method for Registering	Methods Inside Interface
Window events	WindowListener; addWindowListener	windowActivated(WindowEvent) windowDeactivated(WindowEvent) windowIconified(WindowEvent) windowDeiconified(WindowEvent) windowOpened(WindowEvent) windowClosed(WindowEvent) windowClosing(WindowEvent)
Action events	ActionListener; addActionListener	actionPerformed(ActionEvent)
Selection events	ItemListener; addItemListener	itemStateChanged(ItemEvent)
Focus events	FocusListener; addFocusListener	focusGained(FocusEvent) focusLost(FocusEvent)
Text events	TextListener; addTextListener	textValueChanged(TextEvent)
Keyboard events	KeyListener; addKeyListener	keyPressed(KeyEvent) keyRelease(KeyEvent) keyTyped(KeyEvent)
Mouse events	MouseListener; addMouseListener	mouseClicked(MouseEvent) mouseEntered(MouseEvent) mouseExited(MouseEvent) mousePressed(MouseEvent) mouseRelease(MouseEvent)
Mouse move events	MouseMotionListener; addMouseMotionListener	mouseDragged(MouseEvent) mouseMoved(MouseEvent)
List selection events	ListSelectionListener; addListSelectionListener	valueChanged(ListSelectionEvent)
Text-field data change	DocumentListener; addDocumentListener	changedUpdate(DocumentEvent) insertUpdate(DocumentEvent) removeUpdate(DocumentEvent)
Model changes	ChangeListener; addChangeListener	stateChanged(ChangeEvent)

This is not a complete list, but it's more than enough for most applications. All these events pertain to components, except for `WindowListener`, which pertains to a `Jframe` or `JDialog` window. You saw how to use this to make a window closable, back in Listing 12.1:

1. Code `implements WindowListener` in the class definition

2. Code `addWindowListener(this)` in the constructor (the method inherited from `JFrame`).

3. Code the seven method definitions from the `WindowListener` interface, with empty bodies for all but the one you are interested in: `windowClosing`. In this one, add code to close the window (`dispose()`, also inherited) and exit: `System.exit(0)`.

There are more event groups you will need for advanced components, covered later in this chapter. All interfaces in the middle column come from the package `java.awt.event`, except for the last three rows, which come from `javax.swing.event`.

The method to process each event must define a single parameter, which is the name of a class that always ends in "`Event`." These classes are the event classes, and Java sends an object of the appropriate class for each event. You can query information about the event from each object, although you will often get everything you need by calling the `getXXX` methods on your components. One method that all event classes support, which you also need, though: `getSource`. It returns an `Object` object, which is the component object to which the event occurred. For example, if the user presses a push button, the `actionPerformed` method gets called, and `getSource` on the `ActionEvent` object will return the `JButton` object that was pressed by the user. (By the way, the methods in the third column of Table 12.13 all return nothing, `void`, and must all be coded as `public`.)

Imagine you are interested in processing a button-press event for a `JButton` object named `closeButton`. This is an action event, so in your constructor, you would code `closeButton.addActionListener(this)`. The method `addActionListener` is supplied by Java in the `JButton` class, and like all the `addXXXListener` methods, it takes as a parameter any object that implements the `XXXListener` interface required for that event group. Usually, this is the same class that extends `JFrame`, hence you pass `this`. However, you do have the option of putting your event-processing code in a separate class and passing an instance of the other class to the `addXXXListener` method call. This can be handy if you want to share processing logic across windows. In either case, the class that implements ActionListener supplies an actionPerformed method that does the appropriate thing, for example:

```
public void actionPerformed(ActionEvent evt)
{
    if (evt.getSource() == closeButton)
    {
        dispose();
        System.exit(0);
    }
}
```

This method will be called by Java whenever the user presses the closeButton button.

Some of the interfaces, such as WindowListener and MouseListener, require you to code a bunch of methods in your class. Typically, you are only interested in one or two of these, but due to the interface rules, you have to code all the rest too, even if you just make them empty. To save time, Java does supply "adapter" classes, which implement the interface and supply the empty methods already. These classes are named XXXAdapter, as in WindowAdapter and MouseAdapter. You can then simply define a new class that extends the adapter class, and override only the methods you wish to write code for. This can be handy, but since your class is usually already extending JFrame or JDialog, it is rarely usable. However, adapter classes are often used for convenience together with a nested ("inner") class (discussed in Chapter 14). This is only a keystroke-saving convenience. We prefer, instead, to code it properly, making the code easier to read, maintain, and debug.

In summary, then, to process particular events for particular components, you must call the appropriate addXXXListener method and implement the appropriate XXXListener interface. The latter requires you to code the methods in the interface, and it is these methods that Java will call when the event happens. If you register an interest in the same event for many components (such as action events for JButtons), the same method will be called for all components, so you use evt.getSource() to establish which component caused the event to be "fired" (as it is called).

Table 12.14 lists the event groups supported by the basic components. If you define your own model class, you can use ChangeListener to listen for changes to the model (although all components created with the model already do this automatically). Also, all these components support addFocusListener if you want to know when they gain or lose focus.

	Table 12.14: The Usual Events per Basic Swing Component	
Component	Event Interface, Registration Method and Called Method	Description
JButton	ActionListener, addActionListener, actionPerformed	When the user presses the button, process button logic in the actionPerformed method.
JRadioButton, JCheckBox	ItemListener, addItemListener, itemStateChanged	When the user (de)selects the button, call getStateChange on the ItemEvent object. Returns DESELECTED or SELECTED.
JList	ListSelectionListener, addListSelectionListener, valueChanged	When the user selects a list item, use getSelectedIndex on Jlist object to find out the new selected item index.
JComboBox	ActionListener, addActionListener, actionPerformed	When the user selects a list item, Java automatically places the selected item in the text field part. Also supports ItemListener to get control before Java does this.
JTextField, JPasswordField	ActionListener, addActionListener, actionPerformed	This gets fired when the user presses Enter. To monitor keystrokes, extend the model (PlainDocument) and override the insertString method.
JTextArea		The Enter key inserts a new line, so there is no event. To monitor keystrokes, extend the model (PlainDocument) and override the insertString method.

Again, you will see examples of event-processing as you go through this chapter. Also, you'll see more about JTextField programming later, such as how to emulate some of the display-file functionality: restricting the input length, restricting the input characters, auto-advancing to the next field, and even supporting editword-like behavior. First, however, you need to see how all these components are put into your windows and how Java decides to arrange them.

CONTAINERS: JFRAMES, JDIALOGS, AND JPANELS

To see the basic components created in the previous section, you need a window of some kind. This will usually be an instance of the JFrame class. (Remember, frames are considered containers, as they contain other components.) This JFrame class provides a main window with all the usual pieces: a border; a title bar; minimize, maximize, and close buttons; and a system menu in the upper left corner. You create a frame or "main" window easily enough:

```
JFrame myWindow = new JFrame("My First Java Window");
```

This creates an actual window. However, it is not too useful yet, because you cannot see it! You can display it with this:

```
myWindow.setVisible(true);
```

However, it will be a tiny little thing. Prior to calling setVisible, you need to do some typical tailoring:

- *Set the window's size.* This is done using the setSize method, specifying the width and height of the window in *pixels* (a graphical unit of measurement, *very* small). Finding the exact size is a matter of trial and error, but setSize(300,200) will get you going. Alternatively, you can just call the pack method to size the window to match the size of the contents.

- *Set the window's position.* This is done using the setLocation method, specifying the *x* and *y* pixel address relative to the upper left corner of the screen (*x* pixels across, *y* pixels down). Notice that the address is of your window's upper left corner. This, too, is trial and error, but setLocation(200,100) will get you going.

- *Set the window's title.* If you do not specify the title in the constructor to JFrame, you can specify it later using setTitle(String).

- *Optionally, set the window's font, background color, and foreground color.* Setting these once for the window should cause them to be inherited by all the components you add to the window, but so far this doesn't seem to work in Swing. (It did work in AWT.) So, if you want to change the text or color of all your components, use `setFont`, `setBackground`, and `setForeground` for each component, as described in the basic component section earlier in this chapter. By default, your system's current settings for these are used, and most people recommend leaving them that way.

- *Add all the components* you wish to display in the "client area," or middle part of the window. These include the basic components described previously, such as push buttons. We will cover this crucial step shortly.

Before looking at some sample code, let's pause for a word on programming style. We suggest that, for each window in your application, you have a new class that extends `JFrame` (your class is a window, after all), and initializes and populates the window in the constructor. Define all of the component and container objects as private or protected instance variables of the class, and instantiate them in the constructor. These variables will need to be available to your other methods when it comes time to process input, hence the need to make them instance variables.

You will find that you write the same code over and over again when creating new window classes. To help reduce this drudgery, we highly recommend starting with a base class that does some typical stuff (like handling the close event, implementing the common event interfaces, and supplying empty versions of the event interface methods). This way, each new window class you create can simply extend your base class and pick up all that base work for free. Then, it simply has to override the appropriate methods, such as the event methods it is interested in. Further, if you later decide all windows should have a blue background, you have only a single class to change, and all your windows will immediately inherit that change.

This kind of base class for frame windows is shown in Listing 12.3 (without all the `windowXXX` methods, since they haven't changed from Listing 12.1).

Listing 12.3: The Base Window Class

```
import java.awt.*;
import java.awt.event.*;
import javax.swing.*;
import javax.swing.event.*;

public class BaseWindow extends JFrame
        implements WindowListener, ActionListener,
            ItemListener, ListSelectionListener
```

Listing 12.3: The Base Window Class (continued)

```
{
    public BaseWindow(String title) // constructor
    {
        super(title);

        createComponents(); // another method in this class
        addComponents();    // another method in this class

        addWindowListener(this); // we want window events
        setLocation(200,100); // x, y from upper left
        //setSize(400, 200);  // Only used if pack not used
        pack();
        Mnemonics.addMnemonicsForJFrame(this);
        setVisible(true); // Show the window
    } // end constructor

    // instantiate our GUI components
    protected void createComponents() { }
    // add our GUI components to the window by calling add
    protected void addComponents() { }
    // methods required by the listener interfaces we implement

    // WindowListener interface methods
    public void windowActivated(WindowEvent e) { }
    ...
    public void windowClosing(WindowEvent e)
    {
        dispose();
        System.exit(0);
    }

    // ActionListener interfaces methods
    public void actionPerformed(ActionEvent evt) { }
    // ItemListener interface methods
    public void itemStateChanged(ItemEvent evt) { }
    // ItemSelectionListener interface methods
    public void valueChanged(ListSelectionEvent evt) { }
} // end BaseWindow class
```

Look at the constructor. You can't avoid your child classes having constructors, as these are not inherited, but you can reduce them to a simple call to super. However, creating the component objects and then adding them to the window needs to be done in the constructor, and must be done by the child classes. These jobs are abstracted out into two empty methods named createComponents and addComponents. The idea is the child classes will override these and put the code into these methods. The base constructor calls these methods, so for child classes, the child's versions gets called polymorphically.

After these calls, our own handy `Mnemonics` class and its `addMnemonicsForJFrame` method are used to automatically add mnemonics to all the components in the window. The only other methods that child classes might want to override are the appropriate event methods `actionPerformed`, `itemStateChanged`, and `valueChanged`, if the child classes want to process these events. If not, then the methods do not need to be overridden. Notice also that the code calls the `pack` method at the end of the constructor. This method call (inherited from `JFrame`) saves you from having to determine a workable window size yourself. For this to work, however, Java needs to be able to determine the "preferred" size of each component, so you might end up having to explicitly call the `setPreferredSize` method on some components if Java runs into trouble. Also, make sure you specify the number of columns on your `JTextField` components, to help Java do this calculation.

An alternative to a `JFrame` window is a `JDialog` window. This is used when you want to prompt the user for information and "block" while waiting for his or her response. (This is called *modal behavior*.) Typically, dialogs are used to display error messages or prompt for information needed to complete an action, such as prompting for a user ID and password. Coding a `JDialog` class is very similar to coding a `JFrame` class, except that the constructor needs a `JFrame` object to act as the owning parent. (Location is relative to it, and it is locked while the dialog is showing.) Also, you don't call `setVisible` in the constructor. The caller will do that because `setVisible` does not return control until the dialog window is disposed. Finally, in the window-closing code, you do not code `System.exit`, as you never want to exit the whole application just because a dialog window was closed.

Listing 12.4 shows the `BaseDialog` class, but since most of the code is the same as `BaseWindow` in Listing 12.3, only the constructor is given.

Listing 12.4: The Constructor for the BaseDialog Class

```
public BaseDialog(JFrame parent, String title)
{
    super(parent, title, true); // true means modal behavior

    createComponents(); // another method in this class
    addComponents();    // another method in this class

    addWindowListener(this); // we want window events!
    setLocation(250,150); // x, y from upper left
    //setSize(400, 200);// width, height. Only used if pack not used.
    pack();
    Mnemonics.addMnemonicsForJDialog(this);
}
```

Of course, this class is coded to extend JDialog, not JFrame. To test this class, include in it the following main method code:

```
public static void main(String args[])
{
    BaseWindow parent = new BaseWindow("Base Window");
    parent.setSize(300,150);
    BaseDialog dialog = new BaseDialog(parent, "Base Dialog");
    dialog.setSize(50,75);
    dialog.setVisible(true);
    System.exit(0);
}
```

Because the base windows are empty, you have to set their sizes to get a meaningful result. Figure 12.10 shows that result.

Figure 12.10: The JDialog example
using the BaseDialog class

You will see more of JDialog later when you create a dialog. First, let's focus on JFrame.

Adding components to containers: Layout managers

Now the really fun part begins: populating windows with components like push buttons and entry fields. If you think about display files, you'll realize that frame and dialog containers are rather like record formats, and components are like the fields and constants in your record formats. The record formats contain fields.

To lay out your fields in display-file DDS, you specify row and column addresses, and the display-file compiler (CRTDSPF) determines the display length for each field. You must be careful not to overlap fields. In Java, you lay out your components by adding them to your container (frame or dialog). That is, you first instantiate instances of component objects, and then add them to your container, like this:

```
JButton registerButton = new JButton("Register");
getContentPane().add(registerButton);
```

What does this mean? Where does it go? It depends on what *layout manager* you specify for your object. Prior to adding objects to a container, you need to specify a layout manager for that container. Layout managers are classes that define rules about where added components will be placed. To specify a particular layout manager, code the container method setLayout:

```
getContentPane().setLayout(new xxxLayout());
```

Notice for JFrame and JDialog (but not JPanel, as you will see later), you have to call getContentPane() because it is the content pane you are adding to. This is just a special nested container that windows have to hold the components. Having done this with a desired xxxLayout class, your components are added according to the rules of that class, which ensures that the components do not overlap. The layout manager classes are listed in Table 12.15.

Table 12.15: Layout Manager Classes

Layout Manager	Description
BorderLayout	You can only add five components. The window is divided into five regions, each a constant in BorderLayout: NORTH (top), SOUTH (bottom), WEST (left), EAST (right), and CENTER (middle). When adding a component, you must specify which region to place it in. This is great for simple windows.
FlowLayout	Each component inserted after the previous one, with some padding. If it fits horizontally, it goes there; otherwise, it starts on the next line. This is okay for buttons.
GridLayout	The window is divided into evenly sized cells. You must specify in the constructor how many rows and columns to allocate. Each addition then occupies the next sequential cell. Cell size is the largest display size of all the added components. This is great for evenly sized push buttons.

Table 12.15: Layout Manager Classes (cont)	
Layout Manager	**Description**
GridBagLayout	This is the most complex and most flexible class. The window is divided into cells again, but each is sized to be as big as needed for the component in it. It requires the use of the GridBagConstraints helper class to define the attributes of each populated cell. This is great for everything, if you can handle the coding.
BoxLayout	New for Swing, this class is designed to get the benefits of GridBagLayout without the pain. It has one row or column of components, each in its own cell that is uniquely sized for that component. This is great for toolbars or button bars. Our experience, though, is it is tough to get the sizing to come out just right.
CardLayout	Obsolete. The JTabbedPane is the new preferred way, discussed later in this chapter.

In addition to the classes in Table 12.15, there is yet another option: specifying a layout manager of null, like this:

```
getContentPane().setLayout(null);
```

This layout mode indicates that you will hard-code the pixel *x* and *y* address of every component you add. This is not a recommended option and is not covered further in this book, however, because it produces a screen-resolution-dependent window that does not gracefully allow for resizing by the user.

Using BorderLayout

To see what a BorderLayout layout looks like, let's create a class that extends the BaseWindow class from Listing 12.3. It will define, create, and add four components: a list heading, a list, a push button, and a message line (that is, a non-editable JTextField serving the purpose of a message line). The code is shown in Listing 12.5.

Listing 12.5: Testing the BorderLayout Layout Manager

```
// Not shown: usual 4 import statements

public class RegisterWindow extends BaseWindow                    ⟶
```

Listing 12.5: Testing the BorderLayout Layout Manager (continued)

```java
{
    private JLabel       listHeader;
    private JList        list;
    private JScrollPane  listScrollPane;
    private JButton      registerButton;
    private JTextField   msgLine;

    public RegisterWindow()
    {
        super("Registration");
    }

    // Override from parent class: instantiate components
    protected void createComponents()
    {
        listHeader     = new JLabel("Attendees");
        DefaultListModel lModel = new DefaultListModel();
        list           = new JList(lModel);
        listScrollPane = new JScrollPane(list);
        registerButton = new JButton("Register");
        msgLine        = new JTextField(20);
        listHeader.setBorder(BorderFactory.createLoweredBevelBorder());
        for (int idx=1; idx<11; idx++)
            lModel.addElement("Attendee " + idx);
        list.setVisibleRowCount(4);
        registerButton.setBorder(BorderFactory.createRaisedBevelBorder());

        msgLine.setEditable(false);
        msgLine.setBackground(Color.cyan);
        msgLine.setBorder(BorderFactory.createLoweredBevelBorder());
    }

    // Override from parent class: add components
    protected void addComponents()
    {
        getContentPane().setLayout(new BorderLayout());
        getContentPane().add(listHeader, BorderLayout.NORTH);
        getContentPane().add(listScrollPane,BorderLayout.CENTER);
        getContentPane().add(registerButton,BorderLayout.EAST);
        getContentPane().add(msgLine, BorderLayout.SOUTH);
    }
}
```

The code in createComponents first instantiates the components, then does some tailoring of them by calling some of the component methods described earlier. Notice the extra work required for a JList, including creating a DefaultListModel object and then using it to add items to the list. Also notice a JList has to be inside a JScrollPane to see scrollbars, as discussed earlier. This createComponents method will remain the same for subsequent examples in this chapter, as you examine each of the other layout managers (except the obsolete CardLayout).

The important code is in addComponents, which sets the layout manager and subsequently adds the four components. Figure 12.11 shows the result of compiling and running this class. (It has a main method that we didn't bother showing you.)

This example of a border layout turned out so well because there happens to be fewer than five components, and BorderLayout allows up to five. The only unused region is on the left, but you can see that empty regions do not take up any space. If you had more components, you would use "nested containers," discussed in an upcoming section on the JPanel container.

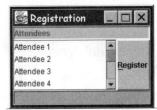

Figure 12.11: The layout produced by BorderLayout

Using FlowLayout

With a FlowLayout manager, you simply add each component to the screen, one after another. If a component fits on the current row, it goes there. If not, it wraps to the next line. If there simply is not enough space left to show a component, it is not shown. Listing 12.6 shows the updated addComponents method to support this manager.

Listing 12.6: Testing the FlowLayout Layout Manager

```
protected void addComponents()
{
   getContentPane().setLayout(new FlowLayout());
   getContentPane().add(listHeader);
   getContentPane().add(listScrollPane);
   getContentPane().add(registerButton);
   getContentPane().add(msgLine);
}
```

Notice this layout manager does not take any parameters to the add method. (Indeed, all others work the same way.) Figure 12.12 shows the new results.

If you resize the window, the components move around automatically to fit the new size. That is, they "flow" as required. It is not a good idea to use pack when using this layout manager, as you can see. Indeed, this layout

Figure 12.12: The layout produced by FlowLayout

manager is not a good choice in this case. However, it can be a good choice when all you are adding is push buttons and you want each to get its own size.

Using GridLayout

The GridLayout manager divides the screen into the specified number of rows and columns. After that, the components are added to the next cell, moving left to right. Each cell is as big as the one necessary to hold the largest-sized component.

This is a tricky layout to use in the example because there is not an even number of components per row. You have one on the first row (the list header), two on the second row (the list and the push button), and one on the third row (the message line). To handle this, specify three rows and two columns, then add a dummy JLabel object to the empty cells so they have something. (Otherwise, all of the components would be shifted inappropriately.) The code for this is shown in Listing 12.7.

Listing 12.7: Testing the GridLayout Layout Manager

```
protected void addComponents()
{
    getContentPane().setLayout(new GridLayout(3,2));
    getContentPane().add(listHeader);
    getContentPane().add(new JLabel(""));
    getContentPane().add(listScrollPane);
    getContentPane().add(registerButton);
    getContentPane().add(msgLine);
}
```

Figure 12.13 shows the result. (It's not pretty!) The problem here is that GridLayout sizes every cell to be as big as the biggest component, which in this case is the JList.

The GridLayout manager is useful only in certain situations, such as for a property-sheet window with label/entry pairs that look good when they are all the same size, as shown in Figure 12.14. It is also heavily used for holding push buttons, when you want all the buttons to be the same size, as shown in Figure 12.15.

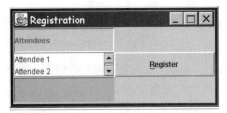

Figure 12.13: The layout produced by GridLayout

Using GridBagLayout

The GridBagLayout manager is by far the most complex of all the layout managers to code. However, when the previously mentioned ones fail to meet your purposes, you can be sure that this one will always work. Like GridLayout, it divides the screen into cells, but not every cell is the same size. You do not specify the rows and columns for the cells when you instantiate the layout object. Rather, it is done implicitly as you add each component. For each component you add, you specify the row and column coordinates (0,0 based), and the number of rows and columns this component is to span. You can also specify information such as whether the component is allowed to grow and shrink with the sizing of the window (horizontally and/or vertically), whether it is to be stretched to fit the cell(s) it is in, and how it is to be aligned in the cell(s).

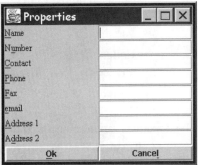

Figure 12.14: Using GridLayout for evenly sized columns in a property sheet

Figure 12.15: Using GridLayout for evenly sized buttons

There is potentially a lot of extra information to be specified with each component as it is added, which is why there is relative complexity. How is all this extra information specified? Not via parameters to the add method, as you might expect. That would make this method too complicated and would require numerous parameters. Rather, in true object-oriented fashion, you instantiate another class, GridBagConstraints, that will contain all this information. With this approach, you can specify all your defaults once, initially. Then, you change only the defaults you need to for each component that you add. The non-object-oriented part of this class, however, is that all this information is specified by explicitly changing variables in the object versus the better approach of using setXXX methods.

Here are the steps needed to use GridBagLayout:

1. Instantiate an instance of GridBagLayout, with no parameters.

2. Instantiate an instance of GridBagConstraints, with no parameters.

3. Specify the GridBagLayout object as the layout manager, via setLayout.

4. Set all your preferred default values in the GridBagConstraints class.

5. For each component to be added:

   ➢ Set the required values of the GridBagConstraints object uniquely for this component (such as the row and column addresses via the gridy and gridx variables).

   ➢ Call the GridBagLayout method setConstraints, passing your component and the GridBagConstraints object.

   ➢ Call the add method of the window to add the component, as usual.

The important variables that need to be set in GridBagConstraints are listed in Table 12.16.

Table 12.16: Important Variables to Set in GridBagConstraints

Variable	Description
gridy, gridx	The row and column position (zero-based) for this component, where 0,0 is the upper left corner.
gridheight, gridwidth	The numbers of rows and columns this component will occupy. The default is one each.
weighty, weightx	Does this component grow in either direction when the window is sized? If yes, specify 1.0, otherwise specify zero. The default is zero. Typically, specify 1.0 for weightx for JTextField, 1.0 for weightx and weighty for Jlist and JTextArea. At least one component should have a nonzero value.
fill, anchor	What should be done when the cell(s) are larger than the component? 1. Stretch the component: set fill to HORIZONTAL, VERTICAL or BOTH. The default is NONE; do not stretch in either direction. 2. Align the component: set anchor to CENTER, NORTH, SOUTH, WEST, or EAST (or NORTHEAST/WEST, SOUTHEAST/WEST). The default is CENTER.

The tricky part (which will eventually come very easily to you) is determining the `gridy/x` and `gridheight/width` to specify for each component. Here is a little algorithm to get you going:

1. Lay out the intended screen in your mind or on paper.

2. Determine how many unique rows there are. In the example, we decided to have four rows because we really want the list box to be taller than the button beside it. We assign the list box to two rows and the button to only one row. Draw a line horizontally across the top and bottom of each component.

3. Determine how many unique columns there are (two, in the example). Draw a line vertically at the start and end of each component.

4. Determine, for each component:

   ➤ The row and column where it should start.

5. If there are no components beside it, its width is the number of remaining columns. The bottom message line in the example will span both columns. If there are components beside it, the width is the difference between this component's starting column and the one beside it.

   ➤ If there are no components beside it, its height is one. If there are components beside it, its height is the number of components, vertically, beside it. For example, a list box with three push buttons vertically beside it would have a height of three (or four, if you wanted a row of padding below the last button).

Figure 12.16 shows how the example is divided up. Notice that the list header should only span one column, not all columns as in the `BorderLayout` example.

The code for this layout is in Listing 12.8. Notice the helper method named `addPart` that handles the tedious but necessary variable assignments.

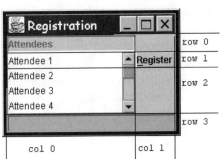

Figure 12.16: Mapping out rows and columns for `GridBagLayout`

527

Listing 12.8: Testing the GridBagLayout Layout Manager

```
protected void addComponents()
{
    GridBagLayout gbl = new GridBagLayout();
    GridBagConstraints gbc = new GridBagConstraints();
    gbc.fill = GridBagConstraints.BOTH;
    gbc.anchor = GridBagConstraints.SOUTH;
    getContentPane().setLayout(gbl);
    addPart(gbl, gbc, listHeader,      0, 0, 1, 1, false, false);
    addPart(gbl, gbc, listScrollPane, 1, 0, 2, 1, true,  true);
    addPart(gbl, gbc, registerButton, 1, 1, 1, 1, false, false);
    addPart(gbl, gbc, msgLine,        3, 0, 1, 2, false, false);
}

protected void addPart(GridBagLayout gbl, GridBagConstraints gbc,
                       JComponent part,
                       int row, int col, int rows, int cols,
                       boolean stretchVert, boolean stretchHorz)
{
    gbc.gridy = row;
    gbc.gridx = col;
    gbc.gridheight = rows;
    gbc.gridwidth = cols;
    gbc.weighty = stretchVert ? 1.0 : 0; // true? = 1 else 0
    gbc.weightx = stretchHorz ? 1.0 : 0; // true? = 1 else 0
    gbl.setConstraints(part, gbc);
    getContentPane().add(part);
}
```

And what does this produce? The result is shown in Figure 12.17.

Remember, users can resize your windows, even if you pack them, so it is important to identify those components you would like to grow when the window is sized, by specifying nonzero values for weightx and weighty. In this example, the list box stretchable in both directions, so when the window is made bigger, the list, and only the list, will grow to absorb the space. If no component has a nonzero weight value, the components will remain clumped in the middle, and all the white space will appear around them.

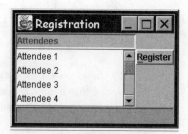

Figure 12.17: The layout produced by GridBagLayout

Using BoxLayout

All the previous layout-manager classes came from the java.awt package and existed in
the AWT days. The BoxLayout class is new for Swing and is in the javax.swing package. Swing engineers (a consortium of companies) invented BoxLayout to handle their
new JToolBar class, which was needed to show evenly sized components in a row, but
without the wrapping behavior of FlowLayout. Unlike GridLayout, they also needed the
ability to place pads between some of the buttons, which you see commonly between
groups of buttons in a tool bar. So they invented BoxLayout, and within it, something
called *struts* for these pads. Having done this, they made it available for you to use.

Table 12.17 compares the attributes of the various layout managers, with the exception of
BorderLayout because its five-region limit is really only applicable in special cases.

Table 12.17: Comparing the Layout Managers (Except BorderLayout)

Attribute	FlowLayout	GridLayout	GridBagLayout	BoxLayout
Non-evenly spaced cells	Yes	No	Yes	Yes
No wrapping	No	Yes	Yes	Yes
Multiple-cell spanning	No	No	Yes	No
Multiple rows or columns	No	No	Yes	No
Easy to use	Yes	Yes	No	Yes

As you can see, GridBagLayout remains the winner in every category except complexity.
It appears that BoxLayout comes in second, but while it is easy to code, it is a pain to finesse so the output is acceptable. Thus, we actually recommend you ignore this layout
manager! For completeness, though, the example in Listing 12.9 shows how to use it.

Listing 12.9: Testing the BoxLayout Layout Manager

```
protected void addComponents()
{
    BoxLayout vertRow =
      new BoxLayout(getContentPane(),BoxLayout.Y_AXIS);
    getContentPane().setLayout(vertRow);
    Box row0 = Box.createHorizontalBox();
    row0.add(listHeader);
```

Listing 12.9: Testing the BoxLayout Layout Manager (continued)

```
        row0.add(Box.createHorizontalGlue());
        getContentPane().add(row0);
        Box row1 = Box.createHorizontalBox();
        row1.add(listScrollPane);
        row1.add(registerButton);
        getContentPane().add(row1);
        getContentPane().add(msgLine);
    }
```

Notice that we BoxLayout is constructed differently than all the other managers. Rather than simply calling setLayout on a new BoxLayout instance, you first have to create a BoxLayout instance and tell it what you intend to use it for (getContentPane in this case, or any JPanel object generically). This is the first pain. To use a BoxLayout for more than one row or column of components, you have to think of your screen as a vertical box, within which each row is another horizontal box, where your actual components are. If any row has only one component, you can just add it to the vertical box. If it has multiple components, you have to first create a horizontal layout box and populate it, and then add that box to the vertical box. Boxes like this can be created either by creating a JPanel and setting its layout manager to a BoxLayout instance, or calling the factory method createHorizontalBox (or createVerticalBox), which returns a container with the appropriate layout manager already set.

The example uses the first way for the vertical box and the second way for the horizontal boxes in the first and third rows. There's only a single component in the first row, but because it should not span the full width, a box is created to hold it and the method createHorizontalGlue is used to create padding beside it. There is also a create HorizontalStrut to create rigid, fixed-sized spaces, but that's not what we want here.

Finally, running this gives Figure 12.18. It's not too bad, but there are a couple of small problems. First, the list header ("Attendees") is not as wide as the list box. Second, the push button ("Register") is centered beside the list, and we prefer it at the top. This should be fixable by setting the minimum size (setMinimumSize) of the list header component and setting the Y alignment of the push button (setAlignmentY) to one. However, everything we tried did not work. It's the little details like this that will get you with BoxLayout. For simple, single-row

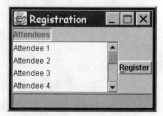

Figure 12.18: The layout produced by BoxLayout

or single-column groupings, though, you might find it works just fine.

Specifying padding between components

When you start to fine-tune your user interfaces, you might be interested in changing the Java-supplied default padding between the components that you add. This can be done with each of the layout managers by specifying horizontal and vertical "gap" values on the constructors, with the exception of GridBagLayout and BoxLayout. Alternatively, you can use the setHgap and setVgap methods supplied by each layout manager class, except for the GridBagLayout class (for which you specify the insets variable in GridBagConstraints object) and the BoxLayout class (where you use struts). The values you specify are in pixels, and you might find that five is a good number if you do not like a "tight" look. In the BorderLayout example, if you change the setLayout line to look like the following, you get Figure 12.19:

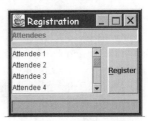

Figure 12.19: BoxLayout
with a padding of 10 pixels

```
getContentPane().setLayout(new BorderLayout(10,10));
```

Padding between the frame of the window and the components requires a different operation. To do that, you simply create an empty border around the content pane, like this:

```
((JPanel)getContentPane()).setBorder(
        BorderFactory.createEmptyBorder(10,10,10,10));
```

You see, the content pane of a JFrame is in fact a JPanel object, which is a special type of component just for holding other components. Like all components, it can have a border. The next section discusses what these JPanels are and how they can dramatically help with your layout decisions.

Nesting layout managers: The JPanel class

You have seen, so far, how you can add components to your JFrame or JDialog window object directly, using one of the layout manager classes to define how the added components will be placed. This is okay, but it does cause some grief choosing the appropriate layout manager, unless you use the complex GridBagLayout. Further, it does not allow for reuse of common GUI constructs. For example, in display files, you typically have one common record format with the Function-key descriptions, which you subsequently write to the bottom of many of your screens. That is reuse. You have this with display files because you can group fields into record formats, which are combined to form a screen. (Indeed, unlike Java, with display files, all fields *must* go into record formats.) The good news is that Java, too, has an easy way to group multiple components into a single entity. That entity is a JPanel object.

A JPanel is a container, like JFrame and JDialog, meaning it allows components to be added to it, and requires a layout manager class to define how the components will be arranged. However, JPanel has no visible borders or other frame pieces because it is meant to be used as part of a window. If you look back at Figure 12.2, you will see that JPanel extends JComponent, which means that anywhere you can add a basic component, you can also add a JPanel object. Thus, by using panels, you can greatly increase your flexibility in choosing a layout manager, because you can add *panels* to a JFrame window instead of adding *components* directly. This way, one area of your screen can use a panel with the layout manager appropriate for it and another can use another panel with a different layout manager appropriate for *it*.

Think about the BorderLayout layout manager. It allows only five components to be added, one each in the north, south, west, east, and center regions. This seems very restrictive, except that each of those components can in fact be a panel that contains many nested components.

Let's go back to the BorderLayout version of the example, from Listing 12.5, and update it to contain not just a single button labeled "Register," but five buttons labeled "Register," "Unregister," "Print," "Save," and "Open." How might you accomplish this? By adding a JPanel object containing these to the JFrame content pane, where you previously added a single JButton object. What should the layout manager of the JPanel object be? Well, you want a column of buttons that are the same size, so you have two easy choices: GridLayout or BoxLayout. Both will work fine, and in fact BoxLayout is best because it allows you to put struts between buttons if you want, adding a visual spacer between groups of buttons. However, to keep things simple here, let's go with GridLayout.

We have decided, by the way, to create a separate class for buttons, named BorderedButton, to make it easier to create buttons that have the border we like. First, then, here is that simple class:

```
import javax.swing.*;
/** Our own button class that simply adds a border to JButton */
public class BorderedButton extends JButton
{
    public BorderedButton(String label)
    {
        super(label);
        setBorder(BorderFactory.createRaisedBevelBorder());
    }
}
```

Listing 12.10 shows the revised addComponents method of the RegisterWindow class. (We don't show you declaring and instantiating the buttons.)

Listing 12.10: The Revised addComponents Method

```
protected void addComponents()
{
    getContentPane().setLayout(new BorderLayout());
    getContentPane().add(listHeader,     BorderLayout.NORTH);
    getContentPane().add(listScrollPane, BorderLayout.CENTER);
    JPanel buttonPanel = new JPanel(new GridLayout(5,1));
    buttonPanel.add(registerButton);
    buttonPanel.add(unRegisterButton);
    buttonPanel.add(printButton);
    buttonPanel.add(openButton);
    buttonPanel.add(saveButton);
    getContentPane().add(buttonPanel, BorderLayout.EAST);
    getContentPane().add(msgLine, BorderLayout.SOUTH);
}
```

You can specify the layout manager object right in the constructor of the JPanel, although calling setLayout separately is also allowed. This method just creates a JPanel object, populates it with buttons, and then adds it to JFrame instead of a single JButton object. Let's see what this looks like, in Figure 12.20.

Not bad! In fact, here's what we usually do with a JFrame or JDialog: We set the layout to BorderLayout, and then we reserve the south region for a message line and the north region for a toolbar (or

Figure 12.20: BorderLayout with a nested GridLayout JPanel

we leave it empty if there is no toolbar). We then always put the "meat" of the window in the center region. The east and west regions usually stay empty, but occasionally we find a good use for them, as in the east region of this example.

If we follow that design pattern here, the list box and its header would go together into their own JPanel, added to the center region. For that JPanel, a good choice is another BorderLayout, as shown in Listing 12.11.

Listing 12.11: The addComponents Method with a Nested Design

```
protected void addComponents()
{
    getContentPane().setLayout(new BorderLayout());
    JPanel listPanel = new JPanel(new BorderLayout());
    listPanel.add(listHeader,BorderLayout.NORTH);
    listPanel.add(listScrollPane, BorderLayout.CENTER);
    getContentPane().add(listPanel, BorderLayout.CENTER);
    JPanel buttonPanel = new JPanel(new GridLayout(6,1));
    buttonPanel.add(new JLabel(""));
    buttonPanel.add(registerButton);
    buttonPanel.add(unRegisterButton);
    buttonPanel.add(printButton);
    buttonPanel.add(openButton);
    buttonPanel.add(saveButton);
    getContentPane().add(buttonPanel, BorderLayout.EAST);
    getContentPane().add(msgLine, BorderLayout.SOUTH);
}
```

A filler JLabel is added to the button panel to push the buttons down to the list area. This gives the result shown in Figure 12.21. As you can see, the layout is as good as you would get with GridBagLayout, but without that layout manager's complexity. The trick is to divide your screen into components that map nicely to one of the layout managers.

Figure 12.21: Using a nested BorderLayout JPanel inside a BorderLayout JPanel

Another benefit of JPanels, beyond the flexibility they give in getting the layout you want, is the ability to encapsulate common UI constructs into reusable objects. When you create a new class that extends JPanel and populate it with components, you can then reuse that object in many windows, as the whole window or as part of a window. You might, for example, need to prompt for a customer number, order number, or part number in many windows. You could put the label, entry field, and "List" push button together in their own class that extends JPanel, and then insert that anywhere in any window you want. Really, you have created a new component!

A simple example is given in Listing 12.12. It is a push-button panel for the bottom of dialogs.

Listing 12.12: A Reusable ButtonPanel Class

```
import java.awt.*;     // AWT components and common classes
import javax.swing.*;  // Swing components and classes

public class ButtonPanel extends JPanel
{
    protected BorderedButton okButton, cancelButton, helpButton;

    public ButtonPanel(boolean evenSized)
    {
        super();
        if (evenSized)
          setLayout(new GridLayout(1,3));
        else
          setLayout(new FlowLayout());
        okButton = new BorderedButton("Ok");
        cancelButton = new BorderedButton("Cancel");
        helpButton = new BorderedButton("Help");
        add(okButton);
        add(cancelButton);
        add(helpButton);
    }
}
```

Again, BorderedButton is just your own class that extends JButton and adds a border. What is nice about this ButtonPanel class is that it allows you to choose between fixed-sized buttons and sized-to-fit buttons. Another example, a message-line class, is given in Listing 12.13.

Listing 12.13: A Reusable MessageLine Class

```
import java.awt.*;
import javax.swing.*;

public class MessageLine extends JPanel
{
    private JTextField msgField;

    public MessageLine()
    {
        super(new GridLayout(1,1));
        msgField = new JTextField();
        msgField.setEditable(false);
        msgField.setBorder(BorderFactory.createLoweredBevelBorder());
        msgField.setBackground(Color.cyan);
        add(msgField);
    }
    public void setText(String text)
    {
        msgField.setText(text);
    }
    public void clearText()
    {
        msgField.setText("");
    }
}
```

Rather than using a JTextField directly as we have been doing (which is preferable to JLabel because the user can manually cursor over to see long messages), we decided to make our own class. We could have extended JTextField, but extending JPanel and putting the JTextField object in it is better, because we can later change the implementation. For example, you might prefer to use a JComboBox, so that, like an AS/400 message subfile, you can write and display multiple error messages. You might also decide to support multiple areas in the message line, as is commonly seen in Windows applications. This is quite easily done by encapsulating the message-line component within a JPanel.

A simple form class

Another example of JPanels for reuse is with form panels. Very often, detail screens prompt for a series of inputs from the user. Typically, you want these to be laid out such the each prompt label is aligned in a column, and each text field or other input component is aligned in another column, and if there are other components beyond that, they are aligned in yet another column. You saw one way to do this earlier, using a GridLayout for a properties-sheet style of window. However, this is not very appealing, as every column ends up the same size.

The very best solution for these types of panels is to use GridBagLayout managers, but they are tedious to code. Instead, let's create a class that extends JPanel to make this easier. The class will have overloaded methods for adding rows of components (each taking different numbers of components to place in the row). The code will then put each given component into the GridBagLayout such that every column is nicely aligned. The class is shown in Listing 12.14.

Listing 12.14: A FormPanel Class that Makes GridBagLayout Easy to Use

```
import java.awt.*;
import javax.swing.*;
public class FormPanel extends JPanel
{
    protected GridBagLayout gbl       = new GridBagLayout();
    protected GridBagConstraints gbc = new GridBagConstraints();
    protected int currRow = 1;
    protected int finalColspan = 1;
    public FormPanel() // constructor
    {
        super();
        gbc.weightx = 0;    gbc.weighty = 0;
        gbc.gridheight = 1; gbc.gridwidth  = 1;
        gbc.anchor  = GridBagConstraints.SOUTHWEST;
        gbc.insets  = new Insets(1,1,1,1);
        setLayout(gbl);
    }
    protected void addPart(JComponent part, int row, int col,
                        int rows, int cols)
    {
        gbc.gridy = row;        gbc.gridx = col;
        gbc.gridheight = rows; gbc.gridwidth = cols;
        if (cols > 1)
          gbc.fill = GridBagConstraints.HORIZONTAL; // stretch
        gbl.setConstraints(part, gbc);
        add(part);
        gbc.gridwidth=1;  // reset
        gbc.fill = GridBagConstraints.NONE; // reset
    }
    // One part, one cell wide
    public void addRow(JComponent part)
    {
        addPart(part, currRow++, 0, 1, finalColspan);
```

Listing 12.14: A FormPanel Class that Makes GridBagLayout Easy to Use (continued)

```
    }
    // Two parts, each one cell wide
    public void addRow(JComponent part1, JComponent part2)
    {
        addPart(part1, currRow,   0, 1, 1);
        addPart(part2, currRow++, 1, 1, finalColspan);
    }
    // One part, spanning given number of cells
    public void addRow(JComponent part1, int cols)
    {
        finalColspan = cols;
        addRow(part1);
        finalColspan = 1; // reset default
    }
} // end of class FormPanel
```

Testing this requires a dialog window class that extends `BaseDialog` from Listing 12.4 (instead of the `BaseWindow` class we've been extending up until now). This dialog, shown in Listing 12.15, uses the `FormPanel` class to prompt for a phone number and a name.

Listing 12.15: A Dialog Window that Uses the FormPanel Class

```
public class AttendeePrompt extends BaseDialog
{
    private JLabel      nbrPrompt, namePrompt;
    private JTextField  nbrEntry,  nameEntry;
    private ButtonPanel buttons;
    private MessageLine msgLine;
    private boolean     okPressed = false;

    public AttendeePrompt(JFrame parent)
    {
        super(parent, "Attendee Prompt");
    }
    protected void createComponents()
    {
        nbrPrompt  = new JLabel("Phone number");
        nbrEntry   = new JTextField(15);
        namePrompt = new JLabel("Name");
        nameEntry  = new JTextField(20);
        buttons    = new ButtonPanel(true);
        msgLine    = new MessageLine();
        buttons.okButton.addActionListener(this);
```

```
        buttons.cancelButton.addActionListener(this);
    }
    protected void addComponents()
    {
        getContentPane().setLayout(new BorderLayout(5,5));
        FormPanel form = new FormPanel();
        form.addRow(nbrPrompt,   nbrEntry);
        form.addRow(namePrompt, nameEntry);
        form.addRow(buttons,2);
        getContentPane().add(form, BorderLayout.CENTER);
        getContentPane().add(msgLine, BorderLayout.SOUTH);
    }
    public void actionPerformed(ActionEvent evt)
    {
        if (evt.getSource() == buttons.cancelButton)
          dispose();
        else if (evt.getSource() == buttons.okButton)
          {
              okPressed = true;
              dispose();
          }
    }
    public boolean okPressed()
    {
        return okPressed;
    }
}
```

The interesting part is in addComponents, where a FormPanel object is created and populated with three rows. The third row is just the ButtonPanel object, and since we want it
to span as many columns as the other rows, we use the version of addRow that lets us
specify a column-span number. To see this, we need a parent window that will bring up
this dialog when some user event happens. So, we change the evolving RegisterWindow
class to do just that when the user presses the Register button.

The code for this is shown in Listing 12.16. Note that the line of code in
createComponent to call addActionListener is not shown, and remember that the parent
class BaseWindow implements the ActionListener interface required to process button
events. This actionPerformed method is required by that interface, and the empty version of it is overridden from the BaseWindow parent class. Note also that the new
MessageLine class is used here, too.

Listing 12.16: Updating RegisterWindow to
Show a Dialog When the Register Button Is Pressed

```
public void actionPerformed(ActionEvent evt)
{
    msgLine.clearText(); // from MessageLine class
    if (evt.getSource() == registerButton)
      {
        AttendeePrompt dlg = new AttendeePrompt(this);
        dlg.setVisible(true);
        if (dlg.okPressed())
          msgLine.setText("Ok Pressed");
      }
}
```

Let's have a look at this thing! Figure 12.22 shows how nicely the components in the dialog have been formatted. That is the beauty of GridBagLayout. The beauty of FormPanel is how very simple the code in Listing 12.15 was to get this. If you do any Swing programming, you will want to use this handy class.

Figure 12.22: A dialog that uses the FormPanel class

You can probably see where we are going with all this: putting a GUI face onto the AttendeeList class from the registration example in Chapter 6. To cut to the chase, you will find all the classes for the fully fleshed-out application on the CD-ROM, in the Listing12-17 subdirectory for Chapter 12. To run it, type java RegisterWindow. This uses the GUI shown in Figure 12.22 to drive the AttendeeList class and its dependent classes Attendee, AttendeeKey, PhoneNumber, PhoneNumberException, and Helpers.

These classes have evolved from when you last saw them in Chapter 9 to include functionality discussed in Chapter 10 (exceptions) and Chapter 11 (threads). The methods the AttendeeList class now supports are register, deRegister, print (to file), write (to disk), and read (from disk). It also still supports display, but since the list is displayed right in the main window, you don't need this one. Note that the file the example reads to and writes from to persist the list is hard-coded for now to event1.dat, and the local stream file printed to is hard-coded to event1.1st. If you are interested in the details of how AttendeeList was enhanced to support these functions, have a look at the code on the CD-ROM.

Listing 12.17 is what the button event-handling method looks like now, to process all the push buttons. Note that attendees is an instance of AttendeeList created in the constructor, while populateList and enableButtons are helper methods created but not shown here. The former populates the list box from the AttendeeList object; the latter enables or disables all the buttons depending on the success of the open operation. Also not shown are the call to addActionListener(this) for all the buttons and the call to addListSelectionListener for the JList object. A new dialog window is created for confirming "unregister" requests. The code for registering is right in the AttendeePrompt class, and the code for unregistering is in the AttendeeDePrompt class. This is necessary to shows errors right in the dialog.

Listing 12.17: The Updated RegisterWindow
Event Methods to Fully Support AttendeeList

```java
public void actionPerformed(ActionEvent evt)
{
    msgLine.clearText(); // from MessageLine class
    if (evt.getSource() == openButton)
      {
        try {
            String filename = attendees.read();
            populateList();
            msgLine.setText("Read in from file " + filename);
            enableButtons(true);
        } catch (java.io.IOException exc) {
            msgLine.setText("Error reading file " +
              attendees.getSaveFileName()+": "+exc.getMessage());
        }
      }
    else if (evt.getSource() == registerButton)
      {
        AttendeePrompt dlg = new AttendeePrompt(this,attendees);
        dlg.setVisible(true);
        if (dlg.okPressed())
          populateList();
      }
    else if (evt.getSource() == unRegisterButton)
```

Listing 12.17: The Updated RegisterWindow
Event Methods to Fully Support AttendeeList (continued)

```
        {
            AttendeeDePrompt dlg = new AttendeeDePrompt(this,
                attendees,(Attendee)list.getSelectedValue());
            dlg.setVisible(true);
            if (dlg.okPressed())
              populateList();
        }
    else if (evt.getSource() == printButton)
        {
          try {
            String filename = attendees.print();
            msgLine.setText("Printed to file " + filename);
          } catch (java.io.IOException exc) {
            msgLine.setText(exc.getMessage()); }
        }
    else if (evt.getSource() == saveButton)
        {
          try {
            String filename = attendees.write();
            msgLine.setText("Saved to file " + filename);
          } catch (java.io.IOException exc) {
            msgLine.setText(exc.getMessage()); }
        }
  } // end actionPerformed
```

The rest of the code, including the `valueChanged` method for processing list-selection events, is on the CD-ROM. Figure 12.23 shows the running application.

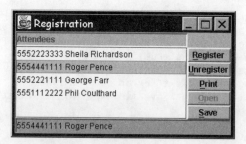

Figure 12.23: A fully functional
AttendeeList GUI application

The key to error-checking is that all of the `AttendeeList` methods throw exceptions, instead of just writing error messages to the console, which is of no value in GUIs. The window code then simply has to catch an exception and query the text of it with getMessage, then write that text to the message line.

EFFECTIVE USE OF JTextFields

The most important aspect of any UI code is getting input from the user. Most of the components in Java for doing this are very straightforward, such as the radio button. However, a text field is actually not that straightforward to use effectively in Java. Because of this, and because you will use them so heavily, and because your expectations are so high from your display-file background, we have to spend a little time here helping you over some hurdles we guarantee you will hit using JTextField.

Component sizing and layout managers

You won't go very far in Swing programming before hitting situations where your components are not sized correctly by Swing. To help you fix that, you have to understand how Java determines the sizes of components. The worst component to get sized correctly is JTextField, so we'll describe the algorithm for it here. With the exception of GridLayout, each layout manager uses the following algorithm to determine the display size of a JLabel, JTextField, or JPasswordField:

- Were columns specified in constructor or via setColumns?
- If yes, use this size.
- If no, was a preferred size set via setPreferredSize?
- If yes, use the size of the letter *m* in the current font, multiplied by the columns.
- If no, use the size of the current contents, computed dynamically on each repaint.

The best answer, then, is to set the size you want by specifying the number of columns on the constructor. You'll find this is actually a tiny bit too small to actually display that many characters, so you should probably add one to it. Remember, this number does not restrict how many characters the user can type; it merely tells Java how big you'd like this field to be. So, if you only want to display 20 characters but allow 100, only specify 20 for the columns. The user can still type 100 characters by cursoring over. Indeed, the user can type a thousand characters if he or she wants! Your error-checking code will check for too-long text when the OK button is pressed.

All components have a preferred, minimum, and maximum size that is either hard-coded by Java or computed depending on contents. You can also query and set all of these, as well as the actual size, via get/setSize. In all cases, the size is specified via a Dimension object, which has height and width public integer fields.

Restricting input in a JTextField

Since JTextField components are the equivalent to named fields in DDS, it will come as a disappointment to you that there is no way to specify "validity checking" information that the runtime can use to restrict what or how much is typed in. There is no data type, no length or decimal positions, no VALUES, RANGE, COMP, CHECK, CHGINPDFT, DSPATR, EDTCDE, EDTWRD, or EDTMSK keyword equivalents. JTextField simply displays String text and returns to you String text. All error-checking is up to you. All formatting is up to you. However, if you want this type of function (and we know you do), you can get it by creating your own class that extends JTextField, and code it yourself.

The first thing you will want to crack is restricting what can be typed in (e.g., only numbers) and how much can be typed (e.g., a maximum of 20 characters). This is easily done by extending the PlainDocument model class, overriding the insertString method to do this error-checking on the given string, beeping (Toolkit.getDefaultToolkit().beep()) if the criteria is not met, or calling the parent's version of this method if it is okay. Java calls this method to update the model with each keystroke the user types. If you reject it, the typed character is rejected:

```
public void insertString(int offset, String newText, AttributeSet as)
        throws BadLocationException
{
    if (getLength() + newText.length() > 20)
        Toolkit.getDefaultToolkit().beep();
    else
        super.insertString(offset, newText, as);
}
```

The getLength method is inherited and is the length of the current text, while newText is the newly typed (or pasted) text. This only shows checking for the length, but by using the RPGStrings class, you could also easily check whether each character in newText is numeric. Of course, you would not hard-code 20 as the maximum length, but rather use an instance variable passed to the constructor.

Next, specify an instance of this model as the first parameter in the constructor to JTextField. This is best encapsulated in your own text-field class:

```
public class SmartField extends JTextField
{
     public SmartField(int columns)
     {
           super (new FieldModel(columns), columns);
     }
}
```

Supporting editword and auto-advance requires rather more work, and is beyond this book. However, the CD-ROM includes a working class that does all this, named SmartTextField. Its model class is SmartTextFieldModel. If you run the TestSmartTextField class, you will see how it works. It restricts users from typing more than the specified number of characters, ensures only digits are typed, and auto-advances to the next field after the maximum number of digits are typed. Further, when the field is not in focus, it formats the text (editword). By default, it does this using a dollar sign and a decimal point at the two-digit location, but you can change that via set method calls.

You will like this class, but for a significantly more robust version with additional capabilities such as range and comparison checking, full editcode and editword support, and even edit masking support, see the JFormattedTextField class that IBM supplies in the "Enterprise Toolkit for AS/400" feature of VisualAge for Java. There is even a JFormattedLabel class for editcode/editword support in labels, and a JFormattedComboBox class the uses the JFormattedTextField for the entry part and a list of JFormattedLabel objects for the list part. These are all way cool! You can even use the model class by itself if you want to format a string with an editcode for printing purposes, say. If you do get into Swing programming, you really cannot live without these classes. They were designed by AS/400 programmers for AS/400 programmers, but they are of value to any Swing programmer.

We also highly recommend looking at all the Java classes at *www.ibm.com/alphaworks*, in the "alphabeans" section. Among other things, you will find text field classes specifically tailored for prompting for phone numbers, dates, zip codes, and so on.

MENU BARS AND POP-UPS

You will be hard-pressed to find a 5250-style traditional menu in a GUI application! Rather, GUIs have menu bars such as the one shown in Figure 12.24.

Figure 12.24: A menu bar with menus of items

This example is comprised of the following:

- A menu bar object of class `JMenuBar`

- Two menu objects of class `JMenu`, for the "File" and "Edit" menus

- A number of objects of class `JMenuItem` for items like "New" and "Open"

Here are the steps to define these menus inside a Java `JFrame` class:

1. Create the `JMenuBar` object.

2. Create the `JMenu` objects for the pull-down menus and nested menus.

3. Add the `JMenu` objects to the `JMenuBar` object.

4. Create the `JMenuItem` objects.

5. Add the `JMenuItem` objects to the `JMenu` objects.

6. Add the `JMenuBar` object to the `JFrame` window, using `setJMenuBar`.

The code to produce the menu bar in Figure 12.24 is shown in Listing 12.18.

Listing 12.18: Creating and Populating JMenuBar

```
private JMenuBar  menubar;
private JMenu      fileMenu, editMenu;
private JMenuItem fileNewMI, fileOpenMI, fileSaveMI, filePrintMI;
private JMenuItem editRegisterMI, editDeRegisterMI;

    menubar = new JMenuBar();
    fileMenu = new JMenu("File");
    editMenu = new JMenu("Edit");
  menubar.add(fileMenu);
```

```
menubar.add(editMenu);
fileNewMI = new JMenuItem("New");
fileOpenMI = new JMenuItem("Open");
fileSaveMI = new JMenuItem("Save");
filePrintMI = new JMenuItem("Print");
fileMenu.add(fileNewMI);
fileMenu.add(fileOpenMI);
fileMenu.add(fileSaveMI);
fileMenu.add(filePrintMI);
editRegisterMI = new JMenuItem("Register");
editDeRegisterMI = new JMenuItem("UnRegister");
editMenu.add(editRegisterMI);
editMenu.add(editDeRegisterMI);

setJMenuBar(menubar);
```

Once you have a menu, processing it is easy. Menus are just like buttons, in that you have to implement the `ActionListener` interface, call `addActionListener` on each `JMenuItem` object, and code the `actionPerformed` method to process the menu-item selection event. You compare the result of `getSource` to each of your `JMenuItem` objects to establish which menu item was selected by the user to cause this event. For example, the `actionPerformed` method is updated as follows:

```
Object part = evt.getSource();
if ((part == openButton) || (part == fileOpenMI))
  ...
else if ((part == registerButton) || (part == editRegisterMI))
  ...
else if ((part == unRegisterButton) || (part == editDeRegisterMI))
  ...
else if ((part == printButton) || (part == filePrintMI))
  ...
else if ((part == saveButton) || (part == fileSaveMI))
  ...
else if (part == fileNewMI)
  ...
```

To have a *cascading menu* (a menu item that, when selected, expands to show yet more menu items), simply add a second populated `JMenu` object to your first `JMenu` object. To show separator lines, simply call `addSeparator` on your `JMenu` object.

Easy stuff, menus. You can enable or disable them just like buttons, and also like buttons, you can put images in them, if you like. Just pass the `ImageIcon` object as the only or second parameter into the constructor. You can even have menu items that visually toggle between selected and unselected, by using the JCheckBoxMenuItem class. Further, the JRadioButtonMenuItem class, together with ButtonGroup, allows you to have a number of menu items, of which only one can be selected. Use setSelected and isSelected to set and query the selection states of these menu item types.

Pop-up menus

In addition to placing JMenuItem, JCheckBoxMenuItem, and JRadioButtonMenuItem objects inside the JMenu objects of a menu bar, you can also add them to a JPopupMenu object to populate a pop-up menu, also called a *context menu*. You can then write code to show this pop-up menu when a user right-clicks on a particular component in your window.

This code is actually a little bit tricky. It involves implementing the mouse listener interface, calling addMouseListener(this) on the target component, and coding the five methods(!) from the interface. Three of these methods need to code a call to isPopupTrigger on the given MouseEvent object to determine if the right mouse button was clicked, and if so, call the show method on the JPopupMenu object. The show method requires you to pass the current object (this) and the x,y coordinates of the mouse click, which you can get by calling getX and getY on the event object.

Let's see an example. First, the RegisterWindow class definition is changed to implement MouseListener:

```
public class RegisterWindow extends BaseWindow
                        implements MouseListener
```

Next, you declare and instance a JPopupMenu instance variable object:

```
private JPopupMenu  popupMenu = new JPopupMenu();
```

Then, you add this object to the JMenuItem objects already in the "Edit" menu, and register your interest in mouse events with the JList component object:

```
popupMenu.add(editRegisterMI);
popupMenu.add(editDeRegisterMI);
list.addMouseListener(this);
```

Finally, you need to code the five methods required by this event interface, and then abstract-out, in method checkForPopup, the common code that three of the methods need to call to ensure the menu is shown. The code for this is given in Listing 12.19.

Listing 12.19: Processing Mouse Events for Showing a Pop-up Menu

```java
public void mouseEntered(MouseEvent evt) {}
public void mouseExited(MouseEvent evt) {}
public void mouseClicked(MouseEvent evt)
{
    checkForPopup(evt);
}
public void mousePressed(MouseEvent evt)
{
    checkForPopup(evt);
}
public void mouseReleased(MouseEvent evt)
{
    checkForPopup(evt);
}
private void checkForPopup(MouseEvent evt)
{
    Component part = evt.getComponent();
    if (evt.isPopupTrigger() && (part == list))
      popupMenu.show(part, evt.getX(), evt.getY());
}
```

When you run the application and right-click in the list area, you get the pop-up shown in Figure 12.25.

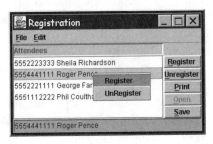

Figure 12.25: A pop-up menu

Menu-item shortcuts

You can assign shortcut keys to your menu items, such as F3 for "Exit" or Ctrl+O for "Open." This is done by calling the setAccelerator method on your JMenuItem object. The only tricky part of this call is the parameters. You have to pass an instance of the KeyStroke class to identify the key-combination to assign. The KeyStroke object is created by calling the factory method getKeyStroke, which requires three parameters: the character or key (F3 or O), any modifier keys (Ctrl), and false. The character is identified by constants in java.awt.KeyEvent, and the modifier keys are identified by constants in java.awt.Event. Here is an example:

```
KeyStroke openKS = KeyStroke.getKeyStroke(KeyEvent.VK_O,
                                 Event.CTRL_MASK, false);
KeyStroke exitKS = KeyStroke.getKeyStroke(KeyEvent.VK_F3, 0, false);
fileOpenMI.setAccelerator(openKS);
fileExitMI.setAccelerator(exitKS);
```

These will show up in the text of your menu item, so users know there are shortcuts. Of course, when a user presses the shortcut key, it will be the same as if he or she had selected the menu item, as far as your event-handling code is concerned.

ADVANCED SWING FUNCTIONALITY

So far in this chapter, you have seen all the basics you need to write user interface applications in Swing. However, Swing offers much more than just these basics. The details of these advanced functions are beyond the scope of this book (you've read enough, right?), but you should be able to read the JavaDoc documentation now to continue on your own. The following sections simply itemize all the additional functionality Swing has, so you know what is available to you.

Default push button

For JFrame and JDialog classes, you can identify a push button as the default push button, so that it is pressed when the user simply presses the Enter key. This is done by calling getRootPane().setDefaultButton and passing a JButton object to it.

Toolbars

There is a JToolBar class for creating a bar of buttons to display across the top of your window. (Actually, you can put it anywhere.) You populate it with JButton objects, so it can show images and/or text. It is typically placed in the north part of a `BorderLayout` layout manager. The toolbar can be "ripped off" by the user and placed elsewhere in the window or floated on the desktop. This is free; no coding is required.

Actions

GUIs often support the same action redundantly in menus, pop-up menus, buttons, and toolbars. This can lead to redundant code and make it a nightmare trying to enable/disable them appropriately. To save you from this nightmare, Swing allows you to define an *action*, which is a class that extends `AbstractAction`, and implements the required `run` method. You pass text and an optional `ImageIcon` object to the parent's constructor.

You can place an action object directly into a menu, pop-up menu, button, or toolbar. The text and optional image from the action will be displayed, and when the user selects the item, the `run` method in your action object will be called. You can also call `setEnabled(true/false)` on the action, and all the GUI places where the action is used will be `enabled/disabled` by that one call.

Multiple-document interface

You can design an application that has a master window with other windows inside it (as in many Windows applications). The classes you need are `JDesktopPane` and `JInternalFrame`. You will use these instead of `JFrame` and `JDialog`.

More components

Here are some other components you can use in Java:

- `JProgressBar`. Moves a bar across to indicate progress.

- `JSlider`. Users can drag a thumbnail to the left or right, much like a horizontal scrollbar.

- `JTree`. A tree with nodes, much like you see in Windows Explorer, on the left side.

- `JTable`. A multiple column list box (a subfile!), much like you see in Windows Explorer, on the right side.

- `JTextPane`. An advanced editor widget that goes beyond `JTextPane`, supporting different colors and fonts for characters.

More containers

The following specialty containers allow for some special effects:

- JSplitPane allows you to put a different component or panel in the left and right panes (or top and bottom panes). User can move the split bar in the middle by dragging it.

- JTabbedPane allows you to create wizards. Put multiple panels in, and cycle through them. Optionally, display a tab at the top of each panel.

Figure 12.26 shows see some of these advanced components and containers. While you can't see it in the figure, the JTextPane shows the prompt, command, and messages in different colors. In fact, two JSplitPanes are used here, one with components on the left (JTree) and right (JTable), and one with components in the top (nested JScrollPane) and bottom (JTabbedPane).

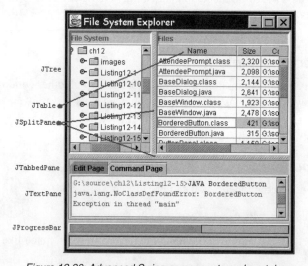

Figure 12.26: Advanced Swing components and containers

Look and feel

The Swing examples you have seen in this chapter so far show the default Swing look, called "Metal." You can change the look and the feel (behavior) to either Windows or UNIX ("CDE/Motif"). With just a few lines of code, your whole application's look changes. Quite cool. You can even write your own look and feel. To set the look and feel, call the static method setLookAndFeel in the UIManager class.

The JavaDoc documentation for this class explains how to use it, but to get you in the "Swing," we have supplied a cool helper class, LookAndFeelMenu. It extends the JMenu class, querying the installed look-and-feel options on your system to create a menu of their names. Further, all the event-processing logic is there to switch the look and feel when the user selects one of these menu items. All you have to do is instantiate the LookAndFeelMenu class, add it to a JMenuBar or a JMenu, and you are done. Figure 12.27 updates the example from Figure 12.26 to show this menu, with the CDE/Motif look and feel selected.

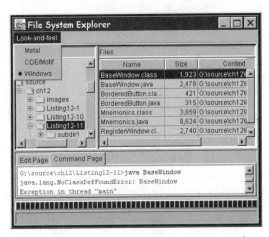

Figure 12.27: Advanced Swing components and
containers, with a Motif look and feel

Predefined dialogs

Swing comes with some predefined dialogs that save you creating them yourself. This is such a great idea, it is a disappointment to learn that there are currently only two provided: an open dialog (JFileChooser) and a color dialog (JColorChooser). The first is very handy, while the second is rarely needed in a business application, unless you sell paint.

Because the open dialog is so important, we'll show you how to use it by changing the Open button in the RegisterWindow class to pop up an open dialog, instead of using a hard-coded file. By default, JFileChooser lists all files in the current directory, but we only want to show files that end with .dat. First, we need a class to do this filtering, as shown in Listing 12.20.

Listing 12.20: A Class to Filter File Names

```
import javax.swing.*;
import java.io.*;

public class EventFileFilter
        extends javax.swing.filechooser.FileFilter
{
    public boolean accept(File f)
    {
        return (f.isDirectory() || f.getName().endsWith(".dat"));
    }
    public String getDescription()
    {
        return "Event files (*.dat)";
    }
}
```

We have to extend FileFilter in the javax.swing.filechooser package, and we have to fully qualify that class name because it collides with a class of the same name in package java.io. The package java.io must be imported because of the File class (discussed in Chapter 14). The class just has to code an accept method that returns true if the given File object should be included in the open dialog list. Java calls accept for every file in the current directory. The File object has a method to determine if the file is a directory or not, and a getName method to return the file's name. It returns true if the file is a directory (to enable drill-down) or ends with .dat. The next method to be coded is getDescription, which returns a string to display in the open dialog for this filter.

Now, let's change the actionPerformed event logic in RegisterWindow to show an open dialog and retrieve from it the name of the file chosen by the user, as in Listing 12.21.

Listing 12.21: A Class to Manage the Open Dialog

```
if ((part == openButton) || (part == fileOpenMI))
  {
    java.io.File currDir = new
        java.io.File(System.getProperty("user.dir"));
    JFileChooser openDlg = new JFileChooser(currDir);
    openDlg.setFileFilter(new EventFileFilter());
    int buttonPressed = openDlg.showOpenDialog(this);
    if (buttonPressed != JFileChooser.APPROVE_OPTION)
    msgLine.setText("Cancelled");
```

$\longrightarrow$

```
    else
      {
        String pathname = openDlg.getSelectedFile().getParent();
        String filename = openDlg.getSelectedFile().getName();
        String eventname =
          filename.substring(0,filename.indexOf(".dat"));
        attendees = new AttendeeList(eventname);
        try {
          filename = attendees.read();
          populateList();
          msgLine.setText("Read in from file " + filename);
          enableButtons(true);
        } catch (java.io.IOException exc) {
          msgLine.setText("Error reading file " +
            attendees.getSaveFileName() + ": " + exc.getMessage());
        } // end catch
      } // end if user didn't cancel open dialog
  }
```

This tells the open dialog what directory to show files in, using the constructor. This is via a File object, and you see the code needed to get a file object representing the current directory. Once there is a JFileChooser dialog, methods are called to tailor it, such as setFileFilter, which takes an object of the previous class to do the filtering by name. Once tailored, it is displayed by a call to showOpenDialog (or showSaveDialog, if this is for the purpose of saving a file). This is a modal call, and the returned value is an integer indicating how the user exited the dialog. The constant APPROVE_OPTION indicates that the Open or OK button was pressed.

The open dialog looks like Figure 12.28. Note that it is in the default Metal look and feel. In the Windows look and feel, it is quite similar to the Windows standard open dialog.

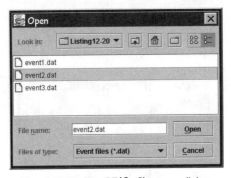

Figure 12.28: The JFileChooser dialog

Message and simple input dialogs

The other help Swing gives you for commonly needed actions is for modal dialogs that display a message or prompt for simple input. The following static methods are supplied in the `JOptionPane` class:

- The `showConfirmDialog` method shows a confirmation dialog with a message and Yes and No buttons.

- The `showMessageDialog` method shows a message dialog with OK and Cancel buttons.

- The `showInputDialog` method shows an input dialog prompting for text or a simple list selection.

- The `showOptionDialog` method creates a generic dialog where you can supply the content.

These methods all take different parameters, which you can read about in the JavaDoc documentation. For now, you will see how to use `showInputDialog`.

The registration example used throughout this chapter has a menu item labeled "New" that prompts the user for the name of the event. This input has `.dat` appended to it to make its file name. Here is the code to prompt the user:

```
String name = JOptionPane.showInputDialog(this,"Enter name of event");
```

Pretty easy stuff! It creates the dialog shown in Figure 12.29.

Figure 12.29: The JOptionPane.
showInputDialog dialog

If the user cancels the dialog, the showInputDialog call will return null. Otherwise, you need to verify that no file with this name already exists. If it does, you should ask the user if it is okay to continue (meaning the file will be replaced). This is the code to do this:

```
java.io.File file = new java.io.File(name+".dat");
if (file.exists())
  {
     int ans = JOptionPane.showConfirmDialog(this,
                           "File exists, override it?");
    if (ans != JOptionPane.YES_OPTION)
      return;
  }
```

Again, the File class is used, this time to test the existence of the file. If it does exist, the showConfirmDialog method is used to pop a message to the user, with Yes and No buttons. If the user does not press the Yes button, the code exits the actionPerformed method. The code above results in the dialog in Figure 12.30.

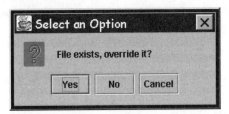

Figure 12.30: The JOptionPane.show ConfirmDialog dialog

APPLETS VERSUS APPLICATIONS

Recall from Chapter 2 the discussion of Java applets versus Java applications:

- Applications can be invoked from a command line, using java MyClass. This first class requires the existence of a public static void main(String args[]) {...} method, which the Java runtime looks for.

- Applets cannot be invoked from the command line. They must be embedded in an HTML Web page, using an APPLET tag. The Web browser, on encountering the APPLET tag, will retrieve the applet from the host server where the Web page came from and run it.

All of the examples to this point have used an application-style `main` method and have been invoked from the command line. All of the non-`main` code is still valid for applets because they use the same language and Java-supplied packages as Java applications do. However, there are some restrictions related to security. Java applets are, by default, restricted to a *sandbox* that prevents them from accessing in any way the workstation or computer the Web browser is running on, or any server other than the one they came from. Applets cannot do the following:

- Access local files in any way, including running local programs

- Access or change local properties, like the current working directory

- Access any server except the one they came from, via any form of communications, including JDBC or the AS/400 Toolbox for Java classes

These restrictions are enforced by the Web browsers, although most allow these to be configured. Java includes the capability of digitally *signing* your applets using the JDK-supplied `javakey` tool. Briefly, this tool allows for mutually consented use of a Java applet that has full access rights. It ensures the following:

- The user knows that the applet came from you and has not been tampered with.

- The programmer knows that only those people identified are allowed to run the applet.

Applets and Swing

Applets are classes that extend the `javax.swing.JApplet` class. This class is a container, much like a `JPanel`, and you write applets exactly as you would write a panel. The only difference is that you must use `getContentPane()` to set the layout and add the components, just as with `JFrame` and `JDialog`. Applets have no frames because they run in the rectangular space of the Web browser frame. Listing 12.22 shows the first example applet.

Listing 12.22: A Simple Applet for Calculating Tips

```
import java.awt.*;
import java.awt.event.*;
import javax.swing.*;
import javax.swing.event.*;
```

→

```
import java.math.*;

public class TipApplet extends JApplet implements ActionListener
{
    private JTextField   input  = new JTextField("100.00",9);
    private JTextField   rate   = new JTextField(".15",2);
    private JRadioButton badRB  = new JRadioButton("Bad");
    private JRadioButton fairRB = new JRadioButton("Fair",true);
    private JRadioButton goodRB = new JRadioButton("Good");
    private ButtonGroup  rbGroup= new ButtonGroup();
    private JTextField   output = new JTextField(9);
    private JButton      calcButton = new JButton("Calculate tip");
    private BigDecimal   badRate = new BigDecimal("0.10");
    private BigDecimal   fairRate = new BigDecimal("0.15");
    private BigDecimal   goodRate = new BigDecimal("0.20");

    public TipApplet()
    {
        output.setEditable(false);
        setOutputFieldColors(false);
        calcButton.addActionListener(this);
        JPanel rbPanel = new JPanel(new GridLayout(1,3));
        rbGroup.add(badRB);  rbGroup.add(fairRB);  rbGroup.add(goodRB);
        rbPanel.add(badRB);  rbPanel.add(fairRB);  rbPanel.add(goodRB);
        JPanel clientPanel = new JPanel(new GridLayout(4,2,0,5));
        clientPanel.add(new JLabel("Enter dollar amount:"));
        clientPanel.add(input);
        clientPanel.add(new JLabel("Select service level:"));
        clientPanel.add(rbPanel);
        clientPanel.add(new JLabel("Press button:"));
        clientPanel.add(calcButton);
        clientPanel.add(new JLabel("You should tip:"));
        clientPanel.add(output);
        getContentPane().setLayout(new BorderLayout(5,5));
        getContentPane().add(clientPanel,BorderLayout.CENTER);
    }

    private void setOutputFieldColors(boolean error)
    {
        output.setBackground(error?Color.red : Color.green);
        output.setForeground(error?Color.white : Color.black);
    }

    public void actionPerformed(ActionEvent evt)
    {
        boolean error = true;
        try
        {
        BigDecimal base =
```

Listing 12.22: A Simple Applet for Calculating Tips (continued)

```
                new BigDecimal(input.getText().trim())
                    .setScale(2,BigDecimal.ROUND_HALF_UP);
            input.setText(base.toString());
            BigDecimal tipRate = fairRate;
            if (badRB.isSelected())
              tipRate = badRate;
            else if (goodRB.isSelected())
              tipRate = goodRate;
            BigDecimal result = base.multiply(tipRate);
            result = result.setScale(2,BigDecimal.ROUND_HALF_UP);
            output.setText(result.toString());
            error = false;
        }
        catch (Exception exc)
        {
            output.setText("** INPUT ERROR **");
            input.requestFocus();
            input.selectAll();
        }
        setOutputFieldColors(error);
    }
}
```

You can see that the applet is a simple tip-calculating tool. You can also see that coding
an applet is identical to coding a JPanel, except for the need to use getContentPane().
To run the applet, you use a little HTML, as shown in Listing 12.23.

Listing 12.23: The HTML that Embeds the Sample Applet

```
<html>
<head>
<title>Tom's Tip Tool</title>
</head>
<body>
<h1>Need help calculating your tip?</h1>
<p>Try this:
<br>
<applet code="TipApplet.class" width=300 height=200>
</body>
</html>
```

At least, this is all you should need to do. However, as of this writing, it will not work
as-is because Web browsers still do not support JDK 1.2 or Swing. To overcome this, you

have to use the *Java plug-in* for the browsers. This comes from Sun for Windows and Solaris, and is shipped as part of the JDK and Java Runtime Environment, so you've already got it. However, to use it, you have to change your HTML APPLET tag to tell it to use the plug-in's JVM instead of the browser's. To do this, you need to download the HTML conversion tool from Sun (*http://java.sun.com/products/plugin/*), which comes as a zip file. Unzip it, and place the zip file and the unzipped directory on your CLASSPATH, then type java HTMLConverter. This will convert your HTML files in place and back them up. After that, you're ready to roll! Just open your HTML file by double-clicking it, and you'll get Figure 12.31.

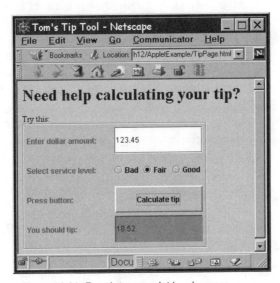

Figure 12.31: Running an applet in a browser

If you can't decide whether to write applets or applications, write everything as applets because you can embed any applet inside a JFrame just as though it really were a JPanel. This gives you the best of both worlds. You'll see how we did that in TestTipApplet.java on the CD-ROM.

For information on the APPLET tag, consult the documentation for the Sun JDK, in the file docs/guide/misc/applet.html in your JDK subdirectory. For information on some of the unique methods available to applets, see the JavaDoc documentation for JApplet and its parent, java.awt.Applet.

TRANSLATION-READY USING RESOURCE BUNDLES

Do you support the translation of your products into different languages, such as German, French, or Japanese? If you do not, yet, you probably will someday, so you should plan your code to allow for this. Preparing for international support usually involves keeping string constants outside of your program so the translators can access them. That way, you can ship only one program object that can display different languages dynamically.

On the AS/400, this is done using display-file objects and message files. You usually let the translators directly edit the text constants in them. You can then simply change your library list to have your programs pick up the different versions of these translated objects. In Java, there are no message files and, as you have learned, no external user interface objects. Up to this point, all of the user-interfaces strings (such as text constants, titles, and button labels) and error-message strings have been hard-coded. The downside of this, of course, is that you'll need to produce redundant copies of your Java programs for each language you want to support. That will create a maintenance nightmare.

Java 1.1 tackled the whole area of internationalization support, including not only translated strings but also the wider topics of currency, collating sequences, and the formatting of numbers, dates, and times. This "internationalization framework" was actually based on code supplied by IBM's Taligent subsidiary. There is a good tutorial on the whole subject in Sun's tutorial on Java. See *http://java.sun.com/docs/books/tutorial/intl/index.html*.

Locales

The main idea behind international support is to allow your program to work in different languages automatically. The trick is to define all your language-sensitive and country-sensitive information (for example, currency is different per country, while language might not be) in a class that is somehow tagged as being for a particular language and/or country. Then, for each language and/or country in which you wish your program to operate, you simply supply a unique version of this class. For Internet applets this is especially important, given the international access they have.

At runtime, then, you need some way to identify the language and/or country in which your user wishes to work. This can be done by asking directly via the user interface (for example, through language and country JComboBox drop-downs), or by simply using the Java system default, which is set up to be the same as the computer, Web browser, or other host in which the Java application or applet is running. Having determined the language and country pair (or optionally, either a language or country, using defaults for the other), your program will choose the appropriate class described earlier, containing language/country-specific information such as translatable strings. How does it do this? Let's look a little deeper....

In Java, the current operating language/country "mode" is captured by a class named Locale in the java.util package. You create a new Locale object by specifying in the constructor the language and the country, as strings. One of these strings can be null, if you are not interested in country-specific languages or language-specific countries. The string values are two-character codes that are predefined by an ISO (International Standards Organization) standard. However, you need not worry about them; rather than instantiating locales, you will probably just use the predefined "constant" locales supplied as helpers in the Locale class, such as Locale.US, Locale.GERMANY, and Local.GERMAN.

What are these mysterious locales, and why do you need them? A number of classes in the java.text package for such things as message/date/number formatting allow you to pass in one of these locale objects so the formatting is done correctly for that place. For example, the appropriate date format and decimal point symbol are used. If no locale is specified, the system-default locale is used, which you can always query by calling Locale.getDefault(). These methods are called *locale sensitive*. They are intended to work correctly for any given locale, or at least the locales they claim to officially support.

To warm up your fingers for more coding to come, here is a simple locale program:

```
import java.util.*;
public class TestLocale
{
    public static void main(String args[])
    {
        Locale defloc = Locale.getDefault();
        System.out.println("name is     : " +
                            defloc.getDisplayName());
        System.out.println("language is: " + defloc.getLanguage());
        System.out.println("country  is: " + defloc.getCountry());
    }
}
```

On our system, this gives the following result:

```
name is     : English (United States)
language is: en
country  is: US
```

Translated strings—Resource bundles

Suppose you want to design your own locale-sensitive classes. The tricky thing is that Locale objects are quite useless on their own—they hold no real information. They are simply objects that your code (and the Java-supplied code in java.text) can use to determine which language to display, or which language/country to support.

Let's write a locale-sensitive version of the little tip-calculator applet. (Note that the following technique is used for Swing or even non-graphical coding, whenever you need to translate strings.)

The class constructor is changed to take an optional Locale object, displaying the window in the language for that locale. If it is a locale into which our strings have not translated, they're simply shown in English. Because this example will only translate into one other language (German), this will often be the case.

The first thing to do is extract all the strings from the program and put them in their own class. You need to put them in a two-dimensional array, where the first string is merely a key for finding the second, translated string. This way, the program will extract the strings by reading them from the array using that key. Java has built-in support for this, in the form of a ListResourceBundle class that is extended in Listing 12.24 to create a new class.

Listing 12.24: A ListResourseBundle Class

```java
import java.util.*;

public class TipStrings extends ListResourceBundle
{
    protected static final Object[][] contents =
    {
        {"LABEL_BAD",       "Bad"},
        {"LABEL_FAIR",      "Fair"},
        {"LABEL_GOOD",      "Good"},
        {"LABEL_CALC",      "Calculate tip"},
        {"PROMPT_AMOUNT",   "Enter dollar amount:"},
        {"PROMPT_SERVICE",  "Select service level:"},
        {"PROMPT_PRESS",    "Press button:"},
        {"PROMPT_TIP",      "You should tip"},
    };

    public Object[][] getContents()
    {
        return contents;
    }
}
```

The getContents method is required to be overridden from the base ListResourceBundle class, since it is defined as abstract. It returns the array of translatable strings, an array called contents in this example.

Now, let's create a German version of this class. Listing 12.25 shows the strings translated into German. The name of the class is also changed slightly to indicate that it is for German locales (with the _de suffix for *Deutsche*, the German word for *German*). We don't actually know German well enough to translate these strings, so we cheated and simply prefixed each one with De_ to test for the right output. This is a good way for you to test you caught every string, prior to the actual translation phase, Ja?

Listing 12.25: The Translated ListResourceBundle Class

```java
import java.util.*;

public class TipStrings_de extends ListResourceBundle
{
    protected static final Object[][] contents =
    {
        {"LABEL_BAD",       "De_Bad"},
        {"LABEL_FAIR",      "De_Fair"},
        {"LABEL_GOOD",      "De_Good"},
        {"LABEL_CALC",      "De_Calculate tip"},
        {"PROMPT_AMOUNT",   "De_Enter dollar amount:"},
        {"PROMPT_SERVICE",  "De_Select service level:"},
        {"PROMPT_PRESS",    "De_Press button:"},
        {"PROMPT_TIP",      "De_You should tip"},
    };

    public Object[][] getContents()
    {
        return contents;
    }
}
```

The code needs to be changed to use these strings and the appropriate version of the class, as opposed to hard-coding the strings:

```java
ResourceBundle strings =
    ResourceBundle.getBundle("TipStrings",locale);
```

This returns an instance of TipStrings_de if the locale is Locale.GERMAN, or TipStrings otherwise. You typically get the Locale object locale by some user prompt, or by calling Locale.getDefault().

Now, all the hard-coded strings are changed to use the getString method from the ResourceBundle object reference variable, as follows:

```
badRB = new JRadioButton(strings.getString("LABEL_BAD"));
```

This takes the key as input and returns the translated value. Simple enough. You can see the complete converted class on the CD-ROM, if you want.

There is more to supporting internationalization than simply factoring out your translatable strings, as you probably know—there are other details like date formats and currency. You can learn about all of this in your JDK documentation, especially in the file D:\jdk1.2.2\docs\guide\internat\index.html.

SUMMARY

In this chapter, you learned the following:

- The basics of Java Swing, and what its advanced capabilities are.

- How to write a Java applet and deploy it in an HTML page.

- How to translate your strings.

- How much you need a break from reading!

DATABASE ACCESS

At this point in this book, you have been exposed to much of the Java language, and should be getting comfortable with Java's syntax and capabilities. However, the primary activity in all of your RPG code is accessing data. Almost all AS/400 RPG applications revolve around database access. They are "based" on "data." Clearly, then, to put Java to use—either on the client or on the server—you need to know how Java programs can access DB2/400 data.

DATABASE ACCESS IN RPG IV

Processing database files has not changed much from RPG III to RPG IV. The operations are still the same (CHAIN, SETLL, SETGT, READ, READP, READE, READPE, WRITE, UPDATE, DELETE, LOCK, UNLOCK, FEOD, OPEN, and CLOSE), although the longer names are now spelled correctly! However, the syntax of the F-spec for declaring database files is different, since F-spec has been redesigned. Here is what the F-spec for a database file looks like in RPG IV:

```
6789012345678901234567890123456789012345678901234567890123456789012
FFilename++IPEASFRlen+LKlen+AIDevice+.Keywords++++++++++++
FProddtl   UF  E          K Disk
```

This declares an updatable, full-procedural, externally described, keyed file named PRODDTL. Note the keyword area from column 44 on. This area allows RPG IV to do away with continuation specifications. Rather, keywords are used to specify additional information, and you can continue coding keywords in positions 44 through 80 on as many subsequent F-spec lines as needed (these lines will have positions 7 through 43 blank). The valid keywords for database files include BLOCK, COMMIT, EXTIND, IGNORE, INCLUDE, INFDS, INFSR, PREFIX, RENAME, RECNO, and USROPN. Some you probably recognize from RPG III, while others such as INCLUDE and PREFIX are new for RPG IV.

V5R1 of RPG IV offers some exciting new capability, via its new EXTFILE and EXTMBR F-spec keywords. With these keywords, you can specify the library-qualified file name and the explicit member to open, respectively. In both cases, the name can be explicitly given as a quote-delimited literal or as a field name. For the latter, when not using USROPEN to defer opening of the file until runtime, the field's value must be available at pre-runtime by using the INZ keyword, or passing the value in as an entry parameter. If no library is given for EXTFILE, then *LIBL is used. For EXTMBR, the special names *ALL and *FIRST are allowed. For explicit library, file, and member name literals or field values, the name must be in uppercase to work properly.

When processing the file, the op-codes now use optional extenders instead of the overloaded column 53 in RPG III. For example, READ(N) means read with no lock. There is also a new E extender that simplifies error processing. When specified, you can do away with result indicators and instead simply test if the %ERROR built-in function equals one (an error) or zero (no error), and use %STATUS to get the file status.

Some RPG programs today still use the RPG cycle to process files. However, this is generally considered an unstructured and obsolete form of database access. If you are writing ILE RPG IV modules in which you specify the NOMAIN keyword on the H-spec, you do not even have the option of using the RPG cycle because it is not permitted. (Note that VisualAge for RPG does not support the RPG cycle at all.)

RPG's built-in database support is sometimes called *direct record access*. It is noteworthy in the database industry because most relational database access is done through some form of *SQL (Structured Query Language)* statements, as you will learn.

RPG DATABASE ACCESS UNDER COMMITMENT CONTROL

If you are conducting sensitive multiple-database transactions, where each transaction consists of multiple database updates, you might also use *commitment control* by following these steps:

- Prepare for commitment control using the CL commands CRTJRN (*Create Journal*), CRTJRNRCV (*Create Journal Receiver*) and STRJRNPF (*Start Journal Physical File*).

- Start commitment control for your application using the CL command STRCMTCTL (*Start Commitment Control*).

- Declare the files on the F-spec as being under commitment control, using the COMMIT keyword. You can specify an optional runtime flag for dynamically controlling the use of commitment control.

- Open the files, either automatically or by specifying the USROPN keyword on the F-spec and using the OPEN operation code.

- Work with the files' records using the usual RPG operation codes.

- Commit the files' changes using the COMMIT operation code, or cancel the files' changes if any error occurs, using the ROLBK (*Roll Back*) op-code.

- End commitment control using the CL command ENDCMTCTL (*End Commitment Control*).

Commitment control can be scoped to either the job or an ILE activation group. It allows you to treat multiple database operations as a single atomic unit of work—either they all succeed, or none succeed. This is the fundamental way in which complex transactions ensure database integrity: you do not want "partial" transactions to corrupt the state of your data.

ACCESSING DATA WITH SQL

SQL is a database industry-standard method of accessing a relational database (one containing records and fields). The current standard is ANSI SQL99. Your SQL code and skills are transferable to other databases and other systems. As you will see, these skills are also directly portable to Java.

The SQL language has a well-defined syntax for creating and manipulating databases. If you use it to create databases on the AS/400, those databases are identical and interchangeable with database files created with DDS. If you have an existing database created with traditional DDS, you can still access that database with SQL's database manipulation statements, as though the database were created with SQL statements, and vice versa. (Note that there are *some* differences.) One restriction, however, is that SQL cannot be used to access multiple-record-format logical files. SQL assumes one format per file and has no syntax for qualifying format names when reading or writing a database.

SQL uses terminology that is different from what you might be used to: *rows* are records, *columns* are fields, and *tables* are files.

When using SQL, you do not use RPG's record-oriented style to access your data. Rather, you use statements where you specify record filter criteria to retrieve, update, or delete all rows meeting those criteria. In RPG, you would code a loop to read through all records (hence record-level access) you wish to view or update, while in SQL you first retrieve all pertinent rows using a filter. You then iterate through each row. Here is an example of a filter:

```
SELECT * FROM CUSTOMER WHERE STATE='PA'
```

This retrieves records from the CUSTOMER table where the STATE field is equal to PA. Note that for each row, all (*) the columns will be returned. Alternatively, you could specify an explicit list of comma-separated field names.

The WHERE clause in this statement is called the *predicate*. It can get as complex as required, using boolean logic and numerous operators to explicitly identify the exact records you are looking for, and functions to apply to the matching rows. For example, you can specify a COUNT column function to count and report the number of rows, or an AVG column function to compute and report the average value for all columns in all applicable rows. There is support for retrieving from multiple tables, for doing "total" calculations, and more.

A SELECT statement can have an ORDER BY clause to sort the returned rows. It can have a GROUP BY clause to apply column functions to sub-groups of the rows. It can also have a

HAVING clause to further filter the rows in the result based on applying a function such as AVG and comparing the output of it. The following is from *DataBase Design and Programming for DB2/400* by Paul Conte (29th Street Press, 1996), a book we recommend:

```
SELECT    ShpCity, COUNT( * ), AVG( Discount)
  FROM    Customer
  WHERE   Discount IS NOT NULL
GROUP BY  ShpCity
  HAVING  AVG ( Discount ) > .01
```

Rather than returning rows of data from the database, this statement returns calculated information based on that data. You get back information about the customers who have an average discount greater than 0.01. This information is grouped by the customer's city, so you'll get back one row of information per city that has customers meeting the criteria. The information you get per row is the name of the city, the number of customers in that city, and the average discount for those customers, as specified on the SELECT statement. Note that customers with no discount value will not be included in the calculations.

As you explore SQL, you will be amazed at the power of the SELECT statement for doing queries and calculations. The result of a query is a temporary *result set* containing all of the returned rows, and there are SQL statements for iterating through each row. (In RPG, FETCH moves you to the next record and places the field values for that row into specified fields). To update records, there is no need for iteration. You simply specify the filter criteria for the affected records and the new value for the field or fields you want to change, like this:

```
UPDATE CUSTOMER SET RATE=2 WHERE STATE='PA'
```

In this case, all records in the CUSTOMER database file where the STATE field is PA have their RATE field changed to two. Is this easier than writing loops?

Deleting records is similar:

```
DELETE FROM CUSTOMER WHERE STATE='WY' AND RATE=2
```

This deletes all records from the CUSTOMER database where the STATE is WY and the RATE field has a value of two. For these types of "apply to all records of this criteria" operations, SQL can offer some coding advantages. In fact, it is similar to creating a logical file view over the database, on the fly. There is also a way to update and delete the current record being processed in a result set that comes from a SELECT statement. This is called *positioned update and delete*.

To insert records into a database you use the INSERT INTO statement, like this:

```
INSERT INTO CUSTOMER (CUSTOMER, STATE, RATE) VALUES('Bobs Bait', 'MA', 1)
```

This inserts a single row into the CUSTOMER table, with values specified for the columns CUSTOMER, STATE, and RATE. There is also syntax to insert multiple rows into the database in a single statement.

Interactive SQL versus embedded SQL

SQL consists of statements such as SELECT, UPDATE, DELETE, and INSERT. On the AS/400, these statements can be run interactively, with the result shown immediately, via the STRSQL (*Start SQL*) CL command. This places you in a shell for submitting SQL statements. You can also code your SQL statements into a source member and run them from there via the RUNSQLCMD (*Run SQL Command*) CL command.

Another option is to embed SQL statements directly into your RPG, COBOL, C, C++, PL/I, or FORTRAN source. Even REXX supports embedded SQL. In these cases, you use special syntax to distinguish between your native source and your SQL source. All SQL source is bracketed by EXEC SQL and END-EXEC, for example:

```
C/Exec SQL
C+ UPDATE CUSTOMER
C+    SET RATE=2
C+    WHERE STATE='PA'
C/End-Exec
```

All SQL statements are coded on C-specs. To continue an SQL statement over multiple lines, use a plus sign in position 7, as shown in the example above with "C+". The SQL statements entered are free-format and case-insensitive.

In embedded SQL, you do not use a SELECT statement directly to retrieve a set of rows. Rather, you have to declare a *cursor* by using the DECLARE CURSOR statement, and specify SELECT there as a statement clause. Then, you can OPEN the cursor (this reads the records from the database that meet the SELECT criteria), FETCH the individual records from the result set (one at a time), process the columns of the currently fetched row, and CLOSE the cursor.

Rather than declaring a file and processing file records as you do in native RPG code, with SQL, you declare a cursor on the file and process the resulting set of records produced by the cursor. The DECLARE CURSOR statement requires you to name the cursor, and this name is subsequently used on the OPEN, FETCH, and CLOSE statements.

When you embed SQL source in RPG source, you no longer use the RPG compiler command. Instead, the compilation is done using the appropriate SQL preprocessor command, such as CRTSQLRPGI for RPG IV. This preprocessor works in two steps. First, it processes the embedded SQL into native RPG statements and an SQL access plan. Then, it compiles the generated intermediate RPG using the traditional compiler, such as CRTRPGMOD. (See the *DB2 UDB for AS/400 SQL Programming* manual for more details.)

Static SQL versus dynamic SQL

SQL statements can be either *static* or *dynamic*. SQL statements you embed in a programming language such as RPG are static. Indeed, static statements can only be embedded in another language and precompiled. Dynamic statements are issued in several ways: interactively, in their own source member, or via APIs. Dynamic statements can be prepared and executed dynamically (depending, say, on runtime information the program has), while static statements are hard-coded into the source program.

Although the statements themselves are hard-coded for static SQL, you can still use program variables to define the parameter values to the statement dynamically. To do this, you specify your program variable name right in the SQL statement, but prefix it with a colon. However, the boolean logic for the filter is still hard-coded. For example, while you can specify a variable for PA in the earlier examples (e.g., WHERE STATE=:MYVAR), you cannot turn STATE= into a variable. For this, you can use embedded SQL EXECUTE IMMEDIATE static statement. This statement submits a character field containing a dynamic statement to the database.

Thus, you can programmatically build up an entire statement, such as an UPDATE or SELECT, based, perhaps, on user-supplied information. Because the preprocessor has no way of knowing the content of that statement field, no optimization is possible on it. It is truly dynamic. This might be slow if you execute statements many times, so there is a way to speed this up. You can first use PREPARE to tell the database about your statement, and then call EXECUTE on it to run it. Calling EXECUTE many times on the same statement can speed things up, as the cycles to verify the statement and build an access path are done only once at PREPARE time.

What are these dynamic statements that you can pass into the EXECUTE IMMEDIATE statement? You will see a list soon, but they are functionally (and often syntactically) the same as those you can statically define in your RPG source.

Dynamic SQL gives you flexibility, allowing you to decide at runtime which SQL statement to run. If your program operates on a specific file, but allows the user or caller to decide what fields will be used in the query, update, delete, or insert action, you should choose dynamic over static SQL.

Dynamic SQL versus CLI APIs

As an alternative to running SQL statements dynamically from RPG using the EXECUTE statement, you could use APIs supplied by the system. These APIs are based on the standard X/Open SQL *CLI (Call Level Interface)* specification, and are similar to Microsoft's *ODBC (Open Database Connectivity)*, which is also based on (and extends) the evolving X/Open standard. Basically, APIs allow you to pass in SQL statements to be executed, although a few APIs perform other functions. For example, there are APIs for connecting and disconnecting from a local or remote database. There are also APIs for querying information about the database itself, such as lists of files and stored procedures.

CLI APIs are designed to be more database-vendor independent than embedded SQL (a more "standard" standard). A CLI program can potentially be written to easily target multiple vendor databases by dynamically connecting to the database, querying database capability information, and passing in SQL statements on the fly. CLI APIs give you the most flexibility. While dynamic statements allow you to decide at runtime which SQL statement to run, CLI APIs go further by allowing you to decide at runtime which local or remote file to operate against.

If your program allows the user to decide the file and the query or manipulation statements to run, you would choose CLI over dynamic SQL. Furthermore, if your program is designed to operate against multiple databases (such as DB2, Oracle, Sybase, and Microsoft) via end-user control, you will need to use CLI.

Table 13.1 summarizes the various "flavors" of SQL.

Table 13.1: The SQL Alternatives			
SQL Statement Type	Run Interactively?	Embed in RPG Source?	Invoke via CLI API?
Static	No	Yes	No
Dynamic	Yes	Yes	Yes

Embedded Static	Embedded Dynamic	CLI APIs
• Best performance	• Need to use prepared statements to get performance	• Hardest to program
• Easiest to code		• Similar to embedded dynamic in performance
• Hard-coded file and field names	• Hard-coded file names, but dynamic field names	• Total flexibility in choice of file and field names

Local versus distributed SQL

SQL can be used by a program to access a database either locally (on the same system) or remotely (on a system other than where the program resides). The latter is called *distributed SQL*. Distributed SQL involves the same set of statements already discussed, plus a few unique statements for accessing remote data, such as CONNECT for connecting to the remote database (something you must do before processing SQL statements for that database).

There are two types of distributed access, as dictated by IBM's *Distributed Relational Database Architecture* (*DRDA*, or "Dr. DA"). The first, called *Remote Unit of Work* (*ROW*), allows you to access a single database on a remote system. The second, called *Distributed Unit of Work* (*DOW*), allows you to access multiple databases on one or more systems, and synchronize transactions (as delimited by COMMIT and ROLLBACK) across the multiple databases. You might know this as "two-phase commit."

Note that ODBC programs, VisualAge RPG, and Java programs running on the client accessing a DB2/400 database on a single AS/400 server do not need to use distributed SQL, despite what you might expect. Rather, they support direct database access as though the database were local, using a database server program that runs on the AS/400 accepting these remote (client) database requests. You only need to use distributed SQL from the client if you want to access databases across multiple AS/400 servers, or if you want to access DB2/400 data by going through another database such as DB2/NT.

That is, when using distributed SQL embedded in your RPG program, for instance, the compiled SQL statements are not stored locally by the precompiler as they are for non-distributed SQL. Rather, they are stored on the remote system where the database exists. How are they stored? By using a *package* object. You identify to the database that your embedded-SQL RPG source is using distributed SQL by specifying a remote or local database name on the RDB (Relational Database) parameter of the CRTSQLRPGI preprocessor command. At that time, you also name the package you wish to create from your embedded SQL statements on the SQLPKG (SQL Package) parameter. This package object is merely a persistent way to store the processed SQL statements (the access plan) from your RPG source.

SQL terminology

As you have seen, SQL uses its own terminology that differs from the native AS/400 terminology. The differences are summarized in Table 13.2.

Table 13.2: AS/400 Versus RPG Versus SQL Terminology		
AS/400 Term	**RPG Term**	**SQL Term**
DB2/400	n/a	Database
Library	n/a	Collection
Library + objects	n/a	Schema
Physical file	Disk file	Table
Logical file (no key)	Disk file	View
Logical file (with key)	Keyed disk file	Index
Record format	Format	Metadata
Record	Data structure	Row
Field	Field	Column

Why the new terms? Because this is a database- and operating system-independent standard language. In SQL, you have one or more *databases*, each with one or more *collections*. Each collection has one or more *tables*, and each table has one or more *columns*. On the AS/400, there is just one database (DB2/400), while in the rest of the world there are many databases. This makes common terminology important. Using this terminology, DB2/400 has collections (libraries) of tables (physical files), and has views (logical files) as well as indexes (keyed logical files). Each table contains one or more columns (fields). When you read from the database, you read rows (records) of data.

Views are like traditional logical files (and they are implemented as logical files). They allow you to filter one or more files. You can access a view from your program as though it were a physical file. However, views provide significantly more filtering capability than logical-file DDS can offer.

Indexes are also implemented as logical files but, unlike views, you cannot access them from your program as though they were physical files. Rather, an index is a tool that you can use to define a permanent access path to your database file for performance reasons. Your code still refers to the original file, but the system recognizes when it is appropriate for an existing index to be used. This saves the overhead of creating a temporary access path on the fly. Mind you, indexes do require some additional system overhead in terms of maintenance, so there is a tradeoff to be considered.

SQL languages: DDL versus DML

You have seen the various flavors of SQL statements, but you have not yet seen what SQL statements actually *do*. SQL is divided into two sub-languages: *DDL (Data Definition Language)* and *DML (Data Manipulation Language)*. DDL statements create and alter entire tables or files. They are equivalent to DDS for defining your database definitions, versus your data. DML statements, in contrast, manipulate actual data—for example, reading, updating, inserting, and deleting rows or records.

Table 13.3 lists common DDL statements, while Table 13.4 lists common DML statements. As you get into Java and its database support, you will use these often, so they are important to know.

Table 13.3: Common DDL Statements

Statement	Description
CREATE SCHEMA/COLLECTION	Create a new schema/collection (library).
CREATE TABLE	Create a new table (file).
CREATE INDEX	Create a new index (keyed logical file).
CREATE VIEW	Create a new view (non-keyed logical file).
ALTER TABLE	Add/delete/change a column (field definition), add constraints, add/delete a key.
DROP XXX	Delete a collection/schema, table, index, view, or package.

Table 13.4: Common DML Statements

Statement	Description
DECLARE CURSOR	Declare a cursor (embedded SQL only).
OPEN	Open a cursor (embedded SQL only).
FETCH	Read the next row of an opened cursor (embedded SQL only).
SELECT	Read one or more rows (CLI only).
INSERT	Insert one or more rows.
UPDATE	Update one or more rows.
DELETE	Delete one or more rows.
CLOSE	Close a cursor (embedded SQL only).
COMMIT	Commit previous transactions (e.g., INSERT, UPDATE, DELETE), with commitment control.
ROLLBACK	Undo previous transactions, with commitment control.

What you need for SQL on the AS/400

To use SQL on the AS/400, including high-level languages like RPG, you must have the IBM product "DB2 Query Manager and SQL Development Kit for OS/400," program number 5716-ST1. You do not need this product to run SQL applications, only to develop them. It includes a Query Manager, the SQL preprocessors, the interactive SQL utility, and the SQL statement processor. This product is not required to use CLI APIs, either; they come free with the operating system. Nor do you need this product for Java database access, although you might find the interactive SQL command very handy for learning SQL.

WHY THE INTRODUCTION TO SQL?

As you get into Java and its database support, you will be using all these concepts, so they are important to know. SQL has undeniably become the industry standard for database access and is supported by every major relational database vendor. If you are not using it already, you almost certainly will be.

When the Java engineers went searching for a standard, portable database access language, they didn't look very far! SQL was the answer, and as you will see, knowing SQL is essential to accessing relational data from Java. There is an alternative to SQL for accessing DB2/400 data from Java, however, which is covered in Appendix A. If you use it, though, you are tied completely to OS/400 and to DB2/400. If that is okay (we don't mind!), you might prefer to jump straight to Appendix A, versus reading further here.

ACCESSING DATA WITH JAVA

Java's built-in support for relational database access is patterned after Microsoft's ubiquitous ODBC standard. ODBC is a C language set of APIs that abstracts-out database access. It allows you to write database-accessing code once and easily target multiple database vendors.

ODBC is a successful attempt by Microsoft to design a standard set of APIs to which programs can code, independent of the database vendor. It is based on the CLI API standard, not embedded SQL, so code written with it can connect to any vendor's database.

Java's database support is patterned after ODBC, but is written entirely in Java rather than C. Like ODBC, it has a framework for database access in which:

- Developers write their database-vendor–neutral code using language-supplied syntax and support.

- The database vendor supplies a piece to be "plugged in" to the infrastructure, allowing database-neutral code to access that particular vendor's product.

Java's framework is called *JDBC*. (It is actually a trademarked name, but it is often referred to as *Java Database Connectivity*). JDBC involves the following:

- A Java package (`java.sql`) with classes and methods for database connectivity, manipulation, queries, and more.

- A Java JDBC *database driver manager*, similar to ODBC's driver manager, that comes with the language.

- Database-vendor-supplied JDBC *database drivers*, which are unique to each database vendor. These "snap in" to allow a single JDBC application to access multiple databases with minimal code changes. The Java-supplied driver manager essentially passes on all SQL statements to the snapped-in database driver supplied by the vendor. While JDBC is database-neutral, you can still exploit unique database vendor functions, if desired.

- A Java-supplied JDBC/ODBC bridge to allow, in the short term, Java access to any database via its ODBC database driver. You will only need and want to use this, however, if your database vendor is one of the few left that does not yet supply a pure Java JDBC driver. This bridge will often be slow, and might only be as portable as the ODBC DLLs it requires.

The key is that you need to write your Java code to the `java.sql` package, not the database vendor APIs. The classes and interfaces in this package pass on the requests to the underlying database on your behalf, as shown in Figure 13.1. This way, you can easily swap in the particular database with minimal impact to your code.

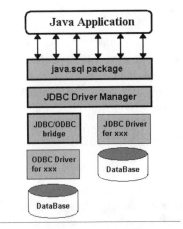

Figure 13.1: The Java JDBC framework

Database vendors can supply any of four types of JDBC drivers:

- *Type 1: JDBC-ODBC bridge.* This is actually supplied with the JDK, and can be used to connect to any existing ODBC driver.

- *Type 2: JDBC native driver.* This is supplied by the database vendor, and under the covers, it uses *Java Native Interface* (*JNI*, which is the Java-supplied way of calling C functions from Java) to call existing C APIs for that particular database. It must be run on the same system as the database, but if the local database can access remote databases, the Java JDBC wrapper will inherit this capability.

- *Type 3: JDBC net drivers.* A pure Java implementation of the JDBC interfaces, this is for use in remote clients. It requires a piece of code running on the server (also supplied by the database vendor) to "listen" for requests sent by the client driver.

- *Type 4: JDBC thin drivers.* This is also a pure Java implementation of the JDBC interfaces, for use in remote clients. The difference from type 3 is that there is no listener code required on the server, as the client communicates directly with the database engine on the server.

JDBC DRIVERS FOR DB2/400

For DB2/400, two JDBC drivers are available. The first is a type-2 driver that comes with the OS/400 JDK. It is a Java JDBC wrapper to the DB2/400 CLI (Call Level Interface) APIs that are part of the operating system. Java code you write using this driver can only run on OS/400 itself, but it is very efficient. Even though it must run on OS/400, it can be used to access databases on other AS/400s. Because this driver comes with the JDK, there is nothing unique you have to do to install it, other than install the JDK (which is on your stack tape, as of V4R2 or higher). The JDK product number is 5769-JV1 for Version 4 releases.

The second driver is a type-4 driver that comes with the AS/400 Toolbox for Java, which is a collection of pure Java classes offering access to many OS/400 services, including data via this JDBC driver. All the Toolbox classes are designed to run either on OS/400 itself or on any client that has a JVM. No prerequisites are needed on any client (and a Web browser is a valid client), other than TCP/IP, which is built into most operating systems these days.

If you are writing client code to connect to OS/400 remotely, this is the driver for you. Because it is Java, it will also run fine on OS/400 itself, but because it uses TCP/IP to talk to the database engine, it is not as efficient as the type-2 driver that comes with the JDK.

To use this driver, you must ensure the Toolbox jt400.jar file is on your CLASSPATH statement. See the installation instructions for the AS/400 Toolbox for Java for details. You can get the Toolbox and documentation by going to www.ibm.com/iseries/java and following the appropriate link. It also comes with your system as of V4R2 or higher, but it must be installed. The Toolbox product number is 5768-JC1 for Version 4 releases, and 5722-JC1 for Version 5 releases.

The jt400.jar file is installed into your Integrated File System, but can then be copied to your workstation, placed on your classpath there, and used to remotely connect to DB2/400, either for production or for testing purposes. You will find it in the IFS directory, /QIBM/ProdData/HTTP/Public/jt400/lib. Of course, it can also be used for code running on the AS/400 itself. For this, set your classpath there to point to it. The details to do this are discussed in Appendix A. Briefly, you create a file named .profile ("dot profile") in your IFS home directory, and put the following statement in it:

```
export -s CLASSPATH=.:/QIBM/ProdData/HTTP/Public/jt400/lib/jt400.jar
```

The Toolbox comes with IBM's WebSphere Development Tools for the iSeries, and it is placed on your classpath automatically.

Appendix A also mentions an alternative direct-record-access option for database access that the Toolbox also supplies. Once the Toolbox has been installed, it is time to start writing your Java database code.

JAVA JDBC PROGRAMMING

The java.sql package that comprises JDBC is Java's equivalent to CLI. Recall that CLI APIs are a set of APIs for executing dynamic SQL statements. For JDBC, these are a set of classes for executing dynamic SQL statements.

The java.sql package that comes with Java consists of a number of public interfaces. (Recall that these are like abstract classes—only method signatures are supplied, not method implementations.) Your code, however, uses them as though they were fully implemented classes because each database-vendor-supplied JDBC driver simply implements each of these interfaces in its own classes. However, by using factory methods, your code only works with the interface names, not the vendor's class names. The main interfaces in the java.sql package are listed in Table 13.5.

Table 13.5: The Main Interfaces in JDBC's java.sql Package

The java.sql Interface	Description
Driver	The main interface, this supplies the connection method for accessing a database. It is the one interface your code never sees directly.
Connection	This represents a specific session with a specific database.
Statement	This is used to execute explicit SQL statements.
PreparedStatement	This is used to prepare repeatedly executed SQL statements and execute them. It extends Statement.
ResultSet	Returned from an SQL query or stored procedure call, this contains the list of returned rows (records) and methods for traversing them, and extracting columns (fields).
CallableStatement	This is used to call stored procedures. It extends PreparedStatement.
ResultSetMetaData	This is used to dynamically determine the column (field) definitions for a ResultSet. It saves hard-coding field attributes.
DatabaseMetaData	This is used to dynamically determine information about the database itself. That is, it finds information about conventions and limits of the database (DB2/400, in your case), as well as information stored in the database's catalog, such as a list of "registered" stored procedures.

In addition to these interfaces that the JDBC driver-provider writes classes to implement, a `DriverManager` class supplied by Java starts the whole process. It contains static methods for registering a particular driver and connecting to that driver's database. The latter method is defined to return a `Connection` interface object, and in reality returns an instance of the JDBC provider's class that implements that interface. Indeed, it is by calling the methods that are defined to return interfaces that you get objects for all the JDBC provider's classes. This is how your code is shielded from explicitly coding the names of the JDBC provider's classes. This way, switching from JDBC driver to JDBC driver is easy.

To write JDBC code, you of course have to import the `java.sql` package, which contains the interfaces and the `DriverManager` class. You then follow the steps in Table 13.6 to work with the database.

Table 13.6: Steps to Writing JDBC Code

Step	Description	Example
1. Register the driver.	Tell Java about your JDBC driver.	DriverManager.registerDriver(new com.ibm.as400.access. AS400JDBCDriver());
2. Connect to the database.	Open a connection. You are allowed more than one.	Connection conn = DriverManager.getConnection ("jdbc:as400://MYSYSTEM");
3. Create statement objects.	Use factory methods to return the appropriate statement object.	Statement stmt = conn.createStatement(); // or PreparedStatement pstmt = conn.prepareStatement("...");
4. Run SQL statements.	Use methods in the statement object to run the SQL statement.	ResultSet rs = stmt.executeQuery("SELECT ..."); int res = stmt.executeUpdate("INSERT ..."); // or pstmt.executeQuery/Update();
5. Process the results.	For queries, walk the returned result set.	while (rs.next()) String column1 = rs.getString(1);
6. Close the statements and the connection.	Use the close method to free up resources as soon as you are done with them.	rs.close(); stmt.close(); conn.close();

For every single JDBC statement you execute, you have to monitor for SQLException, which every single method call can throw. The following sections examine the steps in Table 13.6 in more detail.

Steps 1 and 2: Registering and connecting

The only difference between the Toolbox JDBC driver and the AS/400 Java JDBC driver, from a programming point of view, is the parameters passed to register the JDBC driver and to subsequently connect to the database. Here is how to register each driver:

```
DriverManager.registerDriver(new
    com.ibm.as400.access.AS400JDBCDriver()); // Toolbox driver
DriverManager.registerDriver(new
    com.ibm.db2.jdbc.app.DB2Driver()); // Native AS/400 Java driver
```

Here is how to connect using each driver:

```
Connection conn =
    DriverManager.getConnection("jdbc:as400://system"); // Toolbox
Connection conn =
    DriverManager.getConnection("jdbc:db2"); // Native
```

You must tell Java the database driver you wish to work with. This is the role of the registerDriver method of DriverManager. It takes an instance of a JDBC Driver class as input, and records the address. You need only do this once—when your Java program first starts up, say. You can register more than one JDBC driver. When you subsequently use the getConnection method of DriverManager to start a connection, the DriverManager class will pass the URL (Uniform Resource Locator) given as a parameter to each registered driver, and if the one that returns recognizes that URL, it will be asked to perform the connection. Thus, each JDBC driver is designed to recognize unique URLs, which provide a unique-to-the-world way of identifying something.

So, you register a driver once, but can connect to it more than once. Why connect more than once to the same driver? You might consider this if your code is running on the AS/400 itself, and you want to have one connection per user for security and scalability reasons.

Table 13.6 shows that after registering your driver, you connect to the database using the getConnection method, passing a URL that identifies the driver to connect to, as well as the AS/400 system to connect to. For the Toolbox driver, this is the TCP/IP host name of the system, while for the AS/400 Java JDBC driver, this is the *LOCAL entry from the

WRKRDBDIRE table. For either driver, with code running on the AS/400, you can just supply the special name localhost to represent the current system you are running on (or let it default to this for, the native driver). In addition to this URL, the getConnection method optionally takes two more parameters for the user ID and password. If you specify these, your connection will run under this profile. If you do not specify them, what happens depends on whether your code is running on the AS/400 itself or remotely on a client. On the AS/400, it simply uses the user ID and password of the current job; in other words, it is equivalent to specifying the special value *current for both. For the client, it prompts the user for a user ID and password.

Let's look at a class that does the connection and registration for you, shown in Listing 13.1. It uses the Toolbox driver, but also shows in the comments how to use the native driver instead. It supports three constructors: one takes a system name, user ID, and password; one takes only a system name and defaults or prompts for the user ID and password; and one takes nothing and defaults or prompts for the system name, user ID, and password. Whether the code defaults to the current job or prompts for the missing information depends on whether it is running on the AS/400 itself or on a client machine.

Listing 13.1: A Class for Registering a JDBC Driver and Connecting to the AS/400

```
import java.sql.*;
public class DB2400
{
    private static boolean registered = false;
    private Connection conn = null;

    public DB2400(String systemName, String userId, String password)
        throws SQLException
    {
        if (!registered) // register driver if not already
          DriverManager.registerDriver(
            new com.ibm.as400.access.AS400JDBCDriver());
            //new com.ibm.db2.jdbc.app.DB2Driver());
        registered = true;
        String connectURL = "jdbc:as400";
        // String connectURL = "jdbc:db2";
        if (systemName != null)
          connectURL += "://" + systemName;
        if (userId != null)
          conn = DriverManager.
                    getConnection(connectURL,userId,password);
        else
          conn = DriverManager.getConnection(connectURL);
```

```
    } // end constructor
    public DB2400(String systemName) throws SQLException
    {
        this(systemName, null, null);
    }
    public DB2400() throws SQLException
    {
        this(null, null, null);
    }
    public void disconnect()
    {
        try { conn.close(); } catch (SQLException exc) {}
    }
    public Connection getConnection()
    {
        return conn;
    }
} // end class DB2400
```

You see that the registration need only be done once per JVM session, while you may have multiple connections per session. Thus, the class uses a static variable to tell if you have registered yet, ensuring it is only ever done once.

There is a problem if you want to use the native JDBC driver: you won't be able to compile it on Windows, if that is where you are doing your development. Why? Because the JDBC's driver class will not be found on your CLASSPATH. To get around this, you can use a mapped drive to the AS/400 and add a CLASSPATH entry to the .jar file containing the AS/400 system's Java classes, or use another technique. One alternative is to register the driver by specifying a parameter on the java command, like this:

```
java "-Djdbc.drivers=com.ibm.db2.jdbc.app.DB2Driver" MyApp
```

This is an easy way to do the registration for the native driver, and is also valid for the Toolbox driver. You could supply a CL program for users to run, and specify this value on the JAVA CL command. You can also preset this parameter inside VisualAge for Java on the properties for your main class.

A second way to do this is to dynamically load the appropriate driver after determining if you are running on an AS/400 or not. This is the best solution for two reasons. First, it allows you to run the same code on either the AS/400 or a client, and picks the best driver for each situation on the fly. Second, by dynamically loading the driver class versus explicitly instantiating it, you avoid the compiler verifying the class exists, so you can compile on Windows, yet deploy and run on the AS/400 (or Windows).

How can you determine if you are running on an AS/400? By using the getProperty static method of the System class and passing it the string os.name. This property is hard-coded by each JVM. For AS/400 Java, it is set to OS/400, so you can simply test for this. How do you dynamically load a class in Java, versus using new to instantiate it? By using the forName static method of the Class class, which loads the class into memory at runtime, and then using the newInstance method in it to instantiate an object from the class.

You do not need to understand it fully, but Listing 13.2 gives a revised version of the DB2400 class, which registers and subsequently loads the appropriate JDBC driver depending on which operating system you are running on. Only the first constructor is shown, as the rest of the class is unchanged from Listing 13.1. The changes are shown in bold. Notice how all JDBC driver classes implement the generic Driver interface, and so an object is cast to this. Also notice how the system name is set to localhost if none is given and you are running on the AS/400, as is required there. This is a good class to tuck away and keep!

**Listing 13.2: A Better Class for Registering
and Connecting to the Appropriate JDBC Driver**

```
import java.sql.*;
public class DB2400
{
    private static boolean registered = false;
    private static boolean nativeDriver = false;
    private Connection conn = null;

    public DB2400(String systemName, String userId, String password)
            throws SQLException
    {
        String connectURL = null;
        if (!registered) // register driver if not already
          {
            String osName = System.getProperty("os.name");
            String driverName = null;
            if (osName.equals("OS/400"))
              {
                driverName = "com.ibm.db2.jdbc.app.DB2Driver";
                connectURL = "jdbc:db2";
                nativeDriver = true;
              }
```

```
        else
          {
            driverName = "com.ibm.as400.access.AS400JDBCDriver";
            connectURL = "jdbc:as400";
          }
        try {
          Driver driver = (Driver)
            (Class.forName(driverName).newInstance());
          DriverManager.registerDriver(driver);
        } catch (Exception exc) {
          throw new SQLException(exc.getMessage()); }
        registered = true;
      }
    // connect to the database
    if (systemName != null)
      connectURL += "://" + systemName;
    else if (nativeDriver)
      connectURL += "://localhost";
    if (userId != null)
      conn = DriverManager.getConnection(
              connectURL,userId,password);
    else
      conn = DriverManager.getConnection(connectURL);
  } // end constructor
} // end class DB2400
```

The registration and connection are done in the constructor, and the caller can subsequently call getConnection to get the resulting Connection object. Note that both the registration and the connection can throw an SQLException if anything goes wrong (for example, the driver is not found, the system is not found, or the password not valid). the constructor simply percolates these to the caller, so that anyone instantiating it will have to monitor for SQLException. Here is an example of this, from the main method of the DB2400 class, which is for testing purposes:

```
public static void main(String args[])
{
    System.out.println("Testing DB2/400 connection...");
    try {
      DB2400 me = new DB2400();
      System.out.println("Connected ok!");
    } catch (SQLException exc)
    {
      System.out.println("Error: " + exc.getMessage());
    }
    System.exit(0);
}
```

You have to use `System.exit(0)` because the AS/400 Toolbox for Java spawns non-daemon threads. When running on the AS/400, this code will connect to the current system with the current job's user ID and password. When running on the client, this code will pop up a dialog box, as shown in Figure 13.2.

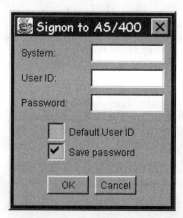

Figure 13.2: A prompt dialog for the AS/400 Toolbox for Java connection

The Toolbox will pop up other dialogs if the user types in invalid information or if the user's password has expired. Note that the Toolbox uses QUSER under the covers, so you have to ensure this user ID is enabled and the password has not expired. Also make sure you have run STRHOSTSRV *ALL on your system to start the system servers, and ensure you have all latest cumulative PTF tapes, especially for earlier releases of OS/400.

The actual syntax for the JDBC connection to DB2/400 is as follows:

```
jdbc:as400://systemName</defaultSchema<;list-Of-Properties>"
"jdbc:db2://systemName</defaultSchema<;list-Of-Properties>"
```

The system name identifies which AS/400 you are going to connect to. The optional `defaultSchema` is the default AS/400 library to access in subsequent operations that do not specify a qualified file name. If no default is specified here, the default library list of your user ID is used to find the file. (Yes, "schema" equals "library" in the JDBC terminology for the AS/400.) The optional list of properties is a semicolon-separated list of `property=value` specifications.

A long list of properties is supported by the DB2/400 JDBC drivers, summarized in Table 13.7. These properties can be specified as part of the getConnection URL, or they can be specified using a Properties object (from java.util) that is passed as the second parameter on the getConnection method call. The Properties class extends Hashtable and supports put and get methods that only support String keys and values.

Table 13.7: JDBC Driver Connection Properties (part 1 of 4)			
Property	Values	AS/ 400	Tool box
user	User name to use in the sign-on	yes	yes
password	Password to use in the sign-on	yes	yes
naming	sql or system: lib.file or library/file Default: sql	yes	yes
access	all (all SQL statements allowed) read call (SELECT and CALL allowed) read only (only SELECT allowed). Default: all	yes	yes
errors	basic (normal AS/400 server error messages) full (detailed AS/400 server error messages) Default: basic	no	yes
blocking	true or false For result set retrieval Default: true	yes	no
block criteria	0 (no blocking) 1 (if FOR FETCH ONLY) 2 (unless FOR UPDATE) Default: 2	no	yes
block size	0/8/16/32/64/128/256/512 Rows per block Default: 32	yes	yes
data compression	true or false Whether to compress the result set data Default: false	no	yes
trace	true or false For simple problem determination Default: false	yes	yes

Table 13.7: JDBC Driver Connection Properties (part 2 of 4)

Property	Values	AS/ 400	Tool box
transaction isolation	none read committed read uncommitted repeatable read serializable For commitment control Default: none	yes	yes
escape processing	true or false Whether to recognize SQL escape sequences; can be faster if you turn it off Default: true	yes	no
libraries	Library used as default for unqualified statements A single name for the native driver, a comma-separated list for the Toolbox Default: *LIBL	yes	yes
translate binary	true or false Treats BINARY and VARBINARY data values as CHAR and VARCHAR Default: false	yes	yes
prompt	true or false Whether a GUI prompt should be shown if no user ID and password given Default: true	no	yes
date format	mdy dmy ymd usa iso eur jis Default: job's date format value	v4r5	yes
date separator	/ - . , " " (space) Default: job's date separator value.	v4r5	yes
decimal separator	. , Default: job's decimal separator	v4r5	yes

Property	Values	AS/400	Tool box
time format	hms usa iso eur jis Default: job's value	v4r5	yes
time separator	: . , " " (space) Default: job's time separator value	v4r5	yes
prefetch	true or false Prefetches rows for SELECT statements Default: true	no	yes
extended dynamic	true or false Caches SQL statements in package on server Default: false	no	yes
package	For extended dynamic, name of package	no	yes
package library, cache, clear, add, error	except warning none For extended dynamic, library of package, whether to cache package in memory, whether to clear package when full, whether to add to existing packages, how to handle package-related errors Default: warning	no	yes
remarks	sql or system Where to get metadata remarks Default: system	no	yes
sort	hex job language table To sort result sets Default: job	no	yes

Table 13.7: JDBC Driver Connection Properties (part 3 of 4)

Table 13.7: JDBC Driver Connection Properties (part 4 of 4)			
Property	Values	AS/ 400	Tool box
sort language, weight	shared or unique For sort=language, the three-character ID of the language to use, and how to handle case Default: shared	no	yes
sort table	For sort=table, the qualified name of a sort sequence table	no	yes
data truncation	true or false Throw exceptions if data has to be truncated when writing to the database Default: false	no	yes
proxy server	hostname:port Middle tier where proxy server is running.	no	yes
secondary URL	JDBC URL for middle-tier redirection. Allows access to another JDBC driver, hence another database.	no	yes
secure	true or false Whether to use SSL for connection Default: false	no	v4r4
lob threshold	Maximum kilobytes that can be retrieved for a large object	no	v4r4

As you see, the user ID and password for the AS/400 connection can be specified in one of three ways:

- Specify it in the connection URL as ";user=uuuuuuuu;password=pppppppp".

- Specify it in the getConnection method call as the second and third parameters.

- Do not specify it at all, in which case the user will automatically be prompted for it when the Toolbox driver is used on the client, or the job's values will be used when using either driver on the AS/400 itself.

Another important property is naming. The default naming convention is naming=sql, but you can also specify naming=system. Using the latter to, for example, qualify a table reference on an SQL SELECT statement, you would specify COLLECTION/TABLE, as in

MYLIB/MYFILE. Using `naming=system` also means that an unqualified table name reference, as in TABLE, is equivalent to *LIBL/TABLE.

As you know already, your library list is used to find the table (that is, the default library list of the user ID that is specified for the connection). If you are not concerned with portability, this is fine. However, if you are thinking about portability to other databases, you might want to leave the default of `naming=sql`. This makes your qualified name syntax consistent with all other databases. This convention is COLLECTION.TABLE, as in MYLIB.MYFILE.

It sounds like a painless enough change—just use a dot instead of a slash. Be careful, however! This also changes where the system looks for unqualified table names. Now, for TABLE, the system will not look in the library list for file TABLE. Instead, it will only look in the library with the same name as the user ID specified in the connection. Therefore, using `naming=sql` implies that you will fully qualify all your table references, or specify a default schema.

Some of the properties can also be specified or at least queried by calling methods on the resulting `Connection` object. Specifically, there are methods for setting and querying commitment-control-related properties, and there are `setReadOnly` and `isReadOnly` methods. You might find it valuable to use `setReadOnly` instead of `access=read only`, since it is more portable. In either case, an entire connection that is read-only is a good idea to ensure no attempt is made to update a database, and possibly to help the database engine with performance tuning. The alternative is to specify the FOR READ ONLY clause on your SELECT statements, but that only prevents positioned updates and deletes, not explicit UPDATE and DELETE statements.

Step 3: Creating SQL statement objects

To use JDBC, you must use SQL statements. The `java.sql` package includes two classes for creating instances to represent SQL statements. When you execute an SQL statement, the database performs two steps:

1. Prepare the statement by effectively compiling it.

2. Run the prepared statement.

The first step can be explicitly done in advance for multiple-use statements, which saves time in the second and subsequent execution of the statement. Thus, the two flavors of SQL statement classes in JDBC are:

- Statement. Use this class to execute statements on the fly. If you have an SQL statement that is to be run only once, this is the class to use. Its executeXXX methods take any string object assumed to contain a valid dynamic SQL statement.

- PreparedStatement. Use this class to prepare a statement that will be executed multiple times. Note that it allows substitution variables, or *markers*, in the form of question marks (?), so that the same statement can be reused multiple times with different values. See the SQL documentation for where you are allowed to use these markers, but essentially they can be used in SELECT statements for the value of a column name (as in WHERE STATE=?), in the SET clause of an UPDATE statement, and in the VALUES clause of an INSERT statement. They cannot be used to substitute in the table or column names themselves, however. That would change the access path of the statement, so it cannot be turned into a variable. You must use separate statements for this. If you cannot hard-code these values, you will have to use a Statement object built up dynamically just prior to execution, instead of a PreparedStatement object.

To instantiate instances of these classes, you do not use the new operator. Instead, you use the createStatement or prepareStatement methods of your previously allocated Connection object to create these objects for you, for example:

```
Statement          stmt  = conn.createStatement();
PreparedStatement pstmt =
    conn.prepareStatement("SELECT * FROM CUSTOMER WHERE CUSTNO=?");
```

Notice how Statement objects do not specify the statement to execute at allocation time, whereas prepared statements do. This is an indication of the longevity of prepared statements. At the time prepared statements are created, they are verified and "compiled" at the DB2/400 server. You must couch your prepareStatement method call in a try/catch block for SQLException, and pay attention to the exception—it usually implies that you have specified an improper SQL statement, or you have not yet connected to the database. It might also be that you are preparing an update statement, and you do not have update authority to the database. Generally, the exception getMessage text is enough to figure it out. However, SQLException also has getErrorCode and getSQLState methods to help programmatically determine the cause of the error.

Having created an instance of Statement or PreparedStatement, you can subsequently execute that statement. Steps 4 and 5, executing an SQL statement and processing the results, are the interesting part, so we'll defer an example until we cover these.

Step 4: Running the SQL statements

Prior to running your prepared statements (PreparedStatement class objects), you have to specify the values for all the "markers" (question marks) in the statement. To do this, use the overloaded setXXX(int, value) method in the PreparedStatement class. The exact method to use depends on the type of the value you want to substitute, which, in turn, depends on the type of the database field or column whose value you are supplying. For example, if you are specifying a value for a decimal field, you would use setBigDecimal. For character database field values, you would use setString.

All of the setXXX variables take two parameters: the relative one-based position of the marker to substitute, and the value to be substituted. These methods are the functional opposite of the getXXX methods you will see in the next section. For example, to set the substitution value for the SQL statement "SELECT * FROM CUSTOMER WHERE CUSTNAME=?" you might specify this:

```
pstmt.setString(1,"George Farr");
```

The number 1 for the first parameter indicates you are substituting for the first question mark. You must substitute for all the question marks before executing the prepared statement. These substitutions stay in effect either for the life of the PreparedStatement object, or until reset, or until cleared via clearParameters. The setXXX methods include those listed in Table 13.8. The "SQL Types" column in that table refers to constants defined in the java.sql.Types class.

<table>
<tr><td colspan="3">Table 13.8: PreparedStatement set Methods for Marker Substitution</td></tr>
</table>

Method	SQL Type	DDS Type
SetBigDecimal	NUMERIC	Decimal
SetBoolean	SMALLINT	binary (4,0)
setByte	SMALLINT	binary (4,0)
setBytes	VARBINARY	character, CCSID(65535)
setDate	DATE	Date
setDouble	DOUBLE	float, FLTPCN(*DOUBLE)
setFloat	FLOAT	float, precision depending on value
setInt	INTEGER	binary (9,0)
setLong	INTEGER	binary (9,0)
setNull	NULL	for null-capable fields (ALWNULL)
setShort	SMALLINT	binary (4,0)
setString	CHAR, VARCHAR	character, VARLEN character
setTime	TIME	Time
setTimestamp	TIMESTAMP	Timestamp
setObject	Any	Any type; specified by one of the java.sql.Types constants

To actually execute an SQL statement, you call one of two methods on the object:

- The executeQuery method if you are running an SQL SELECT statement:

```
ResultSet rs=stmt.executeQuery(String sqlStmt): // Statement
ResultSet rs=pstmt.executeQuery(); //PreparedStatement
```

- This method call sends the statement to the database and returns a ResultSet object. This object has methods for traversing it which are covered in the next section.

- The executeUpdate method if you are running an SQL INSERT, UPDATE, DELETE statement, or SQL DDL (*Data Definition Language*) statements like CREATE TABLE:

```
int res = stmt.executeUpdate(String sqlStmt): // Statement
int res = pstmt.executeUpdate(); //PreparedStatement
```

- This method sends the statement to the database, where it is run. It then returns a count of the affected rows, or zero for DDL statements.

There is also a generic execute method that can return multiple-result sets. This is exclusive to stored procedure calls, however, and is covered later in this chapter.

You use the SELECT statement with the executeQuery method whether you are retrieving one row or multiple rows. The former is just a special case of the latter. For example, the following retrieves all the rows (and all the columns because of the * character) from the MYFILE file:

```
SELECT * FROM MYFILE
```

The following, on the other hand, retrieves a single row from MYFILE—one where the unique key field has a value of *A*:

```
SELECT * FROM MYFILE WHERE KEYFIELD = 'A'
```

This is equivalent to RPG's CHAIN op-code.

What SQL statements can you execute in your execute and executeUpdate methods? Any dynamic one. However, you will primarily use a SELECT statement via executeQuery to read data, and INSERT, UPDATE, and DELETE to manipulate data.

Step 5: Retrieving the information in result sets

After executing an SQL SELECT statement by using the executeQuery method, you have a populated ResultSet object. It contains all the rows that met the criteria specified in the SELECT statement. You iterate sequentially through the result set using the next method, which bumps the implicit cursor ahead by one row.

It is important to note that initially, the cursor is positioned before the first row; you must do one next call to read the first row. The next call will return true as long as there is another row to advance to. When it returns false, you have reached the end of the rows (that is, the end of the file). For example, to iterate through a multiple-row SELECT statement's result set, you code the following:

```
ResultSet rs = stmt.executeQuery("SELECT * FROM MYFILE");
while ( rs.next() )  // while more
    // do processing
```

For single-row SELECT statements, you are expecting exactly one returned row, so your logic might look like this:

```
ResultSet rs = stmt.executeQuery(
              "SELECT * FROM MYFILE WHERE KEYFIELD='A'");
if ( !rs.next() ) // no rows?
    // issue error message
else
    // do processing
```

How do you extract the values for each column of the current row? The trick is to know the following:

- The relative position of the column (the first column is position 1) or the explicit name of the column (the field's DDS name).

- The data type of that column, and its equivalent Java data type.

With this information, you can declare a variable of the appropriate Java data type and assign it by using the appropriate getXXXX method of the ResultSet class. There is one get method for each data type, and it returns the specified column's value of the current row as that data type. All methods support two versions: one in which the first parameter is an integer representing the column position to retrieve, and the other in which the first parameter is a string representing the name of the column to retrieve. These are the functional opposite of the PreparedStatement class's setXXX methods discussed previously, and are listed in Table 13.9.

Table 13.9: The get Methods for Retrieving Column Data from a Result Set

getXXX Method	SQL Types	Description
getBigDecimal (int/String,int)	DECIMAL, NUMERIC1	The second parameter is scale (decimal digits); returns a BigDecimal object
getBoolean	NUMERIC1	Returns a boolean value of true for nonzero; otherwise false
getByte	SMALLINT1	Returns a byte value (one byte, signed)
getBytes	BINARY, VARBINARY	Returns a byte array
getBinaryStream	BINARY, VARBINARY	Returns a java.io.InputStream object
getAsciiStream	CHAR, VARCHAR, BINARY, VARBINARY	Returns a java.io.InputStream object
getUnicodeStream	CHAR, VARCHAR, BINARY, VARBINARY	Returns a java.io.InputStream object
getDate	CHAR, VARCHAR, DATE, TIMESTAMP	Returns a java.sql.Date object
getDouble	FLOAT, DOUBLE1	Returns a double value
getFloat	REAL1	Returns a float value
getLong	INTEGER1	Returns a long value
getShort	SMALLINT1	Returns a short value
getString	any	Returns a String object
getTime	CHAR, VARCHAR, TIME, TIMESTAMP	Returns a java.sql.Time object
getTimeStamp	CHAR, VARCHAR, DATE, TIMESTAMP	Returns a java.sql.Timestamp object
getObject	any	Java decides what java.sql.Types type the column is and creates the appropriate default object.

[1]The recommended type(s) are shown, but this method can actually be used for SQL types SMALLINT, INTEGER, REAL, FLOAT, DOUBLE, DECIMAL, NUMERIC, CHAR, and VARCHAR (and TINYINT, BIGINT, BIT, and LONGVARCHAR, although DB2/400 does not support these SQL types). For more information on data types, see the section "More on data types" later in this chapter.

The Date, Time, and Timestamp classes in java.sql all extend the java.util.Date class discussed in Chapter 8. The Date and Time classes only write the date or time portion in JDBC, versus both values, which their parent java.util.Date holds. Also, Time and Timestamp add nanoseconds, which the SQL standard requires.

As previously mentioned, you can either specify the name or the one-based position of the column. It is recommended that, if your SELECT statement uniquely identifies the columns (as in SELECT COL1, COL2 FROM TABLE), you should use the name again on the getXXX method call. If you specify that you want all columns (as in SELECT * FROM TABLE), use the column numbers because the names are probably not known. If you know the column name but want to specify the column number, you can use the ResultSet method findColumn(String). It is always more efficient to use this once outside the result-set processing loop, and then use the column number versions of the get methods inside the loop. The numeric version is faster than the name version of these methods.

Notice the getBinaryStream, getASCIIStream, and getUnicodeStream methods. They are intended for very large fields, such as bitmap images. (Actually, getUnicodeStream has been deprecated in favor of a new getCharacterStream method discussed later in this chapter.) These methods are alternatives for retrieving these values in smaller, fixed-size blocks, rather than as a single block with the getBytes or getString methods. To use them, you must access the returned java.io.InputStream objects immediately. Otherwise, you face losing them on the next rs.getXXX or rs.next call. The following example is from the *JDBC Guide: Getting Started* document included in the JDK documentation:

```java
java.sql.Statement stmt = con.createStatement();
ResultSet r = stmt.executeQuery("SELECT x FROM Table2");
// Now retrieve the column 1 results in 4 K chunks:
byte buff = new byte[4096];
while (r.next())
{
    Java.io.InputStream fin = r.getAsciiStream(1);
    for (;;)
    {
        int size = fin.read(buff);
        if (size == -1) // at end of stream
          break;
        // Send the newly filled buffer to some ASCII output stream:
        output.write(buff, 0, size);
    }
}
```

If your database uses null values for unset fields (DDS keyword ALWNULL), then the code that processes the result set might deem it important to know if the value for a retrieved column is null or not. To test this, use the ResultSet method wasNull. It returns true if the last column read via a getXXX method call is null.

Recall that when using SQL in RPG programs, your processing for SELECT involves using DECLARE CURSOR and specifying the SELECT statement as a clause of this declaration (using the FOR clause). Thus, in RPG, you name your cursor, whereas in JDBC it is implicit. The ResultSet class and its next and getXXX methods are equivalent to RPG SQL's FETCH NEXT and FETCH NEXT INTO statements. Using JDBC, there might be times when you want to process an UPDATE or DELETE on the current row, instead of specifying a row selection criteria. This is called a *positioned update and delete*. To do this, you need some way in your subsequent UPDATE or DELETE statement to specify the result set and the current row-position within it.

Keep in mind that the result sets are actually implemented and stored in the database. Your Java program only requires memory for one row (or one block of rows if blocking is specified and applicable). The result sets are maintained in the database, so they are given names by the database, even when you do not do so in JDBC. To get a name, you can specify it on your UPDATE or DELETE statement, using the ResultSet method getCursorName. Here is an example:

```
while ( !rs.next() )
{
    ...
    stmt.executeUpdate("DELETE FROM MYFILE WHERE CURRENT OF " +
                rs.getCursorName());
    ...
}
```

There is also a setCursorName method, if you choose to explicitly name the result set. This method is part of the Statement class, however, not the ResultSet class. When you do a positioned update or delete as shown here, you must use a different Statement object than the one used to produce the result set.

A simple query example: Query PDM options

Listing 13.3 is the simplest of examples. It is raw code in a main method that simply connects to the AS/400, prepares a "query all" statement for the PDM user-defined options file QAUOOPT in library QGPL, and then executes that statement and displays the two columns of each retrieved row in the result set.

Listing 13.3: A Class for Querying and
Displaying the PDM User-Defined Options File

```java
import java.sql.*;
public class QueryPDMOptions
{
    public static void main(String args[])
    {
        System.out.println("Welcome to QueryPDMOptions");
        try
        {
            System.out.println("Connecting to AS/400...");
            DB2400 db2400 = new DB2400(); //prompt for sys,Id,pwd
            Connection conn = db2400.getConnection();
            System.out.println("Preparing statements...");
            PreparedStatement queryAll =
              conn.prepareStatement(
                "SELECT OPTION, COMMAND FROM QGPL.QAUOOPT");
            System.out.println("Doing query...");
            System.out.println();
            ResultSet rs = queryAll.executeQuery();
            while (rs.next())
              System.out.println(
                rs.getString(1) + " " + rs.getString(2));
            System.out.println();
            System.out.println("Closing everything...");
            rs.close();
            queryAll.close();
            conn.close();
            System.out.println("Done.");
        } catch (SQLException exc)
        {
            System.out.println("SQL Error......: " +
                                exc.getMessage());
            System.out.println("SQL Error State: " +
                                exc.getSQLState());
            System.out.println("SQL Error Code.: " +
                                exc.getErrorCode());
        }
        System.exit(0);
    } // end main
}
```

Notice the DB2400 class from Listing 13.2 does the registration and connection. The getConnection method does not specify a system, user ID, or password, so when running on Windows, you get prompted for this information. The QAUOOPT file has only two fields, each of type character, so this query is easy. There are no markers to replace, and you simply use the getString method to retrieve each column's data inside the ResultSet processing loop. If you run this simple class either on Windows or AS/400, you get the following output:

```
Welcome to QueryPDMOptions
Connecting to AS/400...
Preparing statements...
Doing query...

AP ADDPRJLIBL PRJ(&ZP) GRP(&ZG) SCAN(&ZH) SCHPTH(&ZS)
 C CALL &O/&N
CC CRTBNDC PGM(&L/&N) SRCFILE(&L/&F) OUTPUT(*PRINT) DBGVIEW(*ALL)
DEFINE(TRACE)
CD STRDFU OPTION(2)
CE CALL QCODE/EVFCFDBK PARM('37' 'Y'                   'OS400'        '
CODEEDIT "&L/&F(&N)"')
CL CHGCURLIB CURLIB(&N)
CM STRSDA OPTION(2) SRCFILE(&L/&F) ??SRCMBR()
CP CRTPGM2 PGM(&L/&N) MODULE(*PGM) ACTGRP(*DFTACTGRP)
CS STRSDA OPTION(1) SRCFILE(&L/&F) ??SRCMBR()
DL DSPLIBL
DM DSPMSG
DO DMPOBJ OBJ(&L/&N) OBJTYPE(&T)
EA EDTOBJAUT OBJ(&L/&N) OBJTYPE(&T)
GO GO &L/&N
IM IMPPART ??OBJ(&L/&F) ??OBJTYPE(*FILE) ??MBR(&N) ??PART(&N)
??LANG(&S) TEXT(&X)
IO IMPPART ??OBJ(&L/&N) ??OBJTYPE(&T) ??PRJ() ??GRP() ??TYPE(&S)
??PART(&N)
JL DSPJOBLOG
MK CRTCMOD MODULE(&L/&N) SRCFILE(&L/C) OUTPUT(*PRINT)
DBGVIEW(*SOURCE) DEFINE(TRACE NONUNIX NONRS6000 ILE AS400)
PL WRKPARTPDM  PRJ(&ZP) GRP(&ZG) TYPE(*ALL) PART(*ALL) LANG(*ALL)
PARTL(&N)
RP RMVPRJLIBL
SL SBMJOB ??CMD(SAVLIB LIB(&N))
SM SBMJOB ??CMD(SAVOBJ OBJ(&F) LIB(&L) OBJTYPE(*FILE) FILEMBR((&F
(&N))))
SO SBMJOB ??CMD(SAVOBJ OBJ(&N) LIB(&L))
SP WRKSPLF
TD STRSDA OPTION(3) TSTFILE(&L/&N)
WS WRKSBMJOB

Closing everything...
Done.
```

A more detailed example: Working with PDM options

The previous example shows how to use the JDBC syntax for connecting and querying data. It's reasonably easy, but it's not the type of robust Java code you probably want you to write. Rather, it is better to put everything that deals with accessing the file via JDBC into a separate class. This way, you have only one place to change if the database changes or you decide to use something other than JDBC. Also, it can make it much easier to write an application that uses the returned data in many places.

Let's look at an example of reading and updating a database, and how you might design the classes to encapsulate that. It again uses the PDM user-defined options database, as everyone has that on their systems. That file is encapsulated in a class named PDMOptions, and its constructor takes a previously created DB2400 object to prepare some statements. Then, methods are supplied for reading the database and populating an internal list, for returning the elements from that list as an Enumeration, for adding a record to the database, for updating a record in the database, and for deleting a record in the database. While not keyed, the reality is no two records can have the same two-character option, and so this enforcement is left to the client code to enforce, which it does.

To encapsulate one record, you need two other classes. The first, named PDMOptionKey here, contains a String object for the option. This class has the usual hashcode and equals methods to allow it to be stored in vectors and hashtables, and have searches done on those. The second, PDMOption, includes a PDMOptionKey object and a String object for the command part of the record. This class has an equals method so that searches can be done for a command, and some helper methods for displaying and printing the record contents. So, the PDMOptions class will create a vector of PDMOption objects on a query, and it will expect a PDMOption object as input to the ADD, UPDATE, and DELETE methods. These will search the vector for matching records, via the indexOf method from Vector.

First, Listing 13.4 shows the PDMOptionKey class. Notice how it supplies a static verify method, so code that takes a new option as user input can test that it is valid. It is a very good idea to encapsulate such error checking in the class for a field, so that it is reusable everywhere.

Listing 13.4: The PDMOptionKey Class,
Encapsulating the Option Part of a PDM Option Record

```java
public class PDMOptionKey
{
    private String option;

    public PDMOptionKey(String option)
    {
        this.option  = option;
    }
    public String getOption()
    {
        return option;
    }
    public void setOption(String option)
    {
        this.option = option;
    }
    public boolean equals(Object other)
    {
        if (other instanceof PDMOption)
          return option.equalsIgnoreCase(
            ((PDMOption)other).getKey().getOption());
        else if (other instanceof PDMOptionKey)
          return option.equalsIgnoreCase(
            ((PDMOptionKey)other).getOption());
        else
          return false;
    }
    public int hashCode()
    {
        return ((String)option).hashCode();
    }
    public static String verify(String newOption)
    {
        String errMsg = null;
        if (newOption.length() == 0)
          errMsg = "No option specified";
        else if (newOption.length() > 2)
          errMsg = "Option more than 2 characters";
        else if (Character.isDigit(newOption.charAt(0)))
          errMsg = "First character of option must not be numeric";
        return errMsg;
    }
    public String toString()
    {
        if (option.length() == 2)
          return option;
        else
          return " " + option;
    }
} // end PDMOptionKey
```

Next, Listing 13.5 is the PDMOption class.

Listing 13.5: The PDMOption Class,
Encapsulating Both Parts of a PDM Option Record

```java
import java.io.*;
public class PDMOption
{
    private PDMOptionKey key;
    private String command;

    public PDMOption(PDMOptionKey key, String ommand)
    {
        this.key = key;
        this.command = command.trim();
    }
    public PDMOptionKey getKey()
    {
        return key;
    }
    public String getCommand()
    {
        return command;
    }
    public void setCommand(String command)
    {
        this.command = command;
    }
    public boolean equals(Object other)
    {
        if (other instanceof PDMOption)
          return command.equals(((PDMOption)other).getCommand());
        else if (other instanceof PDMOptionKey)
          return getKey().equals(other);
        else
          return false;
    }
    public String toString()
    {
        return key.toString() + " " + command;
    }
    public void display()
    {
        System.out.println("--------------");
        System.out.println("Option......: " + key);
        System.out.println("Command.....: " + command);
    }
}
```

```
    public void print(PrintWriter writer)
    {
        writer.println("-------------");
        writer.println("Option......: " + key);
        writer.println("Command.....: " + command);
        writer.println(); writer.flush();
    }
}
```

Finally, Listing 13.6 is the PDMOptions class. (Note that the listing doesn't show all the constructors, since they are just variants of the main one shown.) The helper methods containsKey and getKeyIndex test if a given PDMOption object exists in the file and return its index position in the file. You don't actually have to check the file to do this; you just have to check the internal Vector list, using the indexOf method. You pass it the key part of the option, and Java calls the equals method on this key object for every element in the vector, until one returns true. That is why the PDMOptionKey class's equals method has to recognize a PDMOption object as the parameter and compare keys (the option field) appropriately.

The PDMOptionKey object is used instead of the PDMOption object in the call to indexOf because you want to find a match on the option part, not the command part. You wouldn't need this special version of equals that expects a PDMOption object or PDMOptionKey object if you used Hashtable instead of Vector to store the list of returned rows. However, you will find Hashtable a poor choice for this because its elements method returns the items in a different order than they were placed in the list. Vector preserves the order.

Listing 13.6: The PDMOptions Class

```
import java.sql.*;
import java.util.*;
import java.io.*;
public class PDMOptions
{
    protected DB2400            As400Conn = null;
    protected Connection        conn = null;
    protected PreparedStatement queryAll, addRecord,
                                updateRecord, deleteRecord;
    protected Vector            optionList = null;
    protected String            fileName, librName;

    public PDMOptions(DB2400 As400Conn, String library,
                    String filename)
```

→

Listing 13.6: The PDMOptions Class (continued)

```
        throws SQLException
{
    this.As400Conn= As400Conn;
    conn           = As400Conn.getConnection();
    this.fileName = filename;
    this.librName = library;
    String libFile = library + "." + filename;
    try
    {
      queryAll = conn.prepareStatement(
        "SELECT OPTION, COMMAND FROM " + libFile);
      Statement lockStatement = conn.createStatement();
      lockStatement.executeUpdate(
        "LOCK TABLE " + libFile + " IN SHARE MODE");
      addRecord = conn.prepareStatement(
            "INSERT INTO " + libFile + " VALUES(?,?)");
      updateRecord = conn.prepareStatement(
            "UPDATE " + libFile +
            " SET COMMAND = ? WHERE OPTION = ?");
      deleteRecord = conn.prepareStatement(
            "DELETE FROM " + libFile + " WHERE OPTION = ?");
    } catch(SQLException exc)
    {
        if (queryAll != null) queryAll.close();
        if (addRecord != null) addRecord.close();
        if (updateRecord != null) updateRecord.close();
        if (deleteRecord != null) deleteRecord.close();
        queryAll=addRecord=updateRecord=deleteRecord=null;
        throw(exc); // rethrow
    }
}

public int getAll()
{
    optionList = new Vector();
    try
    {
      ResultSet rs = queryAll.executeQuery();
      while (rs.next())
      {
          PDMOptionKey nextKey = new PDMOptionKey(
                              rs.getString(1));
          PDMOption nextValue = new PDMOption(nextKey,
                              rs.getString(2));
          optionList.addElement(nextValue);
      }
      rs.close();
```

```java
        } catch (SQLException exc) {}
        return optionList.size();
    }
    public Enumeration elements()
    {
        return optionList.elements();
    }
    public boolean containsKey(PDMOption option)
    {
        return (getKeyIndex(option) != -1);
    }
    public int getKeyIndex(PDMOption option)
    {
        return optionList.indexOf(option.getKey());
    }
    public String addOption(PDMOption option)
    {
        String errMsg = null;
        if (getKeyIndex(option) != -1)
          return "Option " + option.getKey() + " already exists";
        try {
          addRecord.setString(1,option.getKey().getOption());
          addRecord.setString(2,option.getCommand());
          int rowsAffected = addRecord.executeUpdate();
          if (rowsAffected == 1) // better!
            optionList.addElement(option);
          else
            errMsg = "No record added";
        } catch (SQLException e) {errMsg = e.getMessage();}
        return errMsg;
    }

    public String updateOption(PDMOption option)
    {
        String errMsg = null;
        int matchIndex = getKeyIndex(option);
        if (matchIndex == -1)
          return "No matching option found";
        try {
          updateRecord.setString(1,option.getCommand());
          updateRecord.setString(2,option.getKey().getOption());
          int rowsAffected = updateRecord.executeUpdate();
          if (rowsAffected == 1) // better!
            optionList.setElementAt(option, matchIndex);
          else
            errMsg = "No record updated";
        } catch (SQLException e) {errMsg = e.getMessage();}
        return errMsg;
    }
}
```

Listing 13.6: The PDMOptions Class (continued)

```
        public String deleteOption(PDMOption option)
        {
            String errMsg = null;
            int matchIndex = getKeyIndex(option);
            if (matchIndex == -1)
              return "No matching option found";
            try {
              deleteRecord.setString(1,option.getKey().getOption());
              int rowsAffected = deleteRecord.executeUpdate();
              if (rowsAffected == 1) // better!
                optionList.removeElementAt(matchIndex);
              else
                errMsg = "No record deleted";
            } catch (SQLException e) {errMsg = e.getMessage();}
            return errMsg;
        }
    } // end class
```

Due to space constraints, Listing 13.6 doesn't show everything in the class. For example, there is an important `close` method that closes all the statement objects. There is also support via one of the constructors for a read-only mode, which does not lock the table or prepare the non-query statements.

You can see in the code we do show that, when this object is constructed, all the potentially often-repeated SQL statements are prepared (SELECT, INSERT, UPDATE, and DELETE). Also, the LOCK TABLE command is used to lock the file member (which is always just the first one in SQL), since this could being used in an edit session, and you can't afford to have the data change underneath you while you work on a local copy of it.

The intended use of this class is to first call the `getAll` method, and then call the `addOption`, `updateOption`, and `deleteOption` methods as many times as desired, and finally call the `close` method. The ADD, UPDATE, and DELETE methods will first update the database and, if successful, update the local Vector list, so it is kept in synch. Note these methods all take a PDMOption object, which you might create from option (opt) and command (cmd) strings like this:

```
    PDMOption newOption = new PDMOption(new PDMOptionKey(opt), cmd);
```

This self-contained class for working with a PDM options file is now ready to be used in one or more applications. To test it, we created a full "work with" GUI for remotely editing any PDM options file. All the code for this is on the CD-ROM included with this book, in Chapter 13's PDMOptions subdirectory.

If you test-drive this application, first copy your PDM options file and open that copy, as this application really does change the file! That is, it actually works, so be careful. Start the application by typing java PDMOptionsWindow. Figure 13.3 shows the main window after opening a file.

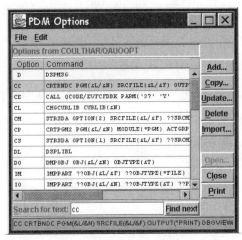

Figure 13.3: A GUI application that uses the
PDMOptions class for database I/O

Note that a JTable holds the list. Chapter 12 did not describe how to code these, but you can read about them in the comments in files OptionsTable.java and OptionsTableModel.java on the CD-ROM. The GUI we wrote simply stores and shows the list of PDMOption objects you get by calling getAll and elements of the PDMOptions class. It then uses the appropriate methods, with the selected objects, for processing the add, copy, update, delete, and import options (for the add option, a new PDMOption object is created).

This example provides a reasonably sized application that works with remote data, yet all database I/O has been encapsulated inside a single class (PDMOptions), rather than being distributed throughout the application. Further, the next application you write can use the same class. As well as encapsulating the I/O in one class, this example encapsulates a single record in one class, and the key part of that record in another (which the first contains). Often, we even go further and encapsulate each field in its own class and then put instances of each in the record class and the key class. This allows us to put the error checking for the fields in one place. However, since the fields in this file are so simple, the basic String class can be used to hold them.

Reading rows a few at a time

A popular question is: "Can I read the database *xx* rows at a time, as I am used to with my subfile processing?" For example, your file probably often contains more than the few dozen records in the PDM options file. The answer is yes, but you have to code this yourself. You simply code your result-set processing to process only the next *n* records at a time. For example, you might have a method named readNextNRows:

```
public short readNextNRows(short n) throws SQLException
{
    short readRows =  0; // return how many rows actually read
    for (boolean more = rs.next();
        more && readRows < n;
        readRows++, more = rs.next())
    {
        // process the current row
    }
    return readRows;
}
```

It is not always necessary to bother with this, though. Instead, you may take a shortcut by placing the result-set processing in a separate thread, so that it runs in the background and can be interrupted by the user. In most cases, this effectively removes the need to only retrieve *n* records at a time because the user is not forced to wait for all records to be read before continuing. Chapter 11 discusses this concept of threads. Simply place the database retrieval code in a class that implements Runnable, and have the run method do your database retrieval. Also, include a private boolean variable that can be set to true to stop any operation.

Putting your database access code into a thread is important if the access is done on the client and from a GUI because your GUI will be locked waiting for the operation to complete, and users won't know what is going on. For this reason, the PDM options example is threaded by creating a PDMOptionsThreaded class and duplicating all the database access methods from PDMOptions in it (constructor, getAll, addOption, updateOption, deleteOption, close). These end up calling the corresponding methods in the PDMOptions class, but they do so from a thread.

The example uses a common trick in GUI applications for this: it pops up a status dialog showing progress and provides a Stop button so the user can stop the action. (We don't burden you with all the code required to do this, but if you are interested, you will find it on the CD-ROM in the PDMOptionsThreaded directory of Chapter 13.) The basic steps are to first create (but don't show) the dialog, then start the thread running, and then show the dialog. This last step won't return control to you until the dialog is closed, and this is done by the thread as its last step.

In the example, a dialog class named DBAccessStatusDialog shows the name of the operation being performed, along with a Stop push button. A JProgressBar gives the idea of something happening, as shown in Figure 13.4.

Figure 13.4: The status dialog shown while accessing the database

If you do decide to process your database access in a thread, you should look at two methods in the Statement, PreparedStatement, and CallableStatement classes that will be of use:

- The cancel() method can be called by another thread to cancel a long-running query prior to executeQuery returning.

- The setMaxTimeout(int seconds) method can set an upper limit in seconds for how long to wait for the SQL query to end. The default is zero, meaning no time limit.

Another potentially useful method is setMaxRows(int max) to set an upper limit on how many records to be retrieved in a result set. Again, the default is zero, no limit.

Handling warnings

There are cases where JDBC (actually SQL) issues warnings, not errors, due to data truncation, implicit commits, and so on. To be thorough, or for SQL statements that you know could result in SQL warnings, you can check for warnings after executing an SQL statement (via execute, executeQuery, or executeUpdate) using the method getWarnings in the Statement class. This returns the first warning in the form of an instance of the SQLWarning exception class. This object has a getNextWarning method for retrieving additional warning messages, if any. You should always call your Statement or PreparedStatement object's clearWarnings method before executing to be sure that any subsequent warnings are actually issued for that statement execution:

```
stmt.clearWarnings(); // stmt == Statement object
stmt.execute(sqlString); // execute sqlString SQL statement
SQLWarning warning = stmt.getWarnings();
while (warning != null)
{
  warning = warning.getNextWarning();
  System.out.println("Warning: " + warning.getMessage());
}
```

Rather than checking the warnings at the statement object level, you can check them at the Connection level itself, to retrieve all the warnings posted for a number of statement executions. Note that the method names and usage are identical:

```
conn.clearWarnings(); // conn == Connection object
// execute one or more statements
SQLWarning warning = conn.getWarnings();
while (warning != null)
  warning = warning.getNextWarning();
```

If this is still not enough flexibility, you can even check them on the ResultSet object, again using the identical methods.

Truncation warnings actually have their own Java exception class, DataTruncation, which inherits from the SQLWarning class. In fact, SQLWarning also inherits from SQLException, so you get access to all the methods in all these classes for DataTruncation exceptions. The DataTruncation class includes methods such as getDataSize to return how many bytes should have been processed, and getTransferSize to return how much data actually was processed (on a read or write). Another useful method is getIndex, which returns the column number of the truncated field. If you suspect a truncation warning, you can use the inherited getSQLState method of your SQLWarning object to check for truncation state 01004, and then cast your object to a DataTruncation object to access the unique methods in that class:

```
if (warning.getSQLState().equals("01004"))
   {
     DataTruncation t = (DataTruncation)warning;
     int colIdx = t.getIndex();
     int truncd = t.getTransferSize();
     System.out.println("Column " + colIdx + " truncated at "
                        + truncd + "bytes");
   }
```

This exception can happen if you use the setMaxFieldSize(int) method on a State-ment or PreparedStatement object. This method places an upper limit on how many bytes will be read or written to the database for any column.

Step 6: Close, close, close

There's nothing new here, just a gentle reminder to *always* close your result set, state-ment, and connection objects as soon as you are done with them! They hold valuable da-tabase resources, and you don't want them held any longer than absolutely necessary. (Any currently open ResultSet is closed implicitly when you execute another statement with the same Statement or PreparedStatement object.)

More on data types

When using SQL, whether embedded in RPG code through CLI APIs or through JDBC, you use predefined SQL data types. These ensure consistency and portability from one database vendor to another. When using SQL in RPG, these data types are mapped to and from RPG-native data-type variables by the database.

The operation is similar for JDBC. You have seen how the getXXX methods in the ResultSet class allow you to equate an SQL column's data type to a Java basic data type or a Java object data type (like java.math.BigDecimal). You have also seen how the setXXX methods in the PreparedStatement class allow you to equate a Java basic data type or Java object. The conversion between the AS/400 EBCDIC values and Java's ASCII values happens automatically for you, including codepage conversions.

Table 13.10 summarizes the SQL data types and their AS/400 DDS and RPG equivalents. (The data-type mapping shown is merely the preferred or most common mapping. You can easily map to and from various types—as you saw, for example, in the setXXX methods.)

Table 13.10: SQL, DDS, and Java Data Types			
SQL Type	**DDS Type (Len)**	**Default**	**Java Type**
BIGINT[1]	B=Binary (9,0)	B (9,0)	int
BINARY[2] (n)	A=Character (n) CCSID(65535)	A (1) CCSID (65535)	String
BIT[1]	B=Binary (4,0)	B (4,0)	short
CHAR (n)	A=Character (n)	A (1)	String
DATE	L=Date (10)	L	java.sql.Date
DECIMAL (n, m)	P=Packed (n,m)	P (5,0)	java.math.BigDecimal
DOUBLE (n)	F=Float FLTPCN(*DOUBLE) (x,x-1)	F (17,16) *DOUBLE	double
FLOAT (n) n=1-14	F=Float FLTPCN(*SINGLE) (x,x-1)	F (17,16) *DOUBLE	float
FLOAT (n) n=25-53	F=Float FLTPCN(*DOUBLE) (x,x-1)	F (17,16) *DOUBLE	double
INTEGER	B=Binary (9,0)	B (9,0)	int
LONGVARBINARY[1]	A (n=max size) VARLEN CCSID(65535)	A (n=max size) VARLEN CCSID(65535)	String
LONGVARCHAR[1]	A (n=max size) VARLEN	A (n=max size) VARLEN	String
NUMERIC (n, m)	S=Zoned (n,m)	S (5, 0)	java.math.BigDecimal
REAL	F=Float FLTPCN(*SINGLE) (8, 7)	F (8,7) *SINGLE	float
SMALLINT	B=Binary (4,0)	B (4,0)	short
TIME	T=Time (8)	T	java.sql.Time
TIMESTAMP	Z=Timestamp (26)	Z	Java.sql.Timestamp
TINYINT1	B=Binary (4,0)	B (4,0)	short
VARBINARY[2] (n) ALLOCATE (m)	A =Character(n) CCSID(655634) VARLEN(M)	A (1) CCSID(65535) VARLEN	String

Table 13.10: SQL, DDS, and Java Data Types (cont)			
SQL Type	DDS Type (Len)	Default	Java Type
VARCHAR (n) ALLOCATE (M)	A+Character (n) VARLEN(m)	A (1) VARLEN	String

[1]These data types are not actually supported by JDBC for DB2/400 (as you will see by perusing the SQLTypes.html documentation file in the Toolbox). However, they are mapped to reasonably equivalent SQL types, which is reflected here. The BIGINT type is actually supported in V4R5 or higher.

[2]DB2 for AS/400 does not actually support BINARY and VARBINARY SQL types; however, the JDBC for DB2/400 driver does tolerate them simply by equating them to DB2/400's CHAR/VCHAR CCSID(65535) values, which is perfectly reasonable.

In addition to those in Table 13.10, DB2/400 supports three SQL types that JDBC does not explicitly support: GRAPHIC, VARGRAPHIC, and LONGVARGRAPHIC for "pure DBCS" fields. These map to the G (Graphic) data type in DDS, with VARLEN where appropriate. For Java, you should map to Java's String class type.

Null-value considerations in JDBC

As you probably know, both DB2/400 and SQL allow "null-capable" fields, which you can explicit set to null to identify an un-set value. This is in place of the old method, which involved using your own hard-coded "special" values to indicate un-set values. Of course this implies that your program needs a way to indicate a column should be set to null on a write (or on a query, if it is null on a read). RPG IV has this now, and of course JDBC also has it.

In Java's JDBC, you can call the ResultSet method wasNull for the previously read column (via getXXX method) of the current row. It will return true if that column value is null.

To write a null value to a field, use PreparedStatements and the setNull method. This method takes as the first parameter the integer position of the marker, and the SQL type of the column that marker represents, for example:

```
pstmt.setNull(1,Types.INTEGER);
```

Further, any of the setXXX methods that take an object accept a null parameter for that object, and will write an SQL null to the database for that column in that row.

Commitment control in JDBC

JDBC supports commitment control, of course, because it is a major part of the SQL standard. To use commitment control with JDBC, you first must specify a *transaction isolation* level. By default, this is none, but you can specify it either as a property on the connect statement, or later via a call to the Connection object's setTransactionIsolation method. The property values correspond to the COMMIT parameter on the CRTSQLxxx preprocessor commands, while the setTransactionIsolation parameter is a constant integer defined in the java.sql.Connection class. The former is a DB2/400-friendly way to do it, while the latter is a database-portable way. The transaction isolation affects how database objects, like selected rows, are locked for the life of a transaction (one or more SQL statements executed between calls to commit), relative to other concurrent transactions. The transaction isolation options are listed in Table 13.11. (See the DB2/400 SQL reference documentation for more information on these.)

Table 13.11: Commitment-Control Transaction Isolation Options		
The Transaction Isolation Property	setTransactionIsolation Method	CRTSQLXXX COMMIT Parameter
none	TRANSACTION_NONE	*NONE or *NC
Read committed	TRANSACTION_READ_COMMITTED	*CS
Read uncommitted	TRANSACTION_READ_UNCOMMITTED	*CHG or *UR
Repeatable read	TRANSACTION_REPEATABLE_READ	*RS
Serializable	TRANSACTION_SERIALIZABLE	*RR

Once you choose and specify a transaction isolation level, you must next decide whether to do explicit commit/rollback calls, or use the default setting of autoCommit. In the default mode, all SQL statements are automatically committed after their last result set row has been read (for executeQuery) or the statement has been executed (for executeUpdate). A statement is also implicitly committed when you execute another statement, if it has not been already. You can, and probably will, turn off autoCommit mode by calling setAutoCommit(false) on your connection object. In this case, you explicitly code your own calls to the commit or rollback methods on your connection object.

Retrieving database metadata in JDBC

One thing you are sure to miss in Java is the lack of externally described files. That is, you cannot simply code the equivalent of an F-spec and have all the file's field names automatically defined in your program. In terms of this function, Java goes back a number of years in usability, into a world where you have to hard-code field names, types, lengths, and so on into your program, and manually keep those in sync with the database. There is no comforting level-check support to ensure that you have done that job properly. And you cannot rely on clever "impact analysis" tools to identify programs affected by a field definition change. Furthermore, because there is no externally described language for user interfaces like display files offer, you lose the benefits of reference fields, as well. This is not Java's fault! It is just that this exceptional productivity and quality advantage is unique to the AS/400 and DB2/400. So what's a poor portable language to do?

Don't despair. There is *something* Java can do, and it has done it. JDBC, and in fact SQL in general, provides a way to at least query this information at runtime, so you do not have to hard-code it. This information is known as *metadata*, and includes everything you need to know about a field or column definition. Of course, using this dynamic approach results in a performance hit, but if you are really concerned about maintenance and integrity, you might decide that it is worth the sacrifice. Actually, if you are writing a truly dynamic application where you cannot predict the file or fields that will be used, you will *have* to use this technique.

You need to use the ResultSet class's getMetaData method, which returns a ResultSetMetaData object containing information about the columns of the result set. To get the information out of it, you use the isXXX and getXXX methods, including those listed in Table 13.12. As you can see, all the methods except getColumnCount take an integer parameter to identify the column number (one-based) to return the information about. If you want to try this out, look at the class TestMetaData on the CD-ROM, which queries and displays this information for the file CUSDATA in library QPDA.

621

Table 13.12: The ResultSetMetaData Methods

Method	Description
isCaseSensitive(int)	Always true for text types such as CHAR, and always false for numeric types like DECIMAL.
isNullable(int)	True if null-capable (ALWNULL).
getColumnCount()	The number of columns.
getColumnDisplaySize(int)	For decimal columns, the total length plus two for point and sign.
getColumnName(int)	The column name (DDS field name).
getColumnType(int)	The column data type, from java.sql.Types .
getColumnTypeName(int)	Same as above, but as a readable string.
getPrecision(int)	The total length (including decimals).
getScale(int)	Decimal positions.

The idea behind metadata is that you can query this information, rather than hard-coding it. That allows your Java code to automatically handle any changes in your database definition.

Another class, named DatabaseMetaData, offers a vast amount of information about the database itself (that is, DB2/400). An instance of this is returned using the Connection object's getMetaData method. The information returned in the large number of methods in this class can be categorized as in Table 13.13. The last two categories are the ones you might need. The others are only needed for completely portable, database-neutral, and dynamic applications, such as a generic database query tool.

Table 13.13: The DatabaseMetaData Methods

Category	Example	Description
Database support information	supportsFullOuterJoins(), getDateTimeFunctions()	The SQL functionality this database (DB2/400, in our case) supports.
Database terminology information	getCatalogTerm(), getProcedureTerm()	What terminology this database uses for common items.
Database name and version information	getDatabaseProductVersion() , getDriverVersion()	The version of this database or JDBC driver.
Cataloged information	getProcedures(), getTables(), getSchemas()	The database-related objects from the system.
Specific information	getColumns(), getProcedureColumns(), getCrossReference(), getExported/ImportedKeys(), getIndexInfo()	Explicit information about a given database object.

The method you might need to use the most is getColumns, if you want to retrieve the field description (TEXT column in DDS) for a column. This method returns a ResultSet object containing the metadata for every column (by default) in the specified table.

For every column in the file, you get one row in the result set. The row contains 17 pieces of information (one piece in each column of the result set), much of it useful: (1) catalog name, (2) schema name, (3) table name, (4) column name, (5) data type, (6) type name, (7) column size, (8) buffer length, (9) decimal digits, (10) numeric precision radix, (11) nullable, (12) remarks, (13) column definition, (14) SQL data type, (15) SQL date/time substitution, (16) character octet length, and (17) ordinal position. Phew! To get the field description, use column 12, the REMARKS column, like this:

```
DatabaseMetaData dbmd = conn.getMetaData();
rs = dbmd.getColumns(null, "QPDA", "QCUSDATA", null);
while (rs.next())
     String description = rs.getString(12);
```

This returns the TEXT value, not the COLHDG value. There is no metadata method for retrieving this, as COLHDG is an AS/400-unique value. However, the DDS compiler will default the TEXT value to the COLHDG value if TEXT is not specified.

THE GOOD STUFF: STORED PROCEDURES, TRIGGERS, AND RI

As part of the evolving SQL standard, new database constructs have been defined, including these three:

- *Constraints*, which are rules about key validation, also called *Referential Integrity* or *RI*.

- *Triggers*, which are programs called when records are added, changed, or deleted.

- *Stored procedures*, which are programs called directly via SQL statements.

These are all part of an effort to allow you to move your database rules out of each of your programs and into the database itself. This is a very important concept. It means that you can increase the number of ways in which your users can access your data, without compromising the data's integrity.

Currently, much of the input validation for a database is done by your RPG program logic. This logic is often duplicated across multiple programs and is subject to multiple maintenance problems. (ILE can help here by allowing you to code a single, reusable *MODULE or *SRVPGM object that all your programs can share.) It also means that, to allow access to the data from, say, a Java client or even a Java server program, you have to either duplicate that logic again, or code your Java programs to call your RPG programs in order to manipulate the data. By centralizing all these validation rules into the database itself, you can ensure that, no matter how your data is accessed, it will remain valid.

With DB2/400 (and the rest of the DB2 family), stored procedures and triggers can be written in any high-level language, and can include embedded SQL. Further, stored procedures can also be written in SQL itself. (The SQL stored procedure language adds basic HLL constructs such as looping and variable assignment.) Or, as of V4R5, stored procedures can be written in Java!

For constraints and triggers, there is nothing to say in JDBC except that if they exist, then they will be executed when you access your data from JDBC. For stored procedures, however, you need to learn how to call them from JDBC.

STORED PROCEDURE CALLS IN JDBC

Stored procedures are simply programs on your server that you can call via SQL statements. This means, ultimately, that the database itself actually calls the program. Stored procedures can be passed parameters, those parameters can be updated, and the new values made available to the calling program. Stored procedures can also be coded to return an SQL result set to the calling program. They are often used by enterprising programmers for two reasons:

- They provide a standard (that is, portable) means of calling any existing non-interactive program on the server, even if that program was not designed as a stored procedure.

- They provide a terrific way to improve database access performance compared to multiple remote SQL statements.

To call an AS/400 program object as a stored procedure, use the class `CallableStatement`, which extends `PreparedStatement`. You acquire an object instance of this via the `Connection` class's `prepareCall` method. When you call an AS/400 program object as a stored procedure, you can pass in parameters to the program as follows:

- *Input-only.* Read, but not updated, by the called program.

- *Output-only.* Updated, but not read, by the called program.

- *Input-output.* Read and updated by the called program.

Further, your stored procedure program can optionally return a result set if it is used to retrieve a list of rows from the database. Some databases support a return code from a stored procedure call, but DB2/400 does not. Instead, simply update one of the output or input/output parameters.

To invoke a stored procedure program from JDBC, first create a `CallableStatement` object by calling `prepareCall`, specifying an SQL CALL statement as the parameter, and specifying a marker (a question mark) for each parameter:

```
CallableStatement proc1 =
  conn.prepareCall("CALL MYLIB/MYPROG(?, ?, ?)");
```

The syntax of the program name is `lib/program` for system naming, or `lib.program` for SQL naming. The resulting object can be executed multiple times. For each execution, do the following:

- Specify the parameter data types *and values* for each input-capable (input or input-output) parameter, using the setXXX methods that your `CallableStatement` object inherits from the `PreparedStatement` class:

```
proc1.setInt(1, 1);
proc1.setString(2, parm2String);
```

The first parameter is a relative number of the marker you are setting, and the second parameter is the value to set it to. These values remain until you change or clear them via `proc1.clearParameters();)`.

- Specify the parameter data types for each output-capable (output or input-output) parameter, using the `registerOutParameter` method:

```
proc1.registerOutParameter(2, java.sql.Types.CHAR);
```

The first parameter is the relative number of the marker you are registering, and the second parameter is the SQL type of the parameter. For input and output parameters, you must do this *and* the previous step, and the types specified for both must be consistent.

- Call the stored procedure program using the `execute` or `executeQuery` methods that your `CallableStatement` object inherits from the `Statement` class. Use the former only if your stored procedure returns multiple result sets. Use the latter if it returns one result set or no result set (the result set will simply be empty):

```
ResultSet rs = proc1.executeQuery();
```

- Retrieve the values of each output-capable parameter using the appropriate getXXX method if the stored procedure program does not return a result set:

```
String returnedValue = proc1.getString(2);
```

- Process the result set as usual if the stored procedure does return a result set:

```
while (rs.next())
    System.out.println("Returned value: " + rs.getString(2));
```

One last thing to note: You cannot just call any program object this way, without first registering the program in the DB2/400 SQL *catalog*. This is done using the SQL statement CREATE PROCEDURE. This need only ever be done once, either from your Java program by executing a Statement object with this command, or through interactive SQL on the AS/400 itself.

Your program can both return a result set and update parameters for maximum flexibility. In fact, your program can return multiple result sets! This is handled in JDBC by using the execute method and iterating through the result sets via the methods getResultSet and getMoreResults that the CallableStatement class inherits from the Statement class.

There is a good example of using stored procedures, including a sample RPG stored procedure program, in the IBM redbook *Accessing the AS/400 with Java*, SG24-2152.

WHAT'S NEW IN JDBC 2.0

What you have read about in this chapter to this point is JDBC as it was originally designed and known as JDBC 1.0. Coincident with JDK 1.2.0, Sun made available JDBC 2.0 (built into the JDK 1.2.0). This adds some exciting new functionality to JDBC 1.0, summarized briefly here. For more details on both the 1.0 and the 2.0 specifications, look at the HTML file index.html in the JDK subdirectory \docs\guide\jdbc.

Data type enhancements

In JDBC 2.0, the following SQL type constants are added to the java.sql.Types class:

- BLOB (Binary Large Objects). Often used to store graphics and other multimedia files.

- CLOB (Character Large Objects). Often used to store documents.

- ARRAY. An SQL array.

- DISTINCT. A user-defined type (UDT), based on a built-in data type.

- STRUCT. A UDT that can have any attributes.

- REF. An SQL reference object.

- JAVA_OBJECT. Used to store Java objects in your database.

To support these new types, there are new setXXX methods for substituting the markers in PreparedStatement objects and for setting the input, output, or both parameters of stored procedures in CallableStatement objects. These are setBlob, setClob, setArray, and setRef. There are also new corresponding getXXX methods in the ResultSet and CallableStatement classes. Note that DISTINCT types are really existing built-in types, so appropriate existing setXXX/getXXX methods are sufficient. Also, STRUCT types simply use the existing setObject/getObject methods.

To support the new get and set methods, new classes have been defined in java.sql named Blob, Clob, Array, and Ref. These are actually interfaces, not classes, but the JDBC driver suppliers implement these and supply real classes. If you decide to use these new types, have a look at the JavaDoc for help.

ResultSet enhancements

The new methods in Table 13.14 are added to the ResultSet class. As you can see, some significant capability has been added to result sets. You can scroll any direction, jump to any row, easily insert/update/delete the current row in the database, refresh the current row's contents from the database, and work with new data types. Phew!

Table 13.14: The ResultSet Enhancements in JDBC 2.0

Method	Change	Description
absolute, relative	New	Moves the cursor to an explicit one-based row number, or a given number of rows forward or backward (using a negative number), respectively.
afterLast, beforeFirst	New	Moves the cursor to just after the last row or just before the first row, respectively.
cancelRowUpdates	New	Cancels updates made to the row via new updateXXX methods but before updateRow.
deleteRow, updateRow, insertRow	New	Deletes or updates the current row from the database or inserts the current row into database.
first, last	New	Positions the cursor at the first or last row.
getArray, getBlob, getCharacterStream, getClob, getRef	New	Supports new data types, as mentioned.

Table 13.14: The ResultSet Enhancements in JDBC 2.0 (cont.)

Method	Change	Description
getBigDecimal	Updated	No second parameter is needed for the scale anymore.
getDate	Updated	You can now specify a GregorianCalendar object as the second parameter, which is used to construct a millisecond value if the database does not store time zone information.
getObject	Updated	You can now specify a Map object as the second parameter.
getFetchDirection, setFetchDirection	New	Returns or sets the fetch direction: FETCH_FORWARD, FETCH_REVERSE or FETCH_UNKNOWN.
getFetchSize, setFetchSize	New	Returns or sets the fetch size for this result set. This is a hint of the block size to the database.
getStatement	New	Returns the Statement object that produced this result set.
getType	New	Returns the type of the result set: TYPE_FORWARD_ONLY, TYPE_SCROLL_INSENSITIVE / SENSITIVE.
isAfterLast, isBeforeFirst, isFirst,isLast	New	Returns true if the cursor is after the last row, before the first row, on the first row, or on the last row, respectively.
previous	New	Moves the cursor to the previous row.
refreshRow	New	Refreshes the current row from the database.
rowDeleted, rowInserted, rowUpdated	New	Returns true if the row has been deleted, inserted, or updated.
updateXXX	New	Just like all the getXXX methods, but these update the values in the result set. The database is not updated until updateRow or insertRow is called.

Something new: Batch updates

We think batch updates are pretty cool. The Statement, PreparedStatement, and CallableStatement classes all now support a new method named executeBatch. This method is similar to execute, but rather than simply executing the one statement represented by the statement object, it executes all the statements that have been specified with the addBatch method of the statement object. The following example is from the JDBC 2.0 specification:

```
conn.setAutoCommit(false);
Statement stmt = conn.createStatement();
stmt.addBatch("INSERT INTO employees VALUES (1000, 'Joe Jones')");
stmt.addBatch("INSERT INTO departments VALUES (260, 'Shoe')");
stmt.addBatch("INSERT INTO emp_dept VALUES (1000, 260)");
// submit a batch of update commands for execution
int[] updateCounts = stmt.executeBatch();
```

This example was for unprepared statements, while the following is for prepared statements:

```
conn.setAutoCommit(false);
PreparedStatement stmt = conn.prepareStatement(
  "INSERT INTO employees VALUES (?, ?)");
stmt.setInt(1, 2000);
stmt.setString(2, "Kelly Kaufmann");
stmt.addBatch();
stmt.setInt(1, 3000);
stmt.setString(2, "Bill Barnes");
stmt.addBatch();
// submit the batch for execution
int[] updateCounts = stmt.executeBatch();
```

Only DDL and DML SQL statements that do not return result sets are valid candidates for batch execution. The batched statements are executed until the first one fails. To determine how many succeeded, call getUpdateCounts to get an integer array. The number of elements in the array tells you how many batch statements succeeded.

Optional JDBC 2.0 enhancements

A new package named javax.sql has been designed as well, to support some advanced functionality, such as database connection pools and interfaces to other optional Java initiatives like *Java Naming and Directory Services* (JNDS) and *Java Transaction Services* (JTS). This package is not part of the core JDK as of this writing. Instead, it is separately downloadable from the JavaSoft Web site. It is only of value if a database vendor implements it. You will probably see advanced implementations as part of the Enterprise JavaBeans offerings, such as in IBM's WebSphere Application Server product, Advanced and Enterprise editions.

WHAT'S NEW IN JDBC 3.0

With the release of the Java 2 SDK, Standard Edition, version 1.4, Sun released version 3.0 of JDBC. This third version of JDBC adds yet more new functionality. The following is from the JDK documentation for JDBC 3.0:

"The JDBC 3.0 API, comprised of packages java.sql and javax.sql, provides universal data access from the Java programming language. Using the JDBC 3.0 API, you can access virtually any data source, from relational databases to spreadsheets and flat files. JDBC technology also provides a common base on which tools and alternative interfaces can be built.

New features include the ability to set savepoints in a transaction, to keep result sets open after a transaction is committed, to reuse prepared statements, to get metadata about the parameters to a prepared statement, to retrieve keys that are automatically generated, and to have multiple result sets open at one time. There are two new JDBC data types, BOOLEAN and DATALINK, with the DATALINK type making it possible to manage data outside of a data source. This release also establishes the relationship between the JDBC Service Provider Interface and the Connector architecture."

EMBEDDED SQL IN JAVA: SQLJ

You have seen the Java-supplied and industry-supported way of accessing data: JDBC. This has proven popular every since Sun (with help from IBM, Oracle, and others) defined it and made it available in JDBC 1.0, with JDK 1.1.0. However, some have found it a bit unnatural for programmers accustomed to accessing their data via embedded SQL in other languages. To this end, Oracle began work on an embedded SQL specification for Java. Today, it is available not as part of the standard JDK, but by database vendors who wish to offer some value-added. Even though it is not part of the JDK, it is still reasonably portable, as more and more database vendors support it. IBM supports it across its DB2 family, for example.

Embedded SQL in Java is called *SQLJ*. It is very similar to embedded SQL in other languages, but we think it is still valuable for you know to know JDBC even if you choose to use SQLJ. Further, you can mix both SQLJ statements and JDBC calls in the same program.

SQLJ allows you to embed SQL statements directly inside Java source code, prefixed by the special string #sqlj. Such source code must exist in files that end in .sqlj versus .java. They are preprocessed into .java files by the SQLJ preprocessor (called a *translator*), which also produces a .ser file, which is known as a *profile*. This contains information about the embedded SQL statements, such as the database schema and the particular data that is accessed. As of V4R5, this is subsequently used to produce a database plan.

The manual *Application Programming Guide and Reference for Java (S/390)*, SC26-9018, lists the following differences between JDBC and SQLJ:

- SQLJ follows the static SQL model, and JDBC follows the dynamic SQL model.

- SQLJ source programs are smaller than JDBC because much of the JDBC code is generated.

- SQLJ does more data type checking during the program preparation process.

- SQLJ allows use of embedded Java host expressions inside SQL statements versus separate JDBC calls for variable binding.

- SQLJ executes statements under the authorization ID of the plan or package owner, checked at bind time. By contrast, JDBC does not know the authorization ID until runtime and so no checking is done until then.

Although this is all true, JDBC is quite easy to use and is getting better. We find the added simplicity of SQLJ to be offset by the fact it is yet another thing to learn (again, knowing JDBC anyway helps), and it requires more complexity to compile and run because of the extra step needed to preprocess the .sqlj file into a .java file, and ultimately a database plan. Obviously, we haven't cornered the market on this opinion, though, or SQLJ would not be so popular! So, it's your choice.

SQLJ is available as of V4R4 of OS/400, but that release only converts the embedded SQL statements into JDBC. As of V4R5, it actually creates database access plans, so it is in fact a better performer than JDBC because it is truly embedded static SQL versus dynamic SQL.

The following is a very brief introduction to SQLJ. The Java documentation for the AS/400 Developer Kit for Java offers more information. Follow the links for the ADK from *www.ibm.com/java*. Also, see *www.sqlj.org* for a reference manual and user guide.

Writing embedded SQL in Java

Your .sqlj files will all start by importing the JDBC and SQLJ packages, like this:

```
import java.sql.*;
import sqlj.runtime.*;
import sqlj.runtime.ref.*;
```

You must also declare a *connection context*, often right after the import statements:

```
#sql context MyCtx;
```

Think of this as defining a new class, which represents a database connection. However, to instantiate an instance of this class, you need to do a traditional JDBC driver registration and connection first, passing the Connection object to the context constructor, as follows:

```
DB2400 db400 = new DB2400();
Connection conn = db2400.getConnection();
conn.setAutoCommit(false); // required for sqlj
MyCtx ctx = new ctx(conn);
```

To subsequently work with embedded SQL, for the most part, you simply embed your SQL statements by prefixing them with #sql and using braces. You can also use the traditional :variable syntax to bind Java variables to variable parts of the SQL statements, for example:

```
try {
  String state = "PA";
  #sql { DELETE FROM CUSTOMER WHERE STATE=:state };
} catch (SQLException exc) {
  System.out.println("Failed: " + exc.getMessage());
}
```

Notice that you must still put all your statements inside try/catch blocks for SQLException. Further, you should subsequently use the Connection's commit method to commit your transactions, and ultimately close the Connection object.

By default, the SQL statements are associated with your connection context. However, you can create multiple connection-context objects. If so, you must identify which one you want to use for each SQL statement, like this:

```
#sql [ctx] { DELETE FROM CUSTOMER WHERE STATE=:state };
```

Note that the :variable can actually be a Java expression if you want to compute the value at runtime.

Where things get more interesting is with queries via the SELECT statement (multiple row queries, not single row SELECT INTO queries, which can simply be embedded). For this, you need to first declare an *iterator*, which is very similar to a cursor in embedded SQL inside RPG. This is also done at the top of the file, after the import statements and before the class definition, and looks like this:

```
#sql iterator MyIter(String name, BigDecimal balance);
```

This also effectively declares a new class, which will have methods matching the variable names you declare as parameters. You declare one variable per column you will be accessing in your database, and the methods are used to retrieve the data for that column in the current result set row, as you will see. The names are arbitrary. They do not need to match the column names, but they should be similar for easy maintenance. To create an instance of your iterator class, you embed a SELECT statement:

```
MyIter myIterObj;
#sqlj myIterObj = { SELECT NAME, BALANCE FROM CUSTOMER };
```

This actually does the query, and under the covers, gets you a result set. To walk that result set, use the supplied next method in the iterator object, and for each element, use the methods you identified in the declaration to get each column's data:

```
while (myIterObj.next())
{
    String name = iter.name();
    BigDecimal balance = iter.balance();
}
myIterObj.close();
```

Got it? Note the iterator object must be closed by you, too.

If you don't want to use column names, there is a variant of iterators known as *positioned iterators* that we leave to you to explore. Further, if you wish to do positioned updates or deletes to the current result set row, you use *updatable iterators*.

There is a lot more detail to be discussed with SQLJ, but we do not cover it here in the same detail as JDBC. Rather, we leave the detailed reading to you, if you decide to use it. However, a full example of what is covered here is shown in Listing 13.7. It is the same example as in Listing 13.3, redone with SQLJ instead of JDBC.

Listing 13.7: A SQLJ Program for Querying the PDM Options File

```
import java.sql.*;
import sqlj.runtime.*;
import sqlj.runtime.ref.*;
#sql context PDMctx; // connection context declaration
#sql iterator PDMiter (String option, String command);

public class QryPDMOptions
{
    public static void main(String args[])
    {
        System.out.println("Welcome to QryPDMOptions");
        try
        {
          System.out.println("Connecting to AS/400...");
          DB2400 db2400 = new DB2400();
          Connection conn = db2400.getConnection();
          conn.setAutoCommit(false);
          System.out.println("Preparing context...");
          PDMctx connCtx = new PDMctx(conn);
          System.out.println("Doing query...");
          PDMiter iter;
          #sql [connCtx] iter =
            { SELECT OPTION, COMMAND FROM QGPL.QAUOOPT };
        System.out.println("Displaying results...");
```

Listing 13.7: A SQLJ Program for Querying the PDM Options File (continued)

```
            while (iter.next())
            {
                String option = iter.option();
                String command = iter.command().trim();
                System.out.println(option + " " + command);
            }
            System.out.println("Closing everything...");
            conn.commit();
            iter.close();
            conn.close();
            System.out.println("Done.");
        } catch (SQLException exc) {
            System.out.println("SQL Error......: " +
                exc.getMessage()); }
        System.exit(0);
    } // end main
}
```

Preparing and compiling embedded SQL in Java

Having coded a .sqlj file, you run the translator to get the runnable class and its required profile:

```
java sqlj.tools.Sqlj QryPDMOptions.sqlj
```

For this to work, you must ensure your CLASSPATH includes the following:

```
/QIBM/ProdData/Java400/ext/runtime.zip
/QIBM/ProdData/Java400/ext/translator.zip
```

With this successfully done, you are ready to run your Java class as usual:

```
java QryPDMOptions
```

We did this on our AS/400 and got the same results as for Listing 13.3 (Here's a tip for working inside QSHELL: use redirection to capture output, as in java QryPDMOptions > pdm.out.)

SUMMARY

This chapter, admittedly, covered lots of different topics, including the following:

- A brief discussion of RPG and SQL database access and commitment control.

- The architecture of JDBC for database access in Java: Java supplies a driver manager, and database vendors supply their own JDBC database drivers. You code the Java-supplied JDBC classes only; the database drivers "snap in" underneath them.

- The steps needed to use JDBC classes in Java programs to access and manipulate DB2/400 data: load the driver, connect to the database, create statement objects, execute the statements, process the results, and finally close the necessary objects.

- An overview of what is new in JDBC 2.0 and 3.0, the new generations of JDBC.

- An overview of SQLJ, IBM, and Oracle's support for embedded SQL inside Java.

You might not be an expert yet at programming database access in Java, but you are certainly on your way!

REFERENCES

For more information on the subjects discussed in this chapter, you are referred to one of the many competent references, including these:

- *Accessing the AS/400 with Java*. IBM redbook: SG24-2152-00.

- *AS/400 Client/Server Performance Using the Windows Clients*. IBM redbook: SG24-4526-01.

- AS/400 Java home page: *www.ibm.com/iseries/java*.

- Conte, Paul. 1997. *Database Design and Programming for DB2/400* Duke Press, ISBN 1882419065.

- DB2 Product Family home page: *www.ibm.com/software/data/db2*.

- Fisher, Maydene, et al. 1999. *JDBC API Tutorial and Reference, Second Edition: Universal Data Access for the Java 2 Platform.* Addison-Wesley, ISBN 0201433281.

- Hamilton, Cattell, and Fisher. 1997. *JDBC Database Access with Java—A Tutorial and Annotated Reference.* Addison-Wesley, ISBN 0201309955.

MORE JAVA

While Java continues to change dramatically from version to version, most of the changes involve the introduction of new packages, classes, interfaces, and methods. The actual core syntax of the language is very stable, with the last major revision being the introduction of inner classes "way back" in JDK 1.1.0.

We want to ensure that this book provides a complete introduction to all the syntax in Java, and to all the major functionality in the JDK-supplied packages. The latter is reviewed later in this chapter, but first, some basic syntactical aspects of the language still need to be covered. For completeness, the following sections offer a very brief tour of the remaining syntax elements, although our feeling is the majority of RPG programmers moving into Java will not need to know them. (By "syntax," we mean any functionality that requires a modifier, keyword, operator, or other basic language element.)

INNER CLASSES

As discussed in Chapter 2, Java applications contain packages that contain classes (or interfaces), which contain static and instance variables and methods. Methods, in turn, contain parameters, local variables, and finally executable code. Chapter 2 doesn't mention, though, that classes themselves can contain other classes. That is, Java classes can have subordinate classes nested inside them, which are known as *inner classes*. A simple example is shown in Listing 14.1.

Listing 14.1: An Inner Class (EnumerateDept) Inside an Outer Class (Dept)

```java
import java.util.*;

public class Dept
{
    private int      deptNbr;
    private Emp      deptMgr;
    private Vector   deptEmps = new Vector();

    public Dept(int nbr, Emp mgr)
    {
        deptNbr = nbr;
        deptMgr = mgr;
    }

    // Dept methods not shown
    public Enumeration getEnumeration()
    {
        return new EnumerateDept();
    } // end method getEnumeration

    class EnumerateDept implements Enumeration
    {
        private int pos=0;

        // end-of-list test...
        public boolean hasMoreElements()
        {
            return (pos < deptEmps.size());
        }
        // retrieve next element...
        public Object nextElement()
        {
            Object retobj = null;
            if (hasMoreElements())
                {
```

```
                    retobj = deptEmps.elementAt(pos);
                    pos = pos+1;
              }
           return retobj;
        }
     } // end EnumerateDept class

  } // end class Dept
```

The full example of this class, including its helper Emp, is not shown here, but is available on the CD-ROM included with this book. The key part of this class is its nested or inner class, EnumerateDept. It is declared right inside the "outer class," Dept, which is the only class that ever needs to see it. The Dept method getEnumeration returns an instance of it, but defines the return type to be the interface Enumeration that the inner class implements.

Inner classes bring nothing new to the table. They offer no functionality that you can't get by simply coding the same class by itself, outside of its outer class. An inner class is just for programmer convenience, as it saves the trouble of working with a separate class, and hence a separate source file, for those classes that are truly nothing more than implementation details.

Inner classes can access all the variables of the outer class, including those marked private. The opposite is not true—the outer class cannot access the variables of the inner class. Further, inner class *instances* are scoped to the current *instance* of the outer class in which they were instantiated. They can directly access the instance variables of the outer class and can use the syntax "this.this" to refer to the outer class instance they are contained in.

Inner classes can also be defined inside blocks or methods. In these cases, they can also access the local variables and method parameters of their enclosing block or method. Java insists that you mark the local variables and methods final if you want to allow the inner classes to access them. This is because an instance of the inner class might "live on" long after the block or method has completed execution, and thus the value of the referenced local variables and parameters need to live on as well, and that means they need to be unchanging.

Listing 14.2 shows a modified version of Listing 14.1, with the inner class moved to be directly inside the only method that uses it. In addition to moving the inner class to be entirely within the getEnumeration method, this example also defines a local and final variable named empsCopy to hold a copy of the current contents of the employee Vector.

The inner class code is changed to use this copy. This is a good idea, since you want a returned enumeration object to be impervious to changes made to the department after you get the object. It should be a snapshot in time. In this example, the same effect could have been achieved by declaring empsCopy as an instance variable of the inner class.

Listing 14.2: An Inner Class Defined Directly Inside a Method

```
import java.util.*;

public class Dept
{
    // ... same as Listing 14.1 ...
    public Enumeration getEnumeration()
    {
        final Vector empsCopy = (Vector)deptEmps.clone();

        class EnumerateDept implements Enumeration
        {
            private int pos=0;

            // end-of-list test...
            public boolean hasMoreElements()
            {
                return (pos < empsCopy.size());
            }
            // retrieve next element...
            public Object nextElement()
            {
                Object retobj = null;
                if (hasMoreElements())
                {
                    retobj = empsCopy.elementAt(pos);
                    pos = pos+1;
                }
                return retobj;
            }
        } // end EnumerateDept class
        return new EnumerateDept();
    } // end method getEnumeration
} // end class Dept
```

ANONYMOUS INNER CLASSES

In an effort to save even more typing, Java also allows you to define an inner class right on the new operator. You simply place the class definition immediately after the new statement, just prior to the semicolon. In this case, you don't even bother to name the class, hence the term *anonymous inner class*.

Listing 14.3 shows yet another revision of the example, using an anonymous inner class instead of a named inner class. Notice that the new operator in this case names the existing class or interface to create a new instance of, followed by a class body ended with a semicolon. The name given on the new operator must be a class or interface that already exists. If it is a class name, the subsequent class body is considered to extend that class. If it is an interface name, the subsequent class body is considered to implement that interface and extend java.lang.Object. The keywords extends and implements are not permitted on anonymous classes. Further, anonymous inner classes are not permitted to define constructors. If any parameters are given between the parentheses on the new operator, they are passed to the parent's matching constructor.

Listing 14.3: An Anonymous Inner Class

```
public Enumeration getEnumeration()
{
    final Vector empsCopy = (Vector)deptEmps.clone();

    return new Enumeration()
    {
        private int pos=0;

        // end-of-list test...
        public boolean hasMoreElements()
        {
            return (pos < empsCopy.size());
        }
        // retrieve next element...
        public Object nextElement()
        {
            Object retobj = null;
            if (hasMoreElements())
              {
                retobj = empsCopy.elementAt(pos);
                pos = pos+1;
              }
            return retobj;
        }
    }; // end anonymous inner class Enumeration
} // end method getEnumeration
```

Anonymous classes are most often seen in GUI and JavaBean coding, where you want to register your interest in a particular event. For example, the examples in Chapter 12 use addActionListener to register GUI components for action events, implement the ActionListener interface in a class, and supply an actionPerformed method that checks for the particular component that fired the event. Alternatively, for each addAction Listener call, you could use new with an anonymous class to pass an instance of an anonymous class that implements the `actionPerformed` method for just that component, for example:

```
okButton.addActionListener( new ActionListener ()
{
    public void actionPerformed(ActionEvent evt)
    {
        System.out.println("OK pressed");
    }
}; );
```

Inner classes, both named and anonymous, should only be used for very small classes that can be digested at a quick glance. Anything bigger, and they actually have a negative affect on the readability and maintainability of the code, completely defeating their purpose. Some programmers don't like to use them at all, but you will see them used heavily in the JDK documentation and examples.

STATIC INITIALIZERS

You have seen static variables, or class variables, since Chapter 2. These are class-level variables defined with the modifier `static`, indicating they have one memory location for the life of the application, versus one per instance of the class. Recall that you can initialize the static variables, like all variables, at the time they are defined, as follows:

```
static int nextAvailableID = 100;
```

When the JVM first loads your class into memory, it immediately allocates storage for all the static variables in the class, and then runs the initialization expression, if there is one (otherwise, it assigns the default initial value based on the variable type). Quite often, other things are of value to do at that initial-load time, as well. For example, you might want to open a connection to a database, or read an initial value from a file. Java allows for this. It allows you to define any block of code at the class level (that is, not inside a method) inside the usual curly braces, as long as you preface the block with the keyword `static`. The JVM will run these blocks of code at the time the class is first loaded into memory, for example:

```
static { MyOtherClass.doStuff(); }
```

Any references to methods must, of course, be static methods, unless you include code to instantiate an object, as usual. These blocks of code are called *static initializers*, and they are the static equivalent of a constructor. The alternative to a static initializer is simply a static method, which you explicitly call at the beginning of your application.

Because static initializers are run so early in the life of an application, there are restrictions on exactly what you can do in them. For example, you can't call any methods that throw exceptions unless you use try/catch to monitor for those exceptions. In general, you don't see too many people coding elaborate static initializers. They tend to heavily clutter a class. Further, it just doesn't sit well with some people to write executable blocks of code outside of a formal method. As with anonymous classes, the increment and decrement operators, and the conditional operator, you can avoid using them, but you probably can't avoid seeing them.

JAVA NATIVE INTERFACE (JNI)

We hate to admit it, but occasionally there are times when there is something you just cannot do in Java, and you are forced to revert to another language, such as C. As the packages supplied with the JDK get increasingly richer, this becomes less and less of an issue. However, Java does have built-in support for calling out of the language. One option is to call an external executable object, which is done using a supplied method and is covered shortly. This is not very efficient, though, and it does not allow you to exchange parameters. The other alternative is to call a function in a DLL (or a service program on OS/400). This runs in the same address space as the virtual machine, so it is usually more efficient and offers more opportunity to interoperate with the called function.

Java comes with built-in support for calling C functions in DLLs, using *Java Native Interface* or *JNI*. This is done by actually wrapping the C function in a Java method that uses the modifier native. This modifier is similar to abstract, in that when you use it, you don't define a method body, for example:

```
public native String getEnvironmentVariable(String name);
```

The modifier native tells Java that this method is not implemented in Java at all, but rather in C (usually), in a DLL somewhere. What DLL exactly? Well, you have to tell Java that, by coding a static initializer (now you know why these exist) in your class that loads that DLL into memory, for example:

```
static { System.loadLibrary("MyDLL"); }
```

This will use the static method loadLibrary in class System in package java.lang, to find the named DLL (or *SRVPGM) on disk and load it into memory. What function (or procedure) in the DLL is called when someone calls your native method? The function with the same name as your native method name. What parameters are passed to it? The same parameters that were passed to your native method. Of course, some data type mapping has to occur between the Java and C language data types, and that is done for you automatically. These mappings are well defined and documented in the JDK documentation.

Can the C function update the parameters? You bet! It is quite cool how Java does all of this underlying plumbing for you so seamlessly. Well, not that seamlessly, actually. There are APIs you will have to call to map the data types and "call back" from C to Java.

So, you "don't do C"? Not to worry. You can call any DLL (or service program on OS/400) written in any language that is compatible with C. That is, if you can call a procedure in a service program from ILE C, you can call it from Java, too. Yes, that means RPG IV procedures, too, but only as of V4R4, when the RPG IV runtime was made thread-safe. You could also call a C function that, in turn, calls an RPG program. However, if your goal is to call an RPG program instead of an RPG procedure inside a service program, the best answer is either to call it as a stored procedure as discussed in Chapter 13, or to use the AS/400 Toolbox for Java program-call class discussed in Appendix A.

JNI involves some other stuff, too. For example, it specifies a set of C APIs that can be called to go the other way. That is, from a C program (or any program that can call C APIs), you can instantiate a Java class and call methods on that class. These APIs are a core part of the JDK, so while they are not written in Java, all operating systems that support Java are required to support them as well. This is one way for RPG to call Java. Another is to use the command-analyzer API to run the RUNJVA command, and then perhaps use a data queue or data area to exchange data. (The AS/400 Toolbox for Java has Java classes for working with these from Java, as discussed in Appendix A.)

If you want to pass parameters, the JNI APIs provide the best option, but they are a bear to code using these C APIs. The good news is that V5R1 of RPG IV adds language support in RPG to make calling Java relatively easy. This includes language syntax for instantiating a Java object and calling methods in that object. Under the covers, the RPG runtime uses the JNI APIs to do this.

There is much more to know about JNI. To get the details, refer to the JDK documentation in jdk1.2.1\docs\guide\jni\index.html, and the RPG IV reference manual for V5R1 or higher.

JAVA REMOTE METHOD INVOCATION (RMI)

Imagine that you have Java code running on a client (for example, Windows or a Web browser), and you want to call Java code running on a server. Perhaps that server Java code uses JNI for accessing an existing application or transaction, and you want to get the results to the client for display to the user. The options for this very common requirement are plentiful.

The Java-designed and defined way is via something known as *Remote Method Invocation*, or RMI. RMI is a means to do a remote procedure call (RPC), but in an object-oriented way. In the days of client/server, RPC was a popular way of remotely calling a function on the server, from the client (as defined in the Distributed Computing Environment, or DCE, world). In an OO world, the preferred way to do client-to-server communications is via *distributed objects*. This is a simple concept: a distributed object lives on the server, but has a thin *proxy* for client code. This proxy object appears to have all the same methods as the "real" object on the server, but when client code calls one of those methods, the call is actually shuttled to the server, where it is executed using the real object. Any updated parameters or returned values are returned to the caller. Preferably, the client code does not know or care that the object it appears to be working with is actually a proxy.

To do distributed object programming, somebody has to give you the engine to enable the magic shuttling across the network (officially called *marshalling*). This, for example, is what OMG's (Object Management Group) CORBA (Common Object Request Broker Architecture) is all about, and what Microsoft DCOM (Distributed Common Object Model) is all about. Java's answer is RMI, and it is a core part of the JDK, so it is available on every system that supports Java. By the way, the client can be any operating system, Web browser, or device that supports Java. And so can the server! It is up to you to decide what is the client and what is the server, although almost always the server is the system where our data, applications, or transactions are.

To use RMI to create a distributed object, you must do the following:

- Create an interface that describes the methods you want to make available remotely on clients. This interface must import `java.rmi.*` and extend `Remote` (from `java.rmi`). Further, every method signature must be defined with `throws RemoteException`.

- For the server side, create a class that implements your interface and code it as needed to perform the functions you desire. As per interface rules, you must supply implementations for all the methods in your interface. Your class must import java.rmi.* and java.rmi.server.*, and extend UnicastRemoteObject from package java.rmi.server. (If you can't extend, that's okay, but you have to do some extra work in your constructor.)

- Your class must supply a main method that instantiates an instance of this class and does some work to make that object "distributable." This includes giving the object a name by which clients will refer to it (since classes can and usually do have multiple objects, each object needs a unique name, since the clients work with objects, not classes), and "registering" the object in the RMI registry. This is all done using the static method rebind in the Naming class in package java.rmi. Prior to this, you must also call the setSecurityManager method in the System class and pass it an instance of RMISecurityManager. By convention, you name your class the same as the interface, but add Impl (for implementation) to the end of the name.

- For the client-side code that will use the distributed object, you declare an instance variable to be the interface type from step 1. Then, rather than using new to instantiate your class from step 2, you call the static method lookup in class Naming in package java.rmi. This method takes a URL that defines the name or IP address of the remote system containing the remote object, and the name given your server class object in step 2. It gives you back the reference to an object instance of a class that implements the client interface from step 1. This object is a proxy of the server object from step 2. That proxy object is automatically downloaded for you by Java. It finds this object on the server by looking in the RMI registry on the server, using the name as a key. Now, you simply call the methods in the proxy as though it were a normal local object, but taking care to monitor for RemoteException exceptions.

So, where does the class for that proxy object come from? You create it using the rmic tool from the JDK. Give it your class name, such as XXX , and it will give you back two class files: XXX_stub.class and XXX_skel.class. The former is the proxy class for the client, and the latter is the "gorp" or skeleton version of the server class, which does all the ugly communications code for each method. You simply place both of these on your server, and RMI takes care of finding and using them appropriately. You never refer to them explicitly in your code.

On the server, then, you have the following:

- The actual server class that you wrote and want to distribute. It implements the interface you wrote that describes all the methods you want to expose to client code.

- A `main` method for instantiating your server class into an object, and registering that object with the RMI registry. This method can either be in your server class itself or in a separate class altogether; it's your choice.

- Additional classes, as needed. The key thing is that you only need to distribute a single object of a single class. After that, you can instantiate and return to the client as many objects of as many classes as you like. You simply supply a method in your distributed class that will return these objects.

- A proxy stub class for your server class, generated via `rmic`. This will be located on disk and instantiated automatically by the RMI registry when your `main` method registers your object. It will also be sent to the client automatically via the RMI registry, when a client calls `lookup`. It handles the communications on the client side.

- A skeleton class for your server class, generated via `rmic`. An instance of this class is automatically created when you register your object with the RMI registry and is run automatically by the RMI registry. Its job is to wait for method-call requests from the client stub object, turn those into method calls to your actual server object, and return the results to the client. That is, it handles the communications on the server side.

On the client, you have the client code you wrote that remotely uses an instance of your server class. It does this by calling `lookup` and getting back an instance of that client proxy stub class. This contains methods of the same name and signature as your server class, but marshals calls to these methods across the wire to your actual server object, via the corresponding server-side skeleton object.

What about that RMI registry? This is executable code that you must start running on your server for everything to work. To start it, simply enter the JDK command `rmiregistry`, or on Windows, type the following:

```
start rmiregistry
```

The registry waits for requests from server Java applications to register objects (using the Naming.rebind method), and for requests from client Java applications or applets to find and retrieve object stubs (with Naming.lookup).

With the registry running, you can run your server-side class by calling it from the command line using the java command, as usual. Unlike the usual way of running Java classes from the command line, however, you have to specify the -D option (to *d*efine an important "property") on the Java command line. Specifically, you have to define the name of a little security-policy file containing information about which classes on the server can be distributed:

```
java -Djava.security.policy=d:/rmi/mysrc/policy examples.hello.HelloImpl
```

Note there should be one space after java and one space after the final policy. In this case, a class named HelloImpl is running from the package examples.hello. The policy property fully qualifies a local policy file.

Here is an example of a policy file (named simply policy, with no extension) that gives all classes access to all distributed server objects:

```
grant {
  // Allow everything for now
  permission java.security.AllPermission;
};
```

Once your Java server class runs, its main method will set the security manager (a necessary detail) and instantiate an object and register it in the registry, as discussed in step 2 earlier, and shown here (taken from the JDK-supplied RMI tutorial):

```
// create and install a security manager
if (System.getSecurityManager() == null)
  System.setSecurityManager(new RMISecurityManager());
try {
  HelloImpl obj = new HelloImpl(); // create our distributable object
  // Bind this object instance to the name "HelloServer"
  Naming.rebind("//myhost/HelloServer",obj);
  System.out.println("HelloServer bound in registry");
} catch (Exception exc) {
  System.out.println("HelloImpl err: " + exc.getMessage());
}
```

This makes the object available to client code, as follows:

```
Hello remoteObj = null; // Hello.java is the remote object interface
try {
  remoteObj = (Hello)Naming.lookup("//myhost/HelloServer");
} catch (Exception exc)
  System.out.println("Remote communication failed with: " +
                     exc.getMessage());
  System.exit(0);
}
System.out.println(remoteObj.sayHello());
```

Note that only the initial object stub typically needs to be remotely downloaded using lookup, and hence the registry. After that, methods in the remote server object can return instantiated objects to the client code as they would normally return objects to local code. If you test an RMI example on Windows running the registry, with your server and client classes on the same system, use localhost for the host name in the rebind and lookup calls. However, beware that lookup will fail if your PC is configured for DHCP!

We don't cover further details of RMI, since there is sufficient information in the JDK documentation. For these details, see the file \jdk1.2.2\docs\guide\rmi\index.html, where \jdk1.2.2 is the directory where you installed the Windows JDK. (This assumes you have installed the JavaDoc documentation for the JDK.) Further, Daniel Darnell's excellent book *JAVA and the AS/400* (29th Street Press, ISBN 1-58304-033-1) contains an example of using RMI on the AS/400. For an in-depth look at RMI, see *Mastering Java 1.2*, by John Zukowski (Sybex, ISBN 0-7821-2180-2).

What is important for you to take from this introduction to RMI is that it is a relatively easy way to write distributed objects in Java. It is a great way to write code that runs on a server, and hence has easy access to all your resources there, and then to distribute that code to a client, such as a Web browser, where it can be displayed to the user. The underlying communications protocol is TCP/IP by default, but RMI in JDK 1.3 does allow you to choose *IIOP* (*Internet Inter-Orb Protocol*) for a CORBA flavor. If you are only interested in doing Java-to-Java communications (versus, say, Java to C++), this is an easy way to achieve that.

JAVA OBJECT SERIALIZATION

If you think about the RMI discussion, you will realize just how much work is being done for you. This is especially true when client code calls a remote method and passes objects as parameters. How does it pass these objects? Well, there really is only one way to pass data between any client and server: as a stream of bytes. That means all object parameters must be converted or flattened to a stream of bytes first, then sent across the network to the server method, which in turn must convert or unflatten the stream of bytes into an object. The conversion from an object to a byte stream and back again is referred to as *serialization*.

It gets even more complicated with objects that contain other objects as instance variables. Each contained object, and every object inside the contained object, must be serialized in order to send the entire main object across the network. On the other side, the server must know exactly the algorithm used to do this, so it can do exactly the same thing in reverse, to re-create the contained objects and the main object from the byte stream.

Serializing an object to a byte stream, and de-serializing it from a byte stream, is not only of value in RMI communications. You will often need to save the current state of an object to disk, and then retrieve it from disk later. The "old" way of doing this was to create your own code to write each of the variables out to disk manually, using your own conventions. For example, you might use a special character to denote the end of each element in an array, so that when you subsequently read it in again, you would know where each record ended. The built-in Java support for serialization makes saving the data in any object, and subsequently restoring it, trivial. The official term for this is called *persistence*. Via serialization, you persist an object to disk.

Whether serializing an object to pass as a parameter in an RMI method call or to persist it to disk, the important step is generating the byte stream. After that, it is a simple matter to send the stream to disk or over the network. So how do you produce this stream? Any class that you want to be able to serialize must be defined to implement the `Serializable` interface from package `java.io`. This interface contains no methods; it is only used as a flag to the compiler and runtime.

To actually write your object to disk, then, use the `ObjectOutputStream` class from the `java.io` package. Instantiate it, passing a `FileOutputStream` object for the target file (a class from `java.io` for writing streams to disk), and then use the `writeObject` method to write objects to the stream, and therefore to the file. After writing, call `flush` to force the buffer to disk, and then `close` the file output stream.

For example, Listing 14.1 showed a class named `Dept`, and you will see on the CD-ROM that it has a `main` method, which creates an instance of the class and populates it with data. We have changed that class to be named `DeptSerializable`, and implemented the `Serializable` interface:

```
import java.io.*;
public class DeptSerializable implements Serializable
```

The only wrinkle is that all instance variable objects in the class must also be of a serializable class type. Thankfully, almost all the JDK-supplied classes are serializable. However, this class contains instances of another class, Emp, which we also had to change to implement Serializable, and which we renamed to EmpSerializable. Next, to test writing to disk, we changed the main method of DeptSerializable to serialize the instance of DeptSerializable it creates and populates. We serialized it to file Dept.ser, using a FileOuputStream object, an ObjectOutputStream object, and calling the method writeObject in ObjectOutputStream, as shown in Listing 14.4.

Listing 14.4: The Serializable Dept Class (main Method Only)

```
import java.util.*;
import java.io.*;

public class DeptSerializable implements Serializable
{
    // .. same ...
    public static void main(String args[])
    {
        int mgrDeptId = 100;
        int empDeptId = 200;
        EmpSerializable mgr =
          new EmpSerializable(1, "Jim Bean", mgrDeptId);
        DeptSerializable dept =
          new DeptSerializable(empDeptId, mgr);
        dept.addEmployee(
          new EmpSerializable(20, "George Farr", empDeptId));
        dept.addEmployee(
          new EmpSerializable(20, "Phil Coulthard",empDeptId));
        dept.addEmployee(
          new EmpSerializable(21, "John S Page", empDeptId));
        dept.addEmployee(
          new EmpSerializable(22, "Sam Let", empDeptId));
        dept.addEmployee(
          new EmpSerializable(22, "Eli J Bean",empDeptId));

        try
        {
        FileOutputStream ostream = new FileOutputStream("Dept.ser");
        ObjectOutputStream serStream = new
ObjectOutputStream(ostream);
        serStream.writeObject(dept);
```
⟶

Listing 14.4: The Serializable Dept Class (main Method Only) (continued)

```
            serStream.flush();
            ostream.close();
            System.out.println("Dept written to Dept.ser");
        }
        catch (Exception exc)
        {
            System.out.println("Error serializing: " +
                               exc.getMessage());
            exc.printStackTrace();
        }
    } // end main method
} // end class DeptSerializable
```

Note how the serializing code is enclosed in a try/catch block, as it can throw exceptions. When you run this class, it runs to completion, creating a file named Dept.ser in the current directory. To test reading this file in from disk, do the functional opposites of everything: a FileInputStream class, ObjectInputStream, and readObject, as shown in Listing 14.5.

Listing 14.5: Code to Re-Instantiate a Serialized DeptSerializable Class

```
import java.util.*;
import java.io.*;

public class TestDeptSerializable
{
    public static void main(String args[])
    {
        try
        {
            FileInputStream istream = new FileInputStream("Dept.ser");
            ObjectInputStream serStream = new ObjectInputStream(istream);
            DeptSerializable dept =
                (DeptSerializable)serStream.readObject();
            istream.close();
            printDept(dept);
        }
        catch (Exception exc)
        {
            System.out.println("Error reading from disk: " +
                               exc.getMessage());
        }
    } // end main method
```

```
    public static void printDept(DeptSerializable dept)
    {
        Enumeration allEmps = dept.getEnumeration();
        System.out.println();
        String hdr = "Employees of dept " + dept.getNbr() + ":";
        System.out.println(hdr);
        for (int idx=0; idx<hdr.length(); idx++)
           System.out.print('-');
        System.out.println();
        System.out.println(dept.getMgr().getName()+" (mgr)");
        while (allEmps.hasMoreElements())
        {
            EmpSerializable currEmp =
               (EmpSerializable)allEmps.nextElement();
            System.out.println(currEmp.getName());
        }
    }
} // end TestDeptSerializable class
```

Notice how a `printDept` method is supplied and called to verify that all the data was read in properly. Running this gives the following:

```
Employees of dept 200:
-----------------------
Jim Bean (mgr)
George Farr
Phil Coulthard
John S Page
Sam Let
Eli J Bean
```

Listing 14.4 saved an object to disk, including all its data, while Listing 14.5 read that object in from disk and brought it back to life. You must admit, this is pretty good. It is a very easy way to save state or data persistently between runs of an application, with only five lines of code to save it and four lines of code to restore it (not including the try/catch code). You could also use it with the JDK-supplied classes for writing TCP/IP or HTTP communications code, for sending objects across the network. All of this is done for you when using RMI. If you have variables that are sensitive (such as password or salary), you can use the `transient` modifier on them. Any transient variables are not saved when their enclosing object is serialized, and they are set to their type's default value when the object is de-serialized.

There are other capabilities in Java's serialization support, such as dealing with parent classes that are not serializable, and dealing with multiple versions of an evolving class.

For more detailed information, see the JDK supplied documentation in the file \jdk1.2.2\docs\guide\serialization\index.html, where \jdk1.2.2 is the directory in which you installed the Windows JDK.

JAVA-SUPPLIED PACKAGES

The Java language is often referred to as a platform. Why? Because the intention is for you to write code that is operating-system independent. Keep in mind that the Java "compiler" (javac) generates byte code for the Java Virtual Machine. It does not generate machine code for the specific machine it happens to run on. Furthermore, to achieve the Java "write once, run anywhere" goal, you need to be able to write Java code that successfully avoids calling operating-system APIs or services.

That is certainly the case for applets; they are not even permitted by the Java security manager to call out to system services and APIs, or to any local program or DLL. Java applications and servlets have more options, of course, including the option to invoke native system commands and C code. Again, though, the intent is to decrease (as much as possible) your dependence on the underlying operating system. That will increase the portability of your code. To this end, the Java language must supply to the programmer as much functionality as possible to avoid the need to call operating-system services. This is the root of the reference to Java as a "platform": programmers are programming to Java and its set of supplied functions. This is in contrast to the traditional style of programming to the target operating systems' APIs.

By now you will surely agree that the Java language itself deserves credit for being a reasonably good language because it has the power of object orientation, but is not too complex. On top of this base, further functionality is provided by the class libraries, or packages, supplied with the language, as shown in Figure 14.1. This shields you from the need to "break out" (access the operating system). The richer these packages are (and they are getting richer with each release), the more function you have built-in. Another big advantage is that, because the packages are ported everywhere with the JVM, you can depend on having an impressive amount of functionality available wherever you go.

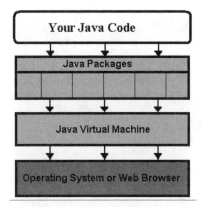

Figure 14.1: Java's application architecture

You are already familiar with some of the class libraries or packages that follow the naming convention java.xxx. For example, you have seen java.sql (for JDBC), java.math (for BigDecimal), and javax.swing and javax.swing.event (for user interfaces). You have used java.util for Date, Vector, HashTable, and Enumeration, and java.text for SimpleDateFormat. You have also used many of the classes in java.lang, the "default" package that is automatically imported by Java. You have seen such classes as java.lang.Object, java.lang.Class, java.lang.Thread, and java.lang.String.

Table 14.1 lists the interesting "core" packages supplied with Java up to 1.4.0. The package names that start with java. were designed to be part of the core Java specification. The package names that start with javax. started out as optional, separately downloadable packages. The packages not described in Table 14.1 are probably not relevant to your first business application.

Table 14.1: JSDK 1.4.0-Level Packages (part 1 of 3)

Package	Description
javax.accessibility	Assistive technologies, including alternative user inputs.
java.awt	An abstract windowing toolkit for user-interface components.
java.awt.color	Support for color spaces.
java.awt.datatransfer	For transferring data between different applications and within the same application; most commonly used for drag-and-drop and the clipboard.
java.awt.dnd	Drag-and-drop support.
java.awt.event	An abstract windowing toolkit for user input events.
java.awt.font	Support for Type 1,2 Multiple Master fonts; OpenType; and TrueType fonts.
java.awt.geom	2-D geometry for advanced graphics manipulation.
java.awt.im java.awt.im.spi	Input Method framework for alternative DBCS input.
java.awt.image java.awt.image.renderable	For images and creating rendering-independent images.
java.awt.print	General printing classes and interfaces.
java.beans java.beans.beancontext	JavaBean classes and interfaces. A bean context is a container for beans, and defines the execution environment for the beans it contains.
javax.crypto javax.crypto.xxx	For cryptographic operations; part of the core JSDK as of 1.4.0.
javax.imagio javax.imagio.xxx	New for 1.4.0, a pluggable architecture for working with images stored in files and accessed across the network.
java.lang.ref	Provides weak references to objects so they'll still be garbage collected.
java.lang.reflect	For getting reflective (dynamic) information about classes and objects.
java.math	Math classes. (Hey, just like high school!)
javax.naming javax.naming.xxx	For naming and directory services, such as LDAP.

Table 14.1: JSDK 1.4.0-Level Packages (part 2 of 3)

Package	Description
java.net	Networking classes for those interested in writing their own communications code, versus using the AS/400 Toolbox for Java, for example. Makes TCP/IP and HTTP communications relatively easy.
javax.net javax.net.ssl	Factories for client and server socket creation, both normal and secure. Allows encapsulation of socket creation.
java.nio java.nio.xxx	New for 1.4.0, these I/O (NIO) APIs provide new features and improved performance in the areas of buffer management, character-set support, regular-expression matching, file I/O, and scalable network I/O.
javax.print javax.print.xxx	New for 1.4.0, a framework, like JDBC. The Java Print Service enables clients and servers to discover and use print services for report writing.
java.rmi java.rmi.xxx	For remote method invocation (RMI).
java.security java.security.xxx	For security, including certificates, digital signatures, and message digests. See docs/guide/security/index.html.
javax.sound.midi javax.sound.midi.spi	New for 1.4.0, for working with MIDI recorded sound and a framework for service providers.
javax.sound.sampled javax.sound.sampled.spi	New for 1.4.0, for sampled audio data and a framework for service providers.
javax.swing javax.swing.xxx	New User Interface controls, layout managers, and models, plus supporting packages; discussed in Chapter 12.
javax.transaction javax.transaction.xa	For transaction managers.
java.util	Utility "value-added" classes like Vector, HashTable, and Date.
java.util.jar java.util.zip	For reading and writing .jar files and .zip files.
java.util.logging	New in 1.4.0, for logging messages during runtime.
java.util.prefs	New in 1.4.0, for saving and restoring preferences.
java.util.regex	New in 1.4.0, for regular expression support (pattern matching).

Table 14.1: JSDK 1.4.0-Level Packages (part 3 of 3)	
Package	Description
javax.xml.xxx org.xml.sax.xxx org.w3c.dom	New in 1.4.0, for XML parsing and generation. Now part of the JSDK, it was previously available from www.alphaworks.com and www.w3.org.
org.omg. CORBA org.omg.xxx	For the mapping of OMG CORBA to Java, including an ORB, plus supporting packages.

COMMON "HOW DO I?" QUESTIONS

To round out your introduction to Java, the following sections answer some questions that we have been asked by AS/400 programmers who were learning Java, or that arose as we were learning and writing in Java. Although this information refers to packages and/or classes not included in this book, once you know where to look, you can easily refer to online documentation.

Note that the following sections answer the questions in the context of Java running on Windows. For Java running on OS/400, the answers are the same, but pertain to the Integrated File System (IFS) versus the Windows file system. If you want to have similar functionality when accessing the IFS file system from a remote client, see the AS/400 Toolbox for Java, which offers IFS classes that extend these built-in JDK classes, but which work against the OS/400 Integrated File System, even when run from a remote Windows or any other client. The classes shown in the following sections also work against the IFS, but only for Java running on the AS/400 itself.

How do I determine the working directory?

To determine the working directory, use the System.getProperty("user.dir") static method call. This returns a String object that contains your current working directory. For example, see Listing 14.6.

Listing 14.6: Querying the Current Directory-System Property

```
public class TestWorkingDir
    {
        public static void main(String args[])
        {
            String currDir = System.getProperty("user.dir");
            System.out.println("Current directory: " + currDir);
        }
    }
```

Compiling and running this gives something similar to the following:

```
>java TestWorkingDir
Current directory: F:\JavaForRPGProgrammers\source\ch14
```

When running on the AS/400, this is the current directory of your QSHELL environment if running there, or as set by the CHGCURDIR CL command. The initial value for this comes from the HOMEDIR value of your user profile, which, if not set, defaults to /, or the root directory. If you don't have a user directory in the IFS yet, you should create one with CRTDIR, and change your profile to point to it.

How do I change the working directory?

The getProperty method inside System is very handy. It has a well-defined list of the properties you can query. Some of them, such as user.dir, are dynamic, while others are hard-coded by the JVM vendor, such as os.name. In addition to getProperty, there is also a setProperty method for changing a property, but only for those that make sense, such as user.dir to change the current directory, as shown in Listing 14.7.

Listing 14.7: Changing the Current Directory-System Property

```
public class TestSetWorkingDir
{
    public static void main(String args[])
    {
        System.out.println("Was: "+System.getProperty("user.dir"));
        System.setProperty("user.dir","c:\\phil");
        System.out.println("Is : "+System.getProperty("user.dir"));
    }
}
```

Notice the double backslash in Listing 14.7. Because the backslash is an "escape" character in Java strings, you must use a double backslash to get just one. This situation is similar to what you find in the C and C++ languages. Compiling and running this example gives something similar to the following:

```
F:\JavaForRPGProgrammers\source\ch14>java TestSetWorkingDir
Was: f:\JavaForRPGProgrammers\source\ch14
Is : c:\phil
```

We do not recommend using the hard-coded backslash character here because not all file systems use it. For example, on UNIX and OS/400 you would need to use a forward

661

slash. A good portable citizen will use the Java-supplied constant pathSeparatorChar in class File in package java.io. This will be defined properly for each system on which you run your Java application.

What are the other system properties you can query? The best answer to this is to write and run a little program that queries and displays them all, as in Listing 14.8.

Listing 14.8: Code to Retrieve and Print All System Properties

```java
import java.util.*;
public class GetAllProperties
{
    public static void main(String args[])
    {
        Properties allProps = System.getProperties();
        allProps.list(System.out);
    }
}
```

If you run this on Windows, you get output like the following:

```
- listing properties -
java.specification.name=Java Platform API Specification
awt.toolkit=sun.awt.windows.WToolkit
java.version=1.2.2
java.awt.graphicsenv=sun.awt.Win32GraphicsEnvironment
user.timezone=America/New_York
java.specification.version=1.2
java.vm.vendor=Sun Microsystems Inc.
user.home=C:\WINNT\Profiles\coulthar
java.vm.specification.version=1.0
os.arch=x86
java.awt.fonts=
java.vendor.url=http://java.sun.com/
user.region=US
file.encoding.pkg=sun.io
java.home=C:\Program Files\JavaSoft\JRE\1.2
java.class.path=F:\IBMDebug\lib\dertrjrt.jar;.;classe...
line.separator=
java.ext.dirs=C:\Program Files\JavaSoft\JRE\1.2\lib...
java.io.tmpdir=C:\TEMP\
os.name=Windows NT
java.vendor=Sun Microsystems Inc.
java.awt.printerjob=sun.awt.windows.WPrinterJob
java.library.path=C:\WINNT\system32;.;C:\WINNT\System32...
```

```
java.vm.specification.vendor=Sun Microsystems Inc.
sun.io.unicode.encoding=UnicodeLittle
file.encoding=Cp1252
java.specification.vendor=Sun Microsystems Inc.
user.language=en
user.name=coulthar
java.vendor.url.bug=http://java.sun.com/cgi-bin/bugreport...
java.vm.name=HotSpot VM
java.class.version=46.0
java.vm.specification.name=Java Virtual Machine Specification
sun.boot.library.path=C:\Program Files\JavaSoft\JRE\1.2\bin
os.version=4.0
java.vm.version=1.0.1
java.vm.info=1.0.1, mixed mode, build g
path.separator=;
file.separator=\
user.dir=F:\JavaForRPGProgrammers\SOURCE\ch14\Listing14-8
sun.boot.class.path=C:\Program Files\JavaSoft\JRE\1.2\lib...
```

We leave it to you to run this on AS/400 to see what you get.

How do I list files and directories?

To list files and directories programmatically, use the `File` class in package `java.io`. It will be worth your while to explore this rich class! The example in Listing 14.9 lists all files in the current working directory.

Listing 14.9: How to List Files in a Directory

```java
import java.io.File;

public class TestList
{
    public static void main(String args[])
    {
        String currDir = System.getProperty("user.dir");
        File listFiles = new File(currDir);
        String[] allFiles = listFiles.list();
        for (int idx = 0; idx < allFiles.length; idx++)
            System.out.println(allFiles[idx]);
    }
}
```

This gives something similar to the following:

```
F:\JavaForRPGProgrammers\source\ch14\Listing14-9>java TestList
TestList.java
TestList.class
```

The File class represents either a directory or a file (a *stream* file as found in Windows or the IFS on AS/400). Which one depends on what name you give it in the constructor. Once you have a File object, there are many cool methods available in it, like isDirectory, exists, mkdir, and delete. The list method used is only valid if the File object represents a directory, and returns an array of names of the files in that directory. There is also a static listRoots method as of JDK 1.2.0 that returns all the root directories in the form of an array of File objects.

To subset the list, specify a FilenameFilter object on the list method call. You must create your own class that implements this interface, and code in an accept method that takes as input a directory name in the form of a File object, and a file name as a String. Java will call this method for each file in the directory, and you have to decide whether to return true, indicating the name should be considered part of the list. For example, to subset the list to retrieve all .java files, you need the class shown in Listing 14.10.

Listing 14.10: A File-Name Filter

```
import java.io.*;

public class JavaFileFilter implements FilenameFilter
{
    public boolean accept(File dir, String name)
    {
        return (name.endsWith(".java"));
    }
}
```

When calling the list method, the next step is to specify an instance of this class in the previous example:

```
String[] allFiles = listFiles.list(new JavaFileFilter());
```

Now, the previous TestList class gives a subset list:

```
F:\JavaForRPGProgrammers\source\ch14\Listing14-10>java TestList
TestList.java
JavaFileFilter.java
```

Here is a final tip regarding the File class: You will often write code that needs to retrieve the name of a file from a File object. There are many methods in the File object for this, but the ones you want are getName to get the unqualified file name, getParent to get just the path name, and getAbsolutePath to get the fully qualified file name.

How do I list drives?

As of JDK 1.2.0, there is now a way to retrieve a list of drives on your current system. This is done using the listRoots static method in the File class. This method returns an array of File objects, as shown in Listing 14.11.

Listing 14.11: Listing Drives Using File's listRoots Method

```java
import java.io.*;

public class TestListDrives
{
    public static void main(String args[])
    {
        File drives[] = File.listRoots();
        for (int idx=0; idx < drives.length; idx++)
            System.out.println(drives[idx]);
    }
}
```

This produces the following on our Windows NT system:

```
A:\
C:\
D:\
E:\
```

How do I create a directory?

To create a directory, you use the java.io.File class once again. The mkdir (make directory) method is the one you want. First, you must instantiate an instance of File that contains the fully qualified new directory name, as shown Listing 14.12.

Listing 14.12: How to Make a Directory Using File's mkdir Method

```java
import java.io.*;

public class TestMkDir
{
```

→

Listing 14.12: How to Make a Directory Using File's mkdir Method (continued)

```
public static void main(String args[])
{
    String currDir = System.getProperty("user.dir");
    String newDir = currDir + "\\newdir";
    File dirObject = new File(newDir);
    System.out.println("mkdir " + dirObject.getAbsolutePath());
    boolean ok = dirObject.mkdir();
    System.out.println("result was: " + ok);
}
}
```

This produces output similar to the following:

```
F:\JavaForRPGProgrammers\source\ch14\Listing14-12>java TestMkDir
mkdir F:\JavaForRPGProgrammers\source\ch14\Listing14-12\newdir
result was: true
```

How do I create or open a flat file and write to it?

Contrary to what you might expect, flat files (such as those on your workstation drives) are not created using the java.io.File class. (Well, there is a way as of JDK 1.2.0 using the createNewFile method in that class, but typically you won't use it.) Instead, you create a file by using the "zoo" of stream classes in the java.io package. This package contains numerous interfaces, classes, and class hierarchies for dealing with streams. (Streams are input or output devices that are read or written bytes at a time.) These classes are designed to be nested. They use one object to create, and another to get the desired input/output interface. Some examples are buffered or unbuffered, random or sequential, byte at a time or line at a time, and binary or text.

What you need to know for our purposes is that, to create a file, you will typically use the FilterOutputStream class. This passes the File object that was created with the file path and the intended file name into the constructor. If the file exists, however, it will be replaced. If you want to first check for the existence of a file, use the File object's exists method. If your intention is to write to the file a line at a time, nest the FileOutputStream object inside a PrintWriter object. That will access that class's println (print line) method, as shown in Listing 14.13.

Listing 14.13: Creating and Writing to a Stream File

```java
import java.io.*;

public class TestWriteFile
{
    public static void main(String args[])
    {
        File outFile =
          new File(System.getProperty("user.dir"),"myFile.tst");
        try
        {
          PrintWriter outFileStream =
            new PrintWriter(new FileOutputStream(outFile));
          outFileStream.println("test");
          outFileStream.flush();
          outFileStream.close();
        }
        catch (IOException exc)
        {
          System.out.println("Error opening file " +
           outFile.getAbsolutePath());
          System.exit(1);
        }
        System.exit(0);
    } // end main method
} // end TestWriteFile class
```

The next step is to write lines to this file with the `println` method. As you have seen all along, use the following `System.out.println`:

```java
outFileStream.println("Hey, I get it now!");
```

Because `PrintWriter` is a "buffered" stream, `println` does not immediately write to disk. For performance reasons, that happens only when its internal buffer is full. If this causes a problem, specify `true` as a second parameter to its constructor, or explicitly call its `flush` method after every call to `println`. Finally, you should make it a habit to call `close` when you are done with a file to unlock it and free its resources.

How do I read a flat file?

For both writing to an output flat file and reading from an input flat file, use the plethora of classes in the `java.io` package. We assume that you want the file to be read efficiently (buffered) and to be read as text, not binary. If that is the case, you open an existing file using a nested-class approach, as shown in Listing 14.14. Notice in the listing that the readLine method was used to read the file a line at a time.

Listing 14.14: Reading the Contents of a Stream File

```
import java.io.*;
public class TestReadFile
{
    public static void main(String args[])
    {
        File inFile = new File(
          System.getProperty("user.dir"),"TestReadFile.java");
        try
        {
          BufferedReader inFileStream =
              new BufferedReader(
                new InputStreamReader(
                  new FileInputStream(inFile) ) );
          boolean done = false;
          while (!done)
          {
            String line = inFileStream.readLine();
            if (line != null)
              System.out.println(line);
            else
              done = true;
          } // end while loop
          inFileStream.close();
        } catch (IOException exc) {
          System.out.println("Error reading " +
            inFile.getAbsolutePath());
        }
        System.exit(0);
    } // end main method
} // end class TestReadFile
```

How do I call another program or command?

While not heartily recommended for portable applications, there are times when you might find it necessary to invoke a local program object on your Windows system. You learned earlier in this chapter about using JNI for calling a DLL or service-program entry point, but sometimes you want to run an executable, not call a DLL function. There is a way to do this in Java that uses the Runtime class in the java.lang package. This class represents your Java runtime system. To get an instance of this class, code `Runtime.getRuntime()`. This returns an object of type `Runtime`, appropriately enough.

You will find a number of useful features in this class for performing functions such as tracing calls, querying available memory, and forcing the garbage collector to run. This is also the class where you find the `exec` method, which you can use to execute other programs or commands. It is, then, roughly equivalent to the command analyzer API (`QCMDEXEC`) on the AS/400. There are actually a number of versions of `exec`, but typically you need only the one that takes one string, which contains the command and its parameters.

This discussion is really only for calling executables on clients from Java running on clients. While it can be used by Java running on the AS/400 to call a CL command, you would only consider doing so if you were concerned about portability to other server platforms. The reason we say this is that the AS/400 Toolbox for Java provides a much richer way to do this, via its program-call class, which includes support for parameter updates and easy retrieval of logged messages. Indeed, the Toolbox has *PCML* (*Program Call Markup Language*) to simplify this even more. In fact, you can now even use this to access procedures in a service program, so the JNI discussion earlier was really only applicable to non-AS/400 Java code. The other benefit of using the Toolbox is that your Java code can run either on the AS/400 or remotely from any client. However, if you are interested in how to call non-AS/400 executables, read on.

The `exec` method in `Runtime` returns an object of type `Process` for managing the running command. The command will be started as soon as you use the `exec` method, but there are methods in the returned `Process` object you can use to wait for the command to finish running and to query its returned value. One such method gets the return code the command specifies when it exits. Also, you will probably want to capture and query any messages it issues to standard output or standard error. `Process` has methods for retrieving these as well.

You can use the ready-made class in Listing 14.15 to run a given command string. It runs the command and captures its standard output and standard error lines as `Strings` in a `Vector` object, which you can subsequently cycle through.

Listing 14.15: A Class for Running Any Local Executable and Capturing Messages

```java
import java.util.*; // for Vector
import java.io.*;
public class TestRunCmd
{
    Vector output = new Vector();

    public boolean runCmd(String cmd)
    {
        boolean ok = true;
        System.out.println(cmd);
        Process process;
        try {
            process = Runtime.getRuntime().exec(cmd);
        } catch (IOException exc) {
            System.out.println("Error running command: " + cmd);
            return false;
        }
        String line;
        // capture standard error
        DataInputStream err =
            new DataInputStream(process.getErrorStream());
        BufferedReader berr =
            new BufferedReader(new InputStreamReader(err));
        try {
            while ((line = berr.readLine()) != null)
                output.addElement(line);
        } catch(IOException exc) {}
        // capture standard output
        DataInputStream in =
            new DataInputStream(process.getInputStream());
        BufferedReader bin =
            new BufferedReader(new InputStreamReader(in));
        try {
            while ((line = bin.readLine()) != null)
                output.addElement(line);
            int rc = process.waitFor();
        } catch(Exception exc) {}
        return ok;
    } // end runCmd method
    public void processOutput()
    {
        if (!output.isEmpty())
        {
            for (int idx = 0; idx < output.size(); idx++)
                System.out.println((String)output.elementAt(idx));
            output.removeAllElements();
        }
    }
} // end class TestRunCmd
```

The main method included for testing this is as follows:

```
public static void main(String args[])
{
    if (args.length != 1)
      System.out.println("Syntax: TestRunCmd command-to-run");
    else
      {
        TestRunCmd me = new TestRunCmd();
        if (me.runCmd(args[0]))
          me.processOutput();
      }
} // end main method
```

This takes any command as a parameter and executes it from Java. If you try the following, the Windows Notepad editor will come up:

```
java TestRunCmd notepad
```

Try the following to see the javac compiler compile the file:

```
java TestRunCmd "javac TestRunCmd.java"
```

If there are errors (try making some), you will see them written out to the console.

We went back to the PDM options application discussed in Chapter 13, in the PDMOptionsThreaded directory, and used the new TestRunCmd class to process the Print button there. We were already printing the PDM options to a local file, so we subsequently used this class to run the command "CODEEDIT filename /C LP_PRINT" on that file. This opened the CODE/400 editor on the file and brought up the print dialog so that we could select a printer and print the list.

How do I save and restore user-profile information?

In your programs, you will probably often want to record user-profile information, such as preferences. To do this in Java, use a class named Properties from the java.util package. The Properties class is a handy utility class for storing key/value pairs, which Java refers to as *properties*. The Properties class extends the Hashtable class, adding the methods setProperty and getProperty. These just call their parents' put and get methods, but are defined to accept String values, for convenience (since no casting is required). It also adds methods for saving the contents to disk and reading them back from disk.

Properties is a table of Strings that can hold any information you want to put in it. Each String object is indexed in the table using another String value for the key. So, you might store information like this about a user:

Name (Key)	Value
"LIBRARY"	"MYLIB"
"NUMBER"	"0011001"

These might represent, for example, the values previously entered into entry fields. That will allow you to default these entry fields with the same values on the next use of your application.

To store this information, create an instance of the Properties class and use the setProperty method, like this:

```
Properties profile = new Properties();
profile.setProperty("LIBRARY", libraryEntryField.getText());
profile.setProperty("NUMBER", numberEntryField.getText());
```

At this point, the information only exists in memory. To save it to a local flat file, use the store method. (JDK 1.1.x used a save method, but this is deprecated now.) Specify a FileOutputStream object for the file to save it to and a header String to be placed as the first line in the file for documentation. We have already discussed how to create or replace an output flat file as follows:

```
File outFile = new File("c:\\", "preferences.ini");
try {
  profile.store(new FileOutputStream(outFile), "User Preferences");
} catch (Exception exc) {
  System.out.println("Error saving profile: " + exc.getMessage());
}
```

You can be as creative as you want to be with the file name and extension. Some common extensions are `.dat`, `.txt`, `.ini`, and `.prf`, but the choice is yours.

When saving to a local file, it is often safe to assume that there is only one user per workstation, so any file name will do. However, if you decide to store the files on a common server, you should probably name the file with the user's ID.

Now that you have this information saved, you need to know how to read it in again. That's a piece of cake. Define a `Properties` object and use its `load` method, specifying a `FileInputStream` as a parameter. This will populate the `Properties` object from disk, after which you can use the `getProperty` method to read individual values from it. Here is an example:

```
Properties profile = new Properties();
try {
  File inFile = new File("c:\\", "preferences.ini");
  profile.load(new FileInputStream(inFile));
  String libName = profile.getProperty("LIBRARY","QGPL");
  String number = profile.getProperty("NUMBER");
} catch (Exception exc) {}
```

The `getProperty` method allows an optional second parameter to return if the asked-for property does not exist. Again, you ask for a property by passing the key value for that property, and get back the value for that property.

When defining a `Properties` object, you can also specify another `Properties` object in the constructor. Here is an example:

```
new Properties(defaultProperties);
```

The values in the other object are used as defaults that "prime" the new object. This is a convenient way to specify default values for those entries not found in the file on disk.

You have seen the `Properties` class before. Recall that Chapter 13 mentions that the JDBC `getConnection` method allows you to specify a `Properties` object as input for giving all the property values. Although we didn't show it, we also used `Properties` in the PDM Options GUI application in Chapter 12. The `PDMOptionsWindow` class uses this to save the name of the last edited PDM options file, and to restore it and use it as the default on subsequent runs of the application.

JAVABEANS

Now that you have seen examples of some common programming situations in Java, let's turn to some common Java-related terms you might have heard. For example, can you define *JavaBeans*? If not, don't be afraid that you don't know beans! JavaBeans are not very mysterious; they are simply "dressed up" Java classes. In other words, they are Java classes that follow a few conventions and, in some cases, add a little functionality to a typical class. Their purpose is to make it easier for tools like VisualAge for Java to work with a class.

As you will see, JavaBeans are classes that have a default constructor, *properties* (any value settable by setXXX or gettable by getXXX), and *methods* (any non-get/set method defined as public). In addition, beans can have *bound properties* (monitorable for changes) and *events* (monitorable triggers, such as a button pressed or an inventory threshold exceeded). Further, your bean classes can also supply property editors and customizers that tools will launch when programmers work with your beans.

Properties

Java is all about reuse. One way to get reuse is to design good base classes that can easily be extended, as you have seen from Chapter 9 on. Another way—just as important and needed—is to design a class that can be adapted easily by setting variable values. For example, imagine writing a GUI class that is a drop-down list showing all the fields from a particular database file, record, and field. To tailor this for another database, you could write a new class that extends the first and overrides this information. Alternatively, you could simply supply methods to set the name of the file, record, and field to list from.

In many cases, you can design highly adaptable classes simply by supplying methods to change key information. By "variablizing," you can make a class that is highly reusable in many situations. The "variables" are probably actual instance variables, but you usually mark them as private, and supply methods to set and get them. So, you might have methods named setDatabaseName and getDatabaseName, for example. These variables are called "properties" in JavaBeans. Simply supplying get and set methods makes the class JavaBean-compliant.

In VisualAge for Java and other tools, when you drop a class onto the GUI Builder window, an instance of the class is created (using the default constructor), and you can subsequently double-click on that object to see and set its properties. The property sheets simply list all getXXX methods, but without the "get" part. For example, you might see a property named databaseName on this sheet. You would be allowed to directly edit those values that have a corresponding setXXX method. When you do change a property value, most tools generate a call to setXXX with your value as the parameter. Note that if your property is a boolean value, you should name the method isXXX instead of getXXX, as in isEnabled, isVisible, or isConnected.

Sometimes your property is actually a list, not a single value. For example, your Department class might have an Employee property that is, internally, an array of employees. In this case, your set and get methods will require an integer index value as a parameter indicating which employee to set or get (an index into the list). These types of properties are known as *indexed properties*.

One last point about properties: They can be stored internally as private instance variables, or they can be computed on the fly. Because you always access them by getXXX and setXXX, what happens under the covers is not important. So, for example, a getPay method might compute the pay property from salary and payPeriod variables.

Listing 14.16 shows a simple JavaBean class that records the current amount of stock in inventory. The class is a JavaBean because it has a default constructor and set and get methods, meaning it has properties (specifically, it has one inStock property). It also has other public methods that users of the bean can call, namely incrementInStock and decrementInStock.

Listing 14.16: A Simple JavaBean-Compliant Class for Tracking Inventory Stock

```
public class Inventory
{
    protected int inStock = 0;
    protected static final int INITIAL_STOCK = 100;

    public Inventory()
    {
        inStock = INITIAL_STOCK;
    }

    public int getInStock()
    {
        return inStock;
    }

    public void setInStock(int newInStock)
    {
        inStock = newInStock;
        if (inStock < 0)
```

Listing 14.16: A Simple JavaBean-Compliant Class for Tracking Inventory Stock (continued)

```
            inStock = 0;
        return;
    }

    public int incrementInStock(int increment)
    {
        setInStock(inStock + increment);
        return inStock;
    }

    public int decrementInStock(int decrement)
    {
        setInStock(inStock - decrement);
        return inStock;
    }
}
```

We wrote a GUI class InventoryWindow to use and test this Inventory bean, which you can see on the CD-ROM. It is quite straightforward. When you run it, you will see something like Figure 14.2.

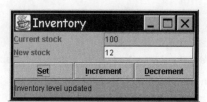

Figure 14.2: A GUI window to test the Inventory bean

There is a problem with the GUI application, however. It does not update the value displayed for "Current stock" after you make changes. You can fix this by monitoring for changes to the inStock property and reflecting the new value in the window.

Bound properties

So, a default constructor and proper use of get and set methods makes your class a bean. That's easy enough. However, if you want to go further, you can, with some additional coding using classes in the java.beans package. For example, if you want to allow other classes to monitor for changes in one of your properties, you can make that property a *bound property*. To do this, you need to supply a method for others to call to register their interest in being notified. You will record every interested object in an array, and when the setXXX method is called, you walk the array and call a method in each of the objects to tell it about the change. Of course, you are going to have to define an interface that callers implement, so you can define the array to be of that type, and to define the method, you will call back to when the property changes.

Luckily, much of this work is done for you. The `java.beans` package has an interface named `PropertyChangeListener`, which defines one method named `propertyChanged`. Further, there is a class supplied for easily recording the references of callers who register: `PropertyChangeSupport`, which has two methods `addPropertyChangeListener` and `removePropertyChangeListener`. Both take an object that implements the `PropertyChangeListener` interface. So, to turn a property into a bound property, follow these steps:

1. Declare an instance variable of type `PropertyChangeSupport` and instantiate it, passing `this` as the parameter.

2. Supply methods for callers to register and un-register their interest. These should be named `addPropertyChangeListener` and `removePropertyChangeListener`, and take as a parameter an object of type `PropertyChangeListener`. These will call the appropriate methods in the `PropertyChangeSupport` object.

3. Change the `set` method to call the `propertyChanged` method on each registered object. This is easy to do using the `firePropertyChange` method in the `PropertyChangeSupport` object. The `firePropertyChange` method requires you to give a name to your property, in the form of a string. This is necessary in case you have multiple bound properties in one bean; registered listeners need to be able to decide which property changed. You also have to pass both the old and the new values, as it will only call listeners if the value actually changes.

Let's put this to work by changing the `Inventory` class to make `inStock` a bound property, as shown in Listing 14.17 (only the new or changed methods are shown).

Listing 14.17: Updating the Inventory Bean to Support a Bound Property

```
import java.beans.*;
public class Inventory
{
```

Listing 14.17: Updating the Inventory Bean to Support a Bound Property (continued)

```java
        protected int inStock = 0;
        protected static final int INITIAL_STOCK = 100;
        protected PropertyChangeSupport listeners =
          new PropertyChangeSupport(this);

        public void addPropertyChangeListener(
            PropertyChangeListener listener)
        {
            listeners.addPropertyChangeListener(listener);
        }
        public void removePropertyChangeListener(
            PropertyChangeListener listener)
        {
            listeners.removePropertyChangeListener(listener);
        }
        public void setInStock(int newInStock)
        {
            int oldValue = inStock;
            inStock = newInStock;
            if (inStock < 0)
              inStock = 0;
            listeners.firePropertyChange(
              "inStock",oldValue,inStock);
            return;
        }
    }
```

Since the incrementInStock and decrementInStock methods call setInStock, as you saw in Listing 14.16, they too will fire a property-change event. Now you have a bound property, so users of this bean can call the addPropertyChangeListener method to be informed of changes to the inStock property. How are they informed? Well, to call the method they must implement the PropertyChangeListener interface and so supply a propertyChange method, which will get called when the inStock property changes. They must also call addPropertyChangeListener(this) on their Inventory object to register interest.

Their propertyChanged method defines a parameter object of type PropertyChange Event, which Java creates for you when you call the firePropertyChange method. This event object has the methods getPropertyName, getOldValue, and getNewValue. The first returns the inStock property name, while the latter two return the old and new values for that property. However, since the property is a primitive int type, getNewValue returns an Integer object. To see this in action, look at the revised InventoryWindow class in the Listing14-17 directory on the CD-ROM. In it, we coded all this so that we can update the value of the inventory displayed in the window. Here is what our propertyChange method looks like:

```
public void propertyChange(PropertyChangeEvent evt)
{
    if (evt.getPropertyName().equals("inStock"))
        currStock.setText(((Integer)evt.getNewValue()).toString());
}
```

The variable currStock is a non-editable JTextField part that shows the current stock level. When you run the window now, this value is kept up-to-date, as shown in Figure 14.3.

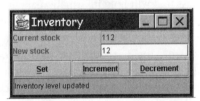

*Figure 14.3: An updated GUI window
that tracks changes in inventory level*

Although very rarely used, bound properties can also be defined as *constrained properties*, which are properties whose listeners can "veto" or reject the change. These are coded using add/removeVetoableChangeListener methods and the VetoableChange Listener interface, and the VetoableChangeSupport class. Listeners reject a change by throwing an agreed-upon exception, which your bean must monitor for and handle by undoing the change.

Events

Bound properties are really a special form of events. An *event* is something that happens during the life of a bean, in which other classes might be interested. Like a bound property, other classes register their interest in an event and are called back when that event happens. You have complete freedom in deciding what events you might like to support. You have seen events already, in GUI programming in Chapter 12. For example, a JButton object will fire an actionPerformed event when the user clicks on the button.

Events are usually associated with GUIs, and reflect something that a user can do. They are a way to inform interested code about a user-initiated event. However, you can define events for anything. For example, let's enhance the Inventory bean to fire an event when the stock gets below a given threshold property, which defaults to 10, but can also be set by callers. To create an event from scratch like this, you must do the following:

1. Define an interface that callers can implement, such as ThreshholdListener-Interface, which contains a method to be called when the event is fired. We name ours threshholdExceeded. By convention, all event-listener interfaces should be defined to extend the EventListener interface in java.util. This is an empty interface whose only role is to tag event interfaces so that tools can identify these interfaces as "event interfaces."

2. Define an event class that will hold information about the event, and which an object of that event will be passed as a parameter to the interface call-back method. We name our event class ThreshholdEvent, and supply methods in it named getThreshholdValue, getOldValue, and getNewValue. By convention, all non-GUI event classes extend EventObject in package java.util and require the object that fires the event as a parameter to the constructor. This is subsequently retrievable by calling getSource.

3. Supply addXXXListener and removeXXXListener methods in the class, which take an object that implements XXXListener, and records (or removes) that object in a list. Our methods are named addThreshholdListener and removeThreshholdListener, and they take a ThreshholdListener object as a parameter.

4. Change the appropriate code in the bean to check for the event happening. When it does, walk the list of registered listeners and call the call-back method (threshholdExceeded) in each one. This requires the creation of an instance of the event (ThreshholdEvent) to pass to the call-back method as a parameter.

Tedious, but not too difficult. Let's start with the event class, shown in Listing 14.18.

Listing 14.18: A New Event Class for Threshold-Exceeded Events

```
import java.util.*;

public class ThreshholdEvent extends EventObject
   {
```

```
    protected int threshholdValue, oldValue, newValue;

    public ThreshholdEvent(Object source, int threshholdValue,
                           int oldValue, int newValue)
    {
        super(source);
        this.threshholdValue = threshholdValue;
        this.oldValue = oldValue;
        this.newValue = newValue;
    }
    public int getThreshholdValue()
    {
        return threshholdValue;
    }
    public int getOldValue()
    {
        return oldValue;
    }
    public int getNewValue()
    {
        return newValue;
    }
}
```

Here is the new interface that listeners must implement:

```
public interface ThreshholdListener extends java.util.EventListener
{
    public void threshholdExceeded(ThreshholdEvent evt);
}
```

Finally, the changes to the Inventory bean class are shown in Listing 14.19 (again, only changes are shown).

Listing 14.19: The Updated Inventory Bean with Support for Threshold Events

```
import java.beans.*;
import java.util.*;
public class Inventory
{
    // ...
    protected int threshhold = 10;
    protected Vector eventListeners = new Vector();

    public synchronized void addThreshholdListener(
```

Listing 14.19: The Updated Inventory Bean with Support for Threshold Events (continued)

```java
      ThreshholdListener listener)
{
    eventListeners.addElement(listener);
}
public synchronized void removeThreshholdListener(
  PropertyChangeListener listener)
{
    eventListeners.removeElement(listener);
}
protected void fireThreshholdEvent(int oldValue)
{
    ThreshholdEvent event = new ThreshholdEvent(
      this,oldValue,inStock,threshhold);
    ThreshholdListener listener;
    for (int idx=0; idx < eventListeners.size(); idx++)
    {
        listener = (ThreshholdListener)
          eventListeners.elementAt(idx);
        listener.threshholdExceeded(event);
    }
}
public int getThreshhold()
{
    return threshhold;
}
public void setThreshhold(int newThreshhold)
{
    threshhold = newThreshhold;
}
public void setInStock(int newInStock)
{
    // ... same ...
    if (inStock < threshhold)
      fireThreshholdEvent(oldValue);
    return;
}
```

Notice the code does its own tracking of registered event-listeners, using a simple Vector. The add and remove methods simply use the addElement and removeElement methods of the Vector class. These methods had to be made synchronized to ensure they work properly in a threaded environment. The threshhold value is made into a property so that callers can query and change it. Finally, the setInStock method now has code at the end to check if the inventory is below the threshold value; if so, it fires the event. This is done by calling the helper method fireThreshholdEvent, which walks the list of registered listeners and, for each one, calls the threshholdExceeded method dictated by the interface. A ThreshholdEvent object is created to pass to that method.

To test this, we updated the InventoryWindow class to implement the ThreshholdListener interface, call the addThreshholdListener method on the Inventory object, and code the threshholdExceeded method. In that method, we used JOptionPane.showMessageDialog to display a warning message to the user, as shown in Figure 14.4. The event we invented supports multiple listeners, which is called a *multi-cast event*. You could support a single listener only, which is known as a *unicast event*.

Figure 14.4: The updated GUI window that issues a warning for threshold events

Serializing beans

One last thing you should do in the bean class is make it serializable. This is because many tools support the user changing a bean instances' properties by serializing the bean to disk. This is very easily done, as shown in Listing 14.20.

Listing 14.20: The Updated Inventory Bean, Now Serializable

```
public class Inventory implements java.io.Serializable
{
    protected int inStock = 0;
    protected static final int INITIAL_STOCK = 100;
    transient protected PropertyChangeSupport listeners =
      new PropertyChangeSupport(this);
    protected int threshhold = 10;
    transient protected Vector eventListeners = new Vector();

    // ... same ...
```

⟶

Listing 14.20: The Updated Inventory Bean, Now Serializable (continued)

```
public void addPropertyChangeListener(
  PropertyChangeListener listener)
{
    if (listeners == null)
      listeners = new PropertyChangeSupport(this);
    listeners.addPropertyChangeListener(listener);
}
public synchronized void addThreshholdListener(
  ThreshholdListener listener)
{
    if (eventListeners == null)
      eventListeners = new Vector();
    eventListeners.addElement(listener);
}
}
```

All you have to do is implement `Serializable`, but the example also flags instance variables that store the property and event listeners as `transient`, since it makes no sense to save them between sessions. (You can't assume those listener objects will exist tomorrow or on a different system.) Because of this, though, these variables will be `null` after the bean is restored from disk, so you have to check for this in each of the add methods, and create new objects, if necessary.

For testing, we updated the `InventoryWindow` class in the `Listing14-20` directory on the CD-ROM to have two new buttons: Save and Restore, as shown in Figure 14.5. These will serialize the `Inventory` bean to disk and restore it from disk, respectively.

Figure 14.5: The updated GUI window that supports saving and restoring the `Inventory` bean

The BeanInfo class

Once you have a beautiful JavaBean created, you make it available for users. They will usually use it in a Java tool such as VisualAge for Java. These tools use a Java-supplied process called *introspection*, using the `getBeanInfo` method in the `java.beans.Introspector` class, to get a `BeanInfo` object containing information about the bean. This object includes lists of its public methods, properties, bound properties, constrained properties, and events. It deduces the property names from the get/set method names,

the bound properties from the existence of add/removeProperty
ChangeListener methods, the constrained properties from the existence of
add/removeVetoableChangeListener methods, and events from the existence of
add/removeXXXListener methods.

If you want to refine this process, you can supply your own explicit BeanInfo class,
which must have the same name as your bean class, but with BeanInfo appended. This
class will extend the SimpleBeanInfo class in java.beans, and you can implement as
many of the methods as you want from that class. Every method shown in Table 14.2 is
designed to give tools more information, which is often reflected in the tool's UI to subsequently help developers who are writing code that uses the bean.

Table 14.2: Methods in the BeanInfo Class

Method	Description
getBeanDescriptor	Returns a BeanDescriptor object, which contains two methods: getBeanClass and getCustomizerClass. The latter is a class you can supply that will be launched by tools when users double-click on your bean. This is usually a GUI window for setting the properties. Without this, tools will show a standard property-sheet editor.
getDefaultEventIndex	An index into EventSetDescriptors of the most common event. Tools can display this event more prominently.
getDefaultPropertyIndex	An index into PropertyDescriptors of the most common property. Tools can display this property more prominently.
getEventSetDescriptors	An array of EventSetDescriptor objects, one per event supported by this bean. The EventSetDescriptor class describes each event with methods like getListenerType to get the listener interface for this event.
getIcon	Returns an ImageIcon object that contains a .gif file to show for this bean when tools display it.
getMethodDescriptors	Returns an array of MethodDescriptor objects describing each method to be exposed to users. Use this if you only want to expose a subset of the public methods.

If you decide to supply a BeanInfo class, you don't have to supply all these methods.
Whatever you don't supply will be queried via introspection. Clearly, a BeanInfo class is

not necessary for most in-house beans, but if you intend to sell or publicly distribute a bean, it is a nice touch to supply one. However, only someone who enjoys pain would write this by hand, versus using a tool like VisualAge for Java to generate it.

Beans and tools

Let's find out what a bean looks like when used in VisualAge for Java, version 3.5.3. In Figure 14.6, we have added an instance of the bean to the Visual Composition Editor (VCE) and double-clicked on it to get the property sheet. As you can see, the properties are displayed and editable.

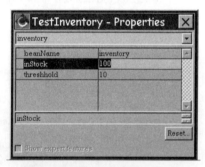

What's great about tools like VisualAge is that they make it easy to create applications by linking events from one bean to methods from another (the firing of that event causes the method to be called), or by linking the bound properties of one bean to the properties of another (changes in the source property cause changes in the target property).

Figure 14.6: The VisualAge for Java property sheet for the Inventory bean

For example, we re-created the test window in VisualAge for Java's VCE, and linked the `actionPerformed` events of the buttons to the appropriate methods in the `Inventory` bean, getting the parameter from the entry field. We also linked the `Inventory` bean's `inStock` property to the top entry field's `text` property, such that any change in the former is automatically displayed in the latter. This was all done visually, with no coding on our part, although the code produced is very similar to what we coded by hand.

Another great benefit of tools like VisualAge is the tremendous help they offer in creating and refining JavaBeans. For example, Figure 14.7 shows the BeanInfo window for the `Inventory` bean. Notice how easy it is to work with all the properties, events, and methods. The *P*, *E*, and *M* superscripts identify which is which, and the *R*, *W*, and *B* superscripts identify readable, writable and bound properties, respectively. You can change any attribute of a property by simply editing the values at the bottom of the page. The code is updated automatically. Also, a `BeanInfo` class is created for you.

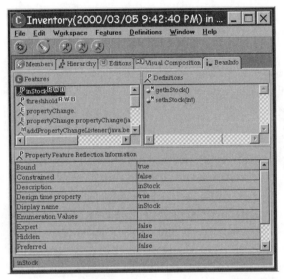

Figure 14.7: The VisualAge for Java BeanInfo window

Rather than doing all the work we did to define properties and events, we could have just used this window. For example, clicking on the P button on the toolbar launches a SmartGuide for creating a new property, as shown in Figure 14.8. You have to admit, this is much easier than coding this stuff by hand!

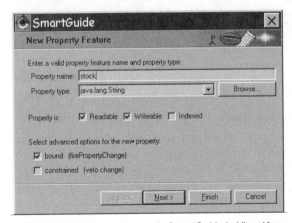

Figure 14.8: Create a property SmartGuide in VisualAge for Java

More beans

To find JavaBeans, go to the VisualAge Developer Domain at *www.ibm.com/software/ad/vadd*. This contains many third-party beans for sale. For free beans, go to IBM's alphaworks Web site, at *www.ibm.com/alphaworks* and follow the links for AlphaBeans. For more technical information on JavaBeans, go to Sun's Web page dedicated to them, at *www.java.sun.com/beans*.

Now you know beans!

NEXT STEPS: OF SERVLETS, JSPS, EJBS, AND MORE

The world of Java is exploding at an unprecedented rate. You have been given a very brief tour of the core Java language as of JSDK 1.4.0. With this under your belt, you can move on to some of the more exciting uses of Java beyond beans, applications, and applets. This includes Java servlets, JavaServer Pages and Enterprise JavaBeans. These are not part of the Standard Edition JSDK, but rather the Enterprise Edition JSDK, also known as *J2EE*. You do not download this, but instead you get or buy a platform that implements it. WebSphere Application Server is one such platform. It offers the runtime classes and implementations of the runtime frameworks for these and the other components that define the J2EE.

At a minimum, servlets and JSPs are part of your future. You will need to learn them. However, they beyond the scope of this book. Please do continue your Java journey, though, and get books on the elements of J2EE. We are confident that you are now very well-positioned to pick up any Java book and easily read and understand it. Whatever you do, do not stop learning now!

SUMMARY

This "wrap up" chapter, briefly covers the following topics:

- Inner classes

- Static initializers

- The Java Native Interface

- Java Remote Method Invocation

- Serializing objects

- The packages in the JSDK, Standard Edition

- Working with local stream files and file system

- JavaBeans

Thanks for coming along for the ride! We are big believers in Java as a single technology that can span all your information technology requirements—from personal devices to rich GUIs to mission-critical enterprise applications. We are big believers in RPG, too, especially RPG IV. However, eventually, Java will play some role in all your new applications.

Java is changing the face and impressions of OS/400—and now you will be there, putting your new Java skills and enthusiasm to work! Never forget, though, that your RPG "heritage" is your strength, and knowing both RPG and Java is your biggest asset. Now it's time to talk to your manager about that raise!

APPENDIX

USING JAVA ON THE AS/400

This appendix is a brief tour of getting, installing, and using Java on OS/400. You might start your Java journey on your personal computer, or by adding a GUI to your existing OS/400 applications. However, OS/400 is committed to being a first-class Java platform based on its own merits, so you can run Java applications on OS/400 itself. Because Java is so portable, there are not too many special instructions for doing this, but the following additional information will give you a leg up.

Using Java on OS/400 involves at least a passing knowledge of the following:

- *AS/400 Developer Kit for Java* (the *JDK*)

- *Integrated File System* (*IFS*), where Java files live and run on the AS/400

- *QShell Interpreter*, the UNIX shell required for working with the JDK commands

- *AS/400 Toolbox for Java*, a set of pure Java classes for accessing OS/400 resources from OS/400 Java or client Java

- *VisualAge for Java*, or its follow-on; IBM's premier development product for Java

Each of these is covered in the following sections, except for VisualAge for Java, which at the time of this writing was on the brink of a major new generation. Further, if you decide to use Java servlets and JavaServer Pages, you need to read up on WebSphere Application Server and the IBM HTTP Server. As of V4R3, everything you need to run servlets and JSPs is built into OS/400.

You might also wish to explore Enterprise JavaBeans, available with the Advanced edition of WebSphere Application Server. This is not part of the base operating system, but an optional product. Beyond what has been covered in the rest of this book, we leave the topic of servlets, JSPs and Enterprise JavaBeans for your own research. You can start at *www.ibm.com/iseries/websphere*.

INSTALLING THE COMPONENTS

Table A.1 shows the information for installing the various pieces, as of Version 4. Note that versions after V4 will have a different number than 5769, such as 5722 for Version 5.

Table A.1: Installation Information for OS/400 Java and Related Products

Product	Product Number	Notes
AS/400 Developer Kit for Java	5769JV1	You can choose from multiple JDKs to install and use. Each is a different option.
Qshell Interpreter	5769SS1, Option 30	
AS/400 Toolbox for Java	5769JC1	

To find out if these products are installed, use GO LICPGM, and select F11 after finding the products in the list. They will show *COMPATIBLE in the Installed Status field. If they are not in this status, use option 1 to install them. If they are on the list, use RSTLICPGM to install them from the OS/400 CD-ROM.

THE AS/400 DEVELOPER KIT FOR JAVA

As mentioned in Chapter 1, the JDK was originally written for Sun Solaris and Microsoft Windows operating systems by Sun Microsystems. IBM licenses the JDK, and the IBM Hursley, England laboratory ports it to all operating systems. The OS/400 team in Rochester, Minnesota then pushes it deep into the operating system to get great performance. Because the JDK is standard, and by the terms of the licensing agreement, IBM and others can only add to it, not take away from it, you will find that all the standard JDK commands are available on OS/400. These include java, javac, javap, javadoc, and jar, among others.

Of course, these are not the standard OS/400-style command names that you are used to. Furthermore, they have to work on Java source files and class files that are ASCII-based, not EBCDIC-based as your RPG source and programs are. This is because the goal is to be able to run any Java class file from anywhere without changing or even recompiling it. Enabling all this—that is, making OS/400 Java support as industry-standard as possible—requires that the JDK be based not in the library/file native file system, but rather on the Integrated File System.

Using the Integrated File System and QShell Interpreter

RPG development uses the native OS/400 file system, which involves libraries inside QSYS, files and other objects inside libraries, and members inside files. Files, and hence their members, are either data files (physical file or logical file) or source files (Source Physical Files). There are other file types, too, like display files and printer files. The underlying collating sequence is EBCDIC, which differs from the ASCII sequence used on most other operating systems (except for OS/390, which is also EBCDIC-based).

The Integrated File System (IFS) is an alternative to the native file system. It is actually multiple file systems in one, but the one you are most interested in is the "root." This is very similar to the file system on Windows. It has directories that can contain other directories and stream files, much like Windows. Stream files are simply flat files that contain a sequence of bytes, with no record partitioning and no relational database constructs—just like files on Windows.

The highest-level directory, the root, is designated by a single forward slash: /. Unlike Windows, the IFS uses a forward slash for path names, not a backward slash. So, if you have a file named HelloWorld.class in directory myJava which is in directory Phil, the fully qualified path name is /Phil/myJava/HelloWorld.class. Note that directory and file names are case-tolerant in the IFS, as with RPG IV. However, all names in Java commands are case-sensitive, as always. If a given path name does not start with a forward slash, then it is "relative" to the current directory.

Prior to Java coming along in V4R2, you could only work with the IFS through OS/400 CL commands. For example, to create a directory, you would use the CRTDIR command, like this:

```
CRTDIR DIR('/Phil')
CRTDIR DIR('/Phil/myJava')
```

You have to create the parent directory before creating the child directory. Each job has a "current directory" that can be determined by the CL command DSPCURDIR, and changed by CHGCURDIR or CHDDIR. To list files and work with them in a given directory, you would use the command WRKLNK. To see all the IFS CL commands, you would type GO FILESYS.

These CL commands are still of value. For example, the first thing you need to do is create a directory for your Java files. First, check to see if the administrator has created one for you in \home\UserID, where *UserID* is your user ID. Use WRKLNK to look for this directory. If one doesn't exist, use CRTDIR to create it. Then, to always make it your default current directory, use CHGPRF (Change Profile) and the HOMEDIR parameter, like this:

```
CHGPRF HOMEDIR('/Phil/myJava')
```

Of course, you might need to get the system operator to do this for you if your profile lacks the necessary authority.

Once you have a directory, and have made it your current directory, you can use the new (as of V4R2) QShell Interpreter. To start it, use the CL command STRQSH or QSHELL. This puts you in a command shell where you can enter standard UNIX commands, instead of OS/400 CL-style commands. This will be more comfortable if you are familiar with UNIX. It is also where you enter the familiar JDK commands, as you'll soon see.

Table A.2 lists some of the common commands you might do on Windows, and their equivalent in IFS—both the CL version and the QShell version. This little table should be enough to get you going with IFS. More detailed information is available online at the iSeries information center.

Table A.2: Windows, IFS CL, and Qshell Commands

Command	Windows	CL	QShell
Show current directory name	cd (no parameters)	DSPCURDIR	pwd ("present working directory")
Change current directory name	cd path or \path	CHGCURDIR	cd path or /path
Make a directory	md or mkdir	CRTDIR	mkdir
Delete a directory	rd or rmdir	RMVDIR	rmdir
Rename a directory	rename		
Display or change directory owner	Windows explorer		chown
Display or change directory authority	attrib	DSPAUT, CHGAUT	chgrp, chmod
List files in directory	dir	WRKLNK	ls
Display file contents	type		pr, cat, tail, head
Copy a file	copy	COPY	cp
Move a file	move	MOVE	mv
Delete a file	erase	WRKLNK	rm
Rename a file	rename	RENAME	mv
Display or change file owner	Windows explorer	WRKOBJOWN	chown
Display or change file authority	attrib	DSPAUT, CHGAUT	chgrp, chmod
Create link		ADDLNK	ln
Define an alias (shortcut) command			alias
Exit shell or prompt	exit		F3
Run CL command			system
Search files for a string			grep

Table A.2: Windows, IFS CL, and Qshell Commands (cont)

Command	Windows	CL	QShell
Set environment variable	set	WRKENVVAR	export
Display commands previously entered			history
Compress/uncompress files	WINZIP or jar		tar/untar or jar
Get online help for a command	help		man

Working with Java on OS/400

Now that some of the basics are out of the way, it's time to focus on working with Java. To run a Java class on OS/400, you enter the QShell Interpreter, ensure you are in the directory containing the Java class file, and then run it using the java command. It's that simple. All the JDK commands are there and are identical to their Windows counterparts—well, actually their UNIX counterparts, but other than remembering to use a forward slash instead of a backslash for path names, it is the same.

So, the first order of business is to get a Java class to run. You have two choices for doing that: either create the .class file using javac on Windows (say) and copy it to the OS/400 IFS, or copy the .java source file from Windows (say) and use javac on OS/400 to create it. Note that in either case, development of Java is done on a workstation running Windows (say) and Java development tools like VisualAge for Java. You don't use the old workhorses PDM and SEU to create Java applications because these tools work on EBCDIC-based native file system objects, and Java is a new breed of ASCII-based IFS objects. If you really are addicted to minimalist green-screen tools, you could use SEU to edit a source member containing Java, and then use CPYTOSTMF (*Copy To Stream File*) to copy that member to an IFS file.

So, how do you get your .java or .class files from Windows to OS/400 IFS? A few options are listed in Table A.3.

Table A.3: Options for Copying Java Files to OS/400 IFS	
Option	Description
Use ftp (File Transfer Protocol)	If your TCP/IP configuration allows this, using ftp from the Windows command line is an easy way to copy any file to OS/400.
Use a mapped drive	Using Windows Explorer, map a network drive to your system and simply use the Windows copy command to copy any file to OS/400 via the mapped drive.
Use CODE/400	If you use CODE/400 anyway for your RPG, CL, and DDS programming (and you should!), it has support under File for saving source to an IFS file and support under Actions for exporting any file to the IFS.
Use VisualAge for Java	The Enterprise Toolkit for AS/400 has easy-to-use support for exporting your Java source or class files to OS/400 IFS, directly from the IDE. You only specify the target location once, and it remembers it every time. This is the easiest option!

Pick whatever you like, or whatever is handy. The only one that you might need help with is ftp, so here is a sample script from a Windows command-prompt window as an example:

```
c:\Phil\myJava>ftp MYSYSTEM
User: coulthar
Password:
230 COULTHAR logged on.
ftp> cd /Phil/myJava
250 "/Phil/myJava" is current directory.
ftp> binary
200 Representation type is binary IMAGE.
ftp> put HelloWorld.class
467 bytes sent in 0.02 seconds
ftp> ascii
200 Representation type is ASCII
ftp> put HelloWorld.java
206 bytes sent in 0.03 seconds
ftp> quit
```

The first cd into your IFS directory is important. When using ftp to the AS/400, it decides whether you are working with the IFS or the native file system based on the syntax of the first place you "cd" into. If the location starts with a forward slash, IFS is assumed; otherwise, QSYS is assumed. Also, it is important to switch into binary mode for class files and ASCII mode for source files. By the way, for multiple files, use the mput (multiple put) command, instead of put. There are also get and mget commands for going the other way.

Setting your classpath in QShell

Your Java files are now in the IFS and you know how to find your way to them and run them, using QShell. You're on our way. The last thing you really need to know is how to set your CLASSPATH so that Java can find your Java classes. By default, it only looks in the current directory, which is not very useful, since you'll probably have classes spread over multiple directories.

The first important note about the CLASSPATH environment variable on OS/400 is that it is based on UNIX, so it uses a colon to separate the entries, not a semicolon as in Windows, for example:

```
/Phil/myJava:/George/myJava
```

To set your CLASSPATH dynamically—that is, each time you run Java—use the -classpath parameter to the java command, like this:

```
java -classpath /Phil/myJava:/George/myJava HelloWorld
```

This is nice, but a pain to remember each time. To make it more permanent, you can set it once for your QShell session using the export command, much like the set command on Windows, for example:

```
export -s CLASSPATH=.:/Phil/myJava:/George/myJava
```

If you type this in your QShell session, that classpath remains in effect for the duration of the session. To see all current environment-variable settings, type export with no parameters. The -s option tells QShell to make this not only a variable for use by QShell scripts, but also for use by applications like the Java interpreter.

This, then, is a little better, but only marginally. To get a little more permanence, create a file named .profile ("dot profile") in your directory in the IFS and put the export command in it:

```
export -s CLASSPATH=.:/Phil/myJava:/George/myJava
```

Use the same options discussed for .java files to create your .profile file, and copy it to the appropriate IFS directory. This is an example where SEU and CPYTOSTMF might be just fine. The "dot" (.) included in the above example represents your current directory. We recommend always putting this on your CLASSPATH, even in Windows. For this .profile to work correctly, it must be in your home directory, as specified on the HOMEDIR of your user profile. By convention, your home directory should be /home/userID, where userID is your user profile name.

You will most often use the .profile option for your own personal Java exploration. However, eventually, you or your system operator might install a Java application for general use on your system, and the time will come to set the CLASSPATH globally for all users. To this, just place that .profile file in a special directory, specifically /etc/profile, where it will be applied to all users on the system.

Actually, this file probably already exists, so you will want to append to it, not create it. To do this, use CPYFRMSTMF to copy into a source member for editing by SEU. Alternatively, just use CODE/400, which has support for directly editing IFS source files. When running a Java program, the CLASSPATH specified in /etc/profile/.profile is checked first for Java classes, and the CLASSPATH specified in your home directory .profile is searched if the class is still not found. Thus, these two files are cumulative, not mutually exclusive.

Using CL commands for Java and the Java Transformer

If you could only run Java classes from QShell, you might be in trouble if you wanted to mix RPG and Java in the same application. For example, how could RPG call Java if there is no CL command to invoke via the command analyzer API? Well, an alternative to the java command in QShell is the RUNJVA (*Run Java*) CL command, or its identical twin the JAVA CL command. These commands allow you to run a Java class directly from the OS/400 command line, a CL program, or any of the traditional ways of running CL commands. Note the Java class files still exist in the IFS. These CL commands will run the QShell java command behind the scenes.

To use them, specify the class file on the CLSF parameter, using the usual fully qualified syntax for IFS files, for example:

```
RUNJVA CLSF('/Phil/HelloWorld')
```

The only tricky part is specifying the CLASSPATH in this situation. The answer is to use the CLASSPATH parameter to specify it dynamically, similar to the -classpath option on the java QShell command. If specifying dynamically doesn't cut it, specify it in the CLASSPATH environment variable using the ADDENVVAR or CHGENVVAR commands. The syntax for the path itself is the same as discussed for QShell.

Note that the CL CLASSPATH environment variable only pertains to you, and only lives as long as your job (much like the QTEMP library). This means you have to add the ADDENVVAR command to a CL program that is run when you sign on, if you want permanence. Also note that this CLASSPATH is only searched after the CLASSPATH in the export -s classpath statement in /etc/profile/.profile, as was the case for .profile in your home directory. And by the way, that profile will be run too, since RUNJVA will invoke QShell and hence this .profile file will be run if it is in your home directory. Really, then, the .profile file in your home directory is the best option for setting up your own persistent and unique classpaths.

When you use RUNJVA, it actually does a little bit more than the java command in QShell. It actually *transforms* your Java class into OS/400 machine code (PowerPC instructions) the first time you run the class. This is the work of the Java Transformer. On subsequent runs, that machine code is executed, instead of the bytecode. This truly compiled Java is much faster than interpreted Java. Behind the scenes, a new object is created—a *JVAPGM (Java Program) object, which is referred to as a *direct execution* (*DE*) object. The .class file remains untouched, so it can still be copied to another operating system and run there, which means portability is not affected. So, you get the best of both worlds: the performance benefits of compiled Java and the portability of interpreted Java. Note that if you subsequently change the .class file by replacing it with a new version, the *JVAPGM is invalidated and so is re-created when you next use RUNJVA.

You can explicitly compile a single class or an entire .jar file of classes in a separate step, if you prefer, using the CRTJVAPGM command. In both commands, you can specify the optimization level, anywhere from 10 to 40. The lower number is best for debugging, while the higher number offers the most optimization.

Two other commands to use with Java Program are DLTJVAPGM and CHGJVAPGM (for example, to change the optimization). Note that DLTJVAPGM only deletes the hidden *JVAPGM object, not the original class file. Finally, there is a DSPJVAPGM command that displays attributes about Java Program, such as its optimization level.

By the way, you can use the green-screen system debugger to debug a Java application. You might want to use interpret mode versus compile mode for this, in which case you can specify INTERPRET(*YES) on the RUNJVA command. To actually debug your Java program, use the RUNJVA command and specify OPTION(*DEBUG), which puts you in a source-level debug session. For this to work, your class must have been compiled with the -g option (javac -g MyJava.java), and the source must exist in the same directory as the class file.

Another option for debugging Java running on the AS/400 is the IBM Distributed Debugger that comes with CODE/400 and VisualAge for Java. It runs on Windows while debugging your interpreted or transformed Java program on the AS/400.

One last point on the Transformer: If you use the java command in QShell, it will use the direct execution object if it exists. Otherwise, it will interpret the class. Thus, many people first explicitly transform their class files using CRTJVAPGM, and then subsequently run them in QShell using java.

AS/400 TOOLBOX FOR JAVA

The Java Program that the Java Transformer creates is not an ILE service program because Java is not an ILE language. You cannot bind or link a Java Program into a non-Java ILE program or service program. Thus, to "get out" of Java, and access you data, other programs, data queues, message files, and so on, you have to rely on some unique-to-OS/400 Java code written by the IBM Rochester team. These classes are called the AS/400 Toolbox for Java.

You are going to love these! They are well-designed, well-written, and come free with the system (and with CODE/400, VisualAge for Java, and Inprise J/Builder). Furthermore, because they are written entirely in Java using only industry-standard TCP/IP sockets for their communication layer, they run everywhere. By extension, so does your code that uses them. This means you can write Java code to access your DB2/400 files or your RPG programs, and run that code anywhere. Run it on the same AS/400, a different AS/400, on Windows, on Linux, on UNIX, in a Web Browser, in a network station, in a personal device. Anywhere. This is the ultimate OS/400 middleware!

The downside (there is always one, isn't there?) is that while your code will run any-where, it will always be trying to talk to an AS/400 somewhere in the world. So, if you are interested or worried about server portability, you will have to forgo the Toolbox, or carefully isolate its usage so that your move to OS/390, for example, is easy. The one ex-ception to this rule is the JDBC driver inside the Toolbox, as described in Chapter 13. It is the one portable set of classes in the Toolbox, as JDBC is industry standard, not unique to OS/400. To switch databases, you need only change the code to register the driver and connect to the database (assuming your SQL statements are standard).

At the time of this writing, there were more than 500 classes in this product, and there are more to come. A brief description of the functionality that these classes provide follows. Refer to the IBM redbook *Accessing the AS/400 System with JAVA* (SG24-2152) for a well-done and more detailed introduction to these classes. Also see the documentation for the AS/400 Toolbox for Java, available at *publib.boulder.ibm.com/html/as400/ infocenter.html*.

Table A.4 lists the functions offered by the AS/400 Toolbox for Java, in their likely order of importance for most Java applications.

Table A.4: AS/400 Toolbox for Java Functions as of V4R5 (V3R2M3) (part 1 of 3)	
Function	Description
Data access via JDBC	SQL access, as described in Chapter 13.
Data access via record-level access	Much like RPG's chain, setll, read, write, update, and delete statements.
Command call	Runs an OS/400 command in batch. Any messages sent by the command are returned to your Java application.
Program call	Runs any program object in batch. Parameters can be passed and updated. Any messages sent by the program are returned to Java.
Data queues	Your Java application can create, read, write, and delete data queues, both sequential and queued. It can also work with the attributes of a data queue.
Data areas	Your Java application can create, read, write, and delete data areas. It can also work with the attributes of a data area.

Table A.4: AS/400 Toolbox for Java	
Functions as of V4R5 (V3R2M3) (part 2 of 3)	

Function	Description
User space	Your Java application can create, read, write, and delete user spaces. It can also read and write the attributes of a user space.
IFS file system	Your Java application can access directories and files in the IFS. This is a superset (and super classes) of java.io in the JDK, tweaked specifically for local or remote IFS access.
Network print	Allows your Java application to work with spooled files, output queues, printers, printer files, writer jobs, and AFP resources. Yes, you can create reports, but it's pretty scary stuff, as you have to create SCS data streams. Reading a spool file is pretty cool, though!
System values	Your Java application can read and change system values and network attributes.
Jobs	Your Java application can retrieve lists of jobs (all, or by name, number, or user) and job log messages, and read the details about a particular job.
Users and groups	Your Java application can retrieve lists of users and groups.
System status	Your Java application can retrieve system status information. It can also access system pool information.
Permissions	Your Java application can retrieve and change OS/400 object authorities.
Digital certificates	Manages digital certificates, which are used for secure transactions over the Internet. For example, they are used by the Secure Socket Layer (SSL).
ftp	Allows you to connect, run ftp commands, and get/put files from Java.
Java application call	Allows you to remotely run Java classes on the AS/400.
Service program call	Allows you to call ILE service program procedures from Java.
Security	Support for the SSL and user authentication.
HTML classes	Classes can be used and run from a servlet or JSP, and generate common HTML tags that can be tedious to code by hand.
Servlet classes	These classes are specifically for use in servlets, for generating HTML output from the other Toolbox classes.

Table A.4: AS/400 Toolbox for Java Functions as of V4R5 (V3R2M3) (part 3 of 3)	
Function	**Description**
Proxy classes	This thin client-side proxy of the full Toolbox allows Toolbox classes to be used locally, yet actually executed remotely.
System properties	For configuring properties that affect certain Toolbox functions.

These major functions are offered through a myriad of classes. To use these classes, numerous other helper classes are supplied that are quite useful in their own right. They are listed in Table A.5. All of these classes are in a package named com.ibm.as400.access. (Notice that the JDBC classes do not require or use these explicitly. They are used under the covers.)

Table A.5: AS/400 Toolbox for Java Helper Classes	
Helper Classes	**Description**
AS/400 object	All service classes except JDBC require one of these as input into their constructor. This class manages OS/400 logins, optionally prompting the user for ID and password (on GUI clients).
AS/400 data types	These classes help you easily translate OS/400 values to and from appropriate Java data types.
AS/400 messages	This class represents an OS/400 message returned from a program or command call.
AS/400 record format information	These classes represent DB2/400 field definitions, record formats, and actual data records. They are used when doing record-level data access, and can be used when working with program calls and data queues.
AS/400 QSYS object path name	This represents objects in the IFS. Because the QSYS file system can be accessed through the IFS, you can use IFS objects to get at your library-based objects, for example: /qsys.lib/mylibr.lib/myfile.fil The helper class QSYSObjectPathName makes it easy to convert native file system object names to IFS-style path names, which all the Toolbox classes expect. Specifically, the static method toPath takes library, object, and object type names and returns a string of the form above.

Table A.5: AS/400 Toolbox for Java Helper Classes (cont)	
Helper Classes	**Description**
Exceptions	The Toolbox has a rich set of its own exception objects.
Trace	Using the Trace class, you can enable logging to help with problem determination. There are five levels of tracing you can enable: information, warning, error, diagnostic, and data stream.

The AS/400 Toolbox for Java also contains a number of *visual classes*, which are Java Swing GUI components that use these base non-visual classes. The visual classes are found in the package com.ibm.as400.vaccess, and they are designed to allow you to easily embed them inside your own Swing GUI applications, saving you some time you would otherwise spend writing them yourself. They all leverage the concept of reusable panels, as discussed in Chapter 12. The GUI classes have to run on a client, so regardless of your OS/400 level, you can always use the latest level of the Toolbox when running Java code on a client. The only thing to beware of is that some newer functions might not apply to a back level of OS/400.

The following are the GUI functions available as of V5R1:

- Function
- Command call
- Data queues
- Error events
- IFS
- JDBC
- Record-level access
- Jobs
- Messages
- Network print
- Permissions
- Program call
- System status
- System values
- Users and groups
- Java application call

We do not describe these classes here because you will probably not be writing Java GUIs. (Instead, we believe you will probably be writing HTML UIs via servlets and JSPs.) We leave them to your own exploration.

In addition to all this, the Toolbox comes with some other functionality:

- *Program Call Markup Language* (*PCML*), an XML language that makes it is easy to code calls to *PGM objects from Java, and even procedures inside *SRVPGM objects from Java. This allows you to define the target program or procedure and its parameters via a simple tag-based language. This is interpreted and turned into the appropriate ProgramCall and ServiceProgramCall classes.

- *Panel Definition Markup Language* (*PDML*), an XML language for defining GUIs that is arguably easier to write than Swing classes, although in the end that is how it is rendered.

- *GUI Builder*, a tool for visually defining PDML windows and panels, generating the PDML tags for you. Also included is a conversion tool to convert Windows resource files into PDML.

Getting the AS/400 Toolbox for Java classes

To use the AS/400 Toolbox for Java, you must first get it. If you have V4R2 or later, it is on your system CD-ROM or tape. To install it, use GO LICPGM, select option 11, and install 5769 JC1 (for a Version 4 operating system). This places the files jt400.jar and jt400.zip in your IFS, in the directory /QIBM/ProdData/HTTP/Public/jt400/lib. You don't need both of these files; either one will do. We prefer the .jar file because it is smaller.

There is also a file jt400doc.zip, which contains the English JavaDoc detailed help for the Toolbox classes. (The jt400mri.zip file has the other languages). To see the JavaDoc help, download this file to your workstation and unzip it. You can use the jar tool in the JDK to unzip a file, as in jar -xvf jt400doc.zip. This gives you many HTML files, so start with the one named Index.htm in the doc_en subdirectory. If you prefer to get the very latest version of the Toolbox, go to *www.ibm.com/iseries/toolbox*. The Toolbox is an open-source product, meaning you can even get the source code for it! Alternatively, you can simply get the Toolbox as part of WebSphere Development Tools for iSeries, which also includes CODE/400, VisualAge for Java, VisualAge for RPG, WebSphere Studio, and WebFacing.

If you are going to use the Toolbox classes from Java code running on a client, and you don't have it as part of one of the products listed above, simply copy the jt400.jar file from the IFS to your workstation. Use any number of methods for this, such as ftp. Once on your workstation, add it to your CLASSPATH. You do not have to unzip this file.

If you are going to use the Toolbox classes for Java code running on the OS/400 itself, you will have to add the /QIBM/ProdData/HTTP/Public/jt400.lib/jt400.jar file to your OS/400 CLASSPATH, using one of the methods described earlier in this appendix. As of V4R4, there is also a jt400access.zip file, which is a smaller version containing only the non-visual classes. You probably want to use that on OS/400. This file has already been optimized for you with the CRTJVAPGM command.

As of this writing, the Toolbox had just been transformed into an open-source product. This means that anyone can get its source and contribute to its functionality, as is the case for other popular open-source products like the Apache Web Server and the Linux operating system. It also means that in order to get the very latest version of the Toolbox, you have to register at the Toolbox Web site for the open-source version and download it. This product is known as *JTOpen*.

Most of the additional functionality described above, such as PCML, is not part of the base jt400.jar file. Therefore, you will need to get JTOpen to get the additional necessary .jar files needed to compile code that uses this functionality. After installing JTOpen, you will find all the .jar files in the lib subdirectory.

Finally, the Toolbox requires the QUSER user ID, so ensure its password has not expired. Also, be sure to start all the host servers (STRHOSTSVR *ALL) and the TCP/IP DDM server (STRTCPSVR SERVER(*DDM)). By the way, ensure you have the TCP/IP Connectivity Utilities for AS/400 installed (5769-TC1).

Using the AS/400 Toolbox for Java classes

The following discussion is independent of the JDBC classes, described in Chapter 13.

To write code that uses the AS/400 Toolbox, import the package com.ibm.as400.access. Your first job is to create an instance of the AS400 class. This class will manage a connection to your local or remote AS/400 and is required as a parameter into the constructor of all the other primary Toolbox classes. The AS400 class can be instantiated with no parameters, or you can specify the AS/400 host name, user ID, and/or password. If you run your Java class on the AS/400 itself, and don't specify any parameters, the object will implicitly use localhost for the system and *CURRENT for the user ID and password. When running on a client, however, the user will be prompted for any of the missing three values:

```
AS400 systemHome = new AS400();
AS400 systemNY = new AS400("NYC","NYCID,"NYCPWD");
```

For a Secure Socket Layer (SSL) connection, use the SecureAS400 subclass of AS400 instead. Once you have an AS400 or SecureAS400 object, it can be used with any of the classes. All the primary classes, like CommandCall and ProgramCall, take an AS400 object as a parameter on their constructor. It is at this time, when running on the client, that the user is prompted for any missing information. It is also at this time that the actual connection is established. You can explicitly force the connection at any time by calling the method connectService. This takes one parameter identifying the type of connection you desire, which in the end tells the Toolbox which AS/400 server subsystem to connect with. The parameter value constants are shown in Table A.6.

Table A.6: AS400 Connection Constants			
Constant	Service	AS/400 Subsystem	AS/400 Job
FILE	Access Integrated File System	QSERVER	QPWFSERVSO
COMMAND	Run AS/400 commands or call AS/400 programs	QSYSWRK	QZRCSRVS
PRINT	Access AS/400 spool files	QSYSWRK	QNPSERVS
DATAQUEUE	Access AS/400 data queues or data areas	QSYSWRK	QZHQSSRV
RECORDACCESS	Access DB2/400 via record-level access	QSYSWRK	QRWRTSRVR

It's your choice whether to have only a single AS400 object with multiple connections for different services, or a separate AS400 object for each service. When you are done with your connection, you must use the method disconnectAllServices to disconnect from OS/400. To end your application, you must use System.exit(0) to kill the daemon threads created by the Toolbox.

The following sections look briefly at the most popular Toolbox classes.

The CommandCall class

Assuming you have an AS400 object named (say) system400 already, you can use it to call one or more non-interactive commands on that AS/400. Just instantiate a CommandCall object with the AS400 object as a parameter, and then call the run method for each command to be run. This will return true if the command ran successfully. To get any AS/400 messages that resulted from the command, call the getMessageList method. It returns an array (possibly null) of AS400Message objects, which you can simply walk and call the getText method on. Listing A.1 shows an example.

Listing A.1: An AS/400 Command Call via the Toolbox

```
import com.ibm.as400.access.*;

public class TestCommandCall
{
    public static void main(String args[])
    {
        AS400 system400 = new AS400();
        CommandCall cmdObj = null;
        try
        {
            System.out.println("Connecting...");
            system400.connectService(AS400.COMMAND);
            System.out.println("Creating CommandCall object...");
            cmdObj = new CommandCall(system400);
        } catch (Exception exc)
        {
            System.out.println("Error connecting: " +
                               exc.getMessage());
            System.exit(1);
        }
        runCmd(cmdObj, "ADDLIBLE CUSTLIB");
        runCmd(cmdObj, "ADDLIBLE CUSTLIB");
        system400.disconnectAllServices();
        System.exit(1);
    }

    public static boolean runCmd(CommandCall cmdObj,
                                 String cmdString)
    {
        boolean cmdOK = false;
        try
        {
            System.out.println("Calling command "+cmdString+"...");
            cmdOK = cmdObj.run(cmdString);
            System.out.println("Command returned. Result = "+cmdOK);
        } catch (Exception exc) {}
        AS400Message msgs[] = cmdObj.getMessageList();
      if (msgs != null)
```

──→

Listing A.1: An AS/400 Command Call via the Toolbox (continued)

```
        {
            for (int idx=0; idx < msgs.length; idx++)
                System.out.println("Message: " +
                                        msgs[idx].getText());
        }
        System.out.println();
        return cmdOK;
    } // end runCmd method
}
```

The static method runCmd is created in this example to run any given command string, given a previously instantiated CommandCall object. The main method creates the AS400 object and explicitly does the appropriate connection, then calls the runCmd method twice with the same ADDLIBLE command, so you can see what happens when the command works and when it does not.

The result of running this command from Windows is that you are prompted for your system, user ID, and password values (at the time of the connectService method call), after which you get the following:

```
ListingA-1>java TestCommandCall
Connecting...
Creating CommandCall object...
Calling command ADDLIBLE CUSTLIB...
Command returned. Result = true
Message: Library CUSTLIB added to library list.

Calling command ADDLIBLE CUSTLIB...
Command returned. Result = false
Message: Library CUSTLIB already exists in library list.
```

The ProgramCall class

It's easy to call any *PGM object on OS/400, but only if the program does not take any parameters. We'll cover this scenario first, then show how to handle parameters.

Again, first instantiate an AS400 object and optionally explicitly connect to the COMMAND service. Then, instantiate a ProgramCall object, passing it the AS400 object, and call any AS/400 program using the ProgramCall method run. Specify as parameters to this method the name of the program to run (in IFS style syntax) and an empty array of type ProgramParameter. (You will see later that, to pass parameters, you simply pass a non-empty array for the second parameter.) Again, run returns true if the call went okay, and you can retrieve program-queue messages using the getMessageList method.

Listing A.2 shows an example of calling program PRINTRPT in library CUSTLIB.

Listing A.2: Calling an AS/400 Program without Parameters

```
import com.ibm.as400.access.*;
public class PrintRpt
{
    protected AS400        system400 = null;
    protected ProgramCall pgmObj     = null;
    protected String       pgmLib, pgmName, pgmIFSName;
    protected ProgramParameter[] parms= null;
    protected boolean      pgmRanOk  = false;

    public PrintRpt(AS400 system400)
    {
        this.system400 = system400;
        pgmName = "PRINTRPT";
        pgmLib  = "CUSTLIB";
        pgmIFSName =
            QSYSObjectPathName.toPath(pgmLib,pgmName,"PGM");
        pgmObj = new ProgramCall(system400);
        parms = setPgmParms(); // call our helper method
    }
    protected ProgramParameter[] setPgmParms()
    {
        parms = new ProgramParameter[0]; // empty array
        return parms;
    }
    public boolean callPgm()
    {
        try {
            System.out.println("Calling pgm "+pgmName+"...");
            pgmRanOk = pgmObj.run(pgmIFSName, parms);
            System.out.println("Result = " + pgmRanOk);
        } catch (Exception exc) {
            System.out.println("Exc: " + exc.getMessage());
        }
        AS400Message msgs[] = pgmObj.getMessageList();
        if (msgs != null)
          for (int idx=0; idx < msgs.length; idx++)
            System.out.println("Message: "+msgs[idx].getText());
        System.out.println();
        return pgmRanOk;
    } // end callPgm method
}
```

Listing A.2 does not show its main method, which exists only for testing purposes. Here it is:

```
public static void main(String args[])
{
    AS400 system400 = new AS400();
    try {
      system400.connectService(AS400.COMMAND);
    } catch (Exception exc) {
      System.out.println("Error connecting: "+exc.getMessage());
      System.exit(1);
    }
    PrintRpt printRpt = new PrintRpt(system400);
    printRpt.callPgm();
    system400.disconnectAllServices();
    System.exit(1);
}
```

Notice how we designed this class. It has the same name as the program itself, and it contains a constructor that prepares the ProgramCall object and the parameter list (an array of ProgramParameter that has zero elements for no-parameter calls). Callers simply pass an AS400 object into the constructor. They then simply call the method callPgm, which actually calls the program, returning true or false to indicate its success. The main method shows how easy it is to use the class. Your team can simply use this class anytime they want to call this program, rather than having to write their own Toolbox code every time. It nicely encapsulates the program as a Java class.

The program called in this example does nothing. Its source is on the CD-ROM included with this book (PrintRpt.irp), if you are interested in running the example. Use File->SaveAs in CODE/400 to save it to an AS/400 source member, then compile it with CRTBNDRPG in library CUSTLIB (which you will have to create, of course).

Running the Java program gives this result:

```
ListingA-2>java PrintRpt
Calling pgm PRINTRPT...
Result = true
```

If you have any trouble running this example or any of the following examples, be sure to use WRKACTJOB on the AS/400, prompting it to specify subsystem QSYSWRK. Look for jobs named QZRCSRVS, in status *MSGW. Use option 7 to look at the message, and you'll probably find the job is waiting on a response to an inquiry message, indicating a library list or authority error.

When you pass parameters, you enter the world of data conversion. Basically, the difference is that the `ProgramParameter` array will be populated with actual `ProgramParameter` objects, one for every parameter the program expects. These objects require you to specify the length of the parameter in bytes, and the actual data for input parameters in the form of a byte array. The tricky part, then, is determining the length and producing the byte array. After you call the program, the next trick is to retrieve the updated parameter values as byte arrays and then convert those arrays to actual Java objects.

The reason the data is passed back and forth as byte arrays is that all data sent across a network must be send as a byte stream, as that is how computers communicate with each other. You need help to determine the byte length given the data type and digit length of a parameter, and you need help to convert the data to a byte stream and back again (and from Unicode to EBCDIC, for text). As it turns out, the Toolbox supplies all this help, in the form of a set of helper classes, one per AS/400 data type.

A Java class named CUSTBAL, which calls an RPG program, will illustrate all this. This program takes a 10-digit (four-byte), unsigned integer value representing a customer ID, and a 7.2 packed decimal parameter that will be updated to hold this customer's current balance. The first parameter is input-only, while the second parameter is output-only. Here is the simple RPG program, just for testing purposes:

```
H DFTACTGRP(*NO) ACTGRP('QILE')
D*------------------------------------------
D* Prototype for main entry
D*------------------------------------------
D CUSTBAL         PR                    EXTPGM('CUSTBAL')
D Id                            10U 0
D Balance                       7P 2
D*------------------------------------------
D* Actual main entry
D*------------------------------------------
D CUSTBAL         PI
D Id                            10U 0
D Balance                       7P 2
C                   EVAL      Balance = 76543.21
C                   EVAL      *INLR = *ON
```

As you can see, RPG IV prototyping defines the parameters, and the return value is hard-coded, but this is enough to test calling an RPG program with parameters from Java. You are welcome to create and populate a database, and enhance this example to use a CHAIN operation to get the requested record.

The Java class that calls this program will need to have two elements in its ProgramParameter array. To create a ProgramParameter object, you need to pass to its constructor the length for that parameter, in bytes. The helper classes from the Toolbox help with that. For the four-byte unsigned integer (10 digits equals four bytes), use the AS400UnsignedBin4 class, and for the packed decimal, use the AS400PackedDecimal class. The former is instantiated with no parameters, while the latter requires you to specify the total length and decimal digits (seven and two in this example).

Here are two instance variables for this:

```
protected AS400UnsignedBin4 parm1Converter = new AS400UnsignedBin4();
protected AS400PackedDecimal parm2Converter = new AS400PackedDecimal(7,2);
```

All the data-type helper classes contain a method named getByteLength that returns the number of bytes a parameter of this type will require in the resulting byte stream. This makes it easy to create the ProgramParameter array entries, as you can see here:

```
protected ProgramParameter[] setPgmParms()
{
    parms = new ProgramParameter[2];
    parms[0] =
        new ProgramParameter(parm1Converter.getByteLength());
    parms[1] =
        new ProgramParameter(parm2Converter.getByteLength());
    return parms;
}
```

The next requirement is to actually set the data for input parameters. The data-type helper objects help here, as well. In the example, only the first parameter (customer ID) requires input, as the other is output-only.

To set data, use the setInputData method of the ProgramParameter object. However, this takes only a byte array as input, so use the AS400UnsignedBin4 helper object parm2Converter to convert the data into a byte array. All these helper classes support a toBytes method, which takes a Java object as input and gives back a byte array version of that object. The type of that Java object input is different for each of the helper classes.

For AS400UnsignedBin4, it requires a Long object. This might surprise you, since long integers are eight bytes in Java, but this is because unsigned four-byte numbers won't fit in *signed* four-byte fields, so the next size up is required.

To allow callers of the Java class to set the customer ID, you'll need to supply a method that takes an int value, converts it to a Long object, and finally uses the toBytes method of the helper object to turn that into a byte array. That byte array is subsequently passed as input into the setInputData method on the ProgramParameter array entry for the first parameter. Here is the method:

```
public void setCustId(int custID)
{
    custIdObj = new Long(custID);
    try {
      parms[0].setInputData(parm1Converter.toBytes(custIdObj));
    } catch (Exception exc) {}
}
```

The setInputData method can throw exceptions, so you have to use a try/catch block.

Now you are ready to call the program, with a parms array. You can do this by simply using the same callPgm method from Listing A.2. After callers call the program, they will want to retrieve the customer balance, which is now sitting in the second ProgramParameter array element. To get this value out, you only have a getOutputData method, which gives the result in a byte array—that's not very useful!

What you want instead is a BigDecimal object, Java's equivalent to RPG's packed decimal. Again, use a helper object, this time the AS400PackedDecimal object named parm2Converter. You simply use its toObject method, which converts a byte array into (in this case) a 7.2 BigDecimal object. Once again, a method hides the complexity from callers:

```
public BigDecimal getCustBalance()
{
    BigDecimal custBalance = null;
    if (pgmRanOk)
      custBalance = (BigDecimal)
        parm2Converter.toObject(parms[1].getOutputData());
    return custBalance;
}
```

The assumption is that callers will call this method right after callPgm, in which case you need to be sure that was successful. That's the reason for the code to check the pgmRanOk instance variable. Also, the toObject method requires you to cast the result.

Listing A.3 is the full class, named consistently with the target program. The idea is to instantiate the class, call the setXXX methods for each input parameter, call the program via the callPgm method, and then extract the results by calling the getXXX methods for each output parameter.

Listing A.3: A Java Class Encapsulating
the CUSTBAL Program, which Takes Parameters

```
import com.ibm.as400.access.*;
import java.math.*;
public class CustBal
{
    *** SAME INSTANCE VARIABLES AS IN LISTING A.2 ***
    protected AS400UnsignedBin4 parm1Converter =
        new AS400UnsignedBin4();
    protected AS400PackedDecimal parm2Converter =
        new AS400PackedDecimal(7,2);

    public CustBal(AS400 system400)
    {
        this.system400 = system400;
        pgmName = "CUSTBAL";
        pgmLib  = "CUSTLIB";
        pgmIFSName =
          QSYSObjectPathName.toPath(pgmLib,pgmName,"PGM");
        pgmObj = new ProgramCall(system400);
        parms = setPgmParms(); // call our helper method
    }
    protected ProgramParameter[] setPgmParms()
    {
        parms = new ProgramParameter[2];
        parms[0] =
          new ProgramParameter(parm1Converter.getByteLength());
        parms[1] =
          new ProgramParameter(parm2Converter.getByteLength());
        return parms;
    }
    public void setCustId(int custID)
    {
        Long custIdObj = new Long(custID);
        try {
        parms[0].setInputData(parm1Converter.toBytes(custIdObj));
        } catch (Exception exc) {}
    }
    public BigDecimal getCustBalance()
```

```
    {
        BigDecimal custBalance = null;
        if (pgmRanOk)
          custBalance = (BigDecimal)
            parm2Converter.toObject(parms[1].getOutputData());
        return custBalance;
    }
    public boolean callPgm()
    {
        *** SAME AS LISTING A.2 ***
    }
}
```

As usual, a main method is supplied to test this:

```
public static void main(String args[])
{
    AS400 system400 = new AS400();
    try
    {
      system400.connectService(AS400.COMMAND);
    } catch (Exception exc)
    {
      System.out.println("Error connecting: " + exc.getMessage());
      System.exit(1);
    }
    CustBal custBal = new CustBal(system400);
    custBal.setCustId(123456);
    custBal.callPgm();
    BigDecimal balance = custBal.getCustBalance();
    System.out.println("Customer Balance: " + balance);
    system400.disconnectAllServices();
    System.exit(1);
}
```

When you run the class, you get the following:

```
ListingA-3>java CustBal
Calling pgm CUSTBAL...
Result = true
Customer balance: 76543.21
```

It worked!

Did you notice a lot of redundant code between the first program-call class in Listing A.2 and the second in Listing A.3? As you write more of these, you'll get more redundancy. What is the answer to redundancy in Java? Inheritance! We recommend you create an abstract base class that all your program-call classes extend. It can supply all the common instance variables, the common constructor code, and even the common callPgm method. Your unique child classes per program will override the setPgmParms method and add the appropriate setXXX and getXXX method for the input and output parameters. Also, each child class would supply its own main method for testing. This isn't shown here, but you can see it on the CD-ROM in the UsingCommonParent subdirectory of the ListingA-3 directory. The parent class is named AS400Program.

Also included in the parent class is a method named addLibraryListEntry that takes a library name as input and adds it to the library list, using the CommandCall class. Most programs you call require the library list to be set up properly. You might want to supply a similar method for doing file overrides. Each child class can call these inherited methods in their constructors. You might also want to supply a default constructor so the class can be used as a bean, for example in the Visual Composition Editor of VisualAge for Java. To support a default constructor, put the code currently in the constructor into its own init method that takes an AS400 object as a parameter. Callers will then have to be instructed to call the init method immediately after instantiating the object.

By the way, the other data-type helper classes (besides AS400UnsignedBin4 and AS400PackedDecimal) are listed in Table A.7.

Table A.7: Data Conversion Classes in AS/400 Toolbox for Java

Toolbox Class	OS/400 Data Type	Java Data Type
AS400Bin2	Signed two-byte numeric	short
AS400Bin4	Signed four-byte numeric	int
AS400ByteArray	Hexadecimal, or any type	byte[]
AS400Float4	Signed four-byte floating-point	float
AS400Float8	Signed eight-byte floating-point	double
AS400PackedDecimal	Packed-decimal numeric	BigDecimal in java.math
AS400UnsignedBin2	Unsigned two-byte numeric	short
AS400UnsignedBin4	Unsigned four-byte numeric	long
AS400ZonedDecimal	Zoned-decimal numeric	BigDecimal in java.math
AS400Text	Character	String (Unicode)
AS400Array	Array	An array of other data types
AS400Structure	Structure	A structure of other data types

PCML for easy calling of programs and service programs

As you have seen, manually coding to the `ProgramCall` class is tedious. The Toolbox designers have recognized this and added an option that makes it significantly easier. They have invented an XML-based language named PCML, or Program Call Markup Language. It is a simple, tag-based language that can be typed into a source file, where tags are used to define the program to call and the parameter attributes for that call. Having typed this in, you can then simply use the `ProgramCallDocument` class in the Toolbox to read and parse that PCML file and automatically convert it into the necessary `ProgramCall` and related objects. You can do this for every call, or do it once and serialize the results for better performance.

Let's look again at the example program `CUSTBAL` in library `CUSTLIB`, which takes one input parameter and one output parameter. The input parameter is a 10-digit, unsigned integer value holding the customer ID. The output parameter will be updated to hold the packed-decimal 7.2 customer balance value. Listing A.4 shows what the PCML file `CustBal.pcml` will look like to describe this program call.

Listing A.4: A PCML File CustBal.pcml for Calling an AS/400 Program

```
<pcml version="1.0">
<!- PCML source for calling CUSTLIB/CUSTBAL ->
  <program name="CUSTBAL"
           path="/QSYS.LIB/CUSTLIB.LIB/CUSTBAL.PGM">
    <data name="custId" type="int" length="4"
          precision="32" usage="input"/>
    <data name="custBal" type="packed" length="7"
          precision="2"  usage="output"/>
  </program>
</pcml>
```

It is reasonably straightforward. The file starts and ends with the `pcml` tag, and each program-call description starts and ends with the `program` tag (you can describe multiple program calls per file). Comments are bracketed between `<!-` and `->`. On the beginning `program` tag, you identify the name of the program you wish to call, via the `name` attribute. Unless the program is in the QSYS library, you must also identify the program via a fully qualified IFS-style name on the `path` attribute.

Between the beginning and ending `program` tags, you describe the parameters by use of the `data` tag. One `data` tag is required per parameter. These tags take `name` (which will become the `ProgramParameter` object name), `type`, `length`, `precision`, and `usage` attributes. The length attribute is the number of bytes for the int data type, and must be two or four. By default, it is assumed to be signed unless you specify a precision of 16 or 32.

For the packed data type, length is the total number of digits, and precision is the number of decimal places. The precision attribute identifies the number of decimal places. The usage attribute is relative to the called program, not the calling program, so if the program updates a parameter, flag that parameter as usage="output". If it only reads the parameter, flag it as usage="input". If it both reads and updates the parameter (or you are not sure), flag it as usage="inputoutput". Input-capable parameters should be supplied a value prior to the call.

Finally, the type attribute indicates the data type of this parameter. The valid types for non-structure parameters are char, int, packed, zoned, float, and byte. There is also an init attribute for initializing parameter values, and a ccsid attribute for identifying the Coded Character Set ID of this character parameter, and a few other rarely used attributes: maxvrm, minvrm, offset, offsetfrom, outputsize, and passby. The JavaDoc help that comes with the Toolbox describes all these parameters.

This example uses the short form to end the data tag, by just putting an ending front-slash character inside the ending greater-than bracket, versus the formal </data> ending tag. This is legal XML syntax whenever a tag has only attributes and no text between the beginning and ending tags.

The Java code to call the program is now much simpler. The usual AS400 object is still necessary, but now you just instantiate the ProgramCallDocument class, passing the AS400 object and the name of the PCML source file without the .pcml extension:

```
AS400 system400 = new AS400();
ProgramCallDocument pcmlDoc =
    new ProgramCallDocument(system400, "CUSTBAL");
```

This instantiation finds the PCML source file, parses it, and converts it internally into all the Toolbox objects you saw earlier. Once instantiated, you are ready to prepare and actually call the program. Prior to the call, you must set the input value for each of the input or inputoutput parameters, using the setValue method of the ProgramCallDocument class. Identify a parameter via its <data> tag name attribute, dot-qualified with the <program> tag's name attribute, and pass the actual value for the parameter in the second parameter. Use callProgram to call the program (identifying the program via its program tag name attribute), and finally use getValue to get the value of each of the output parameters (identifying the parameter via its <data> tag name attribute, dot-qualified with the <program> tag's name attribute):

```
pcmlDoc.setValue("CUSTBAL.custId", new Long(123456) );
boolean pgmRanOK = pcml.callProgram("CUSTBAL");
// Retrieve list of AS/400 messages
AS400Message[] msgs = pcmlDoc.getMessageList("CUSTBAL");
for (int m = 0; m < msgs.length; m++)
    {
        String msgId = msgs[m].getID();
        String msgText = msgs[m].getText();
        System.out.println(" " + msgId + " - " + msgText);
    }
if (pgmRanOK)
    BigDecimal value = (BigDecimal)pcml.getValue("CUSTBAL.custBal");
```

In the ListingA-4 directory on the CD-ROM, you will find an updated version of the CustBal.java class from Listing A.3, which uses PCML instead of ProgramCall. You will also find in the UsingCommonParent sub-directory from there an updated version of the common parent class, renamed to AS400PCMLProgram, and redesigned to use PCML instead of ProgramCall.

This is much simpler than manually writing the tedious code to call ProgramCall directly. This shows how to call a *PGM object with simple non-structure, non-repeating parameters.

This is the simplest scenario, but PCML can also be used to call ILE procedures within *SRVPGM objects versus manually coding to the ServiceProgramCall class directly. To do this, you still use the <program> tag and specify the name of the *SRVPGM on the name="xxx" attribute. However, to identify the procedure within the service program that is to be called, you use the entrypoint="yyy" attribute. The entrypoint attribute is the only difference between calling a program versus an ILE procedure (in any language).

Declaring structures in PCML

In addition to the <program> tag, a <struct> tag is required if you are passing structure parameters instead of simple scalar fields. The idea is to name and define the structure first, and then simply refer to this structure definition in the <data> tag. This is done by specifying a type attribute value of "struct" for that <data> tag, and identifying the name of the structure on the struct attribute of the <data> tag. By allowing externally described structures like this, you can easily reuse them in multiple parameters, program calls, and service program calls.

The <struct> tag goes at the same nesting level as the <program> tags. It has a required name attribute for giving the structure definition an arbitrary name. Within the beginning <struct> and ending </struct> tags, you use <data> tags to define the subfields of the structure, exactly as you do for defining non-structure parameters on the <program> tag.

Imagine, in the previous example, you decided to place both the customer ID and the customer balance parameters into a single structure, and use that structure as a parameter. Here is an example of the PCML <struct> tag to define that structure:

```
<struct name="custInfo">
  <data name="custId" type="int" length="4"
        precision="32" usage="input"/>
  <data name="custBal" type="packed" length="7"
        precision="2"  usage="output"/>
</struct>
```

A <struct> tag is simply defined with an arbitrary name attribute value, and the <data> tags previously specified within the <program> tag are placed into it. To update the <program> tag, you now change its <data> tags to have only a single tag identifying the structure parameter. To identify a parameter whose type is a structure, simply set the type attribute to "struct" and name the structure on the struct attribute:

```
<program name="CUSTBAL"
         path="/QSYS.lib/CUSTLIB.lib/CUSTBAL.pgm">
  <data name="customerInformation" type="struct" struct="custInfo"
        usage="inputoutput"/>
</program>
```

Notice the usage is set to "inputoutput", since the structure is both read and updated. Of course, it is possible for a single <program> tag to have both structure and non-structure parameters.

When writing the Java code to process a program call or procedure call with a structure parameter, everything is the same except the code to set and get the subfield values. All you have to do is further qualify the subfield name with the name of the structure parameter, as shown here:

```
pcmlDoc.setValue("CUSTBAL.customerInformation.custId", new Long(123456) );
boolean pgmRanOK = pcml.callProgram("CUSTBAL");
// Retrieve list of AS/400 messages
AS400Message[] msgs = pcmlDoc.getMessageList("CUSTBAL");
for (int m = 0; m < msgs.length; m++)
    {
        String msgId = msgs[m].getID();
        String msgText = msgs[m].getText();
        System.out.println(" " + msgId + " - " + msgText);
    }
if (pgmRanOK)
    BigDecimal value =
        (BigDecimal)pcml.getValue("CUSTBAL.customerInformation.custBal");
```

Declaring arrays and multiple-occurrence structures in PCML

It's easy to declare arrays and multiple-occurrence structures in PCML. For arrays of
non-structure fields, simply specify the size of the array on the count attribute of the
<data> tag. For arrays of structure fields, or multiple-occurring data structures, simply
specify the number of occurrences on the count attribute of the <data> tag of the <pro-
gram> tag (versus the <struct> tag). Sometimes, you might pass the size in as another parameter instead of hard-coding it. In that case, rather than hard-coding the array size on the
count attribute, specify the name of another <data> tag parameter on the count attribute.

To use PCML, you must import com.ibm.as400.data, and monitor for exception
PcmlException for all the APIs shown here. Further, you might find that the PCML
classes are not on your CLASSPATH. If so, you will have to get the data400.jar and
x4j400.jar files and place them on your CLASSPATH. Remember, all the Toolbox .jar
files now come as part of the Toolbox open-source product, and are also shipped as part
of WebSphere Development Tools for iSeries. You can also read in the Toolbox JavaDoc
documentation about how to serialize a parsed PCML file to improve performance.

The DataQueue class

If you are familiar with data queues on OS/400, you know they are an excellent mechanism for inter process-communication (IPC). They are like mailboxes that any program
can put mail (messages) into and read mail out of. Readers can access messages in
last-in-first-out (*LIFO*), *first-in-first-out* (*FIFO*), or *by-key* sequence. Readers and writers
can communicate via the queue synchronously or asynchronously. Data queues are
heavily used on OS/400, which indicate the usefulness of such a mechanism—and there
is the huge success of their grown-up, many-platform cousin, IBM's Message Queue Series ("MQ Series"), which we strongly recommend you take a look at.

Data queues, via their Toolbox class, have also become a great mechanism for communicating between a Java program and an RPG program, where that Java program can be running anywhere in the world on any machine that has a JVM. For Java code running on a remote machine or client, it is a nice architecture to use a data queue to get at your data versus going directly against the database from the client. This allows you a level of indirection and the potential benefit of changing either the client code or the server code at any time, without affecting the other. For example, your server code that writes data to the data queue might be an RPG program today, but if you switch it to a Java program tomorrow, all those clients reading the queue will not know the difference. It's that encapsulation idea again—hiding details behind some kind of wall.

To use data queues from Java, use the `DataQueue` and `KeyedDataQueue` classes from the Toolbox. The former is for sequential (LIFO or FIFO) access, the latter for reading and writing data by a key. Both classes extend, and hence inherit, much of their behavior (methods) from the `BaseDataQueue` class.

An example will illustrate a sequential data queue. We will use a typical design pattern for data-queue usage: a client and a server are communicating using two data queues. The first is an input data queue, where the client puts in a request for some type of function. The server program monitors this data queue for a request (by reading, and waiting forever on that read). Once the request is put in by the client, the server reads it, processes it (probably by reading one or more database files), and then puts the result into the second data queue, which the client by now is waiting on. Usually, the output is one or more records of information.

Let's assume the input queue exists in library `ALIB` and is named `INPQ`. The output queue is also in `MYLIB` and is named `OUTQ`. Typically, these queue names are generated by the client and made to be unique per client, and are passed to the server program via parameters. Also typically, the client creates the queues initially.

As with `CommandCall` and `ProgramCall`, you instantiate an instance of `DataQueue` and pass to it an `AS400` object. However, for data queues, you must also pass the name of the queue, as in `/QSYS.LIB/ALIB.LIB/INPQ.DTAQ`. You again use the `toPath` method in `QSYSObjectPathName` to create this IFS-style name.

Let's start with the preliminaries, creating the `DataQueue` objects, and from them creating the actual AS/400 *DTAQ objects:

```
AS400 system400 = new AS400();
String inpqName = QSYSObjectPathName.toPath("ALIB","INPQ","DTAQ");
String outqName = QSYSObjectPathName.toPath("ALIB","OUTQ","DTAQ");
DataQueue inpq = new DataQueue(system400,inpqName);
DataQueue outq = new DataQueue(system400,outqName);
inpq.create(2000); // max length
outq.create(2000); // max length
```

Of course, `try/catch` blocks are needed, which aren't shown here for simplicity.

Now it is time to communicate. Assume the RPG program running on the AS/400server has already been started, perhaps by using the `CommandCall` class already discussed. (You have to use the `SBMJOB` command, since if you call the program directly, the call won't return, as the program will be waiting on the data queue. Alternatively, you could use the `ProgramCall` class, but do so in a separate thread.)

Let's also assume that the client wants to tell the server to retrieve a customer information record. This requires you to put a one-character field onto the queue, the letter *C*, which the server program is designed to interpret as "read a customer record." You also have to put a six-digit numeric value indicating the customer ID. The program on the server will then put onto the output queue a record of information including a result code, the customer ID again, the customer name (a 30-character string), the customer phone number (a 15-character string, to be safe), and the customer account balance (a packed-decimal number in the format 7.2). This indicates a need for the record formats described in Table A.8 for input and Table A.9 for the output.

Table A.8: The Input Data Queue Format

Queue Position	Description	AS400 Data Type	Java Data Type
1-1	Request type	One character	String
2-5	Customer ID	Four-byte integer	Integer

Table A.9: The Output Data Queue Format			
Queue Position	Description	AS400 Data Type	Java Data Type
1-2	Return code	Two-byte integer	Short
3-6	Customer ID	Four-byte integer	Integer
7-36	Customer name	30 characters	String
37-51	Phone number	15 characters	String

To write to a DataQueue object, use the write method, which requires an entire array of bytes. You can't write individual fields, only the entire record. This means you need to use the conversion classes to convert each field to a byte array, and then concatenate all the byte arrays for all the fields together. To read from the queue, use the read method, which returns an object of a class named DataQueueEntry. To get the data out of it, use the getData method, which just gives an entire array of bytes. It is up to you to know how to partition this into fields and use the appropriate conversion classes to convert those fields to data. This is possible, but way too much work! The Toolbox will help.

To work effectively with an entire record of individual fields, you can use a combination of classes from the Toolbox. First, there are field-description classes whose objects wrap objects of the conversion classes you saw for program calls. They allow you to name each field, which will come in handy. There is one field-description class for each of the DDS data types on OS/400, and they all take an instance of the corresponding conversion class, plus a field name of your choosing, in their constructor.

Table A.10 lists all of the field-description classes. Keep in mind for the "Java Type" column of this table, the primitive types shown must be wrapped in an object of their class wrappers, such as Integer for int.

Table A.10: Field-Description Classes in the AS/400 Toolbox for Java

OS400 Field Type	Field-Description Class	Conversion Class	Java Type
	FieldDescription: base class		
Binary 4	BinaryFieldDescription	AS400Bin2	short
Binary 8	BinaryFieldDescription	AS400Bin4	int
Character	CharacterFieldDescription	AS400Text	String
Date	DateFieldDescription	AS400Text	String
DBCS graphic	DBCSGraphicField- Description	AS400Text	String
Float 4	FloatFieldDescription	AS400Float4	float
Float 8	FloatFieldDescription	AS400Float8	double
Hexadecimal	HexFieldDescription	AS400ByteArray	byte[]
Packed-decimal	PackedDecimalFieldDescription	AS400PackedDecimal	BigDecimal
Time	TimeFieldDescription	AS400Text	String
Timestamp	TimestampFieldDescription	AS400Text	String
Zoned-decimal	ZonedDecimalFieldDescription	AS400ZonedDecimal	BigDecimal

These field-description classes are only remotely interesting by themselves. They become very interesting, however, when you group instances of them together to define an entire record, such as the format of the record you want to put on the input queue, and the format of the record you want to read from the output queue. The Toolbox supplies a class that allows you to do just this, named, appropriately enough, the RecordFormat class. You can create a RecordFormat object and then place a field description object in it (via the addFieldDescription method) for each of the fields in the record layout.

Here is how you do this for the input and output data queues, so that you know what the format for each looks like:

```
RecordFormat inpqFmt = new RecordFormat();
inpqFmt.addFieldDescription(
   new CharacterFieldDescription(new
AS400Text(1,system400),"request"));
inpqFmt.addFieldDescription(
```

```
  new BinaryFieldDescription(new AS400Bin4(), "custID"));

RecordFormat outqFmt = new RecordFormat();
outqFmt.addFieldDescription(
  new BinaryFieldDescription(new AS400Bin2(),"retCode"));
outqFmt.addFieldDescription(
  new BinaryFieldDescription(new AS400Bin4(), "custID"));
outqFmt.addFieldDescription(
  new CharacterFieldDescription(new AS400Text(30,system400),
                                "custName"));
outqFmt.addFieldDescription(
  new CharacterFieldDescription(new AS400Text(15,system400),
                                "custPhone"));
outqFmt.addFieldDescription(
  new PackedDecimalFieldDescription(
      new AS400PackedDecimal(7,2),"custBal"));
```

This is just like using physical-file DDS to define the fields inside a record format. Note that the AS400Text constructor requires an AS400 object, while the other classes do not. This is for the retrieval of CCSID information, to aid in codepage mapping. Also notice the Toolbox (as of this writing) has no XXFieldDescription class for wrapping unsigned binary numbers like AS400UnsignedBin4. So, you just use the AS400Bin4 and AS400Bin2 classes, which take and return Integer and Short Java objects. This will work fine even though the host program is expecting unsigned data, as long as you don't use really big numbers that would set the sign bit on. The key thing is that the number of bytes is correct between Java and RPG.

Just as you have to compile physical-file DDS so that you can read and write records of actual data, you have to instantiate an instance of something new in the Toolbox—a Record object—to read and write actual data that conforms to the RecordFormat layout. Start by creating a Record object to hold the data you wish to write to the data queue, using the inpqFmt RecordFormat object from above:

```
Record inpqData = new Record(inpqFmt);
Integer custID = new Integer(123456); // ID of customer to retrieve
inpqData.setField("request",  "C");   // Type of request ("C"ustomer)
inpqData.setField("custID", custID); // Set ID of customer to
retrieve
inpq.write(inpqData.getContents());   // Put data record on the queue
```

The record format object is used in the constructor of the Record object. The setField method is then used on the Record object to put each field's value into the record. The first parameter of setField is the field name of the field in the xxxFieldDescription constructor. Alternatively, you could specify a zero-based number representing the field position in the record format. The second parameter is the object that is the value for that field. Finally, the getContents method is used on the Record object to return a single-byte array containing all the field values, and it is placed on the data queue using the write method of the input DataQueue object.

Now you finally have data on your input queue, which should awaken the host program (not shown) to read the database and put the results into our output queue. The Java client code now needs to read the results from that output data queue. To do this, simply use the read method on the outq DataQueue object, which returns an object of type DataQueue Entry. This class is just a thin wrapper for a byte array, not very interesting by itself. What you really want is to get the data into a Record object that uses the outqFmt RecordFormat class, so that you can easily retrieve individual fields using getField from the Record class. You can do this using the getData method of the DataQueueEntry object, which gives a byte array. This byte array can then be used to create a populated Record object, by passing it into the constructor of the Record class along with the RecordFormat object:

```
Record outqData = new Record(outqFmt, outq.read(-1).getData());
Short      outReturnCode  = (Short)outqData.getField("retCode");
Integer    outCustID      = (Integer)outqData.getField("custID");
String     outCustName    = (String)outqData.getField("custName");
String     outCustPhone   = (String)outqData.getField("custPhone");
BigDecimal outCustBalance = (BigDecimal)outqData.getField("custBal");
```

The first line of code here creates the new Record object by passing the output queue RecordFormat object, created earlier, and the byte array read from the output queue. To get that byte array, read is called to get the DataQueueEntry object, and then getData is called on that to get the actual byte array. Finally, getField is called for each field in the record format, specifying the name you gave each field. Notice the result of getField is cast to the appropriate target type.

What happens if the call to read on the output queue happens before the host program has done its work and put the result on the output queue? Nothing. The program will simply wait until data is put on the queue before returning from the read call. This is because of the -1 passed for the parameter to read. Alternatively, you could pass a positive integer representing the number of seconds to wait.

While we have not shown it for simplicity, many of the methods called in this data queue example throw exceptions, and you will have to place them inside try/catch statements. A full data-queue example is available on the CD-ROM in the file CustReq.java in the ListingA-5. It uses the RPG program CUSTREQ.IRP in the same directory, which you should upload and compile into the CUSTLIB library (using CRTBNDRPG). Listing A.5 shows this RPG program.

Listing A.5: A Simple RPG Program for Processing Client Requests via a Data Queue

```
D* Prototype for main entry
D CUSTREQ         PR                      EXTPGM('CUSTREQ')
D dqIn                          10A
D dqOut                         10A
D* Data Structure for input DQ information
D in_data         DS
D  in_request                    1A
D  in_custId                    10U 0
D* Data Structure for output DQ information
D out_data        DS
D  out_retCode                   5U 0
D  out_custId                   10U 0
D  out_custName                 30A
D  out_custPhone                15A
D  out_custBal                   7P 2
D* Size of data-in and data-out data queues
D in_data_size    S              5  0 inz(%size(in_data))
D out_data_size   S              5  0 inz(%size(out_data))
D* Library containing data queues
D CUSTLIB         S             10A   inz('CUSTLIB')
D* How long to wait on a data queue read: -1 = forever
D WAIT_TIME       S              5  0 inz(-1)
D* Actual main entry
D CUSTREQ         PI
D dqIn                          10A
D dqOut                         10A
C                   DOW       NOT *INLR
C                   call      'QRCVDTAQ'
C                   parm                        dqIn
C                   parm                        CUSTLIB
C                   parm                        in_data_size
C                   parm                        in_data
C                   parm                        WAIT_TIME
C                   IF        in_request = 'E'
C                   EVAL      *INLR = *ON
C                   ELSE
C                   IF        in_request = 'C'
C                   EVAL      out_retCode = 0
C                   EVAL      out_custId  = in_custId
C                   EVAL      out_custName= 'Phil Coulthard'
C                   EVAL      out_custPhone='555-111-2222'
```

```
C                       EVAL          out_custBal = 76543.21
C                       call          'QSNDDTAQ'                          98
C                       parm                        dqOut
C                       parm                        CUSTLIB
C                       parm                        out_data_size
C                       parm                        out_data
C                       ENDIF
C                       ENDIF
C                       ENDDO
```

To run the Java code that drives this RPG program, run the CustReq Java class. Here is what this class does:

- In the constructor, it prepares the parameter list (the name of the input and output queues) for calling the RPG program. It also prepares the RecordFormat objects for the input and output queues. (Note we extend AS400Program, the class we invented as a common parent for all classes that call programs on the AS/400.)

- The createDataQueues method creates the input and output data queues.

- The callPgm method spawns a thread in which the RPG program is called. The RPG program starts running, waiting and looping on the input queue.

- The requestCustomer method writes the given customer number to the input queue, together with the request code C, indicating we want customer information. It then waits indefinitely on the output queue for the result. When the RPG program has written the customer information to the output queue, the requestCustomer method reads that information and packages it up into a Customer object, a class that stores all the information about a customer. It then returns this to the caller.

- The requestExit method writes request code E to the input queue, which causes the RPG program to set on LR and exit.

- The deleteDataQueues method deletes the input and output queues.

Note that the input queue and output queue names are hard-coded, but you actually need to generate unique names per client and create unique queues per client. We suggest using the client's IP address or the user ID as the root for these generated names. To get the former, use the static method getLocalHost in class InetAddress in package java.net.

These RecordFormat and Record classes are very handy. They can also be used with the ProgramCall class. This is useful when the program you call returns a record of information. They are also used when doing direct record access to the database, as you will see next.

Record-level database access

Now that you have seen the basics of the AS/400 Toolbox for Java, we will wrap up this introduction with a look at a way to directly access your DB2/400 data. This is an alternative to using JDBC or SQLJ, as presented in Chapter 13.

The Toolbox gives you classes for working with your DB2/400 database files directly, a record at a time, as you are used to in RPG. The classes are AS400File, which is the parent class, the KeyedFile child class for files accessed by key, and the SequentialFile child class for files accessed sequentially. The parent AS400File class offers a lot of functionality for the management of files, such as creating and deleting them, locking them, and managing commitment control on them. We don't cover this functionality here, but the Toolbox documentation does cover it, if you need it. This section just focuses on using the KeyedFile class to read and write an existing keyed file.

The steps to working with data in an existing DB2/400 file are a superset of what you have seen for calling commands and programs and accessing a data queue:

1. Create an AS400 object, as usual.

2. Create a KeyedFile (or SequentialFile) object, passing the AS400 object as a parameter and identifying the name of the DB2/400 file using IFS style syntax.

3. Identify to the Toolbox the layout of the records in the file, by associating a RecordFormat object with the file object.

4. Open the file, specifying if it is to be accessed read-only, write-only, or both; the record-blocking factor to use (ignored for read-write access); and the commitment control to use.

5. Optionally, use the appropriate methods to position the cursor.

6. Use the appropriate read methods to read a record (Record object).

7. Use the appropriate methods to add, update, or delete records in the database.

8. Close the file object.

Let's look a little closer at these steps. As you can see, the RecordFormat and Record classes play prominent roles. This is not surprising, as DB2/400 record-level access works with records of data, and those records need to be defined field by field. However, the great thing about the record-level access functionality of the Toolbox is that you do not have to define the RecordFormat by hand, unless you really want to. Instead, the Toolbox supplies another class, AS400FileRecordDescription, to create these objects for you, based on the existing database record format itself.

You have two options for creating a RecordFormat object directly from an existing database. You can do it every time, dynamically, as your program runs, or once, statically, at development time, and then reuse the generated class at runtime. In both cases, you first have to instantiate an instance of the AS400FileRecordDescription class, passing in an AS400 object and the IFS version of the file name. Again, you can get the latter using the static method toPath of the QSYSObjectPathName class, but for files, you use the four-parameter version, like this:

```
AS400 system400 = new AS400("MYSYSTEM");
String fileName = QSYSObjectPathName.
                   toPath("MYLIB","MYFILE","MYFILE","MBR");
AS400FileRecordDescription frd = new
AS400FileRecordDescription(system400, fileName);
```

The third parameter to toPath is the member name of the file to access. You can specify "%FIRST%" to indicate the first member or "%LAST%" to indicate the last member. The fourth parameter is always "MBR", representing the type of object.

The dynamic retrieval of a record format is done by calling the method retrieveRecordFormat, which returns a populated RecordFormat object:

```
RecordFormat[] myFileFmt = frd.retrieveRecordFormat();
```

Notice that this method returns an array because of the possibility that the file is a multiple-record-format logical file. In most cases, you will only be interested in the first entry in this array. This is very nice, but if you want to squeeze more performance out of your application, you should do this just once and save the result in a class that extends RecordFormat. The Toolbox allows for this, by using its createRecordFormatSource method on an AS400FileRecordDescription object:

```
frd.createRecordFormatSource(null, null);
```

This creates a .java source file in the current directory, which you can subsequently compile via javac and reuse again and again. The file name will be the name of the record format in the database file (you get multiple .java files for multiple-record-format logical files), with the term Format appended. The two parameters the method takes are a target directory to place the resulting java file(s) in, and the name of the package that generates package statements in the generated files. These default to the current directory and no package, respectively, if null is passed.

To use the generated file (after compiling it), simply instantiate an instance of it. For example, if the file above contained a record format named RECORD1, you would use this output (after compiling it with javac):

```
RecordFormat myFileFmt = new RECORD1Format();
```

Once you have a RecordFormat object, call the setRecordFormat method on the KeyedFile or SequentialFile object, and then call open on that object.

Let's look at an example that reads a keyed database file on OS/400. Assume the file CUSTOMER exists already and holds customer information data keyed by customer ID. The "on the fly" method is used to create the RecordFormat object here:

```
AS400 system400 = new AS400("MYSYSTEM");
String fileName =
QSYSObjectPathName.toPath("CLIB","CUST","CUST","MBR");
AS400FileRecordDescription frd = new
AS400FileRecordDescription(system400, fileName);
RecordFormat[] custFileFmt = frd.retrieveRecordFormat();
KeyedFile custFile = new KeyedFile(system400, fileName);
custFile.setRecordFormat(custFileFmt[0]);
custFile.open(AS400File.READ_ONLY, 100,
AS400File.COMMIT_LOCK_LEVEL_NONE);
```

This creates a KeyedFile object, tells the Toolbox what the record format for it is (queried dynamically from the Toolbox), and opens the file. If this is too much work, there is a no-parameter version of setRecordFormat in all XXXFile classes that will call retrieveRecordFormat for you and use the first one. This is the easiest to use if you decide to retrieve it on the fly, but we have had trouble getting it to work with our version of the Toolbox. (We get "Protocol Error Occurred.")

The file is opened using constants defined in the parent class AS400File to specify whether it is to be accessed by READ, READ_WRITE, or WRITE_ONLY, and what the commit level is. The second parameter to open specifies what the blocking factor is, which in this case is set to 100 records. The blocking factor is ignored when the file is opened READ_WRITE.

Now that the file is open, it is time to read from it. This is done by simply calling the read method on the KeyedFile object and specifying the key to use. The key is an Object array, since many files have multiple fields defined for the key. The objects put in the array are instances of Java classes that are compatible with the data type of the key fields in the database (for example, Integer, String, or BigDecimal).

Assume this file is keyed only by the customer ID field, which is a four-byte numeric field. Here is the code to read a particular customer record:

```
Object[] keys = new Object[1];
keys[0] = new Integer(123456);
Record custData = custFile.read(keys);
```

The read method returns a Record object (or null, if no record is found). Recall, then, that getting field data from a Record object is simply a matter of calling the getField method on that object. The getField method expects as input either the name of the field, which in this case is the uppercase field name from the file itself, or the zero-based field position number within the record. The following code reads each field from the retrieved record, using the latter method:

```
if (custData != null)
  {
    Integer    outCustID     = (Integer)custData.getField(0);
    String     outCustName   = (String)custData.getField(1);
    String     outCustPhone  = (String)custData.getField(2);
    BigDecimal outCustBalance = (BigDecimal)custData.getField(3);
  }
```

Using the field positional number is more efficient, but also less resilient to change if fields are added, removed, or repositioned in the record format. When you are done accessing the file, take care to close using the close method on the file object.

There are alternatives to the read method, which just retrieves the first record that matches the given key (or partial key). These are readAfter and readBefore, which return the first record after or before the record matching the given key. Subsequent reads use other methods, relative to the current cursor position: readNextEqual or readPreviousEqual. These do not take a key array, due to their relative nature.

You might also want to position the cursor without doing that initial read. This is possible via the methods positionCursor, positionCursorAfter, and positionCursorBefore. These all take the key array like read, readNext, and readPrevious, but they don't have the overhead of doing an actual database record retrieval. Finally, the read, readNext, readPrevious, positionCursor, positionCursorAfter, and positionCursorBefore methods all allow an optional second parameter, which is a constant from the KeyedFile class. These constants allow you to specify matching criteria for the key, versus just accepting the default, which is "equal." The self-explanatory constants are KEY_EQ, KEY_GT, KEY_GE, KEY_LT, and KEY_LE.

Suppose you have a keyed file and want to retrieve all the records in it, ordered by key. This common requirement is done by using the KeyedFile class, and the readNext method with no parameter. This returns a populated Record object as long as there is another record, and null when you are at the end of the file. You don't have to specify any key objects in this case, and the database will be read by key, by default.

Of course, your applications don't always just read data. Sometimes, they have to update it as well. This is also possible via the Toolbox. Just be sure to specify AS400File.READ_WRITE or AS400File.WRITE_ONLY on the open method call. Then, you can subsequently use the update or deleteRecord methods to update or delete records identified by the usual array of key objects. The update method also needs a Record object containing the new data to put in the fields. The KEY_XX constants are also allowed on these method calls. Here is an example of updating the previously read custData record:

```
custData.setField("CUSTNAME", "ABC Company");
custFile.update(keys, custData);
```

Of course, most of the methods shown here throw exceptions, and so they will have to be wrapped in try/catch statements. A full example of reading the fictitious keyed customer file is in the supplied source TestKeyedRecordAccess.java on the CD-ROM.

In many cases, these record-level-access classes should offer performance gains over the JDBC classes, except for applications that can exploit the expressive power of SQL.

As an example of how to write applications that use the direct-record-access classes described here, we have written a little application that works with a customer database. This application is on the CD-ROM in subdirectory ListingA-6 in AppA, and we invite you to look at it. We don't describe the code here, but we do point out which files are behind which windows. The first file to edit is CUST.PF, in Listing A.6. It is the DDS source for the customer file.

Listing A.6: Physical-File DDS for a Customer Database File

```
A              R CUSTREC                    TEXT('Customer Info')
A                CUSTID        6B  0         TEXT('Unique customer ID')
A                CUSTNAME      30
A                CUSTPHONE     15
A                CUSTBAL       7P  2         EDTCDE(A)
A                                            DFT(0)
A              K CUSTID
```

You should upload this to an AS/400 source member in an AS/400 source file (using File->Save As in CODE/400's editor, for example). Once it is on the AS/400, compile it with CRTPF into library CUSTLIB, say. Now you are ready to populate it with data, and then work with that data. Run the Java class BldCustDB, and you will be presented with the window in Figure A.1.

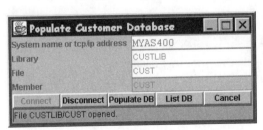

Figure A.1: The BldCustDB Java database example's main window

Type in the name of your AS/400, and press the Connect button. You are prompted by the Toolbox for your user ID and password, then connected to the AS400. The connect method in the BldCustDB class also creates a KeyedFile object, sets the record format for it, and opens it for read/write. Press the Populate DB button, and the populateDB method uses KeyedFile's write method to write 100 records of randomly generated data into the CUST database. Then, press the List DB button, and you will see the window in Figure A.2.

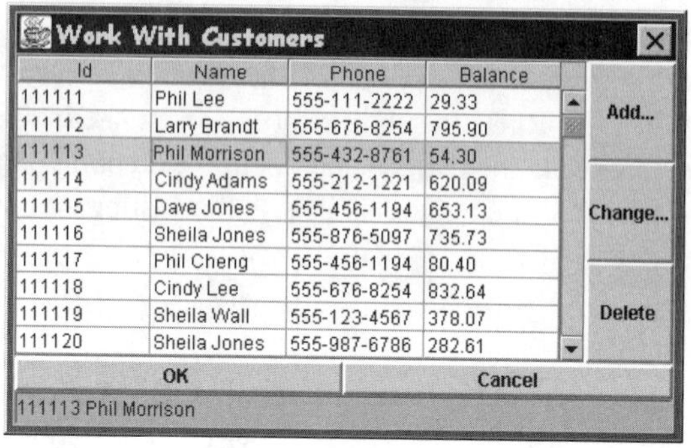

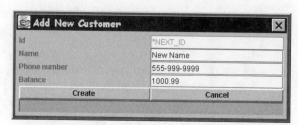

Figure A.2: A window for seeing and working with customer database records

This is a classic "Work With" window for seeing, adding, changing, and deleting records. The class behind this window is DisplayWindowInTable. Its constructor spawns a thread to read all the records from the database into a Vector of Customer objects. This vector, and the code to populate it, is in the class CustomerList (in its populate method). This vector is then passed to the Swing JTable's model class (DisplayWindowModel), which uses it to populate the table. This is done via methods in the DisplayList class, which extends Swing's JTable class and ties that table to our model. (We found it significantly faster to close the KeyedFile object and reopen it for read-only with a blocking factor of 150 records, and then subsequently close and reopen it for read/write.)

If you now press the Add button, you will see the dialog in Figure A.3. This is driven by the CustomerPrompt class. We create a new empty Customer object and pass it to this dialog class, which populates it with user data from the entry fields and returns it. Then, the DisplayWindowInTable class calls the addCustomer method in CustomerList to add that Customer object to both the in-memory Vector and the actual KeyedFile database via its write method.

Figure A.3: A window for adding a new customer record to a database

To determine the next unique ID, the getNextUniqueId method in CustomerList positions the cursor to the last record, reads it, and increments its ID value by one. Finally, we call a method in our table model class to refresh the list to display that new entry.

If you press the Change button, you get the dialog window in Figure A.4. This is also driven by the CustomerPrompt class, but in this case, the entry fields are preloaded with the contents of the selected Customer object in the list. We actually pass a copy of the selected Customer object. On return from this dialog, we pass the updated Customer object clone to the updateCustomer method in CustomerList to update the data in the selected Customer object in the in-memory vector and to update the record in the KeyedFile database via KeyedFile's update method.

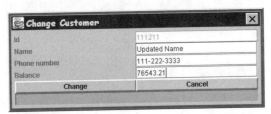

Figure A.4: A window for changing an existing customer record in a database

Finally, the Delete button asks you to confirm your request, and then calls the deleteCustomer method in the CustomerList class, which removes the selected Customer object from the in-memory vector and the KeyedFile database via its deleteRecord method. The confirmation dialog is shown in Figure A.5.

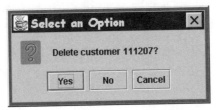

Figure A.5: The confirmation dialog when deleting records

This example shows how to prepare and open a database; read with blocking from a database; write, update, and delete records in a database; and position the cursor in a database. Of course, it also shows how to close the database, as the BldCustDB class does when it ends. It also shows a typical design pattern for classes you will create for each database you wish to access from Java:

- An XXXKey class containing fields that make up the key for this database.

- An XXX class containing non-key fields in this database, with a reference to an XXXKey object.

- An XXXList class for getting and maintaining an in-memory list of records from the database. This is typically an array or vector of XXX objects, populated by reading the database. It also supplies the methods for inserting, updating, and deleting records in the database and keeping the in-memory list in sync.

This should be enough to get you going quickly with your own database-accessing code.

OTHER AS/400 TOOLBOX FOR JAVA FUNCTIONALITY

In addition to the non-visual and visual classes, the Toolbox comes with a number of utility programs such as JarMaker, which can strip the Toolbox .jar file down to a bare minimum if you don't need all the functionality. All the additional functionality is well documented in the Toolbox documentation, and we direct you to it for more information. You can get to this documentation from CODE/400's editor when editing any .java file, by selecting the Help menu, then Java help, then AS/400 Toolbox for Java. It is also available from the Help pull-down of VisualAge for Java.

We think the AS/400 Toolbox for Java is awesome, and we highly recommend it to you and your team. The fact that it is now an open-source product, meaning you can contribute enhancements to it, is even more reason to use it.

APPENDIX B

MIXING RPG AND JAVA

This appendix is a brief tour of the new capabilities added to RPG IV as of V5R1, which makes it easier to use Java Native Interface to call Java from RPG and to call RPG from Java. Appendix A discusses how to use the AS/400 Toolbox for Java to call RPG from Java, using either hand-crafted code to the `ProgramCall` and `ServiceProgramCall` classes or using the Program Call Markup Language (PCML).

While the Toolbox remains the option of choice for calling RPG from Java for many people, there is now an alternative. Specifically, the Toolbox calls RPG programs and service programs in a separate job from that running the Java Virtual Machine. The advantage of this is that there are no worries about thread safety, and it is a tried and trusted application architecture. The alternative is to use Java Native Interface, as Chapter 14 hints at, to call ILE procedures inside service programs, within the same job as the Java Virtual Machine. The advantage to this approach is strictly performance, as it saves the overhead of starting that second job. If your service program does not turn on LR, then the advantage is perhaps minor. The downside of JNI for RPG calls has always been coding complexity, but as of V5R1, RPG has been enhanced to reduce this complexity.

On the other hand, if your goal is to call Java from RPG, you really are tied to JNI. Remember, JNI comes with C APIs for starting the JVM, instantiating objects, calling methods on those objects, and translating data between compiled languages and Java. Thus, it can be used to go either way. The historical problem with using JNI to call into Java has always been that of complexity, which is increased when using RPG versus C. Once again, however, the enhancements in V5R1 of RPG IV have significantly reduced this complexity, hiding much of it behind new RPG-native syntax.

One alternative to using JNI to call Java from RPG is to launch the Java application by calling the JAVA CL command from the RPG program, and then use a data queue or data area to communicate between the two programs. Another alternative is to use an embedded SQL call to invoke the Java class as a stored procedure, leveraging the database. Both come with their own advantages and disadvantages, but this appendix focuses exclusively on the new RPG IV built-in support to call Java directly via Java Native Interface.

RPG CALLING JAVA

To call Java from RPG, the following enhancements needed to be added to the RPG language syntax:

- A new data type to hold an object reference, which is nothing more than a memory address. Since RPG is a strongly typed language, this also requires a means to identify the package-qualified name of the class the referenced object will be an instance of.

- A way to prototype methods in a class. Because RPG does not have Java's late binding capability, the compiler needs to be told about a method, to know how to make calls to it. This means you must tell RPG the method's name, its return type, and each parameter's data type.

- A way to call methods in an object. There needs to be syntax to make the call, pass the actual parameters, and get the returned value, if any. Further, there needs to be a way to identify the particular object for which the method is being called, as opposed to just the class containing the method.

- A way to instantiate an object and store the resulting reference in a field defined with the new object reference data type from above. This requires a way to identify the particular constructor to use and to define the parameters to the constructor, if any.

- A way to prototype and call static methods, which as you know do not require an object in order to call. The compiler only needs to know which class contains the static method.

You might also expect the ability to access public variables in an object, but this support was not added to the RPG language. If you need to access a variable, you must create a Java class with methods that return the variables you are interested in, and optionally create methods to set them, if you want write access.

The enhancements added to V5R1 of RPG IV to enable calling of Java includes the following:

1. A new object data type, o, holds references to instantiated Java objects. Any field defined to be of type o must also specify the new CLASS keyword on the D-spec to identify the object's class type. The syntax for CLASS is CLASS(*JAVA:'package.class'), where both parameters are required. The first parameter, *JAVA, identifies this as a Java object and allows support for non-Java objects in the future. The second parameter is a character literal or constant identifying the package-qualified class name for this object. This name is case-sensitive, just as in Java.

2. An extension of the existing procedure prototyping and calling syntax allows prototyping and calling Java methods as though they were regular RPG procedures. This involves new syntax for the EXTPROC keyword specified on a D-spec prototype, to identify the class that contains the method: EXTPROC(*JAVA:'package.class':'method').
The first parameter, *JAVA, again identifies this as a prototype for a Java method. The second parameter is a character literal or constant field that identifies the package-qualified class that contains the method. The third parameter is a character literal or constant field that identifies the name of the method being prototyped. Both the second and third parameters are case-sensitive. When you prototype a method, use a D-spec with PR in positions 24 and 25, exactly as you do when prototyping a procedure. On the PR spec, specify the EXTPROC keyword, and also specify the return type of the method, if it returns something. The sub-

sequent D-specs that have blanks in columns 24 and 25 identify the parameters of the method, again just as with regular RPG procedure prototypes. For the return type and the parameters, if the data type is a primitive, use the corresponding native RPG data type, as shown in Table B.1. You must also specify the VALUE keyword on the parameter D-specs, as all Java primitives are passed by value. If the return type or parameter type is an object, use the new o data type and specify the CLASS keyword in the keyword area of the D-spec. This keyword has the syntax described in the previous step.

3. Once you have a method prototyped, and you have created an object instance of the class containing the method (described in step 4), you can call the method the same way you call any RPG procedure. This is an elegant mapping of RPG's syntax to Java. Use the CALLP op-code to call a method if you do not care about the returned value, or the EVAL op-code to assign the returned value to an RPG field, or call the method as part of an expression just as with RPG procedures, by using the method name in place of a field name. If the method takes parameters, place them inside parentheses and use a colon to separate them. The only tricky part is identifying the object upon which the method is being invoked. This is done by specifying the object's reference field (type o) as the first parameter. Thus, even methods that do not take parameters will always have a least one parameter in the call to them. While the target object is required as the first parameter in the call, you do not prototype it.

4. A special flavor of the method prototyping syntax is needed for prototyping constructors. To instantiate objects, simply prototype the constructor as though it were a method, and call it as you call any method. This "method" returns a reference to the instantiated object, just as though you had used the new operator in Java. Indeed, RPG is doing this for you under the covers. Because these constructor methods return objects, you *must* specify the CLASS keyword on a constructor prototype, using the syntax described in step 1. Further, you must tell RPG that this is a constructor method, so that it knows to call the new operator. Do this by specifying *CONSTRUCTOR for the method name, in the third parameter of the CLASS keyword. If the constructor takes parameters, simply prototype them exactly as you prototype parameters to regular Java methods.

5. If you wish to call a static method, it is very easy. You do not need to define an object reference field to hold an object, you do not need to prototype the constructor, you do not need to call the constructor to instantiate an object, and you do not need to specify an object as the first parameter to the method call. You do

still need to prototype the method as described in step 3, and you must specify an additional keyword, STATIC, to tell RPG this is a static method. Once prototyped, you can directly call a static method using the usual procedure-call syntax, but you do not need to specify an object field as the first parameter.

Prior to discussing the important topic of data type mapping, let's see an example of this new syntax. Imagine you want to use a Vector object from within RPG. You want to instantiate an instance of Vector and access the methods addElement, size, and elementAt within that object. To keep the example simple, instantiate and store two Integer objects in the vector. Then walk the vector, extracting each Integer object and converting it first to a String object and then to an RPG character field for the purposes of displaying its value on the console.

This example requires the following fields:

- A Vector object reference field to hold the Vector object
- Two Integer object reference fields to hold the Integer objects
- A String object reference field to hold the Integer objects converted
- Miscellaneous RPG data type fields to hold native RPG values

This example also requires the following prototypes:

- The constructor method for the Vector class (for this example, the empty constructor).
- The addElement, size, and elementAt methods for the Vector class.
- The constructor method for the Integer class (for this example, the constructor that takes a primitive int value as a parameter).
- The toString method of the Integer class. This takes no parameters, but returns a String object.
- The getBytes method of the String class. This returns a byte array version of the target String object, which can be assigned directly to a character field in RPG, with all translation to EBCDIC taken care of automatically. It is best to define such RPG character fields with the VARYING keyword so that their content length can vary, just as Java String contents do.

Once the fields are declared and the constructors and methods prototyped, you can write RPG logic to do the following:

- Instantiate a Vector object by calling its constructor, and save the resulting object.

- Instantiate two Integer objects by calling the Integer constructor, saving the results.

- Add the Integer objects to the Vector object by calling its addElement method.

- Walk the elements of the Vector, displaying each object, using the size and elementAt methods of the Vector, and the toString method of the Integer objects.

Start with the field declarations and method prototypes, as shown in Listing B.1. This declares prototypes for two Java constructors and five methods. You do not need to prototype the String constructor because you will not be instantiating a String object directly. Instead, you will get a String object back from a call to the toString method of the Integer class.

Listing B.1: Declaring Object Fields and Java Method Prototypes

```
D* Declare fields to hold Vector and Integer objects...
D VectorObj       S                   O    CLASS(*JAVA : 'java.util.Vector')
D IntegerObj1     S                   O    CLASS(*JAVA : 'java.lang.Integer')
D IntegerObj2     S                   O    CLASS(*JAVA : 'java.lang.Integer')
D* Declare field to hold a String object...
D StringObj       S                   O    CLASS(*JAVA : 'java.lang.String')
D* Declare primitive fields to hold int values...
D IntegerField    S             10I 0 INZ
D Idx             S             10I 0 INZ
D VectorSizeFld   S             10I 0 INZ
D* Declare primitive field to hold RPG version of String values...
D StringField     S             10A   VARYING
D*_____
D*
D* Declare Vector constructor prototype...
D VectorCtor      PR                  O    EXTPROC(*JAVA : 'java.util.Vector' :
D                                           *CONSTRUCTOR)
D                                          CLASS(*JAVA : 'java.util.Vector' )
D* Declare Integer constructor prototype...
D IntegerCtor     PR                  O    EXTPROC(*JAVA : 'java.lang.Integer'
D                                           : *CONSTRUCTOR)
D                                          CLASS(*JAVA : 'java.lang.Integer' )
D** Parameter prototype declaration for Java type: int
D IntegerCtorParm1...
D                               10I 0 VALUE
```

```
D*----------------------------------------------------------------
D*
D* Prototype for addElement method in Vector class...
D VectorAddElementMethod...
D                 PR              EXTPROC(*JAVA : 'java.util.Vector' :
D                                 'addElement')
D** Parameter prototype declaration for Java type: java.lang.Object
D   addElementParm1...
D                              O  CLASS(*JAVA : 'java.lang.Object' )
D* Prototype for size method in Vector class
D VectorSizeMethod...
D                 PR        10I 0 EXTPROC(*JAVA : 'java.util.Vector' :
D                                 'size')
D* Prototype for elementAt method in Vector class...
D VectorElementAtMethod...
D                 PR           O  EXTPROC(*JAVA : 'java.util.Vector' :
D                                 'elementAt')
D                                 CLASS(*JAVA : 'java.lang.Object' )
D** Parameter prototype declaration for Java type: int
D   elementAtParm1...
D                          10I 0  VALUE
D* Prototype for toString method in Integer class...
D IntegerToStringMethod...
D                 PR           O  EXTPROC(*JAVA : 'java.lang.Integer'
D                                 : 'toString')
D                                 CLASS(*JAVA : 'java.lang.String' )
D* Prototype for getBytes method in String class...
D StringGetBytesMethod...
D                 PR        10A   EXTPROC(*JAVA : 'java.lang.String'
D                                 : 'getBytes')
D                                 VARYING
```

The hard part is prototyping the constructor and method calls, and declaring fields to hold object references. Once that is done, simply write code to call the constructors and methods as though they were procedures written in RPG. The mainline code to do this is shown in Listing B.2.

Listing B.2: Instantiating, Populating, and Traversing a Java Vector from RPG IV

```
C* Instantiate Vector object...
C                 EVAL      VectorObj = VectorCtor()
C* Instantiate first Integer object, with 10 for the value...
C                 EVAL      IntegerField = 10
C                 EVAL      IntegerObj1 = IntegerCtor(IntegerField)
C* Instantiate second Integer object, with 20 for the value...
C                 EVAL      IntegerField = 20
C                 EVAL      IntegerObj2 = IntegerCtor(IntegerField)
C* Add the two Integer objects to the Vector object...
```

Listing B.2: Instantiating, Populating, and Traversing a Java Vector from RPG IV (continued)

```
C                   CALLP      VectorAddElementMethod(VectorObj:IntegerObj1)
C                   CALLP      VectorAddElementMethod(VectorObj:IntegerObj2)
C* Walk all elements of the Vector object, displaying each element...
C                   EVAL       VectorSizeFld = VectorSizeMethod(VectorObj)
C                   FOR        Idx = 0 to (VectorSizeFld-1)
C** Retrieve Integer object using elementAt method of Vector...
C                   EVAL       IntegerObj1 =
C                                 VectorElementAtMethod(VectorObj:Idx)
C** Convert Integer object into String object using toString method...
C                   EVAL       StringObj =
C                                 IntegerToStringMethod(IntegerObj1)
C** Convert String object into RPG character field using getBytes method
C                   EVAL       StringField =
C                                 StringGetBytesMethod(StringObj)
C** Display converted String field on console...
C        StringField DSPLY
C* End FOR loop
C                   ENDFOR
C* Exit
C                   EVAL       *INLR = *ON
```

This code starts by calling the Vector constructor method to instantiate a Vector object. It next calls the Integer constructor method twice, to instantiate two integer objects. It passes an RPG integer field as a parameter to the constructor, first with the number 10 and then the number 20. It next calls the addElement method of the Vector object twice to add each Integer object to that Vector object. (For non-constructor and non-static method calls, you must pass the target object as the first parameter, even though you do not prototype this first parameter. It is implicit, and simply a 3GL alternative to Java's "dot" operator.)

An RPG FOR loop visits each element in the Vector object, from zero to the size minus one, as the Vector class uses zero-based element access. The code calls the size method of the Vector object to get the element count, and stores the result in an RPG field of type integer. Each iteration of the loop first calls the elementAt method to retrieve a reference to the Integer object at that index, and then calls the toString method of the Integer object to convert the Integer to a String object, to which it is given a reference. This String object is converted to an RPG character field by calling the toBytes method on the String object, which returns a byte array of individual characters. When you assign a Java byte array to an RPG character field, RPG takes care of converting the data to an EBCDIC RPG character field. Finally, this value is displayed to the console. The result of running this program is the values 10 and 20, as you would expect.

This example illustrates how to deal with casting Java objects when calling Java from RPG. The methods in the Vector class accept and return objects of type java.lang.Object, as shown in the prototypes of the addElement and elementAt methods. However, the code passed an object of type java.lang.Integer when calling the addElement method, and assigned the result of calling elementAt to an object field of type java.lang.Integer. This is legal in Java, but the assignment would require you to cast the result, using java.lang.Integer. There is no such syntax in RPG because the casting is done for you implicitly.

The code for accessing Java from RPG can be a bit tedious to write, due to the requirement to prototype all the constructors and methods and fully describe the class types of object fields. To help with this drudgery, a wizard in the CODE editor will generate these declarations for you, given the package, class, and method you wish to call. Another wizard in CODE converts RPG IV fixed-form logic to the new free-form style. Listing B.3 shows the logic from Listing B.2 in free-form style.

Listing B.3: The Logic from Listing B.2 in Free-Form RPG style

```
         // Insttantiate Vector object...
         /FREE
          VectorObj = VectorCtor();
          // Instantiae first Integer object, with 10 for the value...
          IntegerField = 10;
          IntegerObj1 = IntegerCtor(IntegerField);
          // Instantiate second Integer object, with 20 for the value...
          IntegerField = 20;
          IntegerObj2 = IntegerCtor(IntegerField);
          // Add the two Integer objects to the Vector object...
          VectorAddElementMethod(VectorObj:IntegerObj1);
          VectorAddElementMethod(VectorObj:IntegerObj2);
          // Walk all elements of the Vector object, displaying each
    element...
          VectorSizeFld = VectorSizeMethod(VectorObj);
          FOR Idx = 0 to (VectorSizeFld-1);
            //* Retrieve Integer object using elementAt method of
    Vector...
             IntegerObj1 =
                VectorElementAtMethod(VectorObj:Idx);
          //* Convert Integer object into String object using toString
method...
```

Listing B.3: The Logic from Listing B.2 in Free-Form RPG style (continued)

```
        StringObj =
            IntegerToStringMethod(IntegerObj1);
        //* Convert String object into RPG character field using
getBytes method
        StringField =
            StringGetBytesMethod(StringObj);
        //* Display converted String field on console...
        DSPLY StringField;
        // End FOR loop
     ENDFOR;
     // Exit
     *INLR = *ON;
    /END-FREE
```

Mapping data types

When prototyping method and constructor calls, you specify RPG data types for the parameters and the return type, not Java data types. For each of the eight primitive data types in Java, there is a corresponding RPG data type you should use, and the RPG runtime takes care of the data mapping between the two languages. For objects, use the object o data type together with the CLASS keyword to specify the class type of the object. For arrays, use RPG arrays of fields with the appropriate type for each element. Table B.1 shows the mappings from each of the Java types to their corresponding RPG types.

Table B.1: Data Type Mapping between RPG and Java

Java Type	RPG Type	Comment
Boolean: boolean	Indicator: N	True/false versus one/zero.
Byte: byte	Integer: 3I 0 Character: 1A	If using byte to hold a numeric value, use a three-digit integer in RPG. Otherwise, use a one-digit alpha.
Byte array: byte[]	Character length > 1: nA Array of char length=1: 1A DIM Date: D Time: T Timestamp: Z	An array of bytes can be mapped to a fixed-length alpha field or an array of alpha characters in RPG. It can also be mapped to a date, time, or timestamp if it holds date values
Short: short	2 byte integer: 5I 0	A Java two-byte integer maps to a five-digit integer.

Table B.1: Data Type Mapping between RPG and Java (cont)		

Java Type	RPG Type	Comment
Character: char	UCS length = 1: 1C	Java characters are two-byte Unicode.
Character array: char[]	UCS length > 1: nC Array of UCS len=1: 1C DIM(x)	Straight mapping of Unicode characters or choose an array of single characters.
Integer: int	4 byte integer: 10I 0	A Java four-byte integer maps to a 10-digit int.
Long: long	8 byte integer: 20I 0	A Java eight-byte integer maps to a 20-digit int.
Float: float	4 byte float: 4F	Single-precision floating-point.
Double: double	8 byte float: 8F	Double-precision floating-point.
Any object: Object	Object: O CLASS("x.y")	Holds an object reference.
Any array: xxx[]	Array of equivalent type: x DIM	Choose the type from above for an array type.

Some Java data types, such as byte, map to more than one RPG data type. The one you use depends on your knowledge of the contents. If the byte variable or array contains a character or characters that are the result of calling toBytes on a String object, then use a character field in RPG. On assignment, RPG will do the necessary codepage mappings. If the Java byte variable contains numeric data, assign it to an RPG three-digit integer field, so that no such mapping is done.

In Java, you can only convert characters or strings to single-byte variables and arrays if the Unicode contents can, in fact, be converted to a single-byte codepage. This will not be the case if the character or string contains true double-byte data, such as Chinese or Japanese characters. In these cases, you need to assign the Java character field to an RPG Unicode character field. For Java strings, you first need to use the toCharArray method to convert the String object into a Java character array. This, in turn, can be assigned to an RPG Unicode character field (data type c) or an array of RPG Unicode characters.

When assigning to a field versus an array, set the length to be as big as the string might possibly be (or 32,767 if you don't know how long the Java string might be), and then specify the VARYING keyword to indicate that the length may vary. Keep in mind that, while RPG Unicode characters are two bytes long internally, you specify the length in terms of number of characters, not bytes.

Java exceptions when calling Java from RPG

When you call a Java method from RPG, that method might throw an exception. For example, when RPG does its implicit casting from one object type to another, if the object types are not compatible (as discussed in Chapter 9), you will get a ClassCastException thrown. RPG intercepts all Java exceptions and converts them to standard RPG runtime errors, with one of the program status codes shown in Table B.2. (For a complete and up-to-date list of status codes, see the "Program Status Data Structure" section of the *ILE RPG Reference* manual.)

Table B.2: Java-Related Program Status Codes	

Status Code	Comment
0301	Class or method not found in method call, or error in method call
0302	Error while converting a Java array to an RPG parameter on entry to a Java native method
0303	Error converting an RPG parameter to a Java array on exit from an RPG native method
0304	Error converting an RPG parameter to a Java array in preparation for a Java method call
0305	Error converting a Java array to an RPG parameter or return value after a Java method
0306	Error converting an RPG return value to a Java array

Java Virtual Machine considerations

When calling Java from RPG, the RPG runtime takes care of starting the Java Virtual Machine, if it is not already started. To explicitly start or explicitly destroy the JVM, call the JNI (Java Native Interface) procedures JNI_CreateJavaVM or JNI_DestroyJavaVM, respectively. (You first have to call JNI_GetCreatedJavaVMs.) Calling operating-system JNI methods like these requires you to use /COPY for the copy member JNI in file QSYSINC/QRPGLESRC. The details of making these calls is beyond this book, but are well documented in the *RPG Programmer's Guide*, in the section on RPG and Java.

At the time of this writing, a problem exists when the JVM is used in an interactive job. Specifically, the JVM for the job is destroyed when an ILE activation group ends, and it does not start again cleanly for the same job. This is a known problem, and work is being done to address it in V5R2, and possibly V5R1 via a PTF.

Classpath considerations

When RPG starts the JVM or you start it explicitly using a JNI call, the default CLASSPATH is used. This allows access to all the Java-supplied classes. To access other classes, you need to set your CLASSPATH prior to running your RPG program. This is most easily done using the ADDENVVAR CL command, specifying ENVVAR(CLASSPATH) and a colon-separated list of IFS folders for the VALUE parameter. This command sets the CLASSPATH for the life of this job only.

CALLING RPG PROCEDURES AS RPG NATIVE METHODS FROM JAVA

In addition to calling Java from RPG, there is also RPG support for calling RPG from Java. This support simplifies the effort to code and call Java native methods that are written in RPG as ILE procedures inside service programs. The Java language standard defines a common way to access C functions from Java, by defining a method signature with the keyword native. Such a method has no body, much like methods defined with the keyword abstract. Rather, the method is implemented in C, as a function, within a DLL or service program on iSeries. The DLL or service program containing the function (with the same signature as the Java method definition) is identified using a static initializer, as described in Chapter 14.

While it has always been possible to implement these functions using ILE RPG procedures, the effort required has been daunting without the special syntax and runtime support added to RPG IV as of V5R1. It is very easy, on the other hand, to call any iSeries program or ILE procedure within a service program using the Program Call Markup Language (PCML) supplied in the AS/400 Toolbox for Java. While easy, this means of calling RPG from Java does involve the overhead of starting a new job for the program or service program on the first call, and marshalling the parameter data between the jobs. In many cases, it can be more efficient to use RPG native method support, as the RPG procedures are called within the same job. You might or might not consider it easy.

The first important note about RPG native method support is that you must remember to specify the THREAD(*SERIALIZE) keyword on your RPG H-spec at the top of each module in which you wish to call procedures. Because Java is a threaded language, and you are calling RPG within the same job and possibly within multiple threads, you must use this keyword to avoid corrupting your data if two threads use the same database-accessing RPG logic simultaneously.

Writing an RPG native method is very easy. Simply code a RPG IV procedure as normal, being sure to specify the EXPORT keyword on the P-spec, and export it when creating the service program. (For example, use EXPORT(*ALL) on CRTSRVPGM.) You must also specify the EXTPROC keyword on your procedure prototype, with *JAVA for the first parameter, the package-qualified Java class containing the Java native method definition for the second parameter, and the Java name by which you want to refer to this method as the third parameter. When you create your service program, it is best to specify a named activation group such as QILE or your own name, versus using the default activation group or even *CALLER, since the caller in this case is Java.

To be able to access the procedure from your Java code, simply code a Java native method signature with exactly the same name (including case) as specified on the EXTPROC keyword of your procedure, and the same number of parameters. Each parameter and return type should be the Java equivalent of the RPG data type, as described in Table B.1. To tell Java the name of the service program containing the RPG native method, code the following static initializer at the top of your Java class:

```
static
{
    System.loadLibrary ("MYSRVPGM");
}
```

Replace MYSRVPGM with the name of your service program. Repeat the System.loadLibrary statement for each service program containing native methods you wish to call.

With this, your Java code can now call that Java method as though it were written in Java! All data-mapping of the parameters will be done for you by the RPG runtime. At runtime, ensure that the library containing your service program is on your library list.

Let's look at an example, adapted from the *ILE RPG Programmer's Guide*. It starts with an RPG module that contains a single, simple procedure named checkCust. Given a customer ID, it does a chain operation to that record and returns true if the record was found, and false if it was not. This uses the CUSTDB database file from Listing A.3 in Appendix

A, which contains a record format named CUSTREC. The key is the customer ID field, CUSTID, which has six integer digits and zero decimal places.

In the procedure in Listing B.4, the input parameter is defined as a 10-digit integer field, which maps to the int primitive data type in Java, as shown in Table B.1. The keyword CONST for the parameter indicates the parameter value does not change in the procedure. The procedure simply does a chain to that key, in the database file, and returns an indicator value of one if the chain was successful. The RPG indicator data type maps to the boolean primitive data type in Java. Notice that EXTPROC is specified, but the class name is not qualified with the package name because for this simple example, the class is in the unnamed package.

Listing B.4: An RPG Procedure to Be Used as an RPG Native Method

```
     H NOMAIN THREAD(*SERIALIZE) DFTACTGRP(*NO) ACTGRP('QILE')
ALWNULL(*USRCTL)
     FCUSTDB    UF   E                DISK
       * _____
       * PROCEDURE checkCust prototype
       * _____
     D checkCust        PR              N
EXTPROC(*JAVA:'MyClass':'checkCust')
     D   custId                   10I 0 CONST
     D*
       * _____
       * PROCEDURE checkCust
       * _____
     P checkCust        B                       EXPORT
     D checkCust        PI              N
     D   custId                   10I 0 CONST
      /free
         chain custId  custREC;
         return %found;
      /end-free
     P checkCust        E
```

The Java code to call this procedure as a native method is shown in Listing B.5. A static initializer identifies the service program, and there is a very simple native method declaration. The main method tests instantiating the class and calling the native method.

Listing B.5: A Java Native Method to Call an RPG Procedure via JNI

```
public class MyClass
{

    static
    {
        System.loadLibrary ("RPGNTVMTD");
    }

    /**
     * The declaration of the RPG native method.
     * Calling this calls the RPG procedure checkCust
     *  in service program RPGNTVMTD in library list.
     */
    native boolean checkCust (int custId);


    /**
     * Command line control. Tests the RPG native method.
     */
    public static void main(String args[])
    {
        MyClass testObj = new MyClass();
        // call the native method
        boolean found = false;
        int custId = 123;
        found = testObj.checkCust(custId);
        System.out.println("Result of native method = " + found);
    }

}
```

To other Java code, a native method is no different than a regular Java method. Very nice! When dealing with character strings, it is best to define your RPG procedure to accept either a character or Unicode field, with the VARYING keyword. From the Java side, declare the native method to accept a byte array or a character array, respectively. Then, when you call the method with a String object, use the getBytes or getCharArray method, respectively. The RPG runtime will handle all the codepage conversions. Also very nice!

If your RPG procedure wants to "call back" and execute Java methods within the same object, use the %THIS built-in function to return a reference to the current object. This can then be passed as the first parameter to the Java method, using the syntax described for RPG calling Java.

There are some considerations when writing native methods. One is the CLASSPATH, which must be set properly to find your class, as usual. Another consideration involves exceptions. If your RPG native method ends in an error for some reason, the RPG runtime will throw a Java exception of class type java.lang.Exception, and getMessage on that exception object will return a string of the form "RPG nnnn" where nnnn is the status code from the RPG runtime.

Another consideration regards telling Java when you are done using a Java object, so that the JVM can cleanly dispose of that object, reducing memory leaks. This is done by calling the JNI API DeleteLocalRef. These and other considerations are described well in the *ILE RPG Programmers Guide*, in the section about RPG and Java. We leave them to your additional reading pleasure when you need them.

FINALLY

We hope you take these RPG enhancements as an indication of IBM's commitment not only to Java, but also to RPG. Indeed, IBM believes both languages have a long future and will live happily together for a long time to come!

APPENDIX

OBTAINING THE CODE SAMPLES

All of the code samples shown in the listings in this book are available on the accompanying CD-ROM. To get them, insert the CD and copy the entire "Java For RPG Programmers" folder to a local disk drive.

Within the Java For RPG Programmers folder there is a samples folder, and within that there is a subfolder for each chapter and appendix in the book. Within each chapter folder is a folder per listing from the book, containing the source files for that listing. Where appropriate, there is enough source per such folder to allow for a full compile and run. To do this, you will need to download and install the Java 2 Platform, Standard Edition SDK from the Sun Web site *www.java.sun.com/products*.

The CD-ROM also contains a full Java development environment, for your convenience. This is the Eclipse product, release 1.0, which is also available at on the Web. Eclipse is an open-source project from IBM, for building software around an Integrated Development Environment. It includes Java tooling as part of its base offering. You will enjoy exploring the power of Eclipse, and eventually you may decide to even write your own tools within Eclipse. These are written in Java, and are called *plugins*. There is built-in support in Eclipse for writing plugins for Eclipse. If you use Eclipse, you do not need to download a Java SDK. Eclipse only needs a Java Runtime Environment, and one is supplied for one on the CD-ROM and will automatically be used by Eclipse. However, you may still wish to download the SDK documentation.

To see, edit and run the book samples within Eclipse, first start Eclipse by double clicking on the `eclipse.exe` executable file in the Eclipse1.0 folder. Note that it cannot be run from the CD, only from a writable local disk. Once Eclipse is up, you can import the book samples by using the File menu and selecting the Import option. The import option will create one Java project per chapter. To work with the samples for a given chapter, simply expand the chapter and drill down to the source files. Double click to open a source file. If this file is a Java file with a `main` method, you can run it by selecting the file and then the Run action from the toolbar (the running man icon). As you save your edit changes with Ctrl+S, Eclipse automatically compiles for you. There is also a very nice feature in the Java editor for finding members. After typing an object name and a dot, you can press Ctrl+Space to get a list of members within that object.

This version of Eclipse is the same version that is the basis of the first release of the IBM products WebSphere Studio Application Developer, WebSphere Studio Site Developer and WebSphere Development Studio Client. If you have any of these products, you can copy the `com.j4r` plugins folder to the plugins folder within these products. Once copied, you will see the the Java For RPG Programmers Samples import option when you next start the product. Please note however, this may not work on subsequent releases of these products, as they step up to future releases of Eclipse.

Also on the CD-ROM, for your convenience, is the AS/400 Toolbox for Java. The documentation is in the Toolbox folder, while the Jar files are in the Eclipse subfolder *\plugins\com.j4r\runtime*. These are ready to use within Eclipse for the imported chapter projects. To use them in your own projects, create variable entries to the Jar files. Do this by selecting the project, right-clicking, selecting Properties, then the Java Build Path entry. Go the Libraries tab, and press Add variable. Enter ECLIPSE_HOME for the variable name, and use the Browse button to find the `jt400.jar` file in the runtime folder.

ABOUT THE AUTHORS

Phil Coulthard and George Farr are also co-authors of the book *Java for S/390 and AS/400 COBOL Programmers.*

Phil Coulthard joined the IBM Toronto Laboratory in 1986 and has specialized in tools for the OS/400 programmer (and System/36 before that). He has worked as a developer and team leader on a number of products, including Sort, Character Graphics Utility, Screen Design Aid, and his pet project, CODE/400, the Windows-based follow-on to ADTS (Application Development ToolSet, which includes PDM, SEU, SDA, RLU and DFU). He has been the manager of many OS/400 application-development products, and his current role is lead architect for iSeries application-development products. He works closely with his OS/400 and OS/390 counterparts in strategy and architecture development in Rochester, Toronto, and Silicon Valley.

Phil has a specialized honors degree in mathematics and computer science from the University of Toronto. He is a frequent speaker at COMMON and local user groups, and a frequent author of articles in industry and user-group magazines. He also works closely with iSeries customers on architecture, strategy, and tooling decisions. Phil can be reached at *coulthar@ca.ibm.com*.

George Farr joined the IBM Toronto Laboratory in 1985 and has specialized in the RPG language compilers. He has worked as a developer and team leader on all the RPG compilers on OS/400, including RPG III, RPG IV, and VisualAge for RPG. He has also spent time working in an architecture and planning role for RPG. If it says "RPG," George is the development manager of it. He is also the development manager for the core Integrated Development Environment for iSeries. George's language and IDE focus brings him in constant communication with his iSeries and S/390 COBOL and Java counterparts in Rochester, Toronto, and Santa Teresa.

George has a specialized honors degree in computer science from York University in Toronto. He is a frequent and very popular speaker at COMMON and local user groups, and a frequent author of articles in industry and user-group magazines. George is also the co-author of the books *ILE: A First Look* and *RPG IV by Example*. George can be reached at *farr@ca.ibm.com*.

INDEX

Note: boldface numbers indicate illustrations

instantiating an object, new operator, 54
int data type, 46, 187, 188, 189, 207, 223, 618
/%INT, 219
integrated development environment (EDE), 2
INTEER data type, 618
Integer class, wrappers and to/from, 220-221
integer data type, 183, 184, 188, 189, 207
integrated development environment (IDE), 8
Integrated File System (IFS), 33
    Java on AS/400 and, 691, 693-696
integrated language environment (ILE), 27, 29, 423
interactive vs. embedded SQL, 572-573
interface keyword, 389
interfaces, 187, 226, 360, 387-409, 419
    abstract, 389
    call backs as, 400-401
    casting and, 391-392
    Cloneable, 401, 402-403
    Comparator, 401
    compilers and, 388-389
    constants and, 401
    contracts as, 398
    copy members and, 389-409
    database access and for, 630-631
    Enumeration, 401, 403-409
    extending classes and, 387-409
    graphical user interface (GUI), 402
    helper classes and, 392, 405
    implementing, 361, 390-391, 398-399, 400-401
    interface keyword in, 389
    introspection in, 389
    Iterator, 407
    Java Database Connectivity (JDBC), 402, 583
    Java-supplied examples of, 401-409
    object reference variables and, 391
    pointers and, 400-401
    polymorphism and, 399
    procedure pointers vs., 400-401
    prototyping vs., 387-409
    public, 389
    reuse of code, 394-399
    Runnable, 401

search in, 399-401
service programs vs. ., 387-409, 400-401
signatures and, 389, 404
sort method and, 399-401
threads and, 454-456, 461, 462, 463, 485
in user interface, Swing classes and, 489
international characters, 304
internationalization of user interface, resource bundles, 562-566
Internet, 5, 12-19
Internet Information Server (IIS), 18
Internet Inter Orb protocol (IIOP), 651
Internet service providers (ISPs), 14-15
interpreters, 6, 7
%INTH, 219
introspection, 389, 684
INZ, 51, 191, 192, 193, 194, 195, 224, 288, 289
is a relationship, 415, 417
is method, 223, 621-622
isAlive, 482-483, 486
isDigit, 437
isDirectory, 664
isEmpty, 258, 272
iSeries (see AS/400)
isLeapYear, 354, 357
ISO, 338, 339, 344, 345, 348
isolation levels, 620
ITER, 144, 145, 172-174, 179
Iterator interface, 407
iterators, SQLJ, 634, 635

J

J2EE, 688
jar files, 7, 90-91, 693
    JarMaker and, 740
JarMaker, 740
jarsigner, 8
java command, 7, 37, 650, 693
JAVA command, 37, 742
Java Database Connectivity (JDBC) (see also database access), 402, 558, 580-581, **581**, 583-603
Java development kit (JDK), 7-10, **8**
Java Naming and Directory Services (JNDS), 630-631

Note: boldface numbers indicate illustrations

Note: boldface numbers indicate illustrations

Note: boldface numbers indicate illustrations

Note: boldface numbers indicate illustrations